THE ANTITRUST IMPULSE

COLUMBIA UNIVERSITY SEMINAR SERIES

The University Seminars at Columbia University welcomes this study of *The Antitrust Impulse: An Economic, Historical, and Legal Analysis* by Theodore P. Kovaleff to the Columbia University Seminars Series. The study has benefited from Seminar discussions and reflects the advantages of scholarly exchange provided by the Seminar Movement.

Aaron W. Warner
Director, University Seminars
Columbia University

THE FUTURE OF AMERICAN BANKING
James R. Barth, R. Dan Brumbaugh, Jr., and Robert E. Litan

THE EVOLUTION OF U.S. FINANCE, VOLUME I
Federal Reserve Monetary Policy: 1915–1935
Jane W. D'Arista

THE EVOLUTION OF U.S. FINANCE, VOLUME II
Restructuring Institutions and Markets
Jane W. D'Arista

HOW CREDIT-MONEY SHAPES THE ECONOMY
The United States In a Global System
Robert Guttmann

THE ANTITRUST IMPULSE, Volume I and Volume II
An Economic, Historical, and Legal Analysis
Theodore P. Kovaleff

FROM MALTHUS TO THE CLUB OF ROME AND BACK
Problems of Limits to Growth, Population Control, and Migrations
Paul Neurath

THE ANTITRUST IMPULSE

Volume I

An Economic, Historical, and Legal Analysis

Theodore P. Kovaleff
Editor

M.E. Sharpe
Armonk, New York
London, England

Library of Congress Cataloging-in-Publication Data

The Antitrust impulse: an economic, historical, and legal analysis /
[edited by] Theodore P. Kovaleff.
p. cm. — (Columbia University seminar series)
Includes index.
ISBN 1-56324-180-3 (V. 1) 1-56324-181-1 (V.2) 1-56324-085-8 (set)
1. Antitrust law—United States.
I. Kovaleff, Theodore Philip, 1943–
II. Series.
KF1649.A2A419 1994
343.73'0721—dc20
[347.303721]
94-5618
CIP

Printed in the United States of America

The paper used in this publication meets the minimum requirements of
American National Standard for Information Sciences—
Permanence of Paper for Printed Library Materials,
ANSI Z 39.48-1984.

∞

BM (c) 10 9 8 7 6 5 4 3 2 1

Contents

VOLUME I

VOLUME II

PART III

Economic Perspective

List of Tables and Figures

Chapter 11

Tables

Chapter 12

Tables

Chapter 16

Figure

Contributors

VOLUME I

WALTER ADAMS / JAMES BROCK

A member of the economics faculty of Michigan State University since 1947, Walter Adams also served as its President (1969–1970). A prodigious writer, he quickly became known for his work on the theory of competition and monopoly; as a result, he was appointed to the Attorney General's National Committee to Study the Antitrust Laws (1953–1955). He is the author of *Monopoly in America* and an editor and contributor to *The Structure of American Industry*. Recently, with James W. Brock (see below), he has written *The Bigness Complex: Industry, Labor, and Government in the American Economy*; *Dangerous Pursuits: Mergers and Acquisitions in the Age of Wall Street*, and a devastatingly satirical play, *Antitrust Economics on Trial: A Dialogue on the New Laissez-Faire*.

James Brock has been a member of the economics faculty of Miami University (Ohio) since 1979. Promoted to full professor in 1989, the following year, he was named to the prestigious Moeckel professorship. In addition to the aforementioned coauthored books with Walter Adams, he has writtten *Antitrust, the Market and the State: The Contributions of Walter Adams*.

DONALD DEWEY

Donald Dewey has been a member of the Economics faculty at Columbia University since 1960. He is the author of many scholarly works, including *The Theory of Imperfect Competition*; *Monopoly in Economics and Law*; *Modern Capital Theory*; and *The Antitrust Experiment in America*.

ELEANOR M. FOX / LAWRENCE A. SULLIVAN

Since 1976 Eleanor M. Fox has been a Professor at the School of Law, New York University, where she has taught courses in all aspects of antitrust law. The author of several widely used texts, many articles, and a number of books, including *Industrial Concentration and the Market System: Legal, Economic, Social and Political Perspectives*, she served as a member of President Jimmy Carter's National Committee for the Review of Antitrust Laws and Procedures and is a member of the Advisory Board of *The Antitrust Bulletin*.

Lawrence A. Sullivan has taught courses on antitrust, international transactions, and patents at the University of California Law School, Boalt Hall since 1967. He coauthored *Cases and Materials on Antitrust* with Eleanor Fox. He, too was a member of the Carter committee to review the antitrust laws.

ERNEST GELLHORN / CHARLES A. JAMES / RICHARD POGUE / JOE SIMS

Before becoming a partner in the Cleveland law firm of Jones Day Reavis & Pogue, Ernest Albert Eugene Gellhorn had been a Professor of Law at Duke University and the University of Virginia. Subsequently, he was Dean at the law schools of Arizona State University, Case Western University, and the University of Washington. An expert in the administrative and regulatory fields, he is the author, with Glen O. Robinson, of a casebook on the topic. He is a member of the Advisory Board of *The Antitrust Bulletin*.

Charles A. James received his law degree in 1979 from the National Law Center of George Washington University. He spent six years at the Federal Trade Commission in the Bureau of Competition. He then entered private practice in the Washington office of Jones, Day, Reavis & Pogue where he remained until joining the Antitrust Division as Deputy Assistant Attorney General. In early 1992, he was appointed Acting Assistant Attorney General in Charge of the Antitrust Division. With the change of administrations, he rejoined his former law firm where he chaired the Antitrust and Trade Regulation Section of the Government Regulation Group.

Richard Pogue has been a partner specializing in antitrust enforcement in Jones, Day, Reavis & Pogue since 1961. He chaired the American Bar Association's Antitrust Section. (1983–1984) and is a member of the Advisory Board of *The Antitrust Bulletin.*

Joe Sims began his legal career with the Antitrust Division of the Department of Justice in 1970, starting as a trial attorney but quickly being advanced to Special Assistant and then Deputy Attorney General for Policy Planning and Legislation. In 1979 he left his last governmental position, Deputy Attorney General for Regulated Industries and Foreign Commerce, to become a partner at the law firm of Jones, Day, Reavis, & Pogue. He has remained professionally active, having chaired the Sherman Act Section 1 (1988–90) and the Civil Practice and Procedure committees (1990 to the present) of the Antitrust Section of the American Bar Association. With William Kovacic, he is the author of *The Antitrust Government Contracts Handbook.*

MILTON HANDLER

Immediately after being graduated from the School of Law at Columbia University in 1926, Milton Handler was invited to join its faculty; he remained there until his retirement in 1972. Starting with his stint as General Counsel to the National Labor Board (1933–1934), he was active in government service. He served as Special Assistant to the General Counsel of the Treasury Department (1938–1940), as Assistant to the General Counsel, Lend Lease (1942–1943), as a member of the Attorney General's National Committee to Study the Antitrust Laws (1953–1956) and as Chair of the Special Committee to Study the New York State Antitrust Laws (1953–1956). Intricately involved with the Temporary National Economic Committee and its investigation of the concentration of economic power, he wrote *A Study of the Construction and Enforcement of the Federal Antitrust Laws.* In addition to having written a number of case books, he is the author of *Reforming the Antitrust Laws; Antitrust in Perspective;* and *Antitrust in Transition,* a three-volume collection of his most important articles.

THOMAS EUGENE KAUPER

Thomas Eugene Kauper interrupted a teaching career that had begun in 1964 at the University of Michigan Law School to join the Department of Justice in 1969. His first assignment was in the Office of Legal Council, where he held the rank of Deputy Assistant Attorney General. From 1972 until 1976, he was Assistant Attorney General in Charge of the Antitrust Division of the Department of Justice. Since that time he has been a member of the University of Michigan Law School faculty specializing in antitrust and trade regulation.

THEODORE P. KOVALEFF

After having taught economic and legal history at St. John's University, New York University, and Barnard College, Theodore P. Kovaleff was Assistant Dean at the Columbia University School of Law from 1977 to 1992. He is the author of *Business and Government During the Eisenhower Administration: A Study of the Antitrust Policy of the Antitrust Division of the Justice Department.* He is a member of the Advisory Board of *The Antitrust Bulletin* and was Guest Editor of its volume marking the centennial of the Sherman Act.

ROBERT H. McGUCKIN, III

Robert H. McGuckin, III, served with the Antitrust Division of the Department of Justice from 1974 to 1986, rising to Director of Research, Economic Analysis Group before leaving to become the Chief of the Center for Economic Studies of the Bureau of the Census. Editor of a special issue of *The Antitrust Bulletin* celebrating the tenth anniversary of the Economic Policy Office of the Antitrust Division and author of *Empirical Methods in Economic Analysis: An Innovative Approach to Statistical Techniques*, he has also been been recognized by the Justice Department with its "Award of Distinction" and with the "Unusually Outstanding Award" given by the Bureau of the Census.

STEPHEN A. RHOADES / JIM BURKE

While working on his doctorate in economics at the University of Maryland, Stephen A. Rhoades served as a staff economist at the Federal Trade Commission. Upon receipt of the degree, he joined the Federal Reserve Board. He is currently Chief of the Financial Structure Section of the Division of Research and Statistics. His research is primarily directed in the fields of industrial organization, banking, and antitrust. He is the author of *Power, Empire Building, and Mergers*.

Jim Burke received a Ph. D. in economics from the University of Maryland in 1973. Since that time, he has been primarily involved with regulatory policy matters in the Division of Re search and Statistics at the Federal Reserve Board. His research has been related to the structure and performance effects of consolidation in banking.

JAMES FRANKLIN RILL

James Franklin Rill spent the first thirty years of his legal career in private practice with the firm of Collier, Shannon, Rill & Scott. During this period he was instrumental in founding the Antitrust Law Section of the American Bar Association, which he subsequently chaired. In 1989 President George Bush appointed him as the Assistant Attorney General in Charge of the Antitrust Division of the Department of Justice. He served in that position until early 1992, when he returned to his law firm. He is a member of the Advisory Board of *The Antitrust Bulletin*.

CHARLES F. RULE / DAVID L. MEYER

After graduating from the University of Chicago Law School and serving as law clerk to Daniel M. Friedman, chief judge of the United States Court of Claims (now the Court of Appeals), Charles F. Rule joined the Antitrust Division of the Department of Justice in 1982. Starting as a Special Assistant to Assistant Attorney General William F. Baxter, he was soon appointed Deputy Assistant Attorney General, first being responsible for Policy Planning and Legislation and then Regulatory Affairs. After a stint as Acting Assistant Attorney General in charge of the Antitrust Division, he was confirmed to the post in September 1987; he remained until the end of the Reagan administration. He is now a partner in the law firm of Covington & Burling in Washington, D.C.

David L. Meyer is also an attorney with Covington & Burling, where he has practiced since 1989. Between 1987 and 1989 he was Special Assistant to the Assistant Attorney General in Charge of the Antitrust Division. After graduating from the Yale Law School, he clerked for the Honorable Ralph K. Winter, on the United States Court of Appeals for the Second Circuit.

LOUIS B. SCHWARTZ

Louis B. Schwartz began his career serving on the staffs of the Securities and Exchange Commission and the Criminal and Antitrust Divisions of the Department of Justice. He joined the faculty of the University of Pennsylvania Law School in 1946, remaining there until he became a member of the 65 Club at the University of California, Hastings College of Law in 1984. A member of the Attorney General's National Committee to Study the Antitrust Laws (1953–1955), and Director of the National Committee on Reform of Federal Criminal Laws (1967–1971), he is the author of *Antitrust and Regulatory Alternatives* (with John J. Flynn and Harry First).

JOHN J. SIEGFRIED / MICHELLE MAHONY

John J. Siegfried has been Professor of Economics at Vanderbilt University since 1972. An economist with the Federal Trade Commission, a Senior Staff Economist for the Council of Economic Advisors, and member of the Board of Editors of *Review of Industrial Organization*, *The Quarterly Review of Economics and Business*, and *Journal of Economic Education*, he is also the author of *Empirical Studies in Industrial Organization* (with David Audretech), *Economic Analysis and Antitrust Law* (with Terry Calvani), and of nearly 100 articles.

Michelle Mahony is working on her doctoral dissertation in economics at Northwestern University.

JERROLD G. VAN CISE

An internationally respected authority on the administration and enforcement of the antitrust corpus, Jerrold G. Van Cise was a member of the Attorney General's National Committee to Study the Antitrust Laws (1953–1955). With fellow Cahill, Gordon & Reindel partners, William T. Lifland and Laurence T. Sorkin, he is author of *Understanding the Antitrust Laws; The Antitrust Laws from the Point of View of a Private Practitioner*, (with Sigmund Timberg); *The Federal Antitrust Laws*, and *Understanding the Antitrust Laws*.

JAMES R. WITHROW, Jr.

A member of the law firm of Donovan Leisure Newton & Irvine for a career which lasted from 1935 to 1987, James R. Withrow, Jr., specialized in the areas of antitrust and management.

EDWIN MORTON ZIMMERMAN

After graduating from law school in 1959, Edwin Morton Zimmerman was appointed to the faculty of the Stanford Law School. In 1965 he took a leave of absence to join the Department of Justice. Subsequently, President Lyndon B. Johnson appointed him Assistant Attorney General in Charge of the Antitrust Division in 1968, where he remained until the end of the administration. He has been a partner in the Washington law firm of Covington & Burling since 1969.

VOLUME II

DOMINICK T. ARMENTANO

Dominick T. Armentano is Professor of Economics at the University of Hartford, where he specializes in antitrust, industrial organization, and the relationship between business and society. He is the author of *Antitrust and Monopoly: Anatomy of a Policy Failure*; *Antitrust Policy: The Case for Repeal*; and *Myths of Antitrust: Economic Theory and Legal Cases.*

TERRY CALVANI / MICHAEL L. SIBARIUM

Terry Calvani has been a member of the faculties of Law at Stanford University, Vanderbilt University, and the University of Virginia. The Chair of the American Bar Association's Special Committee to Study Antitrust Penalties and Damages from 1979 to 1982, he then worked as a Commissioner on the Federal Trade Commission until 1990, serving as Acting Chairman from 1985 to 1986. Thereafter, he joined the Washington D. C. office of the law firm of Pillsbury, Madison, & Sutro. With John Siegfried, he is the author of *Economic Analysis and Antitrust Law*. He is a member of the Advisory Board of *The Antitrust Bulletin*.

Michael L. Sibarium served as an Attorney Advisor to Terry Calvani from the time Calvani became acting chairman until 1990. He is presently a member of the Washington law firm of Winston and Straun, specializing in business litigation, antitrust, and trade regulation; he is also a faculty member of the National Law Center, George Washington University.

WILLIAM J. CURRAN III

William J. Curran III was an attorney in the Antitrust Division of the Department of Justice from 1969 to 1975 and has continued to specialize in the field since then. He has served as Editor of *The Antitrust Bulletin* since 1983.

JOEL DAVIDOW

Joel Davidow is a partner in the Washington D.C. law firm Ablondi, Foster, & Sobin where he specializes in the fields of antitrust, international trade, technology transfer, and unfair competion law. He has held various positions at the Federal Trade Commission and is a former Director of Policy Planning and Chief of the Foreign Commerce Section of the Antitrust Division of the Department of Justice. He is Foreign Antitrust Editor of *The Antitrust Bulletin* and a Member of the Advisory Board of the *BNA Antitrust and Trade Regulation Reporter*.

HAMILTON FISH, Jr.

Hamilton Fish, Jr., has been a member of the U.S. House of Representatives since 1969. He is Vice Chairman of the House Judiciary Committee and member of the House-Senate Joint Economic Committee.

JOHN J. FLYNN

John J. Flynn has been a faculty member of the University of Utah College of Law since 1963, specializing in antitrust and business organization. He has served as a consultant to the U.S. Senate Antitrust and Monopoly Subcommittee of the Judiciary Committee and the Bureau of Competition of the Federal Trade Commission and as President of the Section on Antitrust and Economic Regulation of the Association of American Law Schools. He is the author of *Federalism and State Antitrust Regulation*; *Antitrust and Regulatory Alternatives* (with Louis B. Schwartz); *Free Enterprise and Economic Organization: Antitrust* (with Louis B. Schwartz and Harry First); and *Free Enterprise and Economic Organization: Government Regulation* (with Louis B. Schwartz and Harry First). He is a member of the Advisory Board of *The Antitrust Bulletin*.

RALPH H. FOLSOM

With the exception of a stint at the Federal Trade Commission in the late 1970s, Ralph H. Folsom has been a faculty member of the University of San Diego School of Law since 1975, where he specializes in antitrust and law in the People's Republic of China. He is author of *State Antitrust Law and Practice; Antitrust Laws and Trade Regulation, Corporate Competition Law in the European Communities*; and *International Business Transactions* (with Michael Wallace Gordon and John A. Spanogle).

DOUGLAS GINSBURG

In 1983 Douglas Ginsburg left Harvard Law School to become Deputy Assistant Attorney General for Regulatory Affairs. Before being appointed Assistant Attorney General in Charge of the Antitrust Division of the Department of Justice in 1985, he served in the Office of Management and Budget. In 1986

President Ronald Reagan appointed him to the Court of Appeals, District of Columbia Circuit. He is the author of a number of books, including *Antitrust, Uncertainty, and Technological Innovation* and *Regulation of the Electronic Mass Media: Law and Policy for Radio, Television, Cable and the New Video Technologies.*

VALENTINE KORAH

Valentine Korah is Professor of Competition Law at University College, London; she has visited at the Fordham University School of Law on several occasions. She is a member of the Advisory Board of *The Antitrust Bulletin* and the author of *Competition Law of Britain and the Common Market*; *Franchising and the EEC Competition Rules: An Introductory Guide to EEC Competition Law And Practice*; and *Know-how Licensing Agreements and the EEC Competition Rules: Monopolies and Restrictive Practices*.

WILLIAM KOVACIC

William E. Kovacic has experience in government, private practice, and teaching. He served as a Legislative Assistant to the Antitrust Subcommittee of the Senate Judiciary Committee, in the Federal Trade Commission in the Planning Office of the Bureau of Competition, and as Attorney-Advisor to Commissioner George W. Douglas, and then joined the law firm of Bryan, Cave, McPheeters & McRoberts in Washington, D.C. In 1986 he was appointed to the faculty of the George Mason University School of Law, where he specializes in antitrust and government contracts. He has been Chair of the Antitrust and Trade Regulation Section of the Federal Bar Association since 1990. With Joe Sims, he is the author of *The Antitrust Government Contracts Handbook.*

WILLIAM H. PAGE

William H. Page joined the Antitrust Division of the Department of Justice under the Attorney General's Honors Program after graduating from the University of New Mexico School of Law. After three years in the Chicago office he was appointed to the faculty of Boston University School of Law. Since 1981 he has been a member of the faculty of Mississippi College School of Law, where he was named J. Will Young Professor of Law in 1991.

ALMARIN PHILLIPS

Almarin Phillips has taught Economics at the University of Pennsylvania since 1948, specializing in the regulatory process. Codirector of the President's Commission on Financial Structure and Regulation (1970–1971), he also has been a member of the Board of Governors of the Federal Reserve System (1962 –1973). He is the author of *Market Structure, Organization and Performance: An Essay on Price Fixing and Combinations in Restraint of Trade* and *Promoting Competition in Regulated Markets*; and, with Oliver Williamson, he edited *Perspectives on Antitrust Policy*. He is a member of the Advisory Board of *The Antitrust Bulletin*.

PETER WALLACE RODINO, JR.

A member of the U.S. House of Representatives from 1949 to 1989, Peter Wallace Rodino, Jr., was Chairman of the influential House Committee on the Judiciary. After leaving government service he entcred private practice, joining the New Jersey law firm of Rodino and Rodino. He served as a member of President Jimmy Carter's National Committee for the Review of Antitrust Laws and Procedures.

WILLIAM G. SHEPHERD

William G. Shepherd is Chair of the Department of Economics at the University of Massachusetts in Amherst. In 1967–1968, he was Economic Advisor to Assistant Attorney General Donald F. Turner. He has served as President of the Transportation and Public Utilities Group of the American Economic Association (1976) and the Industrial Organization Society (1990) and is a member of the Advisory Board of *The Antitrust Bulletin*. He is the author of *The Treatment of Market Power*; *Public Enterprise: Economic Analysis of Theory and Practice*; *Public Policies Toward Business*; and *Market Power and Economic Welfare*.

RICHARD M. STEUER

Richard M. Steuer has been a partner in the New York City law firm of Kaye, Scholer, Fierman, Hayes & Handler since 1973. He is the author of *A Guide to Marketing Law.*

HANS B. THORELLI / JAMES M. PATTERSON

The publication of his doctoral dissertation, *The Federal Antitrust Policy—Origination of an American Tradition*, in 1955 established Hans B. Thorelli as an authority in the field. Since then, however, most of his work has been in the fields of business planning, marketing, and consumer rights in the North Atlantic Community of nations. His current research efforts are concentrated in the area of strategic planning and structure-strategy-performance relationships in international as well as domestic business. Since 1964 he has been Professor of Business Administration at Indiana University. He served as a member of the President's Advisory Council (1975–1977) and has represented the United States in a number of international negotiations.

James M. Patterson has been Professor of Marketing at the School of Business, Indiana University since 1960. An expert on the structure and performance of the petroleum industry, he is the author of *Marketing: The Firm's Viewpoint* (with S. F. Otteson and W. G. Panschar); *Competition, Ltd.: The Marketing of Gasoline* (with Fred C. Allvine); and *Highway Robbery: An Analysis of the Gasoline Crisis* (with Fred C. Allvine).

DONALD F. TURNER

After a stint in private practice, Donald F. Turner joined the faculty of Harvard Law School in 1954. With the exception of his tenure as Assistant Attorney General in Charge of the Antitrust Division of the Department of Justice (1965–1968), he remained there until his retirement in 1987. Subsequently, he taught at the Georgetown University Law Center (1987–1988) and was a Senior Fellow at the Brookings Institution (1988–1989). With Carl Kaysen, he is the author of *Antitrust Policy.*

Introduction

BY MILTON HANDLER*

In 1982 in an article in the *Columbia Law Review*[1] I urged that, in anticipation of the Sherman Act's centennial, our antitrust jurisprudence be intensively examined in an effort to develop a consensus "on such clarifications and revisions as might be necessary for antitrust to cope with the changing conditions of the remaining years of this and the ensuing ones of next century."[2] In 1987, under the aegis of my lectureship at the Association of the Bar of the City of New York, I arranged a symposium consisting of two sessions, each of which ran an entire day. The addresses delivered at the first session by a galaxy of antitrust luminaries were published in the May 1987 issue of the *California Law Review*.[3] The second session took place in November 1987.

---

* Senior Partner, Kaye, Scholer, Fierman, Hays & Handler.

1 Handler, *Reforming the Antitrust Laws*, 82 COLUM. L. REV. 1287 (1982); N.Y.L.J., April 5–13, 1982, at 1, col. 2.

2 Handler, *Foreword to Symposium: Anticipating Antitrust's Centennial*, 75 CAL. L. REV. 787 (1987).

3 *Symposium: Anticipating Antitrust's Centennial*, 75 CAL. L. REV. 787 (1987). The participants and the titles of their addresses are set

This time the papers were published in the March 1988 issue of the *Cardozo Law Review*.[4]

---

forth in the Table of Contents of the CALIFORNIA LAW REVIEW as follows: *Foreword*, Milton Handler; *The Durability, Relevance, and Future of American Antitrust Policy*, Donald F. Turner; *Comment: Antitrust in the Next 100 Years*, Robert Pitofsky; *The Viability of the Current Law on Horizontal Restraints*, Lawrence A. Sullivan; *Comment: The Sullivan Approach to Horizontal Restraints*, Thomas E. Kauper; *Comment: The Battle for the Soul of Antitrust*, Eleanor M. Fox; *Comment: Horizontal Restraints in Antitrust: Current Treatment and Future Needs*, Harvey J. Goldschmid; *The Viability of Vertical Restraints Doctrine*, William F. Baxter; *Comment: Vertical Restraints and the Secularization of Antitrust*, Earl E. Pollock; *Comment: The Future Viability of the Current Antitrust Treatment of Vertical Restraints*, Sanford M. Litvack; *Monopolization, Mergers, and Markets: A Century Past and the Future*, Phillip Areeda; *Comment: Comparative Advantage and Antitrust Law*, Frank H. Easterbrook; *Comment: Market as Mirage*, Frederick M. Rowe; *Comment: Some Thoughts on Monopoly, Markets, and Mergers*, Michael Malina; *Antitrust, Deregulation, and the Newly Liberated Marketplace*, Stephen G. Breyer; *Comment: Some Additional Safeguards for the Newly Liberated Marketplace*, Louis B. Schwartz; *Comment: Deregulatory Schizophrenia*, Alfred E. Kahn.

4 *Symposium: Anticipating Antitrust's Centennial*, part II, 9 CARDOZO L. REV. 1135 (1988). The participants and the titles of their addresses are set forth in the Table of Contents of the CARDOZO LAW REVIEW as follows: *The Proper Role for Antitrust in a Not-Yet-Global Economy*, Donald I. Baker; *Antitrust in Today's World Economy*, Barry E. Hawk; *The Coexistence of Antitrust Law and Trade Law With Antitrust Policy*, Harvey M. Applebaum; *The Role of Antitrust in an Age of Technology*, Ira M. Millstein; *The Insignificance of Macroeconomics in Patent Antitrust Law: A Comment on Millstein*, Richard A. Posner; *Complex Tradeoffs in Patent Antitrust Law: A Comment on Millstein*, F. M. Scherer; *Balancing the Benefits and Detriments of Private Antitrust Enforcement: Detrebling, Antitrust Injury, Standing, and Other Proposed Solutions*, David Klingsberg; *Federal and State Antitrust Enforcement: Constitutional Principles and Policy Considerations*, Daniel Oliver; *The Appropriate Role of the Antitrust Enforcement Agencies*, Douglas H. Ginsburg; *The Appropriate Enforcement Role of the Government Antitrust Agency*, Sanford M. Litvack; *Open Letter to the New President of the United States*, John H. Shenefield; *Where Do We Go From Here—An Overview*, Milton Handler.

In my overview, which was entitled "Where Do We Go From Here,"[5] I stated:

> Our aim in the symposium was a modest one. The last word has not and cannot be said about any subject which is as pliable and responsive to changing conditions as is our specialty. A law which has been on the books for almost a century—particularly one regarded as part of our unwritten Constitution—is entitled to celebratory proceedings. But it is more important for us to appraise its pluses and minuses—its accomplishments and its shortcomings—its virtues and its deficiencies. Ours is just a beginning. As we approach the centennial, it is to be hoped that the bar associations and universities will place antitrust under the microscope and help in the restatement of its purposes and doctrines so as better to advance the public interest.

I am thus delighted that Dean Kovaleff, my Columbia colleague, has organized the present volume in which a constellation of outstanding specialists and scholars have placed antitrust under the microscope and have endeavored to restate its purposes, its doctrines, and its future. From these and other studies that have been undertaken in the past several years, there should emerge the consensus that I hoped would develop on what antitrust goals should be preserved and what role antitrust should be expected to play in the years ahead.

As well as peering into the future, it is desirable and illuminating to turn to the past to take account of the vicissitudes encountered by antitrust as well as to note its singular accomplishments. The contrast of where antitrust stood five or six decades ago and its situation today helps to put our present inquiry into proper perspective.

The first case book on trade regulation did not appear until 1923.[6] While my own teaching materials were initially circulated in mimeograph form in the late twenties, it was not until 1937 that my *Cases and Materials on Trade Regulation* was published. For years my and Oppenheim's case books were the only two on

---

[5] Handler, *Where Do We Go From Here—An Overview*, 9 CARDOZO L. REV. 1305 (1988).

[6] H. OLIPHANT, CASES ON TRADE REGULATION (1923).

the market.[7] This is to be contrasted with the increased number of case books that are now in active use in the law school world.[8]

Although there were some studies of the various aspects of antitrust,[9] there was no handbook until Sullivan's work came out in 1977[10] and no authoritative treatise until the publication of the various volumes of the Areeda-Turner and Areeda-Hovenkamp treatise starting in 1978. For some years my TNEC No. 38 was the only available brief study of our antitrust doctrines.[11] The first symposium occurred in December 1931 at Columbia.[12]

---

7 M. Handler, Cases and Other Materials on Trade Regulation (1st ed. 1937, Supp. 1947; 2d ed. 1951; 3d ed. 1960, Supps. 1965; 4th ed. 1967, Supps. 1968, 1970). S. C. Oppenheim, Cases on Trade Regulation (1936).

8 M. Handler, H. Blake, R. Pitofsky, H. Goldschmid, Cases and Materials on Trade Regulation (2d ed. 1983); S. C. Oppenheim & G. Weston, Cases and Materials on Unfair Trade Practices (4th ed. 1983); L. Schwartz, J. Flynn, H. First, Free Enterprise and Economic Organization: Antitrust (6th ed. 1983); S. C. Oppenheim & G. Weston, Federal Antitrust Laws, Cases and Comments (4th ed. 1981); P. Areeda, Antitrust Analysis (3d ed. 1981); R. Posner & F. Easterbrook, Antitrust Cases, Economic Notes, and Other Materials (2d ed. 1981).

9 *See, e.g.*, H. B. Thorelli, The Federal Antitrust Policy (1954); M. S. Massel, Competition and Monopoly (1962); C. Kaysen & D. F. Turner, Antitrust Policy (1959); A. D. Neale, The Antitrust Laws of the United States of America (1959); H. Kronstein, J. T. Miller & I. E. Schwartz, Modern American Antitrust Law (1958); E. S. Mason, Economic Concentration and the Monopoly Problem (1957); G. W. Stocking & M. W. Watkins, Cartels or Competition? (1948).

10 L. A. Sullivan, Handbook of the Law of Antitrust (1977).

11 Temporary National Economic Committee, Investigation of Concentration of Economic Power, A Study of the Construction and Enforcement of the Federal Antitrust Laws, 76th Cong., 3d Sess. (Senate Comm. Print, Monograph No. 38, 1941).

12 *The Columbia Symposium on the Anti-Trust Laws*, 18 A.B.A.J. 265 (1932).

Let us pause for a moment to compare the situation today. Abundance has superseded scarcity. There has been a virtual explosion of writings and symposia, the number of which is almost incalculable. Our library shelves are now crowded with books, pamphlets, brochures and articles dealing with the almost infinite combinations and permutations of antitrust rules. No aspect of this corner of the law has escaped the most minute scholarly inquiry. The four issues of the present volume are thus a fitting culmination of the stream of publications that have flowed from the pens of antitrust scholars and practitioners.

In addition to noting this vast explosion of knowledge, it is worth pausing to review the evolution of our antitrust jurisprudence and the cycles of enforcement during its first century. There was meager enforcement in the early years. During the Coolidge administration, the staff of the Justice Department's Antitrust Division was about the size of a corporal's guard. As late as President Roosevelt's first term, when antitrust was temporarily abandoned by the enactment of the National Industrial Recovery Act, there were only a handful of lawyers in the Division whose task then was to enforce the New Deal regulatory measures. It was only with the advent of Thurmond Arnold as Assistant Attorney General in 1938 that antitrust enforcement became a reality. Appropriations increased in almost geometric progression and the size of the staff of both the Antitrust Division and the Federal Trade Commission multiplied to the point where a veritable army has replaced the earlier corporal's guard.[13]

Notwithstanding the sparseness of public enforcement and the fact that the private action did not come into its own until the middle of this century, by 1911 a remarkable *corpus juris* had been developed by the Supreme Court. We normally think of the

---

13 The annual appropriations for the Antitrust Division in the twenties hovered around $250,000, W. HAMILTON & I. TILL, ANTITRUST ACTION 23 (T.N.E.C. Monograph No. 16, 1940), while that for 1988 was $44,937,000. Dept. of Justice Appropriation Act of 1988, Pub. L. No. 100-202, 101 Stat. 1329, 1329-9 (1987).

period prior to 1911 as having been concerned primarily with the initial rejection and ultimate adoption of the rule of reason in the interpretation of section 1. But by that time there were the following solid and substantial contributions to our substantive antitrust law. Horizontal arrangements amongst sellers or buyers fixing prices, dividing markets, or allocating customers had been declared unlawful; concerted boycotts had been outlawed; vertical price agreements had been forbidden; stock acquisitions by major competitive factors lacking any monopoly power had been condemned; the recovery of the overcharge in private treble damage actions based on price-fixing had been upheld; price restrictions in patent license agreements were held permissible and restrictive conduct permitted by the laws of foreign lands in which the act occurred had been excluded from the purview of antitrust.[14]

In subsequent years, these bare-bone rulings were greatly amplified. It is estimated that by 1945 (the year that Chief Justice Stone's tenure ended) the number of Supreme Court antitrust rulings aggregated 156. From that time until the end of the most recent term of Court, the number of decisions had mounted to 396.

In my article on the Supreme Court and the antitrust laws[15] I divided the work of the Court into five periods: (1) the period before 1911; (2) from 1911 to 1920; (3) the years of normalcy and inaction; (4) the New Deal days through the forties; and (5) the years 1950–1967. I noted the important doctrinal developments during these periods which I do not pause to repeat here.

---

14 This paragraph is taken bodily from my paper, *The Supreme Court and the Antitrust Laws: a Critic's Viewpoint*, 1 Ga. L. Rev. 339 (1967), *reprinted in* volume I of my Twenty-Five Years of Antitrust, 89 (1973). In the first chapter in my Antitrust in Perspective (1957), entitled *The Judicial Architects of the Rule of Reason*, I list all of the antitrust decisions either written or participated in by Justice Peckham, Chief Justices White and Taft, and Justices Holmes, Brandeis and Stone.

15 *Id.*

As to section 1, modern antitrust law begins with Justice Stone's seminal opinion in *Trenton Potteries v. U.S.*[16] Justice Douglas built upon that decision in *Socony-Vacuum*.[17] These two cases provide the basis for effectively ridding the economy of classic cartel-types of restraints. There is a vast literature on the varieties of conduct that have been challenged and condemned, based on the invigorated principles derived from these landmark rulings on horizontal collusion.

A word, however, is warranted about the Court's position in regard to vertical restraints. It has stood steadfast in its outlawry of vertical price agreements.[18] The ingenious devices by which businessmen sought to evade the Court's rulings, encouraged at times by its decisions, have ultimately been unsuccessful.[19] The other vertical restraints have had a more checkered history. At first the Court felt that it lacked the information necessary to pass judgment on their validity.[20] Then it applied a strict rule of illegality.[21] Finally, realizing the error of its ways, it put vertical restraints on a sound footing, subjecting them to a rigorous rule of reason of inquiry to determine whether, in point of fact, the restrictions had a serious anticompetitive impact.[22] The Antitrust

---

16 United States v. Trenton Potteries Co., 273 U.S. 392 (1927).

17 United States v. Socony-Vacuum Oil Co., 310 U.S. 150 (1940).

18 *See, e.g.*, Dr. Miles Medical Co. v. John D. Park & Sons Co., 220 U.S. 373 (1911); Monsanto Co. v. Spray-Rite Serv. Co., 465 U.S. 752, 761–762 (1984).

19 *See, e.g.*, United States v. General Elec. Co., 272 U.S. 476 (1926); United States v. Line Material Co., 333 U.S. 287 (1948); Simpson v. Union Oil Co., 377 U.S. 13 (1964); Monsanto Co. v. Spray-Rite Serv. Co., 465 U.S. 752 (1984).

20 United States v. White Motor Co., 372 U.S. 253, 261 (1963).

21 United States v. Arnold, Schwinn & Co., 388 U.S. 365, 379 (1967).

22 Continental T.V., Inc. v. GTE Sylvania, Inc., 433 U.S. 36, 59 (1977).

Division has carried this trend even further with its vertical restraints guidelines.[23]

The merger story is quite different. Before 1950, the Court shifted from one theory to another, leaving the law of mergers under the Sherman Act and original section 7 of the Clayton Act in shambles.[24] Its final decisions before the enactment of the Antimerger Act of 1950, permitted acquisitions with a market share of as much as 65%. This led to the enactment of the Celler-Kefauver Act in 1950.[25] Here again we have a rather sorry spectacle of judicial extremism, best summarized by Justice Stewart's famous pronouncement that the only thing consistent about the Court's merger jurisprudence was that the government always won.[26]

In general terms, the Court initially developed a per se interpretation of the Antimerger Act, holding unlawful any substantial increase in concentration.[27] As a result, this act became an anticoncentration statute rather than an act forbidding mergers that were likely to substantially lessen competition.[28] Since the Court's reading imposed undue fetters on the merger process, a reaction was inevitable. Without overruling its earlier

---

23 U.S. Dep't of Justice Vertical Restraints Guidelines, 50 Fed. Reg. 6263 (Feb. 14, 1985), *reprinted in* 48 Antitrust & Trade Reg. Rep. (BNA) No. 1199, at 3 (Special Supp. Jan. 24, 1985).

24 Handler, *Industrial Mergers and the Antitrust Laws*, 32 COLUM. L. REV. 179, 183 (1932).

25 Celler-Kefauver Act of December 29, 1950, Ch. 1184, 64 Stat. 1125 (codified as amended at 15 U.S.C. § 18 (1982 & Supp. III 1985)).

26 United States v. Von's Grocery Co., 384 U.S. 270, 301 (1965) (Stewart, J., dissenting) ("The sole consistency that I can find is that in litigation under § 7, the Government always wins.").

27 United States v. Pabst Brewing Co., 384 U.S. 546 (1966); United States v. Von's Grocery Co., 384 U.S. 270 (1966).

28 United States v. Philadelphia National Bank, 374 U.S. 321 (1963).

decisions or qualifying its conclusions as to the purposes of the legislation, the Court in due course liberalized the statutory prohibitions in favor of a more realistic assessment of the anticompetitive potential of the mergers that it was called upon to review.[29]

With the advent of the Reagan administration, a 180-degree change in merger enforcement policy occurred. The Turner Guidelines were replaced by those drafted by Assistant Attorney General Baxter. Then those guidelines, which ostensibly codified the new Supreme Court approach, were applied by Prof. Baxter's successors to sanction integrations that plainly contravened Supreme Court precedents that have never been overruled. The pendulum swung from one extreme to another, thus encouraging a merger movement of unprecedented dimension. The test was not whether competition was seriously compromised but whether efficiency was affected. The Celler-Kefauver amendment was thus converted from an anticoncentration to a proefficiency measure, and the public was given the feeling that anything goes.

In their emphasis on efficiency and the absence of any barriers to entry, the enforcement authorities ignored the fact that the statute had as one of its purposes the preservation of small business. When considering the effect of an acquisition on horizontal competition, the plight of suppliers, customers, and the small competitor was disregarded. After all, the small businessman, when competing against the members of a tight oligopoly, may be seriously disadvantaged even though not subjected to unlawful predatory competition. A supplier, again without any illegality, may be put at a substantial disadvantage when his principal customers are four oligopolists in a market depleted of small units. The choices available to consumers can be seriously limited when there are only a handful of suppliers. The legislative history of Celler-Kefauver plainly indicates that these kinds of oligopolistic structures were not what Congress meant to favor, while the atomization of industry, which some of the Black-Douglas decisions encouraged, were likewise not what Congress had in mind.

---

29 United States v. General Dynamics Corp., 415 U.S. 486 (1974).

In my recent annual lecture I inveighed against the present policy of nonenforcement, which I cannot justify either as a matter of policy or under the constitutional principle of the separation of powers.[30] In my view, the executive branch of the government has no veto power over the laws of Congress after their enactment or the decisions of the High Court once they are promulgated. Rather, it is its constitutional duty to enforce both, whether or not they are to its liking.

There was a time when we heard only paeans of praise of antitrust's virtues although to be sure there was always a vocal minority that ascribed all of our economic ills from inflation to our loss of foreign markets to that piece of legislation.

Today, the critics, encouraged by the disfavor with which the Reagan administration held antitrust, now assert that the antitrust laws are obsolete and ought to be repealed. They claim that the fear of antitrust liability within the business community has inhibited the ability of American industry to compete effectively in global markets. We hear that overseas companies, unfettered by antitrust constraints, operate at a distinct advantage over their American counterparts.

The facts do not support these criticisms. There is no question that American firms increasingly face international competition, both in domestic markets and abroad. This does not mean, however, that markets in this country no longer need protection from anticompetitive or monopolistic practices. The antitrust laws are designed to protect markets, and if they are not doing the job effectively, they should be improved. That is what this volume and the symposia that preceded it are all about.

---

30 Handler, *Antitrust Review—1988*, N.Y.L.J., Dec. 15, 1988, at 1, col. 1. My general assertions are documented in a forthcoming paper by James M. Clabault, *Hang Fire: Criminal Antitrust Enforcement 1981–1988*.

I do not burden this introduction with my own views of the adjustments that should be made of our antitrust policies and doctrines. I refer merely to *Reforming the Antitrust Laws*, *supra*, note 1, and my *Foreword and Overview* in the symposia above referred to.

The critics' refrain that foreign companies enjoy the advantages of antitrust-free legal systems is something of a myth. Antitrust enforcement has become more vigorous than ever in the European Community and in Canada, and to a lesser degree in other parts of the world. Most of the foreign companies that have thrived in international competition have done so not because they belong to cartels, but because they have learned to compete in the rough and tumble of rivalry at home and worldwide.

The answer is to insure that antitrust forbids only those practices that threaten competitive markets without discouraging conduct and arrangements that allow American companies to improve their performance and thus to compete to the best of their ability. This in a word is the consensus we are striving to achieve.

I end as I began: A good doctrine has been given to us by Congress and the courts. Following the Biblical injunction, we should not forsake it. The executive branch has the tools to enable our Nation to enjoy the fruits of a viable and salutary *corpus juris* that is designed to safeguard our economic liberties. What is needed is fair, vigorous and effective enforcement.

Dean Kovaleff and his associates have rendered a singular service to the Nation by their vital contribution to our antitrust learning. I salute them and hope that their efforts will bear good fruit.

Part I

Historical Perspective

1
Historical perspective: an introduction

BY THEODORE KOVALEFF

In 1990, the United States celebrated the 100th anniversary of the Sherman Act and the 75th anniversary of the Clayton Act. At such a milestone it is instructive to step back, to attempt to gain the broadest possible perspective, to evaluate the achievements while assessing the failures before setting the course for the next 100 years. In these two volumes, 43 experts in the field of antitrust scrutinize the subject and offer insights into the future of the antitrust impulse. Many of the chapters were published originally in a special volume of *The Antitrust Bulletin*, the leading journal of thought and opinion in the field; they have been revised and expanded, and several additional selections have been included. An especial debt of gratitude is due to the Columbia University Seminars, whose aid allowed this publication to come to fruition.

We have subdivided the topic into three parts: The part that is more historically oriented is contained in volume I; Volume II consists of the more economically and philosophically directed parts. In many ways it is fitting that a contribution by Milton Handler should open the project. No one in any area of the law or legal education

---

For many years, Theodore Kovaleff was an Assistant Dean at the School of Law, Columbia University. He is now Chair, Community Board 9 in the City of New York.

has done more to "put antitrust on the map," no one did more to recognize the anniversaries, and no one has kept the antitrust torch burning more brightly than the Columbia Law School professor who has probably taught the subject to more students than has any other person. The two sections of Volume II are introduced by William E. Kovacic, author of a number of trailblazing analyses of various aspects of the legal system, and William J. Curran III, the extremely able and incisive editor of *The Antitrust Bulletin*.

The antitrust impulse did not suddenly appear in the United States in 1890, like Zeus from the head of Athena, fully developed and a potent force with which to be reckoned. Rather, one can trace the roots of American trade regulation back thousands of years to the reign of Hammurabi. The Babylonian leader's code protected the populace from the unscrupulous who might seek unreasonable profit at the expense of the weak. This usually was in the form of regulating the price that could be charged for a necessity, such as bread. Although archaeologists believe that Hammurabi's Code was not original, but rather a compilation of existing jurisprudence, no earlier evidence of such measures has yet been discovered.

Monopoly, price-fixing, and market division were not unknown in the New World, but almost from the first, drawing on their common law heritage, the English colonists promulgated statutes against regrating, forestalling, and engrossing.[1] As was the economy of the day, the laws were locally oriented. Native Americans do not appear to have shared the antimonopolist outlook, for the Nipmuck Indians went so far as to name a lake near present-day Webster, Massachusetts, Chargoggagoggmanchauggagogg-chaubunagungamaugg, which, in rough translation, means, "You fish on your side, I fish on my side, we both fish in the middle."[2]

---

1 A person who engrossed was one who intercepted goods on the way to market in order to fix the price when he arrived there to sell his goods. An engrosser purchased a commodity wholesale (in gross) and later sold it at a profit, although the goods in question could still be in the wholesale lot. Regrating was buying a necessity in one market with the intent of selling it again at a profit in another market.

2 Recently another translation of the word has been brought to my attention: "You fish on your side; I fish on my side; no one fish in the middle."

The rationale for settlement in what was to become the Thirteen Colonies was unique. Whereas earlier colonization efforts throughout the New World had been based on extractive enterprise, such as those in Latin America that focused on labor- and capital-intensive gold and silver mining, after initial disappointments in Virginia and North Carolina the peopling of British North America was much more individually based. Although certainly not a classless society and although the divisions grew more distinct the farther one traveled southward, there was much less social stratification in the Thirteen Colonies than in contemporary Europe. For the most part a self-selected group of ambitious people, the colonists were independent minded and goal oriented. Both their religious beliefs and their physical environment emphasized personal responsibility. The colonies were thus a fertile breeding ground for the free market concepts Adam Smith would espouse in *The Wealth of Nations.*[3] Although Smith's book was first published in 1776, one cannot cite it as a causal factor in the rush to Revolution. Instead, it highlighted the already extant colonial dissatisfaction with the British mercantile system and its restrictions on individual initiative, be it legitimate or not.

It was in this context that in 1773 mobs in several colonial ports, including Boston, protested a monopoly granted by the British king to the East India Company. The protest took the form of organized boycott, use of substitutes, and, in more than one location, the dumping of the offending product into the harbor. The Tea Party in Boston is better known than its counterparts in New York City or Charleston, South Carolina, where tea was also destroyed or seized, most likely because the British chose to punish the City upon a Hill as an example.[4] The resultant events lead inexorably to the Revolution, causing many historians to cite antimonopoly feelings as one of the roots of the struggle for American independence.

---

3 A. SMITH, THE WEALTH OF NATIONS (Pergamon, ed: 1982).

4 The tea in Charleston was seized and stored for several years until it was finally sold, with the proceeds being used in the Revolutionary effort. In New York, some tea was also thrown into the harbor. The chests in which the tea had been contained were used to fuel a bonfire in front of a building ironically known as the Coffee House. *See* LAWRENCE H. GIPSON, THE BRITISH EMPIRE BEFORE THE AMERICAN REVOLUTION Vol. XII *The Triumphant Empire: Britain Sails into the Storm* (1965) 66–137.

The architects of the central government of the new nation clearly distrusted unchecked centralized power. Be it the short-lived Articles of Confederation or the Constitution, they attempted to divide the bases of power so that no one person or branch could prevail. Not only did the Constitution share authority with the states, but within the federal government responsibilities were divided so as to check and balance functions. The constitutions of the various states were similarly designed to facilitate a permissive and decentralized society, one that would be hospitable, in turn, to economic individualism and to initiative.

The vast expanse of open land to the west beckoned the entrepreneur. As Frederick Jackson Turner later recognized, the existence of the frontier helped to shape the development of the nation.[5] Distant farms and largely isolated cities precluded centralized economic planning. A national infrastructure, made up of a poor transportation network and a virtually nonexistent communications system, stimulated the growth of many local markets served by small concerns. The small size of the enterprises meant that entry was relatively easy, and the large number of firms yielded significant innovations. Furthermore, the lack of any highly profitable, easily transportable product precluded most absentee ownership, thus ensuring on-site proprietorship and further stimulating the already vigorous capitalist impulse.

The Industrial Revolution with its attendant technological advances united tiny localities into regions. As machinery supplemented hand labor in the factory, the building of railroads and canals created the conditions for the amalgamation of local markets into regional ones. The invention of the telegraph facilitated communication, in turn further stimulating economic initiative.

---

5 The first version of his famous paper appeared as *Problems in American History* in a University of Wisconsin publication, The Aegis Nov. 4, 1892. The following summer he delivered a slightly different version of the paper, "The Significance of the Frontier in American History," at a meeting of the American Historical Association held in connection with the Chicago World's Columbian Exposition in July 1893. Subsequently, he explored the ramifications of the thesis in THE FRONTIER IN AMERICAN HISTORY (1920).

The Civil War has been characterized as the Second American Revolution. In that the war induced explosive industrial growth and transformed the economy, the description is valid. The war not only necessitated the deployment of vast armies stretching across the continent, it also demanded a rational system of supply. To this end, Eli Whitney's vision of interchangeable parts was refined to a system of uniform production and standardization. Additionally, the requirements of the war stimulated industrial concentration.

With peace, the lessons of the conflict were not forgotten; and as the American economy began to assume national parameters, consolidation continued at an ever faster rate. Although consolidation was not limited just to railroads, this segment of the economy was more obvious to the general public than were others. With the hammering of the Golden Spike at Promontory Point, Utah, in 1869, the first transcontinental railroad was completed, and the East and West coasts were united. A cause for celebration by some, the rapid growth of railroads was a mixed blessing to others. For many farmers, railroads were the only way to deliver goods to market, and when the railroads merged or formed pools that divided customers, prices rose at a time when farm revenues were declining. Thus it is no surprise that the early efforts at broad-based regulatory action were directed at the railroads and the adjacent storage facilities. Action began on the state level, and when it was tested in the Supreme Court in *Munn v. Illinois*,[6] the right of the state of Illinois to regulate prices of what was in essence a public utility was upheld. Shortly thereafter, the Anti-Monopoly Party ran a candidate for president in 1884, and although it garnered a minuscule total of 175,370 votes [less than 2 percent of the total national vote], its influence was considerably greater than its ballot count.

Although in the *Wabash Case*[7] of 1886 the Supreme Court had invalidated state attempts to regulate interstate rail traffic, within a year the Interstate Commerce Act was enacted, opening the way for

---

6 94 U.S. 113 (1877).

7 Wabash, St. Louis & Pacific Railway. Co. v. State of Illinois, 118 U.S. 557 (1886).

the first non-banking federal regulation of business. Scarcely a year later, in the next presidential election, the Republican Party declared in its platform "opposition to all combinations of capital organized in trusts or otherwise to control arbitrarily the condition of trade among our citizens; . . . [we recommend] to Congress and the State Legislatures . . . such legislation as will prevent the execution of all schemes to oppress the people. . . ." The Democratic Party was slightly less forceful but included a plank opposing trusts: "Judged by Democratic principles, the interests of the people are betrayed, when, by unnecessary taxation, trusts and combinations are permitted and fostered, which, while enriching the few that combine, rob the body of our citizens."[8]

In the same year, Ohio Senator John Sherman introduced his first antitrust bill. Between 1888 and the middle of 1890, many bills and petitions were submitted to Congress; and it was a compromise bill, the work of many that finally bore the name "Sherman Act," which was eventually passed overwhelmingly by a legislature nominally controlled by the Republicans.[9] The House vote of 242 to 0, with 85 abstentions, and the single nay vote in the Senate emphasize the broad-based support for the legislation.[10] Despite the near

---

8 K. PORTER & D. B. JOHNSON COMPS. NATIONAL PARTY PLATFORMS: 1840–1956 (1956).

9 H. THORELLI, THE FEDERAL ANTITRUST POLICY: ORIGINATION OF AN AMERICAN TRADITION 176 (1955). It is interesting to note that very little of Senator Sherman's original work was included in the Act. According to Thorelli, Republican Senator George F. Edmunds of Vermont drafted sections 1, 2, 3, 5, and 6; Senator James Z. George (Democrat, Mississippi) was responsible for section 4; Senator George F. Hoar (Republican, Massachusetts) contributed Section 7; and Senator John J. Ingalls (Republican, Kansas) wrote Section 8. (*Id.* at 212). This situation prompted a rather embittered Senator Hoar to write ironically, "In 1890 a bill was passed which was called the Sherman Act, for no other reason that I can think of except that Mr. Sherman had nothing to do with framing it whatsoever." (*Id.* at 210, quoting from 2 G. F. HOAR, AUTOBIOGRAPHY OF SEVENTY YEARS 363 (1903). It is, however, understandable why the bill was not named for the Massachusetts Senator!

10 The single dissenter was Senator Rufus Blodgett, a Democrat from New Jersey. No explanation of the vote is recorded. *See* vol. 21, pt. 4, CONG. REC. 3153 (1889).

unanimity of the support, the rationale for passage of the statute has been debated for decades. Before he died, James Withrow, Jr., provided the outline of an article for this project detailing some of the intentions of Senator John Sherman; included are new and disturbing but undocumented revelations. Before analyzing the present state of antitrust and its historic goals as a model for the future, Jerrold Van Cise provides his interpretation. He demonstrates that not only were there economic foundations to the laws, there were also social and political bases to the enactment of the Sherman, Clayton, and Federal Trade Commission Acts.[11]

John Siegfried and Michelle Mahony describe the first Sherman Act case, *U. S. v. Jellico Mountain Coal and Coke Company*.[12] Filed by a United States District Attorney in the relatively insignificant Middle District of Tennessee in 1890, the case was won by the Government and not appealed, thus relegating it to near oblivion and denying it the fame and influence likely to have been confirmed upon the first antitrust case to have been heard before the Supreme Court. Had the authors not unearthed the records of the case in the Federal Archives, it would likely have remained no more than a seldom cited, unimportant footnote added to an article by an overly conscientious author. Instead, we now have an analysis of the case and interesting material for comparison with later events.

For the next quarter century additional provisions were added to the antitrust corpus, strengthening it to some extent. In 1894 the Wilson Tariff Act included sections that extended the Sherman Act prohibitions to the importation of goods into the country.[13] In 1908 and 1910 infraction of the Sherman Act was made the basis for cancellation of the rights to certain lands conferred by Congress. In 1912 the Panama Canal Act contained a section that denied the use of the waterway to any transgressor of the law: "No vessel permitted to engage in the coastwise or foreign trade of the United States shall be permitted to enter or pass through the Panama Canal if such ship is

11 15 U.S.C. § 1–11 (1890); 15 U.S.C. § 12–27 (1914); 15 U.S.C. § 41–51 (1914).

12 46 F.432 (C.C.M.D. Tenn. 1891).

13 28 Stat. 570 (1894).

owned, chartered, operated, or controlled by any person or company which is doing business in violation of sections 1 to 11 of this title. . . . "[14]

Probably not by accident, organized labor and farm cooperatives were left vulnerable by the new regulatory legislation; indeed, four of the eight cases filed by the Cleveland administration were directed against some aspect of labor union activity. Only once in the first decade of the 20th century did a bill with provisions designed to provide exemptions to the groups make it through Congress; and that bill was vetoed by President William Howard Taft. Not until the Clayton Act was passed in 1914 did labor unions gain protected status for many, but not all, of their activities.

Despite all the legislative rhetoric and the extensions of the reach of the Sherman Act, the enforcement record was spotty until the presidencies of Theodore Roosevelt and Taft. Eleanor Fox and Lawrence Sullivan analyze actions of TR and trace the growth of differentiation between "good" and "bad" trusts. They demonstrate that politics and power did enter into the equation because by attacking trusts with "bad reputations . . . [he] could maximize the symbolic effect of the prosecutions and assert the administration's executive authority over the enforcement of the antitrust law." They then show how the differentiation between the good and bad trusts evolved or developed into the rule of reason. Briefly, bringing the question to the contemporary period, they note the *Alcoa*,[15] the *United Shoe Machinery*,[16] and finally the *Aspen Skiing*[17] cases to suggest that the law has "circle[d] back to draw upon the old critical distinction between the good and the bad 'trust.' " In *Alcoa* the mere possession of a monopoly position, albeit a sizable one, was found to be illegal; in *Aspen Skiing* a dominant firm may risk anti-

14 15 U.S.C. 31.

15 United States v. Aluminum Company of America, 148 F.2d 416 (2d Cir. 1945).

16 United States v. United Shoe Machinery Co., 110 F. Supp. 295 (D. Mass. 1953), *affirmed* 347 U.S. 521 (1954).

17 Aspen Skiing Co. v. Aspen Highlands Skiing Corp., 495 U.S. 585 (1985).

trust liability when it takes actions which harm a rival if it cannot show that they serve consumers and promote efficiency.

In 1912 the platforms of the three most important political parties all included planks that advocated the strengthening of the antitrust laws. The Democratic platform, branding private monopoly as "intolerable" and "indefensible," backed vigorous enforcement and demanded "the enactment of such additional legislation as may be necessary to make it impossible for private monopoly to exist in the United States."[18] After claiming credit for having "placed upon the statute book . . . the antitrust act of 1890," the Republican platform proclaimed its support of

> the enactment of legislation supplementary to the existing antitrust act which will define as criminal offenses those specific acts that uniformly mark attempts to restrain and to monopolize trade. . . . The same certainty should be given to the Law prohibiting combinations and monopolies . . . in order that no part of the field of business opportunity may be restricted by monopoly or combination. . . . [19]

Although President Taft did not appear to want to increase the certainty or severity of punishment under the law, he did wish to widen the breadth of its coverage.[20] The Progressive Party, led by Roosevelt, was more to the point, favoring "strengthening the Sherman Act" by prohibiting certain trade practices which were legal but "unfair." Furthermore, both the Progressive and the Republican platforms specifically urged the establishment of a strong federal administrative commission to maintain permanent active supervision over corporations engaged in interstate commerce, as, quoting the Progressive platform, "is now done for the railroads by the Interstate Commerce Commission."[21]

The Clayton Act was designed to supplement and extend the

---

18 Porter and Johnson, *supra* note 8, at 169.

19 *Id.* at 178.

20 W. H. Taft, The Anti-Trust Act and the Supreme Court 132–33 (1914).

21 Porter and Johnson, *supra* note 8, at 178.

Sherman Act. With the exception of including exemptions for farm and labor organizations, it did not alter the prohibitions of the Sherman Act; rather, it expanded its ambit, interdicting activities Congress felt had been left uncovered. Most important was the idea of halting problems in their incipiency. Thus whereas the Sherman Act had been directed at present evils, the Clayton Act was aimed against potential problems, whether or not they were currently illegal under the original antitrust statutes.

Almost simultaneously with the approval of the Clayton Act, Congress passed the Trade Commission Act, which created the Federal Trade Commission [FTC] to serve as an administrative body. Congress also endowed it with certain quasi-legislative powers so that it could define unfair competition more exactly and thus determine the areas of its own jurisdiction. The FTC was also given the responsibility of enforcing several sections of the Clayton Act. Since the Department of Justice had also been assigned that task, the two bodies had to coordinate their enforcement activities, a task they have shared to this day.

Despite the fact that the first wave of antitrust fervor reached a high pitch during the first years of Woodrow Wilson's tenure as President, it quickly waned. In reality, antitrust was not high on his agenda; more important was tariff reduction and revision of the banking system. Furthermore, events in Europe cast a shadow over reform opportunities in the New World. Several critics have noted wryly that within hours of the birth of the Federal Trade Commission, World War I began.[22]

As the antitrust ardor waned, the number of exemptions to the corpus grew. Beginning with the labor and farm cooperative exemptions included in the Clayton Act, the trend continued with the Webb-Pomerene Act of 1918,[23] exempting export associations, and the Merchant Marine Act of 1920, sheltering marine insurance.[24] During the 1920s the immunities gained by farmers, dairymen, ranchers, and

22 Lowell B. Mason to author (Apr. 22, 1971). Mason had been a member and critic of the FTC during the Truman administration.

23 40 Stat. 516 (1918).

24 41 Stat. 988 (1920).

fruit growers presaged the National Recovery Administration [NRA] experiment in cartelization. Although the Schechter decision.[25] is commonly credited with ending the NRA, its "Blue Eagle" philosophy was not retired. Subsequent legislation covering aspects of farming, bituminous coal mining, labor activities, oil production, trucking and air transportation was better drafted and therefore survived the Supreme Court test.[26] There was also another side to the New Deal, however, for at the very same time as the Civil Aeronautics Act was being enacted, Thurman Arnold was establishing the Temporary National Economic Committee [TNEC]. Historians have tended to ignore the implications of the regulatory legislation and have concentrated instead on the TNEC, citing it as the beginning of a second wave of antitrust enforcement. The Arnold-led hearings and reports focused national attention on the subject; had World War II and "preparedness" not intervened, the shape of the American economy might well have been changed significantly. On the other hand, one can also argue that the pendulum might just as well have swung back to the "associationalism" of the 1920's and early 1930's.

After World War II many people feared the return of the Depression; with this climate of opinion, the chances for a return to the vigor of the TNEC were dim. But antitrust was not to die. Even during this period, Representative Emanuel Cellar and Senator Estes Kefauver were able to amend the Clayton Act, closing a loophole that had precluded the successful utilization of the statute up to that time. Although the election of Dwight Eisenhower in 1952 seemed to presage a "vacation from antitrust," the record of his administration demonstrates that the corpus was still supported equally by both major political parties.[27]

---

25 295 U. S. 495 (1935).

26 Some historians note that the Court-packing struggle may well have played a role in the deliberations. Thus while Roosevelt may have lost the Court battle, he actually won the war. *See, e.g.,* W. LEUCHTENBURG, FRANKLIN ROOSEVELT AND THE NEW DEAL: 1932–1940, 233–39 (1963). Leuchtenburg goes on to note that in another way, FDR actually also *lost* the war because the struggle with Congress produced scars that did not heal for many years.

27 *See, e.g.*, T. P. KOVALEFF, BUSINESS AND GOVERNMENT DURING THE EISENHOWER ADMINISTRATION: A STUDY OF THE ANTITRUST POLICY OF THE ANTITRUST DIVISION OF THE JUSTICE DEPARTMENT (1980).

The role of economics and antitrust have always been intertwined; yet it was not until the *United Shoe Machinery* case[28] that economists gained warranted recognition as a young scholar named Carl Kaysen advised Judge Wyzanski throughout the deliberations. Donald Dewey briefly analyzes the role of economists in the area of antitrust and then views it inversely, inquiring into the influence of antitrust on the national economy. His conclusions will satisfy neither those who believe that the laws have played a positive role in America's economic development nor those of the Chicago School, some of whom go so far as to suggest that the corpus serves no positive purpose whatsoever and, thus, should be repealed. Edwin Zimmerman, a former chief of the Antitrust Division during the last days of the Carter presidency, traces the infusion of economic theory into Clayton Act enforcement beginning with the *Brown Shoe*[29] case. From the Eisenhower era onward, each administration had its own ideas about what made a merger illegal; although they were not secret, they had to be gleaned from speeches of the Assistant Attorney General, from press releases, and from informal rulings. Such a situation bred uncertainty and may actually have stimulated corporate marriages that might not have been consummated had there been concrete guidelines. Not until 1968 did the Department of Justice actually publish its first set of rules. As time passed (and administrations changed), the guidelines evolved and were subsequently replaced in 1982, in 1984, and again in 1992. Edwin M. Zimmerman analyzes the first three redactions, noting that they have changed faster than the Supreme Court precedent which should have been driving the policy, thus creating new and different uncertainties for all concerned.

In the 1960's and early 1970's, although enforcement was uneven, the record in litigated cases carried up to the Supreme Court was a hitherto unmatched series of victories for antitrust enforcement. Indeed, in his devastating dissent in *Von's Grocery*, Justice Stewart would write:

---

28 *Supra* note 16.

29 United States v. Brown Shoe Co. 370 U.S. 294 (1962).

> In a single sentence and an omnibus footnote at the close of its opinion, the Court pronounces its work consistent with the line of our decisions under § 7 since the passage of the 1950 amendment. The sole consistency that I can find is that in litigation under § 7, the Government always wins.[30]

Nevertheless, breakthroughs in many areas began to change the patterns of world trade during this period. Markets that were previously defined in national or regional terms began to assume global parameters. As railroads had united the country in the post-Civil War period, so now cheap, easily available, and reliable air transport broadened many a market. Disciples of the Chicago School quickly found a home in the Reagan administration, and enforcement policy changed course as the antitrusters factored the ever-shrinking world into their equations.

Whether Chicago School analysis was correct or whether its disciples may have overreacted is a matter of debate. Charles Rule, Reagan's last Antitrust Chief, and David Meyer present the administration side of the argument and seek to demonstrate that "merger enforcement under the Sherman and Clayton Acts has never been more effective." One of the best explanations of the Reagan policy in the area, it details the effects of increased foreign competition on the American economy and on Justice Department enforcement policy.

In my offering I attempt to provide a nonpartisan assessment of the Reagan record. Certain to disappoint the stalwarts of all political stripes, I reject the idea of there having been a "Reagan Revolution" in the field. Rather, I submit, it was an "evolution albeit speeded up," as the foundations for many of the changes had been laid during the Carter administration.

James Rill, the first Assistant Attorney General in charge of the Antitrust Division for President George Bush sets forth his philosophy: Chicago School, modified to avoid some of the excesses of the previous years. The pendulum continued its swing back toward the center as Charles James, who assumed the helm at the Division for

---

30 384 U.S. 270, 301.

the final year of the Bush administration, followed onward in his philosophical footsteps. Clearly, with the appointment of Anne Bingaman, the evolution will continue during the Clinton administration.

Over the years not only the interpretations but also the legal foundations of the corpus have evolved. Robert McGuckin analyzes the changes wrought with the passage of the Hart-Scott-Rodino Antitrust Improvements Act.[31] He describes how after a merger was initially proposed, explanatory papers and forms had to be filed, paving the way, if necessary, for negotiations to be conducted between the companies and the enforcement agencies. A major question today is whether the proposed merger fits into the most recent set of guidelines. Only if the bargaining between the government and the merger partners fails does the government have to resort to court action. McGuckin describes it succinctly: "merger enforcement left the court room after 75 years"; it has now entered the conference room. The lower number of cases filed, therefore, does not mean that enforcement has been relaxed; rather, it means that as policy is better defined and the parameters more clearly drawn, specific rules can be scrutinized beforehand and legal confrontations can be avoided more easily.

The statement, "The past is prologue," leads a number of the contributors to consider the future of antitrust enforcement and how to make certain it is efficiently implemented.

The quartet of Ernest Gellhorn, Charles James, Richard Pogue, and Joe Sims analyzes the Department of Justice and FTC's shared enforcement arrangement and concludes that it is neither efficient nor fair. They believe that one agency should have total responsibility. After analyzing the history of enforcement and considering all the alternatives, they conclude that the simplest solution would be to place the enforcement responsibility with the Department of Justice. From a slightly different perspective, former Assistant Attorney General Thomas Kauper also offers his ideas on the problem. He argues that a new agency would not be the answer, that "Few

---

31 PL 94–435 (1976).

believe that the Federal Trade Commission's procedures have been superior to those of courts in antitrust cases," and that the Antitrust Division will, and should, remain the leading actor.

Stephen Rhoades and Jim Burke see the change in enforcement patterns as the result of much different factors. They demonstrate that a "confluence of economic and political thinking" was the primary cause of the "remarkable turnabout in enforcement of section 7 during the 1980s." They proceed to dissect the economic foundations of the new thinking, and they then conclude that many questions remain, thus suggesting that the pendulum may yet swing back to a more vigorous enforcement policy as we enter antitrust's second century.

Louis Schwartz expands upon the pendulum theory, adapting Arthur M. Schlesinger's cyclical approach to American political history[32] to an evaluation of antitrust ardor and enforcement. Not as optimistic as Schlesinger, who sees a probable liberal recrudescence in the 1990s, Schwartz predicts that the Supreme Court will come to wield great influence over the future direction of antitrust enforcement. He sadly notes that the earliest prospective retirements will be "pro antitrust" jurists, thus precluding the chance for "positive change" emanating from the High Court for some time.

Walter Adams and James Brock are keenly interested in the question of power relationships and expand here on their treatment of this topic in *The Bigness Complex*.[33] As the Constitution was meant to be the model for a system of governance designed to control power, so, too, they view the Sherman Act as designed to prevent "the autocrats of trade from fashioning an *economic* [sic] feudalism" and to preserve the competitive market as the primary regulator of economic affairs. One hundred years after the passage of the first act, seventy-five years after the Clayton Act, they dissect the anatomy of economic power in America. They conclude that the need for controlling power is as persistent today as it was in 1890,

---

32 A. M. Schlesinger, THE CYCLES OF AMERICAN HISTORY 23–48 (1986).

33 W. ADAMS & J. W. BROCK, THE BIGNESS COMPLEX: INDUSTRY, LABOR, AND GOVERNMENT IN THE AMERICAN ECONOMY (1986).

1914, or 1950. The economic fallout of unregulated power ranges from unreasonably high prices to a lack of innovation or technological advance. There are negative consequences in the geopolitical arena as corporate interests may sway public policy. As it was in the past, the task for antitrust today and tomorrow is to help fetter this power for the public good.

As we celebrate the centennial of the Sherman Act, it has been nearly a decade since any divestiture occurred as a result of the statute. And the breakup of the American Telephone and Telegraph Company, in simple dollar measure the largest action in history, has received mixed reviews from the American public. Additionally, there has been little or no outcry against the wave of mergers that have been consummated over the same period. Ironically, it seems as if more voices have been raised against the recent flood of leveraged buyouts; yet, in most instances, these have resulted ultimately in some deconcentration in their industry. Usually after a "restructuring," divisions are spun off or sold to raise cash to pare down the debt incurred in the transaction. Perhaps the publicity of the anniversary will awaken the public perceptions and facilitate the focusing of their reactions to the ongoing changes in the American economy.

It is to be hoped that these contributions will play a part in stimulating thought and debate concerning the role of antitrust in its next century. Out of this must result a blueprint for the future. Clearly, times have changed and the old tested answers, no matter how valid they were in the past, may not meet the new requirements of the 21st century. Whereas once there may have been a good antitrust argument for the breaking up of General Motors, today, with the changed market, it is neither necessary nor would it be sound policy. (Instead, ironically, today there may be a legitimate corporate argument for a "restructuring" which might ultimately have a similar effect.) Nevertheless, in the new world market there is indeed a need for a policy which will protect the American consumer and, at the same time, enhance the ability of American business to compete and prosper in the new environment. The Sherman and Clayton Acts will continue to have an important role to play in this process.

2
Did Sherman want to break the "trusts"?

BY JAMES R. WITHROW, JR.

In this day of scandal, bribes, and paybacks I am moved to add to the folklore surrounding the Sherman Act enactment in 1890. It fell to my lot to have as a friend and client an elderly but active financial man who often reminisced about his first job. In the 1880's and 1890's he was a special messenger/office boy for John D. Rockefeller at 26 Broadway in New York City. Among his duties was to ride down in the elevator eavesdropping on persons who had just left an important meeting with J. D. Rockefeller. Having performed this service he was given other sensitive jobs. He told me that on one occasion he was given an envelope that he was to deliver to Senator Sherman. John D. told him that it contained $10,000 and that the Senator had assured him that the antitrust law to be passed would be quite mild and without real teeth.

My client has been dead for a quarter of a century, and until now I have respected the confidential (but nonpriviledged) nature

EDITOR'S NOTE: *Prior to his death, Mr. Withrow was planning to develop this outline into a full-blown article.*

of his communication. I can, of course, not vouch for the accuracy, but I certainly believed it at the time I was told.

In view of the two decades that passed before the full attack on the Standard Oil Trust (221 U.S. 1 (1911)), it would seem that the Sherman Act appeared to be and was in fact quite toothless.

While reminiscing, I would like to add another more personal experience. At Christmas time in 1934 I was pounding the pavements looking for a job. I had an introduction to Charles Wesley Dunn, a leader of the Antitrust Bar in New York. In the interview, which one of his clients had set up, he flatly said that he was not hiring anyone because "the Sherman and Clayton Acts were dead." Little did he foresee the *Schechter* decision and the revival that these laws would receive under the leadership of Thurman Arnold and his dedicated small band of Division lawyers.

If there is any conclusion to be shown from the Senator Sherman and Charles Wesley Dunn incidents, it is that the Sherman Act has a basic effective vitality which emerges from time to time in an effort to safeguard competition in America. Those who believe that the antitrust laws have lost their vitality had best beware. The older belief in unfettered competition may again replace the structured concepts so popular with some economists and used as a part of the philosophy of the Antitrust Division of recent years.

Based upon history, business communities should well be aware of a return to a more simple and straightforward concept of workable competition.

3
Antitrust past—present—future

BY JERROLD G. VAN CISE*

The life of the law "has not been logic: it has been experience."[1] In antitrust, accordingly, the law has reflected its experience in pursuing the social and economic goals of Congress. Presently, however, it is urged to follow the logic of an economic theory. In the future, therefore, antitrust must choose between its past experience with legislative goals and the present logic of a theory.

The past

The law

RESTRAINT OF TRADE. In his 1888 Message to Congress, President Cleveland warned that trusts, combinations and monopolies were becoming "the people's master."[2] A year later, President

---

* Retired member of the New York and D.C. bars.

1 OLIVER WENDELL HOLMES, JR., THE COMMON LAW 1 (1881).

2 Fourth Annual Message of President Grover Cleveland (Dec. 3, 1888), *reprinted in* E. KINTNER, THE LEGISLATIVE HISTORY OF THE FEDERAL ANTITRUST LAWS AND RELATED STATUTES, part I at 57, 58 (1978) [hereinafter KINTNER].

Harrison requested Congress to take action with respect to these restraints.[3] Thereafter, the Senators who drafted the Sherman Act reported that the "popular mind" had become agitated by the "inequality of condition, of wealth, and opportunity" which had resulted from this concentration of capital into "vast combinations,"[4] and called them a "menace to republican institutions themselves."[5]

Sherman bill In 1890, Senator Sherman introduced a bill that he described as a "bill of rights, a charter of liberty."[6] His proposal was said to have two legislative goals:

(1) Initially, the bill sought to prohibit combinations that tend to "prevent full and free competition."[7] Its purpose was to incorporate into federal law a common law principle that condemned combinations that "affect injuriously the industrial liberty" of citizens. "Industrial liberty" was defined by the Senator as "the right of every man to work, labor and produce . . . on equal terms and conditions. . . . This is industrial liberty . . . ."[8]

(2) Next, the bill prohibited combinations that tend to "advance the cost to the consumer."[9] The objective of this further provision was to adopt as federal law another common law principle that outlawed combinations that "increase the

---

3 First Annual Message of President Benjamin Harrison (Dec. 3, 1889), *reprinted in* KINTNER, *supra* note 2, at 60.

4 Remarks of Senator Sherman, 21 CONG. REC. 2460 (1890), *reprinted in* KINTNER, *supra* note 2, at 123.

5 Remarks of Senator Hoar, 21 CONG. REC. 3146 (1890), *reprinted in* KINTNER, *supra* note 2, at 282.

6 Remarks of Senator Sherman, *supra* note 4, KINTNER at 126.

7 Amendment to S.1, 51st Cong., 1st Sess. (1890), *reprinted in* KINTNER, *supra* note 2, at 112.

8 Remarks of Senator Sherman, *supra* note 4, KINTNER at 116.

9 S.1, *supra* note 7, at 2, KINTNER at 112.

profits of the producer at the cost of the consumer."[10] The Senator denied that increased efficiency through better methods of production could justify such combinations, because "all experience shows that this saving of cost goes to the pockets of the producer."[11]

Sherman Act Eventually, Senators Edmunds and Hoar revised the Sherman bill, and their revision was enacted into law as the Sherman Act.[12] The first section of the revision solved a jurisdictional issue raised in the debates on the original bill, and used language from the common law to prohibit contracts, combinations and conspiracies "in restraint of trade." A new section 2 then provided that "every person," either alone or with "any other person," was prohibited from monopolizing or attempting to monopolize.

The Senators explained that their revision, like the Sherman bill, was intended to "extend," to interstate commerce, the "old" common law principles[13] that had condemned the use, whether by a single person or by a combination, of "means which prevent other men from engaging in fair competition."[14]

UNFAIRNESS OF TRADE In 1913, presidential candidate Woodrow Wilson declared that the "ideals of absolutely free opportunity" in our economy were now being undermined by big business. While trusts and monopolies had been abolished, the laws "do not prevent the strong from crushing the weak" and so "dominate the industry and the economic life of this country."[15] Upon his election, therefore, the House Committee on the Judiciary responded with a report that the "great and powerful" were

---

10 Remarks of Senator Sherman, *supra* note 4, KINTNER at 116.

11 *Id.* at 122.

12 26 Stat. 209, 15 U.S.C. §§ 1-2 (1890).

13 Remarks of Senator Hoar, *supra* note 5, KINTNER at 282.

14 *Id.* at 293.

15 R. CURRENT & J. GARRATY, WORDS THAT MADE AMERICAN HISTORY 214, 219 (1962).

using price discrimination, exclusive dealing and tying practices to destroy independent competitors, and recommended the adoption of legislation to prohibit "unfair" use of these practices.[16] Subsequently, the Senate Committee on the Judiciary likewise urged the enactment of such legislation which, "by making these practices illegal," will "arrest the creation" of trusts, conspiracies and monopolies "in their incipiency."[17]

Clayton Act The Clayton Act was enacted into law,[18] therefore, which provided in sections 2 and 3 that discrimination, exclusive dealing and tying were prohibited "where the effect . . . may be [not "is"] to substantially lessen competition."[19] In addition, the Federal Trade Commission Act was passed empowering the Commission to proceed against both these and other "unfair methods of competition."[20]

In approving the two acts, President Wilson stated that their common purpose was "to make men in a small way of business as free to succeed as men in a big way," and thereby to insure that "American genius and initiative are not guided by a few men" exclusively "but made rich by the activities of a multitude."[21]

1936 Amendment Two decades later, section 2 of the Clayton Act was amended by the Robinson-Patman Act[22] to prohibit

---

16 H.R. Rep. No. 627, 63d Cong., 2d Sess. 8-10 (1914), *reprinted in* Kintner, *supra* note 2, at 1090–92.

17 S. Rep. No. 698, 63d Cong., 2d Sess. 1 (1914), *reprinted in* Kintner, *supra* note 2, at 1744.

18 38 Stat. 730, 15 U.S.C. §§ 12–27 (1914).

19 Remarks of Senator Chilton, 51 Cong. Rec. 16001 (1914), *reprinted in* Kintner, *supra* note 2, at 2629.

20 38 Stat. 717, 15 U.S.C. §§ 41–51 (1914).

21 Letter from President Woodrow Wilson to Representative Oscar Underwood (Oct. 17, 1914), 51 Cong. Rec. A1187, *reprinted in* Kintner, *supra* note 2, at 2838–39.

22 49 Stat. 1526, 15 U.S.C. § 13 (1936).

discrimination in price or certain practices when its effect might be injurious to competition either between big and small buyers or between national and local sellers, in order further to preserve "equality of opportunity" in the nation's markets.[23]

STRUCTURE OF TRADE In 1949, the House Committee on the Judiciary reported that acquisitions and mergers had been contributing to a "high level" of "economic concentration" that threatened "capitalism" itself, by placing "great economic power" in the hands of "a few corporations."[24] The committee therefore proposed amending section 7 of the Clayton Act to bar acquisitions and mergers involving either stock or assets where their effect would not be "so far-reaching" as to amount to a violation of the Sherman Act.

1949 bill The House Judiciary Committee intended, by its proposed section 7 amendment, to prohibit acquisitions and mergers that would (1) eliminate a "substantial factor in competition," or (2) increase the relative size of an acquiring company "to such a point that its advantage over its competitors threatens to be decisive," or (3) unduly reduce "the number" of competitors, or (4) establish relationships between buyers and sellers that "deprive their rivals of a fair opportunity to compete."[25]

1950 Act The Senate Committee on the Judiciary approved the House bill, with minor changes, and it was enacted into law as a new section 7 of the Clayton Act.[26] The committee agreed with a report of the Federal Trade Commission that had opposed the conversion of markets, through successive small acquisitions, from " 'one of intense competition among many enterprises' "

---

23 H.R. REP. No. 2287, 74th Cong., 2d Sess. 3, 6, *reprinted in* KINTNER, *supra* note 2, at 3183, 3186.

24 H.R. REP. No. 1191, 81st Cong., 1st Sess. 2–3, 13 (1949), *reprinted in* KINTNER, *supra* note 2, at 3463, 3472.

25 *Id.* at 8, *reprinted in* KINTNER, *supra* note 2, at 3468.

26 64 Stat. 1125, 15 U.S.C. § 18 (1950).

to one with only " 'three or four large concerns' ";[27] and it stressed that the Clayton Act language (*i.e.*, where the effect "may be" substantially to lessen competition) would enable section 7 to limit "future increases in the level of economic concentration" and thereby aid in "preserving small business as an important competitive factor in the American economy."[28]

The courts

RESTRAINT OF TRADE The Supreme Court, in its famous 1911 *Standard Oil* interpretation of the Sherman Act, ruled that "the main cause" that led to the Sherman Act was the "vast accumulation of wealth in the hands of corporations and individuals" and a "widespread impression that their power had been and would be expected to oppress individuals and injure the public generally."[29] It then held that the provisions of the Act were intended to apply common law principles to federal law, in order to insure that (1) an "individual" had the "right to carry on his trade or calling,"[30] which right was not to be "unreasonably" restrained,[31] and (2) the "public" was to be protected from "enhancement of prices and other wrongs."[32]

In subsequent cases, the Supreme Court has stressed that the Act was designed to be a "comprehensive charter of economic liberty aimed at preserving free and unfettered competition."[33] The statute seeks "to secure equality of opportunity, and to

---

27 S. REP. No. 1775, 81st Cong., 2d Sess. 5 (1950), *reprinted in* KINTNER, *supra* note 2, at 3524.

28 *Id.* at 3, *reprinted in* KINTNER, *supra* note 2, at 3522–23.

29 Standard Oil Co. v. United States, 221 U.S. 1, 50 (1911).

30 *Id.* at 51.

31 *Id.* at 56.

32 *Id.* at 52, 58.

33 Northern Pac. Ry. v. United States, 356 U.S. 1, 4 (1958).

protect the public'';[34] and the "freedom guaranteed each and every business, no matter how small, is the freedom to compete."[35]

Rule of reason In applying these Sherman Act principles to alleged restraints of trade, the courts have resorted to a "rule of reason" (also originating in the common law)[36] to determine, case by case, whether the "main" purpose of a challenged restraint of trade was lawful, and, if it was, whether the resulting effect was "reasonably" ancillary to this lawful purpose.

Application of rule The Court, in applying this rule of reason, has approved both horizontal[37] and vertical[38] restraints where efficiency was the "main" purpose of the parties, and any ancillary effect did not "unreasonably" conflict with the two goals of antitrust.

But it has condemned any restraint involving the rights of competitors when either its purpose[39] or subsequent effect[40] "restricts . . . the liberty of a trader to engage in business,"[41] even though he might be only one small merchant.[42] Again, it has prohibited any restraint affecting the rights of consumers where

---

34 Chas. A. Ramsay Co. v. Associated Bill Posters, 260 U.S. 501, 512 (1923) and United States v. American Linseed Oil Co., 262 U.S. 371, 388 (1923).

35 United States v. Topco Assocs., Inc., 405 U.S. 596, 610 (1972).

36 United States v. Addyston Pipe & Steel Co., 85 F. 271, 380–3 (6th Cir. 1898), *aff'd*, 175 U.S. 211 (1899).

37 Broadcast Music, Inc. v. Columbia Broadcasting Sys., Inc., 441 U.S. 1 (1979).

38 Continental T.V. Inc. v. GTE Sylvania, Inc., 443 U.S. 36 (1977).

39 Otter Tail Power Co. v. United States, 410 U.S. 366 (1973).

40 Associated Press v. United States, 326 U.S. 1 (1945).

41 Loewe v. Lawlor, 208 U.S. 274, 293 (1908).

42 Klor's, Inc. v. Broadway-Hale Stores, Inc., 359 U.S. 207, 213 (1959).

either its purpose[43] or effect[44] was unduly to injure buyers of goods or services, in rulings condemning even the "ethical" restrictions imposed by the legal profession.[45]

UNFAIRNESS OF TRADE The Supreme Court, in its interpretations of the Clayton Act, has recognized that section 2 seeks to "assure, to the extent reasonably practicable, that businessmen at the same functional level would start on equal competitive footing as far as price is concerned."[46] On the one hand, volume purchases that yield cost savings to the seller could justify a lower price to the buyer,[47] and discrimination to meet competition in good faith is also lawful.[48] On the other hand, territorial discrimination intended "to eliminate a competitor"[49] and preferential treatment whose effect is to give "a competitive advantage" to large buyers[50] are unlawful.

With respect to section 3 of the Clayton Act and section 5 of the Federal Trade Commission Act, the Court has condemned the use of exclusive dealing as a "device" to sew up a market "for the benefit of a few."[51] A long-term requirement contract making possible reductions in costs and affecting an insubstantial share of the market has been approved.[52] But, a network of exclusive dealing contracts whose effect is to foreclose "opportunity" for

---

43 United States v. Socony-Vacuum Oil Co., 310 U.S. 150 (1940).

44 National Soc'y of Professional Eng'rs v. United States, 435 U.S. 679 (1978).

45 Goldfarb v. Virginia State Bar, 421 U.S. 773 (1975).

46 FTC v. Sun Oil Co., 371 U.S. 505, 520 (1963).

47 United States v. Borden Co., 370 U.S. 460 (1962).

48 Great Atl. & Pac. Tea Co. v. FTC, 440 U.S. 69 (1979).

49 Moore v. Mead's Fine Bread Co., 348 U.S. 115, 118–19 (1954).

50 FTC v. Morton Salt Co., 334 U.S. 37, 42–43 (1948).

51 FTC v. Motion Picture Advertising Serv. Co., 344 U.S. 392, 394–95 (1953).

52 Tampa Elec. Co. v. Nashville Coal Co., 365 U.S. 320 (1961).

competitors,[53] and tying contracts that have a similar competitive impact,[54] have been disapproved.

Generally, the Court has ruled that both the Clayton and the Federal Trade Commission Acts were intended to advance the public interest "by securing fair opportunity for the play of the contending forces ordinarily engendered by an honest desire for gain."[55]

STRUCTURE OF TRADE Concerning the application of the Clayton Act to acquisitions and mergers, the Supreme Court has explained that the "dominant theme pervading congressional consideration" of the 1950 revision of section 7 was the fear of a "rising tide of economic concentration" and the desirability of "protection of small business." Congress, therefore, had rejected the "standards" of the Sherman Act and instead had adopted the stricter "may be" prohibition of the Clayton Act in order to bar mergers with a "probable anticompetitive effect."[56]

Accordingly, the Court has held that two small rivals may justify their merger where this creates a more efficient and viable competitor in an industry dominated by large companies,[57] and that a large company may acquire substantial competitive assets that it must have in order "to compete effectively."[58] But it has decided that "[p]ossible economies" cannot be used as a defense of an acquisition, by a powerful potential competitor, of a smaller but dominant firm in a related market.[59]

---

53 Standard Oil Co. v. United States, 337 U.S. 293, 314 (1949).

54 International Salt Co. v. United States, 332 U.S. 392, 396 (1947).

55 FTC v. Sinclair Ref. Co., 261 U.S. 463, 475–76 (1923).

56 Brown Shoe Co. v. United States, 370 U.S. 294, 315 *et seq.* (1962).

57 *Id.*

58 United States v. General Dynamics Corp., 415 U.S. 486 (1974).

59 FTC v. Procter & Gamble Co., 386 U.S. 568, 577–80 (1967).

In other decisions, the Court has prohibited (as the House Judiciary Committee had intended in drafting revised section 7) horizontal mergers whose effect was (1) to eliminate a substantial competitor,[60] or (2) to increase substantially the relative size of a major competitor in a concentrated market,[61] or (3) to contribute to a trend toward an undue reduction in the number of competitors,[62] and has also barred both vertical and conglomerate mergers involving buyers and sellers that (4) deprive rivals of a fair opportunity to compete.[63]

The present

The law

RESTRAINT OF TRADE In 1981, Attorney General William Smith announced that the policy of the Department of Justice would continue to be the "promotion of competition." But he cautioned that "bigness in business does not necessarily mean badness" and emphasized that "efficient firms should not be hobbled under the guise of antitrust enforcement."[64]

Thereafter, Assistant Attorney General William Baxter, in charge of the Antitrust Division, declared: "Although not always . . . corporate size would seem to be a symptom of efficiency and success,"[65] and that the "sole goal of antitrust is economic

---

60 United States v. Philadelphia Nat'l Bank, 374 U.S. 321 (1963).

61 United States v. Phillipsburg Nat'l Bank & Trust Co., 399 U.S. 350 (1970).

62 United States v. Aluminum Co. of America, 377 U.S. 271 (1964).

63 United States v. E. I. du Pont de Nemours & Co., 353 U.S. 586 (1957); Ford Motor Co. v. United States, 405 U.S. 562 (1972); FTC v. Consolidated Foods Corp., 380 U.S. 592 (1965).

64 *Attorney General William French Smith's Remarks to D.C. Bar (June 24, 1981)*, Antitrust & Trade Reg. Rep. (BNA) No. 1021, at H-1, H-2 (July 2, 1981).

65 *Interview with Assistant Attorney General William F. Baxter*, Antitrust & Trade Reg. Rep. (BNA) No. 1025, at AA-2 (July 30, 1981).

efficiency."[66] His successor, in turn, reported that currently "the sole basis of antitrust enforcement" should be based "on economic efficiency notions."[67]

In 1987, Assistant Attorney General Charles Rule explained this stress on "efficiency" as follows: " 'Consumer welfare' is the guiding principle of this Administration's antitrust enforcement policy." The objective of such a "consumer welfare standard" is to "efficiently" allocate resources, and thus to "maximize the well-being of society," *i.e.*, to "maximize total surplus." As Congress prohibited "economic conduct that violates economic criteria," the antitrust laws should be construed to prohibit "commercial conduct that threatens the economic fruits of competition," namely, "consumer welfare." He added: "The Chicago School" of economics is "the mainstream."

Subsequently, he conceded that the result of this "effort to anchor antitrust to sound economic principles" has been the "decrease in civil enforcement statistics"; but he stated that this merely "reflects the fact that federal enforcement agencies no longer file cases based on unsound theories."[68]

UNFAIRNESS OF TRADE In 1983, Chairman James Miller of the Federal Trade Commission in his turn announced that—with respect to every initiative proposed to this agency—the Commission now asks: (1) "would we prevail in the courts?" and (2) "would our action increase economic efficiency and benefit consumers?" Only if "the answer to both questions is in the affirmative should we proceed."[69]

---

66 Taylor, *A Talk with Antitrust Chief William Baxter*, Wall S. J. Mar. 4, 1982, at 28, cols. 3, 5.

67 *60 Minutes with J. Paul McGrath, Assistant Attorney General*, 54 ANTITRUST L.J. 131 (1985).

68 Remarks of Charles F. Rule, Assistant Attorney General, at the 21st New England Antitrust Conference, 3-10 (Nov. 13, 1987), and Charles F. Rule, Assistant Attorney General, Criminal Enforcement of the Antitrust Laws, 36th Annual Antitrust Spring Meeting, ABA, 1 (March 24, 1988).

69 *Interview with James C. Miller, III, FTC Chairman*, 51 ANTITRUST L.J. 1, 5 (1982).

A year later he explained that the Commission's goal of efficiency was also derived from the Chicago school of economics, and he candidly revealed that its economic approach emphasized "economic efficiency and consumer welfare . . . as key antitrust objectives, as opposed to 'fairness' or protection of small business."[70]

His successor, Chairman Daniel Oliver, specifically applied this Chicago school approach to the Robinson-Patman Act amendment of section 2 of the Clayton Act. He stated that the present Commission views the 1936 Act as a " 'protectionist, non-efficiency oriented' statute."[71]

STRUCTURE OF TRADE In 1981, Assistant Attorney General Baxter, in discussing mergers, stated that "I do not read Section 7 of the Clayton Act to say anything different from Section 1 of the Sherman Act." In his view, "one decides whether a merger substantially lessens competition in a line of commerce and brings Section 1 into account."[72] Two years later, he summarized the approach of the Department as follows: "We *presuppose* [italics his] that there are efficiencies present. . . . Then, if it's likely to be anticompetitive, we say it can't go forward without any further incremental case-by-case reference to particular economies. . . ."[73]

The Department thereafter, in its 1984 Merger Guidelines, stated that in analyzing acquisitions and mergers "subject to Section 7 of the Clayton Act or to Section 1 of the Sherman Act," it assumes that the "primary benefit . . . is their efficiency-enhancing potential which can increase the competitiveness of firms and result in lower prices. . . . As a conse-

---

70 *Interview with James C. Miller, III, FTC Chairman*, 53 ANTITRUST L.J. 5, 8 (1984).

71 *60 Minutes with Daniel Oliver, FTC Chairman*, 56 ANTITRUST L.J. 239, 241–42 (1987).

72 *Interview with William F. Baxter, Assistant Attorney General*, 50 ANTITRUST L.J. 151, 158–59 (1981).

73 *Interview with William F. Baxter, Assistant Attorney General*, 52 ANTITRUST L.J. 23, 32 (1983).

quence, in the majority of cases, the Guidelines will allow firms to achieve available efficiencies through mergers without interference from the Department."

The Guidelines then advise that if there are mergers which the Department "might challenge," but the parties are able to establish "by clear and convincing evidence" that their mergers will achieve "significant net efficiencies," the government "will consider those efficiencies in deciding whether to challenge the merger." The Guidelines list some of the potential efficiencies that the Department would consider, with the assurance that "[c]ognizable efficiencies" are "not limited to" these suggestions.[74]

The courts

RESTRAINT OF TRADE The Supreme Court, however, has stressed that the words "restraint of trade" in the Sherman Act originated in the common law and thus that whether conduct violates the Act is to be "determined through case-by-case application of the so-called rule of reason—that is, 'the factfinder weighs all of the circumstances.' "[75] Accordingly, it has denied that a single "circumstance" such as efficiency should be the "sole" criterion of antitrust legality. Thus, it has held that a horizontal agreement by doctors fixing maximum fees for health care services was unlawful per se, despite the defense that the doctors could more "efficiently" limit those fees and thereby enable consumers to have low-cost insurance coverage.[76] Also, the Court has refused to overrule its many decisions that tying agreements may be illegal per se,[77] despite the argument by the Department that "cost efficiencies" should justify the practice

---

74 *Department of Justice 1984 Merger Guidelines* § 3.5, 4 Trade Reg. Rep. (CCH) ¶ 13,103, at 20,564.

75 Business Elec. Corp. v. Sharp Elec. Corp., 108 S. Ct. 1515, 1519 (1988).

76 Arizona v. Maricopa County Medical Soc'y, 457 U.S. 332 (1982).

77 Jefferson Parish Hosp. Dist. No. 2 v. Hyde, 466 U.S. 2 (1984).

"[e]ven if the tying arrangement can be shown to reduce the number of the supplier's competitors."[78] Likewise, the Court declined to reconsider its repeated rulings that resale price maintenance is unlawful per se, when the Department advanced the claim—not argued below—that both price and nonprice vertical restrictions may promote efficiency in distribution and thereby have significant procompetitive effects.[79]

The Court, rather, has upheld the defense of efficiency, under the rule of reason, only where the purpose and effect of the transaction were consistent with the original legislative goals of antitrust with respect to competitors and consumers. For example:

Competitive opportunity The Court has denied that the expulsion of a member by a purchasing cooperative was unlawful per se where the purpose of the concerted activity was "designed to increase economic efficiency"; but it remanded the case with instructions that the exclusion could be illegal under the rule of reason if it were shown that the effect was to foreclose the member from a supplier possessing "market power or an exclusive access to an element essential to effective competition."[80] Thereafter, it ruled that a conspiracy by physicians to use peer review proceedings to exclude a competitor from the area's only hospital facilities could not be defended on the ground that "effective peer review [was] essential to the provision of quality medical care."[81] It has also held that the refusal of an operator of three ski facilities to deal with a competitor was not unlawful per se; but it ruled that the former's termination of a joint ticket program with the latter in this case could not have been moti-

---

78 Brief for the United States as Amicus Curiae in Support of Reversal, at 25 n.29, Jefferson Parish, 466 U.S. 2 (1984) (No. 82-1031).

79 Brief for the United States as Amicus Curiae in Support of Petitioner, 12-29, Monsanto Co. v. Spray-Rite Service Corp., 465 U.S. 752, 761–2 (1984) (No. 82-914).

80 Northwest Wholesale Stationers, Inc. v. Pacific Stationery and Printing Co., 472 U.S. 284 (1985).

81 Patrick v. Burget, 108 S. Ct. 1658, 1665 (1988).

vated by reason of "efficiency." Rather, it found that the defendant's purpose was "a deliberate effort to discourage its customers from doing business with its smaller rival"; and, therefore, held under the rule of reason that the termination was unlawful.[82]

Consumer welfare The Court has further ruled that the purpose of a challenged joint selling of TV rights was not per se illegal, because the efficiency of this restraint was "essential if the product is to be available at all"; but it has condemned the effect of its ancillary restrictions on "price and output" under the rule of reason, finding that: "[i]ndividual competitors lose their freedom to compete" and "[p]rice is higher and output lower," so "unresponsive to consumer preference."[83]

UNFAIRNESS OF TRADE Our highest Court has also stressed that "efficiency" may be relevant—but only if consistent with "fair" competition—in proceedings brought under the Clayton and Federal Trade Commission Acts. Thus, it has ruled again that the Robinson-Patman amendment of section 2 of the Clayton Act was intended to curb the "discriminatory preferences" gained by larger buyers over small buyers solely by virtue of the former's greater purchasing power,[84] unless they were affirmatively justified by cost savings or in responding "realistically" (query: efficiently?) to competition.[85] Also, in holding that tying may be illegal per se, despite possible efficiencies,[86] it has cited the "great concern" of Congress with respect to the unfair use of this practice by the "great and powerful," when it enacted section 3 of the Clayton Act.

---

82 Aspen Skiing Co. v. Aspen Highlands Skiing Corp., 472 U.S. 585, 610 (1985).

83 National Collegiate Athletic Ass'n v. Board of Regents, 468 U.S. 85, 101, 106–107 (1984).

84 Jefferson County Pharmaceutical Ass'n v. Abbott Laboratories, 460 U.S. 150 (1983).

85 Falls City Indus., Inc. v. Vanco Beverage, Inc., 460 U.S. 428 (1983).

86 *Jefferson Parish*, *supra* note 77, 466 U.S. at 9–10 n.15.

Again, the Supreme Court has held that a parent corporation is unable to conspire with its subsidiary in violation of section 1 of the Sherman Act (because "efficiency of control" requires parent and subsidiary to be considered "one" person); but it has ruled that harassment of a competitor by a corporation and its subsidiary would be "fully subject" not only to section 2 of that Act, but also to the prohibition of unfair competition in section 5 of the Federal Trade Commission Act.[87]

STRUCTURE OF TRADE A comparison of the approach to antitrust by the Department of Justice with the current Supreme Court is provided by an illuminating section 7 case.[88] Here, a small company had sued to enjoin the acquisition, by its second largest competitor, of the third largest rival. Plaintiff claimed standing to sue by reason of the probability that predatory pricing would result. The district court ruled that "the proposed acquisition violates Section 7 of the Clayton Act," and upheld plaintiff's standing to sue, in part, because otherwise this "might leave a significant antitrust violation unremedied without a single voice calling attention to the potential harm." The court of appeals affirmed.[89]

The Supreme Court granted certiorari, and the Department of Justice filed an amicus brief in which it requested two rulings: (1) that the plaintiff in this case lacked standing to challenge the acquisition, and (2) that "an allegation of threatened future predatory pricing" should "never" be sufficient to give any other plaintiff, if a "competitor," standing to challenge an acquisition.[90]

---

87 Copperweld Corp. v. Independence Tube Corp., 467 U.S. 753 (1984).

88 Cargill, Inc. v. Monfort, Inc., 107 S. Ct. 484 (1986), *rev'g* 761 F.2d 570 (10th Cir. 1985).

89 Monfort, Inc. v. Cargill, Inc., 591 F. Supp. 683, 693, 707 (D. Colo. 1983), *aff'd* 761 F.2d 570 (10th Cir. 1985).

90 Brief for the United States and the Federal Trade Commission as Amici Curiae 9–10, Cargill, Inc. v. Monfort, Inc., 107 S. Ct. 484 (1986) (No. 85-473).

The Supreme Court agreed with the Department that, in this case, the plaintiff had not made a sufficient showing of probable competitive injury to give it standing to sue; but the Court refused to rule that a small competitor should never have standing to challenge an acquisition on a predatory theory. It found that there exists "ample evidence" that predatory pricing "does occur," in our markets, and held that "nothing in the language or legislative history of the Clayton Act suggests that Congress intended this Court to ignore injuries caused by such anticompetitive practices as predatory pricing."[91]

The future

Two roads now diverge, and antitrust cannot travel both. Straight ahead continues the experience of the past. Turning right, is the logic of economic theory, concerning efficiency, urged by the present administration.

A scholarly map[92] describes how the logic of the second alternative "diverges" from the experience of the first.

Goals of antitrust

Initially, the logic of the proposed turn to the right differs from the past in assuming that the "only goal that should guide interpretation of the antitrust laws is the welfare of consumers."[93] It reviews the intent of the sponsors of the Sherman Act and concludes that "other policy goals" are not to be found "in the legislative history."[94] It also assumes that "competition" and "monopoly" in the Clayton Act are "models derived from economics" that "rule out all but economic goals."[95]

---

91 Cargill, Inc. v. Monfort, Inc., 107 S. Ct. 484, 495 (1985).

92 R. Bork, The Antitrust Paradox (1978).

93 *Id.* at 405.

94 *Id.* at 20–21.

95 *Id.* at 58.

The road of antitrust experience, however, has followed the congressional goal of equality of opportunity as well as the economic objective of consumer welfare. See the discussion of legislative history, *supra*. Its road signs marked "competition" and "monopoly," moreover, use words derived from the common law and not from economic models.[96] Accordingly, the economists and lawyers selected by the Eisenhower administration to study the antitrust laws agreed that the "use" of these words by economists "does not necessarily carry any legal significance" or "provide a standard of legality under any of the antitrust laws."[97]

The road of experience, therefore, has assumed that judicial interpretations should be based upon the "original" two, rather than only one, of the dual goals of those who drafted the Sherman Act "bill of rights," and should apply their principles, pursuant to the "rule of reason," to facts that are derived from "the real economic world rather than an economist's hypothetical model."[98]

Efficiency of competition

Next, the proposed turn to the right differs from the road of past experience by relying on the logic of its economic theory on efficiency to advance the goal of consumer welfare.[99] It claims that to "abandon economic theory is to abandon the possibility of a rational antitrust law."[100] Its "antitrust methodology" is derived, in part, from the "Darwinian theory of natural selection," whereby a firm's efficiency is said to be shown by its

---

96 Remarks of Senator Sherman, *supra* note 4, KINTNER at 113–16; Remarks of Senator Hoar, *supra* note 5, KINTNER at 293.

97 REPORT OF THE ATTORNEY GENERAL'S NATIONAL COMMITTEE TO STUDY THE ANTITRUST LAWS 316 (1955).

98 Hanover Shoe, Inc. v. United Shoe Mach. Corp., 392 U.S. 481, 493 (1968).

99 BORK, *supra* note 92, at 90–91.

100 *Id.* at 117.

success in coping with the economic environment and forwarding consumer welfare.[101] The logic of this theory leads us to the conclusion that antitrust should permit all "tying arrangements, exclusive dealing . . . , 'predatory' price cutting, price 'discrimination,' and the like."[102]

The logic of the theory then admits that it is consistent with the Act's section 7 and the goal of consumer welfare to say that "size by internal growth demonstrates superior efficiency, but mergers that create real market control . . . may or may not create new efficiencies." Therefore, it is "intelligible" social policy to apply "stricter standards to mergers." But it further argues that the existence of a trend toward concentration indicates "that there are emerging efficiencies or economies of scale."[103] Accordingly, logic nevertheless dictates that section 7 should be interpreted as "making presumptively lawful all horizontal mergers" that "leave three significant companies" in an industry[104] and "all vertical and conglomerate mergers."[105]

The road of antitrust, however, recalls that a post-Civil War theory of economics known as "Social Darwinism" also claimed that the survival of the biggest represented the survival of the fittest.[106] Congress then rejected this theory when it enacted the Sherman Act to insure that the biggest must prove its superior efficiency in "fair" competition, and it subsequently passed the Clayton Act to prevent the "already great and powerful" from paying or coercing distributors to handle only the products of a "Big Three," so as to exclude smaller independents from our markets. The lesson to be drawn from antitrust history, therefore, is that *internal growth* leading to large size by lawful means is encouraged by our laws, because Congress recognized that

---

101 *Id.* at 105, 118–24.

102 *Id.* at 406.

103 *Id.* at 199, 205–207.

104 *Id.* at 221–22.

105 *Id.* at 406.

106 H. Thorelli, The Federal Antitrust Policy 113–16 (1954).

"considerable size is often essential for efficient operation," but that this "commercial success" must not involve " 'means which made it impossible for other persons to engage in fair competition.' "[107]

The road of experience, moreover, has indeed found it necessary to erect far stricter and higher barriers to *external* growth, as we have noted previously. Congress observed that combinations and mergers more readily lead to the concentration of market power in a few hands, and that the adverse effects of this reduction in the vigor of competition are likely to far outweigh any possible gains in efficiency. As Senator Sherman observed, "all experience" shows that the savings achieved through efficiency by a combination in restraint of trade "goes to the pockets of the producer."[108] Accordingly, antitrust views an intent to gain in efficiency through an acquisition or merger to be lawful; but it requires an affirmative showing that its probable effect will be to promote—not reduce—the vigor of competition.[109]

Over the years, antitrust experience found that new products and services, which result in higher employment and increased national wealth, are best created by a mix of small, medium and large companies. As a White House Task Force (chaired by the Dean of the University of Chicago Law School), reported, the antitrust laws "assume" that "a large number and variety of decision-making units in the economy is important to ensure innovation, experimentation and continuous adaptation to new conditions." And experts are said to have concluded that this increase in the number of competitors "will not be offset by losses in efficiency."[110]

---

107 United States v. E. I. du Pont de Nemours & Co., 351 U.S. 377, 386, 390 (1956).

108 Remarks of Senator Sherman, *supra* note 4, KINTNER at 122.

109 United States v. General Dynamics Corp., 415 U.S. 486, 503–504 (1974).

110 WHITE HOUSE TASK FORCE ON ANTITRUST POLICY 4, 6 (1969).

In particular, the importance of small competitors in our economy was recognized in the most recent report of the President on the state of small business, as follows:

> A wider appreciation of the innovation, the competitive strength, and the quality of life that small firms bring to our economy is an important goal for all who are interested in the long-term economic health of our Nation. We need to understand the small business sector, because ignorance of its contributions and inattention to the effect of government activities on it will result in politics that squelch the vitality of small firms.[111]

Welfare of consumers

The logic of the proposed road to the right, finally, differs from the experience of the past by encouraging further concentration of market power in our economy. A "major component of a firm's efficiency" in concentrated industries is claimed to be the "ability of its management to make decisions" about products, manufacturing, distribution, etc., that "lead" to consumer "acceptance."[112] This decision-making by "three significant rivals in any market"[113] is said to allocate society's economic resources more efficiently, and thereby contributes to "[c]onsumer welfare"—which is assumed "in this sense" to be "merely another term for the wealth of the nation." The logical conclusion, therefore, is that antitrust should have "nothing to say" about the way "prosperity" is distributed.[114]

The "Consumer Welfare Model" of this theory concedes that "[t]hose who continue to buy after a monopoly is formed pay more for the same output, and that shifts income from them to the monopoly and its owners. . . ." But, it reasons, the latter

---

111 1987 State of Small Business: A Report of the President, vii, Transmitted to Congress, 1988.

112 BORK, *supra* note 92, at 194.

113 *Id.* at 406.

114 *Id.* at 90.

"are also consumers."[115] Accordingly, even if the parties to a merger resulting in control of a substantial share of the market "have monopoly profit in mind," antitrust "should never concern itself with equity in income distribution."[116] Any resulting "social discontent" arising from "income redistribution" is not an antitrust "problem" for the "federal judiciary to address."[117]

The road of experience, however, led Congress to decide that consumers should be entitled by the Sherman Act to purchase in markets where "every man" has the right to offer his products in "free" and "fair" competition.[118] It later caused Congress to provide that the "millions of American consumers" are to be guaranteed by the Clayton Act a comparable right to decide from whom to buy the "particular commodities desired" without being led by exclusive dealing contracts[119] to limit their choices to a few firms in "any market." Congress has consistently opposed "the regimentation of men by concentrated economic power" as "the antithesis of liberty."[120]

A conservative administration observed some years ago that "the freedom" of an "open marketplace" is the most "efficient" guarantor of economic prosperity, and noted that, in contrast, when leading firms in our most "highly concentrated industries" were free of competition from others, they had preferred efficient management of "the status quo," and only reluctantly "offered the American consumer important new products" (available abroad) when forced to do so by "foreign competition."[121]

---

115 *Id.* at 110.

116 *Id.* at 219–20.

117 *Id.* at 112.

118 Remarks of Senator Sherman, *supra* note 4, KINTNER at 116.

119 H.R. REP. NO. 627, *supra* note 16, KINTNER at 1093.

120 FINAL REPORT AND RECOMMENDATION OF THE TEMPORARY NATIONAL ECONOMIC COMMITTEE 7 (1941).

121 Address of Attorney General John Mitchell Before the Georgia Bar Ass'n. 1, 8 (June 6, 1969).

The goal of "consumer welfare" in the Sherman Act, moreover, was not intended to be an economist's "model." Senator Sherman *was* concerned with equity in "income distribution." He specifically sought to prohibit combinations that "increase the profits of the producer at the cost of the consumer"[122] (whether or not such combinations, through better methods of productions, achieved "saving of cost").[123] And the road of experience leads to the conclusion that "social discontent" with price increases that "redistribute" the income of consumers in order to profit producers often becomes a very real antitrust "problem" for the federal judiciary, in the form of class actions brought by direct purchasers in order to recover damages in the amount of three times these price increases, plus "reasonable" counsel fees.

Conclusion

The "Past" and "Present" of antitrust, above reviewed, are in agreement at least that, in choosing the road into the "Future," we must "resurrect the original meaning of . . . statutes as the only reliable guide for judgment."[124] The "original meaning" of our basic Sherman Act, fortunately, was "resurrected" by a great dean of the antitrust bar when, in his youth, he joined the Department of Justice during the administration of President Taft. He concluded that:

> . . . those who see in the passage of the Antitrust Act nothing but the purely economic motive . . . fail utterly to grasp the purpose of its framers or the revolutionary character of the trust movement itself.
>
> While, of course, these economic evils had their weight, nevertheless it is equally clear that the Act was aimed at certain social and political evils as well. It was feared that if these combinations were permitted to continue, without limit, a small group of men would acquire

---

122 Remarks of Senator Sherman, *supra* note 4, KINTNER at 116.

123 *Id.* at 122.

124 Address of Attorney General Edwin Meese before the American Bar Ass'n. 17 (July 9, 1985).

absolute control of all industrial affairs. . . . Individual initiative, opportunity and independence would be destroyed.[125]

He also researched the Darwinian theory of efficiency and further concluded that:

Large-scale-production seems to reach its maximum efficiency—in a country as large as the United States at least—long before monopoly is attained.

Thus the Antitrust Act does not prevent the survival of the fittest, as has sometimes been supposed. *It makes efficiency in public service the test of fitness, and prevents the survival unfairly of the unfit.*[126]

Should we now diverge from the "original meaning" and subsequent experience of antitrust, and proceed in the future to follow solely the "less traveled" logic of economic theory, the resulting "change" in direction would indeed make a "dramatic" difference.[127] Possibly, the 1990 Department of Justice is currently returning antitrust to its original intent. But to prophesy is difficult, particularly as to the future.

---

125 Thurlow M. Gordon, Combinations Unduly Restrictive of Competitive Conditions Within the Meaning of the Federal Antitrust Act 2–3 (unpublished manuscript written by Mr. Gordon shortly before leaving the Department of Justice in 1916).

126 *Id.* at 36–37 (emphasis in original).

127 Miller, *supra* note 70, at 7–8.

4
The first Sherman Act case: *Jellico Mountain Coal*, 1891

BY JOHN J. SIEGFRIED* and MICHELLE MAHONY**

I. Introduction

President Benjamin Harrison signed the Sherman Act into law on July 2, 1890.[1] His Attorney General, William Miller, did little to enforce the Act, as his small staff of attorneys was already overburdened. A year after the Sherman Act became law no special instructions regarding its enforcement had yet been issued to the U.S. district attorneys.[2]

---

* Professor of Economics at Vanderbilt University, Nashville, Tennessee.

** Graduate Student in Economics at Northwestern University.

AUTHORS' NOTE: *We thank George Bittlingmayer, Rudolph Blitz, Kenneth Elzinga, Oliver Grawe, David Kaserman, Fred McChesney, George Sweeney and Leonard Weiss for helpful comments on an earlier version of this article. We also thank Mary Ann Hawkins of the National Archives: Atlanta Branch for her assistance in locating the original trial court documents.*

1 Sherman Antitrust Act, 26 Stat. 209, An Act of July 2, 1890.

2 *See* WILLIAM LETWIN, LAW AND ECONOMIC POLICY IN AMERICA 107–108 (1965).

John Ruhm, U.S. district attorney for the Middle District of Tennessee, initiated the first federal action under the new law. Ruhm's effort was the only federal attempt to enforce the Sherman Act during its first year of existence, and it was only with considerable difficulty that he managed to receive official authorization and funding.[3] Despite administrative obstacles, however, Ruhm filed a petition in the United States Circuit Court for the Middle District of Tennessee against the members of the Nashville Coal Exchange [NCE] on September 25, 1890. The petition argued that the Nashville Coal Exchange was an illegal combination in restraint of trade and asked that its members be "enjoined and restrained from further monopolizing and carrying on the coal trade in Nashville."[4]

The NCE included several Kentucky mine operators and large Nashville coal wholesalers who conspired to fix the price of domestic coal in the Nashville market.[5] These wholesale dealers purchased coal from mine operators and resold it to retailers in Nashville as well as selling directly to large-volume final customers. The Exchange controlled about 80% of the coal sold for

---

3 *Id.* at 106. *See also* Hans B. Thorelli, The Federal Antiturst Policy 374 (1955).

4 Petition, 12. *U.S. v. Jellico Mountain Coal and Coke Company* (1890) from the complete set of trial documents of the Middle District Circuit Court, Tennessee, Docket No. 2820, hereinafter referred to as *Jellico*. Our interest in this case began when Siegfried, on a sabbatical, decided to finally read William Letwin's classic (*supra* note 2). Letwin's report on the *Jellico* case (pp. 106–107) would have passed without notice except that the events occurred in Nashville, Tennessee, Siegfried's current residence. Anticipating an advantage in locating the case record (and only later, upon learning more about the federal court archives, realizing that no such advantage existed) he began the search that eventually resulted in this article. The actual court records of the case are in the Atlanta Branch of the federal archives. What appeared to be century-old coal dust on the file jackets containing the record led the assisting archivist to conclude that this case has not been subject to careful examination (or, indeed, *any* examination) for a very long time.

5 Petition, *Jellico*, Exhibit A.

residential heating in Nashville in 1890. Although all Exchange members were defendants in the case, Jellico Mountain Coal & Coke Company was named first and consequently the case is usually identified by its name. Ruhm specified Jellico first because he intended to use Jellico's operations to establish interstate commerce. Jellico mined its coal in eastern Tennessee and shipped its supply to Nashville via Kentucky.[6] Ironically, it was later revealed that Jellico had abandoned its Exchange membership prior to the filing of the petition, but the case title continued to bear its name despite subsequent dismissal of the charges against Jellico itself.

At a preliminary hearing in Nashville on October 13, 1890, Judge E. S. Hammond,[7] sitting in for Judge Howell Jackson,[8] denied the government's petition for a preliminary injunction to bar the Exchange from operating until the case could be tried because "the case was a most important application of the new Act and that if, on the final hearing it should turn out that the case does not fall within the Act, it would more injure the defendants to grant this preliminary injunction than it would injure the public to withhold it."[9]

---

6 Letter from Ruhm to Miller, August 30, 1890, Department of Justice File 8247, Number 8782 (1890).

7 Judge Hammond was born April 27, 1838. He fought for the Confederate Army and in 1868 returned to Nashville to practice law. In 1878, President Hayes, as a symbol of goodwill, appointed him as the first circuit judge of the Western District of Tennessee. He served until his death in 1904.

8 It is unclear why Judge Howell Jackson, the Sixth Circuit court judge for Tennessee did not hear either the preliminary injunction hearing or trial of the case. The court journal reports he did not participate in either proceeding due to "incompetency." In 1892 Jackson issued the circuit court decision for In re Greene, 52 F. 104 (6th Cir. 1892), another important early Sherman Act case. Jackson was appointed to the Supreme Court in 1894 and died in 1895.

9 43 F. 899 (1890).

The trial court hearing occurred the following year, with Judge David M. Key substituting for Judge Jackson.[10] In his decision of June 4, 1891, Judge Key ruled for the government, commencing federal enforcement of the Sherman Act. His decision was not appealed. Had the case gone to the Supreme Court, *U.S. v. Jellico Mountain Coal and Coke Company* might today have a more prominent place in antitrust casebooks than the *Trans-Missouri Freight Association* or *Addyston Pipe and Steel Company* cases.[11]

Nonetheless, *Jellico Mountain Coal* was both the first U.S. case filed under the Sherman Act and the first government victory under the new law. It also turned out to be one of the very few government victories in Sherman Act litigation in the early 1890's.

In this article, we describe the facts of *U.S. v. Jellico Mountain Coal and Coke Company* and report the trial court's conclusion. We evaluate the decision on the basis of economic analysis. *Jellico* illustrates the application of modern cartel theory to a price-fixing episode that occurred nearly a century ago.

II. The coal industry in Nashville: 1890

The coal mining industry serving Nashville in 1890 was depressed despite a stable population in the city and despite the fact that coal was the leading energy source in the United States

---

10 Judge Key was born January 27, 1824. He was admitted to the Tennessee Bar in 1859 and fought with the Confederate Army during the Civil War despite his beliefs against secession. After the Civil War, he returned to Chattanooga, Tennessee to practice law. In 1875, he was appointed to fill the U.S. Senate vacancy left by Andrew Johnson. The Washington exposure led to his appointment as President Hayes' Postmaster General in 1878. Although he was not a Republican, Hayes appointed him in 1880 to the position of circuit judge for the Middle and Eastern District for Tennessee. He held the position until his retirement in 1894.

11 Trans-Missouri Freight Association, 166 U.S. 290 (1897). Addyston Pipe & Steel, 175 U.S. 211 (1899).

at the time.[12] Fierce competition and price wars among mines in the western Kentucky coal fields prior to the organization of the NCE reduced profits earned by mine operators. The price of coal barely covered the short-run incremental cost of production, the result being either significantly lower shipments to Nashville or abandonment of the market altogether by some of the mines.[13] This situation enabled the wholesale coal dealers of Nashville to organize their Kentucky suppliers as participants in the NCE, which would guarantee a fixed price to both dealers and mines.

The industry's market structure facilitated formation of the cartel. The coal industry had two types of ultimate consumers, domestic and industrial. Domestic, or residential, coal the type the cartel tried to control, was bought by individual residential consumers and some larger organizations such as the public school system, Vanderbilt University, and the state hospital, which used it to heat buildings. Industrial (steam), or commercial, coal was used predominantly by large manufacturers, such as cotton and grain mills, and by steamboat owners to power machinery.

Exchange members agreed not to attempt to control the commercial coal market until those nonmember mines "tributary to [Nashville]" became Exchange members, implying that limiting competition in commercial coal was beyond the perceived capacity of the cartel members. Several factors account for the greater competition in commercial vis-à-vis domestic coal. First, there was a "diversity of opinions" about the quality of the various steam coals, making a price agreement more difficult. More importantly, however, coal used for steam generation was "easily reached and was used in large amounts."[14] Often steam generation consumers possessed the ability to bypass the wholesale dealer and buy directly from mines due to the customers' location either on rail lines or along navigable portions of the

---

12 Coal accounted for 61% of U.S. energy consumption in 1890. *See* Robert Romer, Energy Facts and Figures 49 (1985).

13 Deposition of A. J. Kellar, February 16, 1891, *Jellico.*

14 Deposition of J. R. Love, February 5, 1891, *Jellico.*

Cumberland River. Consequently, mines that were not "members of the Exchange were an active source of competition" for industrial coal sales.[15] Furthermore, commercial consumers may have pursued alternative coal supplies to take advantage of lower prices offered by other mine operators and dealers had the cartel tried to dictate supracompetitive industrial coal prices.[16] Steamboats, in particular, could conveniently alter their fuel source in reaction to geographic price differentials.

Finally, many Nashville manufacturers competed with manufacturers in Memphis, Louisville and Cincinnati. If the Nashville firms paid more for their coal than did their competitors, the manufacturing base in Nashville (and the commercial coal business) eventually would have eroded as competitors from other cities acquired a higher market share. Thus coal prices for steam generation in Nashville could not be sustained at a level above those in other regional cities for very long without hurting the wholesale dealers who organized the cartel.[17]

The supply substitutability that characterized the commercial coal market was absent, however, in the domestic coal market, where users did not possess the same supply options. The Nashville public school system, for example, was not located on a rail line and obviously could not move to another city in search of lower energy costs.

Domestic consumers could not switch to steam coal if the price of domestic coal were raised. Physically, steam coal was a poor domestic coal substitute because it was much softer and tended to "slack" when used for domestic heating. Furthermore, Exchange member wholesale dealers would not sell steam coal to domestic consumers. Selling steam coal for domestic purposes forced the wholesaler, whether an Exchange member or not, to

---

15 *Id.*

16 Deposition of Stuart R. Knott, March 13, 1891, *Jellico.*

17 *Id.* This interpretation is supported further by the Louisville and Nashville Railroad's rebates on industrial coal shipments.

forfeit a freight rebate the L&N Railroad paid on industrial steam coal (but did not pay on domestic coal).

The mine operator members of the Exchange were located predominantly in the western Kentucky coal region near Earlington, with the exception of the Jellico and Bon Air mines which were in eastern Tennessee. Although coal for heating purposes could have been brought by barge from Pittsburgh to Nashville, witnesses testified that very little ever arrived.[18] There are several reasons why little coal arrived in Nashville by river, the most important of which was the pricing policy of the L&N Railroad, the exclusive supplier of rail services to Nashville. The L&N was intent on eliminating river competition,[19] and accordingly set rail shipping prices to Nashville with an eye to beating the price of competing products arriving by river. Second, terminal facilities for steamboats and barges in Nashville were terrible.[20] They usually had to pull up to the bank, and unload through the mud.[21] Drayage charges would be high for a relatively low value product like coal.[22] Third, the expansion of L&N lines into rural areas of Tennessee and western Kentucky in the 1880's reduced the backhaul business for river traffic. Until that time, steamboats and barges brought raw materials up the Cumberland to Nashville, a manufacturing and distribution point, and delivered manufactured goods along the Cumberland as they returned down river. But eventually the railroads took over the delivery of manufactured goods, and without the backhaul business, river transportation on the lower Cumberland, between Nashville and

---

18 Deposition of E. W. Hill, February 3, 1891, *Jellico*.

19 *See* BYRD DOUGLAS, STEAMBOATIN' ON THE CUMBERLAND 212 (1961). *See also*, more generally, MAURY KLEIN, HISTORY OF THE LOUISVILLE & NASHVILLE RAILROAD (1972) and WILLIAM H. JOUBERT, SOUTHERN FREIGHT RATES IN TRANSITION (1949). This conclusion is also supported by the deposition of E. W. Hill, *id.*

20 E. W. Hill, *supra* note 18.

21 *Id.*

22 BYRD DOUGLAS, *supra* note 19, at 203, 211.

Paducah, Kentucky eventually dried up.[23] In his documentation of steamboating on the Cumberland River, Byrd Douglas[24] hardly mentions coal.

Pittsburgh was not the only place alternative coal supplies could be secured. But the other coal mines in the Midsouth produced different types of specialized coal. Northern Alabama coal was used in Nashville, but it was best suited for gas and coke production.[25] Sewanee coal, from southeastern Tennessee, was imported for blacksmithing purposes.[26] And while some coal seams in eastern Tennessee produced residential coal, apparently little or none was shipped into Nashville because more lucrative markets existed elsewhere[27] and because of the distance from the mines to Nashville (250 to 325 miles).[28]

In addition to excluding coal imports from other regions, a successful price agreement had to eliminate the qualitative differences in coal produced by the mines that actually did supply Nashville. Coal was universally classified into four general categories—lump, nut, run-of-the-mine, and slack. The Exchange divided it further into five classes, No. 0, 1, 2, 3, and 4, and assigned each mine's coal to a specific class, making agreement on prices within each class possible. The assignments were based on (a) quality, (b) the loss of coal in shipment, (c) the amount of slack and the original mining cost, and (d) potential competition from other coal likely to compete in the Nashville market.[29] Run-of-the-mine and slack coal were used exclusively by

---

23 *Id.* at 227–29.

24 *Id.* at 278–80.

25 Deposition of George W. McCormack, January 8, 1891, *Jellico.*

26 Deposition of J. H. Kendrick, January 6, 1891, *Jellico.*

27 A. J. Kellar, *supra* note 13.

28 E. W. Hill, *supra* note 18.

29 *Id.*

industrial consumers. Practically all of the lump coal and approximately 75% of the nut coal shipped to Nashville were consumed for domestic purposes. The standard coal sold in Nashville to domestic consumers was coal classed as No. 1. Nos. 2, 3, and 4 were used domestically but were higher priced.[30] The percentage breakdown among the five classes of domestically used lump and nut coal is reported in table 1.[31]

Table 1
Distribution of Domestically Used Lump and Nut Coal Among the Classes Sold in Nashville in 1890

Class	*Percentage of total domestic consumption sold in Nashville: 1890*
No. 0	3%
No. 1	60%
No. 2	25%
No. 3	2%
No. 4	10%

SOURCE: Answers of E. W. Hill and J. H. Kendrick, in depositions filed February 3, 1891 and January 6, 1891 respectively, *U.S. v. Jellico Mountain Coal and Coke, et al.*, Docket No. 2820.

III. The Nashville Coal Exchange

The NCE was formed in August of 1889, by agreement of 14 Kentucky coal mining firms and 14 Nashville wholesale coal

30 Brief for the United States, *Jellico*, at 36.

31 Very little No. 0 lump coal was shipped to Nashville and No. 0 nut coal was used exclusively for steam production. No. 4 nut coal was almost exclusively domestic while the nut coal of classes 1, 2, and 3 was pretty well divided between the two sectors. J. H. Kendrick, *supra* note 26 and George W. McCormack, *supra* note 25.

dealers.[32] *Articles of Agreement* were drawn up and printed in a small blue-covered booklet, which apparently served as the conspirators' rulebook. The stated purposes of the organization were to (a) advance the interest of the coal business at Nashville, (b) treat all parties to the agreement in a fair and equitable manner, and (c) establish prices of coal in Nashville and to change them from time to time as occasion may require.[33] The Exchange declared it was organized to "act in a conservative manner, and to sell coal at a fair and reasonable price so as to allow all parties a fair profit for their product."[34] On the other hand, one member of the Exchange described its purpose to "be to restore peace and put an end to the [coal] war [in Nashville]."[35]

Membership in the Exchange was open to all firms owning or operating mines shipping coal to Nashville and all wholesale coal dealers in Nashville. Members paid a $100 membership fee, monthly dues and fines for any violation of the rules.[36] All monies collected were held in a permanent fund from which dividends, when and if declared by a two-thirds vote of the members, were paid.[37] At the monthly meetings held in Nashville, each attending member received $1 and was allowed one vote.[38]

Members retained the right to withdraw from the Exchange and continue to trade in Nashville, although they then forfeited all investment in the Exchange. At least two mine operators did

---

32 Exchange member coal dealers were wholesale dealers, who arranged for the shipment of coal to Nashville, and subsequently resold to either small retail dealers who served individual residences or to large institutions.

33 *Articles of Agreement*, § 3, *Jellico.*

34 *Id.* at § 4.

35 A. J. Kellar, *supra* note 13.

36 *Articles of Agreement*, §§ 5, 6, 7, and 15, *Jellico.*

37 *Id.* at §§ 8 and 9.

38 *Id.* at §§ 14 and 21.

withdraw.[39] Retiring members could transfer their membership or receive a refund of the membership fee, but accumulated dues or a prorated share of fines collected by the Exchange were not reimbursable.[40]

The organization agreed that members who were "owners or operators of mines shall not sell or ship coal to any person, firm, or corporation in Nashville, or West Nashville, or East Nashville, who is not a member of [the] Exchange; and dealers shall not buy coal from any one not a member of the Exchange."[41] This rule was the core of the agreement.

Two years earlier, in 1887, the Nashville dealers had formed an organization to fix prices of residential coal in Nashville. That cartel, however, soon dissolved.[42] The record does not indicate why the 1887 cartel failed, but the reason must have been either price chiseling by the dealers or entry of new dealers to the market. There were no apparent barriers to entry into trading coal. If the cartel had successfully maintained a price sufficient to secure economic profits, the entry attracted by those profits would have soon eroded the cartel price.

While coal wholesaling is an intrinsically competitive industry, the concurrent frustrations of the mine operators serving the Nashville market created an opportunity for the wholesale dealers in Nashville. If the dealers could persuade the Kentucky mine operators to join their scheme, it was more likely to achieve success. Because of geological conditions and transportation costs, the Kentucky mines serving the Nashville residential market possessed (as a group) market power. The mines, however, had not been able to organize themselves into a cartel. Quite the

---

39 Jellico Mountain Coal and Coke Company in east Tennessee transferred its membership to the Southern Jellico Coal Company in about March 1890. Both Standard Coal and Coke Company and the Eureka mine in Kentucky withdrew from the Exchange.

40 *Articles of Agreement*, §§ 10 and 11, *Jellico.*

41 *Id.* at § 24.

42 A. J. Kellar, *supra* note 13.

contrary, the mine operators had been engaged in fierce competition.[43] If the wholesalers could orchestrate a successful cartel among the mine operators, they could reasonably expect the mines to share some of the resulting monopoly profits with them. The wholesalers could provide a valued service to a mine operators' cartel. They could monitor adherence to the agreement, detecting cheating by mine operators. In return the mine operators, by agreeing to sell only to member dealers in Nashville, would effectively limit entry into coal wholesale dealing.

Our interpretation of the events in 1889 is that the wholesalers set out to orchestrate and monitor a mine operators' cartel, and for their contribution to the scheme the wholesalers earned compensation. Compensation might have taken the form of a direct payment to the wholesalers. Instead, however, compensation actually took the form of a reduction in the price charged by mine operators for coal supplied to NCE member dealers. The price to nonmembers rose to infinity in the short run, as the Kentucky mine operators agreed not to sell coal to any nonmember dealer in Nashville. The price to the members was apparently lower than the profit maximizing monopoly price that the mine operators' cartel could have charged the wholesalers if the wholesalers had not been involved in the cartel (which, of course, couldn't have been successfully organized without them). The mine operators could have raised the price of coal offered wholesalers to the price, including transportation, of the next best alternative source of coal available to the Nashville wholesalers. Instead, the evidence in the case suggests that the cartel's transfer price of coal from the Kentucky mines to the Nashville dealers was below the short-run profit-maximizing price level of a successful independent (of the wholesalers) cartel of mine operators, thereby allocating some of the monopoly profits to the dealers in return for their assistance in orchestrating the mine operators' cartel.

This "deal" between the mine operators and wholesalers had the effect of providing coal to the Exchange member dealers at

---

43 *Id.*

prices lower than those available to potential entrants into wholesaling of coal in Nashville, ostensibly "raising rivals' costs" and providing the dealers with a cost advantage over likely new competitors.[44] The same effect, could have been achieved by charging the Exchange member wholesalers a price for coal that reflected the wholesalers' next best alternative source while simultaneously providing compensation for the orchestration services by direct payment. If the cartel members had elected this method of compensation, then there would have been no appearance of a cost advantage to member dealers (vis-à-vis nonmembers and potential entrants), and no "raising of rivals' costs." But direct compensation to the wholesalers for cartel management services would have eliminated the impediment to enter the wholesale market. With a limited number of dealers, and undisrupted commercial relationships between each mine and the few dealers it supplied,[45] the Exchange was in a better position to detect cheating on the agreement by dealers. Were a dealer to chisel on the agreed wholesale markup, the additional orders induced might have been detected by the mine operators traditionally supplying the cheating dealer.[46]

---

44 *See* Krattenmaker & Salop, *Antitrust Analysis of Anticompetitive Exclusion: Raising Rivals' Costs to Achieve Power Over Price*, 96 Yale L.J. 234 (1986).

45 E. W. Hill, *supra* note 18.

46 During its latter days of operation the British Newcastle-Sunderland Coal Cartel of 1770–1840 was strikingly similar to the NCE. The Newcastle-Sunderland Coal Cartel, whose primary market was London, set the price of coal just high enough to limit competition. The northern England cartel established production quotas, and enforced them with the help of the London "factors." London "factors" had a legal monopoly on the importation of coal into London until 1832. Then Parliament abolished their monopoly. But in practice the monopoly of the 14 London "factors," called the Coal Ring, continued with the help of the northern coal cartel. In 1832 the cartel agreed to sell to no merchants in London other than members of the Coal Ring, in return for which the Coal Ring members regulated supply into London and agreed to boycott shipments of coal into London from cartel competitors. *See* Hermann Levy, Monopolies, Cartels and Trusts in British Industry 106–42 (1927).

To discourage cheating, a system of fines was established for members who violated the rules of the Exchange, with the most severe penalty being expulsion and loss of all accumulated capital investment. The penalty for the first offense was $10 plus 2 cents per bushel of coal sold at an unauthorized price or to an unauthorized dealer. A second violation carried a fine of $20 plus 4 cents per bushel of coal sold in violation of the Agreement. Expulsion resulted from a third offense.[47]

The significance of the fines is revealed in table 2. The first offense penalty, 2 cents per bushel, allowed the dealer to break even but the fine for the second offense, 4 cents per bushel of the coal in question, would have caused a substantial loss. The court record indicates that charges of violating the Agreement were sustained against only one member, the Eureka Mine in Earlington. Eureka then withdrew from the NCE, and continued to sell in Nashville as one of the two nonmember Kentucky mines that sold residential coal in Nashville.[48]

Table 2

Dealer Revenue Distribution of One Bushel of No. 1 Domestic Coal Sold in Winter, 1890, in Nashville

Expense incurred	
Price to dealer at the mine	5 cents
Cartage	2 cents
Loss by waste and shortage in loading and unloading	1/2 cent
Yard expense (telephone, employees, etc.)	1/2 cent
Freight expense	6 cents
Dealer's profit	2 cents
Final selling price	16 cents

SOURCE: Answer of John D. Anderson in deposition filed February 2, 1891. *U.S. v. Jellico Mountain Coal and Coke Company, et al.*, Docket No. 2820.

47 *Articles of Agreement*, §§ 17 and 18, *Jellico.*

48 E. W. Hill, *supra* note 18.

A minimum pricing schedule was devised monthly for each grade of coal.[49] The prices guaranteed a fixed amount to both dealer and mine operator exclusive of freight charges, with any increase beyond rail rate advances to be divided equally between them.[50] The record reports that the mine operators and wholesalers initially divided downstream revenues from No. 1 coal equally, 4.5 cents per bushel to each in the summer months and 5 cents per bushel to each in the winter months,[51] and planned to split price increases similarly. These data, summarized in table 2, suggest that the dealers were earning a gross margin of 40% on their revenues, which seems quite high for a wholesaling business. There is no explicit information in the record about the level of margins earned by mine operators selling coal at 5 cents per bushel. It is possible, however, to infer that the margins received by mine operators in western Kentucky on coal shipped to Nashville were at least 20 percentage points (1 cent) higher than margins earned on coal shipped by the same mines to Memphis. There was a 3 cent per bushel differential in the price of western Kentucky domestic coal in Nashville and Memphis. During the 12 months between August 1889 and August 1890 the average price per bushel of domestic coal in Memphis was 12 2/9 cents while in Nashville it was 15 1/6 cents.[52]

Table 3 shows that rail transport costs to Nashville and Memphis were virtually identical. If operating costs of wholesale

---

49 All price changes were subject to a two-thirds vote of the members attending the monthly meeting. *Articles of Agreement*, §§ 16 and 22, *Jellico*.

50 The division of revenues appears to be a formula price contract where the intermediate product price is made a function of the final output price in order to achieve a predetermined split of the maximized joint profits. Such contracts may facilitate agreement among cartel members. *See* Blair & Kaserman, *A Note on Bilateral Monopoly and Formula Price Contracts*, 77 AM. ECON. REV. 460 (1987).

51 Total selling price minus freight expense equals 10 cents per bushel, divided equally between mine operator and dealer. E. W. Hill, *supra* note 18.

52 Brief for the United States, *Jellico*, at 39.

coal trading in Memphis were similar to Nashville, then Nashville wholesalers and the mines that supplied them enjoyed a combined 3 cents per bushel revenue advantage on coal sold in Nashville vis-à-vis coal sold in Memphis. Since the evidence indicates that Nashville wholesalers' profit margin was 2 cents per bushel, western Kentucky mine operators must have enjoyed *at least* a 1-cent advantage on coal shipped to Nashville vis-à-vis Memphis. To the extent that (Nashville and Memphis) wholesalers would have enjoyed margins above zero in a competitive market, the mine operators would have received an even greater (than 1 cent) margin advantage on coal shipped to Nashville through the Exchange.

Table 3
Domestic Coal Rail Rates From Earlington, Kentucky to Nashville and Memphis during 1890

	Nashville	*Memphis*
January	$1.50/ton	$1.40/ton
February	1.50/ton	1.40/ton
March	1.50/ton	1.40/ton
April	1.00/ton	1.40/ton
May	1.00/ton	1.40/ton
June	1.00/ton	1.40/ton
July	1.10/ton	1.20/ton
August	1.20/ton	1.20/ton
September	1.30/ton	1.20/ton
October	1.40/ton	1.20/ton
November	1.50/ton	1.20/ton
December	1.50/ton	1.20/ton
Average:	$1.29/ton	$1.30/ton

SOURCE: Answer of Stuart R. Knott in deposition filed June 27, 1891. *U.S. v. Jellico Mountain Coal and Coke Company, et al.* Docket No. 2820.

Members were required to present at the beginning of each month in which price advanced, a "written statement showing orders they had on hand undelivered, that had been sold during the previous month, such statement to give names of purchasers, number of bushels and kind of coal sold."[53] The purpose of this rule undoubtedly was to prevent members from chiseling by offering to sell coal to new customers at a previous month's lower price.

The Exchange was run along the lines of a "formally organized industry trade association with chairman, rules of order, agendas and regularly scheduled meetings."[54] The rules provided an operating structure that reduced the chance the price-fixing scheme would collapse under either the pressures to cheat on the agreed prices or arguments about the distribution of the gains.

IV. The role of the railroad

Nashville provided an attractive location for a residential coal cartel. The absence of low-cost river transportation to Nashville in the latter part of the 19th century distinguished the city from, for example, Memphis and Louisville, which both enjoyed a coal market influenced by considerable river competition.[55] While the Cumberland River was navigable to Nashville during portions of the year, dangerous stretches of the river during low water periods made barge transportation of coal relatively expensive and unpredictable. The sensitivity of the Cumberland River's navigability to water levels is evident from the monthly variation in rail rates for shipping coal from Earlington, Kentucky to Nashville reported in table 3. Rail rates declined in late spring, when winter snow melt would raise the water level and make river transportation a viable alternative to rail, only to recover from midsummer until late fall of each year, as the river level receded. Ultimately, however, "after the railroads entered the coal fields, [the coal] trade left the river and never returned."[56]

---

53 *Articles of Agreement*, By-Laws, § 3, *Jellico*.

54 *Id.* at 19.

55 Stuart Knott, *supra* note 16.

56 *See* BYRD DOUGLAS, *supra* note 19.

The L&N Railroad never belonged to the Exchange but its rail structure provided benefits. The western Kentucky and eastern Tennessee coal fields were the most accessible to the lines of the L&N and the Nashville market. Shipping coal by rail from other resource-abundant regions such as Pennsylvania was too expensive to permit competition from those areas.

When the NCE was formed, the L&N Railroad enjoyed the advantage of selling its services, for which good short-run substitutes did not exist, to a market of coal dealers that must have numbered at least two dozen (including wholesalers and those final consumers of steam coal who purchased directly from mines). The practice at the time was for the dealers to purchase coal at the mine, and thus it was the wholesale dealers rather than the mines who were the Railroad's customers.

A monopolist supplier of an input, like the L&N Railroad, would prefer to sell to firms that compete with one another.[57] If it sold to a cartel, the cartel's output restriction would reduce the demand for the Railroad's services, thereby diminishing the Railroad's profits.

While the L&N would have preferred to deal with competitive customers, this may not have been an option for the Railroad. Once the NCE had formed, the L&N found itself in a bilateral monopoly relationship with its Nashville coal shippers. While bilateral monopoly should yield a determinate price of the downstream product, the intermediate product price (here, transport services) is indeterminate.[58] Freight rates *might* have remained at the level a monopolist railroad selling to competitive wholesalers would have set, or they might have declined as the wholesalers flexed their monopsonistic muscle.

---

[57] *See* Roger D. Blair & David L. Kaserman, Antitrust Economics 301 (1985) for a modern exposition of the idea, originally articulated by Spengler, *Vertical Integration and Antitrust Policy*, 58 J. Pol. Econ. 347 (1950).

[58] *See* Blair, Kaserman & Romano, *A Pedagogical Treatment of Bilateral Monopoly*, 55 S. Econ. J. 831 (1989).

The record suggests that coal freight rates from Earlington to Nashville remained above short-run marginal cost even after the cartel was organized. Prior to the formation of the cartel the L&N had engaged in third-degree price discrimination (as was common of railroads of the period) that allowed *it* to profit from the relatively more inelastic demand of domestic coal consumers than industrial consumers. The Railroad initially charged the same rates for all coal shipments. But, when sufficient documentation was produced verifying that the coal was ultimately used for industrial (steam generation) purposes, the manufacturer (buyer of steam coal) or its representative (the wholesale dealer) received a rebate on the freight charge. These discounted transport rates for industrial coal must have at least covered short-run marginal cost, or the Railroad would have declined to carry the coal. Consequently, assuming the costs to the Railroad of transporting coal for different uses were the same, the nonrebated rates for domestic coal must have *exceeded* short-run marginal cost. Since rail rates did not decline after the NCE was formed,[59] the L&N Railroad must have continued to enjoy prices above short-run marginal cost even while negotiating with the monopsonistic NCE.

This implies that the cartel did not exercise (all of) its monopsony power in order to end the Railroad's third-degree price discrimination. The NCE appears to have shared with the Railroad at least some of the benefits from its cartelization of Nashville's domestic coal market. It might have done this in recognition of the advantages that the 1890 railroad structure provided the cartel, namely, a barrier to shipping coal into Nashville from alternative mines. If the L&N were squeezed too hard, it might have been tempted to initiate new lines into areas that could provide domestic coal supplies alternative to Earlington, Kentucky. The L&N would have been the most likely railroad to construct such lines because it could have integrated them with its existing lines and Nashville terminal facilities. The Railroad's share of the cartel's monopoly profits may have exceeded its expected profits (less costs of developing new rail lines) were it to have promoted (by opening new rail lines) an

---

59 A. J. Kellar, *supra* note 13.

environment where the shippers competed vigorously against one another.

V. Does the Nashville Coal Exchange fit cartel theory?

Cartels are more likely to develop in industries where structural conditions make collusion easier and where the rewards to price fixing are greater. The Exchange was fortunate to enjoy several such conditions.[60]

Collusion is more likely the fewer the number of sellers, because policies are then more easily coordinated and cheating is more readily detected. It is not impossible, however, for a large group to collude, but then a more formal organization is usually necessary to coordinate the agreement. An agreement among 14 mines and 14 coal dealers is one of large numbers. Consequently the formality of the Exchange organization and its rules and by-laws is to be expected. It is consistent with the findings of Hay and Kelley, and Fraas and Greer in their empirical analyses of cartel behavior.[61]

An agreement on price is easier to reach and monitor the more homogeneous is the product.[62] Coal sales in Nashville were based on an easily observed unit: a bushel. Differences in quality were controlled by the classification scheme. This system simplified pricing and facilitated the detection of cheaters, since price differentials then could not be rationalized on the basis of product differences. Furthermore, there is no indication that the heterogeneity induced by high rates of technological change hampered the cartel's effectiveness.[63]

---

60 For an extensive discussion of the factors facilitating collusion *see* Stigler, *A Theory of Oligopoly*, 72 J. Pol. Econ. 44 (1964); and Hay, *Oligopoly, Shared Monopoly, and Antitrust Law*, 67 Cornell L. Rev. 439 (1982) at 439.

61 *See* Fraas & Greer, *Market Structure and Price Collusion: An Empirical Analysis*, 26 J. Indus. Econ. 21 (1977) and Hay & Kelley, *An Empirical Survey of Price-Fixing Conspiracies*, 17 J.L. & Econ. 19 (1974).

62 *See* Hay, *supra* note 60, at 448–49.

63 *Id.* at 449–50.

The more inelastic the demand for a product at the competitive price the more rewarding is collusion since consumer resistance to price increases is then less.[64] The 1890 domestic coal market in Nashville was characterized by inelastic demand. Product substitution was not a major concern of the cartel because no good alternative source of domestic heat was available. Because competition was more significant for commercial coal, it makes sense that the cartel reached agreement on domestic prices rather than commercial coal prices.

The 1890 Nashville coal market was stable. There is no sign of unexpected changes in demand, which might have destabilized the cartel.[65] The coal business was seasonal but that was anticipated and reflected in prices.

Cartels are easier to police against member cheating when there is open bidding.[66] Residential consumers usually bought from retail coal dealers in Nashville who did not ship coal to the city but rather purchased it from wholesale dealers like the Exchange members. The retail dealers in turn resold it to the general public at posted prices. Consumers who bought larger quantities of domestic coal, on the other hand, often purchased directly from wholesale (Exchange member type) dealers. Some of the customers conducted trade using an open bidding policy (presumably to deter corruption among purchasing agents). Many of the buyers like the public school system and county hospitals conducted their bidding through the city government while private institutions like Vanderbilt University asked for bids that were later made available for public inspection.

Table 4 illustrates the effect of the cartel on bidding for a large *domestic* coal contract, coal used by the Nashville public school system from 1886 to 1890. The public school coal contract was renewed annually in June, at which time any dealer in the

---

64 *See* McElroy & Siegfried, *The Economics of Antitrust Enforcement*, 20 SURVEY OF BUS. 17 (1984).

65 *Id*. at 47.

66 *See* Hay, *supra* note 60, at 451.

Table 4
Number of Bidders on the *Domestic* Coal Contract for the Nashville Public School System, Selected Dates

	Total bidders	*Nashville Coal Exchange members bidding*	
June 1886	8	5	
June 1887	8	7	Average = 4.75
June 1888	5	4	
June 1889	3	3	
June 1890*	3	1	

* Period the Exchange was in operation.

SOURCE: Deposition of F. E. Kuhn filed January 24, 1891. *U.S. v. Jellico Mountain Coal and Coke Company, et al.*. Docket No. 2820.

city could bid on it. The number of annual bids by cartel members declined substantially when the cartel was active. For contrast, table 5 reports the number of bids for the annual Nashville City Works *steam* coal contract. No decline in the number of bids from Exchange members in 1890 is evident for the City Works *steam* contract in contrast to the public school system *domestic* coal contract, where only one Exchange member (the designated one) bid in 1890. While this evidence is suggestive rather than conclusive, it is at least consistent with effective operation of a domestic coal cartel during 1889–1890.

Recent research has found that firms may be more apt to collude when their industry is experiencing hard times because the opportunity cost of not colluding is less than it would be were the industry enjoying the fruits of expansion.[67] The Nashville coal market of 1890 was becoming less profitable, to the point that many mines no longer wanted to sell their product there.[68] The NCE was allegedly formed in response to this deteriorating environment, in order to "stabilize" prices and output.

67 *See* Asch & Seneca, *Is Collusion Profitable?* 58 REV. ECON. & STAT. 1-8, 11–12 (1976).

68 A. J. Kellar, *supra* note 13.

Table 5
Number of Bidders on the *Steam* Coal Contract for the Nashville Water Works

	Total bidders	*Nashville Coal Exchange members bidding*	
June 1886	3	2	
June 1887	3	2	
June 1888	6	2	Average = 2/yr.
June 1889	3	2	
June 1890*	4	3	

* Period the Exchange was in operation.

SOURCE: Deposition of F. E. Kuhn filed January 24, 1891. *U.S. v. Jellico Mountain Coal and Coke Company, et al.*, Docket No. 2820.

A successful cartel must somehow control entry to protect itself from external competition.[69] The Exchange resembled a partial conspiracy because it did not include all firms supplying and selling coal to Nashville consumers. Theoretically, nonmember suppliers could have provided an effective competitive environment. This prospect seems to have induced the Exchange to set prices that would limit the response of potential entrants into mining and/or wholesaling. In addition, the cartel incorporated devices into its rules and practices to impede entry and minimize the threat of external competition.

The Exchange had no restrictions on membership, thus giving the appearance of a cartel with free entry. Under these conditions members might have expected to enjoy short-run disequilibrium monopoly profits, but in the long run a successful (*i.e.*, no cheating) free-entry cartel could expect to earn only normal profits, albeit at a price above the competitive level.[70]

69 *See* McElroy & Siegfried, *supra* note 64, at 17.

70 Patinkin, *Multiple Plant Firms, Cartels and Imperfect Information*, 61 Q.J. ECON. 173 (1947).

Independent mines and dealers could join the Exchange, but none apparently did so after the Exchange initially was formed. Exchange members would obviously have preferred a new market entrant to join the cartel rather than the competitive fringe. Joining the Exchange carried with it certain costs, however. Membership bestowed upon independent firms no benefits they were not already receiving, and constrained their sales because they would have had to have sold at the established Exchange price. In contrast, nonmembership allowed considerable sales at prices minimally below the cartel price. The few nonmember mines in western Kentucky sold through two or three nonmember wholesale dealers in Nashville. Neither the dealers nor the mines alone could have joined the Exchange and maintained their historical commercial relationships without violating Exchange rules. The necessity of both mines and dealers to join simultaneously might have deterred entry. The nonmember mines apparently sold their coal at the same price as member mines.[71]

If production from existing nonmember mines and wholesalers was limited by capacity constraints, then Exchange members were left with the task of defending their profits against the effects of entry by independent mine operators. In the short run, delay, the costs of opening new mines, and the need for a rail spur to the mine protected the western Kentucky coal mines from new local competition. High transportation costs protected them from competition from other coal fields (*e.g.*, Pennsylvania). The wholesalers, who received their compensation from the mine operators by means of a lower than profit maximizing transfer price, did not have to fear sharing their portion of the monopoly profits with new wholesalers because the Exchange member mines agreed not to sell to nonmember wholesalers. So long as entry by new mine operators was impeded, entry into wholesaling also would be limited.

Seventy-five percent of all grades of domestic coal sold in Nashville originated in western Kentucky. Specifically, 60% was shipped from the region around Earlington, Kentucky alone where all the mines belonged to the Exchange. With the inclusion

---

71 A. J. Kellar, *supra* note 13.

of eastern Tennessee mines, the Exchange members accounted for approximately 80% to 85% of the domestic No. 1 coal sold in Nashville. The remaining 15% to 20% originated from two independent Kentucky mines located along the lines of the L&N but not situated near Earlington, one of which (Eureka) had at one time belonged to the Exchange.[72] The Eureka mine produced a low grade of heating coal, and supplied 8% to 10% of Nashville's consumption, selling mostly to schools, hospitals and the penitentiary.[73] The McKinley and Stanley mine produced residential No. 1 coal and reportedly supplied 5% to 12% of Nashville's consumption.[74] Both mines appear to have been operating at capacity. Apparently they shipped coal only to Nashville, unlike the mines belonging to the Exchange, which additionally supplied coal to both the Memphis and Louisville markets. Consequently, once the independents reached short-run capacity, they had no additional coal supplies they could divert to the (now higher priced) Nashville market. Furthermore, no mines "adjacent or convenient to the Nashville market, except those in Western Kentucky yielded No. 1 coal."[75] Practically all of the mines from which it was possible to ship *additional* domestic coal to Nashville at competitive prices were actually members of the Exchange.

The wording of the Agreement itself suggests that very few mines not members of the Exchange shipped domestic coal to Nashville. The exemption of steam coal from the price-fixing scheme because of excessive competition in the industrial sector indicates that "enough of the mines producing domestic coal" had joined the Exchange to give it the power to control price and entry.[76]

---

72 The above figures were obtained from the Brief for the United States, at 36, *Jellico*. The Peacock mine, near Earlington, was also a nonmember, but its owners were members of the Exchange.

73 E. W. Hill, *supra* note 18; and J. H. Kendrick, *supra* note 26.

74 E. W. Hill, *supra* note 18.

75 Brief for the United States, at 37, *Jellico*.

76 *Id.* at 14.

VI. Economic behavior of the Exchange

The Nashville coal market of 1890 can be characterized by what is commonly called the dominant-firm–price-leadership or partial-conspiracy model. The figure illustrates our interpretation of the situation. Industry supply, S, is divided into two components; that supplied by the cartel, S_c, and that supplied by nonmember or competitive fringe firms, S_f, here the Eureka, and McKinley and Stanley mines. We assume the supply of the competitive fringe to be initially fairly elastic due to low-cost expansion of mine output until quantity Q_f^* is reached. At Q_f^*, the nonmember mines who can supply Nashville at the cartel price are operating at full capacity, causing the competitive fringe supply curve to become vertical. The supply curve of the cartel is also fairly elastic initially and becomes vertical at maximum capacity, but we have assumed that level of output to be irrelevant to market demand (D_oD_o). The member mines were much larger and their combined capacity greatly exceeded that of the nonmember mines. This characterization of the situation assumes the cartel members expected nonmember mines to behave as price takers, and therefore perceived the cartel's demand (d_cd_c) to be the residual remaining after the nonmember mines sold what they wished at the cartel price. The reported conduct of the Eureka and McKinley and Stanley mines supports this assumption.[77] To maximize profits, the cartel would have set price by balancing its members' aggregate short-run marginal cost (S_c) against the additional revenue induced by reductions in the cartel price (mr_c). The cartel would have priced at P^*, as if it were the only firm in a market with demand d_cd_c, and short-run marginal cost, S_c. The nonmember fringe would have sold Q_f^* at the price P^*. At P^*, nonmember firms receive a "free-ride" from the cartel because they too enjoy the excess profits the cartel provides by restricting output. Cartel output would have been Q_c^*, and total industry supply of coal to Nashville would have been Q_t^*, with the cartel's market share exceeding the market share of the nonmember mines.

---

77 A. J. Kellar, *supra* note 13.

Figure

Partial Conspiracy Model of Nashville Coal Exchange, Circa 1890

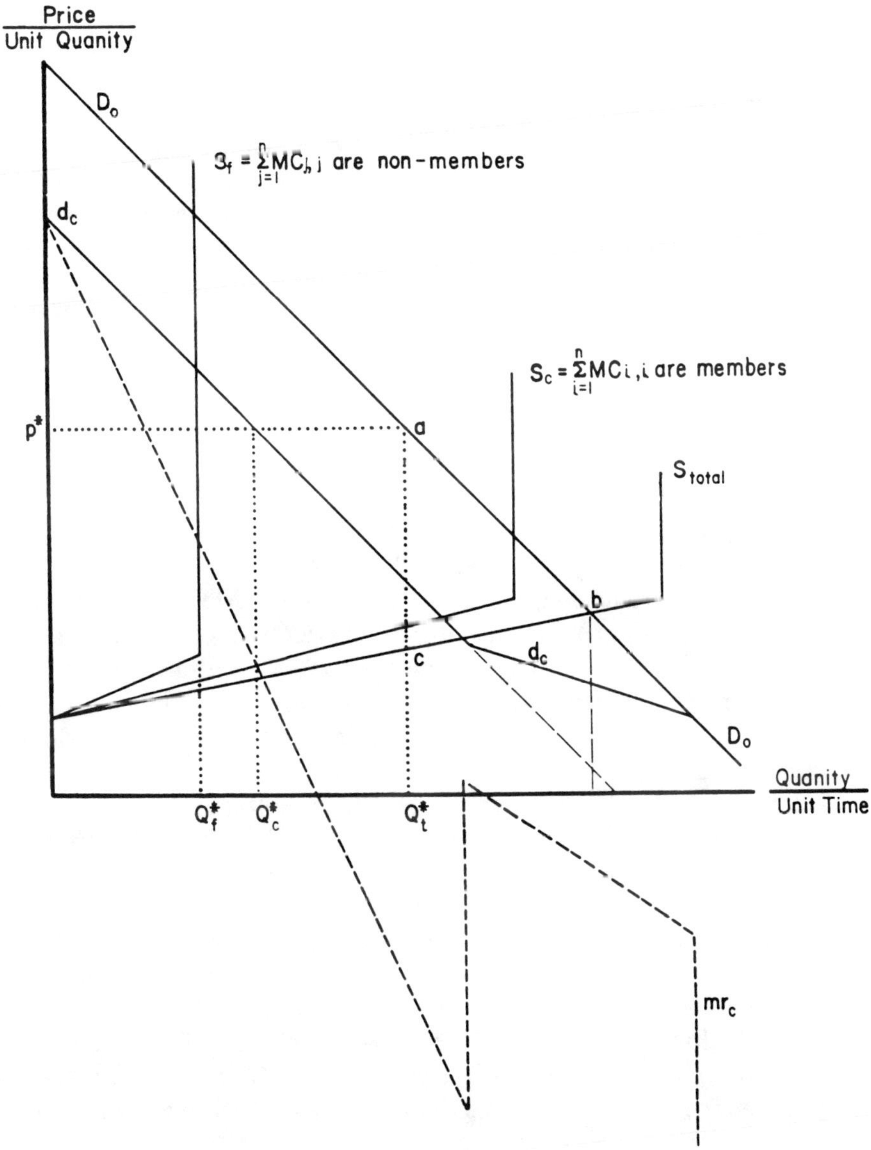

Overall, price is higher and output lower than what would have existed in the absence of the Exchange. Some residential consumers who value heat derived from coal more than the short-run marginal cost of mining it in the member mines either endure lower temperatures or switch to less valuable substitutes, *e.g.*, wood. The deadweight welfare loss caused by the cartel is represented by area *abc* in the figure. It is quite large compared to the usual welfare loss in a partial-conspiracy model because of the assumed limited capacity of nonmember firms to continue to expand supply as price is elevated. A significant increase in price occurs relative to what one usually expects from this type of market structure. In addition, the fringe firm's marginal cost exceeds the marginal cost of member mines, causing aggregate mining costs to be higher than necessary.

Data from the trial record show that the Exchange raised price (at least initially) above the competitive level. The average price per bushel (of 80 pounds) of domestic No. 1 coal in Nashville exceeded the comparable price in Memphis by almost 3 cents over the 12-month period, August 1889 through August 1890. The same western Kentucky coal fields supplied both cities.[78] Prices in Nashville were more than 20% higher than in Memphis. Coal was sold on a sliding scale in Nashville, price varying with quantity purchased, but typically sold by the ton. No sliding scale existed in Memphis, where coal was sold in units of a barrel of 180 pounds. If anything, the typically larger lot sizes in Nashville should have led to lower, not higher, prices there. The only defense the Exchange cited for the price discrepancy was monopolistic rail rates, but the data in table 3 cast doubt on that explanation. There was practically no difference in average rail rates *per trip* from Earlington, Kentucky on the L&N Railroad to Memphis and Nashville. Memphis and Nashville are 267 and 103 miles respectively from Earlington. The freight rate *per mile* was approximately 60% greater to Nashville, revealing price "discrimination by the railroad."[79] However, higher rail rates per mile do not explain the price difference between Memphis and Nashville as the total cost of coal delivery to each of the two cities was

---

78 Brief for the United States, at 36, *Jellico*.

79 *Id.* at 15.

virtually identical. The higher price of coal in Nashville, therefore, seems attributable to the Nashville Coal Exchange.

The partial conspiracy model describes only a short-run situation. In the long run, entry may occur in response to the cartel's attractive profits. Entry would increase the nonmember fringe supply and reduce the cartel's perceived residual demand correspondingly. This process would continue until excess profits were dissipated, at which time the cartel would no longer serve its intended purpose. The entry impediments devised by the Exchange, however, prevented such a situation from developing before Judge Key dismantled the cartel.

VII. Legal arguments and trial court decision

U.S. v. Jellico Mountain Coal was a test case for the new Sherman Act.[80] The government tried to establish that the behavior of the NCE members violated both sections 1 and 2 of the Act; the defendants argued that the Act was unconstitutional.

The evidence in the case consisted primarily of the published Agreement governing the actions of the NCE. The government argued that the Exchange, controlling 80% of Nashville's domestic coal market, restrained trade by denying nonmember mines and dealers access to the market.

The Exchange hinged its defense on constitutional claims. First, it argued that the Sherman Act was unconstitutional because it "confers jurisdiction in equity over controversies other than controversies between citizens of different states."[81] Second, the defendants claimed that section 4 of the Sherman Act, which confers jurisdiction in equity to the United States circuit court in

---

80 *See* William Letwin, *supra* note 2, at 107.

81 This argument had no foundation since section 2 of article III of the Constitution "provides that the judicial power shall extend to all cases in law and *equity* arising under the Constitution and the laws of the United States as well as providing that such jurisdiction shall extend to controversies between citizens of different states." *See* Alan Walker, History of the Sherman Law of the United States 67 (1910).

such situations, was unconstitutional because the Act prescribed criminal penalties upon conviction,[82] and the Constitution requires that "trials of all crimes, except in cases of impeachment, shall be by jury."[83] Finally, the defendants argued that the interstate commerce condition was not satisfied. The contracts between mine operators and wholesale dealers required the dealers to purchase coal at the mines. Transportation and distribution costs were then the responsibility of the wholesalers. The defendants argued that the transactions were separate and unrelated events; the mine operators played no role in transporting coal to another state and the dealers had done "nothing relevant to coal outside the State of Tennessee."[84]

In the trial court (and, ultimately final) decision, Judge Key ruled for the government and issued a permanent injunction against all firms who were members of the NCE at the time the bill was filed. He concluded that "the intentions of the association could hardly have been more successfully framed to fall within the provisions of the Act had the object been to organize a combination, the business of which should subject it to the penalties of that statute."[85] Judge Key avoided the constitutional

---

82 *Id.* at 65.

83 *Jellico* was a case in *equity,* not a criminal proceeding. A case tried in equity does not carry criminal penalties; rather, a petitioner may seek an injunction. The Constitution only mandates the application of the right to a jury when in the absence of such, a person "might be convicted and punished (fine or imprisonment) without the benefit of a say of his peers." *Id.* at 66. This protection does not extend to injunctions. Thus it seems legitimate for a circuit court judge to decide a Sherman Act case brought in equity.

84 *Id.* at 66. Judge Key interpreted the situation otherwise and rejected the defense's claim. He concluded that the transportation of coal between Kentucky and Tennessee was necessary to the execution of the contract. *Id.* at 67. In spite of this early victory on the interstate commerce issue, the government was to encounter considerable judicial resistance to a liberal interpretation of the interstate commerce requirement in Sherman Act litigation for most of its first decade. U.S. v. E.C. Knight, 156 U.S. 1 (1895).

85 46 F. 432, 436 (C.C.M.D. Tenn. 1891).

issues, because he believed that a trial court did not have the authority to question an Act of Congress that had been so carefully considered and argued before its final passage.[86] With constitutional issues set aside, Key concluded that the evidence was easily interpreted as a violation of the law.

Judge Key did not invoke the explicit per se doctrine, which, before the turn of the century, became an integral part of Sherman Act section 1 interpretation. He did, however, recognize that a defense based on reasonable and justified prices was not relevant to the issue, thus anticipating the eventual per se doctrine.[87] He concluded that "the statute condemned the 'attempt to monopolize,' and the Exchange Agreement was in itself such an attempt" regardless of whether and to what extent prices were raised.[88]

It is unclear why the defendants did not appeal. A higher court might have been more inclined to entertain constitutional arguments,[89] but then appeals are also expensive. *Jellico* stimulated a burst of energy with regard to Sherman Act enforcement, especially in the area of coal distribution.[90] The law seemed to have been successfully upheld.

---

86 *Id.* at 435–36.

87 *See*, however, recent exceptions to the per se approach to the Sherman Act: N.C.A.A. v. Board of Regents of the University of Oklahoma and University of Georgia Athletic Association, 464 U.S. 253 (1983); ASCAP et al. v. Columbia Broadcasting System, 441 U.S. 1 (1979); United States v. U. S. Gypsum, 538 U.S. 422 (1978).

88 *See* William Letwin, *supra* note 2, at 145.

89 During the reconstruction period, "states' rights" dominated the political ideology of the South. The defense in *Jellico* questioned the federal government's power under the Sherman Act. Perhaps because the court *in Tennessee* had been unpersuaded by the arguments, the defendants judged further effort in the federal court system unlikely to produce a more favorable verdict.

90 *See* William Letwin, *supra* note 2, at 109.

VIII. Conclusion

Jellico Mountain Coal was the first case filed under the Sherman Act and the first government case decided by a trial court (a private action filed in Louisiana after *Jellico* was decided before the final verdict in *Jellico*). The government's victory in *Jellico* gave initial credibility to the new law. Interestingly, the court applied an approach similar to the subsequently adopted per se standard for conspiracies in restraint of trade. Judge Key made no distinction between good and bad price-fixing but decided that any combination in restraint of trade was an attempt to monopolize the market and was, therefore, illegal under the law.

Analysis of the *Jellico* case suggests that tacit collusion is difficult to organize when the number of sellers is large. Indeed, without the cooperation of the western Kentucky mines Nashville's coal wholesalers could not maintain an agreed price even in a favorable legal environment (*i.e.*, in 1887, prior to passage of the Sherman Act). On the other hand, with the use of organizational devices to facilitate adherence to a price agreement, and a formula to divide the profits earned by the cartel, the members of the NCE appear to have benefitted at the expense of coal consumers until government intervention terminated their agreement. In the right circumstances cartelization may be feasible and worth the effort. Whether Sherman Act section-1 enforcement is efficient in such cases depends on the costs of enforcement, how long the cartel would have survived absent intervention, and the value of the enforcement action as a deterrent to attempts by others to restrict competition.

5
The good and bad trust dichotomy: a short history of a legal idea

BY ELEANOR M. FOX* and LAWRENCE A. SULLIVAN**

Antitrust is not a set of economic rules but institutional policy based on changing economic reality and expressed in changing historical forms. It is rooted not in deductive theory but in law and politics. Each of its major ideas has a history. Each can be identified (albeit sometimes in obscure and often in developing forms) in legislative debates, in the enforcement programs of sequential administrations, and in the holdings and dicta—the normative resolutions, the compromises, and sometimes the evasions—that make up the work product of courts. Our purpose here is to take a single antitrust idea—the notion that there are good trusts and bad trusts, identify its origin, and trace its evolution. To begin, we will recall how the trusts developed and how the public and Congress responded to them; and while we find little support for a good trust-bad trust conception in the public reaction to trusts in the late 19th century, we do find indications that Congress indirectly anticipated the dichotomy.

---

* Professor of Law, New York University School of Law.

** Earl Warren Professor of Public Law, Boalt Hall School of Law, University of California, Berkeley.

After noting that enforcement against trusts during the first decade of the Sherman Antitrust Act was weak, we turn to antitrust enforcement during the presidency of Theodore Roosevelt. During the Theodore Roosevelt administration the good–bad trust dichotomy first came to prominence, though only as a guide to prosecutorial discretion. The idea of such a dichotomy, was predicated more on political goals and commitments than on analysis either of the legislative history or of the common law tradition. Nor was it informed by deductive theory, of the kind sometimes brought into play today. Rather, it was a mechanism or promise that tended to legitimate enforcement. In a brief conclusion we show how the good trust–bad trust idea was transformed at later stages of antitrust development, and may have reappeared in contemporary authority.

The rise of the trusts

Between 1865 and 1910, industrial structure and conventional ways of doing business were immensely and rapidly altered. Changes in corporate structure, first through cartelization and then consolidation and vertical integration, transformed chains of small firms into a complex network of oligopolies and monopolies. By the end of the period of big, bureaucratic corporation had fully emerged and an urban, wage-earning labor force had taken the place of the independent artisans who had previously thrived.[1]

Salient features of that development might be noted. In post-Civil War America resources were abundant. The invention of alloys and new sources of energy made mass production feasible. Over the last decades of the century innovations in communication and transportation provided the needed infrastructure for

---

[1] For a detailed description of the traditional business enterprise, *see* A. D. CHANDLER, THE VISIBLE HAND: THE MANAGERIAL REVOLUTION IN AMERICAN BUSINESS chs. 1–2 (1977). For a general description of the growth of big business, *see* G. PORTER, THE RISE OF BIG BUSINESS, 1860–1910 (1973), and H. N. SCHEIBER, H. S. VATTER, & H. V. FAULKNER, AMERICAN ECONOMIC HISTORY 159–61 (1976).

widening markets. The influx of almost 30 million immigrants provided both a labor force and consumer demand.

The states, in the post-Civil War years, took on a role in promoting and regulating enterprise that differed in kind from prior experience. Special charters, the primary method of incorporation before mid-century, were gradually replaced by general incorporation laws. The states possessed the power to "determine the very structure of the corporate enterprises doing business within their jurisdiction,"[2] but they did not anticipate the speed and scale of the new incorporation movement that would take place during the 1880's and 1890's. Businesses intent on capturing larger shares of the markets for their goods not only took advantage of general incorporation laws and other new legal devices but also did not hesitate to do what seemed expedient to evade remaining state-imposed legal restraints.[3] The older concept of a state role in private decisions about the economy faded.

The changing legal status of the corporation was but one factor in a much larger, ongoing process, a movement to centralize many or all aspects of production, marketing, and distribution. Incentives existed for combining units engaged in production and marketing through both horizontal consolidation and vertical integration. First, some businesses (the Singer Sewing Machine Company, for example) manufactured new, complex products that required special marketing services such as demonstrations and maintenance.[4] Second, traditional outlets were sometimes not able to dispose of the great volume of manufactured goods. Perhaps most importantly, corporations wanted to escape from ruinous competition and declining prices.

The railroads—the nation's first "big business"—were the first to confront the problem of ruinous competition. Railroads

---

2 McCurdy, *The Knight Sugar Decision of 1895 and the Modernization of American Corporation Law, 1869–1903*, 53 Bus. Hist. Rev. 304, 305 (1979).

3 McCurdy, *American Law and the Marketing Structure of the Large Corporation, 1875–1890*, 38 J. Econ. Hist. 631, 637–41 (1978).

4 A. D. Chandler, *supra* note 1, at 402–03.

required a high initial investment for construction and maintenance. To offset the high cost of fixed assets and of operations, railroad companies sought a large volume of business at low rates. Often, railroads adopted the unpopular strategies of setting differential rates for certain large volume shippers and localities and charging less for long hauls than for short hauls. During the construction boom competing roads were forced to lower rates to stay in business.[5]

Responding to these conditions, railroads formed "pools"—horizontal combinations of competitors joining forces to create large, regionally dominant systems, that, today, would be called cartels.[6] These were unstable, however. For example, schemes to apportion the petroleum transportation among the railroads collapsed. When oil refiners and shippers refused to participate, railroads either cheated on other pool members by giving secret rebates[7] or dropped out altogether. Likewise, a pool formed to allocate coal production and establish shipping rates favorable to the railroads was short-lived due to fluctuations in the economy during the 1880's and 1890's. Although railroads pursued legislation to give pools legal sanction, they remained legally unenforceable; under pressure they quickly fell apart.[8]

Pools were attempted in other industries as well, with a similar fate. The collapse of pools led industry to closer forms of horizontal consolidation, to vertical integration (by which a firm or group of competitors attempted to create large organizations that controlled the entire production process from obtaining raw materials to structured marketing systems) or to both. The early trusts were created when a number of corporations, erstwhile pool members, "turned their stock over to a board of trustees

---

5 G. Miller, *Railroads and the Granger Laws* 16–23 (1971); A. D. Chandler, *supra* note 1, at 140–42, 148–51, 156–64.

6 A. D. Chandler, *supra* note 1, at ch. 5.

7 *Id.* at 136–37.

8 E. C. Kirkland, *Industry Comes of Age: Business, Labor, and Public Policy, 1860–1897*, at 203 (1961).

receiving in return trust certificates of equivalent value."[9] As markets gradually expanded despite recurring periods of overcapacity and depression, vertical integration increased. Vertical combination was more successful than were purely horizontal pools in reducing costs, increasing productivity, and eliminating competition.[10] Vertical integration could yield cost-reducing efficiencies; it, like horizontal cooperation or consolidation, could also yield market power.

Standard Oil, the first and best known of the great trusts, was formed in 1882. It successfully captured the petroleum industry and maintained its control for many years. Other refining and distilling companies imitated this new form of organization.[11] After consolidating horizontally, trusts would often attempt to gain control over the input resources and the marketing system needed for their particular industry.[12] Again, Standard Oil was the model that many imitated.

Political and social reactions to the trusts

The trust movement grew out of the problems of overcapacity caused by the industrial revolution.[13] Large-scale, commercialized agriculture and a comprehensive transformation in the means of productivity helped the nation prosper as never before, but overcapacity and overproduction revealed structural flaws in the economy. Business leaders increasingly viewed the trust as a solution. Using combinations and mergers they hoped to attain and solidify market control. "[T]he real intangible was the earning power of the combination, presumably enhanced by the

---

9 A. D. CHANDLER, *supra* note 1, at 319.

10 *Id.* at 285–89.

11 *Id.* at 320.

12 *Id.* at 315.

13 Scheiber, *Property Law, Expropriation, and Resource Allocation by Government, 1789–1910*, 33 J. ECON. HIST. 232 (1973).

economies it brought about and the degree of market control it exerted."[14] But the trust, ostensibly designed to preserve economic stability, was an uncertain instrument. If stability was not apparent as a consequence of trustification, the concentration of wealth and economic power was. While it may be difficult to tell the extent to which the trust movement led to monopoly, "many of the combines came close enough to inspire widespread public concern about the trust movement."[15]

The rise of trusts in the oil, steel, electric power, and other public utility industries during the 1880's fed widespread fears about the economic implications of the combination movement. Economic change during this period had wrought a new social order. Traditional values had been upended. The individual worker and independent artisan were displaced by a specialized, wage-earning industrial labor force. The very nature of private enterprise required redefinition—prompting public reaction and regulatory responses from government.

Political, editorial and other commentators did not at once express the conviction that some trusts were good and some were not. They tended, rather, to be for or against trusts. It was widely recognized that the new order carried both advantages and disadvantages and people tended to be opinionated about the rapid changes they were witnessing. On the one hand, the industrial economy expanded at a rapid rate, bringing a general increase in wealth and productivity. Those who focused their attention on the great industrial expansion affirmed the trusts as a cause or facilitator of progress. They predicted a bright future with even higher production levels, incomes, and standard of living. However, the economic gains in the decades after the Civil War were coupled with "increasing inequalities in the distribution of wealth, a drift toward monopoly, railway abuses of various sorts, unemployment on an unprecedented scale, and health and

---

14 E. C. KIRKLAND, *supra* note 8, at 211.

15 L. GALAMBOS, *The Public Image of Big Business in America, 1880–1940: A Quantitative Study in Social Change* 9 (1975).

housing problems in the rapidly growing cities.''[16] Commentators who focused on the inequalities and abuses were hardly enamored of the trusts. "The promised land,'' said social commentator Henry George,

> flies before us like the mirage. . . . [I]n factories where labor-saving machinery has reached its most wonderful development, little children are at work; wherever the new forces are anything like fully utilized, large classes are maintained by charity or live on the verge of recourse to it; amid the great accumulations of wealth, men die of starvation, and puny infants suckle dry breasts, while everywhere the greed of gain, the worship of wealth, shows the force of the fear of want.[17]

During the 1880s, people became more focused on negative economic developments and began to look to law and government to remedy what had gone wrong in the economy.

The trust became a symbol of the new order. To its supporters, it signified wealth, cooperation, and progressive development. To its detractors, these impersonal, centrally administered monoliths represented greed, inhumanity, and economic stratification. Consequently, despite the fact that only eight industrial consolidations during the 1880's actually took the form of trusts,[18] the term "trust'' came to denote more than a specific legal device for corporate combination. It was the catchphrase in a public debate over the course of economic growth and the distribution of wealth.

It was widely believed in the 19th century that free competition is essential to a thriving, efficient economy. This belief was both a rallying point and a dilemma for both sides of the debate. Business owners argued that competition was the great regulator: It led to economic natural selection, the survival of the most efficient. Because competition was governed by natural laws, any

---

16 S. Fine, Laissez-Faire and the General Welfare State 289 (1956).

17 H. George, Progress and Poverty 8 (1958 ed.).

18 A. D. Chandler, *supra* note 1, at 320.

attempts to impose "artificial" restraints would hinder progress.[19] But this argument was contradicted by the reality that large businesses were consolidating to avoid the rigors of the assertedly immutable law of competition.

Many business people and some economists seeking to reconcile the contradiction argued that trusts were inevitable growths, dictated by the same forces that governed the evolution of the biological world. The evolutionary argument affirmed the positive nature of the trust. The appearance of this new business form signaled that social evolution had reached a new stage. Most who adopted this schema saw the trust eliminating only excessive competition and thus restoring balance and efficiency to the economic order. To some, however, the trust augured the decline of governance by competition and the rise of a new age of cooperation.[20]

Many people—consumers, farmers, laborers, small business owners—rejected these justifications. Newspapers published exposés of unscrupulous methods used by the leaders of trusts in quashing their competitors and forcing smaller businesses to cooperate with them. Henry Demarest Lloyd argued that the trusts achieved their size and power through secret, illegal means. He fueled the growing antitrust movement with tales of the corrupt methods used by the leaders of the first trust—the Standard Oil Company.[21] The reaction to such disclosures was not a demand that trusts reform their conduct; it was a demand that the nation rid itself of the trusts.

Indeed, opponents of the trust turned the evolutionary argument on its head. For example, populist leader William Jennings

---

19 S. Fine, *supra* note 16, at 100–03. For an interesting review of economic views during this period, and for a useful bibliography, *see* May, *Antitrust Practice and Procedure in the Formative Era: The Constitutional and Conceptual Reach of State Antitrust Law, 1880–1918*, 135 U. Pa. L. Rev. 495, 535-53 (1987).

20 *See generally*, S. Fine, *supra* note 16, at 110-11, 221-25, 338; and W. Letwin, Law and Economic Policy in America 75–77 (1965).

21 H. D. Lloyd, Lords of Industry 1–46 (1910).

Bryan labeled trusts as unnatural growths: "Every trust rests upon a corporation and every corporation is unnatural, a man-made creature of law."[22] Many opponents of trusts also rejected outright the claim of classical theorists that when a business services its own interest it inevitably serves the public.[23] Others observed that, whatever the case for smaller firms, the threat of potential competition did not constrain trusts; they responded to potential competition by increasing their efforts at absorbing or eliminating competitors and restricting entry.[24]

In the end, public opinion turned strongly against the trusts. Small business owners viewed the expansion of big business with apprehension, fearing that the trusts would either absorb them or drive them out of business. Small retailers, jobbers, and traveling salespeople found their businesses severely challenged by the new chain stores and mail-order firms.[25] Many shippers, angered by the discriminatory railroad rates, agitated for local and national government regulation.[26] Farmers, plagued by the high costs of farm machinery and consumer products and the low prices of their crops, claimed that their situation was "aggravated by various trusts, such as those that sold farmers bags and bought their linseed oil and cottonseed,"[27] and by "middlemen and commodity speculators who handled their crops."[28] Various farm organizations—the Grange, the Farmers Alliance (precursors of the Populists)—rallied around proposals to control big business. The emergence of national labor unions by the 1880's and the

---

22 CHICAGO CONFERENCE ON TRUSTS 511 (1900).

23 Lloyd, *Wealth Against Commonwealth*, in THE POPULIST MIND 496, 501–02 (N. Pollack ed. 1967).

24 A. EICHNER, THE EMERGENCE OF OLIGOPOLY 124 (1969).

25 A. D. CHANDLER, *supra* note 1, at 233.

26 L. BENSON, MERCHANTS, FARMERS AND RAILROADS 13 (1955); *see also* G. MILLER, *supra* note 6.

27 W. LETWIN, *supra* note 20, at 59.

28 H. N. SCHEIBER, H. S. VATTER, H. V. FAULKNER, *supra* note 1, at 214.

more frequent occurrence of strikes attested to the economic problems of the new industrial workers.[29] Also, the trust's ability to obtain favorable political treatment rekindled the traditional American hostility toward monopoly and special privilege. As William Letwin has commented, "Hatred of monopoly is one of the oldest American political habits."[30]

Reaction to the trusts was not monolithic. These new business organizations had supporters as well as challengers. But despite manifest benefits in the new economic order and despite emphasis on the offensive manipulations that particular trusts had initiated, the tendency was for most people to be against trusts; the public mood was not one that encouraged efforts to separate good trusts from bad ones or to regulate the conduct of trusts in order to assure that they contributed more benefits than harms.

Passage of the Sherman Act

By the election of 1888, which brought William Henry Harrison to the presidency, it was commonly acknowledged that "the public had found the trusts to be a growing and intolerable evil."[31] In view of the strong public feeling, the candidates of the major political parties supported a national antitrust law. Even big business advocates reconciled themselves to a law against the trusts, perhaps convinced that Congress would not vote for the tariff they wanted unless domestic competition was protected by such a law.

In 1889, Senator John Sherman introduced the Sherman Antitrust Bill, which was redrafted largely through the efforts of

---

29 D. Brody, Steelworkers in America: The Nonunion Era 159–60 (1960); A. Paul, Conservative Crisis and the Rule of Law: Attitudes of Bar and Bench, 1887–1895, at 128–30 (1960).

30 W. Letwin, *supra* note 20, at 59.

31 *See* W. H. Taft, The Anti-Trust Act and the Supreme Court 2 (1914); *see also* H. Thorelli, The Federal Antitrust Policy: Organization of an American Tradition 129 (1955).

Senators Edmunds and Hoar. During congressional debate, Senator Sherman gave as the purpose of the bill the need to contain the concentration of economic power:

> The popular mind is agitated with problems that may disturb social order, and among them all none is more threatening than the inequality of condition, of wealth, and opportunity that has grown within a single generation out of the concentration of capital into vast combinations to control production and trade and to break down competition. These combinations already defy or control powerful transportation corporations and reach State authorities. They reach out their Briarean arms to every part of our country. They are imported from abroad. Congress alone can deal with them, and if we are unwilling or unable there will soon be a trust for every production and a master to fix the price for every necessity of life.[32]

The legislative history of the act is replete with such rhetoric. As Judge Robert H. Bork wrote:

> In looking to the legislative history, one discerns repeated concern for the welfare of consumers and also for the welfare of small business and for various other values—a potpourri of other values. So far as I'm aware, Congress, in enacting these statutes, never faced the problem of what to do when values come into conflict in specific cases. Legislators appear to have assumed, as it is most comfortable to assume, that all good things are always compatible.[33]

Although legislative purpose in the Sherman Act may be difficult to pinpoint, the Act features important goals that rely on both judicial authority and common law doctrine to control the trusts. One explicit congressional purpose, emphasized repeatedly, was to protect consumers from unreasonable price increases. Others included protecting small businesses from coercion and assuring that markets remained open to entry and participation.[34] Moreover, Congress did more than indicate gen-

---

32 21 Cong. Rec. 2460 (1890).

33 Bork, *The Role of the Courts in Applying Economics*, 54 Antitrust L.J. 21, 24 (1985).

34 There is, of course, an ongoing debate about the purposes of the Sherman Act. Chicago theorists argue that the goal is allocative efficiency (*e.g.*, R. H. Bork, The Antitrust Paradox, ch. 2, esp.

eral purposes and give the courts an utterly free hand. Judge Bork remarked that Congress gave "no specific directions to judges other than to preserve competition."[35] Yet, while Congress did not actually mention the word "competition" in the statute, it did link the statute to a common law tradition by using the common law phrase, "restraint of trade" and the common law term, "monopoly." To some extent the common law tradition must supplement the statute. Drawing from this tradition, Congress first formulated a concept hardly found in the earlier popular debate: the idea that some conduct by economically powerful firms is acceptable, some not.[36]

---

pp. 61–66 (1978)), but this contention cannot be maintained except by the most strained reading of the legislative history. Disinterested historians are convinced that the Act had several goals; protecting consumers from exploitation by producers, shielding competitors from predation and intimidation, and safeguarding the right of entry. *See* H. THORELLI, *supra* note 31, at 225-32; W. LETWIN, *supra* note 20, at 95–99. *See also* Lande, *Wealth Transfers as the Original and Primary Concern of Antitrust: The Efficiency Interpretation Challenged*, 34 HASTINGS L.J. 65, 96-106 (1982); Kaplow, *The Accuracy of Traditional Market Power Analysis and a Direct Adjustment Alternative*, 95 HARV. L. REV. 1817, 1822 (1982). For a study more nearly contemporaneous with the passage of the Act, *see* A. WALKER, HISTORY OF THE SHERMAN LAW OF THE UNITED STATES OF AMERICA (1910).

35 Bork, *supra* note 33, at 24.

36 It bears noting that there was no single, consistent common law tradition, but variations within England at various points in time, between England and America, and within America from state to state. (*See* HANDLER, TEMPORARY NATIONAL ECONOMIC COMMITTEE MONOGRAPH NO. 38, 76TH CONG., 3D SESS. A STUDY OF THE CONSTRUCTION AND ENFORCEMENT OF THE FEDERAL ANTITRUST LAWS 4–8 (Comm. Print 1941) (hereinafter TNEC No. 38). The English common law, at least after the *Case of Monopolies*, decided in 1602, was hostile to monopolies created by royal grant, but there is little indication either in England or America of hostility to power gained in the marketplace except where bad conduct such as targeted exclusion of competitors or concerted price-fixing was involved. *See* Letwin, *The English Common Law Concerning Monopolies*, 21 U. CHI. L. REV. 355, 367–70 (1954); TNEC No. 38; Jones, *Historical Development of the Law of Business Competition*, 35 YALE L.J. 905, 907–09 (1926). Certainly distinctions were drawn on the basis of the conduct. Dewey, *The Common-Law Background of Antitrust Policy*, 41 VA. L. REV. 759, 770–71 (1955).

True, little in the legislative history illuminates what Congress meant by restraint of trade or by monopolization. Virtually every reference suggests that the courts should interpret the common law concepts in the context of specific cases. As to monopolization specifically, Letwin argues that this law's vagueness reflects a very loosely conceived policy aim: to preserve both competition and combination without destroying the trusts.[37] This illustrative exchange, among others, occurred during debate in the Senate:

> Mr. GRAY. . . . I shall offer . . . [an] amendment now. It is to strike out of section 2, in lines 1 and 2, the words "monopolize, or attempt to monopolize or," so that the section shall read:
>
> "Every person who shall combine or conspire with any other person or persons to monopolize any part of the trade or commerce among the several States, ..."
>
> We will avoid by that amendment the [problem that we] do not know what definition the courts of the United States have ever given to the word "monopoly" or "monopolize."
>
> . . .
>
> Mr. HOAR. I put in the committee, if I may be permitted to say so (I suppose there is no impropriety in it), the precise question which has been put by the Senator from West Virginia, and I had that precise difficulty in the first place with this bill, but I was answered, and I think all the other members of the committee agreed in the answer. . . . that the word "monopoly" is a merely technical term which has a clear and legal signification, and it is this: It is the sole engrossing to a man's self by means which prevent other men from engaging in fair competition with him.
>
> Of course a monopoly granted by the King was a direct inhibition of all other persons to engage in that business or calling or to acquire that particular article, except the man who had a monopoly granted him by the sovereign power. I suppose, therefore, that the courts of the United States would say in the case put by the Senator from West Virginia that a man who merely by superior skill and intelligence, a breeder of horses or raiser of cattle, or manufacturer or artisan of any kind, got the whole business because nobody could do it as well as he could was not a monopolist, but that it involved something like the use of means which made it impossible for other persons to engage in fair competition, like the engrossing, the buying up of all other persons engaged in the same business.

---

37 W. LETWIN, *supra* note 20, at 16.

Mr. KENNA. If the Senator will permit me, I should like to ask him whether a monopoly such as he defines is prohibited at common law. . . .

Mr. HOAR. I so understand it.

Mr. KENNA. Then why should this bill proceed to denounce that very monopoly?

Mr. HOAR. Because there is not any common law of the United States.

Mr. KENNA. There is common law in nearly every State in the Union.

Mr. HOAR. I know. The common law in the States of the Union of course extends over citizens and subjects over which the State itself has jurisdiction. Now we are dealing with an offense against interstate or international commerce, which the State cannot regulate by penal enactment, and we find the United States without any common law. The great thing that this bill does, except affording a remedy, is to extend the common law principles, which protected fair competition in trade in old times in England, to international and interstate commerce in the United States.

Mr. EDMUNDS. I have only to say, in regard to the amendment suggested by my friend from Delaware and the suggestions of the Senator from West Virginia, that this subject was not lightly considered in the committee and that we studied it with whatever little ability we had, and the best answer I can make to both my friends is to read from Webster's Dictionary the definition of the verb "to monopolize."

"1. To purchase or obtain possession of the whole of, as a commodity or goods in market, with the view to appropriate or control the exclusive sale of; as, to monopolize sugar or tea."

Like the sugar trust. One man, if he had capital enough, could do it just as well as two.

"2. To engross or obtain by any means the exclusive right of, especially the right of trading to any place, or with any country or district; as, to monopolize the India or Levant trade."

The old definition. So I assure my friends that although we may be mistaken (we do not pretend to know all the law) we were not blind to the very suggestions which have been made, and we thought we had done the right thing in providing, in the very phrase we did, that if one person instead of two, by a combination, if one person alone, as we have heard about the wheat market in Chicago, for instance, did it, it was just as offensive and injurious to the public interest as if two had combined to do it.

The PRESIDENT *pro tempore*. The question is on the amendment proposed by the Senator from Delaware [Mr. GRAY].

Mr. HOAR. Let it be read.

The PRESIDENT *pro tempore*. The amendment will be stated.

The CHIEF CLERK. In lines 1 and 2 of section 2 it is proposed to strike out the words "monopolize, or attempt to monopolize, or," so as to read:

Every person who shall combine or conspire with any other person or persons to monopolize any part of the trade, etc.

The amendment was rejected.[38]

Post-Sherman "trustification"

During its first decade or so the Sherman Act may have discouraged cartelization and certainly precluded open cartels. But none of the great trusts was directly challenged, and the Act did not check further consolidations. In fact, most of the 20th century's giant firms emerged in the 1890's. The giant integrated industrial firm had been the exception rather than the standard in 1890, but by the end of the post-Sherman merger wave, "the modern multiunit industrial enterprise became a standard instrument for managing the production and distribution of goods in America."[39]

The merger movement, or the "trustification" process as historian Hans Thorelli calls it, came in two spurts, one lasting from 1890 to 1893 and the other, larger wave beginning in 1895 and ending about 1904.[40] The high point of the merger activity

---

38 21 CONG. REC. 3152 (1890).

39 A. D. CHANDLER, *supra* note 1, at 345.

40 R. NELSON, MERGER MOVEMENTS IN AMERICAN INDUSTRY, 1895–1956, at 34 (1959). Statements of the periods of merger movements vary among historians.

was in 1899 when 1,208 firms disappeared because of mergers.[41] In 1897, only eight industrial companies existed with over $50 million in capital, but by 1903, 40 such companies existed.[42] By the end of the merger movement in 1904, 318 corporations owned 40% of all manufacturing assets.[43]

The shift was so marked and rapid that the second merger wave has been labeled "the corporate revolution."[44] Businesses combined to stabilize prices, to gain control over entry, and to create new marketing systems to serve their unique needs. These motives alone, however, are not sufficient to explain the tremendous merger activity in the late 1890's. Three other factors encouraged business combination: (1) the economic success of the trusts formed in the 1880's; (2) the maturation of the industrial finance system; and (3) the favorable legal and political climate for consolidation.

The success of the 1880's trusts strongly influenced the "consolidation craze." At the time the Sherman Act was passed, according to Chandler, only eight trusts actually existed.[45] In part, the small number of trusts was due to the conservative nature of many business people. Businesses hesitated to adopt an organizational device that had yet to prove economically sound. But the early trusts, reorganized as holding companies under accommodating state law, proved their resiliency in the 1893–1895 depression. As independent businesses and loose combinations fell by the wayside, business owners "could not help but notice that prices fell less rapidly and that their fellow capitalists suffered less severely in those industries which had been successfully consolidated."[46] The apparent success of the trusts

---

41 *Id.* at 37.

42 T. Cochran, The American Business System 58–59 (1957).

43 A. Eichner, *supra* note 24, at 1.

44 *Id.* at 2.

45 A. D. Chandler, *supra* note 1, at 320.

46 A. Eichner, *supra* note 24, at 17.

prompted many businesses to combine when the economy began to recover.[47]

Those keeping a nervous eye on antitrust enforcement in the first few years soon discovered that, except for challenging blatant cartels, the government was not likely to do much to preserve competition. As historian Arthur Johnson puts it, the government followed a "policy of drift" because it was generally well-disposed toward business and did not want to impede growth.[48] President Harrison was no trustbuster; under his administration, only seven Sherman Act suits were prosecuted. Cleveland and McKinley, who succeeded him, were also indifferent, if not hostile, to antitrust. Their Justice Departments filed eight and three Sherman Act suits, respectively. It is emblematic that Richard Olney, the Attorney General in the Cleveland administration, had defended the whiskey trust against the government's prosecution the year before he took office. The McKinley administration's ties to business help to explain why, at the height of the merger movement and a rekindling of popular opposition to trusts, it prosecuted the fewest cases of any administration during the 1890's.[49]

Nor did Congress react adversely to this weak enforcement. Many members apparently preferred not to pursue the issue once the Sherman Act had passed and the "trustbusters" had been temporarily appeased. Even those less disposed toward favoring big business apparently thought private enforcement of the Act would be sufficient. At any rate, Congress failed to allot additional money to the Department of Justice to implement the law. In reality, however, private parties instigated few antitrust suits

---

47 *Id.*; L. Hacker, The Course of American Economic Growth and Development 247 (1970).

48 Johnson, *Antitrust Policy in Transition, 1908: Ideal and Reality*, 48 Miss. Valley Hist. Rev. 415, 416 (1961).

49 H. Thorelli, *supra* note 31, at 398–410; W. H. Harbaugh, Power and Responsibility: The Life and Times of Theodore Roosevelt 158 (1961).

and the lack of federal funding hampered the prosecution of the few cases the Department of Justice did pursue. During election years, the political parties usually wrote an obligatory statement favoring antitrust into their platforms, but the tariff, free silver, the poor state of the economy, and the Spanish-American War were the lightening rods for real political concern.

The Supreme Court, too, facilitated the "policy of drift." It did so by its narrow construction of antitrust and other regulatory legislation.[50] Relying on the freedom of contract doctrine and an elaboration of the due process clause, the Court consistently protected private enterprise from government interference throughout the 1890's.[51] In antitrust, the Court's early decisions tended to encourage businesses to abandon loose combinations such as price-fixing agreements and pools—especially after *Addyston Pipe*—but did little to discourage combinations of competitors into single legal enterprises.[52] The antitrust case that probably had the greatest effect in facilitating combination was the *Knight* case of 1895; by holding that the manufacture of sugar was not commerce, and that consolidation of that industry was not within reach of the Act, the Court released any residual hope or fear that antitrust would impede trustification.[53]

---

50 H. THORELLI, *supra* note 31, at 254; J. W. HURST, LAWS AND THE CONDITIONS OF FREEDOM IN THE NINETEENTH-CENTURY U.S. 34–70 (1956).

51 For example, in 1890 the Court retreated from Munn v. Illinois, 94 U.S. 113 (1876), which held that a state could regulate the rates of businesses that were "clothed with the public interest." The Court ruled in Chicago, Milwaukee & St. Paul Railway v. Minnesota, 134 U.S. 418 (1890) that the reasonableness of rates was ultimately a matter for judicial review, thus weakening the states' regulatory power. For further analysis, *see* Paul, *Legal Progressivism, the Courts, and the Crisis of the 1890s*, in AMERICAN LAW AND THE CONSTITUTIONAL ORDER 283 (L. Friedman & H. Scheiber eds. 1978); McCurdy, *Justice Field and the Jurisprudence of Government Business Relations: Some Parameters of Laissez-Faire Constitutionalism, 1863–1897*, 61 J. AM. HIST. 970, 971–73 (1975); and S. FINE, *supra* note 16, at 128, 141.

52 A. D. CHANDLER, *supra* note 1, at 332–33.

53 United States v. E. C. Knight Co., 156 U.S. 1 (1895).

The new century—trustbusting under T.R.

Ten years after passage of the Sherman Act, trusts continued to thrive. The election of 1900 brought the antitrust issue again into public debate; both the candidates and the national political parties again took stands in opposition to industry-dominating firms. Showing no inclination to distinguish between good and bad trusts, the Democratic Party denounced the trusts for robbing producers and consumers, reducing employment, arbitrarily dictating the terms of jobs, and, in general, benefiting a few at the expense of many. Its platform pledged "an unceasing warfare in nation, state, and city against private monopoly in every form."[54] Less adamant in its stance, and at least suggesting the possibility of distinguishing one trust from another on the basis of intent and conduct, the Republican Party stated that it recognized

> the necessity and propriety for honest cooperation of capital to meet new business conditions, and especially to extend our rapidly increasing foreign trade; but we condemn all conspiracies and combinations intended to restrict business, to create monopolies, to limit production, or to control prices.[55]

If the Republican platform was cautious, the party's successful vice-presidential candidate, Theodore Roosevelt, who became President on McKinley's assassination six months into his second term, was by all accounts an adroit politician who understood the importance of the antitrust issue. Roosevelt was especially attuned to the widespread fear of the noneconomic power possessed by the large corporations. He was also attuned to the need for unencumbered economic progress. With passionate rhetoric he sought to assure the public of the government's power to control the trusts.[56] Roosevelt is sometimes characterized as a

---

54 K. Porter & D. Johnson, National Party Platforms: 1840–1956, at 114 (1961).

55 *Id.* at 122. This brief statement might well have been an antitrust plank for the Reagan presidency.

56 R. Hofstadter, *What Happened to the Antitrust Movement?* in The Paranoid Style in American Politics 203, 204 (1965).

shrewd opportunist, primarily interested in antitrust for its political mileage; but other historians, while recognizing his political motivations, see him as having stirred the nation into a state of indignation against the trusts.[57]

But Roosevelt was no enemy of big business. It may be true that he did not want to antagonize people who had contributed to his campaign and who were vital to his future political ambitions.[58] But, more fundamentally, he believed in the "good intentions and social value of the vast majority of businessmen."[59] This, paired with his recognition of the need, both as a matter of politics and a matter of principle, to attack trusts, led him to a simple and vivid dichotomy. While roundly condemning the unscrupulous tactics of certain "bad" trusts, Roosevelt balanced his attack with praise for "good" trusts. "Good" trusts made great material development possible and increased the nation's international prestige. The country should accept "bigness" as an unavoidable characteristic of the new economy.

At the same time, Roosevelt argued, government should break up the "bad" trusts—those that grew not from inevitable economic forces but from unconscionable business practices.[60] Outlining his criteria for antitrust offenses, Roosevelt stated that conduct was the determining factor; wealth or size alone (and, at least implicitly, the degree of market control) were not alone objectionable.[61] Indeed, Roosevelt criticized both the Sherman Act and court decisions interpreting it for failing to distinguish between good and bad trusts and for endangering the vitality of efficient businesses. He claimed:

---

57 *Compare* G. Kolko, The Triumph of Conservatism 65–67 (1963) *with* A. Link, Woodrow Wilson and the Progressive Era: 1910–1917, at 2 (1954).

58 Johnson, *supra* note 48, at 416.

59 L. Hacker, *supra* note 47, at 263.

60 Theodore Roosevelt, *1st Annual Message to Congress*, in The Progressive Movement 1900–1915, at 141–44 (R. Hofstadter ed. 1963). *See also* W. H. Harbaugh, *supra* note 49, at 163.

61 Quoted in G. Kolko, *supra* note 57, at 127–28.

> Very many of the antitrust laws which have made their appearance on the statute-books of recent years have been almost or absolutely ineffective because they have blinked at the all-important face that much of what they thought to do away with was incidental to modern industrial conditions, and could not be eliminated unless we were willing to turn back the wheels of modern progress.[62]

But to accept bigness, even consolidation, did not mean to accept badness, Roosevelt thought. Rather, the country "must recognize concentration, supervise it, and regulate it."[63]

Roosevelt's interest in discriminating between good and bad trusts is reflected in his unsuccessful program seeking legislative reform.[64] In addition, Roosevelt thought a spirit of cooperation should guide the informal relationship between business and government. Rather than prosecuting an errant industry, Roosevelt favored informal resolutions where possible. He envisaged corporate leaders and lawyers meeting with the President at the White House and negotiating "gentlemanly agreements" delimiting the future activities of a suspect combination.[65] Given the content of Roosevelt's views it would not be surprising if, during his administration, decisions whether or not to prosecute were sometimes based upon idiosyncratic judgment, if not political considerations. Politics would inevitably become an ingredient if the idea of the bad trust was not delineated in objective terms and if badness became primarily a matter of a trust's public reputation. Indeed, politics might intrude even more grossly; on what may be slim evidence, Roosevelt's decision not to prosecute International Harvester is sometimes attributed to support given to Roosevelt's campaign.[66]

---

62 Quoted in W. LETWIN, *supra* note 20, at 199.

63 Quoted in *id.* at 247.

64 Roosevelt's proposals included: Federal regulation of interstate corporations that would still allow states power to promulgate their own rules, and a cabinet-level position to oversee commerce and labor. H. THORELLI, *supra* note 31, at 420.

65 R. WIEBE, BUSINESSMEN AND REFORM 42–43 (1962).

66 Johnson, *supra* note 48, at 417–27.

However imprecise his views, Roosevelt's prosecution record reflects his desire to maintain a vigorous antitrust image in the public mind, to attack bad trusts and, at the same time, to remain a friend of business (at least of "good" business). Roosevelt, the so-called trustbuster, prosecuted fewer cases than one might expect. Still, his Attorney General, Philander C. Knox, initiated more suits than preceding administrations and deliberately targeted some of the bigger, better-known trusts. Roosevelt's administration of nearly 8 years brought 18 suits in equity and 25 indictments under the Sherman Act.[67] This was over twice as many as were brought during the entire period from 1890 to 1901, but only half as many as Taft would later prosecute during a single term in office. By suing trusts with poor public reputations, the Roosevelt administration could maximize the symbolic effect of prosecutions and assert the administration's executive authority over the enforcement of the antitrust law.

Interestingly, antitrust enforcement during the Roosevelt years did not attempt to introduce the good-bad trust distinction into the interpretation of the Sherman Act. The view of the administration apparently was that unless Roosevelt's legislative proposals were enacted, the desired distinction would have to be made through prosecutorial discretion. The administration was not very old when its position on the law, and on the way it would exercise discretion, became manifest.

In the *Northern Securities* prosecution, begun in February 1902, Roosevelt seemed to reverse the governmental passivity toward consolidation that had characterized national policy throughout the period of industrialization.[68] Through a vigorous application of the Sherman Act—one predicated on the notion

---

67 W. H. Harbaugh, *supra* note 49, at 340, 404–07. *See also* Keller, *The Pluralist State: American Economic Regulation in Comparative Perspective, 1900-1930*, in Regulation in Perspective: Historical Essays 56, 68 (T. McGraw ed. 1981).

68 Two years later the case reached the Supreme Court where the consolidation challenged by the government was held to have violated the Act. Northern Securities Co. v. United States, 193 U.S. 197 (1904).

that any combination of competitors to eliminate competition is vulnerable under the law if the government decides to prosecute—Roosevelt aimed to assert his own presidential style, win middle-class support for the Republican Party, and persuade Congress to drop its opposition to his legislative program.[69] Letwin describes the prosecution as a staged performance, carefully chosen for its ability "to arouse public interest"[:]

> It was the first antitrust case in which those cast as villains were celebrities. . . . James J. Hill, the swashbuckling railroad man who had built the Great Northern . . . and J. Pierpont Morgan, the Goliath of bankers. Each was accompanied by a host of supporting minor moguls. . . . The drama was staged . . . as a conflict between Reason and Extravagance, between the respectable requirements of the common good and the wilfulness of colorful, but dangerous, buccaneers.[70]

The *Northern Securities* case may indeed have been staged, but it also gave the Supreme Court an important opportunity to influence national policy during the Progressive Era. If Roosevelt's strategy of federal lawsuits seemed uncharacteristic, his choice of a defendant engaged in interstate commerce gave the Court undeniable grounds for upholding national authority to regulate the economy without having to intrude on production and corporate structure. By holding the consolidation unlawful, the Court did not draw the good-bad trust dichotomy into the legal doctrine; at least for railroads it accepted almost unqualifiedly the argument of Attorney General Knox that combination for the purpose of avoiding competition violated the law. But in so holding, it equipped the administration with the discretion to discriminate. The Roosevelt administration would decide what combinations to sue. It would be free to separate the bad trusts from the good without the need to specify its normative position with precision or to labor under judicial supervision.

---

69 W. H. Harbaugh, *supra* note 49, at 161.

70 W. Letwin, *supra* note 20, at 182. For a more complete history of the Northern Securities case, *see id.* at 182–95, 200–37.

Conclusion

The good trust–bad trust distinction, absent from the political debate, and no more than hinted at in the legislation, was developed during the presidency of Theodore Roosevelt as a guide to the prosecutorial discretion by which a sweeping anticonsolidation law would be administered. In 1911 when the Supreme Court decided the *Standard Oil* case,[71] the Court adopted a rule of reason that carried the distinction into substantive law. Yet, in *Standard Oil*, the Court was not clear about how a trial court should distinguish between permissible and impermissible monopolies.[72] If power was gained through trade restraints or blatant acts to harm competitors, that was bad. A monopolist's coercive and oppressive tactics were impermissible; like torts, they were wrongs. The wrongs were not necessarily objectively identifiable. The opinion is replete with vague normative statements.[73] In a sense, *Standard Oil* invited the courts to claim for themselves the broad discretion that, in Theodore Roosevelt's time, was exercised at the executive level.

Within three or four decades a new focus emerged. Tortious wrong was no longer the sine qua non of a section 2 violation. By the time of *Alcoa*[74] (and the second *American Tobacco* case,[75] which adopted *Alcoa* doctrine) the serious question was not whether defendant had done wrong. It was merely whether the defendant was a monopoly and had become so deliberately. All monopolies were bad, Judge Hand said, unless they were granted by the government or were economically inevitable, because (among other things) they yielded bad economic performance. *United Shoe Machinery*, which followed, used economic thinking

---

71 Standard Oil Co. of New Jersey v. United States, 221 U.S. 1 (1911).

72 *Id.*

73 *E.g.*, *id.* at 61–62.

74 United States v. Aluminum Co. of America, 148 F.2d 416 (2d Cir. 1945).

75 American Tobacco Co. v. United States, 328 U.S. 781 (1946).

to distinguish socially useful growth and conduct from that which is proscribed.[76] The *U.S. Shoe Machinery* approach was refined, both at the level of prosecutorial discretion[77] and in the courts.[78] Until recently, one might have thought that the good–bad idea was greatly attenuated, and that antitrust liability was largely a matter of perceived economic consequence.

But *Aspen Skiing*,[79] the Court's most recent monopoly case, shows that methodologies for distinguishing the good from the bad monopolist are still open to development. *Aspen Skiing* deals with a monopolist that refused to cooperate with its less well-situated competitor in giving consumer/skiers the service they wanted—a four-mountain pass. Aspen Skiing—owner of three of the four ski mountains in the area—did all that it could to scotch its smaller competitor's efforts to provide skiers with a four-mountain pass; it even refused to accept vouchers to ski the dominant firm's slopes, provided by the small competitor and equivalent to money itself. As the trial judge charged the jury, in terms the Supreme Court approved, if a monopolist's conduct "unnecessarily excludes or handicaps competitors," rather than being related to "a superior product, superior business sense or historic element," the monopolist violates the Sherman Act. Aspen Skiing had unreasonably excluded its competitor, to the consternation of its customers, and with no good business or efficiency justification. Therefore the Supreme Court upheld the plaintiff's verdict.

---

76 United States v. United Shoe Machinery Co., 110 F. Supp. 295 (D. Mass. 1953), *aff'd per curiam*, 347 U.S. 521 (1954).

77 Views of Reagan administration enforcers are suggested in *Memorandum for the Attorney General (Information Memorandum), Re: U.S. v. International Business Machines Corp., Jan. 6, 1982, reprinted in* 60 TEX. L. REV. 587, 639 (1982).

78 *Compare, e.g.*, Berkey Photo, Inc. v. Eastman Kodak Co., 603 F.2d 263 (2d Cir. 1979), *cert. denied*, 444 U.S. 1093 (1980), and Telex Corp. v. IBM, 510 F.2d 894 (10th Cir.), *cert. dismissed*, 423 U.S. 802 (1975) *with* United States v. Aluminum Co. of America, *supra* note 74.

79 Aspen Skiing Co. v. Aspen Highlands Skiing Corp., 472 U.S. 585 (1985).

One can read *Aspen Skiing* narrowly. It could be viewed as a "duty to deal" case, closely related to the essential facilities cases and thus limited in application to situations that can be assimilated to the conventions of essential facility doctrine. But *Aspen Skiing* might also be read as providing broader guidance. So read, the case suggests that a dominant firm will risk antitrust liability whenever it deliberately takes steps with the intent and effect of seriously hurting a rival, where the dominant firm fails to prove that the steps were efficiency-producing and would serve consumers. Thus, while having been modernized to recognize that competition itself is good, the law has circled back to draw upon the old critical distinction between the good and the bad "trust."

6
Economists and antitrust: the circular road

BY DONALD DEWEY*

A question of some importance

While the literature on antitrust is enormous, one question has received astoundingly little careful attention. What economic benefits has the policy conferred and at what costs? There is no mystery about the reasons for this neglect. For most of its history, economists have not had the tools that would permit cost-benefit questions about the Sherman Act to be answered with anything but vague generalities and high-minded platitudes. Indeed, a great part—maybe even the greater part—of what is now called microeconomic theory has been developed in an attempt to throw light on the issues forced on our attention by the antitrust experiment. We shall return to this conjecture presently. Moreover, in politics ambiguity has its uses. As long as

---

* Professor, Department of Economics, Columbia University.

AUTHOR'S NOTE: *I would like to thank Bruce Bassett for his comments on an earlier version of this article. He, of course, bears no responsibility for the final product.*

the economic consequences of antitrust are largely unknown—and therefore probably not too serious—everyone feels free to retain whatever views on antitrust that he is comfortable with.

Nobody has ever maintained that real-world antitrust is ideal. Its most fervent friends have always wanted more and tougher restrictions on freedom of contract and bigger budgets for enforcement. Its harshest critics have long denounced most antitrust rules as welfare-reducing. But the question of tradeoffs is almost never directly addressed. Robert Bork's treatment of costs and benefits is pretty representative of the evasion of the issue in mainstream economics.[1] Most of antitrust is held to be welfare-reducing; however, the rule that price-fixing agreements are illegal per se is held to have conferred enormous benefits on the American economy. Bork nowhere offers an estimate as to whether the good of the per se rule exceeds the bad of (almost) everything else in the policy.

For purposes of this article, antitrust will be treated as a package deal with three components: (1) the rule against price-fixing that has made all but the most primitive and furtive cartels illegal in the American economy; (2) restrictions on mergers and market shares that have reduced concentration ratios in some industries; and (3) restraints on business practices that have had the effect of "softening" real-world competition to some, largely unknown, extent. (There has been nothing comparable to the 1877 war between the Standard Oil Company and the Pennsylvania Railroad, resulting in Pennsylvania's complete rout, since the passage of the Sherman Act.[2]) Antitrust, so defined, is only

---

1 R. Bork, The Antitrust Paradox: A Policy at War With Itself (1978).

2 The Pennsylvania Railroad management, irritated by Rockefeller's hard bargaining tactics but with no great expertise in the oil industry, made the mistake of trying to lure producers of Pennsylvania crude away from their ties to Standard Oil by favorable rates. The well-managed Rockefeller firm had a much deeper pocket and, unlike the Pennsylvania, no labor union problems. The battle ended with the rout of the railroad and the sale of its tank car equipment to Standard Oil. 1 A. Nevins, John D. Rockefeller: The Heroic Age Of American Enterprise 531–46 (1940).

good or bad in relation to the alternatives. We shall follow tradition and limit comparison to a version of laissez-faire in which the three above components have no place. This alternative was, of course, closely approximated by American business law before 1890 and British business law before 1956.

Economists teach that monopoly is welfare-reducing because it misallocates resources. But as a practical matter how does one identify and measure such a misallocation? For it is visible to the naked eye only when there exists an entry barrier that creates a capitalized economic rent. In the case of a business firm, this means when there is an unmistakable discrepancy between the market value of the firm and the replacement value of its physical assets.

Capitalized economic rents are highly visible only in government-regulated industries with strictly enforced entry barriers. In the city of New York a totally demolished legal taxicab has a market value exceeding $100,000. (We assume that the wreck still has the medallion or "tin" that makes it a legal taxicab and that can be transferred to an operable vehicle.) This monstrosity is possible because the number of permits to operate taxicabs has been fixed for over 60 years and because the police department invests resources to harass the thousands of illegal taxicabs that ride the streets in order to preserve the most lucrative sectors of the city for "legal" taxicabs. Likewise, the discrepancy between the market value of a television station and the modest replacement value of its studio and transmitter has an obvious explanation—a government-imposed limit on the number of permits to operate television stations.

In the unregulated, private sector of the economy—the preserve of antitrust—capitalized economic rents are hardly ever "obvious" but must be painstakingly sought in messy accounting data. Some investigators have found that highly concentrated industries tend to have rates of return on equity capital from 10% to 20% above the average rate of return for the economy; other investigators hold that this difference disappears after an allowance is made for the fact that higher returns are associated with higher risk.[3]

---

3 W. G. SHEPHERD, THE ECONOMICS OF INDUSTRIAL ORGANIZATION 130–32 (2d ed. 1985).

I cannot see that, so far as policy is concerned, it makes much difference which interpretation is correct. Any monopoly rents that exist in the private sector are truly puny compared with those in the government-regulated sector. By way of comparison, in the licensed taxicab industry of New York City, the rate of return on "real" capital, which consists almost entirely of partially depreciated vehicles and garage space, has, for three decades, been in the neighborhood of 200%. The value of the license to operate, of course, represents no real value but only "contrived scarcity." No one, to my knowledge, has yet made a plausible case that it would be cost-effective to use the antitrust machinery to eliminate the monopoly rents that can be identified in the unregulated private sector of the economy.

It is sometimes urged, for reasons that have always escaped me, that the (Abba) Lerner index should be used to measure "monopoly power."[4] The Lerner index is the difference of price and marginal cost divided by price. A minor objection to the Lerner index as a monopoly measure is that, since marginal cost is not an accounting category, some proxy must be found for it. The major objection to the Lerner index is that it is really a measure of aggregated market imperfections and includes, for example, those due to transportation costs. Most such imperfections have nothing to do with the kind of market power that creates an economic rent.

Can economic theory tell us anything about the relative merits of antitrust and laissez-faire as alternative rule sets that affect economic welfare? The answer is yes, but for supporters of antitrust it is a disturbing one. Virtually all economic analysis proceeds on the assumption that people ascend to the higher consumer indifference curves of the modern textbooks (and hence attain more welfare) by engaging in exchange. However we sugarcoat it, antitrust is a set of restrictions on freedom of exchange. Hence, when viewed through Richard Posner's "lens of price theory" the presumption must be that antitrust is welfare-reducing. This presumption can only be set aside by

---

[4] Landes & Posner, *Market Power in Antitrust Cases*, 94 HARV. L. REV. 937 (1981).

showing that one party to the exchange is too incompetent, ill-informed, or immature to look after his own interests in a market; or by showing that the exchange agreement has malign externalities, that is, welfare-reducing effects for third parties greater than the welfare gain that it secures for the two parties directly involved. Thus, as a matter of logic, there can be no general argument that justifies antitrust. The case for any particular antitrust rule as welfare-increasing must be based on "special circumstances."

Given the blatant contradictions between the premises of price theory and those of antitrust, how did virtually the whole of the American economics profession ever come to believe that antitrust is welfare-increasing? While the question is a fair one, we evade it for the moment.

Economists properly worry about the effects of policy on economic welfare. It was D. H. Robertson, I believe, who argued that if economists did not concern themselves with economic efficiency, nobody would. Still, this concern should not lead us to read a goal of welfare maximization into the Sherman Act as Robert Bork seems to do in *The Antitrust Paradox*. Bork appears to argue that a policy that was intended by Congress to promote welfare by promoting competition has been subverted by the courts into a policy of reducing welfare by protecting competitors from the consequences of competition.[5]

The irrelevance of "original intent"

Economists can be forgiven for urging that the promotion of economic welfare ought to be the paramount, preferably the

---

[5] Most readers of Bork believe that the "antitrust parodox" described by Bork in his book denotes the inversion of the Sherman Act's original intent at the hands of judges. However, Bork later claimed that he meant nothing so naive. Rather he meant to convey that, whatever the original intent, if the courts had practiced good law, they would have placed the most direct and reasonable interpretation on the language of the statute; and, had this been done, it would have served to promote consumer welfare. Bork, *Economics and Antitrust: Response*, 3 CONTEMP. ECON. ISSUES 35 (1984–85).

only, goal of antitrust.[6] However, the view sometimes urged that Congress intended the primacy of this goal when it passed the Sherman Act in 1890 is historically suspect and can only be supported by a highly selective use of evidence. Even if this view was correct, it would be irrelevant to antitrust decisions of federal courts in 1990.

A close reading of the debates and committee hearings that preceded passage of the Sherman Act can convey a good idea of the fears that inspired it. The Congress of 1890 had quite a few growing out of the appearance of cartels, the plight of farmers, railroad rates, so-called destructive competition, the size of eastern banks, and, above all, the activities of the Standard Oil Company. But the debates and committee hearings do not indicate that Congress in 1890 meant to lay out any detailed agenda for dealing with its worries. The most that we can assume is that Congress wanted some sort of action from the Attorney General and the courts. It did take care to insure that the Supreme Court would not throw out the new law as an unconstitutional invasion of states rights—hence the wise determination to rest it on the Commerce clause with no mention of manufacturing, labor unions or other specifics.

The debates and hearings provide some evidence that the new law was intended to outlaw cartels, for there seems to have been a consensus that it would make illegal the price-fixing agreements that, by (debatable) congressional reading, the common law had only treated as unenforceable. However, the Sherman Act is

---

6 The indignation of economists who discover late in the game that real-world antitrust may actually undermine the economy's efficiency is sometimes quite touching. Thus: "There is a specter that haunts our antitrust institutions. Its threat is that, far from serving as the bulwark of competition, these institutions will become the most powerful instrument in the hands of those who wish to subvert it. More than that, it threatens to draw great quantities of resources into the struggle to prevent effective competition, thereby more than offsetting the contributions to economic efficiency promised by antitrust activities." Baumol & Ordover, *Use of Antitrust to Subvert Competition*, 28 J. L. ECON. 247 (1985).

statute, not Constitution. What Congress intended by it in 1890 is of antiquarian interest only. Every Congress since then has had the opportunity to correct any court decisions that it found objectionable. As we know, Congress has seldom done so.

The very real achievements of antitrust

We should, I think, assume with Justice Holmes that people must be presumed to intend the consequences of their acts; therefore, the goals of antitrust are to be inferred from its consequences, not from the rhetoric of judges and commentators. We do not know much about the welfare consequences of antitrust. But there is no doubt about its organizational impact. Antitrust has prevented the cartelization of the American economy.[7] It has reduced concentration ratios in some industries. It has softened competition to some largely unknown (and probably unknowable) extent. And these achievements have served to make it a sacrosanct symbol in American politics—one that no serious political leader would dare speak against. If the language of the

---

7 Occasionally an economist will question the conclusion that antitrust is necessary to prevent the cartelization of the economy. (I have never heard the doubt expressed by a lawyer.) For the empirically oriented, my proof is an invitation to cite an economy that has operated during the last hundred years without antitrust rules that was not (or is not) cartelized. For the theorists, my invitation is to write down the conditions for efficient production in an industry that is not perfectly competitive. A necessary condition, of course, is that production must be allocated in a way that keeps marginal cost equal in all firms; this condition cannot be realized without a revenue sharing cartel. Absent antitrust, the cartel is a perfectly rational and inevitable form of business organization.

For empirical evidence, dated but still relevant, that the Sherman Act has reduced the availability of the most efficient methods of collusion and thereby reduced the amount and effects of collusion, *see* G. STIGLER, THE ORGANIZATION OF INDUSTRY 259–95 (1968).

What are popularly called cartels vary enormously in their power to affect price. Some are little more than luncheon gatherings where the business outlook is discussed. Others perform most of the functions of a multiplant firm. The economist's expectation is that, when the law does not interfere, firms will invest in collusion so long as the additional expected return is greater than the additional cost.

first two sections of the Sherman Act is not a part of the Constitution, it might as well be.

Antitrust and the populist impulse

For a long time after I began to doubt that antitrust did anything to increase economic welfare, I was puzzled by its immense popularity as an ideal—even with fellow economists. Almost alone among major economic policies, it is a policy without a political constituency of beneficiaries. While antitrust may misallocate resources to the dismay of economists, it creates scarcely any economic rents—the usual raisons d'être of constituencies. The only obvious beneficiaries of antitrust are members of the antitrust bar, a few economic consultants, and businessmen who win in the treble damage suit lottery. Neither the Sherman Act nor any amendment was passed in response to the pressure of these groups.

The popularity of antitrust no longer surprises me. As I have lived and learned, it has come to seem perfectly reasonable in a country that is dedicated to the preservation of bicameral state legislatures (even in Rhode Island), the electoral college, independent sewer districts, township governments, grand juries, popular election of coroners and court clerks, and state constitutions that specify the width of ski trails in state parks. These institutions are popularly thought to disperse power and they undoubtedly do serve to fragment decision making. Only rarely does anyone (most likely some sort of college professor) question whether they are worth what they cost in terms of alternatives that must be sacrificed.

I learned in my college course in historical methods that "inevitable" is the favorite adjective of mediocre historians who write history as apology for the victors and have not the wit to imagine what might have been. But I do believe that there was something very nearly inevitable about the appearance of antitrust on the American scene in 1890. Given the primitive character of the federal civil service, any policy to deal with the concerns of Congress could only have been enforced through the courts. Given the novelty and complexity of some of the problems faced, Congress had no choice but to confer broad discretionary power on the federal courts. I think that we may assume that, in the 1890's, any policy that sought to minimize the role of the judiciary by the enactment of detailed legislation or the creation of a powerful regulatory commission would have been declared unconstitutional.

The policy launched by the Sherman Act was cheap (at least in the beginning) and it delivered a quick and visible payoff with the outlawing of cartels in *Addyston Pipe* (1899).[8] An even more dazzling result came when the Supreme Court directed the breakup of the Standard Oil and the American Tobacco companies in 1911. No significant opposition to the policy developed as it gained momentum; indeed, except for a few Socialists and Social Darwinians, very soon almost all men came to speak well of it. (There was the notable exception of Justice Holmes, though his harshest criticism of antitrust was reserved for private correspondence.[9]) Admittedly, nobody could prove that antitrust was doing anything to benefit consumers. But then nobody could prove that it was doing anything to injure them. Finally, as time passed, antitrust gained the presumption in favor of the status quo that, in stable political systems, is granted to all policies and institutions that offend hardly anybody.

A profession converted

As noted above, given the American bias in favor of decentralized decision making and fragmented authority, I no longer wonder at the popularity of antitrust. However, I still do find puzzling (and fascinating) the way in which the views of economists on antitrust have developed and changed over the years.

---

8 Addyston Pipe & Steel Co. v. United States, 175 U.S. 211 (1899).

9 Holmes' oft-cited judgment that "the Sherman Act is a humbug based on economic ignorance and incompetence" was given in a letter to Sir Frederick Pollock, April 23, 1910. THE HOLMES READER 112 (J. J. Marke 2d ed. 1964).

Let us pass quickly through the decades. Economists had nothing to do with the passage of the Sherman Act in 1890.[10] It was greeted by our then tiny profession with a mixture of indifference, hostility and contempt. True, Alfred Marshall following developments from the other side of the Atlantic had kind words for the new law but I do not believe that he understood the American politics that produced it.[11] He seems to have assumed that an act of Congress is drafted with the same dispassionate precision as an act of Parliament prepared by civil servants. Young American economists recently back from Germany saw it as an impertinent interference with a Zeitgeist that was decreeing ever greater size and centralization. They preferred what they believed to be Bismarck's solution—large firms closely supervised by competent and incorruptible civil servants. Older economists raised on the British classics saw antitrust as a departure from the wisdom of laissez-faire. Since we no longer teach much history of economic thought, it is not widely known that the American Economic Association was founded by young Germanophiles; and that their plainly avowed purpose was to encourage German-style research and give a hearing to critics of laissez-faire. Their bête noire was the Social Darwinism of William Graham Sumner.[12]

---

10 The intellectual origins of the Sherman Act have been exhaustively studied. *See especially* H. THORELLI, THE FEDERAL ANTITRUST POLICY 108–27 (1954) and W. LETWIN, LAW AND ECONOMIC POLICY IN AMERICA 71–77 (1965).

11 A. MARSHALL, REPORT OF THE SIXTEENTH MEETING OF THE BRITISH ASSOCIATION FOR THE ADVANCEMENT OF SCIENCE 898, 905 (1891).

12 The intellectual contest between the young Germanophiles and the older American economists (some of whom like Sumner himself had studied in Germany) was both ideological and a *methodenstreit*. The former were ably led by Richard Ely, Henry Carter Adams, and Simon Patten and the latter by Simon Newcomb, Arthur Hadley, David Wells and, of course, Sumner. Fortunately, in the United States, the struggle between the two positions was not as bitter or inimical to theoretical work as in Germany where the so-called historical school gained nearly complete control of university appointments in economics until after

Somewhere between 1900 and 1920 majority opinion among American economists swung behind antitrust. The acceptance was rapid and total. If Marxists are excepted, I cannot cite a single American-trained economist of any prominence who, in the interwar years, questioned the desirability of the Sherman Act. Even refugee scholars from Europe, notably Joseph Schumpeter,[13] Ludwig von Mises,[14] and Herbert von Beckerath,[15] who clearly disbelieved the assumptions underlying antitrust did not go out of their way to attack it. (I suspect that they regarded antitrust as a puzzling but probably relatively unimportant bit of American folly—far below the evil influence of Marx and Keynes.)

How and why did this very sudden and abrupt change in opinion come about? An uncharitable judgment would be that it was just another case of "if you can't lick them, join them"; for by 1920 it was clear that antitrust was here to stay. I am sure that there was more to the story than this though I am not sure how it should be told. The acceptance of antitrust by economists was so sudden and complete that it resembles a religious conversion and is as difficult to explain. The turning point is marked by the appearance in 1901 of C. J. Bullock's once much-cited survey of the "trust" literature which found virtually no evidence that the great corporate mergers that were attracting attention could be explained by the need to achieve economies of scale.[16] Bullock was an academic economist of standing who had also written a

---

World War II. With John Bates Clark and Francis Walker as peacemakers, both sides were soon able to coexist reasonably well in the American Economic Association. The contest between the old and the new in 19th-century American economics is traced in 3 J. DORFMAN, THE ECONOMIC MIND IN AMERICAN CIVILIZATION, esp. chs. 7 & 9 (1949).

13 J. SCHUMPETER, CAPITALISM, SOCIALISM, AND DEMOCRACY (3d ed. 1950).

14 L. VON MISES, PLANNING FOR FREEDOM (1952).

15 H. VON BECKERATH, MODERN INDUSTRIAL ORGANIZATION (1933).

16 Bullock, *Trust Literature: A Survey and a Criticism*, 15 Q. J. ECON. 167 (1901).

first-rate and widely used introductory textbook. Two years later a leading financial journalist, John Moody, said much the same thing in his widely read, *The Truth About the Trusts*. With the appearance of J. B. Clark and J. M. Clark, *The Control of Trusts* (1912), the necessity and desirability of antitrust became part of the received wisdom in American economics.[17] At this time the elder Clark (J. B.) was the most widely honored economist in the United States. He had never been known to say a good word for populist causes.

In retrospect we know that Bullock and the economists who have followed him in doubting the importance of scale economies, especially those who did the trust studies for the Bureau of Corporations and early Federal Trade Commission, "got it wrong." We have no good reason to question their finding that the scale economies realized in a great majority of the mergers studied were "small" or sometimes invisible and presumably nonexistent. Nor need we question their finding that, in many instances, the promoters of mergers were motivated mainly by the hope of a killing in the stock market or a monopoly rent. This is the way students of my generation were still learning it at the University of Chicago in the early 1940's. The all-important truth that we were expected to accept (as undergraduates we had no way of testing it) was that the only significant economies of scale (and scope) relate to the plant; therefore, multiplant firms—a set that includes virtually all firms on the Fortune 500 list—can have no efficiency justification. The view that all significant economies of scale relate to the plant was later elevated to a "fundamental

---

17 This joint effort of father and son was far more supportive of the antitrust effort than an earlier book by J. B. Clark alone, THE CONTROL OF TRUSTS: AN ARGUMENT IN FAVOR OF CURBING THE POWER OF MONOPOLY BY A NATURAL METHOD (1901). The "natural method" of the elder Clark is little more than laissez-faire purged of "predatory" practices, especially railroad rebates. The change in emphasis was probably due to the influence of the son since, according to the preface of the later book, he did most of the rewriting.

principle'' by Frank Albert Fetter.[18] The clear implication of this teaching was that a position in favor of trustbusting and merger controls is the only possible one for the economist who values economic efficiency. Henry Simons' *Positive Program for Laissez Faire* was the good news to be carried to the world.[19]

What the early trust investigators did not grasp—and the mistake is still regularly made in merger studies—is that the "true" motives behind a merger, even when they can be identified with confidence, have no economic significance. The important question is the fate of the firm that is created or enlarged by merger. Suppose that the post-acquisition enterprise survives for some considerable period, say 15 years. Then the conclusion must be that the merger either improved efficiency or at least left it unchanged. It is of no consequence that afterward the firm may have gone through one or more receiverships and reorganizations. The economic success of a merger is ratified by the firm's ability to survive, not the financial rewards, if any, to stockholders.

In this connection I think it worth noting that the role of scale economies in bringing about the growth of large firms is often misunderstood. The only economies of scale that can be easily measured relate to the plant ("establishment" in Census nomenclature). Here all that one needs for a good approximation are detailed engineering and accounting data. But scale economies "external to the plant and internal to the firm" is an open ended category; the same is true of scale diseconomies. (Quantity discounts on paper clips versus the cost of another copying machine, etc.) Both can be cited ad infinitum but only a highly subjective balance can be struck between them. As noted above, over the years most studies have depreciated the cost savings to be had by increasing the number of plants under common control, and there is no good reason to question their findings. However,

---

18 Fetter, *The Fundamental Principle of Efficiency in Mass Production*, in RELATIVE EFFICIENCY OF LARGE, MEDIUM-SIZED, AND SMALL BUSINESS 398 (TNEC Monograph No. 13, 1941).

19 Simons, *A Positive Program for Laissez-faire*, in ECONOMIC POLICY FOR A FREE SOCIETY (1948).

to validate mergers, such savings need not be "big"; they need only be positive. Paltry cost reductions associated with greater firm size may be sufficient to bring about major changes in concentration ratios.

In fact, we have good reason to believe that, over a wide range of output, most industries operate under conditions of something close to constant unit cost. This assumption is consistent with studies that show that scale economies external to the plant are, at most, small. If it were not so, this country's experiments with trustbusting would not have been politically possible. There would have been too many victims. The ideal corporate candidate for divestiture is the firm that has constant unit cost over a wide range of output and earns only a normal rate of return on capital, *e.g.*, the typical national or regional chain of grocery supermarkets. Here divestiture into a few pieces may not increase economic welfare but then it does not inflict significant capital losses on stockholders (including widows and orphans) or threaten the pensions of workers. The only measurable welfare loss is that imposed by litigation costs.

Economists to the rescue

Antitrust fervor was undoubtedly heightened by the torrent of criticism of businessmen and their world unleashed by the Great Depression, especially after the disillusionment with the self-government in industry experiments of the National Industrial Recovery Act. From this distance in time, it is hard to believe that leading American economists of the 1930's really believed with Gardiner Means[20] that the price rigidities that appeared to characterize highly concentrated industries had been a major factor causing or prolonging the Depression (compared with, say, the contraction of the money supply between 1929 and 1933). But the written record indicates that this is exactly what they did believe.

---

20 MEANS, INDUSTRIAL PRICES AND THEIR INFLEXIBILITY, S. DOC. NO. 13, 74th Cong., 1st Sess. (1935); *Notes on Inflexible Prices*, 26 AM. ECON. REV. SUPP. 23 (March 1936).

In the spring of 1932 a number of the profession's brightest luminaries, led by Frank Albert Fetter and Jacob Viner and fearing that either or both of the political parties would adopt a plank hostile to antitrust, prepared a statement for the national conventions to be held in the summer. The statement, which was circulated and signed by 127 American economists, flatly denied that the Sherman Act had contributed to the Depression by encouraging "over-production" and "destructive competition" in the 1920's. (This seems to have been a widely believed absurdity in the early years of the Depression.) The economists then counterattacked.

> On the contrary, the most competent economic opinion, as well in Europe as in this country, can be cited in support of the view that a strong contributing cause of the unparalleled severity of the present depression was the greatly increased extent of monopolistic control of commodity prices which stimulated financial speculation in the financial markets. There is growing doubt whether the capitalistic system, whose basic assumption is free markets and a free price system, can continue to work with an ever widening range of prices fixed or manipulated by monopolies.[21]

The return of doubt

Over the years, and especially after World War II at the University of Chicago, antitrust issues began to be studied by economists with much better training, tools, and data. The result, as we know, has been increasing skepticism about the economic case for antitrust. My own loss of faith may have gone farther than anybody else's but its path and rate of development are pretty typical of my age cohort.[22] Most of us now accept the

---

21 *Statement of the Economists' Committee on Anti-trust Law Policy*, 22 Am. Econ. Rev. 465, 468 (1932).

22 To date I have had hardly any company in American economics (cartels are more favorably regarded abroad) in questioning the welfare-promoting merits of the rule that cartels are illegal per se. Dewey, *Information, Entry, and Welfare: The Case for Collusion*, 69 Am. Econ. Rev. 587 (1979); and *Welfare and Collusion: Reply*, 72 Am. Econ. Rev. 276 (1982). However, help seems to be on the way.

(footnote 22 continued)

criticism of antitrust as forcefully set forth by such writers as Dom Armentano,[23] George Stigler,[24] Harold Demsetz,[25] and Richard Posner.[26] This criticism sees hardly any merit in the policy other than the rule that price-fixing agreements are illegal per se. The views of Oliver Williamson on antitrust deriving from his emphasis on the firm's effort to minimize transaction costs are not quite so negative.[27] Still, he does make clear that older economists were too quick to label as anticompetitive innovations in business structure and conduct that could have no place in the perfectly competitive market that was their reference point.[28]

Considerable doubt about the merits of the per se rule is indicated in Bittlingmayer, *Decreasing Cost and Competition: A New Look at the Addyston Pipe Case*, 25 J. L. ECON. 201 (1982); D. ARMENTANO, ANTITRUST AND MONOPOLY: ANATOMY OF A POLICY FAILURE 133–66 (1982); and Newmark, *Is Antitrust Enforcement Effective?* 96 J. POL. ECON. 1315 (December 1988).

23 D. ARMENTANO, ANTITRUST AND MONOPOLY, *supra* note 22 and ANTITRUST POLICY: THE CASE FOR REPEAL (1986).

24 G. STIGLER, *supra* note 7, at 5–22.

25 Demsetz, *Economics as a Guide to Antitrust Regulation*, 19 J. L. ECON. 371 (1976).

26 R. A. POSNER, ANTITRUST LAW: AN ECONOMIC PERSPECTIVE (1976).

27 O. E. WILLIAMSON, MARKETS AND HIERARCHIES, ANALYSIS AND ANTITRUST IMPLICATIONS: A STUDY IN THE ECONOMICS OF INTERNAL ORGANIZATION (1975) and *The Modern Corporation: Origins, Evolution, Attributes*, 19 J. ECON. LITERATURE 1537 (1981).

28 Of course the older economists' case for antitrust still has its supporters, perhaps most notably in Walter Adams, J. W. Brock and W. G. Shepherd. I admit to being puzzled by this fidelity. Since large firms, with or without large market shares, are social and even political as well as economic entities, there are understandable reasons for disliking them and wishing to impose additional controls on their behavior.

What I cannot understand is why, in the face of what our profession has learned in a hundred years of antitrust studies, economists who support the old case for antitrust still argue as if economic theory shows that corporate regulation through antitrust benefits consumers—

What I will have the presumption to call blue-ribbon opinion among economists on antitrust has come (nearly) full circle. One can imagine the ghost of William Graham Sumner somewhere out there muttering "I told you so."[29] Since the best work by economists on antitrust has only served to underscore the merits of laissez-faire—and, as we have seen, given the assumptions of price theory, it could not have been otherwise—two questions would seem to require answers. Was this trip necessary? What did we learn along the way? I am most comfortable with the second question.

Microeconomics as an externality of antitrust

I will go out on a limb and argue that a great part of modern microeconomics is the creation of economists working in the United States and that it has developed in response to our efforts to deal with issues forced on our attention by antitrust, most notably issues associated with cartels, oligopoly, price discrimination, mergers, resale price maintenance, vertical integration, tying contracts, so-called predatory competition, free riding, and limit pricing. I would cite the theory of contestable markets as a recent example of a benign externality of the Sherman Act.[30] While antitrust may have done nothing provable for consumers, it has certainly helped to educate economists.

---

or could benefit them if only it was done right. *See* W. G. SHEPHERD, THE TREATMENT OF MARKET POWER: ANTITRUST, REGULATION, AND PUBLIC ENTERPRISE (1975) and W. ADAMS & J. W. BROCK, THE BIGNESS COMPLEX: INDUSTRY, LABOR AND GOVERNMENT IN THE AMERICAN ECONOMY (1986).

29 A representative sample of Sumner's ideology and irascibility can be found in two articles on trusts published in THE JOURNAL OF COMMERCE AND COMMERCIAL BULLETIN on June 24 and 25, 1901. "There is no evil or danger in trusts which is nearly so menacing to society as the measures which are proposed for destroying trusts."

30 Baumol, *Contestable Markets: An Uprising in the Theory of Industrial Structure*, 72 AM. ECON. REV. 72 (1982); and W. J. BAUMOL, J. C. PANZAR, and R. D. WILLIG, CONTESTABLE MARKETS AND THE THEORY OF INDUSTRY STRUCTURE (1982).

In considering the other question, Was this trip necessary? we should remember that many (if not most) of the issues associated with the above economic phenomena appeared in court before they had received the attention of economists. Thus the Supreme Court had the task of trying to figure out the reasons for price leadership in *United States Steel* in 1920.[31] The Justices would have been no wiser if they had consulted the leading economics textbooks of that day.

For the record, the Sherman Act is older than what most of us would regard as "big business." In 1890 most American economists knew their Adam Smith, John Stuart Mill, and Francis Amasa Walker. But their knowledge of economic theory did not extend beyond these writers. When it came to information about the economic system, the representative American economist in 1890 knew little more than the representative Congressman or journalist.

Is it a reproach to our profession that we have traveled from William Graham Sumner by way of Frank Albert Fetter only to wind up with the modern skeptics? I think not. Our education—and the resulting expertise—was obtained at a reasonable cost to the public. For its first 50 years the country's investment in antitrust was so small that its welfare impact, whether positive or negative, had to have been slight. Antitrust became a policy with an unmistakable price tag only after World War II with the rise of the treble damage suit, the class action, and the passage of the Celler amendment.

It is, I believe, an accepted truth in the so-called hard sciences that most experiments are unsuccessful in that they only tell you what not to do in the future. I see no reason why economists should feel sheepish about our rate of learning on antitrust matters. As Frank Knight wrote:

> It requires an astounding amount of painful effort in the original construction and pondering of criticism to reach any justified assurance that an opinion has merit, in a field where terms cannot be objectively defined and results objectively tested. Once a man's mind

31 United States v. United States Steel Corp., 251 U.S. 417 (1920).

is liberated and set to thinking, he becomes an inveterate "theorizer" and is as partial to his own ideas as he is to his own children, or any individual interest whatever.[32]

Mea culpa?

Have the mistakes of economists been costly in the sense that they have led to the adoption of unwise (*i.e.*, welfare-destroying) antitrust rules? On the assumption that judges and legislators at least occasionally paid attention to us, our bad advice undoubtedly did some harm, *e.g.*, in providing fallacious arguments for the merger and tying provisions of the Clayton Act. But here again I see no reason to don ashes and sackcloth. In giving advice that later turned out to be bad, we are hardly alone among the professions. In any event, I think that judges and legislators would have reached most of our incorrect conclusions about antitrust without our help. The most influential were (and are) enticingly plausible, *e.g.*, the theory of "predatory" competition.

The antitrust bandwagon had already acquired most of its momentum before economists climbed on board. However, our ascension did have one result that was probably important: it provided intellectual respectability for a policy that had highly emotional (and suspect) populist origins. While I know of no way of quantifying the effects of this endorsement, it must have had some effect. A policy can only be fortified when Congressmen are being told by professors and civil servants what is pleasing to the ear.

What is the prospect for improving the economics of antitrust? As statistical techniques and computer technology become more sophisticated and data accumulate, we can hope to reach more precise and persuasive conclusions about the welfare impact of antitrust rules. Progress in this direction will be a "scientific advance" and bring deserved credit to our profession. Given the obstacles to empirical work on antitrust, I doubt that progress

---

32 F. H. KNIGHT, THE ETHICS OF COMPETITION 354–55 (1935).

will be striking enough to have much effect on legislation or case law in the next 10 or 20 years. (My crystal ball does not operate beyond two decades.)

In the past I have argued that "antitrust comes at a cost." While I certainly still think so, the statement needs careful qualification. It is true only in the sense that the introduction of antitrust rules that restrict mergers, cartels, and exclusionary pricing into a laissez-faire model must have the effect of reducing economic welfare. This much is certain. But, to say the obvious, we cannot possibly know what would have happened to the real-world American economy without the Sherman Act. Justice Douglas always believed that his agenda for antitrust was the country's only prophylaxis against bureaucratic socialism because, by his reading, Americans would not stand for the kind of business landscape that a laissez-faire legal framework would produce. Without sharing his certainty, we can note that socialists have always been among the most implacable critics of antitrust. There are in this world economic policies far worse than antitrust. Knowing that they exist creates, I think, a presumption in favor of going slow in pushing for change.

Last thoughts

The Reagan administration made a serious and surprisingly successful effort to move antitrust in the direction of modern blue-ribbon opinion in economics. Conglomerate and vertical mergers were left alone as were horizontal mergers involving small market shares; prosecution of price-fixing agreements was stressed; and the Justice Department even sought (unsuccessfully) to overturn the rule in *Dr. Miles* against resale price maintenance contracts.[33] The attack on the state immunity doctrine was revived (though not vigorously pressed). If one believes with Bork that no antitrust rule or decision is justified unless price theory provides a presumption that it will increase output, the administration's effort must be welcomed. If one believes that antitrust is mainly justified as a way of preserving and fostering decentralized

33 Dr. Miles Medical Co. v. Park & Sons Co., 220 U.S. 373 (1911).

decision making, it need not be. (I suspect that there is a touch of the populist in most American economists.)

Will the Reagan course be maintained in future administrations? Do not bet on it. The populist impulse in this country has waxed and waned but it has been with us ever since the pilgrims are said to have stepped on Plymouth Rock. Even with treble damage suits and class actions on the scale of the 1970's antitrust is still a low-cost way of providing an outlet for the impulse. Whatever the welfare losses of antitrust, they are certainly far less than those imposed on the economy by the tax policies and zoning regulations of three levels of government.

An economist is honor bound to give as honest a reading as he can of the costs and benefits of antitrust in relation to proposed alternatives. As we have seen, when the lens employed is price theory, and the alternative for comparison is freer exchange, he will, if his syllogisms are sound, always rule against antitrust—in the absence of some circumstance that justifies setting aside one or more of the fundamental assumptions of price theory. But the economist as citizen has no obligation to preach Bork's output test or Dewey's welfare test.[34] Decentralization of decision making, the dispersion of power, and a higher standard of business ethics are honorable values. Antitrust has done something to advance them in the past and can do so in the future. There is no reason why the economist as citizen should not decide that antitrust, with all its presumptive inefficiencies, is worth the cost.

At the end of my industrial organization course I used to invite the class to speculate on the economic and political consequences of repealing the antitrust laws. While I still like the economic part of the question, I no longer think that the political part has much point. The organizational changes that would follow repeal—widespread cartelization and an explosion of mergers and price wars—would scare the wits out of the country. For the present, repeal, or even much further dismantling, is simply not a serious option in American politics. In any event,

---

34 D. Dewey, *Antitrust and Its Alternatives: A Compleat Guide to the Welfare Tradeoffs*, in Antitrust and Regulation 1 (Grieson ed. 1986).

the corporation is a creature of law whose rights and responsibilities have to be specified somewhere. As an accident of history, the Sherman Act became the statutory basis for much of federal supervision and control of corporations. A repeal of Sherman would have to coincide with new statutory foundations for many of the essential federal oversight functions where corporations are concerned.

And the future? The per se rule against price-fixing seems safe enough into the future. The essentially ad hoc scrutiny of mergers will continue under the guise of applying somebody's merger guidelines. The burden of proof can be expected to shift back and forth between government and defendant as public attitudes to "big business" warm and cool. Much more uncertain is the future of the treble damage suit since its development is more influenced by lower court judges who are less affected by what professors of law and economics are currently writing about antitrust. It is unlikely that we shall see in our lifetimes another decision so disruptive of everyday life as the Bell system break-up (unless the attack on the state immunity doctrine is resumed and successfully pressed).

Economists have learned an immense amount about real-world markets by studying antitrust issues over the last century. I think that the learning experience is pretty far into diminishing returns. In the future I expect that our role in analyzing antitrust will be very similar to our role in analyzing problems of tariff protection. We will point out the costs and, on occasion, try to measure them. Some of us will demonstrate ingenuity by devising scenarios in which, by the careful choice of assumptions, an antitrust rule brought forward by lawyers can be shown to increase economic welfare—just as clever international trade theorists, doing an end run around the law of comparative advantage, can construct models to show that a nation can increase its economic welfare by the correct mixture of tariffs and exchange controls.

The truth is that much of what passes for economic analysis in antitrust cases, is a kind of window dressing. My favorite example is *du Pont-General Motors*.[35] Here the obstensible issue was

---

35 United States v. E. I. du Pont de Nemours & Co., 353 U.S. 586 (1957).

whether du Pont had an unfair advantage over rivals in supplying General Motors with paints and varnishes; the "real" issue was whether because of their size, the corporate tie between the country's largest automobile manufacturer and its largest chemical company should be allowed to continue. The antitrust game required that the court go through the motions of sifting through a mass of feeble statistics on the market for automobile paints, varnishes, and fabrics before concluding that the tie should be cut. So far as I know, nobody has ever suggested that the outcome of the case made any perceptible difference to the prices of cars and trucks.

From the beginning, two presumptions about antitrust enforcement have contended for judicial and congressional favor. One says that all doubts should be resolved in favor of freedom of contract—provided that the cost is not too great. The other says that all doubts should be resolved in favor of decentralized decision making—provided that the cost is not too great. Arguments of great weight and antiquity can be cited to support both. Given the obstacles to measuring cost—and the opportunities that antitrust provides for good and inexpensive political theater—I can see no reason why the contest between these two quite reasonable presumptions should ever be finally decided.

Let us not end on a note that could be mistaken for cynicism. History could have dealt the United States a policy far worse than antitrust for coping with our long-standing fear of great corporate size. In any event, an economist is in no position to chide Congressmen and judges for failing to accept immediately truths that it took his trade the better part of a hundred years to learn.

7
Section 7 and the evolving role of economics

BY EDWIN M. ZIMMERMAN*

Section 7 of the Clayton Act, born 75 years ago into premature desuetude,[1] revised and resurrected in 1950,[2] is typically invoked to prevent consummation of the transaction to which it is applied and requires an evaluation of competitive consequences that have not yet occurred.

Not only is there ordinarily no track record of a merger's impact at the time of a decision to sue, but postmerger behavior during pendency of litigation of the validity of the transaction (assuming the transaction is not enjoined) is probably unreliable,

---

* Covington & Burling, Washington, DC.

1 Act of Oct. 15, 1914, Ch. 322, 38 Stat. 730. Acquisition of assets was not covered and the courts held that mergers were therefore outside the reach of section 7. Arrow-Hart & Hegeman Electric Co. v. FTC, 291 U.S. 587 (1934). *See* United States v. Philadelphia National Bank, 374 U.S. 321, 337–40 (1963).

2 Celler-Kefauver Act of Dec. 29, 1950, Ch. 1184, 64 Stat. 1125, 15 U.S.C. § 18.

and in any event is deemed unreliable, as evidence of the probable competitive effect.[3]

Section 7 thus is peculiarly dependent on prediction of competitive consequences. It also seeks that prediction for a "line of commerce" in any "section of the country," language that appears to connote the product and geographic dimensions of the economist's concept of a "market." Since economics provides help in predicting the competitive impact of a transaction, and since economists are skilled in dealing with market definition issues and economic data, it seems inevitable that economic theory and concepts should play important roles in the development of the jurisprudence of revised section 7. However, the precise dimensions of those roles have been the subject of considerable controversy.[4]

This article will briefly review the evolution of the use of economics in merger enforcement.

I. *Brown Shoe*

Section 7 jurisprudence effectively began with the Supreme Court's 1962 opinion in *Brown Shoe Co. v. United States*, 370 U.S. 294 (1962), when the Court first interpreted the new section 7. Economics and antitrust, of course, were not unknown to one another before 1962. Among many others, Adelman, Bain, Director, Markham, Mason, and Stigler had written astutely on a variety of antitrust issues from the perspective of economics and economists. However, their work was of limited influence, perhaps because, as noted by one reviewer of the state of antitrust research as of 1960:

> So far, there has been very little tendency among economists to translate their policy views into specific suggestions for the guidance of the courts or, failing that, for remedial legislation. The acuteness

---

3 FTC v. Procter & Gamble Co., 386 U.S. 568, 592–93 (1967) (Harlan, J., concurring).

4 *See, e.g.*, Fox & Sullivan, *Antitrust—Retrospective and Prospective*, 62 N.Y.U. L. REV. 936 (1987).

> of economists' analysis of the shortcomings of the legal process contrasts oddly with the thin quality of their constructive suggestion.[5]

This seeming insensitivity of one field for the practical needs of another perhaps reflects the then rarity of interdisciplinary work and the novelty of the idea that economics could play more than a subsidiary role in shaping law. These obstacles were surmounted in Kaysen and Turner's *Antitrust Policy*, the result of the collaboration of an economist who had served as a judicial law clerk and a lawyer with a doctorate in economics.[6] And in 1960, Derek Bok published a lengthy article that focused in detail, in the context of section 7, on the institutional problems that bedevil absorption of economic theory into the law.[7]

After reviewing the debates leading to the 1950 legislation, and evaluating economic theory and research on the nature and effects of mergers, Bok argued for relatively simple merger rules. This position was based on his belief that only such rules were capable of judicial administration and that much of the relevant economic theory might not be well enough understood to assist in predicting the future. He warned that an "unwillingness to recognize the limits of our understanding hardens resistance to simple rules because of the false hope that more information can somehow dispel doubts about the consequences of a disputed merger."[8]

In *Brown Shoe* the Supreme Court ignored Bok's warning about the need for relatively simple rules. It surveyed the legislative history of section 7, stressed that market shares alone would not suffice for an analysis, and stated that "only a further examination of the particular market—its structure, history and probable future—can provide the appropriate setting for judging

---

5 H. PACKER, THE STATE OF RESEARCH IN ANTITRUST LAW at 33 (1963).

6 C. KAYSEN & D. TURNER, ANTITRUST POLICY (1959).

7 Bok, *Section 7 of the Clayton Act and the Merging of Law and Economics*, 74 HARV. L. REV. 226 (1960).

8 *Id.* at 349.

the probable anticompetitive effect of the merger.''[9] It also emphasized the importance of halting trends toward concentration, and the relevance of the merger's probable effects on "the economic way of life sought to be preserved by Congress.''[10]

From the point of view of recourse to economic theory and concepts, and of sophistication in the use of economic data, the opinion is a failure. The Court's analysis of market definition is limited; it gives undue importance to actual usage of the term "market," which may be loose and may or may not refer to economic markets; it introduces the concept of submarkets (which many economists find useless or confusing); disapproval is expressed for mergers achieving a 5% market share (on the ground that approval here would require approval of further mergers by others also seeking 5% market shares, seemingly suggesting that the Court feared oligopoly behavior in a market consisting solely of 5% factors); wholesale and retail data are apparently improperly commingled; and possible efficiencies that result from vertical integration of manufacturing into retailing are relied on as an additional reason for invalidating the merger.[11] As one economist critic noted, the Supreme Court "considered the merger illegal because prices would simultaneously both rise and fall.''[12]

II. The post-*Brown Shoe* cases

Surprisingly, however, 1 year after *Brown Shoe* both economic theory and Bok's warning about the pitfalls of overly complex economic rules emerged importantly to help shape the *Philadel-*

---

9 Brown Shoe Co. v. United States, 370 U.S. 294, 322, n.38 (1962).

10 *Id.* at 333.

11 *Id.* at 344. *See* Peterman, *The Brown Shoe Case*, 18 J. L. Econ. 81 (1975), for a detailed review of the record in the case and of the Court's opinion.

12 Peterman, *supra* note 11, at 138.

phia National Bank decision.[13] There, the majority stressed that the test it advanced—a merger that resulted in a significant increase in market concentration and produced a firm controlling over 30% of a market was presumptively unlawful—was "fully consonant with economic theory." The Court cited Kaysen and Turner, Stigler, Markham, Machlup, Bain, and Mason.[14] The Court also endorsed Bok's view that given the complex and elusive nature of economic evidence, and given the need for certitude in business planning, the test for illegality should be simplified where possible.[15] It stated that the economists' perception of a relationship between an unconcentrated market and vigorous competition "was undoubtedly a premise of congressional reasoning about the antimerger statute."[16] A form of oligopoly theory, for this case at least, thereby became a judicially acknowledged part of the legislative history of section 7.

This express reference to economic theory was not repeated in the subsequent post-*Brown* section 7 majority opinions by the Supreme Court. Although the Justice Department in its briefs to the Court in cases such as *Von's*[17] and *Pabst-Blatz*[18] sought to build on *Philadelphia National Bank* and to rely on a then widely accepted version of oligopoly theory, the majority opinions did not deem it necessary to do so. The opinions merely recite changes in the numbers of competitors over time and changes in market shares of the parties to the transaction without explaining the possible economic significance of those changes. In *Von's* the majority opinion stated that the basic purpose of section 7 "was to prevent economic concentration in the American economy by

---

13 United States v. Philadelphia National Bank, 374 U.S. 321 (1963).

14 *Id.* at 363 & nn. 38, 39, 41.

15 *Id.* at 362.

16 *Id.* at 363.

17 United States v. Von's Grocery Co., 384 U.S. 270 (1966).

18 United States v. Pabst Brewing Co., 384 U.S. 546 (1966).

keeping a large number of small competitors in business." (p. 275) Again, "Congress sought to preserve competition among many small businesses by arresting a trend to concentration in its incipiency . . . ." (p. 277) The *Von's* majority, using these premises, concluded that a merger resulting in a market share of 7.5% was unlawful.[19]

The majority opinion in *Pabst-Blatz* similarly was devoid of economic analysis, again relying primarily on a decline in the number of competitors and a rise in the share of the market controlled by larger companies. This led it to hold, among other things, that a resultant 4.49% share of a national market sufficed for illegality.

The majority opinion in the Court's first market extension case, arising out of the Procter & Gamble acquisition of Clorox,[20] was similarly devoid of reliance on or reference to economic theory, although a proposition begging for some such reference was advanced as one of the bases for decision—*i.e.*, that substitution of a powerful acquiring firm for a smaller but already dominant firm will raise entry barriers and dissuade smaller competitors from aggressively competing.[21]

The majority opinion in *FTC v. Procter & Gamble Co.* also makes the statement that:

> Possible economies cannot be used as a defense to illegality. Congress was aware that some mergers which lessen competition may also

---

19 The dissenters noted: "The Court's opinion is remarkable for its failure to support its conclusion by reference to even a single piece of economic theory." *Id.* at 302 n.35.

20 FTC v. Procter & Gamble Co., 386 U.S. 568 (1967). Justice Harlan, in his concurrence, made heavy use of economic writings, theories, and concepts. He also concluded that resultant efficiencies should be weighed against adverse competitive effects, an approach ultimately incorporated in the Justice Department's 1988 Antitrust Enforcement Guidelines for International Operations.

21 *Id.* at 578.

result in economies but it struck the balance in favor of protecting competition.[22]

III. The 1968 merger guidelines

It is against the background of cases such as these that in 1968 the Justice Department issued its first set of merger guidelines.[23] Given the subsequent proliferation of antitrust guidelines, this event does not now appear significant. But it was significant at the time as the first effort to explicate comprehensively and in detail a whole area of the Antitrust Division's enforcement policy.[24] Moreover, by spelling out the circumstances in which enforcement action could be expected and the rationale for such action, the 1968 Guidelines also provided a good indication of when enforcement action was *not* to be anticipated.

The 1968 Guidelines were formulated under Donald Turner, whose background as a lawyer and economist made him uniquely capable of the effort to incorporate economic reasoning into relatively workable legal rules. The 1968 Guidelines relied heavily on what was perceived to be the predictions of economic theory as to the relationship between market structure and performance. In particular, it relied on the premise of oligopoly theory that "where a few firms account for a large share of the sales" the structure "tends to discourage vigorous price competition by the firms in the market."[25] The Guidelines, accordingly, focused largely on market concentration. The role of entry barriers was acknowledged (although relatively little significance was in fact given to ease of entry). Some significant attention was paid to

---

22 *Id.* at 580.

23 Merger Guidelines, Department of Justice, May 30, 1968.

24 Speeches by enforcement officials advised the bar and others of enforcement policies both prior to and after 1968. The 1968 Guidelines differed from such speeches in the detail, comprehensiveness, and specificity of the statements of the tests to be applied.

25 1968 Merger Guidelines, ¶ 1. Economic writings, such as J. Bain, Industrial Organization, were relied on for this reasoning.

formulating an economically respectable approach to market definition. An effort was also made to express in economic terms, largely in terms of raising entry barriers, a basis for enforcement against vertical mergers.

The 1968 Guidelines did not refer to quasi-social or political aspects of the legislative origins of section 7. However, the Guidelines did not repudiate or ignore existing precedent (much of which was, after all, developed in cases appealed by the Justice Department). They attempted, rather, to explicate and rationalize in economic terms the then-existing body of Supreme Court merger opinions and modestly to shape future development of certain areas of section 7 law. Hence, the 1968 Guidelines retained, with some amelioration, the market share tests of *Von's* (though not of *Pabst-Blatz*), provided for vertical enforcement on the basis of so-called foreclosure, reflected the "entrenchment" theory of *Procter & Gamble*[26] and incorporated a version of the "reciprocity-creating" theory of *United States v. Consolidated Foods*[27] as a foray into the pure conglomerate field. The Supreme Court's expressed concern about mergers that furthered "trends" toward concentration led to a special provision for markets exhibiting such a trend.[28] An effort was made to outline a potential competition theory.[29] The Guidelines only slightly modified the flat rejection of an efficiencies defense in *Procter & Gamble* by stating that an otherwise challengeable merger could not be justified by improvements in efficiencies unless there were "exceptional circumstances."[30]

The Guidelines purported to be written solely as a guide as to the Justice Department's enforcement intent. But the effort to provide some economic cogency to existing precedent was, no doubt, also intended to infuse economic reasoning into the

---

26 1968 Merger Guidelines, ¶ 20.

27 *Id.* at ¶ 19.

28 *Id.* at ¶ 7.

29 *Id.* at ¶ 18.

30 *Id.* at ¶ 10.

further development of merger law. No massive incongruity between the legislative goals and an economically oriented enforcement policy was seen since the oligopoly theories relied upon led to rules that also helped implement noneconomic legislative goals.

IV. The 1982/84 merger guidelines

Some 14 years later, in 1982, the Justice Department issued a new set of merger guidelines. In explaining the reasons for the new rules, Attorney General William French Smith stated that the 1968 Guidelines had become obsolete for several reasons.[31] These included the fact that they were based on the assumption of a very close relationship between concentration and market performance which he characterized as a questionable assumption grounded on "outworn and inaccurate economic literature of the 1930s and 1940s."[32] New developments in economics were said to raise doubts about the 1968 Guidelines' use of economic formulae confined to market concentration and market share. He also stated that the Supreme Court's opinion in the *General Dynamics* case[33] illustrated a broadened analysis that included evidence that market shares may not reflect present and future competitive conditions in the market. He saw a more economic orientation in the Supreme Court's nonmerger antitrust cases, such as that in *GTE-Sylvania*,[34] which suggested that merger cases would also be decided differently once before the Court, and noted that the Department's own enforcement had already changed in recent years, with vertical and conglomerate cases no longer being a major enforcement focus.

---

31 Smith, *Changing Enforcement Policy*, 51 ANTITRUST L. J. 95, 97–100 (1982).

32 *Id.* at 97–98.

33 United States v. General Dynamics Corp., 415 U.S. 486 (1974).

34 Continental T.V. Inc. v. GTE-Sylvania, Inc., 433 U.S. 36 (1977).

This explanation of the reasons for the new guidelines is incomplete. In fact, Supreme Court merger jurisprudence had not materially changed since 1968, and Attorney General Smith had to acknowledge that there had been "no real landmarks."[35] And *General Dynamics* could readily be regarded as standing only for the unremarkable proposition that in using concentration and market share data to determine validity under section 7, the market share data should have predictive and not merely historical significance.

The changes in the Guidelines could better be understood as reflecting the impact of ongoing scholarship that culminated in the publication in 1976 and 1978 of two trenchant critiques of antitrust policy by legal scholars steeped in antitrust economics, particularly as developed by Aaron Director, George Stigler, and others at the University of Chicago—Richard Posner's *Antitrust Law: An Economic Perspective* and Robert Bork's *The Antitrust Paradox.* These works were the condensation of several years of writing by the two authors, and reflected more than two decades of analysis and criticism of antitrust policy and enforcement by economists and law professors, mainly at Chicago and Yale.

The 1982 Guidelines, which were created under the aegis of William F. Baxter, did not purport to reflect existing Supreme Court precedent. They omitted provisions applicable to conglomerate mergers (entrenchment and reciprocity-creating acquisitions) and they omitted a provision addressed to mergers in markets in which there was a trend to concentration. They reached vertical mergers only in extreme situations.

They retained an emphasis on concentration and market shares.[36] But, presumably in response to a recognition by econo-

---

35 *Id.* at 99.

36 The 1982 Guidelines use the Herfindahl-Hirschman index [HHI] method of calculating concentration in place of the four-firm concentration levels used in the 1968 Guidelines. This change had been urged by Richard Posner as long ago as 1969. Posner, *Oligopoly and the Antitrust Laws: A Suggested Approach*, 21 STAN. L. REV. 1562, 1602 (1969). There is considerable correlation between the two measures. An

mists of less correlation between concentration and performance than had previously been supposed, they no longer purported to find problems with mergers involving market shares at the low levels of *Von's*. Rather, they provided for "safe harbors" where concentration and concentration changes were deemed too low to warrant any antitrust concern. Furthermore, they regard concentration and market share data as the beginning, not the end, of analysis. Since concentration is viewed by the 1982 Guidelines as a problem only when it may lead to collusion, unless concentration and the change in concentration are very high an examination of a variety of "other factors" is usually called for to ascertain whether concern with collusion is, after all, plausible.[37]

As originally written the new guidelines, like the 1968 Guidelines, did not accept an efficiencies defense unless exceptional circumstances were present. In the 1984 revision of the 1982 Guidelines, however, the possibility of an efficiencies defense was upgraded. A new provision, paragraph 3.5, was added. It reads:

> If the parties to the merger establish by clear and convincing evidence that a merger will achieve . . . efficiencies, the Department will consider those efficiencies in deciding whether to challenge the merger.

The 1982/1984 Merger Guidelines make significant use of economics, not merely as to methodology and concepts,[38] but in terms of basic policy goals. The upgrading of the efficiencies factor—always a basic concern to an economist—reflects this. And it has been repeatedly asserted by Antitrust Division officials that the ultimate goal of antitrust in general and of section 7

HHI of 1,800 is roughly equivalent to a four-firm concentration ratio of 70%. *See* White, *Antitrust and Merger Policy*, 1 J. Econ. Perspectives 13, 17 (1987).

37 For a detailed comparison of the 1968 and 1982 Guidelines, *see* Fox, *The New Merger Guidelines—A Blueprint for Microeconomic Analysis*, 27 Antitrust Bull. 519 (1982).

38 An economist who coauthored the 1982 Guidelines regards their provision on market definition as the "most important conceptual contribution" of the Guidelines. *See* White, *supra*, note 36, at 14.

enforcement in particular is the purely economic one of maximizing "consumer welfare" (not in Consumers Union sense but in the microeconomic sense of maximizing the efficient allocation of resources to produce the greatest total wealth, without regard to distribution of that wealth).[39]

V. The 1988 international guidelines

The 1982/1984 Merger Guidelines were supplemented by the 1988 Antitrust Enforcement Guidelines for International Operations. These 1988 Guidelines deal with the full scope of antitrust enforcement, not merely mergers. But they are pertinent because they sought to place Justice Department enforcement policy toward mergers in the context of overall competitive policy, because they are candid as to their view of that policy, and because they further upgrade the role of efficiencies. They probably represent a high point in the influence of Chicago school economics upon the formulation of antitrust policy.

The 1988 Guidelines stated that efficiencies would not only "be considered" (as the 1984 Guidelines had it) but if significant can be dispositive on the question of legality, even in the presence of anticompetitive effects.[40] The 1988 Guidelines also make explicit that their underlying assumption is that most mergers play a "beneficial" role in the economy,[41] that a major function of the concentration thresholds in the Guidelines is to identify so-called safe harbors, and that if a merger does not fall in a safe

---

39 Robert Bork argued strenuously that maximization of consumer welfare, as so defined, is the only "legitimate" goal of antitrust, and that other goals, of a quasi-social or political nature, are unworkable or incapable of having intellectual content. *See*, *e.g.*, R. Bork, The Antitrust Paradox 56 (1978).

40 The 1988 Guidelines state a merger will generally not be challenged if there is clear and convincing evidence that it would result in significant procompetitive efficiencies that could not otherwise be achieved "and that the merger would therefore not likely result in a net decrease in consumer welfare." 1988 Guidelines, ¶ 3.3222.

41 *Id.* at ¶ 3.3.

harbor the effect on concentration is but one of several factors that will be examined.[42]

The Department through its 1982, 1984, and 1988 Guidelines gradually shifted from a position of rarely considering efficiencies to a general willingness to evaluate them.[43] Indeed, the 1988 Guidelines list examples of efficiencies it will consider and states the Department, in analyzing whether efficiencies would offset the threat of anticompetitive harm,

> would compare the estimated cost savings from the claimed efficiencies (less the estimated cost of consolidating the operations of the merging firms) with the threat of harm to competition resulting from the merger.[44]

VI. Conclusion

With the 1984 and 1988 Guidelines the Chicago school microeconomic ascendancy in the Justice Department's formal statements of section 7 enforcement policy has become nearly complete.[45] Those Guidelines depict an enforcement policy that differs considerably from possibly antiquated but still extant Supreme Court precedents. The differences go to the question of the type of mergers that may be unlawful, the tests to be applied, the role of efficiencies, and the goals sought to be achieved by the legislation.

Antitrust lawyers are alert and flexible and they and their merging clients have adjusted to the greatly enhanced role of

---

42 *Id.* at ¶ 3.32.

43 The greater the competitive risks, the greater the level of expected efficiencies that must be established. *Id.* at ¶ 3.3222.

44 *See id.* at Case 1.

45 Federal Trade Commission merger enforcement is, of course, as important as Justice Department enforcement. No effort is made here to trace the evolution of economic theory and concepts in merger enforcement by that agency, but the two agencies generally take consistent positions.

economics in federal merger enforcement. Lawyers have become conversant with economic concepts, both analytical and prescriptive; law schools teach economics along with antitrust; use of economic consultants working with lawyers on merger transactions is widespread and conventional. There are, nonetheless, at least three questions posed by the present situation: (1) how to plan, given the as yet lack of uniform acceptability of the microeconomic approach to merger law; (2) how to cope with the fact that the durability of the present policy, if not authenticated by Congress or by the Supreme Court, may be cast in doubt with each change of administration; and (3) how to deal with the complexity and uncertainty inherent in the applicability of an enforcement policy that takes into account a variety of different economic factors.

1. As to the first point, the disparity between federal merger enforcement policy and Supreme Court precedents is a source of continuing uncertainty for business planning. The *Cargill* case[46] limits but does not prevent litigation by private parties who, of course, will invoke existing case law. In most transactions, this possibility may be of less than major consequence. This is because the primary obstacle to consummation of a merger in the ordinary situation is a federal enforcement agency challenge, and where the merger is consensual and no competitor's ox is particularly gored, no one else will engage in expensive, time-consuming section 7 litigation. But in hostile transactions or where a competitor has unusual incentives, private suits cannot be ignored.[47] Lower court judges are still obliged to follow precedent and, thus far at least, the detailed statements of Justice Department merger enforcement policies have not predictably shaped decisions in the appellate courts.

It is this disparity between the announced enforcement policy and precedent that, no doubt, animated the Reagan administration to attempt to secure a congressional revision of section 7 that

---

46 Cargill, Inc. v. Montfort of Colorado, Inc., 479 U.S. 104 (1986).

47 *See, e.g.*, R. C. Bigelow, Inc. v. Unilever N.V., 1989-1 Trade Reg. Rep. (CCH) ¶ 68,398 (2d Cir. Jan. 17, 1989).

would, by eliminating the incipiency provisions of the statute, wipe the judicial slate more or less clean. That legislative effort failed and it is far from clear that a renewed effort along the same lines will succeed in the foreseeable future.

Perhaps a total accommodation will be achieved as the composition of the Supreme Court and courts of appeals gradually changes. But this, too, is speculative. The antitrust views of prospective Supreme Court or court of appeals' appointees may not rank among the primary criteria for nomination. Moreover, the legislative history of the 1950 version of section 7 may, ultimately, defy even the most ambitious of judicial efforts to find consumer welfare in the economic sense as the main goal of the statute.

A related problem of possibly increasing importance in the merger field may be that posed by state attorneys general. The standards they intend to employ, as set forth in their March 10, 1987 statement entitled *Antitrust Enforcement: Horizontal Merger Guidelines of the National Association of Attorneys General*, differ in a number of important respects from those of the Justice Department. They pointedly state that

> it is the legislative function to make basic policy choices, whether or not those choices coincide with the beliefs of a particular administration, enforcement agency, or a particular school of economic theory.[48]

They reject "consumer welfare" in the microeconomic sense as a primary goal of Congress and state that transfer of wealth from consumers to companies with market power "is the major evil sought to be addressed by Section 7."[49] They take a distinctly less expansive approach to market definition that, in most cases, will result in attribution of larger market shares to merging parties; they add to the threshold tests used by the Justice Department the possibility of enforcement on the basis of a smaller increase in concentration if overall market concentration

---

48 *Horizontal Guidelines of the National Association of Attorneys General*, ¶ 1 n.7.

49 *Id.* at ¶ 2.11.

had been increasing over the past 36 months; they limit consideration of efficiencies to transactions which result in HHIs of less than 1,800; and they confine consideration of "other factors" solely to ease of entry, history of collusive behavior, and, as limited above, efficiencies.

Clearly, to the extent state attorneys general are actively engaged in section 7 enforcement or in state merger law enforcement, the difficulties in planning a merger are increased.

What may make the situation less than intolerable is that it is unlikely that state attorneys general will routinely engage in merger litigation. For most transactions, getting by the federal agencies will be dispositive. But there will be a few for whom the accident of state enforcement will be a dismaying experience.

2. The durability of present merger enforcement policy, as articulated in the Guidelines, will remain in doubt as long as it lacks endorsement of Congress or the Supreme Court. As noted above, congressional endorsement is probably not imminent. A shift in Supreme Court decision making is more probable; but should it occur, it may of necessity be only partial and incremental.

The 1988 election probably insured basic continuity of policy for the near-term (although it already appears likely that stricter enforcement within the confines of that policy is to be expected). Moreover, the declining position of the United States in the world market and the growth of foreign competition in the United States may, ultimately, have as much to do with continuity of present merger enforcement policy as economic theory. The world envisaged by Justices Black and Douglas of numerous small entrepreneurs whose opportunity for growth is to be protected seems more and more to be a remnant of a bygone age, particularly if such protection is at the expense of American efficiency and competitiveness.[50] Even the state attorneys general

---

50 In *Cargill*, *supra* note 46, Justice Brennan, author of the *Philadelphia National Bank* opinion, noted that the claim that Congress

do not urge a return to the 1968 Guidelines on horizontal mergers, but rather employ modifications of the Justice Department's 1984 Guidelines. But the ambitious nature of the guidelines' commitment to economic theory and the extent to which they are ahead of case law in that commitment, leaves them vulnerable to the possibility of abrupt change, at least as to particulars.

A different possible challenge to the durability of present policy arises from the fact that economic learning itself changes and evolves. For example, a critical area is the question of the assumed relationship between concentration and performance. The *Philadelphia National Bank* case as well as the 1968 Guidelines were heavily reliant on this assumed relationship. Although the Attorney General, in explaining the reason for the 1982 Guidelines, noted that later studies had cast doubt about the firmness of the relationship, those Guidelines, including the 1984 and 1988 supplements, continue to utilize concentration data and the contribution of the merger to concentration, in various important respects. Yet there have been additional questions raised as to the validity of the "structuralist" theory[51] and a significant number of economists now question whether *any* correlation can be shown between market structure and performance.[52] Conceivably, at some point, this theoretical underpinning of the Department's Guidelines might be eroded to the point where it can no longer be relied upon for any purpose. A different approach will be needed. But then, unless Congress has again spoken in the interim, the tension between what Congress intended in 1950 as to concentration, and what economic theory suggests as sound policy, will become even greater than it now is.

---

intended the courts to apply section 7 to keep small competitors in business at the expense of efficiency was "a proposition about which there is considerable disagreement." 479 U.S. 104, 116, n.11.

51 *See* J. W. MEEHAN JR. & R. J. LARNER, ECONOMICS AND ANTITRUST POLICY, 179–208 (1989).

52 *See* Phillips, *Market Concentration and Performance: A Survey of the Evidence*, 61 NOTRE DAME L. REV. 1099 (1986).

3. The present Justice Department enforcement policy at first blush appears flatly inconsistent with precepts set down by the Bok article. In place of relatively simple rules there are a variety of economic factors that are to be considered, such as ease of entry, homogeneity or heterogeneity of the product,[53] information exchanges and detectability of deviations from agreed-on prices,[54] ability of fringe sellers to increase sales,[55] prior history of collusion,[56] etc. Little guidance is provided on the ordering or weighing of these factors. Nor is much useful guidance provided as to measurement of the important ease-of-entry factor. Moreover, with the full-fledged recognition of an efficiency defense, the 1988 Guidelines indicate that parties may find themselves engaged in a comparison of estimated cost savings from claimed efficiencies less the estimated cost of consolidating the operations of the merging firms, on the one hand, with some quantification of the threat of harm to competition resulting from the merger, on the other. Obviously, such an exercise is replete with uncertainties—*e.g.*, how to quantify the threat of harm, how to predict the cost of consolidation, how to calculate the cost savings from the efficiencies.

On the face of it, this is the nightmare Bok warned of. However, there is an important distinction: the rules are relatively simple and clear as far as the definition of safe harbors are concerned. There, all that is looked at is concentration and market share data. To be sure, even these "simple" rules are loaded with the uncertainty that is attendant on the process of defining the relevant market on the basis of which concentration and market data can be computed. The "market," according to Justice Department Guidelines, is to be defined on the basis of a completely hypothetical exercise—"hypothetical buyers and competitors with perfect information responding to a [hypothetical

---

53 1984 Merger Guidelines, ¶ 3.411.

54 *Id.* at ¶ 3.42.

55 *Id.* at ¶ 3.43.

56 *Id.* at ¶ 3.44.

5%] price rise by a hypothetical monopolist.''[57] But market definition is inevitably a source of complexity, whatever the guidelines.

The present Guidelines are, therefore, helpful in their relatively straightforward approach to safe harbors. For the mergers that can rest in those safe harbors, the Guidelines, except for the unavoidable vagaries of market definition, have the clarity and simplicity that Bok urged. But where safe harbors are not available, the array of economic factors that come into play are many and complex and prediction of enforcement agency positions will not be easy.

As a practical matter, if the choice is between simple but restrictive rules and a full menu of economic factors that may salvage a merger, most would prefer to take their chances with a detailed multifaceted analysis. As an institutional matter, it may be that in the nearly 30 years since Bok wrote his article, economic sophistication of bench and bar, and economic learning, have developed to the point where the 1960 warning of chaotic results can be disregarded. Time will tell.

---

57 Salop, *Symposium on Mergers and Antitrust*, 1 J. ECON. PERSPECTIVES 3, 10 (1987).

8
Toward a merger policy that maximizes consumer welfare: enforcement by careful analysis, not by the numbers

BY CHARLES F. RULE* and DAVID L. MEYER**

As we commemorate the 75th anniversary of the Clayton Act and the 100th anniversary of the Sherman Act, merger policy is the subject of intense controversy. During the last years of the

---

* Partner, Covington & Burling; formerly Assistant Attorney General, Antitrust Division, U.S. Department of Justice.

** Associate, Covington & Burling; formerly Special Assistant to the Assistant Attorney General, Antitrust Division, U.S. Department of Justice.

AUTHORS' NOTE: *This article was prepared as the Reagan administration drew to a close; and it therefore reflects merger policy as it had developed during that period. While there may have been some subtle changes, particularly in rhetoric, it is likely that those changes are primarily at the margins of Department policy toward mergers and that the analysis discussed herein accurately describes the basis for current enforcement decisions.*

We wish to thank George Rozanski, Economist, Antitrust Division, for his contribution to the discussion of the economic theory underlying merger analysis.

Reagan administration, a handful of very large corporate control transactions attracted the attention of the print and television media. That attention in turn offered the critics of antitrust policies a platform from which to broadcast their views concerning the appropriate course that federal antitrust enforcement—under the Sherman and Clayton Acts that we now commemorate—should take in future years.

Much of this criticism was based on a mischaracterization of merger policy as it had evolved under the Reagan administration, reflected a misunderstanding of the purposes and capabilities of the antitrust laws, or amounted to dangerous and counterproductive "business bashing." Properly understood, merger policy, as it is still enforced at the Department of Justice, is carefully tailored to protect consumers against transactions that create, maintain, or facilitate the exercise of market power—that is, the power to raise prices above competitive levels. At the same time, that policy is also designed to avoid otherwise interfering with the market for corporate control.

This article will demonstrate that neither the formulation of merger policy by antitrust enforcers nor the often critical assessment of that policy by outside observers should be based solely on numbers—on numbers of transactions challenged or on concentration statistics, Herfindahl-Hirschman indices [HHIs], of those allowed to go forward. This article will first explain that changes in the relative numbers of mergers challenged by antitrust enforcers in recent years have had more to do with changes in the world economy than in the tolerance of antitrust enforcers to the creation of market power.

The article then turns to a discussion of the operational goals of merger policy—clarity/certainty and accuracy. Achieving these goals requires that government decisions to block mergers not be based on strict, inflexible numerical criteria, pursuant to which every merger yielding certain levels of and increases in concentration will be challenged. Rather, such numbers can only be the starting point.

The final section of the article describes the alternative, more accurate approach to merger enforcement that looks beyond the numbers and determines whether a merger truly threatens to lessen competition substantially. That approach, which has evolved at the federal level over the last 10 years, is based on an understanding of all the scenarios in which a merger among competitors might create, enhance, or facilitate the exercise of market power, and on a careful analysis of the facts to determine whether any such scenario is likely. The article devotes considerable attention in particular to the circumstances in which market power can be exercised in bidding markets.

The current "merger wave"

To be sure, much has changed in the 75 years since the framers drafted the Clayton Act, and in the 39 years since Congress amended it with the Celler-Kefauver Antimerger Act.[1] In recent years, America has experienced what by normal historical standards would have to be considered a merger wave. The number of transactions about which the Department of Justice [Department] was notified under the Hart-Scott-Rodino [H-S-R] Act[2] has increased in each of the last 6 years. In fiscal year 1988 (October 1987 to September 1988), the last full year of the Reagan administration, the Department received filings for 2,747 transactions, a record number. Compared to 1979,[3] when the government received filings for only 859 transactions, the number of reported transactions has increased tremendously.

The wave is reflected in enforcement statistics as well. In fiscal 1988, at least 26 mergers were challenged or abandoned by the

---

1 Pub. L. No. 81-899, 64 Stat. 1125 (1950).

2 15 U.S.C. § 18a. The H-S-R Act facilitates enforcement of the Clayton Act by requiring businesses to notify the Federal Trade Commission [FTC] and the Department of proposed transactions that would exceed certain size-of-parties and size-of-transaction thresholds, provide information relating to those transactions, and wait a prescribed period before consummating the transaction.

3 Fiscal 1979 was the first full year for which the H-S-R Act required filings. *See* 16 C.F.R. § 800.1 (1988) (transitional rule governing H-S-R filings); 43 Fed. Reg. 33,537 (July 31, 1978) (H-S-R rules).

parties after federal investigation, a peak since the merger boom of the late 1960's and early 1970's. Despite this increase in enforcement, however, it is true that the federal government challenges a relatively smaller percentage of mergers today than 10 years ago. One study indicates the Department and FTC are challenging mergers at only about one-third the rate of 10 years ago.[4] While that number may understate the level of enforcement—for example, by not counting instances where parties abandon their transactions after the government expresses concern, but before a complaint is filed[5]—the government does challenge today a smaller percentage of the transactions that it reviews.

The merger wave and the relative decline in merger challenges, however, are not the product of a decreased commitment to accomplishing the consumer welfare goals of the antitrust laws. Rather, the statistics reflect an increasingly sophisticated and accurate enforcement policy that is applied against the backdrop of numerous significant changes in the U.S. economy.

In attempting to evaluate federal merger policy, one must first recognize that there has been significant progress in society's understanding of the economic effects of mergers and in the ability of federal enforcement agencies and courts to isolate those mergers that truly threaten to harm competition. Courts, recognizing the "consumer welfare" focus of antitrust law,[6] have interpreted the law to proscribe only that conduct, including mergers, that truly threatens consumers—that is, conduct that

---

4 *See* 52 Antitrust & Trade Reg. Rep. (BNA) No. 1305, at 451–52 (Mar. 5, 1987) (House Judiciary Committee charts on federal antitrust enforcement), *cited in* Pitofsky, *Antitrust in the Decade Ahead: Some Predictions About Merger Enforcement*, 57 ANTITRUST L.J. 65, 66 (1988).

5 Those instances represent an increasing proportion of all merger challenges.

6 *See, e.g.*, Reiter v. Sonotone Corp., 442 U.S. 330, 343 (1979) (legislative history "suggest[s] that Congress designed the Sherman Act as a 'consumer welfare prescription' ") (quoting R. BORK, THE ANTITRUST PARADOX 66 (1978)).

threatens to raise prices and to restrict output without generating offsetting efficiency benefits. Using the tools of economic analysis and the lessons learned from past misguided merger policy, courts, in league with antitrust enforcers, have vastly improved their ability to identify mergers that create such a threat. Because experience, economic theory, and empirical research provide a much improved basis for accurately predicting the effects of mergers,[7] there is less impetus to block mergers—such as those involving miniscule shares of a market—solely out of a fear of the unknown.[8] As it evolved during the Reagan administration, antitrust enforcement against mergers became much more like a rifle shot than the blunderbuss approach of just a few years ago. The inevitable result has been relatively fewer challenges.

Federal enforcement officials have also taken more care to clarify and publicize their enforcement policy. The Merger Guidelines, which were rewritten in 1982 and revised in 1984,[9] along with the Antitrust Enforcement Guidelines for International Operations, which were rewritten in 1988,[10] provide much clearer guidance regarding how to structure a corporate control transac-

---

[7] Economic analysis of the effects of mergers has improved greatly in recent years, beginning in the mid-1970's with the so-called new learning challenges to the relationship between concentration, firm profitability, and market performance. *See, e.g.*, INDUSTRIAL CONCENTRATION: THE NEW LEARNING (H. Goldschmid, H. Mann, & J. Weston, eds. 1975); Demsetz, *Industrial Structure, Market Rivalry, and Public Policy*, 16 J.L. & ECON. 1 (1973).

[8] *See, e.g.*, United States v. Von's Grocery Co., 384 U.S. 270, 273 (1966) (upholding challenge to merger producing firm with 7.5% post-merger market share); Brown Shoe Co. v. United States, 370 U.S. 294, 343-46 (1962) (upholding challenge to merger producing firm with 5% postmerger market share).

[9] U.S. Department of Justice Merger Guidelines (June 14, 1984) (hereinafter Merger Guidelines), *reprinted in* 4 Trade Reg. Rep. (CCH) ¶ 13,103.

[10] U.S. Department of Justice Antitrust Enforcement Guidelines for International Operations (Nov. 10, 1988) (hereinafter International Guidelines), *reprinted in* 4 Trade Reg. Rep. (CCH) ¶ 13,109.

tion in order to avoid challenge.[11] As discussed below, the two sets of Guidelines provide clear safe harbors for mergers that do not threaten consumers.[12] This increased clarity and the concomitant ability of private parties to understand and comply with the law inevitably has reduced the percentage of reported transactions challenged by the Department. Indeed, in theory, if the Merger Guidelines were perfectly clear and courts were always convinced that the Department's position was correct, then the Department would be required to challenge virtually no mergers because none would be proposed that the Department would disapprove. The number of merger challenges would be equal to zero, regardless of the harshness or leniency of the substantive standards of merger analysis.

It would be wrong, however, to conclude that expanding and clarifying the boundaries of these safe harbors has been the sole, or even the predominant, cause of the increase in corporate control transactions. Rather, the merger wave clearly has much more to do with the healthy, dynamic economy that America has enjoyed for the past several years than with any change in antitrust policy. There are a number of financial reasons for firms to undertake mergers that have nothing to do with the creation, maintenance, or exercise of market power. For example, a merger may be designed to oust incompetent management, to achieve economies of scale or scope, or to achieve favorable tax treatment.[13] When a merger is motivated by one of these aims and does not threaten to raise prices to consumers, the antitrust laws are simply not implicated. Thus, even if, as we argue below, current antitrust enforcement policy succeeds in blocking nearly

---

11 The FTC has issued a Statement Concerning Horizontal Mergers, *reprinted in* 4 Trade Reg. Rep. (CCH) ¶ 13,200 (1982), that sets forth a merger analysis substantially similar to that in the Department's 1982 and 1984 Merger Guidelines. The Statement specifically states that the FTC will give considerable weight to the 1982 Guidelines.

12 *See* discussion at notes 27–28, *infra*.

13 *See, e.g.*, F. SCHERER, INDUSTRIAL MARKET STRUCTURE AND ECONOMIC PERFORMANCE 127–41 (2d ed. 1980).

all truly anticompetitive mergers that are attempted, the number of mergers can still increase dramatically for reasons unrelated to antitrust enforcement.[14] In fact, the dramatic changes within the U.S. economy during the 1980's have created an increasing number of opportunities for firms to merge and/or restructure in order to obtain these not anticompetitive financial benefits.

Perhaps the most significant change in the economy is the increased presence of foreign competition. As deregulation and technological advance have brought down the cost of transportation and communication, and as real exchange rates have adjusted to the post-World War II restructuring of world financial markets, markets have expanded from localities to regions to the nation and, in an increasing number of cases, to the world. In many economic markets foreign products and services today provide a check on anticompetitive behavior of U.S. firms and protect consumers more effectively than any antitrust regime ever could. More significantly in terms of providing the motivation for corporate control transactions, the decline of U.S. economic dominance and the presence of foreign competitors have increased the urgency of efforts by American firms to become as efficient and competitive as possible. As the geographic scope of markets has expanded, new opportunities and dangers have been presented to U.S. firms. Mergers and acquisitions are important means by which to respond to challenges created by foreign competition.

An examination of the types of transactions that have been occurring confirms that the current merger wave cannot effectively be explained by changes in merger enforcement. Perhaps if all the transactions reported under the Hart-Scott-Rodino Act involved competitors—that is, were mergers that conceivably could threaten to increase prices—it might be reasonable to argue that merger challenges should increase in direct proportion to the

---

14 Of course, increased certainty and clarity in enforcement will reduce the cost of engaging in mergers that are not anticompetitive, by reducing the risk that the government will challenge such a merger. *See* discussion at text accompanying notes 27–28, *infra*.

number of transactions reported. Under H-S-R, however, firms must report far more than just mergers with their competitors.[15] Indeed, because a great deal of the recent merger activity has involved something other than the combination of competitors, "merger wave" is in many respects a misnomer for the recent increase in transactions reported under the H-S-R Act. More accurately, the phenomenon has been a "wave of corporate control transactions."

A substantial number of the transactions—at least 200 a year during the period 1983–1987[16]—have been leveraged buyouts [LBOs], no doubt reflecting changes in the capital markets and the "discovery" of high-yield debt instruments (so-called junk bonds). The substance of an LBO generally involves merely "taking a company private"—that is, changing the form of the firm's capital from public equity to private debt. LBOs generally do not combine the assets of any companies, much less competing firms. Moreover, the motivations for true LBOs are almost by definition not anticompetitive. Current management may believe that if given more total control of the company, the firm's value can be enhanced. An outsider may believe the value of the company can be increased if it is broken up into more commercially and financially sensible parts and sold off. Or it may be that the parties are taking advantage of a tax code that is biased in favor of debt and against equity ownership. Of course, it is also possible that the lenders participating in a particular LBO have made a multibillion-dollar blunder. Whatever the reason or reasons for a particular LBO, exercising market power to raise prices to consumers—the raison d'etre of antitrust challenges—is usually not one of them, nor is it the effect of such a transaction.

---

15 For example, the H-S-R Act requires the reporting of virtually all transactions transferring in excess of $15 million in assets or voting securities where one of the parties has annual net sales or total assets of $10 million or more and the other has annual net sales or total assets of $100 million or more, regardless of whether the firms compete in any market. 15 U.S.C. § 18a(a); 16 C.F.R. § 801 *et seq.*

16 Data are from W.T. Grimm & Co. and M & A Almanac, 1987 Profile.

An even larger number of so-called mergers involve divestitures or are pure "conglomerate" transactions. Antitrust enforcers struggled for many years to devise a theory of anticompetitive harm from conglomerate mergers.[17] Even before the advent of the so-called new learning, however, the courts were skeptical, if not downright hostile, toward those theories.[18] And today no respectable antitrust theory exists that could justify the costs of deviating from a rule of per se legality for pure conglomerates.[19]

---

17 *See, e.g.*, F. SCHERER, *supra* note 13, at 335–47, 558–63.

18 On several occasions, the Department's challenges to conglomerate acquisitions were decisively rejected by the courts. *See, e.g.*, United States v. International Telephone & Telegraph Corp., 1971 Trade Cas. (CCH) ¶ 73,619, at 90,546 (N.D. Ill. 1971) (rejecting challenge to IT&T's acquisition of Canteen Corp. on theory of reciprocal dealing); United States v. International Telephone & Telegraph Corp., 324 F. Supp. 19 (D. Conn. 1970) (rejecting challenge to IT&T's acquisition of Grinnel Corp.), *appeal dismissed per stipulation*, 404 U.S. 801 (1971); United States v. International Telephone & Telegraph Corp., 306 F. Supp. 766, 796 (D. Conn. 1969) (denying preliminary injunction against IT&T's acquisition of Grinnel Corp. and Hartford Fire Insurance Co., specifically rejecting theory that merger would contribute to "rising tide of economic concentration in American industry"), *appeal dismissed per stipulation*, 404 U.S. 801 (1971); *see generally* United States v. Northwest Industries, 301 F. Supp. 1066, 1096 (N.D. Ill. 1969) ("The law as it now stands makes the adverse effect on competition the test of validity. . . .").

19 The concern that mergers have led to an increased concentration of economic wealth in society (also referred to as "aggregate concentration") has never been an appropriate concern of the antitrust laws. There is no economic effect on consumers unless the increase in concentration occurs in particular, economically defined product markets. Moreover, the concern that aggregate concentration will corrupt political processes is unsupported in both fact and theory. Indeed, it has been suggested that lobbying groups composed of small businesses have been more effective in Congress than associations of large businesses. The very existence of a perceived public disdain for concentrations of economic wealth serves as a check on the political power of such aggregations. Even if aggregate concentration posed a real problem, however, there is simply no evidence that such concentration is increasing. The most recent information indicates that the percentage of assets accounted for by the largest 100 or 200 U.S. firms is below the 1970

Similarly, the large number of divestitures—involving over 1,000 transactions a year between 1983 and 1987[20]—generally pose no competitive problem. Unless divestitures involve the sale of assets to a competing firm, their most prominent effect is to decrease the concentration of economic wealth in society.

As a result of these changes in the economy, in the economic understanding of enforcers and courts, and in the manner in which corporate control is transacted, there is simply a smaller percentage of merger transactions that are anticompetitive today than in the past. Faced with this reality, critics of the recent wave of corporate control transactions have focused their attacks on perceived harms unrelated to the impact on competition. The fears have been expressed, for example, that companies are burdened with too much debt, that managers are wasting too much time on "unproductive financial shell games,"[21] that ownership is being concentrated in the hands of a few, and that U.S. firms are being gobbled up by foreign interests. There is good reason to believe that these concerns are based on questionable facts,[22] or on even more questionable theory. Even if such

---

level and has been stable in recent years, while the percentage of all employment accounted for by the same firms has been declining. U.S. Department of Justice, March 1987 Update of Aggregate Concentration Figures (measures derived from data obtained from the following sources: Internal Revenue Service, Statistics of Income, Corporate Income Tax Returns; *Fortune*, lists of largest corporations; U.S. Department of Commerce, Survey of Current Business).

20 Data are from W.T. Grimm & Co. and M & A Almanac, 1987 Profile.

21 W. ADAMS & J. BROCK, THE BIGNESS COMPLEX 373 (1986).

22 With respect to the concern that corporations in general are overburdened with debt, see Bernanke & Campbell, *Is There a Corporate Debt Crisis* in 1 BROOKINGS PAPERS ON ECONOMIC ACTIVITY 83, 123 (W. Brainard & G. Perry, eds. 1988) (finding appropriate cause for concern, but no crisis, noting for example that debt-asset ratios of Japanese corporations are twice those of U.S. counterparts). In addition, the available evidence flatly contradicts the notion that economic wealth is becoming increasingly concentrated in the hands of a few

transactions do impose significant costs, these concerns are irrelevant to antitrust enforcement, which must focus solely on the effect of a transaction on competition and the well-being of U.S. consumers.

In addition, even to the extent these nonantitrust concerns are legitimate and society determines that government should address them, the government response should be narrowly focused to avoid interfering with legitimate transactions that can enhance efficiency. It is more appropriate to do nothing unless it is clear that the benefits of a response outweigh its costs. Indeed, creating a new regulatory regime that required the Department or some other bureaucracy to review all transactions and stop those that would violate some new nonantitrust criterion would very likely make matters worse. For example, the investors taking the financial risk by lending their money to an LBO have a much greater incentive than government bureaucrats to be sure that the deal makes financial sense—and thus improves the economic wealth of society. While those investors might make mistakes, it is certain that they make far fewer than would a government bureaucracy performing a screening function without similar financial incentives. The current woes of the market for high yield debt suggest that the market is efficiently dealing with any excesses that may have occurred with respect to leveraged buyouts.

With the decline in the percentage of anticompetitive transactions, the Department inevitably has challenged a smaller percentage of the transactions reported under the H-S-R Act. That is because the Department's merger enforcement has been principled. By enforcing the Clayton Act, and in somer merger cases

---

corporations. *See* note 19, *supra*. Indeed, the number of corporations has grown very rapidly during the past decade, with nearly the entire increase attributable to firms with less than $1 million in sales. *See* Jahr, *Corporate Wealth: More for the Little Guys*, Wall Street J., Jan. 21, 1987, at 20.

the Sherman Act,[23] in accordance with rigorous economic analysis, the Department challenges only those mergers that threaten substantial anticompetitive harm—by creating or enhancing market power—that is not outweighed by expected efficiency gains and procompetitive effects of the merger. Unlike the days when the only consistency in merger law and policy was that the government always won,[24] if the Division is satisfied that such harm is not likely, it will not challenge a merger even if it could bamboozle a court into issuing an injunction. In today's world, all other things being equal, that means the government challenges a smaller percentage of reported transactions.

Of course, there are still anticompetitive mergers, and given that merger enforcement policy can never be stated with crystal clarity and that analysis of mergers will always be more art than science, at least some of the mergers that are attempted will probably always warrant a challenge. In some cases—for example, in markets for hospital care or aggregate rock used in asphalt—there is no foreign competition. In other cases, even accepting the presence of foreign competition, a merger may still create a firm with the power to raise price. And so, even during the Reagan administration, the government has, with some fre-

---

23 While § 7 of the Clayton Act, 15 U.S.C. § 18, explicitly governs mergers and acquisitions, such transactions may also violate § 1 of the Sherman Act, 15 U.S.C. § 1, if they unreasonably restrain trade. On several occasions, the Department has challenged mergers under that provision. *See, e.g.*, United States v. Rockford Memorial Corp., 1989-1 Trade Cas. (CCH) ¶ 68,462 (N.D. Ill. 1989); United States v. Carilion Health System, 1989-1 Trade Cas. (CCH) ¶ 68,451 (W.D. Va. 1989), *aff'd*, 1989-2 Trade Cas. (CCH) ¶ 68,859 (4th Cir. 1989); United States v. Central States Bank, 564 F. Supp. 1478, 1480–81 (W.D. Mich. 1983) (rejecting defendant's claim that court lacked subject-matter jurisdiction under 15 U.S.C. § 1 where defendant gained control of a bank while simultaneously controlling a competing bank); United States v. First National Bank & Trust Co., 376 U.S. 665, 671–72 (1964). The Department has long held the view that the standard of merger analysis under the two statutes is identical. *See, e.g.*, Merger Guidelines § 1.

24 *See* United States v. Von's Grocery Co., 384 U.S. 270, 301 (1962) (Stewart, J., dissenting) ("The sole consistency that I can find is that in litigation under § 7, the Government always wins.").

quency, brought merger cases. In fact, in the last full year of the Reagan administration—fiscal 1988—at least 26 mergers were challenged or abandoned as a result of government investigation. The fact that the Division has not always won its merger cases[25] has not deterred it from continuing to challenge mergers that are demonstrably anticompetitive. With the Department's access to confidential information, increasingly sophisticated economic analysis, and commitment to protect consumers, there is good reason to believe that chances of successfully engaging in an anticompetitive merger have never been lower. Indeed, critics of the Department's merger enforcement have been forced to rely on general (and largely irrelevant or misleading) statistics because they are unable to point to a significant number of specific mergers that were not challenged but that led to higher prices.[26]

---

25 *See, e.g.*, United States v. Carilion Health System, 1989-1 Trade Cas. (CCH) ¶ 68,451 (W.D. Va. 1989), *aff'd*, 1989-2 Trade Cas. (CCH) ¶ 68,859 (4th Cir. 1989). United States v. Waste Management, Inc., 743 F.2d 976 (2d Cir. 1984) (reversing district court's finding that merger violated Clayton Act on ground that ease of entry constrained exercise of market power); United States v. Calmar, Inc., 612 F. Supp. 1298 (D.N.J. 1985) (denying preliminary injunction). *Cf.* FTC v. Owens-Illinois, Inc., 681 F. Supp. 27 (D.D.C. 1988) (denying FTC request for injunction, holding that FTC had sought to define the relevant product market too narrowly), *vacated as moot*, 850 F.2d 694 (D.C. Cir. 1988).

26 In fact, about the only specific example of anticompetitive mergers that critics have been able to identify involve the airlines. At least one study has shown that the recent merger of TWA and Ozark may have resulted in increased prices in certain markets. *See* U.S. Government Accounting Office, Briefing Report to the Hon. John C. Danforth, Committee on Commerce, Science & Transportation, U.S. Senate, Airline Competition: Fare and Service Changes at St. Louis. Since the TWA-Ozark Merger (Sept. 21, 1988) (finding positive impact of merger on TWA fares). *But see* U.S. Department of Transportation, A Comparison of Air Fares and Service at St. Louis Before and After Trans World Airlines Acquired Ozark Airlines (Jan. 1989) (criticizing data used by GAO study and claiming that there is no evidence of an impact of merger on TWA fare structure). Until 1989, however, the Department of Transportation [DOT] had exclusive authority to review and approve airline mergers. Many of the controversial airline mergers

Clarity and substantive accuracy

Having argued that the statistics concerning the percentage of reported mergers challenged by federal antitrust enforcers do not support the proposition that those enforcers have in recent years allowed more *anticompetitive* mergers to be consummated, it is necessary to explain why current enforcement policy can be trusted to block truly anticompetitive mergers. In order to understand current policy, it is first essential that one understand the operational—as opposed to substantive—goals of the policy: clarity/certainty and accuracy. In an economic environment in which literally an infinite variety of circumstances can affect the likelihood that a merger will create, maintain, or facilitate the exercise of market power, perfect clarity and certainty in the application of enforcement policy can only be achieved at a substantial cost in terms of the accuracy of the conclusion. Similarly, maintaining full flexibility and employing the abundant resources that would be necessary to achieve a very high degree of accuracy might generate prohibitively high degrees of enforcement uncertainty and administrative cost.

Thus, in an effort to optimize these two, at least potentially contradictory, operational objectives, merger policy seeks to maximize certainty/clarity when the risk is low that a merger is anticompetitive, and to maximize accuracy when that risk is high. Fortunately, the Department knows from experience, theory, and empirical research that most corporate control transactions involve little if any anticompetitive threat. Where the parties do not compete, or where they do but their collective market shares are small and/or the market is not concentrated, there is little risk that a corporate control transaction will be anticompetitive. The Department's Merger Guidelines provide assurance that mergers occurring under circumstances where the anticompetitive threat is slight—for example, where the postmerger Herfindahl-

---

of the past several years, including the Northwest/Republic and TWA/Ozark transactions, were challenged by the Department before DOT, but were approved by DOT over the Department's objections.

Hirschman index is below 1,000[27]—are within "safe harbors," *i.e.*, will not be challenged by the Department.[28] Even ignoring the cost of the resulting uncertainty to business planners, the resources spent trying to investigate every such merger to guarantee that it in fact poses no competitive threat would be disproportionately greater than the benefits. Therefore, in the safe harbor range below the Guidelines' HHI thresholds, where the competitive threat is virtually nonexistent, the value of certainty—of having bright lines that make enforcement decisions perfectly predictable—predominates. Procompetitive mergers among small market participants or in unconcentrated markets should not be chilled as a result of a fear of challenge by antitrust authorities. In that range, the numerical simplicity and clarity of HHI safe harbors performs a vital function.

As market concentration increases, however, the relative importance of accuracy in merger enforcement also increases. When a merger produces concentration above the Guidelines' thresholds—*i.e.*, above 1,000 with a 100-point increase or above 1,800 with a 50-point increase—enforcers can no longer be confident that the benefits of certainty will clearly outweigh the possibility that the transaction may injure consumers. Only further analysis can accurately assess such a merger's likely effect.

Moreover, it is less important to provide businesses with certainty that particular mergers will *always* be challenged. In order for business planners to avoid unlawful transactions, it should be sufficient for them to know that the Department will carefully scrutinize any merger that "falls" outside the deep safe

---

27 Merger Guidelines § 3.11. The HHI is a numerical index designed to facilitate the interpretation of market data. It is calculated by summing the squares of the individual shares of all the firms included in the market. Merger Guidelines § 3.1.

28 Mergers also fall within safe harbors if they produce a postmerger HHI of between 1,000 and 1,800, but result in an increase in the HHI of less than 100 points, or if they produce a postmerger HHI of over 1,800, but increase the HHI by less than 50 points. Merger Guidelines § 3.11. *See also* International Guidelines § 3.32 (first step of analysis is to determine whether "merging firms compete in the same product or geographic market").

harbors of the Merger Guidelines and to understand the substantive standards governing the Department's analysis and the nature of the factors that are relevant to applying those standards. If, after applying that knowledge, the planners conclude that their merger is not on balance anticompetitive and that the financial benefits outweigh the costs and risks associated with government review of the transaction, then it is appropriate for the government's inquiry into the net effects of the transaction to be as accurate as possible. Society would gain little from a policy that attempted to draw stark lines based on readily observable and objective, but relatively inaccurate, proxies demarcating mergers that are presumed to be anticompetitive and always will be challenged. Such certainty and clarity concerning the invariability of challenge will do little more than shut off avenues that business planners—and society—might otherwise find fruitful and beneficial to explore. As long as it is recognized that the courts can employ special rules to promote judicial economy—for example, *Philadelphia National Bank*'s rebuttable presumption based on concentration and market shares[29]—government merger investigations can stress accuracy over certainty outside the safe harbors.

The fact that the HHI thresholds have been exceeded does not establish that a merger will be anticompetitive. The level of concentration will be an important—at times even predominant—factor in the ensuing analysis that the Guidelines' thresholds trigger. But because concentration statistics are only as good as the underlying market definition and, even if perfectly calculated, are at best a rough proxy of market power, passing the 1,000 or even 1,800 barrier by itself reveals very little about the actual competitive impact of the transaction.

---

29 United States v. Philadelphia National Bank, 374 U.S. 321, 363 (1963) ("we think that a merger which produces a firm controlling an undue percentage share of the relevant market, is so inherently likely to lessen competition substantially that it must be enjoined in the absence of evidence clearly showing that the merger is not likely to have such anticompetitive effects").

First, even if it could be assumed that a merger's effect on competition depended on concentration alone, the predictive value of concentration numbers would depend on the accuracy of the market-share calculations. If markets are misdefined or market shares miscalculated, the concentration numbers that are generated will bear no meaningful relationship to a merger's effect on competition.[30] Yet anyone familiar with the Supreme Court decisions in the early 1960's knows how easy it can be to gerrymander markets.[31] Market definition is an art, not a science, and the metes and bounds of a relevant market may vary depending on the subjective perception of the individual(s) performing the analysis. Even under the Department's Merger Guidelines, which describe a process of market definition as objective and exacting as one can imagine, it is not possible to define markets with scientific precision.

In addition, the market shares are only a proxy for the relative competitive vigor of the market participants. Market shares are a description of how firms have fared competitively in the past, while merger analysis is an attempt to predict the future. Often history provides some guide to the future, but, as the Supreme Court recognized in the *General Dynamics* case, at times it may be clear that the future will be very different from the past and thus that reliance on historical market shares would be misleading.[32] Consequently, other nonquantitative factors must be con-

---

30 *See* FTC v. PPG Industries, Inc., 798 F.2d 1500, 1503 (D.C. Cir. 1986) (if relevant market defined incorrectly, "HHI's computed are meaningless and do not reflect market reality").

31 United States v. Pabst Brewing Co., 384 U.S. 546, 555–56 (1966) (Harlan, J., concurring in result) ("statistics and other evidence bearing upon market shares, market trends, number of competitors and the like" must be considered in any § 7 case, but will vary "depending upon what geographic area is chosen as relevant, and the possibilities for 'gerrymandering' are limitless").

32 United States v. General Dynamics Corp., 415 U.S. 486, 501 (1974) ("Evidence of past production does not, as a matter of logic, necessarily give a proper picture of a company's future ability to compete.").

sidered in order to serve as a check on, or to overcome errors in, market definition, identification of market participants, and market-share calculation. For example, the Guidelines require the examination of market-share statistics in light of certain special considerations relating to foreign competitors and in light of changing market conditions, such as the access of firms to new technology that is important to long-term competitive viability.[33]

Second, even assuming the impossible—that is, that enforcement agencies and courts could define markets and calculate market shares with scientific precision based on perfect information—a policy based on numbers alone would result in challenges to mergers that did not threaten to raise prices and/or restrict output. Theory, experience, and empirical research refute the old notion of a lockstep, absolute correlation between concentration and market power.[34] Rather, concentration is at best only the beginning of the inquiry into whether market power is substantially more likely to be exercised after the merger than before.[35]

---

33 *See, e.g.,* Merger Guidelines §§ 2.34, 3.23 (foreign competition), 3.21 (changing market conditions).

34 The so-called new learning convincingly demonstrated that the supposed link between high concentration and high profitability does not establish a link between concentration and noncompetitive market performance. *See* note 7, *supra.*

35 This principle has been recognized by the courts as well. *See, e.g., General Dynamics,* 415 U.S. 486 (permitting merging firms to show that, irrespective of their market share, other pertinent factors establish that statistics give an inaccurate account of the merger's probable effect on competition); United States v. Waste Management, Inc., 743 F.2d 976, 982 (2d Cir. 1984) (market shares do not reflect ease of entry and thus "may yield market share statistics that are not an accurate proxy for market power"); FTC v. Owens-Illinois, Inc., 681 F. Supp. 27 (D.D.C. 1988), *vacated as moot,* 850 F.2d 694 (D.C. Cir. 1988). *Cf.* Cargill, Inc. v. Monfort of Colorado, Inc., 479 U.S. 104, 120 n.15 (1986) (in connection with likelihood of predatory pricing created by merger, it is "important to examine the barriers to entry into the market, because 'without barriers to entry it would presumably be impossible to maintain supracompetitive prices for an extended time' ") (quoting Matsushita Electrical Industrial Co. v. Zenith Radio Corp., 475 U.S. 574, 591 n.15 (1986)).

Perhaps the most significant factor that must be examined is the ease of entry. If a price increase by the firms in a market—whether the result of leading firm dominance or collusion among market incumbents—would quickly draw new entrants into the market with a significant quantity of output and with a product having sufficient quality, reputation, and all other relevant characteristics to satisfy consumer demand, it is highly unlikely that the price increase would be profitable for any significant period of time. Indeed, the very potential for such entry will constrain the ability of the merged firms to raise price even in the short run.[36] Under these circumstances, consumers will not be hurt by a merger regardless of its effect on the concentration of existing firms in that market. Conditions of entry in a market are therefore highly relevant, and at times of overriding importance, to the significance of concentration and market share numbers.[37]

---

36 *See, e.g.*, United States v. Waste Management, Inc., 743 F.2d 976, 981-84 (2d Cir. 1984).

37 In assessing entry conditions, the Department's focus is on the practical ease of entry—*i.e.*, will new firms actually enter and overcome the merger's effect on prices—rather than on "Stiglerian" barriers to entry. *See* Merger Guidelines § 3.3 ("the Department will consider the likelihood and probable magnitude of entry" in assessing whether "entry is so easy that existing competitiors could not succeed in raising price for any significant period of time"); *see also* "Business and Economic Realities—The Key to Merger Enforcement," Remarks by Judy Whalley, Deputy Assistant Attorney General, Antitrust Division, U.S. Department of Justice, Before the American Bar Association Antitrust Section Spring Meeting (Mar. 23, 1988), *reprinted in* 57 ANTITRUST L.J. 109, 111-14 (1988); "Merger Enforcement Policy: Protecting the Consumer," Remarks of Charles F. Rule, Assistant Attorney General, Antitrust Division, U.S. Department of Justice, Before the 1987 National Institute, ABA Section of Antitrust Law (Oct. 9, 1987) (hereinafter "Rule Merger Speech"), *reprinted in* 56 ANTITRUST L.J. 739 (1987) and 7 Trade Reg. Rep. (CCH) ¶ 50,009. The former approach is in general more restrictive—*i.e.*, less likely to conclude that entry will eliminate the anticompetitive effect of a merger—than the latter. The Merger Guidelines reflect the view that the time lag associated with some entry may allow intolerable supracompetitive pricing that merger enforcement should seek to prevent. *See* Rule Merger Speech, *supra*, 57 ANTITRUST L.J. at 745.

A second important category of factors that affects the relative significance of concentration is the nature of the product and the manner in which it is transacted in the marketplace. If, for example, the commodity comprising the product market is widely differentiated or custom manufactured for individual customers, coordination of pricing and output decisions among competitors will generally be very difficult even in highly concentrated markets. In such markets, competitors must agree not on just one price, but on several.[38] While a carefully orchestrated criminal conspiracy, for example to allocate territories or contracts, might be attempted (and certainly would be criminally challenged if detected), the Department's enforcement of the criminal provisions of the Sherman Act should be sufficient to deter such attempts.[39] The same is true, albeit to a lesser extent, if the relevant product market comprises more than one commodity—*e.g.*, a Ford Taurus and a Jaguar sedan—that are substitutes among which consumers will switch readily in response to a relative change in price, but which are not priced identically. Under these circumstances, a given level of concentration will be of considerably less threat to consumers than in more homogeneous product markets. Other factors—such as the closeness of substitutes and the lumpiness of orders, to name just a few—have similarly important effects on the likelihood that a merger producing a given increase in concentration will facilitate collusion and harm consumers.[40]

The relevance of these factors, and the many others identified in the Merger Guidelines, means that a "magic number" for merger enforcement can never be found. Were the Department automatically to challenge a merger every time HHIs exceeded 1,800 or any other number, inaccurate decisions would often be made: transactions would be prohibited *and* deterred that would not actually have harmed, and might well have benefited, consumers. Moreover, as indicated above, the benefits of clarity and

---

38 *See* Merger Guidelines § 3.411.

39 *See* notes 61–64 and accompanying text, *infra.*

40 *See* Merger Guidelines §§ 3.41, 3.42, 3.43, 3.44.

certainty that such incorrect bright lines provide would not overcome these costs.[41]

The decision to challenge a merger therefore cannot be purely a "numbers game." Instead it must, and does, focus on all of the factors that are relevant to a transaction's effect on market power. With access to confidential data, and the ability carefully to study the actual economic effects of a transaction, the Department's staff can achieve accuracy that would be impossible were it to apply a purely numerical test of a merger's effects. For that reason, the "shadow merger guidelines" alluded to by some of the Department's critics are mere fiction.[42] Rather than a set of shadow guidelines with enforcement thresholds set at some magic number above 1,800, there are only the Merger Guidelines, applied, as their very terms demand,[43] with care and flexibility to the facts of every case to insure that only anticompetitive mergers are challenged.

Even above the Merger Guidelines' thresholds, however, clarity remains important. Merger enforcers should—and in fact do—attempt to employ an analysis of the competitive effects of a merger that is thorough and accurate, yet remains consistent and clearly understood by transacting parties—even though they recognize that the analysis cannot be reduced to a precise set of purely mathematical formulae like the physics calculations required to put a satellite in orbit. Given that the ideal of mathematical precision is unattainable, the Department's merger analysis, as spelled out in the Merger Guidelines and as put into practice, has achieved a high level of accuracy and predictability by focusing on the underlying rationale for antitrust law's concern with mergers: market power and the circumstances under which that power can be exercised.

---

41 *See* discussion at text accompanying note 29, *supra.*

42 *See* Briggs & Calkins, *Antitrust 1986-87: Power and Access (Part I)*, 32 ANTITRUST BULL. 275, 304-05 (1987).

43 *See* Merger Guidelines § 1.0.

Market power and its exercise

There are three basic scenarios under which market power can be exercised—single-firm behavior, explicit collusion, and the noncooperative interaction of firms, in bidding markets and otherwise. Each of these scenarios offers a different set of economically plausible stories of how a merger might be likely to have an anticompetitive effect. It is the applicability of those stories—rather than HHI numbers alone—that the Department's analysis seeks to confirm or deny in a given merger investigation. Although concentration is a central factor in the efforts of antitrust enforcers to determine whether any of these potential scenarios exist in connection with a given merger, concentration alone should never be determinative, and in some cases it may be of little or no ultimate significance.

Single dominant firm

The exercise of market power by a single dominant firm acting unilaterally is perhaps the easiest story to tell because the dominant firm's success requires no cooperation with rival firms, which ordinarily tend to have strong incentives not to cooperate. A single dominant firm that has a far greater share of the market than its rivals may be able unilaterally to raise prices in the market above competitive levels. Even though all of the other firms in the market act as price takers and expand their output until price equals their marginal cost, constraints on their ability to expand output may prevent them from replacing the output withheld by the dominant firm and so from competing price down to the competitive equilibrium. In this way, the competitors price under the dominant firm's "umbrella price," which over time will tend to decline as fringe firms add capacity, expand their output, and erode the dominant firm's market share.[44] Theoretically, a single dominant firm may be able to use threats

---

44 *See* F. SCHERER, *supra* note 13, at 232–43.

of predation to intimidate fringe firms and potential new entrants and deter them from making major inroads into the dominant firm's market share and thereby undercutting the price umbrella.[45]

A merger that creates a firm with the capacity to dominate the market thus threatens consumer welfare and is challenged. The analysis of the dominant firm scenario is somewhat easier than that for the other two scenarios discussed below, primarily because predicting the interaction between the merged firms and the remaining firms in the market is less complex.[46] If the ability of fringe players to expand is constrained—and it is rare that fringe players have infinite supply elasticity—then one can assume that consumer welfare will be harmed by higher prices even under the most optimistic assumption that the fringe will price at marginal cost. Of course, even where the market shares of the merging firms suggest that they will have a dominant or even monopoly position after the merger, the Department does have to consider factors other than concentration, such as ease of entry, the ability of the fringe to expand, and the market shares of fringe firms, that bear on the ability of the dominant firm to exercise market power.[47] Nevertheless, those qualitative factors

---

45 Such predation is under most situations not likely to be economically rational for a dominant firm, particularly if the predatory strategies available require the firm to lower price across its entire output, thus absorbing losses far in excess of those imposed on rivals or new entrants. *See* "Claims of Predation in a Competitive Marketplace: When Is an Antitrust Response Appropriate?" Remarks by Charles F. Rule, Assistant Attorney General, Antitrust Division, U.S. Department of Justice, Before the American Bar Association Annual Meeting (Aug. 9, 1988) (hereinafter Rule Predation Speech), *reprinted in* 57 ANTITRUST L.J. 421, 424 (1988).

46 *Cf.* R. BORK, *supra* note 6, at 221 (suggesting rule that "mergers up to 60 or 70 percent of the market should be permitted" because only then is it clear that a merger would result in a decrease in output).

47 *See, e.g.*, The Echlin Manufacturing Co., 105 F.T.C. 410, 484 (1985) (final order dismissing complaint against merger of two assemblers of automotive carburetor kits where combined market share in excess of 50% and postmerger HHI in excess of 3,000, but barriers to

that reflect the ease (or difficulty) of collusion are irrelevant.[48] Moreover, while in theory the enforcement agencies can and do consider the potential that the merger will generate efficiencies, the fact is that it is very unlikely that efficiencies will offset the competitive threat of such a merger.[49]

At the same time, however, acquisitions by an existing dominant firm may affect concentration only slightly, yet still may raise competitive concerns. If the fringe firm to be acquired can expand output readily were the dominant firm to increase price at the margin, it can serve as an important constraint on the dominant firm's pricing that is not adequately reflected in the fringe firm's small market share. Thus, even if a merger between a dominant firm and one of its much smaller competitors would not significantly increase the likelihood of collusion, it could still—by eliminating a constraining rival—enhance the ability of the dominant firm to wield its power unilaterally.

For this reason, application of traditional standards of concentration may provide a misleading assessment of the merger's likely harm to consumers. Therefore, the Guidelines have

---

entry nonexistent; noting that absence of entry barriers prevents exercise of market power "regardless of the concentration in the nominal 'market,' and indeed even if that 'market' has been 'monopolized' by a single firm").

48 Merger Guidelines § 3.12. These factors include the nature of the relevant product and terms of sale, information about specific transactions and buyer market characteristics, and conduct of firms in the market. *See* Merger Guidelines § 3.4.

49 It is also unlikely that efficiencies explain a merger to monopoly. The fact that no firm grew internally to the monopoly suggests that costs are not such that there are substantial efficiency advantages to the scale achieved by the merger. Moreover, if in fact the market ultimately can sustain only one firm—*i.e.*, it is a market with natural monopoly characteristics—then it is likely to be preferable from the standpoint of consumer welfare to require the identity of the monopolist to be chosen through competition (while prices are constrained) rather than through a merger.

adopted the leading firm proviso,[50] which states that, notwithstanding the general HHI standards, the Department is likely to challenge any merger between a leading firm with a 35% market share and a competitor having at least a 1% share.[51]

Collective exercise of market power

Market power may also be exercised by several firms acting collectively. Such scenarios are the most common focus of merger analysis—because it is much clearer that mergers creating dominant firms are likely to be challenged, firms tend not to waste their time and money proposing such transactions. The evolution of analysis in merger law has in recent years been primarily concerned with identifying those mergers that are likely to result in output and price levels that diverge from the competitive outcome because of behavior that is coordinated by an actual agreement or through the noncooperative interaction of firms. In either case, concern with coordination of pricing and output is greatest in those markets where sales are many and frequent, and thus where firms can more easily share the fruits of their mutual forbearance. An extreme example illustrates this point best: If only one big sale is made in an industry in a given period, firms are likely to compete very vigorously to win that contract,

---

50 Merger Guidelines § 3.12. *Cf.* United States v. Aluminum Co. of America ("Rome Cable"), 347 U.S. 271 (1964) (stating that "if concentration is already great, the importance of preventing even slight increases in concentration and so preserving the possibility of eventual deconcentration is correspondingly great" while condemning a merger between a firm with 27.8% and a firm with 1.3% in a market with a five-firm concentration ratio of 76%).

51 As some quick arithmetic will indicate, however, the leading firm proviso will rarely produce a result inconsistent with the general HHI thresholds. For example, a merger between a 35% leading firm and one of 15 equally-sized fringe firms (each with a 4.33% share) and a merger between a 42% leading firm and any fringe firm with a share greater than 1% would both produce a postmerger HHI of over 1,800 and an HHI increase of more than 50 points. In both instances, therefore, the Guidelines' normal thresholds would indicate that there may be a competitive concern.

because—assuming it is difficult to subcontract the work—there is nothing that can be shared if they agree not to compete.[52]

EXPLICIT COLLUSION The easiest collusion story to tell—and an important traditional concern about mergers—is that a merger may facilitate explicit collusion among firms in a market. Explicit collusion involves actual agreement, a legal concept requiring only a meeting of the minds. By reducing the numbers of firms that need to reach and abide by an agreement, a merger may increase the expected profitability of collusion, and thereby make it more likely that firms will agree to raise prices and restrict output.[53]

Such "naked" agreements among competitors, of course, clearly harm consumers and are both per se unlawful and criminal. Thus it may be that consumers, represented by antitrust enforcers, are willing to suffer some costs in the form of foregone structural efficiencies in order to prevent mergers from making market conditions more conducive to explicit collusion. Particularly where there is evidence that explicit collusion occurred in the

---

52 In addition, even if an agreement is reached, cheating may occur that, in the absence of repeat transactions, would be difficult to punish. On the other hand, of course, firms may find it easiest explicitly to allocate contracts when contracts let for bid are few. Moreover, even when there is only one transaction, the possibility of paying off the firms that do not receive the business—for example, with rigged subcontracts or phony invoices—makes explicit collusion possible. Indeed, similar schemes have often been the target of criminal prosecution by the Department. *See, e.g.*, United States v. MMR Corp., Cr. Docket No. 88-559 (E.D. La. filed Nov. 3, 1988) (indictment charging bid-rigging conspiracy involving "lucrative subcontract" in "consideration for defendant MMR's agreement not to compete"). Nevertheless, it remains impossible to tell a noncooperative interaction story in the absence of repeat transactions.

53 A merger that increases market concentration might make collusive schemes more feasible to enter, easier to police, as well as more difficult to detect. *See* Merger Guidelines § 3.44(a).

past, the Department has challenged mergers with a view toward preventing similar behavior in the future.[54]

On the other hand, there is no strong empirical evidence linking the structure of markets with the incidence of explicit collusion.[55] Indeed, there is substantial anecdotal evidence at least that explicit collusion is attempted in a broad variety of market structures. A substantial number of recent Division criminal cases involve markets into which entry appears relatively easy or in which there are a large number of competitors. For example, it is highly unlikely that the government would challenge a merger between road builders, primarily because of ease of entry, but not long ago the Division uncovered and prosecuted endemic bid-rigging in the industry. Similarly, the Division has recently discovered and begun to prosecute what appears to be widespread price-fixing by purchasers at commercial auctions, even though there are a large number of competitors in the relevant market

54 Evidence of past explicit collusion may be relevant to merger analysis for several reasons. First, such evidence indicates that collusion is not infeasible as a result of easy entry or difficulties of coordinating behavior, and thus that future collusion may be more likely to occur. *See* Merger Guidelines § 3.44(a). Second, such evidence may cast some doubt on the validity of the parties' asserted efficiency-related motivations for their transactions. Finally, it is conceivable that past explicit collusion may become a relevant component of market structure; firms may reach a noncooperative equilibrium at a "traditional," collusively set level of price and output.

55 As indicated above, *see* note 7, *supra*, the old empirical studies that purported to show a close correlation between industry concentration and noncompetitive performance (as measured by profits) have little continuing validity. There are more recent (and somewhat more credible) studies that tend to show, particularly in bidding markets, that as the number of competitors decreases significantly, prices tend to increase. *See*, *e.g*, CONCENTRATION AND PRICE (L. Weiss, ed. 1989) (collecting studies). To the extent those studies are valid, they probably reflect that the likelihood of "noncooperative equilibria," discussed at text accompanying notes 65–81, *infra*, increases as concentration increases, rather than indicating any correlation between market structure and explicit collusion.

(defined as it is on the basis of the ability to sustain a 5% price increase for 1 year[56]).

The fact that the Department does not challenge mergers in such circumstances does not establish that the government's merger policy is too lax. Rather, it simply reflects the fact that, in the case of explicit collusion, market structure is not the sole or even primary determinant of whether collusion will be attempted. Some conspirators may attempt—and at times are able—to "fool" the market through their covert, fraudulent behavior.[57] For example, by getting together all the dealers of commercial machinery who actually attend an auction, determining whether they will agree to rig the auction, and forming agreements on an auction-by-auction basis (so-called auction pooling), explicit collusion can be made to succeed in an industry with many competitors.[58] Moreover, in the case of explicit collusion, extra-legal barriers—for example, destroying a new entrant's equipment or bidding aggressively against bidders who refuse to participate in the illegal pool—can be erected by the conspirators.[59] Thus, merger policy, which of necessity must be exclusively structural with limited supplementation based on evidence of past collusive behavior, can generally decrease to only a limited degree the incidence of explicit collusion.[60]

---

56 *See* Merger Guidelines §§ 2.0, 2.11.

57 Indeed, most cases of price-fixing and bid-rigging involve fraudulent behavior. The schemes typically rely on the deception of the customer for their success, and they therefore likely would be covert even if they were legal. *See* Warren-Boulton, Maricopa *and Maximum-Price Agreements: Time for a New Legal Standard?* 7 J. HEALTH ECON. 185, 187–88 (1988).

58 *See, e.g.,* United States v. Seville Industrial Machinery Corp., 696 F. Supp. 986 (D.N.J. 1988) (upholding indictment of 19 corporate and 17 individual defendants for successfully rigging auction of used commercial machinery).

59 *See* Rule Predation Speech, *supra* note 45, 57 ANTITRUST L.J. at 432.

60 Conveniently, merger policy probably reduces the risk of explicit collusion in the area where explicit collusion and noncooperative inter-

There is, moreover, a better way to eliminate most explicit collusion. A vigorous program of criminal enforcement can deter such conduct without intervening to block efficient transfers of assets or corporate control. If adequate penalties are imposed on criminal collusion, rational economic actors—as most firms are—will no longer perceive price fixing, bid rigging, and similar activity to be profitable, and thus will not engage in such conduct.[61] This form of deterrence, unlike blocking mergers, entails little, if any, costs in the form of foregone productive efficiencies.

Several studies indicate that stiffer criminal penalties and the Department's vigorous program of criminal prosecution are having a real effect on deterring explicit collusion.[62] Unfortunately, the record numbers of price-fixing and bid-rigging cases that the Department has brought during the past several years reveal that a system of optimal deterrence is not yet in place. The stiffer penalties mandated by the Sentencing Guidelines should be a

---

dependence tend to become blurred and where a behavioral solution of criminal prosecution is least effective. If the number of players in the market is few and new entry is unlikely, the degree of explicit coordination required is minimal. In such situations, it is much easier to conceal the collusion and much more difficult for the government to get evidence of an agreement that is sufficient to establish beyond a reasonable doubt that a criminal violation has occurred. However, it is these same market characteristics that merger enforcement tends to prevent.

61 *See generally*, "Deterring Antitrust Crimes Through Stiffer Penalties," Remarks of Charles F. Rule, Assistant Attorney General, Antitrust Division, U.S. Department of Justice, Before ALI-ABA "Antitrust Law" Course of Study (May 6, 1988) (hereinafter Rule Criminal Deterrence Speech) (discussing theory of optimal deterrence in connection with antitrust crimes).

62 *See* E. Snyder, New Insights into the Decline of Antitrust Enforcement (June 1988) (unpublished manuscript, for presentation at 1988 Western Economic Ass'n Meetings); Block & Feinstein, *Controlling Collusion in the Construction Industry: Some Lessons from Recent U.S. Experience*, 28 Swiss Rev. Int'l Competition L. 41, 51 (1986).

major step in that direction.[63] However, certainly in the interim—and likely forever because criminal enforcement, like all enforcement, entails some costs—mergers that enhance the likelihood of explicit collusion will continue to pose some legitimate enforcement concern.[64]

Noncooperative equilibria

The collective exercise of market power need not involve actual agreement. Price and quantity outcomes—or equilibria—that diverge from the competitive outcome can occur at least in theory due solely to the noncooperative interaction of firms in the market. By altering the structure of a market, therefore, mergers can result in anticompetitive outcomes that do not involve explicit collusion. The effect of mergers on such noncooperative market outcomes is highly relevant to merger enforcement policy because these equilibria either are not by themselves unlawful or cannot be proven to involve unlawful agreement, and they thus cannot be effectively deterred by a behavioral enforcement policy. Their prevention therefore requires a structural merger enforcement policy.

A market outcome is noncooperative if each firm in the market chooses a strategy that maximizes its own profits, and each firm chooses its strategy without coordinating that decision with its competitors. The fact that firms choose strategies independently, however, does not mean that they ignore interactions with their competitors. Those interactions—for example, the response of rivals to a firm's price cuts—may be an important

---

63 *See* Rule Criminal Deterrence Speech, *supra* note 61. The antitrust provisions of the Sentencing Guidelines, which apply to offenses committed or continuing on or after November 1, 1987, generally require convicted corporations to be fined a minimum of $100,000 and convicted individuals to be fined a minimum of $20,000 and sentenced to a minimum of 4 months' incarceration. U.S. Sentencing Commission, Sentencing Guidelines and Policy Statement, § 2R1.1 (April 13, 1987).

64 *See* note 60, *supra*.

determinant of the profits that a particular firm can expect to gain from a particular strategy. The equilibria that are achieved in markets through noncooperative firm interaction are sometimes characterized as "Nash" equilibria.[65] The phenomenon of a noncooperative equilibrium above the competitive price achieved through the mutual recognition of interdependence is also sometimes referred to as "tacit collusion."

In many markets the number of firms is sufficiently large, entry is sufficiently easy, and/or predicting the response of other firms is sufficiently difficult that individual firms do not perceive that their profits depend upon the decisions of other firms. Under these circumstances, the information that a firm needs in order to choose a profit-maximizing pricing and output strategy is adequately summarized by the prevailing price in the market and the firm's knowledge of its own costs. Such a firm is known as a price taker, and the noncooperative outcome that results in such a market is the competitive outcome.

In markets with very few firms, high barriers to entry, and little variety among products, on the other hand, interactions between firms are more important, and the noncooperative outcome may depart sharply from the competitive outcome.[66] For example, firms in a tight oligopoly market might recognize that their profits are higher when they all charge higher prices. Although an individual firm could increase its profits in the short term by reducing price, to do so might be expected to cause rivals

---

65 Special cases of Nash equilibria are Bertrand and Cournot equilibria. The Cournot equilibrium concept describes a situation where firms set their quantity levels based on assumptions regarding the quantity strategies chosen by rivals. *See* F. Scherer, *supra* note 13, at 152–56 (traditional Cournot analysis); J. Tirole, The Theory of Industrial Organization 218–21 (1988) (same). The Bertrand concept involves the choice of pricing rather than quantity strategies. Under the Bertrand concept, two competitors will often be sufficient to achieve the competitive equilibrium. *See id.* at 209–11 (Bertrand paradigm).

66 *See* J. Tirole, *supra* note 65, at 206–207, 209–70 (1988); J. Friedman, Oligopoly and the Theory of Games (1977); *see also* F. Scherer, *supra* note 13, at 151–68.

to respond by cutting their prices, thus resulting only in lower profits for all firms.

A merger between firms in such a market can result in a significantly higher price by increasing firms' perceptions of the importance of their interactions or by altering the firms' expectations as to their mutual reactions to a higher level of price. In determining whether an anticompetitive effect is likely in a given case, market concentration and the increase in concentration caused by the merger may be important factors if they reflect the relative competitive significance of the merging firms better than the mere identity of those firms or the number of firms in the market. In general, and all other things being equal, the more concentrated the market, and the greater the market shares of the merging firms, the more likely it is that the combination of the merging firms will increase the perceived importance of the remaining firms' strategic interactions, and thus lead to another noncooperative equilibrium at a higher price level.

Concentration, however, can only be the starting point for this analysis because all other things typically are not equal. The threat of entry might constrain pricing decisions regardless of the increase in concentration achieved by the merger. Moreover, even in markets in which the number of firms is relatively few and entry is difficult, the noncooperative outcome might be close to the competitive outcome. Whether the noncooperative outcome in a market will be affected by the merger's change in market structure depends on the nature of the change in market structure that the merger will create, on the nature of the product, or the manner in which sales are transacted, and on a wide variety of other factors related to the nature of the information available to firms as they make their independent profit-maximizing choices.

As an illustration, consider a market in which a small number of firms compete. Each firm recognizes that sales of its product depend on the prices that competitors charge. If one firm could count on other firms not changing the prices they have set for their products, then the firm would have a strong incentive to shade its price and capture a larger share of the market at the expense of its rivals. Under some circumstances, however, the firm may be discouraged from lowering its price because it anticipates that the response of rivals will be to lower their prices, resulting simply in lower profits for all firms. On the other hand, if the firm believes that it can hide its price reduction from its rivals, it will be more likely to lower its price, because an immediate price reduction on the part of rivals will not be anticipated. As a general matter, therefore, if firms find it difficult to monitor the actions of rivals, perhaps because information about terms and conditions of supply and demand change frequently in unpredictable and unobserved ways, the noncooperative outcome will be closer to the competitive outcome.[67] Firms will be more likely to believe that a price reduction will capture the market and lead to increased profits, rather than leading to an immediate price war.

Other characteristics of the market can also affect the nature of the noncooperative equilibrium. For example, a firm will be more likely to adopt a strategy designed to improve its own position at the expense of rivals (with the result generally being lower prices) if the payoff from the strategy can be realized before rivals are able to respond effectively. If purchases of the product are large and occur infrequently, then the firm has an incentive to lower its price in order to gain a large order today, while forsaking incremental revenues (the difference between the firm's new lower price and the previous equilibrium price) that it might have earned on sales in the distant future.[68]

Alternatively, there may be opportunities for the firm to compete along dimensions other than price—such as quality—that result in increased sales and to which rivals can less easily respond. Competition along these other dimensions will often lead to lower prices, as rivals strive to retain sales in the market.

---

67 *See* Merger Guidelines § 3.42 ("Department is more likely to challenge a merger if [detailed information about specific transactions or individual price or output levels] is available to competitors").

68 *See id.* (Department more likely to challenge merger where "orders for the relevant product are frequent, regular, and small relative to the total output of a typical firm in the market").

For example, a firm might be able to invest in product or process innovations that increase its sales. Rivals will have difficulty monitoring and predicting the success of a competitor's investments in innovation. Moreover, if the firm's investments prove successful, the rivals may not be able to respond quickly because of the lags and uncertainties in the process of innovating. Even if competing rivals were able to imitate the innovation, the firm that introduced the innovation may achieve a lasting advantage simply by virtue of being first.

Finally, of course, a merger may generate efficiencies that promise to yield improvements in consumer welfare that outweigh any potential threat from the increased likelihood of noncooperative interdependence. As Oliver Williamson has pointed out, a relatively small increase in productive efficiency in theory can outweigh a significant price increase.[69] However, proof, measurement, and weighing of efficiencies is a complex process at best: efficiencies are easy to allege, hard to prove, and even harder to balance.[70] While a full discussion of the government's treatment of efficiencies is beyond the scope of this article, two points are worthy of note. First, given the complexity of an analysis of efficiencies, the Department's analysis imposes several conditions—for example, that the efficiencies be based on clear and convincing evidence and not be capable of being achieved just as effectively by some less anticompetitive alternative—that tend to insure that only substantial, verifiable efficiencies will be taken into account.[71] Second, the Department has argued that the courts should give even more limited consideration to efficiencies than the Department, for example, by requiring that cognizable efficiencies be passed on to consumers of the relevant product.[72]

---

69 *See* Williamson, *Economies as an Antitrust Defense: The Welfare Tradeoffs*, 58 AM. ECON. REV. 18, 27–28 (1968).

70 *See, e.g.*, R. POSNER, ANTITRUST LAW: AN ECONOMIC PERSPECTIVE 112 (1976); R. BORK, *supra* note 6, at 122–29.

71 *See* Merger Guidelines § 3.5; International Guidelines § 3.222.

72 *See* Plaintiff's Memorandum of Points and Authorities in Support of Jury Instruction on Efficiencies, United States v. Carilion

The foregoing suggests that, even in the case of noncooperative interdependence, any attempt to reach accurate conclusions about a merger's competitive effects requires an examination of more than just market shares and concentration. Moreover, there is an additional reason for caution in challenging mergers on the basis of concentration alone. With the exception of a limited number of markets—airlines and those involving bidding, discussed below[73]—there is a paucity of reliable empirical data verifying a strong correlation between high concentration and noncooperative interdependence (or even verifying the prevalence of such interdependence).[74] Thus, in the scenario of noncooperative interdependence, the case for challenging mergers is based essentially on the logic of the theory. But markets are complex, and it is difficult for economic theories fully to incorporate that complexity. A focus on concentration alone fails to acknowledge that complexity. Moreover, and perhaps ultimately more important, some cases are sufficiently complex that the logic of the theory tying market performance to concentration itself breaks down. Where the complexity of a market is such that the prospect of a noncooperative equilibrium other than the competitive one is

---

Health System, Civ. No. 88-0249-R (W.D. Va. filed Jan. 9, 1989); Memorandum in Support of Plaintiff's Motion in Limine Relating to Efficiencies, United States v. Archer-Daniels-Midland Co., No. 83-51-D (D. Iowa filed May 4, 1987).

73 With respect to airlines, see note 26, *supra*. *See also* G. Hurdle, R. Johnson, A. Joskow, G. Werden, & M. Williams, Concentration, Potential Entry, and Performance in the Airline Industry 35 (U.S. Department of Justice, Antitrust Division, Economic Analysis Group Discussion Paper Series, Feb. 19, 1988) (finding that in general best predictor of performance in nonstop city pair markets "is a measure of concentration that incorporates both the number and size distribution of incumbents and the number of potential entrants we identify as not significantly deterred by economies of scale or scope"). With respect to bidding markets, see CONCENTRATION AND PRICE, *supra* note 55. *See also* J. Morris, The Relationship between Industrial Sales Prices and Concentration of Natural Gas Pipelines (unpublished manuscript of FTC economist, Nov. 2, 1988) (finding that prices for sales of natural gas to industrial customers are on average inversely related to the average number of competitors that a pipeline faces).

74 *See* note 34, *supra*.

counterintuitive and thus unlikely—because the facts show entry to be easy, expansion of the fringe to be likely, or other factors such as a highly heterogeneous product to be present—then a government challenge of any merger—even one that yields high concentration or significantly increases concentration—would likely be inappropriate.[75]

Bidding and auction markets

The case for concern about noncooperative interdependence is perhaps greatest in the context of "bidding" or "auction" markets.[76] Many products whose market value is not readily determined in advance of a transaction are literally sold by auction, while others are sold through market processes that closely resemble auctions or bidding processes.[77] These products are typically those for which conditions of supply and demand vary significantly over time or for which the exact nature of the product and the conditions of its sale vary from one transaction to the next. Regardless of the impact of a merger in such a market

---

[75] It is largely for this reason that more than 10 years ago then-Professor Bork suggested that mergers should be challenged only when they created the prospect of single-firm market power (combined market shares of more than 60% to 70%), or at least only when they resulted in fewer than three significant companies. *See* R. BORK, *supra* note 6, at 221–22.

[76] For a general discussion of the economic theory underlying auction and bidding markets, see McAfee & McMillan, *Auctions and Bidding*, 25 J. ECON. LIT. 699 (1987). Several empirical studies of bidding markets have found that as the number of competitors decreases significantly, prices tend to increase. *See*, CONCENTRATION AND PRICE, *supra* note 55; J. Morris, *supra* note 73.

[77] Although the analysis of bidding markets discussed herein is geared toward mergers among firms that sell at auction, and thus compete against each other by bidding down the price of the good or service sold, the analysis also applies to firms that buy at auction and compete by bidding up the price.

on the likelihood of explicit collusion,[78] the merger's effect on market structure can have a significant impact on price and output in the market. Moreover, such a merger might have a harmful impact that would not be revealed by casual analysis that began and ended with the calculation of HHIs based on the actual sales of firms in the market.

1/N markets

One kind of bidding market is a "1/N"[79] market. A 1/N market is one in which some number of firms (N) is equally capable of bidding on and performing on contracts. For example, in some markets a small firm, which lacks specialized assets possessed by firms with a larger share of sales, may nevertheless be able to bid on a contract first and then acquire the necessary inputs (possibly by subcontracting) if it turns out to be the winning bidder. While there may be reputational or other barriers to being viewed by customers as a "qualified" bidder, any firm that has cleared those hurdles is an equally credible member of the pool of potential bidders, whether or not the firm has actually bid on contracts in the past.

In such a market, information on the current sales of firms doing business in the market and on the supposed "capacity" of the assets currently held by those firms might not accurately describe the relative competitive significance of existing and potential competitors. Each firm in the pool of potential bidders, regardless of its relative market share and whether or not it bids on any one particular contract, is equally important to the likely profitability and success of explicit or tacit collusion. Accord-

---

78 As discussed at text accompanying note 52, *supra*, the heterogeneous nature of many products sold through an auction process—such as specialized equipment sold infrequently to diverse users—makes such collusion less likely. Merger Guidelines § 3.411.

79 Called one over N.

ingly, each firm should be analyzed as if it had a "market share" equal to that of every other firm—*i.e.*, a share of 1/N.[80]

An important caveat in applying a 1/N analysis is that firms may not be equally capable of supplying the market, either because of different relative efficiencies or capacity constraints. Information gathered from buyers or firms in the market might reveal that the firms actually do differ in ways that are competitively significant. Moreover, market share data may reveal that firms' shares of sales are widely dispersed, with the differences remaining stable over time. In these situations, it would probably not be true that the N firms were equally capable, and it would be inappropriate to assign each an equal share of 1/N.

Potential bidders vs. actual bidders

Before challenging a merger in any auction/bidding market, the Department examines whether the pool of potential bidders is significantly greater than the number of actual bidders for indi-

---

80 *See* International Guidelines, Case 5, 4 Trade Reg. Rep. (CCH) ¶ 13,109.84. In a market composed of eight competitors, for example, each would be attributed a share of 1/8, or 12.5%.

1/N markets can be analyzed within the context of the normal HHI standards, but the HHI must be computed based on equal market shares of 1/N. A shorthand expression of the HHI in such a market is 10,000/N. If N firms have equal shares of 1/N, each firm's percentage share can be expressed as 100/N. The sum of the squares—the HHI—is therefore equal to 10,000/N.

Note that viewing a market as 1/N leads to no a priori conclusion regarding whether traditional HHI numbers overestimate or underestimate the likelihood of anticompetitive collusion. While 1/N analysis will always yield a concentration level below that given by an HHI computed on actual shares, because there is no variation in market shares, 1/N analysis can yield either an increase or decrease in the *change* in concentration resulting from a merger. For example, in a market of five firms, an acquisition by a 10% firm of another 10% firm would create a 25% firm under 1/N analysis rather than the 20% share the merged firm would have been assigned under traditional analysis. On the other hand, if a 50% firm acquired a 20% firm in the same market, 1/N analysis would still indicate that the merger produced a 25% firm, while traditional analysis would view the combination as having a 70% share.

vidual transactions. If bidding is costly, it is likely that not all firms in a market—those capable of bidding—will bid on any one transaction. Bidding may be expensive because firms have to solicit bids from possible subcontractors, fulfill bonding requirements, expend significant personnel resources in evaluating and formulating a bid, or even form consortia to offer a particular product or service. These costs of bidding, moreover, are sunk costs expended whether or not the firm wins the bid.

The need to expend these bidding costs will lead firms not to bid unless they believe their chances of winning at a price above their marginal costs are great enough to justify the investment on bidding. A firm's assessment of that probability will be directly related to the number of other similar firms that are bidding—or are expected to bid—on a given contract. In cases where transactions costs are high, therefore, the bidding market will reach an equilibrium at which significantly fewer than the number of potential bidders will bid on any given contract. In other words, the number of actual bidders, expressed as "*n*", will be significantly less than the number of firms in the market, expressed as "*m*".

If *m* is significantly greater than *n*, a merger in the market would have very little or no effect on the market equilibrium, even if it significantly increases the HHI.[81] The same number of actual bidders will continue to bid even if the total number of potential bidders is reduced, to (m-1). If the Department can establish that the number of bidders usually observed on transactions in a given market is significantly less than the number of potential bidders (such that (m-1) is greater than *n*), it will be unlikely to challenge a merger in that market simply because it has resulted in fewer members of the pool of potential bidders. On the other hand, as discussed below, if the bidding market is one of heterogeneous costs and the merger involves the first- and second-lowest cost firms, there might be an anticompetitive effect even if *m* is greater than *n* after the merger. Similarly, if there is a cost disparity between a group of firms the members of which

---

[81] *See* International Guidelines, Case 5, 4 Trade Reg. Rep. (CCH) ¶ 13,109.84.

consistently bid and win most projects (the *n* firms) and the group of firms the members of which only sporadically bid and win (the (*m-n* firms), then a merger between two *n* firms can result in higher prices because the (*m-n*) firms are in reality a noncompetitive fringe.

Heterogeneous cost auction markets

Not all bidding markets, of course, are 1/N. Generally, firms are not identical in their ability to supply a given product to a given buyer. There is no inconsistency in postulating a market where selling firms have varying costs—or varying efficiencies—of supplying different groups of customers and in which the higher-cost firms manage to remain in the market over time. Firms with lower average costs may move up their marginal cost curves as they near capacity, leaving business for the higher-cost firms at the prevailing price. Alternatively, sellers may be more or less proficient at producing and marketing to particular market segments. For example, while one maker of sophisticated medical imaging equipment may be most proficient at selling to applications that require a more reliable, less-sophisticated configuration, another might be more proficient at supplying a machine to users who need more advanced features but are willing to tolerate a higher failure rate. As a result, even though both firms might compete for both groups of customers, they would possess varying "efficiencies" in satisfying those customers and the identity of the lower-cost seller in the market for medical imaging equipment would be seen to vary from sale to sale.

The auction mechanism

In any bidding market, 1/N or otherwise, the nature of the auction mechanism—and thus the nature of the information that each bidder has about the costs of other bidders—can make an important difference in the assessment of a merger's effect on the noncooperative market equilibrium. In a market employing a sealed-bid auction or a similar procedure by which the price is set by the winning bid (even if there is some renegotiation after the first round of bids), the merger of any two bidders may have some effect on price, even in the absence of explicit collusion. The essence of the problem that confronts a firm bidding at such an auction is that it does not have enough information in advance of the auction to be able to predict with certainty the bid that other firms will submit. In choosing what bid to submit, each bidder faces a tradeoff between its need to bid low in order to win the contract and its desire to bid high in order to increase its profit. The presence of a large number of expected bidders encourages all bidders to bid close to their true marginal costs in order to win the contract. At some point, reducing the number of bidders increases the perceived probability of winning with a higher bid, and thus leads firms rationally to increase the price they bid.

In most cases, of course, such as where there are numerous actual or potential bidders, this effect on price will be insignificant, if not nonexistent, because the elimination of one bidder will only marginally increase the likelihood of winning with a higher bid. Concentration and market share data offer the best initial measure of the effect that the elimination of a given bidder will have on the noncooperative market equilibrium in markets where firms have varying costs. Firms with historically high market shares are likely to be viewed by other bidders as relatively low-cost firms for a substantial segment of the market. A merger that eliminated competition between two of these firms could therefore result in a significant increase in the market price.[82]

On the other hand, if an auction market is more analogous to an open "English" auction (or if competitors' costs are common knowledge), a more than de minimus direct effect on price is only

---

[82] Of course, if firms with large market shares in fact had advantages in competing for different market segments, traditional market-share analysis would tend to overstate the anticompetitive effect of a merger between two firms with large shares and understate the effect of a merger between a large firm and its smaller rival in the same market segment.

possible if the merger combines firms that are the first and second lowest bidders to a significant number of customers. In an English auction, transactions are carried out by some process of negotiations pursuant to which proposed prices are revised until only one seller—the "winning" or lowest bidder—remains. That seller receives a price just below that of the second-lowest bidder, whose bid it has bettered in the auction process. Because every seller has an opportunity to lower its bid in order to win the contract, all sellers can be certain that the lowest-cost bidder on a given contract will win the auction, but that the price it receives will be determined by the bid (and costs) of the second-lowest bidder.[83] Therefore, given the second bidder's presence, the third bidder and every other higher-cost bidder has no direct effect on the price charged by the first bidder. In the absence of collusion, elimination of a competing bidder through merger has a direct effect on the prices offered by the winning bidder *only* if the merger is between the first and second bidders on a significant number of bids.[84]

Under these circumstances, and for these purposes, standard measures of concentration such as the HHI are largely irrelevant. The merger between the first or second bidder and any firm other than those two might be perfectly harmless even if HHI numbers indicated a serious problem. Another way of looking at this

---

83 The same result occurs in auctions—sometimes referred to as Vickrey auctions—where the identity of the winning bidder is determined by the lowest bid, but the price is set by the second-lowest bid. *See* McAfee & McMillan, *supra* note 76, at 702.

84 In the context of transactions that approximate an English auction, it is conceivable that firms with the largest shares of the relevant market as defined according to traditional market definition principles might be the first and second most efficient bidders on only a very small portion of the transactions in the market. That may be the case because their cost structures are complimentary, with the firms each possessing advantages in serving different sets of customers, *see* discussion under heading "Heterogeneous cost auction markets", *supra*, and with the cost structures of other competitors tending to lie on a spectrum between those of the two largest firms. In such a case, a merger between the two largest firms in the "market" might not significantly harm competition.

problem would be to view a customer or group of customers to which the merging firms represent the first and second bidders as comprising a separate market (because they would not switch to the third or subsequent bidders in the face of a 5% to 10% price increase) in which HHI measures *would* indicate a competitive concern. In this sense, the auction market analysis can be viewed as a check on inaccurate market definition.[85]

The application of bidding-market analysis does not, however, rule out the possibility that a merger in such a market might also increase the likelihood of collusion. For example, it is possible that a merger between bidders other than the first and second lowest would still have an effect on the ease and profitability of collusion. If the first bidder acquired the third, collusion among the first and second bidders would be more profitable because it would yield prices constrained by the fourth bidder rather than by the third bidder.

In applying this auction market analysis in merger enforcement decisions, two additional practical problems must be overcome. First, it is often difficult to determine whether a market is appropriately characterized as an auction market, and if so whether it is more like an English auction or a sealed-bid auction. Given the critical nature of this distinction, the inability to distinguish can be fatal to the predictive value of the analysis.

Second, even if it were certain that a market was sufficiently similar to an English auction, the identity of the first and second bidders will inevitably vary from sale to sale. Indeed, if those identities did not vary, only the first bidder would make any sales, and it would be the only firm to remain in business.[86] Therefore, it is often difficult to identify a significant customer or group of customers to whom the merging firms represent the first

---

85 Similarly, viewing auction analysis as a kind of check on market definition, a hypothetical "third bidder" that was merging with the first bidder might appropriately be viewed as not competing in the same relevant market as the first bidder.

86 Strategic behavior by customers under these circumstances could result in purchases from the second bidder, even at higher prices, in order to retain it as an alternative source of supply in the future.

and second bidders, and thus for whom the merger would cause an anticompetitive effect on the equilibrium price. It may not be possible to do more than get a qualitative sense of the overlap between the merging parties' relative strengths. The larger the percentage of the market for which they are the first and second most efficient sellers, the greater the concern created by the merger. Moreover, since efficiencies are likely to be realized across the whole range of output of the merging firms, the smaller the percentage of their output that represents such a first/second overlap, the more likely it is that a strong efficiencies showing will save the merger from challenge.

Conclusion

In these contexts and others, the Department's merger analysis has focused on evidence that reflects an economically plausible story of a merger's likely effect on the creation or exercise of market power, rather than on any purely numerical assessment of that effect. Ordinarily, but not always, market concentration as measured by the HHI will be highly relevant evidence of that effect. But it is only evidence; the HHI is but a starting point if merger enforcement is not to condemn and deter many transactions that do not harm consumers.

While many commentators and critics have measured the nature and success of the Department's merger enforcement by looking at enforcement statistics and the HHIs of the mergers that the Department has and has not challenged, it is crucial to understand that merger enforcement is not simply a "numbers game"—nor should it be in an age when greater economic sophistication enables antitrust enforcers to be more accurate. The intentions of the framers of the antitrust laws are best fulfilled, and consumers are best served, not by the highest possible number of merger challenges or by bright line tests that are inevitably inaccurate. Rather, the optimal merger policy is one that supplies clear rules and carefully applies them to *all* of the economic realities of a given case. In assessing the success of the Department's merger enforcement, an examination of those realities rather than the numbers alone leads inexorably to the conclusion that merger enforcement under the Sherman and Clayton Acts has never been more effective.

9
The Reagan REvolution[1]

BY THEODORE KOVALEFF*

Most facets of the Reagan years have been subjected to careful review and scrutiny from all sides of the political spectrum. In attempting to analyze the relationship of business and government during the period, it is instructive to examine the initiatives in the area of antitrust to gain insight into the broader policy. To this end, we will concentrate on the activity of the Antitrust Division of the Department of Justice, headed by political appointees, rather than analyzing that of the Federal Trade Commission [FTC] which has 5 members, appointed from different political parties for staggered terms. Clearly, the former can move more quickly to reflect the orientation of an incoming administration than can the latter which, by its very

* For many years, Theodore Kovaleff was an Assistant Dean at the School of Law, Columbia University. He is now Chair, Community Board 9 in the City of New York.

1 Earlier versions or portions of this chapter were presented to meetings of the Economic and Business Historical Society, the Western Economic Association International, and Hofstra University's Ninth Presidential Conference: Ronald Reagan, the Fortieth President. In addition to those persons cited throughout the paper, the author would like to thank William Curran III, Alan A. Fisher, Douglas Ginsburg, James A. Langenfeld, Gilbert Mathis, James C. Miller III, John R. Morris, Raymond J. Saulnier, and David P. Scheffman for their helpful comments and useful suggestions. Any errors, however, are solely those of the author.

composition, is forced to take a more bipartisan tack.[2] Finally, we attempt to place the Reagan antitrust record in historical perspective.

Not only will we look at the "numbers," we will attempt to assess the quality behind the quantity. At one time or another every scholar in the field has attempted to quantify the antitrust activity of an administration, but none has succeeded, and most have foundered in their usually ideologically based attempts to justify or castigate the record of the administration in question. Evaluation of the Reagan record is not easy: The concept of "market,"[3] key to any antitrust analysis, changed rapidly in the 1970's and 1980's as a revolution in the economics academy led to its capture by members of the Chicago School (which held that unfettered marketplace action should be the determinant of policy).[4] Additionally, this was a

---

2 By late 1983, one can safely include the actions of the FTC in the analysis, for by that time the majority of the members had been appointed by Reagan. The Reagan-appointed Chair of the FTC, James C. Miller III, stated, however, that before that time he had slowed the actions of the Commission almost to inactivity following the principle of "Do no evil." Miller to author (Apr. 22, 1993).

3 The term has always been difficult to define or understand. Robert Pitofsky bluntly adds that "[u]nfortunately, no aspect of antitrust enforcement has been handled nearly as badly as market definition" (*New Definitions of Relevant Market and the Assault on Antitrust*, 90 COLUM. L. REV., 1807 [1990].)

4 Robert Bork was one of the first to apply what became known as Chicago School theory to antitrust. Laying the foundations in *Legislative Intent and the Policy of the Sherman Act*, 9 J. L. & ECON., 7–48 (1966) (reprinted in The Political Economy of the Sherman Act 39–70 [E. T. Sullivan ed. 1991]) and *Antitrust and Monopoly: The Goals of Antitrust Policy*, 57 PAPERS AND PROCEEDINGS, AMERICAN ECONOMIC ASSOCIATION 242–53 (1966), Bork subsequently expanded upon the idea in THE ANTITRUST PARADOX: A POLICY AT WAR WITH ITSELF (1978). *Also see* Posner, *The Chicago School of Antitrust Analysis*, 127 U. PENN. L. REV. 925–52 (1979). Posner, probably the most prolific of the group, published 22 law review articles in the short span between 1980 and 1983. *Additionally*, Easterbrook, *The Limits of Antitrust*, 63 TEX. L. REV. 1–40 (1984); for the added perspective gained from more than one term of the Reagan presidency, *also see* Easterbrook, *Workable Antitrust Policy*, 84 MICH. L. REV. 1696–1713 (1986). For a comparison of the beliefs of the Chicago School with those of the more traditional structuralists, *see* the appendix to Fox and Sullivan, *Antitrust—Retrospective and Prospective: Where Are We Coming From? Where Are We Going?* 62 N.Y.U. L. REV. 936, 969–88 (1987). Although the concept of two groupings makes for easy, symmetri-

period of massive restructuring. Many corporations, especially those in the banking and transportation industries expanded. Others, on the other hand, contracted and focused their objectives more clearly, partially in response to their protected local, regional, or national arenas that were changing rapidly to a single, solitary world market in which competition—either potential or real—loomed from hitherto undreamed of corners of the globe. Thus quick comparisons with earlier periods are fraught with danger.

The inheritance

Philosophy

Marc Allen Eisner has detailed the rise in influence of economists in the Antitrust Division of the Department of Justice and their subsequent shift in philosophical orientation from structuralist (believing that structure, conduct, and performance should dictate policy) to that of the Chicago School. He notes that much of this change actually transpired in the 1970's.[5] The newly entrenched

---

cal contrasts, the views of the adherents are actually quite individualized. Indeed, the Antitrust Section of the American Bar Association divides each approach into two parts (MERGER STANDARDS UNDER UNITED STATES ANTITRUST LAWS 87–119 [Monograph No. 7, 1981]).

For an easy-to-understand, popular explanation of Chicago School economics, see Meadows, *Bold Departures in Antitrust: Reagan's Chief Guardian of Corporate Competition Believes Bigness Can Be Healthy*, FORTUNE, Oct. 5, 1981, at 180–88.

5 ANTITRUST AND THE TRIUMPH OF ECONOMICS: INSTITUTIONS, EXPERTISE AND POLICY CHANGE, chap. 5 (1991); *also see* Wood & Anderson, *The Politics of U. S. Antitrust Regulation*, 37 AMER. J. POL. SCI. 1–39 (1993). Herbert Hovenkamp traces the influence of economics on antitrust policy to the 1920's (". . . [O]ne must go all the way back to the first thirty years of antitrust enforcement to find a policy that can reasonably be characterized as having little or no economic content" 84 MICH. L. REV. 220–23 (1985)]). Indeed, Robert Bork attempts to unearth an economic welfare root to the Sherman Act in THE ANTITRUST PARADOX, 21; *also see* his earlier *Antitrust and Monopoly, supra* note 3, at 242–53. *Additionally, see* Gattuso, *Antitrust: An Incomplete Revolution*, in ASSESSING THE REAGAN YEARS 261–70 (D. Boaz, ed., 1988); Bickel, *The Antitrust Division's Adoption of the Chicago School Economic Policy Calls for Some Reorganization: But Is the Division's New Policy Here to Stay?* 20 HOUSTON L. REV. 1083–1113 (1983); and Kurdle, *Antitrust*

school would, however, provide much of the ideological underpinnings for the Reagan domestic policy.

After years of tilting toward industrial regulation by the federal government, the tide had turned, and politicians on both sides of the political spectrum had begun to embrace the Chicago School–supported idea of deregulation. Early experiments had begun in the late years of the Carter administration under the able tutelage of Alfred Kahn.[6] The first industries to have been "set free" had been airlines and trucking. Thus, the Chicago School belief in the role of the

---

and the Performance of the U. S. Economy, in REVITALIZING THE U. S. ECONOMY 64–82 (F. Stevens Redburn, T. I. Buss, & L. C. Leckbur eds. 1986).

In 1983, at a symposium commemorating the tenth anniversary of the Economic Policy Office of the Antitrust Division, Lawrence J. White provided a brief review of the rise in importance of economists in the Division. *See* 29 ANTITRUST BULL. 1–2 (1984); many of the papers and comments are included in the issue.

See Correia, *Antitrust After the Reagan administration*, 76 GEO. L. J., 329–35 (1987). Correia was Chief Counsel and Staff Director to the Subcommittee on Antitrust, Monopolies and Business Rights of the Senate Committee on the Judiciary at the time he wrote the article. *See also* Pitofsky, *Does Antitrust Have a Future?*, 76 GEO. L. J., 321–27 (1987). Both works are part of a collection of papers delivered at the Airlie House Conference on Antitrust Alternatives; each argues that the Division's perspective was evolving in the 1970's but that the Reaganauts "overdid it" in the 1980's.

6 If one is to seek the roots of deregulation one must look back at least as far as 1962, when President John F. Kennedy, in his Transportation Message, noted that:

> The management of various modes of transportation is subjected to excessive, cumbersome and time consuming regulatory supervision that shackles and distorts managerial initiative. Some parts of the transportation industry are restrained unnecessarily; others are promoted or taxed unevenly and inconsistently.
>
> Some carriers are required to provide, at a loss, services for which there is little demand. Some carriers are required to charge rates which are high in relation to cost in order to shelter competing carriers. . . .
>
> I am convinced that less Federal regulation and subsidization is in the long run a prime prerequisite of a healthy inter-city transportation network.

Later in the speech, Kennedy proposed

> ". . . greater reliance on the forces of competition and less reliance on the restraints of regulation. . . . And it means that, to the extent possible, the users of

efficient market, coupled with the allied deregulation impulse, were already a well-established part of the national agenda by the time Ronald Reagan was elected to the White House.

Ongoing actions

The Reaganauts inherited from the outgoing Carter administration an Antitrust Division immersed in the prosecution of two cases that were consuming most of the energies of the Antitrust Division. The first, filed against International Business Machines Corp. [IBM] in the last days of the Johnson administration, was getting nowhere despite the amassing of millions of pages of trial testimony, for it was bogged down by unfocused prosecution and complex legal maneuvering on both sides. After thirteen years, the end was no nearer than it had been a decade earlier. The second, the landmark action against the American Telephone and Telegraph Co. [AT&T], though closer to denouement, absent a consent judgment, could easily have been projected to continue for at least another half decade, further eating up valuable Antitrust Division resources. Much of the remaining Division activity was centered on the discovery and prosecution of horizontal price-fixing especially in highway construction.

Leadership and appointments

It is clear that Ronald Reagan entered the presidency with the very clear agenda of slimming down government and getting it "off the people's backs." Not only were all cabinet appointments made utilizing this ideological filter, but all those named to lower positions shared this philosophical outlook; furthermore, all were required to be tough enough to withstand the expected onslaughts of

---

transportation services should bear the full costs of the services they use . . ." (New York *Times*, Apr. 6, 1962, at 18–19.)

Similar sentiments were also voiced by President Dwight D. Eisenhower and can be found in the Transportation Act of 1958 (PL 85–625, 72 Stat. 568). In neither case, however, did any meaningful changes in the philosophical thrust of the laws, or their enforcement, result; thus we must credit the Carter administration with the beginning of the deregulation revolution.

press and political opponents.[7] When Attorney General William French Smith chose Stanford University Law Professor William Baxter to head the Antitrust Division, it was certainly no accident. A brilliant scholar with a record of public service and an impressive list of publications, Baxter's inclinations had been clearly set forth for all to see.[8] Furthermore, no member of the transition team could have ignored the fact that, in the event of the need to make policy decisions on the AT&T case, his im-

---

7 Martin Anderson to author (Apr. 22, 1993); Edwin Meese III to author (Apr. 23, 1993); James C. Miller III to author (Apr. 22, 1993); James G. Watt to author (Apr. 22, 1993). In this regard, I would like to thank Hofstra University for sponsoring the Ninth Presidential Conference treating the Reagan presidency; the meeting facilitated access to a number of important members of the administration.

8 *See especially* his *Antitrust and Regulated Industries Overview: Competitive Principles in Regulated Industries*, 39 ABA ANTITRUST L.J. 427–532 (1969–70). His input on the sections on banking (pp. 446–49) and communications (pp. 488–89) can easily be interpreted as foreshadowing his future actions. Additionally, as an active member of the Neal Task Force on Antitrust Policy, he had had a chance to make his viewpoints well known. In fact, he wrote the section on patents (William K. Jones to author [Mar. 24, 1992]; Professor Jones was also a member of the Commission): His recommendations on ensuring the availability of licensed patents presaged his later stance on telephone line accessibility for long distance carriers. Although originally not released, roughly 1 year later, as a result of congressional inquiry, the Group's report was made public and is reprinted in *The White House Task Force Report on Antitrust Policy*, 2 ANTITRUST L. & ECON. REV. 11 et seq. (1968–69). For a clear exposition of Baxter's thought on the topic, *see* his *Legal Restrictions on Exploitation of the Patent Monopoly: An Economic Analysis*, 76 YALE L.J. 267–370 (1966). *Also see* his *How Government Cases Get Selected—Comments from Academe*, 46 Antitrust L.J. 586–601 (1977), *Placing the Burger Court in Historical Perspective*, 47 ANTITRUST L.J. 803–18, and PEOPLE OR PENGUINS: THE CASE FOR OPTIMAL POLLUTION (1974). THE POLITICAL ECONOMY OF ANTITRUST (R. D. Tollison ed. 1979) consists of a paper of that title written by Baxter, followed by commentary and lively debate on many of the issues he treats.

Michael Isikoff and Merrill Brown even quote Baxter as having described some of the Supreme Court's opinions as "rubbish" based on "whacko" theories (*Baxter's Reign: Evolution, Not Revolution*, Washington Post, Dec. 11, 1983, at F1 [note that he allegedly used the epithets *before* his appointment as AAG]).

mediate superiors were likely to have to recuse themselves due to their prior relations with Mother Bell or her subsidiaries.[9] Thus there could be no check on the Assistant Attorney General; the president would not have dared to involve himself for fear of a public reaction like that which had befallen Richard Nixon as a result of his intemperate involvement in the settlement of the cases against the International Telephone and Telegraph Corp. [ITT] in 1972.

During the Reagan years "there was an enormous continuity in the Division"[10] because Baxter's successors—Paul McGrath, Douglas Ginsburg, and Charles F. Rule—had worked together; and, though they were not ideological clones, they all shared his Chicago-based philosophy which was often described euphemistically as the "maximization of consumer welfare,"[11] or better, as "eco-

---

9 According to Meese, this matter was *not* discussed with him, but, it "might well have been thought of at the lower levels." Meese to author (Apr. 23, 1993).

10 McGrath to author (Jan. 21, 1993), noting that, while he had been Chief of the Civil Division he had worked closely with Baxter's Antitrust Division and that Ginsburg and Rule had both held lesser posts within the Division before being named to head it.

11 *See*, for instance, two pieces by Rule & Meyer: *An Antitrust Enforcement Policy to Maximize Economic Wealth*, 33 ANTITRUST BULL. 677–712 (1988), and *Towards a Merger Policy that Maximizes Consumer Welfare: Enforcement by Careful Analysis*, 35 ANTITRUST BULL. 251–95 (1990), *A Talk with Antitrust Chief William Baxter*, WALL STREET JOURNAL, Mar. 24, 1982, at 28; Baxter, *Separation of Powers, Prosecutorial Discretion, and the "Common Law," Nature of Antitrust Law*, 60 TEX. L.REV. 661–703, esp. 693–94 (1982); and Henderson, *Efficiency Becomes Yardstick for Mergers; Antitrust Chief Says Goals Achieved*, WASHINGTON POST, Mar. 24, 1985, at H1.

An early exposition of the idea of consumer welfare can be found in Williamson, *Economies as an Antitrust Defense: The Welfare Tradeoffs*, 58 AMER. ECON. REV. (1968); Robert Bork popularized it in his oft-cited ANTITRUST PARADOX, *supra* note 4, esp. chapter 5; *also see* Bork, *Consumer Welfare*, NAT'L L.J., Sept. 7, 1987; also see section on "consumer welfare" in R. Collins and D. O'Brien, *Just Where Does Judge Bork Stand?* NAT'L. L.J. 13, 28–29 (Sep. 7, 1987).

For a devastating analysis of this idea *see* Lande, *An Anti-Antitrust Activist?* NAT'L. L.J., Sep. 7, 1987, at 13 et seq.

nomic efficiency."[12] In terms of policy, this had the effect of narrowing the ambit of the antitrust corpus in the realm of Clayton Act merger enforcement. The opposite, however, would prevail when considering such Sherman Act offenses as bid-rigging and price-fixing.

In passing, it should be noted that most of the judges Reagan appointed to the Court of Appeals were sympathetic to the Chicago School and were committed to economic efficiency. The choices of Robert Bork, Douglas Ginsburg, Richard Posner, Anthony Scalia, James Harvie Wilkinson, Frank Easterbrook, and Ralph Karl Winter, Jr.—all academics well known for their ideological purity—contrast somewhat to later Reagan nominations to the Supreme Court.[13]

---

12 Eisner & Meier, *Presidential Control versus Bureaucratic Power: Explaining the Reagan Revolution in Antitrust*, 34 AMER. J. POL. SCI. 273–74 (1990); *see also* U.S. DEPARTMENT OF JUSTICE, OFFICE OF THE ATTORNEY GENERAL, ANNUAL REPORT OF THE ATTORNEY GENERAL OF THE UNITED STATES 3 (1984). For a critique, *see* Shepherd, *Three "Efficiency School" Hypotheses about Market Power*, 33 ANTITRUST BULL., 395–415 (1988).

13 Austin, *Antitrust Reaction to the Merger Wave: The Revolution versus the Counter Revolution*, 66 N.C.L. REV. 947–48 (1988); Graham, *Conservative Academics: Rising Stars*, Legal Times, Mar. 18, 1985, at 1. *Also, Reagan Justice: A Conservative Legacy in the Appellate Courts*, Legal Times, May-June 1988, spec. supp.

Paralleling some of Eisner's findings, William E. Kovacic has shown that the Judiciary began to turn more conservative in the field of antitrust before the election of Reagan; *see* his *Reagan's Judicial Appointments and Antitrust in the 1990s*, 60 FORDHAM L. REV., 49–124 (1991). Even more specifically, Chicago School thought also appears to have begun to influence several members of the Supreme Court, starting as early as 1975. Peter M. Gerhart identifies six cases (*Goldfarb v. Virginia State Bar*, 421 U.S. 773 [1975], *Continental T.V., Inc. v. GTE Sylvania, Inc.*, 433 U.S. 36 [1977], *National Society of Professional Engineers v. United States*, 435 U.S. 679 [1978], *Broadcast Music, Inc. v. Columbia Broadcasting, Inc.*, 441 U.S. 1 [1979], *Reiter v. Sonotone Corp.* 442 U.S. 330 (1979), and *Catalan, Inc. v. Target Sales, Inc.*, 446 U.S. 643 [1980]) in which the "Court seemed to be moving toward a comprehensive, integrated antitrust methodology based upon economic analysis and largely following the writing of the Chicago Schoolers such as Robert Bork and Richard Posner" (*The Supreme Court and Antitrust Analysis: The (Near) Triumph of the Chicago School*, SUPREME COURT REV. 139 [1980]). The dichotomy between the appointments to the different levels of the Judiciary can easily be explained by the collective fates of Bork and Ginsburg when nominated to the High Court.

Holdover actions

United States v. International Business Machines Corporation[14]

After many years of research, discovery, and trial (during which five presidents had appointed nine Attorneys General and seven Assistant Attorneys General [AAG] in Charge of the Antitrust Division), a review headed by AAG Baxter finally resulted in the decision that further efforts would be futile and that the IBM action should be dropped. Baxter reasoned that, despite the fact that the case was already thirteen years old, with 66 million pages of documents entered into the record and 856 witnesses having testified, in the best of all possible worlds, were the case to be allowed to continue, it would require at the least several more years to reach an adjudicated conclusion. Furthermore, no one could hazard how long the appeals process might last. But, alas, even worse, Voltaire had overcome Leibniz and Pope, and it was not the best of all possible worlds: The case had been badly handled, poorly argued, based on flawed economic theory, and, as time passed, much of the government's argument had been made moot by the many advances of the computer revolution. As Baxter stated in a press conference, "In some ways, the ultimate horror . . [would be for the case to stretch on] for another 20 years."[15] The case was, therefore, without merit and should be dismissed.

Rather than viewing the outcome as an IBM victory, it would be more correct to interpret it as a defeat for the government. Robert Bork had already described the action as the "Antitrust [D]ivision's Vietnam."[16] In deciding to end the action, AAG Baxter directed that a

---

14 69 Civ. 200 (S. D. N.Y. 1969–1982). For a good background on the case and the growth of the computer industry in general, *see* two books by Franklin Fisher (with J. McKie & R. Manke): IBM AND THE U.S. DATA PROCESSING INDUSTRY (1983), and (with J. J. McGowen & J. E. Greenwood) and FOLDED, SPINDLED, AND MUTILATED: ECONOMIC ANALYSIS AND THE U.S. v. IBM (1983). *Also see* R. T. DELAMASTER, BIG BLUE: IBM'S USE AND ABUSE OF POWER (1986).

15 Grier, *Impact of AT&T, IBM Decisions*, Christian Science Monitor, Jan. 11, 1982, at 1.

16 New York Times, Jan. 9, 1982, at 1:1; Baker, *Government Enforcement of Section Two*, 61 NOTRE DAME L. REV. 899 n. 13 (1986).

devastating memorandum to the Attorney General, William French Smith, be included with the standard transmittal forms. After weighing "the financial and social costs of continuing the litigation, the government's likelihood of success, and the potential benefits to be obtained if the government should win," the memo concluded that the case must be dismissed. It offered numerous specifics, including:

> 1. It may well be that IBM is a monopolist and controls some segment of the computer market. However, even if that were so, the government's case does not allege that IBM achieved that position illegally. Rather, the complaint alleges that IBM maintained a monopoly position lawfully achieved through a series of illegal actions ("bad acts") against competitors. I have examined the merits of the government's case concerning IBM's "bad acts" and have concluded that, while several may have occurred in the manner and with the intent alleged, the most persuasive episodes concern computer systems that are not included within the market IBM is alleged to have monopolized. . . . Other allegations concern IBM's actions against manufacturers of peripheral equipment designed to operate with IBM systems. Most of these manufacturers sued on their own behalf, and all of them lost either at trial or at the appellate level.
>
> 2. "Whatever the chances that the government will prevail at trial, the likelihood of success on appeal is small. The case would be appealed to the Second Circuit, which recently decided Berkey [*Berkey Photo Inc. v. Eastman Kodak Co.*, 603 F.2d 263 (2d. Cir. 1979), cert. denied, 100 S. Ct. 1061 (1980)]. In that opinion, the court defined the offense of monopolization in a manner which indicates it may be unreceptive to the theory in this case. . . . [T]he sheer length of the trial and the large number of pretrial and trial rulings involved make it possible that there were errors at trial which may in themselves warrant reversal.
>
> 3. "Finally, even assuming that the government could prove IBM's liability, there is no assurance that appropriate relief could be obtained. Where illegal acts have been proven, the purpose of relief is to remove the defendant's ability and incentive to engage in similar acts in the future. This can be done by injunction or divestiture, with courts expressing a preference to avoid structural relief where possible. . . . It could also be done by punitive sanctions in a criminal case. In addition, the United States could attempt to recover any damages it may have suffered as a result of illegal behavior.
>
> In this case, injunctions are likely to be ineffective. The conduct episodes that appear most promising as potential bases for liability are time-bound and highly specific to the immediate context in which they

occurred. It is impossible to fashion injunctions to prevent similar future violations that are neither so specific that they would be meaningless outside those now-extinct circumstances, nor so general that they would simply echo the language of the antitrust laws themselves. . . .

. . . [S]tructural relief in this case would be totally disproportionate to the nature and scope of the violations that we might be able to [prove? (a word is left out)]. Moreover, despite years of effort, no structural relief proposal has been identified that would inject new competition into the industry while retaining the efficiencies necessary to create viable successor companies.

In my view, the most appropriate relief in cases of this nature may be to impose fines or other penalties commensurate with the gravity of any illegal behavior. Such relief could deter illegal conduct by punishing responsible individuals, and by depriving the perpetrator of some or all of the benefits from that behavior. However, the government here precluded the possibility of obtaining fines or incarceration of responsible individuals by pursuing a civil rather than a criminal action in 1969. . . .

Rather than continue the case, I could attempt instead to negotiate a settlement with IBM. While this option has many advantages over continued litigation, it presents some of the same problems. For the reasons discussed above, no appropriate injunction or structural relief can be specified. Accordingly, it is difficult to identify the goals that we would seek in a settlement. Moreover, I am pessimistic that IBM would agree at this point to more than token measures. In negotiations conducted at the end of the Carter Administration, IBM demonstrated its reluctance to settle for structural and injunctive relief measures far short of those proposed in the course of this litigation by the government. While it might have been possible to negotiate a purely cosmetic settlement, to do so would not have been in the best interests of the public."[17]

Why preceding Attorneys General had not subjected the case to similar analysis is unclear; why the waste of governmental energies

17 Memorandum from Abbott B. Lipsky, Jr., "at the direction of Assistant Attorney General Baxter in his absence," to the Attorney General dated January 6, 1982, copies of which were included with the Department of Justice press release dated January 8, 1982, announcing the dropping of the action. *Also see* Legal Times, Jan. 18, 1982, at 29.

and resources was not stopped earlier has never been satisfactorily addressed. Although politically it might have been embarrassing to have dropped the case earlier, the potential dividends in terms of increased Antitrust Division productivity could have been immense, and a good portion of the estimated $20 million of government expenditures could have been saved. A similar, but significantly larger, savings could have been made by IBM.[18]

The almost simultaneous announcement of the settlement of the AT&T case likely muted much of the politically based criticism that would, otherwise, inevitably have occurred.[19]

United States v. American Telephone and Telegraph Company[20]

The story of the filing of the suit against Mother Bell, the tortuous early days of the trial, the coming of Judge Harold H. Greene

---

18 The company has refused to make public the amount it expended in fighting the fourteen year action. In reply to a recent letter addressed to the president of "Big Blue," I was informed that the figures were still "not available" (Whitney Weyant, Media Relations, to author, Mar. 27, 1992). Conservative estimates have placed the costs at $150 million. Nicholas Katzenbach, a former Attorney General in the Johnson administration and General Counsel for IBM during the entire contraposition, has been quoted as saying that he had an "unlimited budget to fight the case, and every year I overspent it" (Harvey Goldschmid to author, Mar. 1992). According to James B. Stewart, Cravath, Swaine & Moore received fees "in excess of $15 million per year" plus lavish expenses for handling the case (THE PARTNERS: INSIDE AMERICA'S MOST POWERFUL LAW FIRMS 92–98 [1983]).

Had all the government's supplemental requests for documents been allowed, some 5 billion additional pages of documents would have to have been produced at the expense to the company of some "62,000 man-years of effort at a cost of more than $1 billion" (Think, Jan.-Feb. 1985, at 7; Think magazine is an IBM house organ published in New York City).

Nevertheless, in the final analysis, the government also suffered further, because legal fees and all the other attendant costs of the action were deductible from the corporate taxes paid by the computer giant.

19 Baker, *supra* note 16, at 909–12.

20 CA No. 74–1698 (D. D. C.); *also see* 524 F. Supp. 1336 et seq., and 552 F. Supp. 131 (D. D. C. 1982).

and how he changed the pace and trajectory of the action has all been described in great detail elsewhere and is germane to our topic only as background.[21] A comparison of the negotiations between the company and the Justice Department in the waning days of the Carter administration with those leading to the settlement in the early Reagan years is much more instructive. January 1981 is a good dividing line in this exercise, because not only was Ronald Reagan to be inaugurated but also the actual AT&T trial was scheduled to commence during that month.

It is noteworthy that after Reagan's landslide victory, but before his inauguration, AT&T appeared most interested in working out a consent judgment with the outgoing administration. The communications giant wanted the government to end its action and to lift the strictures of the 1956 consent decree that prohibited it from entering any business outside the tightly defined communications industry.[22] For its part, although the specifics of the Antitrust Division's wishes ebbed and flowed somewhat, they included:

1. The divestiture of roughly 40% of the Western Electric Co.;
2. Agreement that the Bell Operating Companies [BOC] would have to purchase their equipment on the open market and that all AT&T research for the BOCs would be similarly available to non-Bell operating companies.
3. The spinoffs of three BOCs: usually mentioned were Pacific Telephone and the two in which AT&T was a minority shareholder—Cincinnati Bell and Southern New England Telephone.
4. The reorganization of the other BOCs so that they would be able to make the services of the other long distance carriers avail-

---

21 The best work on the subject is P. TEMIN AND L. GALAMBOS, THE FALL OF THE BELL SYSTEM: A STUDY IN PRICES AND POLITICS (1987). For treatments from widely differentiated perspectives, *also see* S. COLL, THE DEAL OF THE CENTURY: THE BREAKUP OF AT&T (1986); F. HENCK AND B. STRASSBURG, A SLIPPERY SLOPE: THE LONG ROAD TO THE BREAKUP OF AT&T (1988); C. R. KRAUS AND A. W. DUERIG, THE RAPE OF MA BELL: THE CRIMINAL WRECKING OF THE BEST TELEPHONE SYSTEM IN THE WORLD (1988); and A. STONE, WRONG NUMBER: THE BREAKUP OF AT&T (1989).

22 1956 Trade Cas. ¶68,246.

able to their users.[23] (This is similar to the options offered today to all users.)

There was neither the time nor the inclination on the part of presiding Judge Greene, to allow the complex negotiations to progress to a denouement acceptable to both sides. As a result, it became necessary to backtrack somewhat as the new administration assumed control. In the meantime, the long-awaited trial also began.

At once the newly appointed chief of the Antitrust Division, Baxter, set to analyzing the case and the philosophical underpinnings of the proposed settlement. Almost immediately he jettisoned the Litvack plan because it "did not have any theory behind it." Baxter viewed it as punitive, instead of being responsive to the structural problems of the industry. To the Chicago School–oriented AAG, brought in to bring "rationale to enforcement,"[24] what was necessary was to separate the regulated portions from the unregulated; then the free market could rule the fate of the latter.[25]

As time passed it became evident that in the trial there were actually three, not two, separate interests, all pulling in different directions. Not only were there AT&T and the Justice Department, there was also Judge Greene arrayed against the communications giant; and each of the players had a different agenda. Neither Baxter nor the AT&T leadership believed that any settlement resulting from the trial would be satisfactory. And Judge Greene was pressing the case on toward a rapid conclusion. Were there to be an adjudicated verdict in favor of the government, he would play a significant role in framing a decree that would undoubtedly include divestitures.

Nevertheless, the communications giant was not without its

---

23 Material derived from interview with Sanford M. Litvack (June 12, 1990), the Assistant Attorney General in Charge of the Antitrust Division at the close of the Carter administration, and corroborated in part in Temin and Galambos, *supra* note 21, at 208–15, and Coll, *supra* note 19, at 147–58.

24 Meese to author (Apr. 23, 1993).

25 Temin and Galambos, *supra* note 21, at 219–22.

friends. Reminiscent of the behind-the-scenes lobbying during the settlement negotiations leading to the consent decree of 1956, the Department of Defense, this time led by Casper Weinberger, came to its aid, touting national defense considerations. Additionally, the Department of Commerce, led by Malcolm Baldridge, also came forth to attempt rescue. And although Reagan did not personally intervene, he did note publicly that when he was young, it had cost $2.00 to make a call across the continent and 2 cents to mail a letter; that had now changed to 20 cents for both. A recollection such as this clearly had ramifications for *both* AT&T and the "big" government! According to Edwin Meese, III, however, the issue never reached the President for input. It was, nevertheless, discussed at several policy conclaves in which the various departments met to facilitate internal coordination.[26]

The question of uncertainty about the future of the communications giant began to play a more important role in the script. Were the government to prevail, no one had any idea of the extent of the settlement that Judge Greene might attempt to impose. Moreover, AT&T would most likely appeal, and it would take years for the appeals process to be exhausted. Similarly, were AT&T to win, the government would also likely appeal. In either scenario, appeals would expend time and resources for both the company, which wanted to progress, and the agency, which wanted to move down its agenda. A negotiated settlement would obviate many of the uncertainties.[27] With this mindset, the two contenders sought to forge an agreement within the parameters of a revision of the 1956 consent decree.[28] When finally reached, the agreement included the following provisions:

---

26 Meese to author (Apr. 23, 1993).

27 But not all would be resolved, because Judge Greene would still be a factor with which to be reckoned as he would have to oversee any negotiated settlement.

28 Rather than enter a new settlement, the Justice Department decided that a modification of the 1956 Consent Decree would be the correct methodology. Inasmuch as one of the main reasons why AT&T agreed to the new stipulations was the lifting of some of the strictures of the 1956 Decree; this appears to have been the correct blueprint.

1. The BOCs would be split off from AT&T, with the promise that they would never rejoin Mother Bell.
2. AT&T would continue to control its research arms, but they would have to serve the BOCs on a priority basis.
3. Each BOC would offer competing long distance carriers to its customers on a nondiscriminatory basis.
4. The BOCs were to provide local service only.
5. The shackles of the 1956 consent decree were to be lifted, and AT&T would be allowed to enter areas not specifically in the communications field, finally opening the way for it to expand into the computer business.[29]

The resolution was a clear triumph for Baxter and for those in the Antitrust Division who had labored on the case for nearly a decade. Thwarting those who had wanted to drop the action early in the Reagan years, the AAG was instrumental in formulating a decree which was clear and to the point.[30] According to Donald Baker, who, at the time of the filing of the suit had been a deputy Assistant Attorney General in the Antitrust Division responsible for supervising activities in the regulated sector and who later became the AAG, "[i]t accomplished precisely what the government had set out to accomplish, and indeed accomplished it to an even greater degree than we who had filed the case in 1974 could have reasonably hoped."[31]

---

29 Ironically, the 1956 Consent Decree had been attacked by antitrust activists as a sellout; in retrospect, however, it appears that absent the lifting of its restrictions, there could have been no settlement including the divestiture of the BOCs, and the case might still be with us today.

30 Washington Post, July 9, 1981, at D9.

31 *Symposium: Developments in Section Two of the Sherman Act: Article: Government Enforcement of Section Two*, 61 NOTRE DAME L. REV. 917 (1986). The praise was bipartisan: Sanford M. Litvack, President Carter's second AAG in Charge of the Antitrust Division, is quoted as stating, "[The settlement] achieved all the essential goals of the lawsuit. . . . [It] will prohibit cross-subsidization from regulated monopoly service to long-distance services that now face substantial competition and it will eliminate the incentives to discriminate on the part of the Bell operating companies in providing local exchange service and in purchasing equipment and supplies" (Washington Post, Feb. 4, 1982, at D10). Donald F. Turner, AAG for President Lyndon B.

Deregulation

Perhaps as an outgrowth of the opposition to the war in Vietnam and the Watergate scandal, there grew within the country an antipathy to all manifestations of "big government." Nowhere was this better exemplified than in the attitude toward regulated industries. Although, as we have noted, one can trace the beginnings of the deregulation impulse back to the Eisenhower administration, it is not until the Nixon-Ford era that the taproot of the deregulation impulse can be found.[32] In the Carter administration, with the appointment of Alfred Kahn to the chairmanship of the Civil Aeronautics Board [CAB], the movement began to have a positive impact on the American economy.[33] With potent support from influential members of both the political right and left, and partially as a result of the positive impact on airline earnings resulting from the loosening of the tight strictures of the CAB during the waning years of the Ford administration, Congress passed the Air Cargo Deregulation Act of 1977[34] and the Airline Deregulation Act of 1978.[35] Relaxation was also extended to most land-based transportation with the passage of the Motor Carrier Act and the Household Goods Transportation Act in 1980.[36] The election of Ronald

---

Johnson, stated, "Mr. Baxter got what the government wanted. It looks to me like a very good settlement" (Grier, *supra* note 15, at 1).

32 ANNUAL REPORT OF THE COUNCIL OF ECONOMIC ADVISORS 121–30 (1971).

33 M. DERTHICK AND P. QUICK, THE POLITICS OF REGULATION chaps. 1–3 (1985); Eads and Fix, REGULATORY POLICY, in THE REAGAN EXPERIMENT: AN EXAMINATION OF THE ECONOMIC AND SOCIAL POLICIES UNDER THE REAGAN ADMINISTRATION 133–35 (J. L. Palmer & I. V. Sawhill eds. 1982).

34 PL 95–163; 49 U.S.C. § 1,371, 1,388. *Also see* HARDAWAY, TRANSPORTATION DEREGULATION (1976–1984): TURNING THE TIDE, 14 TRANSP. L.J. 137 (1985).

35 PL 95–504; 49 U.S.C. § 1,301, 1302 et seq. In 1980 PL 96–192; 49 U.S.C. § 1,341, n. Conservatives apparently supported deregulation predicated on the belief that economic freedom must be pursued and government control limited; across the aisle, Senator Edward Kennedy supported it as "opposing monopoly." For an analysis of the Kennedy position, *see* Clark, *Some Lessons from Airline Deregulation*, Wall Street Journal, Nov. 22, 1983, at 35.

36 PL 96–454; 49 U.S.C. 10,101 et seq., § 10,734, § 10,526(a).

Reagan, then, found the movement in full force; its momentum continued as, for instance, vast areas of communications and other modes of transportation, most notably bus travel, were deregulated.[37]

The Airline Deregulation Act of 1978 provided for the termination of the CAB in 1985 and for its responsibilities to be handed over to the Department of Transportation [DOT], an agency of the executive branch. A mixed blessing at best, this had the effect, among other things, of further removing the industry from under the antitrust umbrella of the Justice Department. As a result, despite the immediate apparent, if illusory, success of the removal of controls,[38] when airlines began to consider consolidations, there was

---

37 Note the Bus Regulatory Reform Act of 1982 (PL 97–261; 49 U.S.C. § 10,101). Thoms, ROLLIN' ON . . . TO A FREE MARKET: MOTOR CARRIER REGULATION 1935–1980, 13 TRANSP. L.J. 81–82 (1983). For background on the growth of deregulation, *see* two works by Paul Stephen Dempsey: THE SOCIAL AND ECONOMIC CONSEQUENCES OF DEREGULATION: THE TRANSPORTATION INDUSTRY IN TRANSITION (1989) and FLYING BLIND: THE FAILURE OF AIRLINE DEREGULATION (1990). E. E. BAILEY, D. R. GRAHAM & D. P. KAPLAN, DEREGULATING THE AIRLINES (1985) take a more positive, though dated, view of the process, albeit colored by their CAB employment record. S. BREYER, REGULATION AND ITS REFORM (1982) extensively analyzes the deregulation of the airline, natural gas, telecommunications, and trucking industries. Levine, *Airline Competition in Deregulated Markets: Theory, Firm Strategy and Public Policy*, 4 YALE J. ON REG. 393–494 (1987) includes a useful bibliography and provides a good overview of the topic. *Also see* Yandle, *The Evolution of Regulatory Activities in the 1970s and 1980s*, in ESSAYS IN CONTEMPORARY ECONOMIC PROBLEMS, 1986: THE IMPACT OF THE REAGAN PROGRAM 105–45 (P. Cagan ed. 1986).

38 Although it is easy to measure cost per mile and then to suggest that, as the figure had fallen in the years subsequent to deregulation, the public had benefited from the change in policy, a number of other factors must be taken into account. First, the tickets that are compared in the test should be identical. This means that the ticket in question must have the same flexibility (cancelability and utility); that is, one cannot compare average ticket prices before and after deregulation because there are so many different types of tickets post regulation and those with the most stringent requirements pull down the average ticket price. A refundable ticket good any day and a nonrefundable ticket which can only be used for a trip that must have been planned and purchased 21 days in advance and which must include a Saturday night stayover simply are not fungible and thus should not be comparable. Furthermore, the number

little to preclude them, as the DOT was staffed with people who "had never seen a merger they didn't like." Despite prompt opposition by the Antitrust Division in almost every instance, no antitrust-based objections were considered by the DOT to be of sufficient merit to halt the march to increased concentration.[39]

As a result of the climate, there was considerable consolidation in the industry. Not only did Trans World Airlines swallow up Ozark,[40] but also [the "also" is needed—in Latin non solo . . . sed etiam] Republic took over North Central, Southern, and Hughes Airwest only to be merged into Northwest; Texas Air (later to change its name to Continental Airlines) became the holder of Continental, New York Air, Eastern, and People Express, which had, itself, acquired Frontier, Britt, Provincetown-Boston Airline (PBA), and Rocky Mountain; and USAIR absorbed Piedmont,

---

of trips that involve a second or third flight has increased significantly since deregulation. In each of these cases, the mileage traversed and the length of time expended per trip have increased markedly. To compare a prederegulation nonstop trip with one in the postderegulation era that involved a flight into a hub (*infra*, note 42) and then a flight on to the destination and to find that the "cost per mile had fallen" would be incorrect if the mileage flown and not the mileage between destinations had been measured. Finally, the price of fuel, a major ingredient in airline expenditures, fell significantly in the 1980's.

For the Reagan administration analysis *see* COUNCIL OF ECONOMIC ADVISORS, ECONOMIC REPORT OF THE PRESIDENT 199–229 (1988); *also see* FEDERAL TRADE COMMISSION, THE DEREGULATED AIRLINE INDUSTRY: A REVIEW OF THE EVIDENCE (1988).

39 Charles F. Rule to author (Mar. 24, 1990). Rule was the fourth AAG in Charge of the Antitrust Division, serving from 1986 until shortly after President Reagan left office. Apparently the Department of Justice filed no objections to the last of the consolidations, the merger of USAIR with Piedmont. This was probably due to the earlier lack of success in influencing the outcome of similar merger situations.

Interestingly, in the Doles' campaign autobiography, despite her relative longevity at the helm of the DOT, Elizabeth Dole devotes little space to that phase of her career and makes no comment whatsoever concerning the plethora of mergers or the agency's benevolent stance toward them. The topic should have been included on pp. 229–32 of B. and E. DOLE (with R. N. Smith), THE DOLES: UNLIMITED PARTNERS (1988).

40 All starred consolidations were announced in 1986, just one year after the demise of the CAB.

which had previously acquired Henson and Empire.[41] In each case the result of the marriages has been a growth of the power of the surviving airline at one or more of its hubs.[42] Ignoring the growing regionalized concentration, however, the DOT argued that the mergers stimulated national competition, contending that in the "national air transportation market" there was competition among hubs and that the threat of potential entrants in each of the hubs would effectively keep down fares and ensure satisfactory service.[43]

Forgotten or ignored by the DOT was the fact that for deregulation to work, there had to be competition on *all* levels, even *within* the hub cities themselves. For potential competition to be a valid threat to an existing entity, a new entrant has to be able to enter the market. When the number of gates or takeoff and landing slots was limited at an airport and with the majority of them controlled by one or sometimes two airlines, as was the case in most of the affected cities, the chance for new entrants in the field was slim, and the existing carriers could and did act accordingly.[44]

Nevertheless, with the benefit of hindsight it is easy to blame the "subsequent deterioration of the airline industry" solely on de-

---

41 Payne & Ticer, *What's Standing Between USAir and Piedmont*, BUSINESS WEEK, Oct. 5, 1987, at 40; Valente & Rose, *Concern Heightens About the Airline Industry's March Toward Near Domination By Only a Few Major Carriers,* Wall Street Journal, Mar. 10, 1989, at A12. Note that we have not included the Delta merger with Western or American's acquisition of AIRCAL, neither of which appreciably increased the concentration of a single carrier at any specific airport.

42 As a result of deregulation, many airlines opted for a new route system. Whereas before they had flown an interactive nonstop system, afterwards they changed to a "hub and spoke" system. Thus, to go from point *x* to point *y*, the traveller starting from *x* often had to fly to point *z* and change to a plane bound for point *y*. As a result, for many trips the distance traveled and the time spent grew significantly. In a Brookings Institution study, Steven Morrison and Clifford Winston suggest that as a result of the change the average length of a trip increased 5.4%, not including the increased possibility of additional delays (THE ECONOMICS OF AIRLINE DEREGULATION 22 [1986].

43 Rule to author (Mar. 24, 1990).

44 Alfred Kahn to author (Nov. 16, 1990). *Note: The Antitrust Implications of Airport Lease Restrictions,* 104 HARV. L. REV. 548–66 (1990).

regulation, but that unfairly places all the blame in one place, exonerates the often less-than-competent airline management and overlooks the fact that many of the airlines were in poor economic health before deregulation. Ironically, the cutthroat pricing strategy employed in the industry suggests that there may indeed have been a "national market," at least for some routes, and that management adopted poor strategies for gaining or protecting profits and market share. Finally, bigger-is-better is not always true. It is difficult to understand why every airline, with the possible exception of Alaska Air, felt compelled to expand, rather than to concentrate on simply developing and enlarging its existing markets.

The situation was replicated in other areas of the transportation industry, although the results were not so disastrous for those involved in the amalgamations. In the railroad sector, the number of major players decreased by at least one third. Furthermore, several branched out acquiring interests in other companies providing air, truck, or barge service.[45] In trucking there was a parallel amalgamation, but it was not so obvious because the industry was much more fragmented; nevertheless, the market share of the four largest carriers rose roughly 10% during the first Reagan administration alone.[46]

Deregulation also brought greater competition to other indus-

45 CSX Corp. acquired American Commercial Lines (a barge operator), Sea-Land Corp. (an ocean-going hauler), and Texas Gas Transmission (a pipeline operator). Burlington Northern acquired El Paso Natural Gas in addition to various small truckers which it amalgamated into BN Motor Carriers, Inc.; and Norfolk and Southern purchased a controlling interest in Piedmont Aviation which it later sold, allowing the company to be acquired by USAIR; see *supra*. For a discussion of this phenomenon, see Dempsey, *Antitrust Law and Policy in Transportaion: Monopoly Is the Name of the Game*, 21 GA. L. REV. 560–64 (1987).

46 Sacasas & Glaskowsky, *Motor Carrier Deregulation: A Decade of Legal and Economic Conflict*, 18 TRANSP. L.J. 197, 210 (1990); and Dempsey, *Transportation Deregulation—On a Collision Course?* 13 TRANSP. L.J. 329–92 (1984), and *supra* note 45, at 575–6. The subsequent surge in airline bankruptcies was matched only in the area of bus transportation; here, however, several other factors were responsible for the corporate difficulties.

tries. These included, but were not limited to, many aspects of the financial markets,[47] the energy industry,[48] and communications.[49]

For the consumer, then, in most cases deregulation was beneficial, at least over the short term. Longer range, if one were to use the most all-encompassing test—the burgeoning of passenger miles flown on scheduled airlines—even taking into account the ultimate fate of several of the carriers, one should probably label it a success.[50]

Guidelines

Mergers

Background

One of the goals of the Reagan antitrusters was to remove corporate uncertainty from the equation. In the area of mergers, Meese put it succinctly: "We wanted to do away with the 'Russian Roulette' approach to the Clayton Act." He explained that this had entailed companies being told to "go ahead and merge, and if it violates the law, we will bring a case against you."[51]

---

47 For instance, the Monetary Control Act of 1980 (PL 96–221; 12 U.S.C. § 226 n., 248, 261) and the Garn–St. Germain Act of 1982 (PL 97–320; 12 U.S.C. § 226), plus the relaxation of controls on interest rates.

48 For instance, the Department of Energy Organization Act of 1977 (PL 95–91; 3 U.S.C. § 19, 5 U.S.C. § 101 et seq., 7 U.S.C. § 916, 15 U.S.C. § 766 et seq., 42 U.S.C. § 2,201 n., 7,101 et seq., which substituted the Department of Energy's Federal Regulatory Commission for the Federal Power Commission, and the Natural Gas Policy Act of 1978 (PL 95–621; 15 U.S.C. § 330n., 3,311 et seq., 42 U.S.C. § 7,255).

49 For instance, the 1981 and 1982 amendments to the Communications Act allowing lotteries to decide who should receive certain licenses and lengthening the term of a license before the need for renewal. Furthermore, the Federal Communications Commission deregulated cable companies, authorized direct satellite broadcasting, eliminated time constraints on advertising, and terminated content regulations in radio broadcasting.

50 Kahn, *Airline Deregulation—A Mixed Bag, But a Clear Success Nevertheless*, 16 TRANSP. L.J. 229 (1988); Hawk, *Airline Deregulation after Ten Years: The Need for Vigorous Antitrust Enforcement and Intergovernmental Agreements*, 34 ANTITRUST BULL. 267–305 (1989).

51 Meese to author (Apr. 23, 1993).

Until the publication of the *Report of the Attorney General's National Committee to Study the Antitrust Laws* in 1955, no specific statement existed detailing what would lead a merger to be opposed by the Antitrust Division.[52] Many were dissatisfied with the *Report* because, although it set forth a lengthy list of criteria to be utilized in evaluating the legality of a merger, it offered no way to quantify or rank them. Nevertheless, despite the lack of precision, little concerted effort was expended to expand upon the *Report*'s parameters for more than a decade.

The first specific merger guidelines were issued by the Department of Justice in May 1968, and over the succeeding years, they were utilized unevenly.[53] If anything, the criteria were too stringent, and they totally ignored the claim of efficiencies resulting from a proposed consolidation—a fundamental tenet of the Chicago Schoolers.

The Reagan Merger Guidelines

Fourteen years later the Reagan administration issued new, updated, more specific, but less rigorous Guidelines.[54] The 1982 Guide-

---

52 It should be emphasized that the report was not issued by the Antitrust Division and, thus, was not until later incorrectly characterized as a guideline. Before, company planners had had to sift through speeches and interview transcripts to divine what corporate actions might be attacked and what would be ignored.

53 The complete text of all the Guidelines issued from this date through 1984 can be found in the appendices of ABA, HORIZONTAL MERGERS: LAW AND POLICY (Monograph No. 12, 1986). William Blumenthal chaired the task force that wrote the monograph. Also see 2 Trade Reg. Rep. (CCH) ¶ 4,510.

54 Eleanor Fox's application of the new Guidelines to the section 7 Clayton Act cases that had previously been argued in the Supreme Court demonstrates that many of them would not have been brought had the new parameters been in effect at the time of the filing. (*The New Merger Guidelines—A Blueprint for Microeconomic Analysis*, 27 ANTITRUST BULL. 575–91 [1982]). Herbert Hovenkamp notes succinctly that the difference between the 1968 and 1984 Guidelines "is the degree of danger that the Justice Department perceived in market concentration . . . [and] the concentration level at which mergers are considered to be dangerous" (*Antitrust Policy after Chicago*, 84 MICH. L. REV. 220 n. 37 [1985]). On the other hand, John E. Scarbrough and Malcolm R. Pfunder identify situations in which the new Guidelines were at least as strict as their predecessors (*New Merger Guidelines Not Always Less Restrictive*, Legal Times, Jan. 10, 1983, at 19.)

lines also failed to provide a simple litmus test to determine the legality of a specific merger. They included no instant "relevant market" calculation and no magical market computation; they did, however, provide a listing of factors to be considered in attempting to make such determinations.

In an effort to quantify merger effects more precisely, the antitrusters adopted the Herfindahl-Hirschman Index [HHI] to

---

For a thoughtful analysis, *see* Werden, *Market Delineation and the Justice Department's Merger Guidelines*, 1983 DUKE L.J. 514–79 (1983). At the time, Werden held the post of Senior Economist at the Antitrust Division.

The Federal Trade Commission took a parallel action on June 14, 1982, releasing a STATEMENT OF THE FEDERAL TRADE COMMISSION CONCERNING HORIZONTAL MERGERS, *reprinted in* 2 Trade Reg. Rep. ¶ 4,516.

For a good overview of the reactions to the Guidelines, *see Symposium: 1982 Merger Guidelines*, 71 CALIF. L. REV. (1983): among its participants were Eleanor Fox (*The 1982 Merger Guidelines: When Economists Are Kings?*, at 281–302), Stephen Calkins (*The New Merger Guidelines and the Herfindahl-Hirschman Index*, at 402–29); Robert G. Harris and Thomas M. Jorde (*The 1982 Merger Guidelines: Market Definition in the Merger Guidelines: Implications for Antitrust Enforcement*, at 464–96), Phillip Areeda (*Justice's Merger Guidelines: The General Theory*, at 303–10), Louis B. Schwartz (*The New Merger Guidelines: Guide to Governmental Discretion and Private Counseling or Propaganda for Revision of the Antitrust Laws?*, at 575–602), Thomas Kauper (*The 1982 Horizontal Merger Guidelines: Of Collusion, Efficiency and Failure*, at 497–534), and Donald I. Baker and William Blumenthal, (*The 1982 Guidelines and Preexisting Law*, at 311–47). Former AAGs, Kauper and Baker offer especial insights: the former wishing for lower threshold levels, while being prepared to accept a broader efficiency defense so as not to deter "salutary mergers;" the latter identifying the definition of market as the most significant contribution of the Guidelines. Each provide important understanding into the thought patterns of the enforcers as they deal with day to day or crisis determinations.

Also see ANTITRUST POLICY IN TRANSITION: THE CONVERGENCE OF LAW AND ECONOMICS esp. 147–338 (E. M. Fox and J. R. Halverson eds. 1984), including pieces supporting and castigating the new regulations; and a note entitled *An Economic Analysis of the 1982 Justice Department Guidelines for Horizontal Mergers*, 67 MINN. L. REV. 749–92 (1983). In addition, 6 RESEARCH IN LAW AND ECONOMICS: ANTITRUST AND REGULATION (R. O. Zerbe ed. 1984) contains two valuable pieces on the subject: Fisher & Sciacca, *An Economic Analysis of Vertical Merger Enforcement Policy*, at 1–133; and Rogowsky, *The Justice Department's Merger Guidelines: A Study in the Application of the Rule*, at 135–66.

measure the relative concentration of an industry and the market shares of the merging companies.[55] Antitrust Division reaction to a proposed merger would depend on the concentration in its industry and on the size of those involved in the proposed amalgamation; the lower the index, the less a chance of opposition, with 1,000 seen as a threshold.[56] Above 1,000, the chances of governmental action grew more and more certain. Two years later, in an effort to "spell things out and make them more understandable," an update was issued.[57] The growing importance of foreign competition was specifically addressed, and the new Guidelines built

---

55 Without delving into the intricacies of the HHI, it is simply another way of calculating the relative concentration of an industry. Although it is complicated, upon careful study, it can be understood, even by noneconomists. The Department of Justice release announcing the new Guidelines utilized 20% of the 15 page document to describe the HHI. Briefly, were one to add the squares of the market shares of the factors in a specific industry, one would have its HHI. Using the example from the Guidelines, in a simplified market of only four firms, two with 30% shares and two with 20% shares, the HHI would equal 30 squared plus 30 squared plus 20 squared plus 20 squared or 900+900+400+400 or 2,600. The new Guidelines divided markets into "unconcentrated" (HHI below 1,000), moderately concentrated (HHI between 1,000 and 1,800), and highly concentrated (HHI over 1,800). (The complete text of the Department of Justice press release, along with a statement by Attorney General William French Smith on the subject, can be found in 27 ANTITRUST BULL. 619–31 [1982]).

In their useful article on the subject, Neil B. Cohen and Charles A. Sullivan, while noting difficulties with the HHI, view it as helpful for providing "guidance from economic theory" in merger policy decision making (*The Herfindahl-Hirschman Index and the New Antitrust Merger Guidelines: Concentrating on Concentration*, 62 TEX. L. REV., 507 [1983]). *Also see The Herfindahl-Hirschman Index as a Market Structure Variable: An Exposition for Antitrust Practitioners*, 27 ANTITRUST BULL. 593–618 (1982), pp. 593–618. These two explanations of the HHI are probably the best available. *Also see* Peutler, *A Guide to the Herfindahl Index for Antitrust Attorneys*, in 5 RESEARCH IN LAW AND ECONOMICS: ANTITRUST AND REGULATION 167–90 (R. O. Zerbe ed. 1983).

56 Although originally calculated in decimal form, in an effort to make the index easier to understand, AAG Baxter multiplied the figures by 1,000 to yield whole numbers (New York Times, Feb. 2, 1981, at D1).

57 According to McGrath, before 1982, trying to determine the reaction of the Antitrust Division was akin to "reading tea leaves." As "one of the few Assistant Attorney Generals who had actually practiced in the field for an extended period," he wanted to be certain that the Department's position would be

in "enormous additional flexibility for mergers among companies in distressed industries."[58]

The value of the Guidelines cannot be measured by analyzing their content alone; attention must also be paid to whether courts considered them in evaluating mergers, *and* to whether subsequent AAGs would adopt and follow them. In the former instance, they were cited almost immediately;[59] in the latter, it is still too early to draw accurate conclusions.[60]

Vertical restraints[61]

The Reagan guidelines promulgated in an attempt to eliminate uncertainty as to the direction of the enforcement policy of the administration, the Guidelines released in January 1985 focused on three areas that had been the center of significant controversy in the preceding years:

1. Territorial and customer restraints: restrictions on the area in which, or customers to which, a buyer is permitted to resell goods purchased from a seller.
2. Exclusive dealing arrangements: a requirement that a buyer deal only with a specific seller or that a seller deal only with a particular buyer or group of buyers.

---

clear for both lawyers and corporate executives. The Vertical Guidelines were published with the same intentions (McGrath to author, Jan. 21, 1993).

58 McGrath, *Necessary Flexibility Is Already Present Under the 1982 and 1984 Merger Guidelines*, 55 ANTITRUST L.J. 13, 18–19 (1986). *Also see* Bronsteen, *A Review of the Revised Merger & Guidelines,* 29 ANTITRUST BULL. 613–52 (1984); and Salop & Simons, *A Practical Guide to Merger Analysis*, 29 ANTITRUST BULL. 663–703 (1984).

59 *See*, for instance, United States v. American Cyanimid, 719 F.2d 558, 566–7 (2d Cir. 1983); United States v. Waste Management Inc., 793 F.2d 976, 982–3 (2d Cir. 1984).

60 In April 1992 the Bush administration announced "standards that will clarify [the] guidelines" used to determine when mergers will be challenged. Davidson, *U.S. Will Issue Revised Guidelines on Antitrust Issues*, Wall Street Journal, Apr. 1, 1992, at C27. Initial analysis of the new regulations suggests that they will further relax the rules.

61 Vertical restraints are contractual provisions designed to control relationships among firms doing business at different levels of the market distribution system.

3. Tying arrangements: a requirement that a buyer of a product or service purchase another, distinct product or service as a condition for the purchase of the first.[62]

Vertical arrangements deployed by companies with small market shares—where such arrangements would not raise prices—would be lawful. The Guidelines contained a series of tests similar to those that measured merger legality to ascertain the possible competitive effects of an arrangement.[63] A firm or group of firms considering adoption of such a vertical arrangement could submit a request to the Department for screening and for an indication of future enforcement intentions. The quick look would yield a determination of safe harbor or place the arrangement in a suspect category. In the former case, no further action would be taken; in the latter, after informing the company, a more detailed market study would be undertaken before tendering the opinion.

Although the measurements were difficult to make and even harder to agree upon, the importance of the policy in detailing the need to apply the rule of reason to this area of commercial regulation cannot be overemphasized. The Guidelines may be technically flawed, but they must be viewed in the context of their time; thus they were an important step forward because they eliminated some uncertainty.[64]

---

62 For the complete text of the Guidelines, including sample calculations for the various tests, *see* Bureau of National Affairs, *Regulatory and Legal Developments, Justice Department's Vertical Restraints Guidelines*, Daily Report for Executives, Jan. 24, 1985, at B1.

63 If the firm employing the restraint had a share of the market of 10% or less it could take advantage of the exclusion, provided that the Vertical Restraint Index (the VRI is calculated by squaring the market share of each firm in the market party to the arrangement) was less than 1,200 and the coverage ratio (the coverage ratio is the percentage of each market involved in the restraint) was less than 60%.

64 Sims & Lande, Vertical Restraints Guidelines: A Step Forward, Legal Times, Mar. 4, 1985, at 5; *also see* Fisher, Johnson, & and Lande, *Do the DOJ Vertical Restraint Guidelines Provide Guidance*," 32 ANTITRUST BULL. 609–42 (1987). For a less glowing evaluation, see Gellhorn and Fenton, *Vertical Restraints during the Reagan Administration: A Program in Search of a Policy*, 33 ANTITRUST BULL. 543–73, esp. 567–73 (1988).

International operations

The Reaganauts also brought up to date the Division's Guide for International Operations, promulgated in January 1977.[65] Draft Guidelines were first made public for comment in early 1988, but there is no easily available public record of the text. According to AAG Rule, "A lot of the conduct that was condemned in the past turns out to have been efficient conduct that enabled firms to compete more vigorously. . . . The courts are more reluctant to condemn that type of activity today than they were ten or eleven years ago."[66] Finally, in November, the Department of Justice Antitrust Enforcement Guidelines for International Operations were published.[67] They were little changed from those offered in the earlier draft. Although they did not attempt to provide a précis of foreign law, they did provide a blueprint for enforcement during the last months of the Reagan administration.

It should be emphasized that each of the Guidelines simply set forth one administration's interpretation of the antitrust corpus and detailed how it would be enforced. Guidelines lack the power of law and thus were binding neither on future regimes nor on the courts. Not surprisingly, therefore, the Reaganauts also sought to codify the regulations, thereby ensuring that their interpretation of the corpus would endure beyond 1988.

Legislative proposals

Key to understanding the legislative proposals of the Reagan administration is its conclusion that the United States economy had to be able to compete more effectively in the world arena. This

---

65 U.S. DEPARTMENT OF JUSTICE, ANTITRUST DIVISION, ANTITRUST GUIDE FOR INTERNATIONAL OPERATIONS, JAN. 26, 1977 (and revised Mar. 1, 1977) (1977).

66 Washington Post, June 8, 1988, at D3.

67 Even this text is difficult to access. It is included, however, in J. P. GRIFFIN, U.S. INTERNATIONAL ENFORCEMENT: A PRACTICAL GUIDE TO THE JUSTICE DEPARTMENT GUIDELINES B–101–B–147 (Bureau of National Affairs, Inc., Corporate Practice Series, 1989).

belief was enunciated most clearly by the President's Commission on Industrial Competitiveness in January 1985,[68] which suggested that the antitrust corpus be modified to reflect the reality of the global market and to recognize the efficiencies that could be recognized from mergers.[69]

Three relatively minor pieces of legislation were passed during the first Reagan administration. The Export Trading Company Act of 1982 eased antitrust strictures on companies involved in exporting American products.[70] The National Cooperative Research Act of 1984 reduced the possibility of exposure to the laws by companies engaging in joint research ventures.[71] Supported by the administration and backed by a broad bipartisan group in Congress, the Shipping Act of 1984[72] allowed shipping companies to fix prices,

---

68 PRESIDENT'S COMMISSION ON INTERNATIONAL COMPETITIVENESS, GLOBAL COMPETITION: THE NEW REALITY (2 vols. 1985). This prestigious group comprised executives from "blue-chip" American corporations (AT&T, B. F. Goodrich, Deere, Hewlett-Packard, Owens-Illinois, Rockwell, and Westinghouse), trade union leaders (from United Auto Workers and the AFL–CIO), and professors and administrators (from Harvard University and the University of Wisconsin).

69 Vol. 1 at 39–41, 58; vol. 2 at 188–93; *also see Report of the President's Commission on Industrial Competitiveness: Hearing before the Subcommittee on Economic Stabilization of the House Committee on Banking, Finance, and Urban Affairs*, 99th Cong., 1st Sess. 109 et seq. (1985).

70 PL 97–290; 15 U.S.C. § 4,001 et seq. The Act was designed to increase United States export of goods and services by encouraging more efficient provision of trade services to exporters and by reducing the restrictions on financial institutions' relationships with exporters. An exporter could obtain a certificate from the Department of Commerce with the concurrence of the Department of Justice if they could reach a consensus that such an agreement would not adversely affect trade patterns within the United States.

71 PL 98–462; 15 U.S.C. 4,301 et seq. In more legal terms, it required U.S. courts to judge the competitive effects of joint research and development (R & D) under a rule of reason standard that balanced the procompetitive benefits against any potential anticompetitive effects. It also limited relief that might be obtained to actual rather than treble damages where the challenged conduct was within the scope of a notification filed by the joint R & D venture with the Attorney General and the FTC.

72 PL 988–237; 46 U.S.C. § 1,701, 1,701n., 1,702 et seq.

coordinate schedules, and share revenues based on the premise that there existed an inelastic amount of available tonnage. Updating the Shipping Act of 1916, the 1984 Act was designed to eliminate uncertainties arising from the passage of time and from changing judicial interpretations.[73] None of the new legislation altered the major thrust of the antitrust corpus, and each built on a well-established precedent of granting exemptions to sectors of the economy or to groups viewed as requiring special attention. Nevertheless, a large number of companies quickly opted for the protection offered by the legislation.[74]

In February 1986 the administration sent a series of bills to the Congress as part of an antitrust reform package designed to update the antitrust and international trade law by "modernizing the disincentives and incentives" with which antitrust litigants must deal:[75]

1. The Merger Modernization Act, amending section 7 of the Clayton Act to treat only those mergers with the "significant probability" of lessening competition (essentially just replacing the wording "tend to" and "may be"[76]).[77]
2. The Antitrust Remedies Act, designed to restrict treble damage awards to cases involving overcharges or underpayments, to allow

---

73 *Maritime Conferees Near Vote*, New York Times, Feb. 14, 1984, at D24; for a fine treatment of the background of the bill, *see* Giduck, *The Shipping Act of 1984: A Return to Antitrust Immunity*, 14 TRANSP. L.J. 153–77 (1985).

74 Baldridge speech to the Antitrust Section of the American Bar Association Convention, *reported in* 49 Antitrust & Trade Reg. Rep. (BNA No. 1224), at 156 (July 18, 1985).

75 Ginsburg to author (Feb. 2, 1987; Feb. 8, 1989). *Also see* Ginsburg, *The Reagan Administration's Legislative Initiative in Antitrust*, 31 ANTITRUST BULL. 851–69 (1986)

76 In other words, for a merger to be attacked as illegal it would require a significant probability (much more than a "possibility") that competition would be harmed. According to Secretary of Commerce Malcolm Baldridge, the original language was a "mealy mouthful," 50 Antitrust & Trade Reg. Rep. (BNA No. 1268), at 980, 989 (June 5, 1986).

77 S. 2160, 99th Cong., 2d Sess., 132 CONG. REC. 26, 2281–82 (1986).

the United States government to recover treble damages, to allow recovery of counsel fees by some prevailing defendants, in some instances to permit the reduction of treble damages to single, and to set the time at which interest on the award payments should begin (the time of the infraction, rather than the time of the award).[78]

3. The Distressed Industries Bill, allowing the President to grant an antitrust exemption for up to 5 years for mergers in domestic industries injured by competition from imports.[79]

4. The Foreign Trade Bill, facilitating motions to dismiss actions in cases involving trade with foreign nations.[80]

5. A bill relaxing the prohibitions on interlocking directorates in section 8 of the Clayton Act.[81]

In the antitrust perspective, the first three were the most important items on the administration's legislative agenda. The Merger Modernization Act emphasized the thrust of the administration against actions deleterious to the welfare of the consumer. Combinations viewed as anticompetitive increased a corporation's ability to exercise "market power," with market power being defined as the ability of "one or more firms profitably to maintain prices above competitive levels for a significant period of time." Generally, this legislation followed the parameters of the 1984 Guidelines.[82] Thus it is no surprise that the bill also allowed an "efficiencies defense" or excuse. The Antitrust Remedies Act was in part a reaction to the filing of an increasing number of private treble damage suits.[83] Although originally included as a means of

---

78 S. 2162, 99th Cong., 2d Sess., 132 CONG. REC. 26, 2284–87 (1986).

79 S. 2161, 99th Cong., 2d Sess., 132 CONG. REC. 26, 2284–87 (1986).

80 S. 2164, 99th Cong., 2d Sess., 132 CONG. REC. 26, 2288–89 (1986).

81 S. 2163, 99th Cong., 2d Sess., 132 CONG. REC. 26, 2287–88 (1986).

82 For a good analysis of the legislation, *see Reagan Administration's Antitrust Revisions*, BANKING EXPANSION REPORTER, Mar. 3, 1986, at 4; but *also see* Adams & Brock, *The Proposed Emasculation of Section 7 of the Clayton Act*, 65 NEB. L. REV. 813–22 (1986); and Krattenmaker & Pitofsky, *Antitrust Merger Policy and Merger Administration*, 33 ANTITRUST BULL. 211–32 (1988).

83 For a sample of the debate on the subject, *see* Easterbrook, *Detrebling Antitrust Damages* 28 J.L. & ECON. 445–65 (1985); and Hovenkamp, *Treble Damage Reform* 33 ANTITRUST BULL. 233–58 (1988).

stimulating opposition to anticompetitive behavior, supporters of the legislation believed that treble damages had come to have the effect of deterring hard-but-fair competition, in which the consumer benefited from aggressive pricing. Further, AAG Douglas Ginsburg wondered aloud whether some of the filings had been made with the hope of reaching lucrative out-of-court settlements; the prospect of single damage awards would not be as alluring and thus might cut down on such frivolous suits. The AAG often stressed that treble damages would remain in place for all cases in which there had been overcharges that actually had been harmful to the consumer.[84] Overall, the change would probably have resulted in a larger sum of monies accruing to the government.[85] The Distressed Industries Bill would have allowed companies to merge over the following 5 years in areas defined as distressed, in return for refraining from requesting policies defined as "protectionist" for the following 10 years. The brainchild of Commerce Secretary Baldridge (with the exception of the DOT, his arm of government was the least hospitable to antitrust enforcement), this had the least support and, at the time, was recognized as having the least likelihood of becoming law.

The Foreign Trade Bill set forth the standards under which the antitrust corpus should be applied to corporate conduct abroad. Here the idea of efficiency was supplemented with that of stimulating exports. It is noteworthy that no such relaxation of the corpus was considered when dealing with imports.

The amendment to the Clayton Act ban on interlocking direc-

---

84 *See*, for instance, Bureau of National Affairs, *Regulatory and Legal Developments*, Daily Report for Executives, Nov. 15, 1985, at A15; *also id.*, *Regulatory and Legal Analysis*, Jan. 13, 1986, at C–1.

85 For a relatively sympathetic treatment of the detrebling question, *see* Cavanagh, *Detrebling Antitrust Damages: An Idea Whose Time has Come?* 61 TUL. L. REV. 777–847 (1977). By 1987, Donald F. Turner had become convinced that, in some cases, detrebling would be correct (*Anticipating Antitrust's Centennial: The Durability, Relevance and Future of American Antitrust Policy*, 75 CALIF. L. REV. 811–12 [1987]). On the other hand, *see* Correia & Budieri, *Antitrust Legislation in the Reagan Era*, 33 ANTITRUST BULL. 374–83 (1988).

tors actually brought the statute up to date, for it raised the threshold for application of the statute up to inflation-adjusted levels. Additionally, it provided that if companies were not in direct competition, they could have common directors even if their worth surpassed the levels set forth in the bill.

The success rate for the legislation was near zero. A bill relaxing the ban on interlocking directorates was passed by the Senate in 1987,[86] but no similar bill was even introduced in the House. Undeterred, the administration reintroduced most of the legislation in the following session—where it experienced a similar fate.

Procedure and structure

In line with its all-encompassing economic philosophy, the Reaganauts understood that antitrust enforcement had many different ramifications. It is thus not surprising that the responsibility for enforcement activities appears to have become more broadly shared. Although opinions differ as to whether the responsibility became divided or whether the Division was simply more receptive to the input of other government enforcement agencies, there is no doubt that during the Reagan era, antitrust became part of the "Bigger Picture," with its activities brought more into synchronization with the policies of other branches of government.[87]

Internal interaction

In November 1984, on foreign policy grounds, Reagan ordered the Antitrust Division to halt an investigation into the airline passenger traffic market between the United Kingdom and the United States. In fairness, such intercessions were not new: They can be traced back at least to the 1950's, when the Eisenhower administration halted a merger investigation involving the Aluminum Corp. of America and British Aluminum. At roughly the same time there

---

86 S. 1086.

87 Moore, *DOJ Sharing of Antitrust Policy Power Criticized*, Legal Times, Jan. 21, 1985, at 2.

was a Sherman Act case against the United Fruit Co. in which the Department of State became intimately involved.[88]

In early 1984, the Antitrust Division was confronted with the possibility that the country's largest steel producer, United States Steel Corp. would acquire National Intergroup Corp., the parent of National Steel. At about the same time LTV Corp., the nation's third-largest steel maker, requested permission to take over Republic Steel Corp., the fourth-largest producer. Complicating the already difficult task of defining the market was the problem of imports and the effect of restrictive quotas on some of the products in question. Public opposition to the amalgamations focused on the plans of Big Steel, while the Antitrust Division looked at the larger picture. Bowing to pressure, U.S. Steel abandoned its plans and, after loud protestations from well-placed politicians, from Trade Representative William Brock, and from Commerce Secretary Baldridge,[89] a compromise was reached in which LTV and Republic

---

88 The materials on the aluminum investigation are still classified; the closed file (60–0–37–250) is in the Department of Justice papers stored in the Federal Records Center, in Suitland, Maryland.

For background on the United Fruit Co. case, *see* T. KOVALEFF, BUSINESS AND GOVERNMENT DURING THE EISENHOWER ADMINISTRATION 62–65 (1980). Also, *see* the Department of Justice release dated February 4, 1958. A complete set of Department of Justice releases is housed in the School of Law collection of the Libraries of Columbia University in New York City.

89 The differences were not only argued behind closed doors, they also found their way into the press. *See*, for instance, Baldridge, *Halting the LTV-Republic Steel Merger: How to Ruin an Entire Industry*, New York Times, Mar. 11, 1984, at 3:2; Bureau of National Affairs, *McGrath Leaves Antitrust Division after "Redoing" Antitrust, Achieving Enforcement Goals*, Daily Report for Executives, Apr. 9, 1985, at C–1. The rhetoric quickly became heated; in referring to a Baldridge-inspired Commerce Department proposal to repeal section 7 of the Clayton Act, AAG McGrath stated that the proposal, "as a technical matter, does not make sense" (*60 Minutes with J. Paul McGrath, Assistant Attorney General Antitrust Division*, 54 ANTITRUST L.J. 131, 137-[1985]).

Also see Henderson, *"Efficiency" Becomes Yardstick for Mergers; Antitrust Chief Says Goals Achieved*, Washington Post, Mar. 24, 1985, at H1; for a fine note on the subject, *see* Loeb, *Antitrust Implications of Domestic Mergers: A Proposal for the Treatment of Imports and Its Application to LTV-Republic*, 60 N.Y.U.L. REV. 667–701 (1985).

agreed to fix-it-first[90] by selling two mills to eliminate any overlap.[91] Unfortunately, neither the divestiture nor the merger had the desired results. In the former case, the divisions were sold to a weak firm which could do little to strengthen them; in the latter, the two aging steel makers with out-of-date plant and equipment found they could not compete any more successfully combined than they could apart. All too soon after the merger was consummated, the successor company filed for bankruptcy protection.[92]

The reaction to the merger between two corporations whose principal business was rail transportation—the Southern Pacific Co. (SoPac) and Santa Fe Industries, Inc.—illustrates that some of the administrative bodies were concerned with promoting competition. Cooperating with the Antitrust Division while allowing the amalgamation to proceed, the Interstate Commerce Commission [ICC] refused to let the two companies commingle their rail assets and required that the operations of SoPac be placed under the control of independent trustees pending the regulatory body's determination on the merger. As the two had many miles of parallel trackage throughout much of the West and Midwest, the ICC reflected the Justice Department's concern that competition would be diminished in these areas.[93] The ICC's subsequent disapproval of the merger

---

According to McGrath, Baldridge felt very strongly about the U.S. Steel action but did not really care about the LTV amalgamation. Indeed, when Big Steel backed off, "he was so bent out of shape it was unbelievable" (McGrath to author, Jan. 21, 1993).

90 *Infra*, p. 240.

91 Baker, *A Look at the "New" Antitrust Policy; Why Was the LTV-Republic Decision Such a Surprise?* NAT'L. L.J., Mar. 12, 1984, at 13; Behr & Isikoff, *Election Year Threat; Mergers Prompt Administration Split*, Washington Post, (Mar. 11, 1984, at A1; memorandum from McGrath to D. Lowell Jensen, Acting Deputy Attorney General, concerning Department of Justice Clearance of the LTV/Republic Steel Merger (Mar. 20, 1984), *reprinted in* 5 Trade Reg. Rep. ¶ 50,465.

92 Simison & Blumenthal, *LTV Corp. Files for Protection from Creditors Under chapter 11*, Wall Street Journal, July 18, 1986, at 3.

93 The case is extremely interesting for those who specialize in market definition. The railroads argued that the strongest competition emanated not

essentially reflected the Justice Department's position, for it required massive divestiture as a prerequisite to sanctioning the merger. The extent of the required divestiture was so great that the railroad ultimately decided to sell the SoPac division *in toto*. In May 1988 the Justice Department approved its sale to Rio Grande Industries, operator of the Denver & Rio Grande Railroad, noting that the "two carriers . . . serve no competing routes."[94] In August the ICC placed its imprimatur on the transaction.[95]

The contrast in attitudes and interpretation between the ICC and the DOT is most striking; in the former, there was close cooperation with the Antitrust Division; in the latter, the advice and counsel of the Antitrust Division was ignored and it had little possible recourse. As a result, competition was seriously injured in the airline industry.

Growth of interstate banking

As interstate banking began to be legalized, many banks made acquisitions beyond their original market area. The growing concentration of the nation's banking industry was the result not so much of the Reagan administration's more benign view of consoli-

---

from each other but from trucks and barges. Justice countered, saying, "While trucks and other modes compete with railroads for certain traffic, there is overwhelming evidence . . . that, in the region of the merger, trucks are at a distinct competitive disadvantage for large shipments . . . particularly bulk commodities moving in large volumes over long distances" (Feaver, *ICC Urged to Reject Rail Merger*, Washington Post, Oct. 23, 1985, at F3). The DOT testified before the ICC in support of the merger, stating, "Except in those relatively rare situations where competition is reduced [and with divestiture or guarantee of track rights this would be vitiated], the merger is consistent with the public interest" (*Justice Dept. Had Urged Rejection of Deal on Tuesday; DOT Endorses Merger of Santa Fe, SP*, Los Angeles Times, Oct. 24, 1985, at 4:7). For a good analysis of the reaction of the ICC, *see* Dempsey, *supra* note 45, at 567–69.

94 Rosenblatt, *Justice Department Endorses Sale of Southern Pacific*, Los Angeles Times, May 7, 1988, at 4–2.

95 Jouzaitis, *ICC Backs S. Pacific Sale to Rio Grande*, Chicago Tribune, Aug. 10, 1988, at Bus. Sec. 3.

dations as it was of the new definition of markets and the necessity to merge failing institutions with sounder ones to protect depositors. As a result of the latter situation, several banks that had been trying to broaden their horizons were finally able to do so with the blessing of the Federal Deposit Insurance Corporation.

Sale of government assets

One of the Reagan 1980 campaign themes was opposition to "Big Government." Not only did this entail cutting back or eliminating special programs, it also was meant to include the transfer of various federal responsibilities to the private sector. Although it was not until the last years of his second administration that Reagan finally formed a committee to study the ramifications of privatization, from the first he considered various governmental activities and trusts as potential candidates for sale.[96] Additionally, as a means of cutting the deficit such divestitures were most attractive to the administration, for they would generate significant, albeit one-time, revenues useful in closing the budget gap even if the income generated did not count in the Gramm-Rudman Deficit Reduction Act calculations. From the beginning, one of the most attractive candidates for this treatment was the Consolidated Rail Corp. [Conrail].

Although DOT Secretary Elizabeth Dole the wife of Robert

96 PRESIDENT'S COMMITTEE ON PRIVATIZATION, PRIVATIZATION: TOWARD MORE EFFECTIVE GOVERNMENT: REPORT OF THE PRESIDENT'S COMMITTEE . . . (1988). *See also* Cowan, *Calculating the Bottom Line of "Privatization,"* New York Times, Apr. 3, 1983, at 4:5; Ricter, *Private Business Doing Public Tasks*, Los Angeles Times, May 23, 1985, at 1:1. Interestingly, there was no meaningful disposition of the federal land holdings; for a lucid explanation, *see* R. Nelson, *Privatization of Federal Lands: What Did Not Happen*, in REGULATION AND THE REAGAN ERA: POLITICS, BUREAUCRACY AND THE PUBLIC INTEREST 132–65 (R. E. Meiners & B. Yandle eds. 1989).

Despite the rhetoric, however, the privatization of Conrail and Amtrak was not included in the Heritage Foundation's blueprint for the Reagan administration; *see* MANDATE FOR LEADERSHIP: POLICY MANAGEMENT IN A CONSERVATIVE ADMINISTRATION (C. L. Heatherly ed. 1981) and MANDATE FOR LEADERSHIP II, CONTINUING THE CONSERVATIVE REVOLUTION (S. M. Butler, M. Sanera, & W. B. Weinrod eds. 1984).

Dole, the Republican Senate leader, was definitely in favor of the concept of privatization, she acted very slowly in the case of Conrail, and it was not until February 1985 that she finally made public her plans for its disposition. Instead of marketing it to the public—certainly the "free-est" of all free market solutions—she proposed a sale to Norfolk Southern Corp., ignoring the fact that the two firms had many miles of parallel trackage. In fairness, however, there was some method to this proposal. A direct stock sale plan would entail some possible pitfalls: first, the legitimate fear that the market might not be able to absorb the entire offering all at once (there had never before been a stock offering of such a magnitude), thus necessitating a two- or three-stepped sale; second, were it to be sold, its price might be too low, and, whether or not the charge was legitimate, the ramifications of having "played into the hands of the speculators" would be politically unpalatable, especially in view of the Doles' 1988 presidential ambitions. On the other hand, sale to Norfolk Southern would ensure that it would be run by a well-managed, financially secure entity. With the help of her husband, a plan to sell the line to Norfolk Southern was passed in the Senate; in the House, however, it failed due to Democratic opposition led by Congressman John Dingell, who strongly backed the public offering route.[97]

A second major hurdle to the Norfolk Southern purchase was the problem of antitrust concerns. Although the Antitrust Division had been quoted as saying that the divestiture of some competing operations should "on its face" solve the problems, it never formally withdrew its objections.[98] The Heritage Foundation, a conservative think tank which supplied much of the personnel of the Reagan administration, strongly favored the public offering route, for it wanted to replicate the British experience with successful divestitures of such state-owned companies as British

97 Elizabeth Dole ascribes partisan motives to Dingell, noting that he hoped the Democrats would regain control of the Senate in the next election, thus facilitating his plan to re-regulate the railroads (*supra* note 39, at 255–56).

98 Feaver, *Norfolk Southern Scraps Bid to Buy Conrail from U.S.; Plan for Public Sale of Freight Line Gathers Steam*, Washington Post, Aug. 23, 1986, at Bus. Sec. 1.

Telecom.[99] Furthermore, other competing carriers continued to be vocal in their opposition. In the end, these factors, coupled with Dingall's opposition, forced Secretary Dole to alter her plans.

In March 1987, at a price of more than $1.6 billion, in the largest initial public offering up to that time in United States history, the government sold the entire Conrail system to the public. The transaction included a number of restrictions, all of which were designed to ensure that the company would remain a vigorous transportation competitor:

- Capital expenditures had to remain over $350 million per year.
- Common stock dividends were limited to ensure continued corporate health.
- No individual owner could hold more than 7.5% of the common
- stock, and foreign ownership would be capped at 20%.
- Norfolk Southern would be barred from applying to the ICC to merge with or to control the company.[100]

Thus, while in the end the Conrail privatization reached the correct destination, it was due neither to the Reagan agenda nor to the DOT but instead to the combined forces of other potentially affected corporations and to influential Democrats allied with the Reagan Antitrust Division.

Amicus interventions and judgment modifications

The filing of amicus briefs in cases believed to involve important questions of antitrust policy, though not a departure from previous policy, grew in significance during the Reagan years.[101] Clearly,

---

99 Smith, *Is This Any Way to Sell a Railroad?*, FORTUNE, May 25, 1987, at 91.

100 For a complete listing of the stipulations, *see House Panel Approves Measure to Sell Federal Portion of Conrail*, Antitrust & Trade Reg. Rep. (BNA), at 239 (Sep. 18, 1986).

101 *See*, for example, U.S. DEPARTMENT OF JUSTICE, OFFICE OF THE ATTORNEY GENERAL, ANNUAL REPORT OF THE ATTORNEY GENERAL OF THE UNITED STATES 129–30 (1985).

if an administration wishes to expand on the ambit of a statute it can file a case of its own. If, on the other hand, it wants to narrow or alter the focus, it must seize upon opportunities created by private actions. Frustrated in its attempts to change the existing statutes, the Antitrust Division spent significant resources reviewing pending cases in the courts of appeals for possible amicus participation as a means of maximizing the long-term impact of its policy.[102] Additionally, the Supreme Court routinely sought Justice Department and FTC input when treating private cases. This was in keeping with the traditional deference shown in administrative law cases to the opinions of agencies charged with enforcing the relevant statutes.[103] Justice's intervention in *NCAA v. Board of Regents*[104] illustrates the use of the amicus process to alter the thrust of the law: The government brief argued for the use of the rule of reason approach in an area that previously might well have been decided solely on per se terms.[105] While performed to enhance the program of the Division, this policy had the added effect of aiding those parties on whose side the government intervened.

In the area of consent judgment modifications and terminations, as was the case in previous instances when there was a change of party in the White House, the new administration reviewed many of the outstanding decrees. According to Baxter, the Division gave special attention to those that prohibited companies from making

---

102 Litvack, *Government Antitrust Policy: Theory versus Practice and the Role of the Antitrust Division*, 60 TEX. L.REV. 649–60, esp. 652 (1982). Note that he opposes this.

103 Campbell, *The Antitrust Record of the First Reagan Administration*, 64 TEX. L.REV. 354 (1985).

104 104 S. Ct. 2948 (1984).

105 Brief for the United States as Amicus Curia at 13–15. It should be noted that while the NCAA lost the action, it did so on "rule of reason"–based economic analysis, with the Court delving into possible economic alternative schemes. As Campbell noted, "The result is precisely what the Justice Department wanted: an analysis of the economic efficiency underlying a horizontal agreement, an analysis that would have been entirely foreclosed in a *per se* approach" (p. 357). Important precedent was now in place for use in future actions.

vertical arrangements or entering new lines of business. It also attempted to vacate decrees that had barred the sharing of research without the permission of the Division.[106] The average number of modifications and terminations rose in comparison to the number entered during the Carter administration (from an average of 17.5 per year to 21.125 per year), but this was due, in part, to three exogenous factors:[107]

- Carter administration–instigated policy that limited the maximum length of the decrees to 10 years (note that the figures for the terminated decrees include those which expired.[108]
- Provisions of the Hart-Scott-Rodino Antitrust Improvements Act[109] that required companies larger than a specified size to notify the government of any merger plans (note that this duplicated stipulations in many of the decrees, thus rendering them redundant).
- Changes in the judicial interpretation of the corpus. Prior to 1977 all agreements restricting the allocation of territories, distributors, or franchisees had been viewed as illegal per se. In *Continental T.V. v. GTE Sylvania, Inc.*, (1977), the Supreme Court had ruled that such compacts could be legal, thus paving the way for a subsequent rule of reason treatment of each such arrangement.[110]

As is evident from the appended listing, many of the terminations simply brought the agreements into line with the new interpretations.

---

106 Meadows, *supra* note 4, at 188.

107 For exact figures see chart entitled "Work Load Statistics" in Appendix.

108 The standard boiler-plate language utilized read, "Automatic termination after ten years reflects the Government's belief that in most cases the anticompetitive effects from any proscribed practice will likely be eliminated after such a period. Market conditions can, and often do, change a great deal in a decade." It was not possible to break out the number of expirations prior to 1981. (*See* Appendix A, Consent Decrees: Terminations and Modifications; *see*, for instance, case involving Rome and Haas Co.)

109 PL 94–435; 15 U.S.C. § 1,311 et seq.

110 433 U.S. 366, *reversing* United States v. Arnold, Schwinn & Co., 388 U.S. 365 (1967).

In a departure from long-established policy, AAG Baxter had ceased entering companion civil actions with the criminal filings. Although initially the second filing might have appeared redundant, settlement of civil actions can include injunctive relief, violations of which could involve different and sometimes heavier penalties than stipulated in the antitrust corpus. Barter nevertheless argued that, with the increased penalties for antitrust transgressions, this streamlined the process without diluting the deterrent effect. In line with this change, when the only strictures remaining in a consent decree were those reiterating Sherman Act prohibitions, the existence of the statute was viewed as sufficient protection against recidivism.

Staffing and funding[111]

In the 1970's, the authorized staffing of the Antitrust Division had increased by slightly more than one third (see figure), some-

Figure: Staffing and Funding

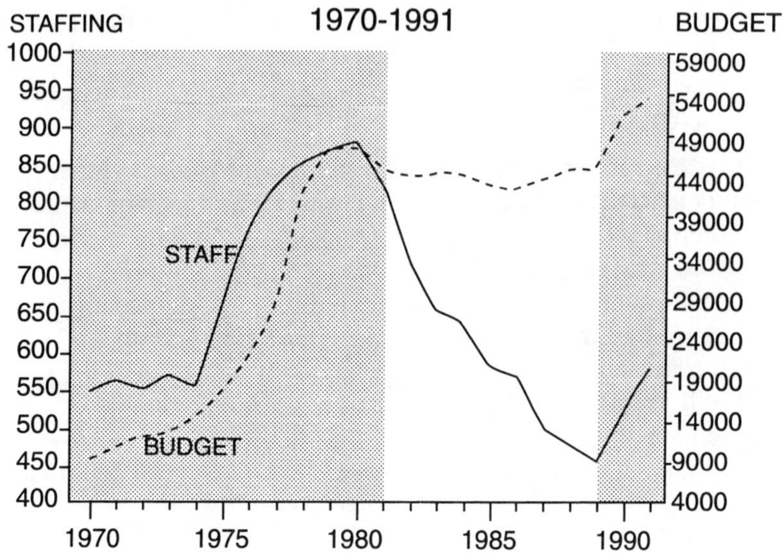

---

111 For exact figures see chart entitled "Staffing and Funding" in Appendix.

what less than the rate of increase for the rest of the Washington bureaucracy. Largely due to more modernized management techniques and equipment, more efficient use of staff, and, in part, the result of the ease of application of the Guidelines, the Division was one of the few branches of government that actually fulfilled the Reagan goal of cutting back in size. Not only did the number of authorized employees fall by 42%, the actual staffing plummeted 46%, indicating that the leadership of the Division must have been in agreement with the overall policy. Additionally, during the Reagan years, the Division's total budget shrank by slightly more than 5%. Considering that the starting salary of lawyers entering the Division rose from $23,566 to $28,852 per year, an increase of 22.4% during the period, and that the annualized average inflation rate was 4.2%,[112] this amounted to a significant cutback.

Economist reviewers

Probably the most conclusive illustration of the growing influence of economists in the Antitrust Division was the change in review procedure implemented by Charles F. Rule when he was Acting AAG. Removing lawyers from the initial screenings of all proposed mergers and replacing them with economists, the move, probably partially designed as an economy measure, also illustrated how intertwined antitrust had become with economic theory. To those who attacked the reorganization as placing the review procedure in the hands of "conservative economists," Rule responded, "A large number of the filings [under the Hart-Scott-Rodino Act] only require someone to read it once and see if it's not a problem. . . . [This will allow] our lawyers to focus on cases that might amount to something."[113]

---

112 Thus, for the period, the Consumer Price Index rose roughly 39%.

113 Kurtz, *Justice Shifts Antitrust Responsibilities; Switching Initial Review to Economists Said to Further Weaken Merger Enforcement*, Washington Post, Dec. 11, 1986, at D9. For a sample of the form required to be completed by merging companies, see T. W. Brunner, T. G. Krattenmaker, R. A. Skitol, & A. A. Webster, Mergers in the New Antitrust Era 273–94 (1985).

The "numbers"

Sherman Act actions

The number of cases alleging violation of sections of the Sherman Act increased dramatically during the Reagan years.[114] During the tenure of J. Paul McGrath, the second AAG, the Division conducted a careful review of the enforcement process. The Division's Criminal Task Force drew up a report that was never made public; in essence, however, the report set forth an agenda that stressed Sherman Act–based activities, an emphasis which continued for the

Figure: Cases Filed

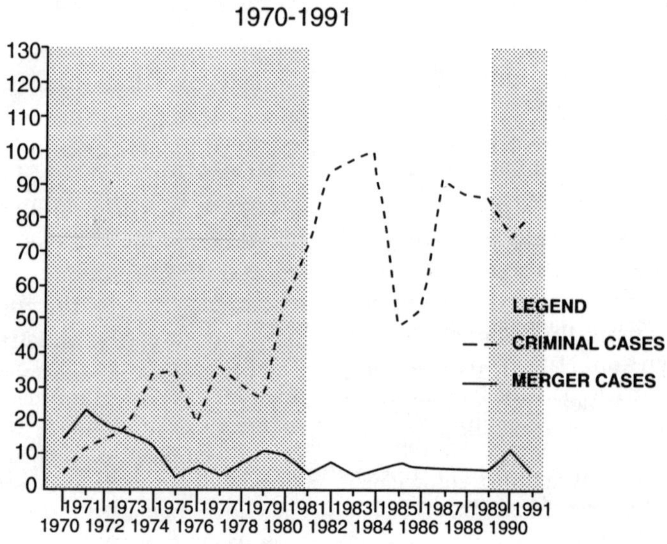

114 In a most thought-provoking piece, William Kovacic notes, however, that the number of actions against truly large firms decreased due mostly to "Modern developments in antitrust learning, doctrine, and corporate counseling," *Federal Antitrust Enforcement in the Reagan Administration: Two Cheers for the Disappearance of the Large Firm Defendant in Nonmerger Cases*, in 12 RESEARCH IN LAW AND ECONOMICS 182–83 (R. O. Zerbe ed. 1989).

rest of the Reagan years.[115] The succeeding AAG, Ginsburg, followed the same path but took an even sterner position, attacking the "tendency of federal courts to treat antitrust felons leniently by fashioning sentences involving community service, instead of sending them to jail." He further pressed for "stiff fines and jail sentences in antitrust persecutions."[116]

Rule, Reagan's last AAG, stressed on many occasions the importance of focusing almost exclusively on bid-rigging and price-fixing cases. His "number one priority . . . [was] simple: criminal cases and more criminal cases," and the policy followed during his tenure reflected this persuasion.[117] And he supported increasing the fine for Sherman Act violations from $1 million per count to $10 million.[118] Even after taking into account the numbers caveat, it is clear there was no letup in this type of antitrust enforcement activity—indeed, as figure on page 236 demonstrates, the number of criminal actions filed in district courts alleging various types of restraint of trade was more than double the average for that of the preceding decade or administration. The results were similar for the results of the filings. For 4 of the 8 years of the Reagan presidency more than 100 individuals were indicted for infractions of the Sherman Act (see figure p. 238), a

---

115 Bureau of National Affairs, *supra*, note 89.

116 Bureau of National Affairs, *Antitrust Chief Stresses Prosecution of Bid Rigging*, Daily Report for Executives, Nov. 15, 1985, at A15. Nevertheless, he too did not preach antitrust simply for antitrust's sake, noting that the Division's objective is "to forestall private conduct inimical to competition and to ensure that antitrust enforcement, both public and private, does not discourage business firms from efficient procompetitive conduct."

117 Rule to author (Mar. 24, 1990); Marcus, *Rule Defends Antitrust Enforcement*, Washington Post, Sep. 4, 1987, at F1; *Antitrust Chief Is New; Policy Isn't*, INDUSTRY WEEK, Sep. 21, 1987, at 6. Cases brought alleging violation of the Sherman Act can be either civil or criminal; all cases treating Clayton Act section 7 violations (mergers) must be tried as civil actions. Allegations of price-fixing or bid-rigging are per se criminal charges.

118 *Antitrust Chief Urges Stiffer Corporate Fines*, Chicago Tribune, Oct. 30, 1988, at 11C.

Figure: Individuals Indicted and Days of Jail Served

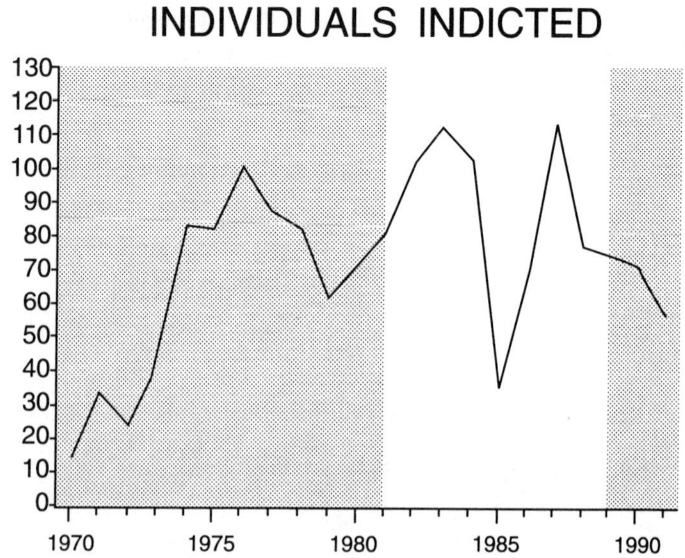

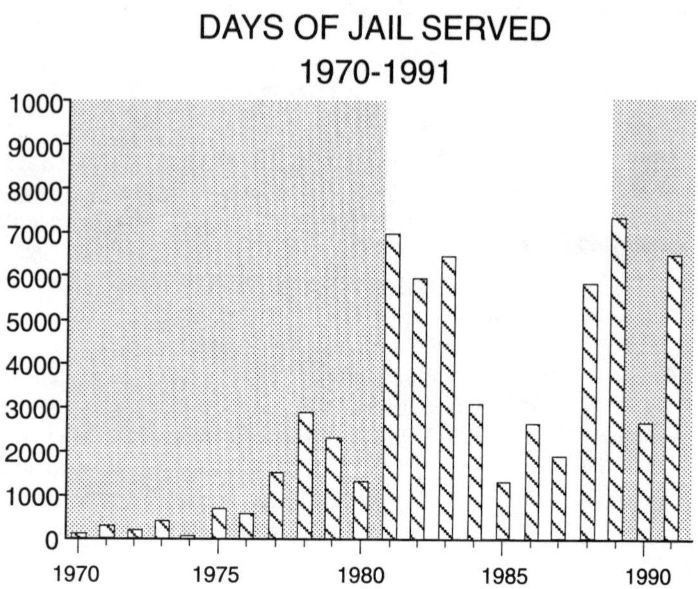

number surpassed only once previously (in 1976); the total fines assessed and paid, even in inflation-adjusted dollars, rose to record levels; and the number of days served in correctional facilities by executives either found guilty or pleading *nolo contendere* (see figure p. 238) was more than double the yearly average during any previous administration.[119]

Clayton Act actions

Perusal of Clayton Act enforcement statistics does not offer a similar yield. For the most part, the Reaganauts believed that takeovers were beneficial, both for those directly involved and for the economy as a whole:[120]

> The evidence is overwhelming that successful takeovers substantially increase the wealth of shareholders in target companies. . . . Economic theory therefore suggests, and available evidence confirms, that merger and acquisition transactions are, on average beneficial for stockholders in both bidder and target firms. . . . The evidence is strong that takeovers generate aggregate net benefits to the economy.[121]

---

119 Statistics for the period vary widely from publication to publication. Indeed, in the Attorney General's annual reports, the numbers are not identical from year to year. For the chart entitled "Workload" included in the appendix, we have chosen to use officially provided Department of Justice Workload Statistics for the period 1970–1990. The author would like to thank Ms. Jackie Frend Vassanelli and Ms. Mary Ann Berry of the Office of Operations of the Antitrust Division of the Department of Justice for their help in assembling the figures. For 1991, the numbers were taken from *Antitrust Division's Workload Data Over the Past 10 Fiscal Years*, Antitrust & Trade Reg. Rep. (BNA), at 79–90 (Jan. 23, 1992).

120 Perhaps the best refutation of this belief can be found in the works of Walter Adams and James Brock. They demonstrate that the most competitive and efficient firms are not necessarily the largest; mergers forming such firms promote neither efficiency nor competition. *See*, for instance, THE BIGNESS COMPLEX; INDUSTRY, LABOR, AND GOVERNMENT IN THE AMERICAN ECONOMY (1986), *The "New Learning" and the Euthanasia of Antitrust*, 74 CALIF. L. REV. 1516–66 (1986), and *Joint Ventures, Antitrust, and Transnational Cartelization*, 11 NW. J. INT'L. L. & BUS. 433–83 (1991).

121 COUNCIL OF ECONOMIC ADVISERS, ECONOMIC REPORT OF THE PRESIDENT 197–98 (1985).

> . . . [A]n active merger market is a health threat to incompetent management. . . .[122]

It is undeniable that during the Reagan era the number of corporate mergers consummated burgeoned, while the number attacked shrank measurably. Many other factors besides governmental benevolence played a role in the growth of corporate marriages. For the most part, the Reagan years were a time of prosperity; during periods of economic expansion the number of mergers increases whether or not the government is in the hands of those amenable to such activities.[123] Furthermore, the increase in certainty brought about by the more clearly defined guidelines allowed corporations to plan their actions with a greater degree of confidence.[124]

Some of the largest mergers in United States history were arranged during this period, with what appears to have been nary a whimper from Washington. In actuality, much more transpired behind the scenes. In a number of cases, fix-it-first avoided legal confrontations.[125] In essence, this involved a process in which companies with merger plans would meet with officials in the Antitrust Division, or in other cases the FTC, and shortly thereafter would receive permission to continue with their plans, provided they fixed-it-first—usually via the divestiture of certain competing portions of the two companies which would have made the marriage illegal under the Clayton Act.[126] Pursuant to the Hart-Scott-Rodino

---

122 *St. Joe-Homestake, Kennecott Deals Highlight Current Antitrust Liberalization*, METALS WEEK, Sep. 22, 1986 at 3.

123 Similarly, in times of recession, the number of mergers decreases; illustrative of this is the falloff in corporate combinations during the latter years of the Bush administration.

124 Langenfeld & Scheffman, *The FTC in the 1980s*, 5 REV. OF INDUS. ORG. 88 (1990).

125 *"Fix it First": The Value of Early Antitrust Planning*, Legal Times, Apr. 7, 1986, at 31.

126 In 1986 Charles Rule, then Deputy Assistant Attorney General, would note: "Unlike any past administration, we've developed a fix it first doctrine for antitrust policy. . . . Why stop an entire merger if simply one-tenth of the assets create an anticompetitive problem?" Quoted in Lewis, *The Reagan Revolution in Antitrust*, N.Y.L.J., Sep. 21, 1989, at 1.

Act, all companies with assets over $15 million had to notify the government of their merger plans at least 30 days in advance of the closure of the deal.[127] Thus there was no chance that a consolidation could be missed. The listing that follows includes the largest mergers of the period, providing likely explanations for why they were allowed to proceed.

E. I. Dupont de Nemours and Co. / Conoco Co. (1981)
Occidental Petroleum Corp. / Iowa Beef Processors, Inc. (1981)
United States Steel Corp. / Marathon Oil Co. USX Corp. (1982)
Chevron Corp. / Gulf Oil Corp. (1984)
LTV Corp. / Republic Steel Corp. (1984)
Texaco Inc. / Getty Oil Co. (1984)
Mobil Corp. / The Superior Oil Co. (1984)
Philip Morris Companies, Inc. / General Foods Corp. (1985)
General Motors Corp. / Hughes Aircraft Co. (1985)
Reynolds (R. J.) Industries, Inc. / Nabisco, Inc. (1985)
Allied Corp. / The Signal Companies, Inc. (1985)
Baxter Travenol Laboratories, Inc. / American Hospital Supply Corp. Baxter International (1985)
Burroughs Corp. / Sperry Corp. Unisys Corp (1986)
Occidental Petroleum Corp. / Midcon Corp. (1986)
General Electric Co. / RCA Corp. (1986)
British Petroleum Co., PLC / The Standard Oil Co. (Ohio) (remaining 45%)
Chrysler Corp. / American Motors Corp. (1987)
Philip Morris Companies, Inc. / Kraft Inc. (1988)
Campeau Corp. / Federated Department Stores, Inc. (1988)
Bridgestone Corp. / Firestone Tire and Rubber Co. (1988)
Grand Metropolitan, PLC / The Pillsbury Co. (1988)

Not included in this compilation are the transactions that were leveraged buyouts [LBOs] but are often listed as mergers due to the necessity of merging the bought-out company into a new corporate entity to complete the transaction. We make this exclusion because there was no increase in the size of the corporation in question; prime examples include the Kohlberg Kravis

127 PL 94–435 (1976); 90 Stat. 1383.

Roberts [KKR] buyouts of RJR Nabisco and Beatrice Foods Corp.[128]

The DuPont, Occidental-Iowa Beef, and U.S. Steel transactions involved companies in fields that were different from those of the acquiring company, making them conglomerate-type mergers.[129] From the 1960's onward, members of the Division had been interested in extending the ambit of the laws to cover conglomerate mergers, but with little success. The closest they ever came was the negotiated ITT settlement, ironically tainted because of the Watergate scandal.

In both the Chevron and the Texaco mergers and the purchase of the remaining portion of the public shares of Standard Oil of Ohio, as part of the fix-it-first mechanism, the resultant companies agreed to sell off portions of their businesses where they had been in direct competition.

The Mobil purchase of Superior Oil was accomplished with no objections from the FTC.[130] Superior Oil was valuable for its reserves, and Mobil made the transaction to supplement its dwindling holdings.

Ironically, the reason that Hughes Aircraft elected to seek a buyer rather than to remain independent was based on the tax laws. Absent Internal Revenue Service pressure, it is unlikely that the Howard Hughes Medical Institute would have felt the need to sell the securities. As General Motors [GM] had no parallel lines and had not previously indicated any interest in entering the field, there was no basis for Justice Department opposition. Had Hughes not been

---

128 See *infra* pp. 246–7. When writing of the LBOs, Joe Sims and Robert Lande note that the leveraged buyouts are "without even a hint of an antitrust problem" (*New Forces Chip Away at Agencies' Policy of Antitrust Abandonment*, Legal Times, Apr. 20, 1987, at 14).

129 There was one small area of overlap: Conoco did have a joint venture with Monsanto Co., a major competitor of DuPont. After opposition from the Justice Department, as part of a consent agreement this was dissolved before the takeover was consummated (1982 Trade Cas. ¶ 64,479).

130 *FTC Permits Mobil to Buy Superior Oil*, Wall Street Journal, May 17, 1984, at 53.

acquired by GM, the company would not have remained independent; instead, it likely would have been taken over by either the Ford Motor Co. or the Boeing Co., other finalists in the bidding.[131]

The R. J. Reynolds and both Philip Morris takeovers were viewed as attempts by the two cigarette giants to cut down on what they considered to be overdependence on a single product supporting their bottom lines—cigarettes. As such, the move was seen as strengthening the two entities while having no ill effects on the consumers.

The Baxter Travenol takeover of American Hospital Supply was complicated by American Hospital's early efforts to resist Baxter's advances, one of which had been the invocation of the antitrust laws, noting that each company had interests in several overlapping fields. Fix-it-first enabled Baxter to dispose of portions of these holdings both before and after the takeover was consummated.[132]

The Allied Chemical acquisition of the Signal Companies was similarly facilitated by an agreement with the Justice Department to sell its air turbine business by the end of the year,[133] thus fixing-it-first.

Although the Burroughs Corporation was profitable, it was not able to compete effectively in the computer industry. Sperry was in worse straits.[134] It was easy to argue that by allowing Burroughs to swallow up the failing Sperry, it would be stimulating competition in the computer industry.

After having taken over Cities Service[135] and Iowa Beef Proces-

---

131 Nag & Harris, *High Tech Drive: GM's Winning Offer for Hughes May Set Heavy Industry Trend*, Wall Street Journal, June 6, 1985, at 1, 14.

132 Wall Street Journal, Aug. 9, 1985, at 31; Nov. 27, 1985, at 14; and Dec. 24, 1985, at 14. According to Ginsburg, "The relief we obtained was substantial" (Ginsburg to author [Feb. 1, 1993]).

133 Wall Street Journal, July 31, 1985, at 28.

134 Ironically, the July 1955 Sperry merger with Remington Rand formed a company larger than IBM. Nevertheless, it was soon surpassed by "Big Blue."

135 See *infra*, 246.

sors, Occidental Petroleum Corp. acquired Midcon, one of the nation's largest pipeline operators, as part of its efforts to become one of the "majors." To "help clear up antitrust problems" it sold Mississippi River Transmission, a unit of Midcon, to Arkla, Inc.[136] There appear to have been no further difficulties after agreement to the divestiture.

The General Electric [GE] takeover of RCA could only transpire after an agreement that the merged entity divest itself of radio and television outlets in the markets in which the two companies competed directly. Several other divisions were also sold as part of a fix-it-first bargain. FCC regulations limiting the number of outlets a company could own mandated the radio and television sales. According to Ginsburg, analysis of other areas of overlap yielded only one of major significance. Here, there was only one customer involved, the Department of Defense. The DOD was "indifferent to the merger."[137] Nevertheless, there was an eerie irony to this consolidation because the 1932 divestiture of RCA from GE has been viewed by many as one of the main ingredients in fostering the competition in the electronics industry that stimulated its stunning growth over the next decades.

Chrysler's absorption of American Motors was allowed because American was a failing company. It was hoped that, with the addition of the Jeep line, the merger would strengthen the nation's third-largest and weakest auto maker so it could compete better with both domestic and foreign rivals.

Federated Department Stores had been in play for some time, with Campeau and R. H. Macy the finalists in the battle over acquisition. After several rounds of increased bids, Macy agreed to withdraw from the contest provided that Campeau sell it the I. Magnum and Bullocks divisions. As Campeau already had exposure in the markets served by the two divisions, this could be viewed as an example of a "preemptive fix it first action."[138] Although it is more

---

136 Moffett, Arkla *Will Buy Unit of MidCon For $305 Million; Sale Should Clear the Way for Occidental's Merger with Gas Pipeline Firm*, Wall Street Journal, Feb. 25, 1986, at 12.

137 Ginsburg to author (Feb. 1, 1993).

138 New York Times, Mar. 29, 1988, at D1; Mar. 30, 1988, at D1; Mar. 31, 1988, at D1; Apr. 1, 1988, at D3; and Apr. 2, 1988, at 33.

difficult to ascertain whether the subsequent disposition of the Brooks Brothers and Filenes' Basement divisions was made to raise cash or for antitrust reasons, the divisions were, nevertheless, quickly sold.

Not all of the consolidations ended so happily for their proponents:[139]

The Coca Cola Co. / Dr. Pepper Co. (1986)
PepsiCo Inc. / Seven-Up Division of Philip Morris (1986)
United States Steel Corporation / National Intergroup Inc. (1984)
Mobil Oil Co. / Marathon Oil Co. (1981–1982)
Gulf Oil Co. / Cities Service Co. (1982)

In each of these instances there were clear-cut infractions of the Guidelines, and the Reaganauts moved to interdict the amalgamations—sometimes with the help of the company being acquired.[140]

Philip Morris had been attempting to shed its slow-moving Seven Up division for some time and was delighted when PepsiCo showed interest in purchasing it. Perhaps as a tactic to thwart its arch rival, Coca Cola attempted to acquire Dr. Pepper. When the FTC indicated its opposition to the deals (they would harm many small independent bottlers), PepsiCo retreated, purchasing only the overseas portion of the company. Coca Cola was more persistent, not surrendering until after the takeover was blocked in Federal Court. Shortly thereafter, Dr. Pepper was taken private in an LBO led by A&W owner Hicks & Haas. Later in the year, the same group bought the domestic Seven-Up properties, making the new entity the third-largest soft drink company in the United States.[141]

---

139 In addition to those mentioned *infra*, the antitrusters attacked a number of smaller mergers. Most illustrative of the Reaganaut philosophy, this group includes the Heinz (H. J.) Co. (Star-Kist) takeover of Bumble Bee (it would result in 53% of the market in the hands of one company) and the Pacific Resources purchase of a Shell Oil Corp. division in Hawaii.

140 Carter, *Yes, Antitrust Can Still Say No*, FORTUNE, Sep. 1, 1986, at 63. Note that in several cases it was the FTC and not the Antitrust Division that actually objected to the mergers.

141 A good treatment of the case can be found in L. J. White, *Application of the Merger Guidelines: The Proposed Merger of Coca Cola and Dr. Pepper*, in THE ANTITRUST REVOLUTION 80–98 (J. E. Kwoka, Jr., & L. J. White eds. 1989).

Marathon Oil's steadfast opposition to Mobil's unfriendly acquisition offer, buttressed by government hostility, set the stage for "white knight" U.S. Steel's purchase of the company.[142]

In the early 1980's, one of the most undervalued of all the oil companies was Cities Service. As such, it became the object of T. Boone Pickens's Mesa Petroleum's interest. To avoid Pickens's clutches, Cities Service sought an alternate and friendly merger partner, Gulf. The government opposed the union on antitrust grounds, and another haven, Armand Hammer's Occidental Petroleum, was finally found.

While companies were increasing their size via acquisition, some were also adjusting to the times by restructuring or divesting parts of their operations. Not only did General Electric acquire, it also shed units, the most outstanding being the disposal of its Utah International Division, as it refocused its efforts on high technology and financial services. Many of the "go-go" conglomerates of the 1960's sold off companies they had previously acquired, in order to concentrate on core businesses. In a trend that continues today, ITT, Teledyne, and Gulf and Western slimmed down, using the proceeds of their divestitures to purchase other more relevant businesses, to pare debt, or to share with their stockholders. Most notable, one of the pioneer conglomerates, Gulf and Western, divested numerous divisions, including those involved in agricultural operations, in cigar manufacturing, industrial and consumer products. Both it and IC Industries actually sold the division around which their companies had originally been formed.[143] Shortly after having disposed of its auto supply businesses, Gulf and Western renamed itself Paramount Communications, Inc. and

---

142 Marathon obtained a court injunction against the Mobil merger (Marathon Oil Co. v. Mobil Corporation, et al., 530 F. Supp. 315 [1981]). Absent this, it is probable that had Mobil been willing to divest previously competing Marathon properties, the government would have, in the end, not opposed the merger. *See* F. M. Sherer, *Merger in the Petroleum Industry: The Mobil-Marathon Case*, *id.* at 19–35.

143 In the former instance, the Michigan Plating and Stamping Co. and the Beard and Stone Electric Co.,

announced its determination to concentrate on movies, publishing, and sports; after selling its railroad interests, IC (Illinois Central) Industries renamed itself Whitman Corp., stating that it planned to emphasize food and consumer goods.

Other companies also refined their interests as they purchased divisions that had been shed because of fix-it first or because of corporate restructuring. Often such transactions reinvigorated the line and in the process injected new potency into the company as a whole. While selling off its domestic animal feed business (in 1986), Ralston Purina acquired Continental Baking from ITT and the Eveready line from Union Carbide. Determined to be more market driven, it then disposed of its other slow-moving, cyclical agricultural commodities divisions and fast-food restaurants. Black & Decker Inc. acquired General Electric's housewares division and added new vigor to the already competitive market.

The LBO was refined during the Reagan years as it achieved mega-deal status with KKR's $6.3 million buyout of Beatrice Foods and its subsequent even larger deal involving RJR-Nabisco. Lost in the rhetoric attacking LBOs was the fact that the object was often subsequently slimmed down as the buyers attempted to raise money to lessen their debt load via the sale of various divisions of their newly acquired company. Many times, divisions were divested to their managers, creating new entrepreneurial opportunities.

Unintended consequences of export enhancement policies

In an effort to stimulate exports, Reagan policy makers sought to lower the cost of the dollar. They were very effective in this regard: by 1986, the value of the yen, versus the dollar, had appreciated to such an extent that instead of requiring ¥ 226 to purchase $1, only ¥ 162 were needed. During the same period, the purchasing power of the French franc increased from 2.385 to 1.475 to the dollar. Although appreciation of foreign currencies was not universal, it is incontrovertible that the dollar depreciation did increase exports as, suddenly, American goods were priced much more competitively on the world market. At home depreciation lowered the cost of American companies themselves; as a result, many were bought by foreign enterprises.

In the first 6 months of 1988, for instance, foreign buyers spent $31.3 billion in 151 transactions to acquire American companies.[144]

The Bridgestone Tire's acquisition of Firestone Tire and Rubber simply substituted a new factor in the American market. Until the transaction, Bridgestone had been an inconsequential player in that market. Had the Japanese company not completed the purchase, it is likely that one of the European tire makers would have bought the company. There appears to have been no Justice Department or FTC opposition, as competition may well have been stimulated by the appearance of an aggressive new entrant in the American market.

Grand Metropolitan Limited's [Grand Met] unsolicited takeover bid for Pillsbury led to one of the most bitter corporate struggles of the era. In attempting to evade the clutches of the British conglomerate, Pillsbury had sought several other possible merger partners, including Unilever, but to no avail. There appear to have been no antitrust objections to the takeover, possibly because Grand Met likely informed Justice of plans to sell a number of divisions after the merger was consummated. Ironically, the event that was, probably, most harmful to competition in this drama was the subsequent sale of the Pillsbury grain-processing operations to a unit of Conagra, already a significant factor in the field.[145]

Conclusion

The question remains: Was there a "Reagan revolution" in the field of antitrust as a whole? Alas, there is no clear answer. As we have seen, the country had evolved markedly in the period since the 1960's; and were one to have posed the question, juxtaposing the record of the 1960's with that of the 1980's, the answer would surely have been different and affirmative. Instead, the question must be posed in the context of the late 1970's and 1980's. In much the same way as Vincent Blasi and William

---

144 *Value of Merger Deals Hits Record High in First Half*, Los Angeles Times, Sept. 27, 1988, at Bus. Sec. 8. C. Michael Aho and Marc Levinson, place this important event in historical context in AFTER REAGAN: CONFRONTING THE CHANGED WORLD ECONOMY, 158–72 (1988).

145 Wall Street Journal, Dec. 5, 1988, at B5.

Kovacic have disappointed many a conservative—the former with his conclusions based on a study of the Supreme Court and the latter with his analysis of judicial appointments[146]—the conclusion of this analysis is certain to dissatisfy many a Reagan backer. In the area of mergers, there was not a revolution but an evolution—albeit significantly speeded up—as mergers were no longer viewed with suspicion. Rather, they came to be seen by many as efficiency enhancing and hence good for the economy. Furthermore, it is noteworthy that after one places the raw numbers into context, in this case as a percentage of gross national product, the value of companies involved in mergers was not record setting; it had been higher in 1968 and 1969. When considering the record of Sherman Act enforcement, there was no change in direction, only an increase in intensity. In a slightly dated statement, Donald F. Turner, a former AAG for Lyndon Johnson and coauthor of a definitive study on the subject,[147] succinctly noted, " Some things are easier now, but anyone who ever thinks antitrust is dead is crazy."[148] Nevertheless, partially as a result of an awareness of the threat of foreign competition, by the end of the Reagan years it was possible to state, "What's good for General Motors is good for America" and not be pilloried[149]—quite a turnaround in the space of 35 years! It is not that there was no policy, it is that there was a change in national attitude—which the Reagan policies more or less reflected. In the process, it may have become too easy for companies to merge.

That there were errors of omission in Clayton Act section 7 enforcement is a proposition from which many, even some of the staunchest Reaganauts, would not dissent. On the other hand, that earlier merger policy might have gone too far is another proposition with which even such an antitrust stalwart as Donald Turner would

---

146 THE BURGER COURT: THE COUNTER REVOLUTION THAT WASN'T (V. Blasi ed. 1983); for Kovacic, *see supra* note 9.

147 C. KAYSEN & D. TURNER, ANTITRUST POLICY: AN ECONOMIC AND LEGAL ANALYSIS (1959).

148 Reilly, *Antitrust Policy After the Steel Veto*, FORTUNE, Mar. 19, 1984, at 85.

149 Contrast this with the uproar following the misquote of the confirmation hearing statement of former General Motors president, Charles Wilson: "I had always thought that what was good for the country was good for General

subsequently come to agree.[150] Regrettably, although some of the Reagan braintrusters had written extensively before entering government, few have been prolific since their return to private life. Sorely lacking are studies that demonstrate the wisdom of the policies of the 1980's, a useful counterbalance to the voluminous critical literature. Thus many a negative evaluation has gone unanswered.

A final question must be asked: Where exactly did President Reagan stand? Had he any thoughts on the subject? Had he left a record on the subject? Alas, it appears not. There was no article written years earlier, similar to that of Eisenhower's piece in the American Bar Association *Journal*,[151] not even a statement or portion of a speech in support of the antitrust corpus; on the other hand, there was nothing attacking the laws. Furthermore, a perusal of Reagan's memoirs, *An American Life*,[152] yields no reflections at all on the topic of antitrust. And it includes nary a comment on the breakup of AT&T, the IBM settlement, or the privatization of Conrail.

Be it revolution or evolution, as antitrust enters its second century, what matters most is that it is not dead. Mergers that were approved based on the premise of actual or foreign competition might, with changes in political agendas (such as, for instance, the imposition of protective tariffs, quotas or embargoes), or external events, become blatantly anticompetitive. Addition-

---

Motors . . . ," which had been turned into ". . . what was good for General Motors was good for the country."

In 1986 the Competitive Enterprise Institute even began to publish a newsletter, the *Washington Antitrust Report*. Shortly thereafter, it began to boast on its masthead that it had been "Busting Trustbusters Since '86." Such a claim would have been unthinkable scarcely a decade earlier.

See C. L. HEATHERLY & B. Y. PINES, MANDATE FOR LEADERSHIP: POLICY STRATEGIES FOR THE 1990s, 326–27 (1989).

150 Turner, *supra* note 85, at 806. *Also see* his *The Virtues and Problems of Antitrust Law*, 35 ANTITRUST BULL. 298 (1990); and Pitofsky, *Anticipating Antitrust's Centennial: Antitrust in the Next 100 Years*, 75 Calif. L. Rev. 818–20 (1987).

151 *The Middle of the Road: A Statement of Faith in America*, 35 A.B.A.J. 810–12, 879–80 (1949).

152 AN AMERICAN LIFE: THE AUTOBIOGRAPHY (1990).

ally, should exchange rates change significantly, foreign goods might well become priced out of the American market. The Sherman Act was not repealed, and the other relevant statutory authority remained essentially unchanged from the Carter days; the Warren Court's Clayton Act section 7 legacy was not overturned; if the amalgamations of the Reagan years were truly as potentially anticompetitive as some critics have charged, when and if the evidence becomes conclusive these mergers will provide the basis for future deconcentration actions. As long as the results of the AT&T settlement, the largest divestiture in history and, for the public, the epitome of antitrust, do not turn into a disaster, leading to an anti-antitrust backlash that erects political barriers to future Sherman Act section 2 and Clayton Act section 7 cases praying divestiture, another wave of antitrust activism will most assuredly begin.[153]

---

153 Naturally, this assumes that the court system will be amenable to the actions.

Shenefield, *An Open Letter to the New President of the United States*, 9 CARDOZO L. REV. 1298 (1988). William G. Shepherd lists a number of possible candidates for potential section 2 actions in *Economic Analysis to Guide Antitrust Enforcement: Prospects for Section 2* 35 N.Y. L. SCH. L. REV. 930–37 (1990).

In fairness, it should be noted that the record of success in previous section 2 Sherman Act deconcentration initiatives has been far from stellar. For a fine overview, see Kovacic, *Failed Expectations: The Troubled Past and Uncertain Future of the Sherman Act as a Tool for Deconcentration* 74 IOWA L. REV. 1105–50 (1989). *Also see* his unpublished paper, "The Rise and Fall of the Deconcentration Vision in American Antitrust Policy," prepared for delivery to the 64th Annual Western Economic Association International Conference, June 20, 1989, Lake Tahoe, NV. Going one step further, Austin, *Antitrust Reaction to the Merger Wave: The Revolution versus the Counter Revolution*, pp. 956–961, states that "Chicago is very close to accomplishing the de facto repeal of Clayton § 7, if not Antitrust." Furthermore, were any deconcentration action to be launched, he suggests that the makeup of the Supreme Court would likely checkmate any such counterrevolution in the foreseeable future. Although it is difficult to look into the future with any degree of certainty, one can just as easily disagree. Were the situation to have become egregious, the Court might well react in a different way than Austin suggests; it would not be the first time the Court changed its direction in reaction to new realities, political or otherwise.

Appendix A

Consent decrees: terminations and modifications[1]

American Cyanamid Co., 8–4–64; 8–6–82

In 1964 it held an overwhelming position in the sale of melamine. By the date of the termination, the market had changed and the agreement allowing it to produce only a limited amount was outdated, as more than 50% of the sales came from imported product.

Motor Vehicle Manufacturers Association of the United States, Inc. *et al.*, 10–29–69; modified 11–18–82

Modification allowed auto manufacturers to cooperate in auto emission equipment as permitted on a case-by-case basis. This included cross-licensing and joint research. A five-year termination date was set for the decree.

Ford Motor Co. *et al.*, 11–15–38; 3–8–83

Terminated a decree requiring Ford to treat all financing companies alike. As a result of the change, the company could attempt to stimulate sales by actions of its finance arm, offering joint promotions, etc.

---

1 The first date listed after the company name is the date of the filing of the original decree; important modifications are then listed. The final date is that of the termination. The description that follows provides background and then gives the Justice Department rationale for the change. Any explanatory material is not to be interpreted as supplied by the author, unless so specified.

The author would like to thank Ms. Laura Marin, Special Assistant to the Assistant Attorney General in Charge of the Antitrust Division (James F. Rill and then Charles James), for her help in assembling the files from which the précis were made. Note that the AT&T divestiture, which was actually a modification of the 1956 Current Decree, is included in the body of the chapter.

Wean Engineering & Foundry Co. (Wean United, Inc.), 12–3–52; 3–16–83

When entered, the judgment forced the company to cease making agreements with foreign producers of steel production equipment via licensing arrangements and territorial divisions that had the effect of allocating markets. By termination, the market had changed and the company wanted to enter into a joint venture with a foreign producer and license technology.

General Motors Corp. *et al.*, 7–28–52; 8–15–83

See Ford action *supra*, at 3–8–83.

Borax Consolidated, Ltd. *et al.*, 8–16–45 and modified on 9–28–45 and 9–25–46; 8–31–83

The consortium had been charged with controlling the world supply of borates, borax, and boric acid, with restrictive selling practices, and with allocating markets. Terminating the decree would allow United States Borax, one of the signatories, to acquire a contiguous area and mine it. In so doing, they would be more efficient "than anyone else." As the rest of the decree simply outlawed practices covered by the Sherman Act, it could easily be terminated with no possible anticompetitive effects.

Timkin Roller Bearing Co., 2–15–50; 9–7–83

The company had been accused of dividing the world market for antifriction bearings with its partially owned British and French rivals. In decree modifications in 1957 and 1958, the company was allowed to purchase the outstanding interests in the British and French entities. As a result the rationale for the decree became moot.

Chrysler Corp. *et al.*, 11–15–38; 10–3–83

See Ford action *supra*, at 3–8–83.

American Can Co., 6–22–50; 10–31–83

The company had been charged with monopolizing the manufacture, distribution, and sale of metal and fiber containers and closing equipment. As part of the agreement it had had to divest itself of its closing machinery business. By termination, the market had changed, as there were many new entrants and many companies were manufacturing for themselves. Therefore, there was no need to continue the strictures of the decree.

Continental Can Co., 6–26–50; 10–31–83

See American Can action *supra*, at same date.

Safeway Stores, Inc., 12–7–57; 11–30–83

The company had been accused of having attempted to monopolize specific markets by selling at "unreasonably low prices," posting different prices in different stores, and operating stores or departments below the cost of doing business. In the decree, the company promised not to do this. By termination, the market had changed, there was a great deal more competition and the company was "no longer in a position to use predatory pricing to dominate the industry."

Rome and Haas Co., 11–18–48; 12–21–83

The agreement, in response to the accusation that the company had participated in a worldwide cartel to fix prices and allocate territories in the sale of acrylic products, had prohibited the company from entering into such agreements, establishing prices or terms of resale, allocating markets or distribution areas, or limiting research. Citing the 10-year policy, the fact that market had changed and the cartel had been broken, and the company was selling on the international market where its competitors had exclusive dealing arrangements, the Justice Department noted that the only other stipulations contained in the decree duplicated those cited as illegal in the antitrust laws. Thus the decree was terminated.

Foster & Kleiser Co. ***et al.*****, 3–13–31; 2–4–84.**

The companies had been charged with attempting to monopolize areas of the outdoors advertising business; the original decree had enjoined the acquisition of competitors or contracting with advertisers at unfair or discriminatory prices. At termination, the Department of Justice cited the 10-year rule, the fact that the market had changed, and that the final decree was "anticompetitive" in that there cannot be aggressive pricing.

Toro Manufacturing Corp., 11–12–71; 3–5–84

The agreement was in response to the accusation that the company had fixed, stabilized, and maintained wholesale and retail prices for lawn care products by establishing and maintaining exclusive distribution sales territories. The judgment enjoined such practices, although it did allow it to " fair trade" where legal The judgment was terminated for several reasons: 1) Market conditions had changed; the company now had only 10% and the agreements could stimulate competition; 2) While, at the time of the filing, the practices were illegal per se, with the overturning of the *Schwinn* decision in *Continental T. V., Inc., v. GTE Sylvania, Inc.*,[2] they must now be judged with a "rule of reason" approach; and 3) The 10-year limit for such decrees.

Owens Illinois, Inc. (formerly Owens Illinois Glass Co.), 9–18–46; 4–4–84

The company had been charged with monopolizing and attempting to monopolize the glass container and closure market by leasing closing machinery with the proviso that only Owens Illinois products be used on the machines. The decree had enjoined such practices and included licensing provisions. By the time of termination, such tying agreements required substantial market power to be found illegal; also, the markets had changed, and another company owned twice the market share of Owens Illinois.

National Ice and Cold Storage Co. of California, Union Ice Co. *et al.*, 6–11–52; 5–21–84

The group had been charged with attempting to monopolize the ice trade in California. The market and the major products of the companies involved had changed since the filing. Instead of the sale of block ice for the transportation and display of fish, meat, and produce, their largest sales item had evolved

2 United States v. Arnold, Schwinn & Co., 388 U.S. 36 (1977).

to "party ice" (cubes). As drafted, the decree had prohibited any sales to supermarkets; thus the termination would stimulate competition. The rest of the stipulations were covered by the antitrust laws and thus were unnecessarily duplicative.

Arthur Murray, Inc. *et al.*, 11–21–58; 7–13–84

The company had tied the sale of financed dance lessons to the use of specific credit companies; in the decree this had been enjoined. Because of truth-in-lending restrictions and the growth in competition, the decree was terminated.

National Broadcasting Co. Inc., 11–28–77; modified 8–31–84

Companion cases had been filed against American Broadcasting Co. (ABC) and Columbia Broadcasting System. The modification brought the regulation governing the amount of in-house prime-time production into line with that controlling ABC.

Inco, Ltd., Electric Storage Battery Co. (ESB, Inc.) *et al.*, 11–24–47; 9–11–84

The group had been charged with having divided the world market for electric storage batteries from 1891 until 1936. The decree had called for the termination of restrictive agreements and had enjoined exclusive territories in the sale of batteries. By the time of the termination, market conditions had changed, foreign companies, hitherto precluded from doing business in the United States, had entered the domestic market, all the patents in question had expired, Inco had left the business, and the distributive arrangements were no longer *per se* illegal.

Bally Manufacturing Corp., 10–2–72; 10–29–84

The decree responded to the charge that Bally had allocated exclusive territory for its amusement and gaming equipment arms. With the overturning of *Schwinn* in *Continental T. V.*, the restrictions were no longer held to be *per se* illegal.

National Lead Co., Titan Co. Inc., E. I. duPont de Nemours and Co., 7–22–47; 11–15–84

The group had been charged with having created a worldwide cartel in the sale and production of titanium compounds. The decree had enjoined the granting of exclusive territories. At the time of the termination, market conditions had changed, National Lead (now NL Corp.) had left the business, exclusive distributorships were no longer necessarily unlawful, and the 10-year rule justified the action.

Elgin Corp., Elgin Sweeper Co., and Leach Co., 2–5–65; 12–13–84

The Elgin Corp. had been the sole agent for both Elgin Sweeper and Leach and had eliminated competition among distributors of the two companies' products. The decree had prohibited exclusive territories. At the time of the termination, because of the overturning of the *Schwinn* decision, such divisions were no longer per se illegal. The 10-year rule was also cited.

Culbro Corp., HavaTampa Corp., HavaTampa Holding Co., HAV Corp., 7–7–78; modified 12–15–84

When HavaTampa Corp., was taken over, Culbro had wanted to purchase debentures of the surviving company. As they were both leading cigar manufacturers, the decree had placed a dollar limit on the amount of cigars that HavaTampa, also a distributor, could purchase from Culbro. When Eli Witt, the successor company to HavaTampa, divested its manufacturing arm, the overlap was removed. The new modification allowed an increased level of purchases from Culbro and, invoking the 10-year rule, set a termination date for the decree in 1988.

Owens Corning Fiberglass Corp., Owens Illinois, Inc. (formerly Owens Illinois Glass Co.), Corning Glass Works, Inc., 6–23–49; 1–31–85

The companies, with Owens Illinois and Corning owning substantially all of Owens Corning Fiberglas, had been charged with sharing patents and facilities as part of a worldwide cartel agreement dividing territories. The decree had included injunctions against territorial and production restrictions and compulsory licensing of patents. Throughout the years the decree had been modified to allow the companies to liquidate their interest in Owens Corning. By the time of the termination, they owned only a 3.6% equity stake; all but three of the patents had expired, and market conditions had changed and the use of exclusive distributors was a common business practice utilized by competing firms.

L. A. Young Spring and Wire Corp. *et al.*, 6–26–51; modified 3–20–85

The companies had been charged with having divided territories and customers and with having fixed prices for wire hangers. The decree had imposed reporting requirements and had enjoined the aforementioned practices. As modified, the decree stipulated that any acquisitions that would otherwise not have to be reported under the Hart-Scott-Rodino Merger Notification Act, for a period of 10 years would have to be reported. All other provisions of the decree were terminated.

New York Great Atlantic and Pacific Tea Co., Inc., 1–19–54; 3–29–85

The company had been charged with having abused its centralized buying power, pricing below cost in specific markets, and manipulating internal transfers. The decree had precluded such practices and stipulated that it could not tell suppliers what to do to get special allowances. According to the Justice Department, the Final Judgment had "outlived whatever utility it may once have had." At the time of the termination, the market had changed and the company's position had eroded and it could not get the discounts it once did. The rest of the decree treated practices covered by the antitrust laws; thus its continuance was unnecessary.

Sargent & Co., 4–8–70; 5–23–85

The company had been accused of having entered into agreements to restrict territories in the sale of master keys. The consent decree had enjoined them not to do so. With the reversal of *Schwinn*, the practice was no longer illegal per se; additionally, it had run for 15 years and the 10-year rule was in effect.

Emhart Corp., 2–24–70; 5–23–85

See Sargent action, *supra*, at 5–23–85.

Eaton Yale & Towne, Inc., 3–2–72; 5–23–85

See Sargent action, *supra*, at 5–23–85.

Standard Oil Co. (New Jersey), 3–25–42 and supplemented 4–7–43; 7–1–85

The company had been charged with dividing the world market in various chemicals with IG Farben. Under the decree, the company was to discontinue all contracts with Farben, to license patents, and not to divide or offer exclusive territories for the sale or distribution of the products. At the time of the termination, Farben had been liquidated, the patents had expired, exclusive territories were no longer held to be per se illegal, and the injunctions had been in effect for more than 10 years. Other possible problems could be handled by the Sherman Act.

National Finance Adjusters, Inc., 8–24–81; modified 8–8–85

The group had agreed that it would not advertise prices for repossession or grant exclusive territories for its services. As a result of the modification, it could still request that members guarantee satisfaction. The time period of the agreement, according to the 10-year rule, was set to begin with the date of the modification.

Borg-Warner Corp. *et al.*, 10–22–62; 8–13–85

The consent decree had been designed to dissolve a patent pool and to restore competition in the jet-process well-servicing industry. This had been accomplished via licensing and sales provisions in the decree. At the time of the termination, many of the strictures had expired and the market had changed, as there were many new entrants in the field. Other possible problems could be handled by the Sherman Act.

Dempster Brothers, Inc. *et al.*, 7–6–62; 9–27–85

The decree had enjoined the company from limiting its distributors' freedom to handle other items, from allocating territories, from forcing purchasers to buy certain items, and from prohibiting its distributors from competing on sales to government agencies. Because of the 10-year rule, the reversal of *Schwinn*, and market change, the decree was terminated.

Radio Corp. of America, 10–21–32; 10–1–85

The decree had responded to a charge that the company had combined with others to restrain trade in the field of radio communications and apparatus. The decree was terminated because of a changed market with the company no longer dominant, the existence of regulatory laws, the passage of the Record Carrier Communication Act of 1981, which precluded the company from excluding competitors, and the reversal of the *Schwinn* decision.

Victor Talking Machine Co. [acquired by RCA in 1929], 5–13–18; 10–15–85

The decree was designed to respond to the charge that the company had attempted to restrain trade in "talking machines" and records, etc. via restraints on price, territories and customers. Noting the reversal of *Schwinn*, the 10-year rule, and the fact that RCA only produced records and tapes, the government terminated the decree.

Radio Corp. of America, 10–28–58; 10–28–85

In response to government action to ensure that the color television market was competitive, the company had agreed to a judgment providing for sharing patents on a nonexclusive, royalty-free basis and promised not to attempt to acquire an exclusive license to any patents in the field. As the patents had expired, the market conditions had changed, and the company was hindered by the strictures of the decree in its ability to compete, the decree was terminated.

Parker Hannifin Corp., 11–1–77; modified 10–30–85

The decree had precluded the company from making further acquisitions of tire hardware manufacturers. The modification was entered so the company could purchase the Schrader Bellows Automation Group from Scovill, Inc.

Volkswagen of America *et al.*, 5–7–62; 11–4–85

The decree had enjoined the company from forcing dealers to adhere to fixed prices for autos and parts. The decree was terminated because of the changed market conditions, the 10-year rule, the fact that "the prohibition duplicated law, but can also prohibit actions falling short of violating it," and other possible problems could be handled by the Sherman Act.

American Smelting & Refining Co. *et al.*, 10–11–57; 11–4–85

In response to the charge that the companies had combined to restrain and monopolize the mining, refining, smelting, and sale of lead, they entered into a decree enjoining them from fixing prices, discounts, or exchanging information. The decree was terminated because it had "accomplished its purpose," it hindered ASARCO from competing for tolling contractions as the negotiations would require government permission in every case, an "expensive and time consuming process," it would be procompetitive, and other possible problems could be handled by the Sherman Act.

Marshall & Ilsley Bank Stock Corp. (Bank Stock Corp. of Milwaukee), Marshall & Ilsley Bank, Northern Bank, and the Bank of Commerce, 12–1–69; 12–6–85

The decree had been entered forcing the company to divest itself of an acquisition [Bank of Commerce], and it enjoined future acquisitions. The decree was terminated due to a change in definition of market and banking practices and needs. For the first time, the HHI index was employed in termination deliberations, and it demonstrated that the takeover of the Northern Bank would have little effect on competition.

Alexander & Baldwin, Ltd., C. Brewer and Co., Amfac, Inc., and Matson Navigation Co., 8–17–64; 2–6–86

The companies had bought stock in Matson and were enjoined by decree from making further purchases. The decree was terminated because of changed market conditions, the existence of additional shippers, the fact that Matson could not handle the shipment of raw sugar, and, finally, other possible problems could be handled by the Sherman Act.

Mead Corp., 5–14–70; 2–7–86

By the decree, the company had agreed to divest all of its paper merchant houses and promise to make no future acquisitions in the field without prior approval. The decree was terminated due to changing market conditions, the 10-year rule, the changed role of paper merchant houses, ease of entry in the field, and the fact that the decree foreclosed possible competitive activities by the company.

Mortgage Conference of New York ***et al.*****, 6–16–48; 3–10–86**

The decree responded to the charge that the industry trade association had set rental policies for mortgaged properties and withheld financing for new construction if it were seen to lessen income from other mortgaged properties. The decree further enjoined the fixing of rates. The decree was terminated for all but a few factors (see below, 6–9–86) because the market had changed, the Conference association had dissolved, and to allow companies to participate in low-cost financing to rehabilitate residential neighborhoods.

Yoder Bros., Inc., Yoder Bros. of California, Inc., BGA International, Inc., 4–20–70; modified 4–28–86

The consent decree had enjoined restrictive agreements on the sale and breeding of chrysanthemums, the division of customers, and horizontal and vertical agreements having the effect of precluding entry by others. The decree was modified to allow Yoder to sell directly through agents rather than just through brokers.

Beech Aircraft Corp., 11–8–65; 5–1–86

The decree had enjoined the company from imposing territorial, resale, product, and price limitations on its distributors. The decree was terminated because the company's competitors were not operating under such strictures, the 10-year rule, and the reversal of the *Schwinn* decision.

Cannon Mills Co. ***et al.*****, 7–31–70; 5–15–86**

The decree enjoined fixing the prices or restricting the sales of sheets to any buyer of class. The decree was terminated because it might "inhibit rather than promote competition," the change in market structure, the 10-year rule, the reversal of *Schwinn*, and other possible problems could be handled by the Sherman Act.

J. P. Stevens & Co. ***et al.*****, 7–31–70; 5–15–86**

See Cannon Mills entry, *supra*, at 5–15–86

Springs Mills, Inc. ***et al.*****, 7–31–70; 5–15–86**

See Cannon Mills entry *supra*, at 5–15–86.

Mortgage Conference of New York ***et al.*** **(remaining defendants), 6–16–48; 6–9–86.**

See *supra*, at 3–10–86.

Waste Management, Inc., and WM Acquiring Corp., 5–6–85; modified 6–17–86

Under the decree, the company had agreed to divest specific properties and not to make any other acquisitions. The modification would let it trade properties with Genstar Corp. New Jersey, the home of the to-be-acquired company, wants larger companies involved in the business; thus the modification fit with its policies while stimulating competition.

Burroughs Adding Machine Co., 3–3–13; 7–2–86

The decree had prohibited the company from acquiring any business in competition with it and attempting to "get customers to stop using a competitor." The decree was terminated because the market had changed, the product lines had changed, and it "binds a small factor in the computer business" with restrictions not designed for the times.

Hughes Tool Co., Inc., ***et al.*****, 4–4–58; 7–30–86**

The company had been accused of attempting to monopolize the manufacture and sale of oil and gas well equipment. The decree had enjoined the company from fixing prices, pooling patents, restricting imports, territorial divisions, and the requirement that Hughes participate in all sales of the equipment. The decree was terminated because the patents and techniques had changed significantly, the market had changed, the company should be able to license its technology for foreign use, and the 10-year rule.

Bendix Aviation Corp., 12–22–48; modified in 1953 to include Westinghouse and Wagner Manufacturing; 8–19–86

The decree had enjoined joint activity, exclusive dealing, the allocation of territories, the threats of price wars and manufacture of products not presently made to discipline other companies, and the practice of resale price maintenance. The decree was terminated because of changed industry conditions, the 10-year rule, and the fact that "joint activity may well be procompetitive."

Toyota Motor Sales, USA, Inc., Toyota Motor Distributors, Inc., 7–28–75; 8–19–86

The decree had enjoined the companies from fixing the prices for their products and from limiting geographic areas in which distributors might operate. The decree was terminated because of the reversal of the *Schwinn* decision, the fact that "prohibitions against nonprice vertical restraints no longer represent current antitrust law," the 10-year rule, and that other possible problems could be handled by the Sherman Act.

Loew's Inc. *et al.*, 2–6–52; 10–10–86 [one of the "Paramount Decrees"]

As part of the consent decree, the company had agreed to divest itself of its movie theaters. It had done so successfully, except for one instance in which the landlord refused to allow a transfer of the lease. In the interim, the company had divested itself of its movie-making assets. Therefore the decree was terminated for the company, as it was "without rationale at the present time."

American Bosch Corp. *et al.*, 12–29–42; modified 6–4–48; 10–30–86

The decree grew out of charges that the company had made sales and patent sharing and manufacturing agreements with its counterpart in Germany. It enjoined price-fixing and limited production, distribution and the allocation of markets. The decree was terminated because of industry and market changes, the agreements between the two companies had been terminated, and other possible problems could be handled by the Sherman Act.

CBS, Inc., 12–10–74; modified 11–19–86

See National Broadcasting Co., Inc. entry *supra*, at 8–31–84.

Nissan Motor Corp. in USA, 2–26–73; 12–12–86

In agreeing to the judgment, the company removed territorial limits on sales territories and prices. The decree was terminated because of the reversal of *Schwinn* and the recognition of the importance of a dealer network in the sales of automobiles.

American Pharmaceutical Association, Michigan State Pharmaceutical Association, 6–18–81; modified 1–21–87

The decree had included provisions in which the groups had agreed not to limit price advertising or to try to limit it. The modification allowed them to attempt to get the government to pass legislation limiting the price content in advertising.

Western Precipitation Corp. (now Joy Manufacturing Corp.) *et al.*, 4–11–46; 2–26–87

The decree had enjoined allocation of territories and markets in the manufacture and use of electric precipitation equipment, products, and procedures. Additionally, the group was not to fix prices, terms, or conditions of sale, or to restrict imports. Finally, it was to license its technology. The decree was terminated because the remedial objectives had been achieved, the patents had expired, all affirmative actions had been fulfilled, the firm was no longer dominant in the field, technology had advanced, and the price treatment was no longer held to be per se illegal.

American Potash & Chemical Corp. *et al.*, 5–21–40; 4–1–87

The decree was in reaction to the companies, having employed basis point pricing, having refused to sell directly to individual farmers, and having been charged with refusing to compete with each other. The decree was terminated because of changes in the pricing structure, more competitive market conditions, many new entrants in the field, and the 10-year rule.

Allied Finance Adjusters Conference, Inc., 5–25–83; modified 4–6–87

See National Finance Adjusters action *supra*, at 8–8–85.
The modification also slightly changed the definition of exclusive territory.

Max Factor & Co., 4–20–67; 4–27–87

The decree responding to the charge that the company had conspired to fix prices of its products enjoined the practice and forbade denying supplies to those who refused to cooperate. The decree was terminated because the methods of distribution had changed, the *Schwinn* decision had been reversed, and the 10-year rule.

Greyhound Corp. and GLI Holding Co., 6–27–57; 5–18–87

The decree had enjoined the company from engaging in exclusive or preferential bus-purchasing practices, discriminatory conduct against other bus companies' use of terminals or sales of buses; additionally, all companies using a terminal had to be offered the same services. Further, it could not restrict access or service to other companies when using non–Greyhound-owned terminals. The decree was terminated because of the change of market; with the growth of the number of bus manufacturers, it would be impossible to restrict competition in the field of bus transportation by limiting sales of vehicles. Additionally, because terminal services were often expensive to provide, often the company had not wanted to lease space in its terminals; therefore the termination would create efficiencies as other smaller companies would be able to use the terminals without Greyhound having to provide the services.

General Tire and Rubber Co., 3–21–44; 5–29–87

In the decree, the company agreed not to tie the use of the patent [the Kraft Tire balancer] to the purchase of "unpatentable materials." The decree was terminated because the item was no longer used, the patents had expired, the market had changed, the 10-year rule, and that other possible problems could be handled by the Sherman Act.

Wall Paper Institute *et al.*, 6–8–50; 5–29–87

The decree enjoined the fixing of prices and availability of credit, restriction of sales, allocation of production, and refusal to sell to those not cooperating in the arrangement. The decree was terminated because the market had changed and "most of the provisos duplicated the antitrust laws."

Association of American Battery Manufacturers *et al.*, 12–10–53; 6–2–87

The decree had terminated contracts covering the sale, purchase, collection, and transportation of used batteries and lead which had the effect of denying access to supplies required by battery rebuilders. The decree was terminated because of the growth of competition in the battery market, the change of industry conditions, the eclipse of the rebuilders and the growth in importance of scrap dealers, the lack of scarcity of lead, and the 10-year rule.

Columbia Artists Management, Inc., Community Concerts, Inc., National Concert and Artists Corp., and Civic Concert Service, Inc. 10–20–55; 6–16–87

The decree responded to the charge that the companies had restrained trade in the management and booking of concerts, enjoining them from dividing markets, exclusive dealing arrangements, and organizing audience associations. The decree was terminated because of the 10-year rule, the changed market conditions, the procompetitive possibility of the organization of new audience associations, and other possible problems could be handled by the Sherman Act.

National Cash Register Co. *et al.*, 2–1–16; 6–22–87

The decree had enjoined the company from attempting to persuade purchasers of competitors' products to switch, from engaging in "espionage," from copying products, and also required it to gain permission to make acquisitions. The decree was terminated because the company was "no longer a monopolist," there was vigorous competition in the market, and some of the provisos put an unjust burden on the company. In that it "levels the field," change was procompetitive.

EKCO/GLACO, Inc., 5–9–66; 7–30–87

Responding to charges that the company had acquired actual or potential competitors, had built to preempt entry into markets by others, had given discounts to customers purchasing from different plants, had received requirements contracts, and had sold at a loss to drive competitors from the market, the decree had enjoined tying contracts, artificially low prices, and further acquisitions, while mandating that the company follow a published list of prices. The termination was based on a changed market, ease of entry, and the hardship that the pricing arrangements had placed on the company in attempting to meet or beat its competition.

Holophane Company, Inc., 2–8–54, modified 11–4–65; 10–14–87

The decree had proscribed market allocation, restrictions on resale, allocations of territories, and had prescribed that the company take actions to promote sales in foreign countries. The decree was terminated because patent licensing was seen no longer as unlawful (after *Continental T.V. v. GTE Sylvania*) but rather as procompetitive, the relative small size of the company, and the fact that the decree had regulated business practice and forced it to do certain specific things when it ought to be allowed to "exercise its own judgment."

Material Handling Institute, Inc., Hoist Manufacturers Institute, Industrial Trade Association *et al.*, 3–21–73; 11–23–87

The decree terminated association membership eligibility restrictions and enjoined "unreasonable" entry requirements and a rule limiting members who deal with foreign companies. Furthermore, all were to be allowed to exhibit at trade shows. With the change in rules allowing nonmembers to exhibit in trade shows, the decree could be terminated because the market had changed, the 10-year rule, that many practices were allowable under a rule of reason treatment that had previously "been illegal *per se*, and that other possible problems could be handled by the Sherman Act."

Parke Davis & Co., Eli Lilly & Co., 9–6–51; 12–18–87

The two had been charged with having conspired to restrain trade in gelatin capsules plus the manufacture and sale of machinery to produce them. As a result, they had agreed to a consent decree which required licensing of the patents, sale of the machinery, and no volume discounts. The decree was terminated because "it had outlived its time," the patents had expired, the markets were changed, and actions had been per se precluded when they should have been evaluated in the context of the rule of reason. Finally, there was "no need for the defendants to be subject to legal constraints beyond those generally applicable to other firms in the industry."

First National Supermarkets, Inc., dba Pick-N-Pay Supermarkets, Fisher Foods, Inc., dba Fazio's, Association of Stop-N-Shop Super Markets, 11–22–85; modified 12–18–87

In the decree, Fisher was enjoined from agreeing on sales terms, prices, sales, or communication with others concerning them; neither Fisher nor First National could become members of the Association. The modification allowed Fisher to become part of the Association due to a change in the market structure, poor financial health of Fisher, and the appearance of new competitors in the industry.

Simplex Time Recorder Co. *et al.*, 11–29–63; 1–21–88

The company had been accused of attempting to monopolize the sales of master clocks by attempting to purchase the assets of a competitor, Stromberg, and by threatening to put Stromberg out of business by underselling it and hiring away its personnel. As a result, it agreed to a decree enjoining it from charging unrealistically low prices, stealing personnel, making comments about the financial background of its competitors, or refusing to sell parts to specific purchasers. Furthermore, it agreed not to make acquisitions without approval. The decree was terminated because the market had changed and shrunk with the advent of computers; the company was precluded by the agreement from taking pro-competitive actions, and now it does not undercut the competition.

National Retail Credit Association, Retail Credit Men's National Association *et al.*, 10-6–33; 3–30–88

The decree enjoined the groups from allocating territories, treating association members differently from nonmembers, and listing those doing business with nonmembers. The decree was terminated because there was a new structure to the field with the coming of the computer; the local bureaus had little control and thus were of little significance.

Studiengesellschaft Kohle, m. b. H., Stauffer Chemical Co., Hercules, Inc., Texas Alkyls, Inc. *et al.*, 12–12–77; 4–7–88

The group had been charged with attempting to monopolize and with restraint of trade in aluminum trialkyls. The decree stipulated that there should be no agreement enforcing a limit on the sale of the product and that patent licenses should be granted in specific situations. The decree was terminated because it had prevented the companies from entering into licensing agreements that would have been procompetitive. In an unrelated court decision (*U.S. v. Studiengesellschaft Kohle, m. b. H.*, 670 F. 2d 1122), the court had reversed strictures against such practices, thus the decree was no longer in line with government policy.

American Body and Trailer, Inc., Utility Trailer Manufacturing Co., Great Dane Trailers, Inc., 6–16–58; 8–19–88

The decree was in response to the charge that the group had allocated territories and fixed prices in the sale of trailers. It enjoined agreements enjoining distributorships, limitations of territories, and referring inquiries to other manufacturers. The decree was terminated because the market had changed, the 10-year rule, and it "inhibits adoption of now lawful practices that can promote competition."

Minute Maid Corp., 9–7–55; 8–27–88

To settle Clayton Act difficulties associated with its acquisition of Snow Crop Corp., the company had made several divestitures and promised not to acquire any further facilities in the orange juice processing field. The company's new owner, Coca Cola, wanted to purchase a processing plant. The decree was terminated because the acquisition would not harm competition as the HHI index would be minimally affected. Continuing the decree would serve no purpose, as the provisions of the Hart-Scott-Rodino Act would preclude acquisitions of any import.

Appendix B

U.S. Department of Justice, Antitrust Division
Staffing and funding

	1970	1971	1972	1973	1974	1975	1976	1977	1978	1979	1980	1981	1982	1983	1984	1985	1986	1987	1988	1989	1990	1991
Authorized staff																						
Attorneys	306	315	325	327	327	367	442	459	464	476	464	464	374	338	314	281	281	281	258	258	303	303
Economists					34	41	51	54	56	58	58	53	58	46	47	47	47	47	32	32	42	42
Paralegals							24	45	46	85	85	85	83	63	61	64	64	64	56	56	64	64
Other	289	295	305	302	268	304	339	349	354	358	332	332	314	295	282	257	257	257	203	203	214	214
Total	595	610	630	629	629	712	856	907	920	977	939	939	829	742	704	649	649	649	549	549	623	623
Actual staff																						
Attorneys	291	307	294	299	296	343	385	421	383	394	429	409	338	292	295	258	256	224	219	209	254	280
Economists	25	23	21	26	24	36	43	40	44	45	45	38	41	43	43	46	44	40	39	36	40	42
Paralegals								46	79	93	83	71	60	56	65	59	59	56	55	50	54	63
Other	237	234	239	245	236	293	345	318	353	340	326	310	283	267	236	218	210	181	167	163	181	200
Total	553	564	554	570	556	672	773	825	859	872	883	828	722	658	639	581	569	501	480	458	529	585
Funding																						
Appropriations	9761	11079	12340	12836	14790	18253	22239	27706	32371	37500	43544	44862	44000	44489	44229	43119	42586	43845	44937	44937	31817	33750
Grant Monies								1000	10000	10000	4000											
Filing Fees																					19749	20000
Total BA	9761	11079	12340	12836	14790	18253	22239	28706	42371	47500	47544	44862	44000	44489	44229	43119	42586	43845	44937	44937	51566	53750

I would like to thank Ms. Mary Ann Berry and Ms. Jackie Freund Vassanelli of the Department of Justice, Antitrust Division, for supplying the official statistics for the period 1970–1989. Note that the numbers differ somewhat from those provided in the annual reports. For 1990 and 1991 we have used the chart entitled *Antitrust Division's Workload Data Over Past 10 Fiscal Years*, Antitrust & Trade Reg. Rep. (BNA), at 79–88 (Jan. 23, 1992).

Appendix C

U.S. Department of Justice, Antitrust Division Workload, 1970–1991

	1970	*1971*	*1972*	*1973*	*1974*	*1975*	*1976*	*1977*	*1978*	*1979*	*1980*	*1981*	*1982*	*1983*	*1984*	*1985*	*1986*	*1987*	*1988*	*1989*	*1990*	*1991*
INVESTIGATIONS																						
Sherman Act §1	232	391	285	307	202	274	263	330	162	225	219	162	139	136	135	130	169	125	115	93	71	77
Sherman Act §2	24	43	20	27	22	14	15	25	21	20	65	8	12	10	5	5	12	4	3	7	4	5
Clayton Act §7	173	133	147	174	107	77	84	110	96	152	59	68	85	79	105	107	128	132	88	108	93	92
Clayton Act §8	16	5	6	7	1	7	4	1	2	1	1	0	0	1	1	0	0	0	0	0	0	0
Clayton Act §3	2	4	4	9	0	3	0	0	0	2	6	0	0	0	0	0	0	0	0	0	0	0
Other	26	17	3	14	6	6	8	18	9	7	27	17	26	19	11	12	6	9	10	12	10	4
BUSINESS REVIEWS																						
Requested	16	14	18	22	18	20	30	30	24	18	26	18	23	26	20	28	27	25	23	13	7	14
Issued	9	10	9	15	14	17	24	20	18	16	18	18	23	26	20	28	52	32	18	15	9	7
PREMERGER NOTIFICATIONS																						
Received									147	859	824	993	1204	1101	1339	1604	1949	2533	2747	2883	2262	1529
Investigations initiated									20	101	56	67	55	62	79	106	85	89	56	64	59	67
Cases filed									0	9	7	3	3	2	5	5	4	4	6	4	6	2
PRELIMINARY INQUIRIES																						
Initiated	375	482	462	361	385	265	311	277	243	329	241	198	285	181	181	180	222	174	134	141	147	149
Terminated	463	417	417	341	362	314	310	387	284	345	367	224	169	184	175	196	237	192	167	144	135	145
Pending	494	531	531	543	574	525	519	365	324	308	183	157	193	190	196	180	165	147	114	111	123	127
GRAND JURIES																						
Initiated	23	43	32	34	37	37	50	48	27	38	46	34	49	48	48	58	51	59	63	47	42	45
Terminated	17	15	27	35	29	44	33	53	52	51	23	34	18	31	28	52	48	42	52	47	62	34
Pending	46	69	67	73	61	75	92	86	61	49	51	51	82	99	119	125	128	145	156	156	139	150
Indictments returned	8	9	28	25	29	25	18	17	32	27	26	53	67	44	57	27	17	38	26	21	20	21
Criminal	5	6	16	17	21	14	12	10	18	18	20	40	61	42	52	23	17	38	26	21	19	19
Civil	3	3	12	8	8	11	6	7	14	9	6	13	6	2	5	4	0	0	0	0	1	2

DISTRICT COURT CASES

Total civil cases																						
Filed	54	52	72	42	33	37	45	34	2[illegible]	31	28	26	18	10	14	11	6	15	11	6	14	17
Terminated	49	44	44	50	48	24	40	36	4[illegible]	32	39	36	42	17	11	19	58	10	22	4	9	21
Won	43	42	41	44	42	13	31	27	3[illegible]	28	32	36	31	15	8	13	44	7	20	3	4	15
Lost	4	1	1	5	3	5	5	4	[illegible]	0	5	0	3	2	1	2	10	0	0	0	1	4
Dismissed	2	1	2	1	3	6	4	5	[illegible]	4	2	0	8	0	2	4	4	3	2	1	4	2
Pending	88	96	124	116	101	114	119	108	87	86	121	111	87	80	83	75	23	28	17	19	15	11
Restraint of trade—civil																						
-Filed	15	14	31	19	10	29	18	19	20	14	14	19	8	5	7	2	0	9	0	0	2	2
-Terminated	17	16	16	21	26	9	14	13	22	26	28	28	31	18	6	10	24	1	12	1	0	5
Won	16	16	16	21	24	7	11	10	20	24	26	26	23	18	4	6	22	1	11	1	0	4
Lost	1	0	0	0	1	1	1	0	0	0	1	1	1	0	0	2	1	0	0	0	0	1
Dismissed	0	0	0	0	1	1	2	3	2	2	1	1	7	0	2	2	1	0	1	0	0	0
Oligopoly/monopoly—civil																						
-Filed	11	15	13	5	6	3	5	2	0	2	1	1	0	1	0	0	0	0	0	0	0	0
-Terminated	8	11	9	7	2	7	7	3	1	2	0	0	2	2	0	0	8	0	0	0	0	0
Won	8	11	9	7	2	2	4	2	1	2	0	0	1	0	0	0	4	0	0	0	0	0
Lost	0	0	0	0	0	2	1	1	0	0	0	0	0	2	0	0	3	0	0	0	0	0
Dismissed	0	0	0	0	0	3	2	0	0	0	0	0	1	0	0	0	1	0	0	0	0	0
Merger cases																						
-Filed	15	24	19	16	13	3	7	4	7	11	10	4	8	4	5	7	6	6	6	5	11	4
-Terminated	14	11	20	18	14	7	15	13	14	1	8	8	9	5	3	8	22	8	5	2	7	10
Won	10	10	18	13	10	4	9	9	10	0	5	5	7	5	3	6	16	5	4	2	3	5
Lost	3	1	0	4	2	3	4	3	3	0	3	3	2	0	0	1	5	0	0	0	0	3
Dismissed	1	0	2	1	2	0	2	1	1	1	0	0	0	0	0	1	1	3	1	0	4	2
Damage actions—civil																						
-Filed	4	1	1	0	2	6	1	1	3	4	1	0	1	0	0	0	0	0	0	0	1	1
-Terminated	0	0	1	1	0	0	1	2	2	3	0	0	0	0	1	0	0	0	0	1	0	1
Won	0	0	1	1	0	0	1	1	1	2	0	0	0	0	1	0	0	0	0	0	0	1
Lost	0	0	0	0	0	0	0	0	0	0	0	0	0	0	0	0	0	0	0	0	0	0
Dismissed	0	0	0	0	0	0	0	1	1	1	0	0	0	0	0	0	0	0	0	1	0	0
Other civil																						
-Filed	14	4	11	5	6	2	15	3	1	5	2	2	1	0	2	1	0	0	5	1	0	10
-Terminated	9	8	1	6	8	2	9	7	11	5	3	0	0	0	1	1	4	1	5	0	2	5
Won	8	7	1	5	8	0	9	6	8	4	1	0	0	0	0	1	2	0	0	0	1	5
Lost	0	0	0	1	0	0	0	0	0	0	1	0	0	0	1	0	1	1	5	0	1	0
Dismissed	1	1	0	0	0	2	0	1	3	1	1	0	0	0	0	0	1	0	0	0	0	0

DISTRICT COURT CASES *(continued)*	*1970*	*1971*	*1972*	*1973*	*1974*	*1975*	*1976*	*1977*	*1978*	*1979*	*1980*	*1981*	*1982*	*1983*	*1984*	*1985*	*1986*	*1987*	*1988*	*1989*	*1990*	*1991*
Total Criminal Cases																						
Filed	5	12	15	20	34	35	20	37	31	27	55	70	94	98	100	47	53	92	87	86	75	81
Terminated	9	8	1	6	8	2	9	7	11	5	61	59	87	94	82	71	59	26	39	140	82	71
Won	8	7	1	5	8	0	9	6	8	4	57	57	78	85	72	64	54	20	34	129	73	66
Lost	0	0	0	1	0	0	0	0	0	0	3	2	7	5	9	5	5	4	4	10	5	4
Dismissed	1	1	0	0	0	2	0	1	3	1	1	0	2	4	1	2	0	2	1	1	4	1
Pending	14	16	19	18	34	50	35	38	35	29	24	35	42	47	65	41	35	101	159	105	88	98
Restraint of trade—criminal																						
-Filed	4	79	14	19	21	29	16	34	27	24	55	69	92	92	96	43	47	77	74	80	66	74
-Terminated	10	8	12	18	17	12	31	23	28	28	58	59	85	91	81	65	52	23	29	123	74	66
Won	9	7	12	16	14	12	30	16	26	28	54	57	76	82	72	58	48	17	28	114	67	61
Lost	0	1	0	2	3	0	1	6	2	0	3	2	7	5	8	5	4	4	1	8	5	4
Dismissed	1	0	0	0	0	0	0	1	0	0	1	0	2	4	1	2	0	2	0	1	2	1
Oligopoly/monopoly—criminal																						
-Filed	0	2	1	1	3	1	2	1	0	0	0	0	0	0	0	0	0	0	0	0	0	0
-Terminated	0	0	1	2	2	3	1	3	0	1	0	0	0	0	0	0	0	0	0	0	0	0
Won	0	0	1	1	0	3	1	1	0	1	0	0	0	0	0	0	0	0	0	0	0	0
Lost	0	0	0	1	2	0	0	1	0	0	0	0	0	0	0	0	0	0	0	0	0	0
Dismissed	0	0	0	0	0	0	0	1	0	0	0	0	0	0	0	0	0	0	0	0	0	0
Other related crimes																						
-Filed	17	5	11	5	15	10	19	5	7	4	0	1	2	6	4	4	6	15	13	6	9	7
-Terminated	1	2	0	1	1	6	4	4	6	7	3	0	2	2	4	6	9	9	10	17	8	5
Won	1	2	0	0	1	3	3	2	3	7	3	0	2	2	3	6	8	8	6	15	6	5
Lost	0	0	0	0	0	3	1	2	2	0	0	0	0	0	0	0	1	0	3	2	0	0
Dismissed	0	0	0	1	0	0	0	0	1	0	0	0	0	0	1	0	0	1	1	0	2	0

APPELLATE CASES

Antitrust Division cases																						
Court of Appeals																						
-Filed	3	4	2	3	3	3	10	15	13	18	15	17	16	11	13	27	26	8	24	32	10	18
-Terminated	1	6	1	6	2	4	3	9	7	18	19	23	13	23	14	19	19	10	21	19	19	16
Won	1	3	1	3	1	4	3	6	4	17	16	19	8	20	9	15	16	7	17	18	15	9
Lost	0	3	0	3	1	0	0	3	1	0	1	4	5	3	5	4	2	3	2	0	4	0
Dismissed	0	0	0	0	0	0	0	0	2	1	2	0	0	0	0	0	1	0	2	1	0	7
Supreme Court																						
-Filed	2	4	5	5	2	3	0	1	5	8	2	6	12	3	3	10	5	[illegible]	4	5	3	3
-Terminated	0	1	4	6	1	3	3	1	5	1	9	9	9	2	2	8	3	2	2	2	0	7
Won	0	1	3	5	1	2	0	0	4	1	9	5	8	2	2	7	3	2	2	2	0	7
Lost	0	0	1	1	0	1	3	1	1	0	0	4	0	0	0	1	0	0	0	0	0	0
Dismissed	0	0	0	0	0	0	0	0	0	0	0	0	1	0	0	0	0	0	0	0	0	0
Amicus—Antitrust Division cases																						
Court of Appeals																						
-Filed	2	2	0	2	4	2	1	1	6	1	8	6	5	8	3	1	1	6	2	1	1	0
-Terminated	0	1	2	4	2	2	3	0	4	1	7	3	0	3	7	2	1	7	4	1	1	1
Won	0	1	2	3	2	2	3	0	2	1	7	3	0	2	6	0	1	5	4	1	0	1
Lost	0	0	0	1	0	0	0	0	2	0	0	0	0	0	1	2	0	1	0	0	1	0
Dismissed	0	0	0	0	0	0	0	0	0	0	0	0	0	1	0	0	0	1	0	0	0	0
Supreme Court																						
-Filed	0	1	5	1	2	1	1	1	6	3	3	10	9	7	9	9	9	3	5	2	4	3
-Terminated	1	0	0	4	2	1	2	2	6	2	3	7	2	3	10	7	8	2	4	1	4	5
Won	1	0	0	4	2	1	2	2	6	2	3	6	2	3	7	5	5	2	4	1	3	3
Lost	0	0	0	0	0	0	0	0	0	0	0	1	0	0	3	2	3	0	0	0	1	2
Dismissed	0	0	0	0	0	0	0	0	0	0	0	0	0	0	0	0	0	0	0	0	0	0
Other Agencies' cases																						
Court of Appeals																						
-Filed	142	145	150	156	182	209	208	190	201	136	312	275	173	311	313	373	248	189	129	124	79	103
-Terminated	147	126	131	176	122	215	122	105	112	50	321	205	158	334	345	319	118	277	96	80	103	93
Won	75	72	60	96	56	107	54	42	62	34	294	132	124	155	208	148	60	94	49	26	66	47
Lost	24	14	17	22	20	59	23	18	21	4	8	11	13	25	28	25	16	76	12	18	13	14
Dismissed	48	40	54	58	46	49	45	45	29	12	19	62	21	154	109	146	42	107	35	36	24	32
Supreme Court																						
-Filed	10	6	1	17	24	6	16	8	12	5	27	21	7	13	6	30	17	11	11	18	7	7
-Terminated	12	7	13	19	23	11	12	15	9	3	24	16	4	6	9	14	10	13	4	7	4	6
Won	10	6	12	17	23	10	10	15	8	3	24	16	3	6	9	13	6	12	4	7	3	6
Lost	2	1	0	0	0	0	0	0	1	0	0	0	1	0	0	0	4	0	0	0	1	0
Dismissed	0	0	1	2	0	1	2	0	0	0	0	0	0	0	0	1	0	1	0	0	0	0

	1970	1971	1972	1973	1974	1975	1976	1977	1978	1979	1980	1981	1982	1983	1984	1985	1986	1987	1988	1989	1990	1991
JUDGMENT ENFORCEMENT																						
Divestitures	7	5	3	5	18	37	21	21	25	2	5	6	7	7	5	5	4	5	4	3	4	3
Compliance reports	62	65	100	112	115	140	140	311	313	360	335	312	215	188	206	287	231	141	155	137	104	82
Consent decrees																						
"Expired"												10	16	11	11	6	2	5	8			
Terminated	2	3	4	1	3	5	2	6	9	7	7	0	0	10	9	14	14	3	4	21	6	1
Modified	8	6	5	11	16	8	12	13	10	5	12	9	6	4	2	8	5	3	0	1	2	
TOTAL	10	9	9	12	19	13	14	19	19	12	19	19	22	25	22	28	21	11	12	22	8	1
Contempt cases	1	1	0	2	4	4	4	5	4	1	1	2	1	1	0	0	0	0	1	1	0	0
Other enforcement inquiries	37	50	46	54	36	50	50	65	73	65	70											
ATTORNEY DAYS IN COURT		1833	1872	1962	2385	5642	6123	4912	5167	4628	4644											
CASE RESULTS																						
Individuals indicted	14	34	24	42	84	82	101	88	83	62	72	83	103	113	104	36	68	115	78	76	72	58
Total individual fines [000]	243	40	203	221	175	645	570	743	1231	2098	667	660	1585	1463	1176	846	1152	1636	1996	2892	917	2806
Total individuals fined [#]	17	18	24	46	32	44	72	87	72	76	27	33	42	46	45	43	44	42	53	54	30	37
# Individuals sentenced [jail]	3	7	1	8	5	8	6	26	29	19	15	49	54	51	32	11	16	15	30	32	17	22
# Individuals sentenced [including probation]	11	7	14	13	26	30	34	58	71	58	47	59	72	83	63	53	50	48	73	76	42	50

Total days of jail served	111	270	180	450	50	690	560	1561	2921	2360	1381	7041	5940	6543	3181	1356	2725	1994	5892	7473	2739	6594
Corporations indicted	16	56	51	69	121	127	110	147	147	102	87	74	113	122	131	50	69	119	89	88	88	70
Total corporation fines [000]	1512	268	977	1208	1263	2200	3135	2597	11224	23328	8601	16178	35223	19430	19218	3533	9570	16265	28830	25600	22658	17573

I would like to thank Ms. Mary Ann Berry and Ms. Jackie Freund Vassanelli of the Department of Justice, Antitrust Division, for supplying the official statistics for the period 1970–1989. Note that the numbers differ somewhat from those provided in the annual reports. For 1990 and 1991 we have used the chart entitled *Antitrust Division's Workload Data Over Past 10 Fiscal Years*, Antitrust & Trade Reg. Rep. (BNA), at 79–88 (Jan. 23, 1992).

10 Directions for antitrust enforment at the Department of Justice

BY JAMES F. RILL*

The Department of Justice celebrated the 100th anniversary of the Sherman Act by inviting prominent members of the antitrust community to speak candidly on the contribution of the Sherman Act over the past century and its likely influence in future years. As we had hoped, the views presented were lively and diverse, representing a spectrum of opinion on the relevance of the Act to modern societal, governmental, and business institutions.

Despite the varied perceptions of our speakers, there was a clear consensus that antitrust enforcement is sure to play a major role in promoting and preserving competition in free market economies, both at home and abroad. Furthermore, the centennial speakers agreed that the Sherman Act could serve as a valuable model for countries that seek to implement a competition policy, for it provides fundamental competition principles rather than a rigid code of prohibited business practices. By design, the Act permits antitrust enforcement to benefit from and adapt to new learning about the nature of business and economics. This design has served the United States well, and it is highly adaptable to the needs of other countries and future decades.

---

* Assistant Attorney General, United States Department of Justice, Antitrust Division, June 1989–May 1992.

The flexibility of the Act also permits a legal climate that is conducive to diverse trends in antitrust theory, policy, and enforcement. Indeed, antitrust has just experienced one of the truly important periods in its evolutionary history. Have we reached the end of the debate? Of course not. It would be rash, probably arrogant, to argue that the period of learning is over and that the current doctrine is necessarily the last word.

It is reasonable to expect further debate over how best to implement the goals and objectives of antitrust, but I doubt that antitrust theory will undergo a radical transformation in the near future. The sweeping changes of the past 20 years have established a rational and solid foundation of current economic and legal theory that is attuned fully to a social welfare objective. This does not mean that antitrust enforcement will be static. On the contrary, current developments in domestic and foreign markets suggest that the next decade will see extensive changes in the way Americans conduct business. Antitrust enforcement will have to respond creatively and rationally to the many forces that have already begun transforming geographic and product markets. The question for the next decade, therefore, is not so much the nature of antitrust theory as it is the contours of enforcement policy.

In general, I expect to see a continued resurgence of confidence in federal antitrust enforcement and an increasing recognition among government officials that antitrust enforcement can provide one of the most effective means of preserving, protecting, and promoting competition. Why antitrust? The national experience with government and economic regulation has led to the widespread understanding that competition rather than regulation is more likely to benefit consumers. With this understanding, there is an increasing appreciation of antitrust enforcement as one of the least intrusive forms of governmental intervention.

In markets determined by competition rather than regulation, the market works as an efficient check on anticompetitive practices. The market is not fully self-policing, however. Competitive abuses must be kept in check. Antitrust enforcement performs this function with a minimum of regulatory control and, therefore, provides an ideal means of selectively protecting the market from anticompetitive conduct.

As I see it, there is only one counterforce to the growing momentum of antitrust enforcement. Congressional support for federal enforcement activities is a prerequisite for success. Without sufficient resources, the Antitrust Division cannot conduct a credible enforcement program. And without credible enforcement, a deterrence program is not likely to succeed.

Fortunately, in 1990 Congress supported the Department's pro-enforcement program with an increased level of funding and with other legislative support. In a major endorsement of antitrust enforcement, Congress raised the maximum fines that can be imposed for antitrust crimes, and it provided the Antitrust Division with increased, stable funding that will allow the Division to begin rebuilding its professional and support staff after a 10-year decline. The current level of congressional support is a very positive development that should allow antitrust enforcement to fulfill its role as a champion of competition.

To gain a better idea of federal antitrust enforcement in the future, it is useful to consider the developments that have already occurred at the Department of Justice in the 1990's. Indeed, change has come at a brisk pace in four major areas of emphasis: criminal enforcement, merger enforcement, competition advocacy, and international competition. Developments in each of these areas point to the future of antitrust enforcement at the Department of Justice.

Criminal enforcement

Enforcement of the federal antitrust statutes thorough criminal prosecution is at the heart of the Department's antitrust program and will continue as one of the Antitrust Division's top priorities. Horizontal conspiracies can have devastating effects on social welfare because they distort the dynamics that determine market structure. If undeterred or undetected, conspiracies by competitors are the single biggest threat to our system of free enterprise. Criminal antitrust enforcement, therefore, will always be a critical component of free and open competition, and recent developments indicate that the Department's criminal antitrust enforcement program will continue its solid record of success.

Increased statutory penalties

The effectiveness of the Department's criminal antitrust program has been greatly enhanced by Congress' enactment of the new $10 million statutory fine for corporate violations.[1] The new statutory maximum means that federal courts finally can impose the full range of monetary penalties recommended by the U.S. Sentencing Commission's Sentencing Guidelines.[2] While the threat of a $10 million penalty is likely to exert a deterrent effect in itself, the actual imposition of higher fines in cases should persuade the business community to reevaluate its calculus of the costs and benefits of taking steps to ensure that antitrust crimes are not committed.

Improved detection and prosecution

The Antitrust Division has become substantially more effective in establishing coordinated investigative networks with other federal agencies and with state enforcement officials, and we expect to continue developing and perfecting a system of regular contacts with state Attorneys General, federal Inspectors General, and U.S. Attorneys. This type of coordination has enhanced the Department's investigative abilities and improved the efficient allocation of resources and expertise. In addition, cooperation has expanded our information base, with federal and state governmental agencies more alert to cartel behavior and encouraged to call on the Division for assistance or direct action in attacking it.

The Department's recent Florida milk bid-rigging investigations

---

1 The Antitrust Improvements Act of 1990, H.R. 29, 101st Cong., 2d Sess., 1990.

2 The U.S. Sentencing Commission's Guidelines for federal sentencing are a critical companion to federal antitrust enforcement. The practical effect of the Guidelines is to greatly increase the cost of committing antitrust crimes. The cost to an individual convicted of an antitrust crime will in all but the rarest of circumstances be incarceration, as well as mandatory fines of up to 10% of his firm's total revenues from goods or services tainted by the criminal act. Organizations face fines of from 20% to 50% of the tainted revenues. U.S. SENTENCING COMMISSION, GUIDELINES MANUAL § 2R.11 (1989).

and prosecutions are an excellent example of the success of a cooperative approach to antitrust enforcement. Closely coordinated investigative work of the Division and the Florida Attorney General's Office uncovered a widespread, possibly multistate, pattern of bid-rigging conspiracies. Working with the information provided by the Attorney General's Office, the Antitrust Division to date has prosecuted successfully 21 price-fixing cases among milk suppliers in Florida, resulting in at least $20 million in federal penalties and the conviction of 23 defendants.[3] In addition, the State of Florida has collected almost $30 million in settlement of related damage suits.

The Antitrust Division's prosecution techniques have kept pace with our enhanced investigative capability. Of course, the Division will continue its policy of prosecuting per se horizontal conspiracies criminally and of charging all crimes that were committed in connection with criminal antitrust schemes—such as wire fraud, mail fraud, tax evasion, or conspiracy to defraud the government. In addition, we have developed charging procedures that allow us to prosecute attempted bid-rigging and price-fixing by charging primary violations of wire and mail fraud.[4] This is an important

---

3 *See, e.g.*, U.S. v. Borden, Inc., Cr. No. 90–61-CR–T–17–C (filed 3/1/90, M.D. Fla.); U.S. v The Southland Corporation, Cr. No. 90–62–CR–T–10–C (filed 3–1–90, M.D. Fla.).

4 In United States v. Ames Sintering Co. (filed 1989, E.D. Mich.) attempted bid-rigging was held to be actionable fraud under the federal wire-fraud statutes.

The defendants were charged with wire fraud in connection with an unsuccessful scheme to defraud a major customer by rigging bids for a contract to supply pressure plates used in power steering systems. The trial court denied defendants' motion to dismiss, which was brought on grounds that a mere inquiry or proposal to rig a bid is not actionable fraud under the statute. The trial court upheld the indictment, stating that the wire fraud statute prohibits "having devised or *intending to devise* any scheme or artifice to defraud. . . ." Thus, the government need only prove a scheme to defraud and the use of interstate wires in furtherance of the scheme. The order was upheld by the Sixth Circuit.

The rationale in *Ames* was applied in an order denying defendants' motion to dismiss in U.S. v. Critical Industries, Inc., Cr. No. 90–00318 (filed 7–24–90, D.C. N.J.), where the defendants were charged with wire fraud in connections with an unsuccessful scheme to fix prices.

expansion of our charging tools, and it is a tool that we will continue to develop.

Emphasis on white-collar crime

The Antitrust Division's participation in the Attorney General's recent initiative to uncover and prosecute "crime in the suites" is a harbinger of future enforcement priorities. Antitrust crimes are as likely to occur in a white-collar context as any other, and, given the emerging dominance of the professional services sector in relation to the nation's GNP, white-collar environments are increasingly the setting of antitrust investigation and prosecution.

United States v. Alston[5] is a prime example of our criminal enforcement program at work in the professional services sector. The case involved a grand jury indictment charging three dentists and two of their professional corporations with conspiring to fix and raise the copayment fees that members of four independent prepaid dental insurance plans were required to pay to the defendants and other dentists.

The dentists who provided services for the four plans were compensated by a capitation schedule—in other words, they were paid a predetermined monthly amount for each subscriber who selected them as the provider. Services provided by the dentists that were not specifically covered by the capitation schedule were compensated by direct payments from the subscriber to the provider at rates independently determined by each plan. These "copayments" were the fees that the dentists wanted to raise.

Led by the three individual defendants, more than 30 dentists sent identical letters to each of the plans for which they provided services. The form letters demanded an increase in copayment fees and attached a new copayment schedule that was 25%–30% higher than the old one.

This was not a situation in which a panel of providers who were

---

5 United States v. Alston, Cr. No. CR 90–042–TUC (filed 9–20–90, D.C. Ariz.).

part of a legitimate joint venture engaged in fee negotiations with third-party payers. Instead, independent dentists banded together for the purpose of forcing a fee hike among the competing plans. Three of the plans did indeed raise copayment rates, and those higher rates are still in effect. The fourth called the federal government.

The case involved clear-cut per se illegal conduct warranting criminal prosecution, and criminal prosecution was the only appropriate course.[6] The dentists' conduct did not relate to any form of efficiency-enhancing economic integration, and it did not result in the introduction of a new product into the market. Moreover, as more than one unindicted coconspirator testified, the primary purpose of the conduct was to set higher copayment fees. With no economic integration and no new product, what we had was a garden variety price-fix, a per se illegal offense.

Merger enforcement

Enforcement of the antitrust laws against anticompetitive mergers or similar consolidations is the Department's other top antitrust enforcement priority. Although the 1990's may have introduced a slowdown in certain types of merger transactions, there has not been a proportional decrease in the number of proposed mergers that require the Division's close attention.[7] In fact, there was a 100% increase in Department of Justice merger challenges in 1990.

---

6 The Antitrust Division's longstanding position is that aggressive *criminal* enforcement is necessary to maintain an effective deterrence program. For that reason it observed a policy of prosecuting per se violations criminally. The Division has the discretion to seek instead a civil remedy for a per se violation, but it exercises that discretion only in very limited circumstances.

7 During an average month, the Antitrust Division reviews the potential competitive effect of 150–200 proposed mergers or acquisition transactions, the majority of which come to our attention through Hart-Scott-Rodino Act premerger notifications. We do not, however, limit our investigations to Hart-Scott-Rodino transactions. The Division also investigates—and will challenge where appropriate—proposed or consummated mergers that do not fall under the Hart-Scott-Rodino premerger notification requirements. In fact, 50 percent of the Division's public challenges in 1990 were the result of the investigatory initiative of the Antitrust Division's staff of lawyers and economists.

But the importance of merger enforcement is not revealed by the volume of transactions we review or the number of cases we bring. The importance of merger enforcement is revealed by the quality of our analysis. We recognize that most mergers are pro-competitive or competitively neutral. Overly zealous merger enforcement, therefore, runs the risk of itself being anticompetitive. Our focus necessarily is on deterring or preventing those mergers that lessen competition without effecting the incentives for pro-competitive or competitively neutral transactions.

Department of Justice merger guidelines

The Antitrust Division's merger policy is driven by the Department's 1984 Merger Guidelines,[8] which ensure a high quality of analysis. In 1990 the number of merger challenges doubled, but each challenge was the result of the rigorous and faithful application of the Guidelines.

Of course, the Guidelines and the merger review process are likely to undergo continuing evaluation and, if necessary, fine-tuning and clarification.[9] At present, the Antitrust Division is considering a revision of the 1984 Guidelines to reflect the theoretical and practical learning that has developed since 1984. We are consulting with the Federal Trade Commission (FTC) during the review process and expect the finished product to be an up-to-date, comprehensive guide to federal merger analysis and enforcement.

Coordination among merger enforcement agencies

The FTC's involvement in the Merger Guidelines project is indicative of the unprecedented cooperation that the Department and the FTC currently enjoy in merger enforcement. Both agencies have worked hard to cultivate this relationship, and we are advancing toward enhanced coordination with the states. The success of

---

8 U.S. DEPARTMENT OF JUSTICE, MERGER GUIDELINES (1984).

9 The Department issued revised Merger Guidelines twice in the 1980s, each time with the intention of providing better guidance.

our movement toward enhanced coordination may be, in part, a result of the commitment of the Executive Working Group on Antitrust (EWG)[10] to opening lines of communication among all antitrust agencies. As a result of dialogue facilitated by the EWG, the antitrust agencies are in general agreement that harmonization of merger enforcement is a worthwhile and necessary goal in order to avoid sending mixed legal and policy statements. The EWG has allowed us to make major strides in that direction, reducing the possibility of conflicting enforcement objectives and standards.

Competition policy and deregulation

In recent years there has been a heightened level of federal antitrust enforcement activity in newly deregulated industries. This is not a surprising development—antitrust enforcement is likely to be a factor in any industry that breaks out of a regulatory regime into the freedoms of a market—and it should not be viewed as a step backward to intrusive governmental regulation. On the contrary, antitrust enforcement is one of the few forms of governmental intervention that can help ensure a competitive market without needlessly disrupting market dynamics.

Of course, the Department's involvement with deregulation is not limited to enforcement. The Department also helps to shape regulatory policy by advising other federal agencies on competition policy.

Competition advocacy

For many years, the Antitrust Division has acted as a competition advocate, formulating advice to help the federal government consider fully the competitive implications of regulatory action.

---

10 The Executive Working Group on Antitrust comprises senior officials of the Antitrust Division, the FTC, and the National Association of Attorneys General who meet on a regular basis to discuss matters of common interest, including improved enforcement

The Division routinely participates in administrative proceedings that require an application and understanding of the antitrust laws or competition policy. Many times, an appearance by the Department of Justice before the appropriate regulatory body has been instrumental in modifying or eliminating outdated and anticompetitive regulation.

Traditionally, the competition advocacy program has been a relatively quiet forum in which the Department addressed and advocated policies that support or promote competition. In 1990 the Department's presence became more extensive and substantial. Two factors contribute to this development.

First, a reinvigoration of the Department's competition advocacy program is a direct response to the agenda of the Bush administration. The President is clearly on the record supporting market solutions and deregulatory initiatives,[11] and the President's strong support is a critical factor in the reinvigoration of our program.

Second, the Antitrust Division brings unwavering attention to the competitive process. Our economists and lawyers are experts in competition policy, theory, and analysis, and they offer to other federal departments and agencies the benefit of skilled and straightforward analysis of the impact of federal policy on competition.

Deregulatory initiatives

As a result, the administration increasingly has called on the Department to help shape and implement the President's important deregulatory programs. The Department of Justice has a seat on the White House Deregulatory Task Force, and it is a member of the White House Council on Competitiveness. The Attorney General serves on a number of cabinet-level working groups that are consid-

---

coordination.

11 Message of the President to the Congress of the United States, Aug. 3, 1990, Preface to REGULATORY PROGRAM FOR THE UNITED STATES GOVERNMENT,

ering plans of action in a wide range of regulated industries.

Of course, in addition to our expanded role as policy advisors, we continue our advocacy program. In fiscal year 1990 the Division participated in numerous administrative proceedings involving agriculture, transportation, financial markets, health care, insurance, energy, ocean shipping, telecommunications, broadcasting, and other areas.[12]

International competition

Antitrust and competition policy in a global context is a rapidly intensifying responsibility of the Department of Justice. In the past 2 years alone the Antitrust Division has greatly increased its international activities with a focus on better understanding and, where possible, coordination of international antitrust and competition policy, and on elimination or reduction of anticompetitive barriers to U.S. business opportunities.

Coordination of international competition policy

With respect to our first area of activity—better understanding and coordination of international antitrust and competition policy—the Department's policy is to establish increased cooperation and interaction among countries that seek to adhere to a competition policy. These countries include our traditional trade partners, as well as countries that have only recently begun to think about the role of antitrust policy.

For instance, the Antitrust Division and the FTC participate in a regular series of consultations with the Canadian antitrust authorities to promote a better mutual understanding of the laws and enforcement programs of our two nations. We have entered into a Memorandum of Understanding with the Canadians that reflects a carefully developed system of notification and information sharing

April 1, 1990–March 31, 1990, Executive Office of the President of the United States.

where bilateral interests are affected.[13] Also of great significance, the United States and Canada have recently ratified a treaty regarding cooperation in criminal investigations.[14] This treaty bodes very ill for price-fixers and bid-riggers on both sides of the border.

Similar regular consultations are held with Japan and the European Community and, of course, meetings take place twice a year at the Organization for Economic Co-operation and Development (OECD). Meetings with the antitrust authorities of other nations are also conducted on a frequent basis. In general, exchanges of this sort are extremely useful in illuminating the similarities and differences in our respective approaches to antitrust and competition policy, for they provide opportunities for shirt-sleeve sessions conducive to the development of a focus on problems of information sharing and legal process.

Cooperative measures, such as those I just outlined, have made it possible to avoid or resolve potential conflicts with our trade partners. But our work has just begun. In the next decade, antitrust officials must address substantive problems, such as limitations on information sharing that stand in the way of international enforcement cooperation or conflicting legal requirements that may pit the remedies of one country against the regulations of another. Procedural inhibitions also remain, such as differing time frames for merger investigations and decisions from country to country. Substantive questions regarding the relationship between market shares and market power, the significance of entry barriers, and the weight to be given to actual and potential import penetration will need to be considered and possibly harmonized.

---

12 During fiscal year 1990, the Antitrust Division filed comments in 54 regulatory agency proceedings.

13 Memorandum of Understanding as to Notification, Consultation and Cooperation with Respect to the Application of National Antitrust Laws, Mar. 9, 1984, United States–Canada, *reprinted in* 4 Trade Reg. Rep. (CCH) ¶ 13,503. This agreement has served as a model for the most recent version of the OECD recommendation on antitrust cooperation, Revised Recommendation of the OECD Council Concerning Cooperation Between Member Countries on Restrictive Practices Affecting International Trade, OECD Doc. No. C(86)44 (Final) (May 21, 1986).

14 U.S.–Canada Mutual Legal Assistance Treaty in Criminal Matters (1985).

Increased cooperation—indeed, harmonization—is, of course, no longer the exclusive concern of the OECD nations. The Division has been active in consulting with the Soviet Union and with Eastern European governments that wish our advice on antitrust matters, including the formation of free market economies. In October 1989, the Attorney General visited the Soviet Union, where one of the topics high on the agenda was a request for advice on competition policy. This meeting was followed by President Bush's offer to President Gorbachev to provide technical assistance on antitrust and other economic matters. Later this year, the Department and the FTC will host a week-long seminar on competition policy for officials of the Soviet Union and its republics who have requested an in-depth look at the United States' experience with free market dynamics.

The formation of democratic governments in Eastern Europe has prompted other requests for technical advice on the formation of competition policy. Antitrust Division and FTC officials have traveled on several occasions to Poland and Czechoslovakia, two countries that are making heroic efforts to introduce competition principles. Both countries have sought the United States' advice and technical assistance on legal and structural barriers to free markets, as well as existing trade opportunities. We have engaged in detailed discussions on the technical problems both countries face in the transition to a market economy, and we hope soon to initiate a long-term technical assistance program that would assign Department and FTC lawyers and economists to one or both countries on an extended basis.

Removal of structural barriers

Our efforts to increase cooperation and trade opportunities in global markets are closely aligned with the Department's second major undertaking—to remove structural barriers to trade by promoting competition principles. During 1990, in that connection, I participated on behalf of the Department of Justice as a principal negotiator in the U.S.–Japan Structural Impediments Initiative (SII) talks. The SII talks were aimed at solving some of the deep-rooted structural problems in both our systems that frustrate open markets, and the talks resulted in commitments on the part of both Japan and the United States that should help reduce the structural barriers to trade that we identified over the course of the year-long negotiations.

Early in the SII process, we identified more effective antitrust enforcement in Japan as an important step that could be taken. By July 1990 the Government of Japan had agreed to stronger enforcement of Japan's Antimonopoly Act, including increased criminal enforcement, tougher penalties for antitrust violations, more effective private remedies, and stronger prohibitions against collusive distribution practices which blockade imports from the United States and other countries.[15]

Implementation of these agreements is now under way. High-level study groups are submitting reports for the consideration of the Government of Japan, particularly the Japanese Fair Trade Commission and the Ministry of Justice. The commitments of these agencies to substantially enhance antitrust enforcement is encouraging, and their progress to that goal will be a centerpiece of follow-up SII discussions.

Conclusion

During the past 100 years, the external look of antitrust has varied, but the fundamental goals of antitrust—preserving a free, competitive economy in which the consumer is benefited and well-managed firms flourish—have remained unchanged. These goals endure because they are basic to the values that underlie our nation's economic system—a system which other countries are now striving to emulate.

---

[15] U.S.–Japan Structural Impediments Initiative, Final Report, June 28, 1990.

11
Merger enforcement: out of the courtroom after 75 years

BY ROBERT H. McGUCKIN, III*

I. Introduction

Merger policy has undergone many changes during the 75 years since the Clayton Act was adopted in 1914. Most commentators now recognize that horizontal combinations are the major concern of antitrust authorities.[1] Reflecting this view, the latest revisions to the Department of Justice [DOJ] Merger Guidelines issued in 1982 and 1984 place enforcement emphasis on horizontal mergers.[2]

---

*AUTHOR'S NOTE: The judgments and conclusions are mine and do not necessarily reflect those of the Census Bureau. Skillful assistance was given by Charles Larrabee, and helpful advice was received from Thomas Abbott, Stephen Andrews, and Timothy Dunne.

1 The correctness of this focus, while widely accepted, is of course not unanimous: Some commentators think that no mergers should be proscribed, while others believe that even conglomerate mergers should not be allowed. I take merger policy to be a part of the general antitrust goal of limiting anticompetitive conduct. Thus restrictions of mergers on the grounds that they disrupt local economies or are unfair to labor are viewed as outside the antitrust debate.

2 U.S. DEPARTMENT OF JUSTICE, ANTITRUST DIVISION, U.S. DEPARTMENT OF JUSTICE MERGER GUIDELINES (1984). The 1984 Guidelines are substantively almost identical to those issued by the DOJ in 1982. They replaced DOJ Merger Guidelines first issued in 1968. *See* Trade Reg. Rep. (CCH No. 4430 (1968).

Even with a consensus on the appropriateness of a merger policy that focuses on horizontal acquisitions, there is still argument about the specific standards and rules used to judge when a horizontal combination is anticompetitive. This is not surprising, for the new enforcement Guidelines issued by the DOJ relax the standards in the 1968 Guidelines they replaced. The DOJ caseload data, consistent with a more liberal enforcement policy, show an enormous decline in the number of merger cases brought by the DOJ in the past 15 years, despite a major merger movement during the period.[3] As one would suspect with the change in policy focus to horizontal mergers, vertical and conglomerate merger cases have been virtually eliminated. But the number of horizontal cases has also dropped significantly.[4]

What inferences can be drawn about antitrust enforcement policy and effectiveness from caseload data? At first glance, the decline in DOJ merger cases would appear to reflect a real cutback in merger enforcement, even for horizontal mergers. But indexes of enforcement policy based on cases filed can provide misleading signals of enforcement objectives and effectiveness. Use of caseload data as a measure of the impact or effectiveness of enforcement is especially suspect in the years following the passage of the Hart-Scott-Rodino Antitrust Improvements Act [HSR] in 1976. Since that time a substantial portion of the enforcement of the Clayton Act was conducted outside the courtroom. Mergers were proposed, papers were filed with the enforcement agencies, evaluations were undertaken, and negotiations were conducted and concluded between enforcement agencies and the merging firms, with the courts only coming into play when negotiations failed. Thus the HSR procedural innovations led to new "internal" review procedures. The caseload data will not reveal such activity unless a divestiture or spinoff is part of a consent order. Moreover, little in the way of administrative information is produced by the DOJ regarding these internal activities. In this

---

3 *See* Johnson & Smith, *Antitrust Division Merger Procedures and Policy, 1968–1984*, 32 ANTITRUST BULL. 967 (1987). Their paper also offers substantial evidence that the new Merger Guidelines formally codified DOJ policy that had actually changed in the 1970's.

4 *Id.*

environment, it is especially difficult to assess the extent of substantive enforcement actions through caseload analysis.

In this article I present new evidence on the nature and extent of horizontal mergers among the largest competitors in 1,500 manufacturing product classes or lines of business classifications during the 1972–1982 period.[5] Before turning to an examination of the data on allowed mergers, I briefly review merger enforcement since the passage of the Clayton Act. This discussion serves to emphasize and illustrate the importance of evidence on the universe of allowed mergers—those not challenged by authorities—in evaluations of current enforcement policy.

II. Merger enforcement

For purposes of exposition I divide merger enforcement into three periods. The first consists of the period from passage of the Clayton Act in 1914 to its amendment in 1950; the second is the period from 1950 until the adoption of DOJ guidelines in 1968, and the third is the period from 1968 to the present.

A. The early years

As described in A. D. Neale's classic treatise, the Clayton Act represented a compromise on procedural grounds.[6] The House of Representatives favored drafting section 7 in such a way as to outlaw specific practices if the effect was to substantially lessen competition. Among the most important practices cited was the acquisition of stock in competing companies. The Senate favored an approach that would have allowed the Federal Trade Commission to operate as an expert body to evaluate and proscribe "unfair methods of competition."[7] The compromise adopted in the law was

---

5 Similar data to judge the effects of mergers in the post-1982 period are not yet available.

6 A. D. NEALE, THE ANTITRUST LAWS OF THE U.S.A., A STUDY OF COMPETITION ENFORCED BY LAW (2d ed. 1970).

7 Section 5 of the Federal Trade Commission Act.

to list several specific practices that were prohibited in cases "where the effect may be to substantially lessen competition or tend to create a monopoly." This qualifying phrase was felt to provide antitrust enforcers with flexibility while sending specific instructions that certain practices were condemned by the Congress.

Unfortunately, because the language of the Act limited it to a narrow class of transaction, section 7 was drafted in such a way that virtually any merger could be consummated. In particular, despite the fact that stock acquisitions had figured prominently in the debate on the Act, by the 1920's the Court had ruled that they were outside the scope of the law.[8] Thus as long as the merger transaction was structured carefully, antitrust enforcers could be circumvented.

The procedural aspects of the law limited its reach, although the substantive goal of the legislation was an area of agreement. Prohibiting trust building or monopolization activity was seen as the primary objective of the legislation. This vision is remarkably similar to today's, even though procedural deficiencies in the law made merger policy ineffective during the 35 years following its passage.

B. The Celler-Kefauver amendment

The enforcement environment changed dramatically after the Celler-Kefauver amendment to section 7 was adopted in 1950. After the Celler-Kefauver Act, the form of the transaction largely became a nonissue as far as enforcement was concerned. The focus of the debate on merger policy centered on the interpretation of the phrase "to substantially lessen competition."[9]

In the second era of merger enforcement, as with the first, the caseload data reflected the limits of merger policy. An examination of the individual cases provides a guide to enforcement standards—very strict in the post–Celler-Kefauver period and lenient in the

---

8 *See* Swift and Company v. Federal Trade Commission, S.C. (1926).

9 *See*, for example, DEPARTMENT OF JUSTICE, THE REPORT OF THE ATTORNEY GENERAL'S NATIONAL COMMITTEE TO STUDY THE ANTITRUST LAWS (1955).

prior period. Unlike the pre-amendment period, the cases represent a rich source of information on enforcement objectives and the practical problems associated with them. The cases illustrate the difficulty in applying economic concepts such as markets and monopoly power, which are hard to measure precisely. The cases also overwhelmingly reflect matters of substance: the appropriate standards for judging a horizontal merger anticompetitive and whether restrictions should be extended to conglomerate mergers. Commentators recognized that determining the likelihood that a merger would reduce competition required careful economic analysis.

Also, unlike the previous period, strict enforcement raised to importance the issue of the extent to which beneficial mergers were deterred.[10] Antitrust enforcers, aided by a supportive Supreme Court, created a policy that had as its essential ingredient a willingness for the courts to stop almost any merger in which an argument could be made that a competitor might be hurt. In the *Von's* case, for example, "substantial" was a 5% share of a relatively unconcentrated market.[11] In the 20 years following the passage of the Celler-Kefauver Act, the Department of Justice and the Federal Trade Commission did not lose a single case at the Supreme Court level. Although enforcement was never quite so constraining for conglomerate mergers as for horizontal or vertical mergers, by the time the Justice Department issued its first set of merger guidelines in 1968, antitrust policy was a significant constraint on firm growth by mergers. The DOJ had virtual carte blanche in deciding when a merger was anticompetitive.

C. The 1970's and beyond

The 1968 Guidelines represented a high-water mark in enforcement against horizontal mergers. The restrictiveness of the

---

10 Posner, *A Statistical Study of Antitrust Enforcement*, 13 J.L. & ECON. 365 (1970). The extent of such deterrence is difficult to measure because one cannot observe mergers that would have been undertaken in the absence of legal prohibitions.

11 United States v. Von's Grocery Company, 384 U.S. 270 (1966).

Guidelines' policy was reduced through changes implemented in the 1970's and codified in new DOJ Guidelines in 1982 and revised in 1984. The new Guidelines reflect a more lenient policy with respect to market share. They also reflect new procedures for determining antitrust markets and include explicit recognition of entry barriers and related economic concepts, such as weighing probable efficiency gains against potential anticompetitive effects. Thus the new policies cannot be adequately described as a simple relaxation of market share standards.

The examination of current enforcement policy through litigated cases is less informative today than in previous years because of procedural changes resulting from passage of the HSR Act in 1976. The HSR Act made it virtually impossible for a merger exceeding a $15 million threshold limit to be consummated before undergoing antitrust review. Before its passage, authorities learned when mergers were about to take place or had taken place from the financial press and related sources. Sometimes the authorities missed mergers altogether. Often enforcers found themselves proceeding against a merger after it had taken place and the assets had been (hopelessly) shuffled. In other cases, difficult injunctive proceedings had to be undertaken to stop a merger while evidence could be obtained through discovery. Once the discovery process was complete, the case often was dropped because the evidence suggested no violation. Unfortunately, there was no mechanism to collect the information prior to the filing of a case.

These problems were greatly reduced, if not eliminated, because the HSR Act required that for most mergers the parties notify and provide information to the enforcement authorities before the merger. In fact, preliminary injunctions and protracted relief proceedings appear to be a thing of the past. Johnson and Smith report that the proportion of cases filed and then dropped declined from a substantial fraction of the total merger cases before the Act was passed to virtually none following its passage.[12]

The Act also made it very difficult to evaluate merger policy. The premerger notification provisions ensured that the enforcement

12 Johnson & Smith, *supra* note 3.

authorities could evaluate the merger before it was consummated. This meant that in addition to providing the merging firms with a statement of their enforcement plans before the merger, the enforcers could provide the merging firms with a description of those segments of the companies that violated antitrust standards. Typically, these segments represented a small part of the merging firms' assets. Thus the firms could often sell off those portions of the firm that raised antitrust concerns and thereby proceed with the merger.

These procedural changes are sensible, because they reduce the required expenditures for all participants in the process. The only problem is that it is now difficult for an outsider to evaluate enforcement. In typical administrative proceedings there is a public record that observers can examine. This is not the case for mergers that are approved via restructuring by divesting some segments of the merging firms' operations. In particular, even though the identity of the merger is known, the details of these negotiations are unavailable. Consequently, current merger policy cannot be fully evaluated without some details concerning those mergers that have been allowed to be consummated. Moreover, because merger policy standards have been relaxed from those in place prior to the early 1970's, an examination of currently allowed mergers provides good evidence of the extent to which previous enforcement standards deterred beneficial mergers. It is to these issues that we now turn.

III. Evaluation of current merger policy

In this section we examine horizontal mergers among large manufacturing firms in the period 1972–1982. After identifying consummated horizontal mergers, we examine each for compliance with the market share and concentration standards in the 1968 DOJ Guidelines. The set of allowed mergers that violate the 1968 standards provides an indication of the leniency of current DOJ policies relative to those in place in 1968. Since the 1968 standards are quite strict, this set of mergers should also encompass most of those that a priori might be anticompetitive. Following this, we ascertain whether those mergers that would have been prohibited under the old standard are anticompetitive, and we thereby evaluate current policy. This is accomplished through an examination of postmerger price-cost margins, market share, and related information concerning conduct and performance.

A. Data

The data for this analysis are derived from the Longitudinal Research Database [LRD] maintained at the Center for Economic Studies at the U.S. Bureau of the Census. This panel of manufacturing establishments is obtained by linking plant-level Census of Manufactures and Annual Survey of Manufactures data from 1972 to 1986.[13] Individual plants or establishments are the basic reporting unit for the data. They are linked through time by a permanent plant identification number. In addition, the LRD contains a code that identifies the firm owning the plant in each year.

Each plant is classified in that industry or product class that accounts for the largest proportion of its shipments. Using this information, I developed a size ranking of producers in each of the roughly 450 4-digit industries and 1,500 5-digit product classes in manufacturing. This was accomplished by combining all establishments with common ownership by product class and then ranking the firms by size, measured by total value of shipments. A firm was separately identified in all product classes in which its plants were classified. Throughout the discussion I refer to a competitor or firm in a specific product class as a line of business.[14]

The analysis is based on all horizontal mergers undertaken among manufacturing lines of businesses during the 1972–1982 period. Mergers are identified by comparing the ownership of each line of business in 1982 and 1977 with its ownership in 1977 and 1972, respectively. Each case in which separate lines of business in the same industry or product class at the beginning of a period had

---

13 *See* McGuckin & Pascoe, *The Longitudinal Research Database (LRD): Status and Research Possibilities*, 69 SURVEY OF CURRENT BUSINESS (1988) for a more complete description of the LRD.

14 This terminology follows that used by F. M. SCHERER & D. J. RAVENSCRAFT, MERGERS, SELLOFFS, AND ECONOMIC EFFICIENCY (1987).

common ownership at the end of the period is counted as a horizontal merger.

There were several reasons for selecting the 1972–1982 period. Of greatest importance was the fact that both years represented census years. In census years data are collected from the complete manufacturing universe. Also, a special survey identifies ownership of establishments for census years.[15] Unless there are substantial divestitures or closures by merging lines of business during the interval over which the changes in ownership are identified, use of census years is an appropriate method for identifying horizontal mergers. Moreover, even if some mergers are missed, they will not tend to be mergers which create large market shares that can be exploited for monopoly profits.

The beginning of the sample period, 1972, was the year in which the Economic Policy Office [EPO] of the DOJ was formed. According to Johnson and Smith, the formation of the EPO represented the beginning of the shift in policy emphasis toward a more liberal view of horizontal mergers and away from enforcement against vertical and conglomerate activity.[16] Although I would have preferred to use 1987 as the end of the period, data for such an analysis will not be available until late 1990. Nonetheless, 1982 is when the new Merger Guidelines were first issued by DOJ, and it marks the end of the period in which the policy had been in place but not officially announced. Moreover, by this time the procedural changes introduced by the HSR Act were in place.

The 5-digit product class is our basic unit of analysis. Though certainly not markets in the antitrust sense, the 5-digit product classes represent a detailed product classification. By way of contrast, there are more than 1,500 5-digit product classes but only 450 4-digit Standard Industry Classification [SIC] codes. Often the industrial classification system is criticized on the grounds that the

15 The data for annual survey years contain more noise because the sampling design is not as focused on ownership changes.

16 Johnson & Smith, *supra* Note 3.

4-digit SIC codes represent too broad an amalgamation of products.[17] This is surely true in many cases, particularly when viewed from the demand side of the market. In fact, even the 5-digit classification may be too broad in some instances. But in some respects the classifications are too narrow: that is, markets can span individual 4- and 5-digit classifications because in some cases rapid changes in the classification of products produced in individual plants are observed to coincide with shifts in relative demand. Despite these potential pitfalls, the 5-digit breakout should give a good idea of the set of potentially anticompetitive mergers.[18]

B. Mergers in manufacturing

I identified 300 separate horizontal mergers among lines of business in 5-digit product classes in the 1972–1982 period.[19] Of this group, 114 took place after 1977. In other words, about 38% of the horizontal mergers took place in the second half of the 10-year period. By way of comparison, there were 14,494 merger transactions in the 1973–1982 period.[20] Of these transactions, 63% took

---

17 *See, for example*, G. J. WERDEN, THE DIVERGENCE OF SIC INDUSTRIES FROM ANTITRUST MARKETS: SOME EVIDENCE FROM PRICE FIXING CASES (Economic Analysis Group Discussion Paper 88–9, 1988).

18 The issue of the broadness of market definition is not confined simply to production technology. Transportation costs are also important in defining the geographic boundaries of the market. Since our data are national, they may represent too narrow (international) or too broad (local) markets for antitrust analysis. Below, I make attempts to look at these factors for particular mergers in the sample.

19 In 9 other instances the data suggested a horizontal merger, but information was missing. It is worth noting that by widening the scope of the market the number of observed horizontal mergers increased. When the 4-digit level of classification detail was employed, the number of horizontal mergers increased by roughly 25%. However, if attention is restricted to just the top 20 lines of business in each industry, the total number of observed horizontal mergers was about the same as reported in the text for the 5-digit classification.

20 Reported in Lichtenberg & Siegel, *Productivity and Changes in Ownership of Manufacturing Plants*, 3 BROOKINGS PAPERS ON ECONOMIC ACTIVITY 643 (1987).

place after 1977. This means that while the number of horizontal mergers among 5-digit lines of business in manufacturing showed a decline toward the end of the 1970's and early 1980's, overall the number of mergers increased.[21]

In contrast to horizontal mergers, the distribution of merger activity among the top 20 manufacturing lines of business in 1972 characterized as conglomerate acquisitions parallelled that found for all merger transactions during the period.[22] These data are in line with a view that a liberalization in merger policy toward conglomerate mergers began with the formation of the EPO in the DOJ in 1972 and was solidified by the end of the decade. They do not suggest any differential leniency toward horizontal mergers.

Of the 300 lines of business sold in the 1972–1982 period, only 133 are in well-defined product groupings for which concentration ratios and similar statistics are developed. The other 167 horizontal mergers represent agglomeration of lines of business classified in miscellaneous or not-elsewhere-classified groupings. These classifications contain lines of business in a wide variety of activities and statistical problem cases. For this reason, further analysis was restricted to the 133 sellers in well-defined product groupings.

Although the identified horizontal mergers involved 133 distinct sellers, they included only 104 buying lines of business. In fact, only 72 of the selling lines of business represented sales to a one-time buyer. Thus a large portion of the mergers involved multiple purchases by a single buyer. This pattern suggests that for some of the mergers the market shares involved could be quite large.

C. The trend of market shares

We begin our examination of the data by comparing the premerger market share of the merging firms with those observed after

21 Based on top 20 lines of business at the 4-digit level, the 1972–1979 and 1977–1982 periods show relatively equal levels of major activity.

22 McGuckin & Andrews, The Performance of Lines of Business Acquired in Conglomerate Mergers (mimeo 1988).

the merger. Horizontal mergers followed by increased market share suggest efficiency gains to a merger, while decreases in market share are consistent with anticompetitive output restrictions. The average combined market share (the sum of the two firms' market shares prior to merger) for the 50 horizontal transactions involving a separate buyer in the post-1977 period are .061 for 1977 and .055 for 1982. The 54 pre-1977 transactions show a different time pattern across the sample period: This group of mergers has mean shares of .055 in 1972, .051 in 1977, and .061 in 1982. The contrast between the increase in combined share for those mergers undertaken before 1977 and the fall in combined share for the post-1977 merger sample is consistent with the view that merger standards were reduced toward the latter part of the period. It is also consistent with the view that mergers toward the end of the 1972–1982 period were anticompetitive or had fewer efficiencies associated with them than did those at the beginning of the period.

There are several reasons for being skeptical about drawing a conclusion that these mean shares reflect anticompetitive mergers. First, the differences in market share are not statistically significant for either grouping.[23] Second, in related work on conglomerate mergers it was found that increased performance, as measured by market share gains, took some time to achieve. In fact, McGuckin and Andrews[24] found a very similar pattern of market share changes for pure conglomerate acquisitions. Third, although my experience with the EPO during the relevant period suggests that the influence of economists increased, the relevant issue is whether this increasing influence led to more anticompetitive mergers. There are explanations other than reduced competition for the pattern of market shares observed in the data. Of particular interest is the possibility that reductions in market shares arose from consolidations of capac-

23 The variances observed for the combined shares in each year were large relative to the mean: The standard deviation of the combined shares was .057 in 1972 and .052 in 1982 for the 50 post-1977 mergers. For the .054 pre-1977 mergers the standard deviations were .061 and .076, respectively. The increase in the variances in the combined market shares observed in 1982 suggests that the performance of the merged firms is difficult to predict.

24 McGuckin & Andrews, *supra* note 22.

ity in declining industries. Also, the mid-1970's saw dramatic increases in foreign competition that would have reduced the value of domestic capacity. Finally, the observed average premerger and postmerger market share is small, less than 7%. This hardly suggests a great weakening of enforcement standards.

D. Mergers violating the 1968 Guidelines

Nevertheless, the mean of the market shares hides a considerable number of mergers that have market shares greater than those allowed by the 1968 DOJ Guidelines. In fact, some mergers also violate the prima facie market share standards in the 1982 Guidelines. Because confidentiality standards are associated with the data, we cannot report any specifics on those mergers whose market shares would not have passed the 1968 Guidelines. But we can classify each of the 104 mergers by comparing the premerger combined market share of the merging firms and the 4-firm concentration ratio of the 5-digit product group in which the lines of business are classified with the published standards in the Guidelines. Of the 104 horizontal mergers observed among the largest lines of business, 17 (9 after 1977 and 8 before 1977) do not pass the prima facie standards in the 1968 Guidelines.[25] There is no concentration of these mergers by industry. In fact, the distribution of all mergers provides no hint of a pattern, with the possible exception of food, which had a disproportionate number of the total mergers.

E. Premerger market structure

Table 1 shows the distribution of the 17 mergers that on prima facie grounds violate the 1968 Guidelines thresholds by market concentration. Even though the concentration classes were chosen with an eye to confidentiality, the results are startling. There were 5 mergers in which the 4-firm concentration ratio was above .50 and 5 in the .40-.49 range. These are relatively concentrated markets. Moreover, the market shares of the merging lines of business are not small. Though not shown in table 1, for the 8 lines of business

25 If the 5-digit product classes are too broad, then this procedure might understate the number of mergers violating the guidelines.

that merged before 1977 the average combined market share is .18, whereas for transactions after 1977 the combined market shares are around .17. These measures of market structure would raise concerns among many antitrust practitioners.

Table 1

Horizontal Mergers with Market Share of Merging Firms and Market Concentration which Exceeded the Thresholds of the 1968 DOJ Guidelines, 1972–1982

Market concentration prior to merger	*Number of mergers*	*Change in market share**	*Change in price-cost margin**
>.50	5	+.011	+.043
.40–.49	5	–.012	–.007
<.40	6	–.043	–.086
Total	17	–.015	–.020
Time of Merger			
Pre-1977	8	+.025	–.003
Post-1977	9	–.051	–.045

* Calculated over the period 1977–1982.

Before drawing any conclusions, I examined the performance of the mergers. As recognized in the 1982 Guidelines, efficiencies, low entry barriers, the amount of capacity that could be brought into production within a year, and related factors can overcome a prima facie case against a merger based on a market structure. Moreover, it is well to remember that the market classifications I use are product class groupings, not antitrust markets. With these factors in mind, I use changes in price-cost margins following the merger as a measure of the firm's performance.[26] The results of this examination are shown in the last two columns of table 1.

26 The price-cost margin was calculated as value of shipments less variable costs, which include labor, materials, and costs of purchased services. They were calculated from establishment data and do not include allocations for advertising and capital services.

What is surprising about table 1 is the postmerger performance of the combined firms. Whether looked at from the standpoint of market shares or price-cost margins, those mergers in markets with high initial concentration ratios show better performance. Thus, the 5 mergers in markets in which the concentration ratio is above .50 showed positive gains in both market shares and price-cost margins. In the 11 other mergers, particularly in markets in which concentration was below .40, both market shares and price-cost margins fell.

The 8 pre-1977 mergers show relatively similar price-cost margins (-.003) to all horizontal mergers (-.008), the 9 post-1977 mergers exhibit significantly greater losses (-.045) in price-cost margins than do all horizontal mergers after 1977 (-.008). This is probably a reflection of the short time involved following the merger.

Together, increases in market shares and profitability together suggest efficiency gains to the mergers. Consistent with this finding is the uniformly better performance in the concentrated markets and the fact that the pre-1977 mergers, those in which the merging firms had some time to integrate the merged facilities, have the best performance.

In table 2, changes in price-cost margins are displayed in three categories: large increases, large decreases (greater than .06 percentage points), and relatively stable (less than a .06 percentage point change). The 17 mergers are not equally distributed across the three groups. Most fell in the large decreases category. The second and third columns of table 2 reinforce the conclusion drawn from table 1 that postmerger performance is best for mergers in relatively concentrated markets and with large market shares.

Finally, in an admittedly subjective exercise I examined those mergers with the greatest prima facie likelihood for anticompetitive impact (high product class concentration and large market shares) according to the characteristics of the product class in which they fell. I was particularly interested in industry demand growth, the existence of foreign competition, and whether the 5-digit product class

Table 2

Distribution of Mergers by Change in Price-Cost Margins, 1972–1982*

Change in price-cost margin (PCMR)	*Number*	*Average product class concentration*	*Average premerger combined market shareof merging lines of business*
PCMR ≥ .06	4	51	.20
–.06 < PCMR < .06	4	40	.17
PCMR < .06	9	45	.16
TOTAL	17		

* Average change in price-cost margin for all 104 horizontal mergers = –.008.

was too narrowly defined. These three factors would tend to offset the likelihood that a merger would lead to anticompetitive performance and would probably be considered by antitrust concerns.

For the five mergers that on prima facie grounds had the most likely anticompetitive impact, I found one in which it appeared that market concentration and market shares were overstated because of intensive foreign competition and two in which the product class appeared too narrow so that there were numerous potential entrants. In these instances the market share standards could reasonably be expected to be adjusted downward. The other two mergers are both in relatively slowly growing markets, but neither could be dismissed on the basis of readily available information as having mitigating factors that would offset Guideline presumptions. For both, performance following the merger was relatively poor.

I also looked at the set of horizontal mergers showing the best performance in terms of increased price-cost margins. With one exception, the data do not suggest an anticompetitive explanation as the source of the gains. In two of the four cases market share increased substantially after the merger. In another the market share was virtually constant. The remaining merger showed a large gain in price-cost margins and a falling market share. This is the most likely candidate for showing that the new policy is too lenient.

IV. Conclusions

Overall, the data do not suggest any move to unchallenged anticompetitive mergers. The percentage of horizontal mergers in manufacturing did not increase after 1977. Moreover, the absolute totals do not indicate a strong movement designed to cash in on lenient enforcement policies. While a significant fraction (10%–15%) of the observed horizontal mergers had market shares greater than those allowed under the 1968 Merger Guidelines of the DOJ, performance measures do not suggest that the mergers had anticompetitive effects. Furthermore, some of the observed violations of the 1968 Guidelines' also violated the 1982 standards. This suggests that special factors overrode the prima facie case against the market share standards. This possibility was supported by information on the product markets associated with those mergers with the most likely competitive impacts. Intensive foreign competition and a too narrowly defined market, indicating that concentration and market share are overstated, characterized these product classes.

These results show that enforcement of the Clayton Act against horizontal mergers remained vigorous in the manufacturing sector despite the relatively low level of observed DOJ cases after 1972. Examination of mergers approved by enforcement authorities during the 1972–1982 period suggests that current policy is not allowing anticompetitive mergers to be consummated. If anything, the evidence suggests that the earlier standards deterred beneficial mergers. The new Guidelines probably encouraged conglomerate and vertical mergers as well as mergers among firms in broadly related activities. But relaxation of the market share standards that characterized enforcement in the 1960's has not led to anticompetitive mergers. I conclude that the Clayton Act is alive and well 75 years after its passage.

12
Economic and political foundations of section 7 enforcement in the 1980's

BY STEPHEN A. RHOADES and JIM BURKE*

I. Introduction

Section 7 of the Clayton Act (1914) finally became an effective antitrust law when the "asset loophole" was closed by the Celler-Kefauver amendment to the act in 1950. Since that time, section 7 has gone through various phases of enforcement, from vigorous enforcement during the 1960's to more cautious enforcement during the 1980's. A good deal of attention has been devoted to the legislative intent, landmark cases, and earlier enforcement of section 7 so we will not discuss these matters in any detail. Instead we explore some of the causes and consequences of the remarkable turnabout in enforcement of section 7 during the 1980's.

---

* Federal Reserve Board, Washington, D.C.

AUTHORS' NOTE: *The views expressed herein are the authors' and do not necessarily reflect the views of the Board or its staff. For helpful comments we thank Dean Amel, Anthony Cyrnak, Timothy Hannan, and Nellie Liang.*

We propose that a strong confluence of economic and political thinking has been the primary cause of cautious enforcement of section 7 during the 1980's. We discuss the evidence supporting this proposition and present tests of one of the key economic theories, contestability theory, underlying cautious enforcement of section 7. In addition, we present (1) findings of a simulation of merger activity in banking based on the Justice Department's 1982 horizontal merger guidelines, and (2) data on recent merger activity in the industrial sector and banking. The simulation and merger data suggest that the economic and political thinking of the 1980's have been effectively implemented as a matter of public policy, resulting in a substantial increase in merger activity and the potential for additional consolidation in the future.

We conclude that the economic foundation for the approach to section 7 enforcement in the 1980's is probably no stronger than it was in the 1960's. Specifically, while technical and interpretive developments in economics since 1970 have raised important questions and doubts about the foundations for enforcement during the 1960's, equally important questions have been raised about the economic underpinnings of section 7 enforcement in the 1980's. Until these questions are resolved, speculation as to the future course of section 7 enforcement, *i.e.*, more cautious or more vigorous, seems especially hazardous.

II. Background and perspective

To place the present course of section 7 enforcement in perspective, it is useful to review briefly the legislative and economic foundations of the Celler-Kefauver amendment to section 7 and its early enforcement. By the 1940's, section 7 of the original Clayton Act was proving to be an ineffective law for inhibiting mergers because of the "asset loophole."[1] The act

---

[1] The discussion in this section is based partly on Bok, *Section 7 of the Clayton Act and the Merging of Law and Economics*, 74 HARV. L. REV. 226–355 (1960); Brodley, *Oligopoly Power Under the Sherman and Clayton Acts—From Economic Theory to Legal Policy*, 19 STAN. L. REV. 285–366 (1967); A. D. NEALE & D. G. GOYDER, THE ANTITRUST LAWS OF THE U.S.A. chap. 7 (3d ed. 1980); and I. M. STELZER, SELECTED ANTITRUST CASES: LANDMARK DECISIONS chap. 2 (3d ed. 1966).

prohibited the acquisition by one corporation of the stock of another where the result would be a substantial lessening of competition between the companies. It did not, however, prohibit *asset* acquisitions, which provided a loophole that was exploited.

In addition to recognizing the ineffectiveness of the original section 7, some members of Congress became concerned with the pace of merger activity and the apparent increasing levels of business concentration in the American economy suggested by a major Federal Trade Commission study.[2] In addition to the ineffectiveness of section 7 of the Clayton Act due to the asset loophole, sections 1 and 2 of the Sherman Act (1890) were also regarded as ineffective in stemming increases in industry concentration. This was because of the law's requirement that a monopoly exist already or that intent to monopolize must be proven in order to challenge a merger. These considerations led to a major push for new antitrust legislation to supplement the Sherman Act. The Senate stated its objective as follows:

> . . . Broadly stated, the bill, in its treatment of unlawful restraints and monopolies, seeks to prohibit and make unlawful certain trade practices which, as a rule, singly and in themselves, are not covered by the act of July 2, 1890 [the Sherman Act], or other existing antitrust acts, and thus, by making these practices illegal, to arrest the creation of trusts, conspiracies, and monopolies in their incipiency and before consummation . . . .[3]

Ultimately, congressional concern with the trend toward rising concentration and the inadequacy of existing antitrust laws led to passage of the Celler-Kefauver Act amending section 7 of the Clayton Act in 1950. The amendment states in part:

> That no corporation engaged in commerce shall acquire, directly or indirectly, the whole or any part of the stock or other share capital and no corporation subject to the jurisdiction of the Federal Trade Commission shall acquire the whole or any part of the assets of another corporation engaged also in commerce, where in any line of commerce in any section of the country, the effect of such acquisition

---

2 FEDERAL TRADE COMMISSION, THE PRESENT TREND OF CORPORATE MERGERS AND ACQUISITIONS (1948).

3 I. M. STELZER, *supra* note 1 at 69.

may be substantially to lessen competition or to tend to create a monopoly.

The unusually lengthy legislative history of the amended Clayton Act indicates that Congress intended this law to extend well beyond the Sherman Act to provide a tool for stopping mergers before a monopoly or near monopoly was created. It is also clear that increasing business concentration raised numerous noneconomic and sociopolitical issues that concerned Congress at that time. It was argued, for example, that (1) maintaining many small businesses and the local control of industry are desirable goals; (2) there are political dangers posed by concentration of business; and (3) there would be a loss of individual independence and initiative with increasing control over the economy by big business. As one student of the legislative history of the Celler-Kefauver Act observed:

> . . . it seems abundantly clear that "competition" meant far more to Congress than prices, costs, and product innovations. Hence, where economic doctrine is to be applied, it must be a doctrine which takes account of the broader range of interests which Congress had in mind if the statute is to be fairly interpreted.[4]

In spite of the various noneconomic arguments supporting passage of the Celler-Kefauver amendment, the new section 7 explicitly mentioned only economic concepts and resulted in the marriage of law and economics to a greater degree than had any earlier antitrust law. The law is explicit as to the need to define and apply basic economic concepts when judging the competitive effects of a merger. Both product and geographic *markets* (*i.e.*, ". . . in any line of commerce in any section of the country . . . .") must be defined, and *competition* must be assessed or measured (*i.e.*, ". . . the effect of such acquisition may be substantially to lessen competition . . . ."). However, the wording of section 7 is very broad, and the Congress provided little guidance regarding the application of these economic concepts. Essentially, Congress expressed its intent regarding competitive effects of mergers but did not address what constitutes a

---

4 Bok, *supra* note 1, at 248.

violation of the law. In any event, the role Congress gave to economics in the enforcement of section 7 suggests that new developments in economics will have a direct effect on antitrust enforcement toward mergers; a point that will be highlighted in later sections.

Regardless of some observations to the contrary, enforcement of section 7 during the 1950's and 1960's had a rather solid foundation in economic theory and evidence. The economic foundation for the enforcement of the amended section 7 during its early years may be traced to theoretical work on oligopoly and monopolistic competition during the 1930's, especially by Chamberlin and Robinson.[5] The key prediction of this body of theory, from the standpoint of antitrust enforcement, is that the structure of a market, as reflected in the number and size distribution of firms, will influence the pricing behavior and ultimately the profit performance of firms in a market. This is the so-called structure-conduct-performance hypothesis.

Empirical work investigating hypotheses suggested by this theory tended to use the case study approach until Joe Bain's initial cross-section statistical tests in the 1950's.[6] Following Bain's work, there was a large amount of statistical research during the next two decades testing the structure-performance hypothesis. Most of these studies yielded results that supported the hypothesis.[7] The large number of empirical studies and the consistency of their results combined with the incipiency doctrine

---

5 *See* E. CHAMBERLIN, THE THEORY OF MONOPOLISTIC COMPETITION (8th ed. 1965) and J. ROBINSON, THE ECONOMICS OF IMPERFECT COMPETITION (1934).

6 *See* Bain, *Relation of Profit Rate to Industry Concentration: American Manufacturing, 1936–1940*, 65 Q. J. ECON. 293–324 (1951) and BARRIERS TO NEW COMPETITION (1956).

7 For a literature review in the industrial sector *see* Weiss, *The Concentration-Profits Relationship and Antitrust*, in INDUSTRIAL CONCENTRATION: THE NEW LEARNING 184–233 (H. Goldschmid, H. Mann & J. Weston eds. 1974), and for banking *see* S. A. RHOADES, STRUCTURE-PERFORMANCE STUDIES IN BANKING: AN UPDATED SUMMARY AND EVALUATION (Staff Study No. 119, Federal Reserve Board, Aug. 1982).

of the amended section 7, apparently provided the antitrust agencies and the courts with what they regarded as a solid economic and legislative foundation for challenging many mergers. This is reflected in a series of Supreme Court decisions during the 1960's.

The early decisions under amended section 7 established the crucial role of economic analysis in antitrust cases. They also highlighted the difficulty of applying even simple economic concepts, such as the market (much less more complex and uncertain concepts, such as competition) to real-world settings.[8] Finally, these early decisions may have reflected the Supreme Court's efforts to account for some of the noneconomic factors appearing in the legislative history, which could explain some of the arguably strained economics in some decisions.

Brown Shoe (1962) was the first case to come before the Supreme Court under the amended section 7 of the Clayton Act.[9] The Court's decision in that case explicitly recognized oligopoly theory and expressed the Court's intention to inhibit the formation of oligopoly. *Brown Shoe* essentially implemented the incipiency doctrine enunciated earlier by the Congress and was followed by *Philadelphia National Bank* (1963),[10] which was important for several reasons. First, the Supreme Court's decision in *Philadelphia* clearly indicated that the antitrust laws apply to banking, a matter that had been in question. Second, the case is notable for the Court's reliance on the structuralist approach to merger analysis.

---

8 Though market definition seemed to be a key issue in many section 7 cases, the issue was not unique to section 7 cases. For a thorough analysis of the complex market definition issue in *U.S. v. E. I. du Pont de Nemours & Co.*, a monopolization case under section 2 of the Sherman Act, *see* Stocking and Mueller, *The Cellophane Case and the New Competition*, 45 AMER. ECON. REV. 29–63 (1955).

9 Brown Shoe Co. v. United States, 370 U.S. 294 (1962).

10 United States v. Philadelphia National Bank, 374 U.S. 321 (1963).

> Specifically we think that a merger which produces a firm controlling an undue percentage share of the relevant market and results in a significant increase in the concentration of firms in that market is so inherently likely to lessen competition substantially that it must be enjoined in the absence of evidence clearly showing that the merger is not likely to have such anticompetitive effects. . . . Such a test lightens the burden of proving illegality only with respect to mergers whose size makes them inherently suspect in the light of Congress's design in section 7 to prevent undue concentration. Furthermore, the test is fully consonant with economic theory . . . .[11]

Finally, the *Philadelphia* decision firmly established the role of economics in section 7 cases. As one legal scholar noted:

> There was perhaps no more striking fact in the Supreme Court's pioneering *Philadelphia Bank* decision than its reliance upon primary economic authority in shaping a new rule of law for testing the legality of mergers. Bain, Machlup, and Mason, all economists, have become authorities alongside prior judicial precedent and legislative history. The economic assumptions of the Court have been based on the current findings of these and other economists, and a rule of law is required to be more consistent with economic theory than with past precedent.[12]

The *Brown Shoe* and *Philadelphia* decisions were followed by the *Alcoa-Rome* and *Continental Can* cases. Both raised very difficult market definition issues that arguably allowed decisions based on the general concern with large firm size and aggregate concentration to appear as though they were based on a strict analysis of competition.[13] These two decisions were followed by the *Von's Grocery* decision that arguably stretched economic analysis beyond reasonable limits.[14] In *Von's Grocery*, the Court appeared to have stepped away from the structuralist approach to analyzing competition, which had a sound theoretical and empirical foundation. Instead, the Court seemed to use economic

---

11 From A. D. NEALE & D. G. GOYDER, *supra* note 1, at 189.

12 Brodley, *supra* note 1, at 297 and 298.

13 United States v. Aluminum Co. of America, 377 U.S. 271 (1964) and United States v. Continental Can Co., 378 U.S. 441 (1964).

14 United States v. Von's Grocery Co., 384 U.S. 270 (1966).

analysis to cloak a broader analysis based on concerns expressed in the legislative history of section 7 of the Clayton Act.

Certainly the 1960's witnessed vigorous enforcement of the amended section 7. However, it may be that the seeds of dissent that would eventually erode some support of section 7 enforcement were planted in the economics profession by the 1960's decisions in *Alcoa-Rome*, *Continental Can*, and *Von's Grocery*. In particular, the wording of section 7 focused narrowly on economic considerations and the Supreme Court appeared to attempt to present its decisions in terms of economics. Thus, economists may have expected the analysis and decisions in these cases to be based strictly on economic considerations. From this perspective, the decisions in cases such as *Alcoa-Rome*, *Continental Can*, and *Von's Grocery* may be regarded as inadequate. To the extent that economists believed that these decisions, presumed to be based on economic considerations, could not be justified using economic analysis, then they might well conclude that the courts had misused economics.[15] In any event, the vigorous enforcement of the amended section 7 by the Justice Department and courts up through *Von's Grocery* (1966) gradually diminished throughout the 1970's.[16] Enforcement entered a new phase in the 1980's as the result of a strong confluence of economic and political thinking.

---

15 In spite of dissatisfaction among economists, these court decisions may have been wholly justifiable on the basis of various noneconomic considerations. Though such considerations are not spelled out in section 7, they are clearly a part of the formal legislative history of the act. It is, therefore, presumably appropriate for the courts to weigh these noneconomic and noncompetition considerations in reaching a decision. We cannot escape the fact that society has legitimate noneconomic goals. It would, however, be useful if the rationale, whatever it may be, for the courts' decisions were made as clear as possible.

16 For an excellent, detailed account and analysis of merger and enforcement activity *see* WILLARD F. MUELLER, THE CELLER-KEFAUVER ACT: THE FIRST 27 YEARS, prepared for the House Subcommittee on Monopolies and Commercial Law of the Committee on the Judiciary, 96th Cong., 1st Sess. (1980).

III. Political foundations

Shortly after the Reagan administration took office in 1981, it became apparent that antitrust policy in general, and especially toward mergers, was on the agenda for significant change. What is particularly remarkable is not so much that an administration wanted to change the direction of antitrust policy but that the efforts to do so were so widespread, vocal, and persistent. The intended change in enforcement was clearly to be in the direction of more caution. The administration's approach was signaled to the press and business community by speeches and interviews, appointments to antitrust agencies, new merger guidelines, and a legislative proposal that would abolish section 7 of the Clayton Act. These developments are outlined below.

The thrust of the administration's position on antitrust policy is perhaps best conveyed by press reportings based on a variety of administration sources. A collage of these reportings is presented below.

> Securities and Exchange Commission Chairman John S.R. Shad said yesterday that, on balance, mergers are good for America—putting money in the pockets of shareholders to reinvest in the economy.[17]

Citing Mr. Baxter's (Assistant Attorney General for Antitrust) 1979 testimony for the oil industry in opposition to proposed antimerger laws and his statement that ". . . he doesn't believe 'conglomerate mergers, or mergers generally, have increased economic concentration to dangerous levels,' " the *Post* observed,

> This contrast has had a significant impact. Wall Street financiers are being told by their lawyers that almost any merger apparently is worth a try.
>
> "Things are being proposed that would never have been proposed" by companies before the Reagan administration took office, said John Shenefield, an antitrust lawyer in the Carter administration.

---

17 Washington Post, July 14, 1981, at E1, col. 2.

This article went on to note: "Office of Management and Budget Director David Stockman has said he 'disagrees with the whole antitrust tradition.' "[18]

> For the first time since the Depression, the federal government is striving to loosen the restraints that antitrust laws place on big business. "Bigness doesn't necessarily mean badness" declares Attorney General William French Smith. Attacking past enforcement of antitrust laws as "misguided and mistaken," he says, "Efficient firms shouldn't be hobbled under the guise of antitrust enforcement."[19]
>
> In general, big mergers don't bother William Baxter, the new chief of the Justice Department's antitrust division. He believes big businesses are "very valuable things" because they tend to be the most efficient.[20]
>
> The Reagan administration today dropped two antitrust suits filed by the Carter administration after acknowledging that it had created "a more favorable atmosphere for mergers" of big business.[21]
>
> He [Mr. Baxter] believes, for starters, that most mergers are a good thing. And he is a proponent of a relatively new and fundamentally different philosophy known as the Chicago School of antitrust law and economics—so named because it first emanated from scholars at the University of Chicago.[22]
>
> James C. Miller headed Reagan's FTC transition team, which proposed killing the commission's antitrust arm.[23]
>
> Attorney General William French Smith, outlining the new administration's more lenient attitude toward business mergers, said yesterday that competition no longer necessarily requires a large number of competitors in each industry.[24]

---

18 *Id.*, Aug. 23, 1981, at G1, col. 1.

19 Wall Street Journal, July 8, 1981, at A1, col. 1.

20 *Id.*

21 New York Times, July 9, 1981, at D1, col. 1.

22 FORTUNE, October 5, 1981, at 180 (brackets added).

23 *Id.* at 184.

24 Washington Post, June 25, 1981, at B1, col. 5.

The Reagan administration yesterday rewrote the antitrust guidelines that have governed business since the Johnson administration signaling a more permissive era for corporate mergers.

"There is no question they are somewhat more permissive," said Assistant Attorney General William F. Baxter, ... "Their underlying philosophy"—one that the Reagan administration has been following even before the guidelines were issued—"is that mergers are a very, very healthy phenomena of the capital market and should not be interfered with except under exceptional circumstances . . ."[25]

Mr. McGrath, who succeeded William F. Baxter as antitrust chief in December, offered a strong defense of mergers in general as increasing competition, raising efficiency, acting as a "healthy threat" to bad management and contributing to the redeployment of corporate assets.[26]

. . . President Reagan would ask Congress for sweeping antitrust law changes. The changes would relax traditional restrictions on mergers between competitors. They would write into law the Reagan administration's relatively tolerant policy toward mergers in all industries, a policy reflecting the view that mergers often enhance business efficiency.[27]

Loosening restrictions on mergers, Mr. Meese [Attorney General] said, would "make the United States more competitive and eliminate hindrances" in the law that have barred joint corporate projects.[28]

As a result of these guidelines, few mergers have been opposed by the Justice Department. "The current Justice Department policy is not much different from what we would seek through legislation," Mr. Speakes [White House spokesman] said. "But we would like to see it codified."[29]

Mr. Baldridge noted ". . . American industry is also impeded by the Clayton Act of 1914 and the Sherman Act of 1890, which are intended to prevent the formation of monopolies and anti-

---

25 *Id.*, June 15, 1982, at D7, col. 1.

26 New York Times, Mar. 9, 1984, at D13, col. 4.

27 *Id.*, Jan. 15, 1984, at D1, col. 6.

28 *Id.*, at D8, col. 5 (brackets added).

29 *Id.*, at D1, col. 6 (brackets added).

competitive trade practices, such as price-fixing.'' Further, ''Secretary of Commerce Malcolm Baldridge said today that he would press for relaxation of the nation's antimonopoly laws to help industry compete with the record tide of imports.'' And also, ''Mr. Baldridge listed trade reorganization and changes in the antitrust laws as the principal items on his agenda for the year.''[30]

> The White House will propose ''substantial'' changes in federal antitrust laws to prevent future administrations or courts from reversing Reagan administration policy favoring corporate mergers and competition, the head of the Justice Department's antitrust division said this week.[31]
>
> In Ginburg's [Assistant Attorney General for Antitrust] view, antitrust laws have been abused and ''perverted'' at times in the past, to prevent mergers that would have created more competition and a stronger economy. ''In the 1960s, there were cases brought by the government to prevent mergers that in retrospect . . . were obviously procompetitive,'' he said.[32]
>
> FTC Commissioner, James C. Miller III, has repeatedly called for an easing of restraint on mergers, including reporting and waiting periods, arguing that we ''need a competitive market for assets and capital.''[33]
>
> ''Many American industries now compete in global markets, and cannot afford to be shackled by outmoded, unduly restrictive antitrust rules,'' Mr. Meese said.[34]

The press reports and quotations of numerous administration officials speak for themselves. It is clear that, beginning in 1981, a strong political foundation was built for more cautious enforcement of the antitrust laws and section 7 of the Clayton Act in particular.

---

30 New York Times, Feb. 8, 1985, at D12, col. 1.

31 Washington Post, Nov. 28, 1985, at F1, col. 3.

32 *Id.*, at F2, col. 1 (brackets added).

33 Washington Post, Sept. 24, 1985, at E4, col. 1.

34 New York Times, Feb. 20, 1986, at D5, col. 2.

IV. Economic foundations

Remarkably, at the same time that changes in the political arena supported more cautious enforcement of section 7, a number of significant developments in industrial organization economics tended to support such a position. By 1980, these developments in economics had raised numerous questions about the meaning and validity of the many earlier structure-performance [S-P] studies. As a consequence, many economists became uneasy about the straightforward use of earlier S-P studies as the basis for enforcing section 7. To many, a more cautious approach was in order though the appropriate degree of caution may be debated.[35]

This section presents an overview of the theoretical and empirical developments in industrial organization economics that we think have had the most direct effect on recent section 7 enforcement.[36] This review serves three purposes. First, it illus-

---

35 It is an interesting historical parallel that the vigorous enforcement of section 7 during the 1960's and early 1970's was based on similarly consistent political and economic developments. The Kennedy and Johnson administrations were generally optimistic about what the federal government could accomplish with the economy, and Keynesian economics provided the guide for macroeconomic policy. At the microeconomic level, the landmark work of Joe Bain had led, beginning in the late 1950's, to a large number of the structure-performance studies. These studies almost invariably found a strong, positive relationship between the level of industry concentration and profit rates. This work provided what appeared to be a solid basis for vigorous section 7 enforcement, and the political leadership at the time was receptive to applying the research in public policy.

36 We have excluded, for example, theoretical work emphasizing the role of transactions costs in influencing firm behavior and recent game theory suggesting the profitability and feasibility of collusion. Work on transaction costs proposes that firm behavior is aimed at reducing transactions costs. To the extent that mergers serve this goal, there is a potential loss of efficiency from preventing mergers. *See, for example*, Williamson, *Transforming Merger Policy: The Pound of New Perspectives*, 76 AMER. ECON. REV., PAPERS & PROC. 114–19 (1986) and OLIVER E. WILLIAMSON, MARKETS AND HIERARCHIES: ANALYSIS AND ANTI-

trates that, aside from the recent political climate and philosophical views opposing antitrust and other forms of regulation, legitimate economic questions have been raised regarding the interpretation and validity of previous S-P studies. Second, it shows that while questions have been raised it has not been proven that the earlier results or interpretations are incorrect. Third, by highlighting the current uncertainty of the economic foundations for section 7 enforcement, this review suggests the difficulty of predicting the future course of enforcement and of determining the appropriate degree of caution to be exercised in enforcement today.[37]

Early interpretive developments and S-P studies

The earliest questions regarding the validity of the S-P relationship had a sharp, critical tone and gave the impression of being based primarily on a philosophical sentiment for unfettered laissez-faire capitalism.[38] The critical and philosophical tone of

---

TRUST IMPLICATIONS (1975). In contrast to many other developments in industrial organization since 1970, very recent work in game theory suggests that collusion and predatory pricing are feasible and profitable, which goes against the work of only a decade ago. This most recent work tends to support less cautious section 7 enforcement. *See, for example*, Geroski, Phlips, and Ulph, *Oligopoly, Competition and Welfare: Some Recent Developments*, 38 J. INDUS. ECON. 369–86 (1985); and Roberts, *A Signaling Model of Predatory Pricing*, OXFORD ECONOMIC PAPERS, NS, 75–93 (Suppl. Nov. 1986).

37 This review focuses rather narrowly on those developments that have been directly relevant to the meaning and validity of structure-performance studies and the structural approach to merger analysis. A much broader review of economic analyses and issues underlying horizontal merger policy may be found in Pautler, *A Review of the Economic Basis for Broad-Based Horizontal Merger Policy*, 28 ANTITRUST BULL. 571–651 (1983).

38 *See, for example*, Brozen, *Concentration and Structural and Market Disequilibria*, 16 ANTITRUST BULL. 241–48 (1971) and *The Antitrust Task Force Deconcentration Recommendation*, 13 J. L. & ECON. 279–92 (1970). The main substantive point in Brozen's papers is

these early challenges to the S-P model tended to elicit a sharp reaction in kind. This type of debate probably did not provide the basis for the kind of constructive debate and developments that would develop later. It may, however, have served the purpose of attracting scholarly attention to the issue.

While the course of the debate over the meaning and validity of the S-P model was subsequently influenced by various substantive developments in industrial organization economics, elements of the philosophical critique persist. Perhaps most notable is the opposition to section 7 enforcement on grounds that since businessmen are profit maximizers and collusive behavior is very uncommon (due to enforcement problems, potential competition, and so forth) mergers will generally lead to efficiency gains and are, therefore, in the public interest. This is more a philosophical than economic foundation for antitrust policy because it is treated as an established principle even though each element of this position embodies one or more hypotheses. Moreover, conflicting hypotheses and evidence may frequently be found.

Since the earliest philosophical attacks on the S-P model, the questions raised have been generally less sharply critical and more constructive. Harold Demsetz' reinterpretation of the results of earlier S-P studies marks the beginning of these developments. In a 1973 paper, Demsetz proposed that the positive statistical relationship found between industry concentration and profits in

---

that the cross-section findings, for individual years, of a positive S-P relationship capture a short-run transitory relationship. Over the long run, Brozen believed that industry profits would not remain abnormally high and supported this position by reexamining the industries used in Bain's landmark study over a longer period. A further examination of the persistence of profits among Bain's industries by Qualls found that high profits tend to persist, thus refuting the Brozen view. A major original empirical study by Mueller also found evidence that high firm profits tend to persist in the long run. At this time, many students of industrial organization would accept the proposition that there is a long-run, positive relationship between industry (firm) profits and concentration. The major debate today is over the source of the high profits. *See*, Bain, Q. J. ECON., *supra* note 6; Qualls, *Stability & Persistence of Profit Margins in Highly Concentrated Industries*, 40 S. ECON. J. 604–12 (1974); and DENNIS C. MUELLER, PROFITS IN THE LONG RUN (1986).

most S-P studies was *not* the result of collusion, which had been the traditional explanation.[39] Instead, he argued that high profits in highly concentrated industries are the result of greater efficiency and superior performance of some firms in an industry. These firms tend to earn high profits and gain market share as a result of their superior efficiency and performance with the results being a relatively concentrated industry and high industry profits.

Demsetz conducted tabular and correlation analyses using IRS profit data and the results supported his argument. While the empirical analysis was rather modest and by no means conclusive, Demsetz' "efficiency" explanation is, a priori, a credible alternative to the traditional "collusion" explanation for the S-P relationship. Moreover, Demsetz' hypothesis has not been disproven on a priori or empirical grounds. Importantly, it has stimulated a growing body of empirical studies aimed at discriminating between the efficiency and collusion hypotheses, a number of which will be discussed later.

Technical developments and early S-P studies

The important contribution of Demsetz is his reinterpretation of results from earlier S-P studies, *i.e.*, attributing the positive profits-concentration correlation to efficiency rather than collusion. Since his reinterpretation, there have been a number of theoretical and empirical developments directly relevant to the S-P relationship.[40] These developments have generally raised questions about the methodology and consequently the validity of

---

39 Demsetz, *Industry Structure, Market Rivalry, and Public Policy*, 16 J. L. & Econ. 1–9 (1973). This paper contains Demsetz' most lucid statement of the efficiency hypothesis even though a subsequent paper is more often cited. *See*, Demsetz, *Two Systems of Belief About Monopoly*, in Industrial Concentration: The New Learning, *supra* note 7, at 164–84.

40 Of course, the Demsetz interpretation also implies a technical problem arising from simultaneity in the S-P studies, but his most important contribution was the reinterpretation of results from previous S-P studies.

the many earlier S-P studies and their use in section 7 enforcement. Several of these studies will be discussed briefly to draw out the main lines of questioning.

A fairly broad critique of the S-P literature was presented by Almarin Phillips in a 1976 paper.[41] While this paper itself might be criticized for not presenting new theory or empirical evidence, subsequent work suggests that Phillips was perceptive and on the mark with his critique. Some of the key points he made were later raised as the result of more formal theoretical and empirical work. Probably most basic was Phillips' observation that in spite of the broad theoretical basis for analyzing the S-P relationship (*e.g.*, Chamberlin's theory of monopolistic competition) none of the studies to date had constructed a formal theoretical model to justify the specific empirical model estimated. In that regard, Phillips was particularly critical of the concentration variable, which he contended was not very sensitive to the number of firms (*N*) in an industry. He noted that *N*, but not concentration, has a fairly solid theoretical basis in the work of Cournot and others. This led Phillips to favor the Herfindahl index over the concentration ratio as a measure of structure.[42] He felt that the barriers to entry and demand variables of early empirical studies could probably be justified by theory. However, he believed that because formal models were not being used in S-P studies, a number of problems with the estimating model could exist.

In addition to citing some data problems, a hazard in all empirical work, Phillips expressed concern with the possibility that the concentration variable is an endogenous variable that is jointly determined with profits. Statistically, the concern is that if concentration is jointly determined with profits, the single-

---

41 Phillips, *A Critique of Empirical Studies of Relations Between Market Structure and Profitability*, 23 J. Indus. Econ. 241–49 (1976).

42 The most appropriate measure of concentration based on theoretical considerations may be debated. For example, while in agreement as to the economic relevance of the number of firms for analyzing competition, Adelman was not receptive to the use of a dispersion measure, such as the Herfindahl index. *See*, Adelman, *Differential Rates and Changes in Concentration*, 41 Rev. Econ. & Statistics 68–69 (1959).

equation models typical of past studies would yield biased estimates of the parameters. This, in turn, could lead to incorrect results. The problem would be eliminated by estimating simultaneous equation models, though we emphasize that the results of simultaneous equation models may not differ substantially from single-equation models, *i.e.*, the results of previous studies are not necessarily incorrect. From a conceptual and policy standpoint, the concern raised by the possibility that concentration is jointly determined with profits is that the single-equation models would not enable us to see the possible feedback effect of profits on concentration. Such evidence would have implications for antitrust policy and provide a basis for discriminating between the collusion and efficiency hypotheses about the S-P relationship.

In retrospect, it appears that the most perceptive observations raised in Phillips' critique of the S-P literature are (1) the potential problems of the usual statistical models tested (because they are not derived from formal theoretical models) and (2) the possible endogeneity of the concentration variable in the typical single-equation model, *i.e.*, profits and concentration may be jointly determined and, therefore, a simultaneous equation model would be required to obtain valid estimates.

Phillips' critique of the S-P literature was followed by a number of empirical studies that accounted for some of the problems he had discussed. At least as early as 1971, the possibility of simultaneity between *advertising* and profitability (or concentration) had led some economists to propose two- or three-equation models for estimating purposes.[43] Strickland and Weiss extended this work by proposing a three-equation model in which advertising, concentration, and profits are endogenous.[44]

---

43 *See, for example*, Greer, *Advertising and Market Concentration*, 38 S. ECON. J. 19–32 (1971). Greer treated advertising, concentration, and growth as endogenous in a three-equation model. Also see Richard Schmalensee, who treated advertising and profits as endogenous in a two-equation model, THE ECONOMICS OF ADVERTISING (1972).

44 Strickland & Weiss, *Advertising, Concentration, and Price-Cost Margins*, 84 J. POL. ECON. 1109–21 (1976).

While their paper was motivated by the debate over the possible simultaneous determination of *advertising* and profits (or concentration), the estimating model used appears as follows:

$$\frac{Ad}{S} = f(C, M, \frac{CD}{S}),$$

$$C = f(\frac{Ad}{S}, \frac{MES}{S}),$$

$$M = f(C, \frac{Ad}{S}, X)$$

where *Ad* is advertising expense, *S* is value of shipments, *C* is concentration, *M* is the price-cost margin, *CD* is consumer demand, *MES* is minimum efficient scale, and *X* is a catch-all of variables affecting *M* but not $\frac{Ad}{S}$ or *C*.

In view of this model specification, even though the possible simultaneity between concentration and profits was not the main focus of the analysis, concentration and profits are indeed treated as endogenous variables in the model and tested in a simultaneous equation model. Arguably this represents a technical improvement in estimating the S-P relationship. Moreover, it is notable that the simultaneous equation test of the S-P relationship showed a positive and statistically significant relationship between concentration and profits. However, the single-equation test found a positive but insignificant relationship. These findings illustrate the kind of differences that may result from using different testing procedures, though such differences will not necessarily result.

Cowling and Waterson can probably be credited with the first empirical study of the S-P relationship to account explicitly for at least some of the recent technical criticisms or developments.[45] In particular, they constructed an explicit theoretical model as the basis for deriving the empirical model they used to estimate the

---

45 Cowling & Waterson, *Price-Cost Margins and Market Structure*, 43 ECONOMICA 267–74 (1976).

relationship between changes in price-cost margins (1963–1968) and changes in concentration. The theoretical model shows the price-cost margin to be determined by a concentration measure and the industry price elasticity of demand. The authors noted that since elasticities of demand generally cannot be measured, S-P studies omit this variable;[46]

> . . . an omission that implies the strong assumption that demand elasticity is constant across industries within the cross-section. However, if we shift our focus to *changes* in structure effecting *changes* in performance, then it may be reasonable to assume that the omitted-variables problem is less severe; i.e., assuming the constancy of industry price elasticities over time may be less heroic then assuming that they are constant across industries.[47]

Cowling and Waterson's test results show a statistically significant positive relationship between structure and performance. This finding is consistent with many earlier S-P studies and indicates that tests based on a better methodological foundation will not necessarily yield different results from the earlier S-P studies. This is an important point because it sometimes seems to be forgotten—the results of earlier S-P studies have been questioned; it has not been demonstrated that they are generally wrong. In any event, the primary reason for discussing the Cowling and Waterson paper is not the empirical analysis per se, which is based on old data, a relatively small sample, and an

---

46 Note that the results based on a model with omitted variables *may* not be valid but this is not necessarily the outcome. The problem is we simply do not know what, if any, affect a properly specific model would have on the results.

47 Cowling & Waterson, *supra* note 45, at 267. This problem of different elasticities across industries suggests the usefulness of conducting such research across local markets within industries where local markets exist, such as grocery retailing and banking. Such samples also substantially avoid the extraordinary problem of holding other factors constant, which is a difficult task in cross-section studies of manufacturing regardless of whether the individual firm or the industry is the unit of observation.

estimating model with a maximum of three independent variables. Rather, this paper stands out as being the first S-P study in which the estimating model was derived directly from a theoretical model. Moreover, it illustrates the problems that may be brought to light by using this approach.

Another paper illustrating the recent technical developments in testing the S-P relationship also illustrates that questions continue to emerge regarding the appropriate methodology and, by inference, the validity of earlier findings.[48] In an extension of Cowling and Waterson's theoretical model, Clarke and Davies conclude that Cowling and Waterson's test results, though corrected for misspecification (elasticity of demand omitted) on the basis of the original Cowling and Waterson model, are likely subject to simultaneous equation bias because profits and concentration are simultaneously determined.

Starting from a simple, firm profit equation, Cowling and Waterson's model led to the result that profits would be directly related to concentration (as measured by a Herfindahl index) as follows:

$$\frac{\Pi}{R} = \frac{H(1+M)}{\eta}$$

where the left side of profits (Π) to revenues (R) and the right side contains the Herfindahl index (H), elasticity of demand (η), and a function of the conjectural variation (M). However, the Clarke-Davis model yields the following:

$$H = (1/N) + (1 - \eta N)^2 V_c^2/N$$

and

[48] Clarke & Davies, *Market Structure and Price-Cost Margins*, 49 ECONOMICA 277–87 (1982).

$$\frac{\Pi}{R} = \frac{1}{N\eta} + \frac{(1 - \eta N)^2 V_c^2}{N\eta}$$

where H, Π/R, and η are defined as above and V_c is the coefficient of variation of marginal costs (indicating cost differences between firms). Very simply, these equations show that *both* H and Π/R are determined by cost and demand conditions, *i.e.*, V_c^2 and η. Consequently, a simultaneous equation estimating model would be appropriate instead of the Ordinary Least Squares [OLS] model. Moreover, Clarke and Davies note that the omission of the elasticity of demand (η) from most estimating models causes a misspecification of the model, as pointed out by Cowling and Waterson. They also note that because H and η are directly related, there is the additional problem of an omitted variable that is correlated with an explanatory variable that is included. Finally, their theoretical model also indicates that H and Π/R are both larger the greater the cost (efficiency) differences between firms (as measured by V_c^2). This theoretical model, is, of course, consistent with the Demsetz explanation of the profits-concentration relationship. The Clarke and Davies paper provides a good example of the explicit theoretical modeling of the S-P relationship and the questions raised as to the validity of early S-P studies. It also illustrates that simply because an estimating model (*e.g.*, Cowling and Waterson) is based on an explicit theoretical model does not insure that the estimating model will be a good one and free of criticism.

Though the Strickland and Weiss paper discussed above adopted the arguably more appropriate simultaneous equation estimation procedure, their estimating model was still subject to criticism. In particular, Martin notes that the Strickland and Weiss estimating model does not satisfy the rank condition for identification.[49] Martin presents a theoretical extension of each of the three equations in the Strickland-Weiss model to construct an estimating model that satisfies the rank as well as order condition for identification. Moreover, Martin makes some limited modifi-

---

[49] Martin, *Advertising, Concentration, and Profitability: The Simultaneity Problem*, 10 BELL J. ECON. 639–47 (1979).

cations to two of the Strickland and Weiss equations (advertising and profitability equations) but fundamentally alters the concentration equation based on his assumption that concentration is a dynamic variable. This latter twist on the Strickland and Weiss model illustrates clearly that even when estimating models are based on formal theoretical models, the incorporation of different assumptions, either because of a different view of the way the economy works or for convenience in modeling, may yield substantially different estimating models. Furthermore, the fact that the Strickland and Weiss paper used a simultaneous equation model but could still be subject to criticism on econometric grounds, highlights the precariousness of any single econometric study. In any event, like Strickland and Weiss, Martin finds a positive relationship between concentration and profitability.

The four studies discussed above are intended to illustrate technical developments in industrial organization economics directly related to tests of the S-P relationship. These studies highlight a number of shortcomings of early S-P studies including (1) failure to derive estimating models directly from theoretical models; (2) misspecification of the estimating equation, *i.e.*, the problem of omitted variables; and (3) the need to use simultaneous equation models instead of single-equation models for testing the S-P relationship if in fact profits and concentration are simultaneously determined. These studies also illustrate that incorporation of various technical advances does not necessarily produce test results different from those based on the earlier studies. It is apparent that the technically improved studies may be subject to shortcomings as were the earlier studies. The discussion above suggests that our knowledge about the organization and behavior of industry is still evolving. It is not clear where we will end up.

Without question, the interpretive developments of Demsetz and subsequent technical developments have raised questions regarding the validity and meaning of the S-P relationship. The usefulness and problems with these developments are widely recognized in the literature. For example, in a recent essay Bresnahan and Schmalensee observe that a trend ". . . in recent work is the growing tendency to exploit contemporary advances in economic theory and econometric methods."[50] Similarly, Morris, Sinclair, Slater, and Vickers note that, "The economics of industrial organization is undergoing major change and development. New methods of analysis are forcing substantial rethinking of the causes, nature and effects of competitive behavior."[51] Importantly, these authors conclude by highlighting the uncertainty of our knowledge.

> . . . the new theoretical approaches have opened up many new possibilities, and as a result Industrial Organization is in a state of some turmoil. There is at the moment even some embarrassment of choice among competing theories, and even within theoretical frameworks there is perhaps still too much freedom to choose one's conclusion by selection among many plausible assumptions.[52]

Empirical evidence on collusion vs. efficiency hypotheses

At the same time that the theoretical foundation for the S-P relationship was changing, efforts were being made to distinguish empirically between the Demsetz and traditional explanations for the positive S-P relationship. Earlier we pointed to Demsetz' 1973 interpretation of the positive S-P relationship as the first in a series of developments in industrial organization directly related to the S-P relationship. His hypothesis that the observed S-P relationship is due to the superior performance and efficiency of some firms rather than to collusion has led to a number of empirical studies that have attempted to discriminate between the alternative hypotheses. Since these two hypotheses have very different implications for section 7 enforcement, it is useful to

---

50 Bresnahan & Schmalensee, *The Empirical Renaissance in Industrial Economics: An Overview*, 35 J. Indus. Econ. 374 (1987).

51 Morris, Sinclair, Slater, & Vickers, *Strategic Behaviour and Industrial Competition: An Introduction*, Oxford Economic Papers, NS, 1 (Suppl. Nov. 1986).

52 *Id.* at 7.

review some of the empirical work to see whether it is possible to draw any reasonably firm conclusions. This brief review is not intended to be an exhaustive review of relevant studies or a detailed critique of the studies covered.[53] Instead this review is intended to direct the interested reader to the literature; provide an indication as to the direction of the findings; and show that the efficiency interpretation proposed by Demsetz has itself been subject to questions and reinterpretations (*e.g.*, product differentiation and strategic groups, rather than efficiency, being proposed as explanators of high profits).

According to Demsetz, the efficiency hypothesis suggests that in high concentration industries the difference in profitability between large and small firms will be greater than in low concentration industries. In a test of this hypothesis, Round used 33 Australian manufacturing industries and data for 1971 and 1972. He analyzed differences in profitability among firms within industries.[54] Test results tend to reveal the hypothesized pattern of results. However, Round also finds that the difference in profits among the large firms in an industry is greater in high concentration markets. This, of course, does not seem entirely consistent with the view that an industry becomes concentrated because some firms are more efficient and become large relative to others. Because of this not easily explicable result, Round concludes that his results provide tentative support for the efficiency hypothesis.

Carter compares the effect of industry concentration on price-cost margins of the top four firms and also the fifth through eighth largest firms.[55] Tests for each of the *Census of Manufac-*

---

53 A fairly detailed critique of Demsetz' empirical work and some other related work may be found in Daskin, Essays on Firm Diversification and Market Concentration (Ph.D. dissertation, Massachusetts Institute of Technology, 1983). This study also conducts an empirical test of the Demsetz hypothesis based on a relatively carefully developed estimating model.

54 Round, *Industry Structure, Market Rivalry and Public Policy: Some Australian Evidence*, 18 J. L. & Econ. 273–81 (1975).

55 Carter, *Collusion, Efficiency and Antitrust*, 21 J. L. & Econ. 435–44 (1978).

tures years 1963, 1967, and 1972 are based on a comparison of price-cost margins (calculated from Census data) for about 700 4-digit manufacturing industries. The price-cost margin based on the top four firms in 350 industries is used as the dependent variable and, in addition, the margin based on the fifth–eighth largest firms in all 350 industries is used. The leading firm and secondary firm equations are pooled and OLS tests conducted. Results show that the concentration variable has a positive and significant effect on leading firms' margins but not on the margins of firms 5–8. Carter concludes that these results strongly support the Demsetz efficiency hypothesis. Though not possible with Census data, one cannot help but wonder what the result would be if the margins of smaller firms, *i.e.*, below number eight, had been examined. This would provide a more convincing comparison of large and small firms.

In an analysis using the Profit Impact of Market Strategy [PIMS] Program of the Strategic Planning Institute product-line data for 4 to 10 years and 1,500 observations, Gale and Branch compare the effect of both concentration and market share on firm rates of return.[56] Their regression results show that when concentration is used in an equation as an explanatory variable but market share is excluded, the concentration variable is positive and statistically significant. This, of course, is the result obtained in so many earlier S-P studies. However, when market share is included in the equation along with concentration the market share variable is positive and significant but concentration is insignificant. This finding with respect to market share and concentration is consistent with other studies that use this methodology. The authors conclude that since market share dominates concentration these results support the efficiency hypothesis, but not the collusion hypothesis. Although these and other authors have drawn similar conclusions based on the market share-profitability results, the reader should be cautious about casually accepting such conclusions. As we will discuss at the end of this section, a simple comparison of the effects of market share and

---

56 Gale & Branch, *Concentration Versus Market Share: Which Determines Performance and Why Does It Matter?*, 27 ANTITRUST BULL. 83–105 (1982).

concentration on firm profits is not an adequate test of the collusion vs. efficiency hypotheses.

Using the Federal Trade Commission Line of Business data for 1975, including observations on 3,200 lines of business in about 260 industries, Ravenscraft compares the ability of market share and concentration to explain profits.[57] OLS and generalized least squares [GLS] estimations yield similar results. Specifically, in tests using 258 industries as the unit of observation (thus no market share variable is included), the concentration variable is positive and statistically significant. However, when the individual lines of business of firms is the unit of observation, and it is possible to calculate and include a market share variable, concentration does not have the hypothesized effect. It is concluded that the positive concentration-profits relationship may reflect advantages (efficiency, etc.) of large firms over small, as Demsetz proposed. Nevertheless, the author expresses some concern that while the competitive process may be allowing superior firms to achieve high market shares, the process does not seem to be eroding away their high profits. This leads one to wonder whether market imperfections, *e.g.*, entry barriers, exist since resources are apparently not moving into high profit product lines.

One recent study uses a Monte Carlo technique to test for the ability of models typically employed to distinguish between price-raising (collusion) and cost-reducing (superiority) effects.[58] The analysis leads Ravenscraft to conclude that, based on individual firms, a model containing both collusion and superiority effects will yield unbiased estimates. In contrast, a model based on industry observations and containing only a concentration variable will tend to yield a concentration effect that is overestimated. These findings clearly lend support to the superiority hypothesis over the collusion hypothesis. The author, however, notes that while this and other recent studies suggest that profit differences among firms reflect differential firm effects rather than industry

---

[57] Ravenscraft, *Structure-Profit Relationships at the Line of Business and Industry Level*, 65 Rev. Econ. & Statistics 22–31 (1983).

[58] Ravenscraft, *Collusion versus Superiority: A Monte Carlo Analysis*, 2 Int'l J. Indus. Org. 385–402 (1984).

effects, the explanation of the firm effects is not clear. Is it due to lower costs, better quality, etc.?

A study using 1971 and 1977 data for about 150 Canadian manufacturing industries attempts to discriminate between the collusion and efficiency hypotheses.[59] Clarke, Davies, and Waterson construct a theoretical model yielding specific predictions as to the empirical results arising from each hypothesis. Their basic tabular analysis, following Demsetz, is a within-industry comparison of the profits of large and small firms. Tests indicate, for most industries, no support for either hypothesis, though for some industries there is evidence that market power and efficiency are both at work. That is, profit differences between large and small firms are no greater in high concentration than in low concentration industries. The authors conclude that collusion and efficiency may both be at work. However, they emphasize their concern with the methodology of within-industry profit comparisons used in many studies. They contend that there is great difficulty in interpreting the results. According to the authors, factors such as product differentiation and scale economies bias the results toward supporting the efficiency hypothesis.

Another recent study used banking as the focus of analysis.[60] Smirlock used data on 2,700 unit banks for 1972 and 1978 to compare the relative ability of firm market share and market concentration to explain firm profits. Test results, as we have seen in other studies, show that, when used alone, concentration is positive and significantly related to firm profits. However, when firm market share is also included in the equation, market share is statistically significant with a positive effect on profits and concentration is insignificant. The author concludes that these results clearly support the efficiency hypothesis and that the positive concentration-profits relationship in earlier S-P studies is

---

59 Clarke, Davies, & Waterson, *The Profitability-Concentration Relation: Market Power or Efficiency*, 32 J. INDUS. ECON. 435–50 (1984).

60 Smirlock, *Evidence on the (Non) Relationship Between Concentration and Profitability in Banking*, 17 J. MONEY, CREDIT, & BANKING 69–83 (1985).

probably simply due to the correlation between concentration and market share.

Another study using the Federal Trade Commission Line of Business data (1975) for 1,775 business units operated by 456 firms in 242 manufacturing industries employs a different testing technique than other studies.[61] Schmalensee uses an analysis of variance procedure to compare market share, firm, and industry effects on firm profits. He finds that (1) firm effects do not exist; (2) industry effects are important and account for at least 75% of the variance of industry rates of return; and (3) market share effects exist but account for a negligible fraction of the variance of business units' rates of return. He concludes that the classical focus on industry-level analysis is appropriate and that difficulties in measuring industry phenomena (*e.g.*, barriers to entry) plus the possible endogeneity of many industry variables in the long run may explain why industry variables often perform poorly. This study is especially interesting for its discussion of various technical aspects of the collusion-efficiency debate.

A second paper by Schmalensee constructs formal models of industry behavior under alternative hypotheses, in the manner of Clarke, Davies, and Waterson.[62] These models, which are designed to predict the different effects arising from collusion and efficiency, are tested for both 1963 and 1972 on 70 IRS industries. Using these industry data, test results are generally weak and inconsistent across years. Specifically, the 1963 results are weakly consistent with a pure collusion hypothesis and with a hybrid collusion/efficiency hypothesis. The author expresses skepticism about econometric problems in using IRS size class data and the sharply different estimates for two different years. While it might be concluded there is some support for both hypotheses, according to the author the results may really indicate that the validity of these hypotheses differs across industries and years.

---

61 Schmalensee, *Do Markets Differ Much?*, 75 AMER. ECON. REV. 341–51 (1985).

62 Schmalensee, *Collusion versus Differential Efficiency: Testing Alternative Hypotheses*, 35 J. INDUS. ECON. 399–425 (1987).

A recent study using 1984 data for about 6,300 unit banks compares the effects of concentration and market share on firm profits in a multiple regression model.[63] Evanoff and Fortier place special emphasis on the role of barriers to entry and conduct tests on two samples: one including firms from low entry barrier markets (*i.e.*, in statewide branching states) and another including firms from high entry barrier markets (*i.e.*, in unit banking states). Essentially, their test results indicate that when a concentration variable is included as an explanatory variable without a market share variable, concentration has a positive and significant effect on profits. However, when a relative market share variable (market share divided by concentration) is also included in the equation, market share is positive and significant but concentration has no effect. Further tests, based on a different measure of concentration, suggest that the effect of concentration holds up when included with a market share variable, at least in high barrier/unit banking markets. Nevertheless, the stronger results here indicate that the firm's market share dominates industry concentration in influencing firm profits.

Whereas most investigations of the S-P hypothesis have used firm or industry profits as the dependent variable, a recent study by Berger and Hannan uses prices instead of profits.[64] They contend that prices are superior to profits for discriminating between the collusion and efficiency hypotheses because high profits may reflect either relatively high prices or relatively low costs. This argument may be true, but we emphasize the necessity of accounting for cost differences in "price" studies. Otherwise,

---

63 EVANOFF & FORTIER, REEVALUATION OF THE STRUCTURE-CONDUCT-PERFORMANCE PARADIGM IN BANKING (Staff Memoranda, SM 87-9, Federal Reserve Bank of Chicago, 1987).

64 Berger & Hannan, *The Price-Concentration Relationship in Banking*, 71 REV. ECON. & STATISTICS 291–99 (1989). *Also see* Timothy H. Hannan, Bank Commercial Loan Rates and the Market for Commercial Loans (mimeo, Federal Reserve Board 1990) and Stephen A. Rhoades, Local vs National Banking Markets: Evidence from an Analysis of Mortgage Loan Rates in 20 Cities (mimeo, Federal Reserve Board 1990).

price differences may simply reflect cost differences. The authors analyze a sample of 470 banks using quarterly observations on various retail deposit interest rates paid (MMDAs, Super NOWs, and various CDs) during the period 1983–1985. If Demsetz' efficiency hypothesis prevails, the price for the same product in concentrated and unconcentrated markets should not differ, or, if there is any difference, the price would be lower in the concentrated markets due to greater efficiency.

OLS test results show that banks in more concentrated markets pay depositors lower interest rates than banks in less concentrated markets based on both quarterly cross-section and pooled equations, and after controlling for wage costs. Moreover, inclusion of a market share variable in the equations along with concentration does not weaken the concentration variable results even though the market share variable is statistically significant. It is suggestive for future research that Berger and Hannan express reservations about the appropriateness of including a market share variable to explain firm profits because of the possible endogeneity of market share. In any case, of the studies reviewed above, this study stands out in two respects. First, it is the only one to unequivocally reject the efficiency hypothesis and accept the collusion hypothesis. Second, it is the only study to use prices rather than profits as the dependent variable. Importantly, it may have consistent support from other "price" studies.[65] This raises questions about the appropriate methodology (*i.e.*, profits or prices as the dependent variable) to be used in tests attempting to discriminate between the collusion and efficiency hypotheses. It certainly seems that a price-concentration relationship, holding costs constant, would unequivocally support the collusion hypothesis.

We have briefly examined 11 papers that have explicitly conducted tests to discriminate between the collusion and efficiency hypotheses of the S-P relationship. It appears that the empirical evidence based on profits as the dependent variable is

---

65 For an overview of many price studies, in which concentration generally has a significant effect on prices whether or not market share is included, *see* CONCENTRATION AND PRICE (L. W. Weiss ed. 1989).

coming down on the side of the efficiency hypothesis. However, studies using price as the dependent variable generally tend to support the collusion hypothesis. Further, a number of technical criticisms have been raised with respect to studies that support the efficiency hypothesis but some also apply to price studies. These criticisms include the crudeness of measuring industry variables compared to firm variables, possible measurement and econometric problems of within-industry studies, inadequacy of profit as opposed to price measures for comparing the collusion and efficiency hypotheses, and the failure of most studies to account for barriers to entry in their models. Moreover, some authors expressed concern about the fact that results consistent with the efficiency hypothesis may also be consistent with other (nonefficiency) factors. For example, the higher profits of larger firms may be due to product differentiation or first mover advantages rather than efficiency. Consequently, it may be market power after all that explains the within-industry differences in profits noted by Demsetz and later confirmed by others. In fact, one study that focused on market share effects on firm profits, with concentration and cost held constant, discussed at some length the product differentiation/market power foundation for the market share–profits relationship.[66] Ravenscraft and Mueller have proposed that the persistence of high profits raises concerns about market imperfections allowing these profits to continue at high levels.[67] Finally, it is arguable that most of these studies are subject to some of the same technical shortcomings of the earlier S-P studies, *i.e.*, endogeneity and lack of a formal theoretical model.

It is notable that individual firm market share has come to play an increasingly important role in empirical studies attempt-

---

66 Rhoades, *Market Share as a Source of Market Power: Implications and Some Evidence*, 37 J. ECON. & BUSINESS 343–63 (1985).

67 Other empirical studies presenting evidence on the collusion-efficiency debate include Smirlock, Gilligan, and Marshall, *Tobin's Q and the Structure-Performance Relationship*, 74 AMER. ECON. REV. 1051–60 (1984); DENNIS C. MUELLER, *supra* note 38; M. A. UTTON, PROFITS AND STABILITY OF MONOPOLY (1986); and Heywood, *Market Share and Efficiency: A Reprise*, 24 ECON. LETTERS 171–75 (1987).

ing to distinguish between the collusion and efficiency hypotheses. The recent emergence of market share as an explanatory variable can probably be attributed to two things. First, it was not until Shepherd, in 1972,[68] provided a rationale for and empirical evidence on the role of market share in determining firm and industry profits that market share became widely viewed as a variable appropriate for consideration in structure-performance studies.[69] Shepherd has since developed the rationale for treating individual firm market share as a source of market power in considerable detail.[70] Second, it has only been fairly recently that firm-level (as opposed to industry-level) have become fairly widely available, which of course permits the calculation of market shares. Today, market share is commonly used in such studies and we suspect that it will be a key element to distinguishing between the collusion and efficiency hypotheses.

It appears to us that results of market share–profitability tests have been fairly widely accepted as supportive of Demsetz' efficiency hypothesis. However, there are credible alternative explanations for these findings that are consistent with the existence of market power due, for example, to product differentiation, first-mover advantages, and dominant firm pricing power. This possibility combined with the persistence of profits over time, which suggests the existence of barriers to entry, indicates that the explanation for the market share–profits relationship is not at all certain. Put simply, the comparison of market share and concentration effects on performance (profits or prices) is not by itself an adequate test of the collusion vs. efficiency hypotheses.

---

68 Shepherd, *The Elements of Market Structure*, 54 Rev. Econ. & Statistics 25–37 (1972).

69 Up until this time, the relatively homogeneous group behavior of firms in a market implied by Edward Chamberlin's work in the 1930's had dominated the traditional approach to industry analysis and structure-performance research.

70 Shepherd, *On the Core Concepts of Industrial Economics*, Mainstreams in Industrial Organization 23–67 (H. W. deJong & W. G. Shepherd eds. 1986).

In addition to the explicit tests to discriminate between the collusion and efficiency hypotheses, a separate body of literature has developed. Specifically, the concept of strategic groups provides an alternative to the Demsetz explanation for observed intraindustry differences in firm profitability. Because of its relevance to the collusion vs. efficiency debate, it is useful to review this literature.

Strategic groups

The concept of strategic groups was developed as an analytical framework that explains why firms within the same industry are often observed to have different strategies.[71] According to the concept, these strategy differences may result in systematic differences in profitability. Consequently, an industry may contain firms exhibiting different profit performance because the industry is composed of two or more sets of firms (strategic groups). Within each group, firms are fairly homogeneous but firms in different groups are relatively dissimilar in terms of strategy and, ultimately, performance. Moreover, profitability differences between firms or groups of firms in an industry may persist due to mobility barriers and product differentiation that inhibit entry from one strategic group into another within the same industry.[72]

It is obvious that by providing an explanation for systematic within-industry differences in profitability among firms, the strategic groups concept provides an alternative to the Demsetz efficiency explanation. Though the concept was not originally developed by Caves and Porter as an alternative explanation, the relevance to the collusion-efficiency debate became obvious.

---

71 Caves & Porter, *From Entry Barriers to Mobility Barriers: Conjectural Decisions on Contrived Deterrence to New Competition*, 91 Q. J. ECON. 241–61 (1977).

72 The authors of the concept fully recognize their intraindustry concept of barriers to entry as an extension of Bain's landmark work on barriers to new competition. *See* Bain, *Conditions of Entry and the Emergence of Monopoly*, in MONOPOLY AND COMPETITION AND THEIR REGULATION 215–41 (E. H. Chamberlain ed. 1954).

Thus, in a later paper Porter observed ". . . this theory provides an explanation both for stable differences in competitive strategies among firms within an industry, and for persistent intra-industry profit differences among firms." Furthermore, based on his empirical results, Porter argues ". . . that the empirically supported theory refutes the Demsetz/Mancke view that large firms earn higher profits because they are more efficient or lucky, and not because they possess market power."[73] Mobility barriers apparently protect the profits of successful firms.

In his paper, Porter develops the notions of strategic groups, mobility barriers, and their relation to firm profits at some length. Porter then tests the strategic groups hypothesis on a sample of 38 IRS, "minor" industries (1963–1965). The attractiveness of IRS industry data for within-industry profitability comparisons is that data are reported by various size classes of firms. Porter assumes that the relative size of a firm in its industry proxies its strategic group membership and proceeds to divide each industry into two strategic groups—a leader group and a follower group. Test results indicate that, while profitability differences do exist between the leader and follower groups, (1) the leader group is less profitable than the follower group in a number of industries (opposite of Demsetz' findings), and (2) the structural determinants of profitability are different for the two groups. This last finding cannot be explained by the Demsetz theory, but can be explained by the use of different strategies in the two groups.

A number of papers have analyzed the concept of strategic groups since the work of Caves and Porter. As a group, these studies have found profit or other performance differences between the strategic groups of firms under analysis. Six of the studies define strategic groups on the basis of a variable selected a priori. Porter, and Caves and Pugel use firm size as the variable

---

[73] Porter, *The Structure Within Industries and Companies' Performance*, 61 REV. ECON. & STATISTICS 214 (1979).

that will distinguish strategic groups,[74] based on the idea that large firms and small firms will employ different strategies, which are hypothesized to yield different performance. Caves and Porter use a measure of industry heterogeneity (greater heterogeneity implying more distinct groups) as their indicator of the existence of strategic groups.[75] Newman defines strategic groups on the basis of the diversification strategies of firms in an industry; those with similar diversification being classified in the same group.[76] Oster argues that strategic groups should be defined on the basis of behavior variables and chooses the advertising to sales ratio as the basis for defining strategic groups.[77] In another study, Tremblay focuses on the beer industry and defines his strategic groups on the basis of whether firms have national or regional distribution of their products.[78]

The six studies of manufacturing industries just noted define strategic groups on the basis of some variable selected a priori (*e.g.*, size or diversification). Three studies of financial industries have attempted to analyze the basic question of whether strategic groups exist. That is, they do not select some variable that is assumed to be the basis along which strategic groups are formed. Hayes, Spence and Marks analyze 18 large investment banks for

---

74 *See id.* and RICHARD E. CAVES & THOMAS PUGEL, INTRAINDUSTRY DIFFERENCES IN CONDUCT AND PERFORMANCE: VIABLE STRATEGIES IN U.S. MANUFACTURING INDUSTRIES (Monograph Series in Finance and Economics, No. 1980-2, New York University Graduate School of Business Administration, 1980).

75 Caves & Porter, *Market Structure, Oligopoly, and Stability of Market Shares*, 26 J. INDUS. ECON. 289–313 (1978).

76 Newman, *Strategic Groups and the Structure-Performance Relationship*, 60 REV. ECON. & STATISTICS 417–27 (1978).

77 Oster, *Intraindustry Structure and the Ease of Strategic Change*, 64 REV. ECON. & STATISTICS 376–83 (1982).

78 Tremblay, *Strategic Groups and the Demand for Beer*, 34 J. INDUS. ECON. 183–98 (1985).

similarities in various performance characteristics.[79] They conclude that there are four strategic groups based on performance vector differences among the firms. In another study, Passmore analyzes balance sheet data for 50 of the largest U.S. banks.[80] He groups the banks into two sets on the basis of the proportions of each bank's portfolio devoted to each balance sheet item. Amel and Rhoades analyze the balance sheet items of all banks in 16 selected large and small markets in 1978, 1981, and 1984 to determine whether strategic groups exist.[81] They find that approximately six strategic groups exist, and that membership in the groups is relatively stable over time.

Studies of strategic groups have yielded consistent results. Strategic groups of firms have been found to exist within industries and profit performance differs between the groups. The consistency of findings is especially notable in view of the differences among the studies in terms of industries examined, the basis for defining groups, and statistical methodology. It is also interesting that while the strategic groups literature has evolved largely independent of the collusion-efficiency debate, it appears to be directly relevant. At this point in the development of the literature, the evidence does not appear to support the Demsetz efficiency hypothesis regarding within-industry profitability differences. However, because studies of strategic groups have not focused primarily on that debate, the implications of the results are certainly not conclusive. Focusing more along these lines would be a fruitful direction for future research into strategic groups.

The main conclusion to be derived from the strategic groups literature is that it provides a credible alternative to the Demsetz explanation for within-industry differences in firm profitability.

---

79 SAMUEL L. HAYES, III, A. MICHAEL SPENCE, & DAVID VAN PRAAG MARKS, COMPETITION IN THE INVESTMENT BANKING INDUSTRY (1983).

80 PASSMORE, STRATEGIC GROUPS AND THE PROFITABILITY OF BANKING (Research paper No. 8507, Federal Reserve Bank of New York, Sept. 1985).

81 Amel & Rhoades, *Strategic Groups in Banking*, 70 REV. ECON. STATISTICS 685–89 (1988).

This alternative story is based on market power and barriers to entry (mobility barriers). Moreover, the empirical evidence on intraindustry performance differences, based on strategic group comparisons, is often not consistent with the Demsetz efficiency hypothesis.

Potential competition/contestable markets: the theory

The last of the economic developments that we think have had the most direct affect on section 7 enforcement during the 1980's is the theory of potential competition. Developed almost 40 years ago by Joe Bain,[82] the theory of potential competition has recently enjoyed a resurrection in a more restricted and formal paradigm referred to by its authors as "contestable markets."[83] The resurrection of potential competition is interesting because after a surge of interest following its development by Bain and others, and its application in a few court cases during the 1960's, interest among economists seemed to fade away during the 1970's. It is certainly possible that the waning interest stemmed from difficulty in empirically testing the theory, particularly its limit pricing hypothesis. However, by the time that the modern version of the theory of potential competition was presented in 1982, it may be that a whole new generation of economists, who had not struggled with the earlier version, was ready and eager to think about this modern version. Like its predecessor, contestable markets is logical and intuitively appealing at least when its extreme assumptions are overlooked.

---

82 The concept was developed in detail in Bain, *A Note on Pricing in Monopoly and Oligopoly*, 39 AMER. ECON. REV. 448-64 (1949). Further development and empirical evidence were presented in JOE S. BAIN, BARRIERS TO NEW COMPETITION (1956). An earlier, more limited discussion of potential competition may be found in Clark, *Toward a Concept of Workable Competition*, 30 AMER. ECON. REV. 241-56 (1940).

83 WILLIAM J. BAUMOL, JOHN C. PANZAR & ROBERT D. WILLIG, CONTESTABLE MARKETS AND THE THEORY OF INDUSTRY STRUCTURE (1982).

Whether or not frustration over problems in testing contestability theory gradually emerge as they did before remains to be seen. In any event, because the notion of contestable markets is an economic concept that has been heartily embraced in section 7 enforcement during the 1980's, it is useful to outline the concept and its policy implications, discuss some critiques of the theory, and present some recent empirical evidence. In addition, we present results of a crude empirical investigation of contestability theory in commercial banking.

The original theory of potential competition was developed to fill a gap in the literature. Microeconomic models of the industry up to that time focused entirely on factors that are internal to an industry, such as the number of sellers and product differentiation, as determinants of price and output decisions. In his 1949 article, Bain proposed that external factors may also play an important role in determining prices and output. He argued that prices and output decisions of established firms in an industry may be significantly influenced by the threat of entry by potential entrants. Bain developed in some detail the concept of limit pricing to explain how and why firms in an industry may price at a level below that which would appear to be profit maximizing.[84] The basic argument is that firms would choose to limit their price below the short-run, profit maximizing level in order to forestall new entry and maximize long-run profits.

In his 1956 book, Bain extended his theory of potential competition by incorporating the concept of barriers to entry.[85] The height of entry barriers in an industry was used to explain how far above the competitive level the limit price could be set without inducing new entry. Firms in industries with relatively high entry barriers could set a high limit price without inducing

---

84 In an interesting contrast to the theory of contestable markets, the theory of potential competition and limit pricing were motivated by empirical observation of a pattern of pricing apparently below the profit maximizing level.

85 This extension of the theory was also motivated by empirical observation.

entry. Firms in industries with low barriers to entry would have to set a price closer to the competitive level to forestall entry.

The theory of contestable markets proposes that factors external to the industry (specifically potential entrants) are the primary determinants of pricing and output decisions. There is basically no role in the theory for internal factors such as the number of competitors, firm market share, product differentiation, or barriers to entry in influencing the behavior of established firms. Thus, while the conjectural variations of firms within an industry had been an important element in theories of firm behavior from Cournot to Bain and beyond, this interdependence of firms is ruled out of the theory of contestable markets. For this reason alone, the theory of contestable markets is a marked departure from previous microeconomics models and has attracted a great deal of attention. Additionally, the assumptions underlying contestable markets and the conclusions drawn from the theory have been a major source of discussion and debate. Baumol has stated that "A contestable market is one into which entry is absolutely free, and exit is absolutely costless."[86] The analysis based on these assumptions and the assumption of no sunk costs leads Baumol to the conclusion,

> Our analysis, in contrast, provides a generalization of the concept of the perfectly competitive market, one which we call a "perfectly contestable market." It is, generally, characterized by optimal behavior and yet applies to the full range of industry structures including even monopoly and oligopoly.[87]

Unfortunately, the theory of contestable markets seems to have been carelessly interpreted to imply that market structure generally is irrelevant for competition and that monopoly/oligopoly pricing does not occur. That is, monopoly profits may not be earned by a monopolist or oligopolist because they would be contested away by new entrants. What often seems to be forgotten in applying the theory is that the competitive outcome

---

86 Baumol, *Contestable Markets: An Uprising in the Theory of Industry Structure*, 72 AMER. ECON. REV. 3 (1982).

87 *Id.* at 2.

of the theory is based on some very strong assumptions (notably no sunk costs and ultrafree entry and exit). This optimistic view of the competitive outcome and policy implications probably stems from the authors' enthusiastic and vigorous dissemination and defense of the theory. This vigorous presentation has probably caused one of their own warnings to be frequently overlooked. Specifically, Baumol has cautioned,

> First, let me recall the observation that real markets are rarely, if ever, perfectly contestable. Contestability is merely a broader ideal, a benchmark of wider applicability than is perfect competition. To say that contestable oligopolies behave ideally and that contestable monopolies have some incentives for doing so is not to imply that this is even nearly true of all oligopolies or of unregulated monopolies.[88]

Because the theory of contestable markets suggests such a different approach to analysis of section 7 cases and because the theory may have been carelessly interpreted as to its policy implications, it is useful to examine various professional evaluations of the theory. Of particular interest, is the usefulness of the theory for policy purposes. It is also useful to look at results of early tests of the theory as well as some new evidence we have developed.

The theory of contestable markets has spawned a large literature. We have selected for discussion several reviews, critiques, and empirical tests more or less randomly to get some indication as to how comfortable one should feel in using this theory as the primary economic foundation for section 7 enforcement.

The assumption of no sunk costs plays a critical role in contestability theory in that it allows completely free entry and costless, frictionless exit. In a brief theoretical critique, Weitzman rejects the assumption of no sunk costs. He argues that there is no such thing as pure fixed costs and unless sunk costs exist somewhere in the production technology, all costs are variable.[89] He concludes that contestability cannot provide the basis for a

---

88 *Id.* at 3.

89 Weitzman, *Contestable Markets: An Uprising in the Theory of Industry Structure: Comment*, 73 AMER. ECON. REV. 486–87 (1983).

general theory of market "forms." Another early critique of the theory also attacked underlying assumptions. Schwartz and Reynolds argue that perfect contestability requires two implausible assumptions.[90] First, an entrant can enter instantaneously with absolutely no entry lag. Second, an entrant can cut price, exit, and incur no loss of fixed costs before the incumbent can even adjust its price. Schwartz and Reynolds note that the early limit price models of entry deterrence, such as Bain's, were criticized and replaced for the very reason that established firms can adjust price and output rapidly in response to entry. They conclude that ". . . Baumol's theory is not robust; once we deviate even slightly from the strict assumption of contestability, pricing and entry decisions depend on the nature of firm interactions. There is no escaping the 'reaction functions and the other paraphernalia of standard oligoloply models' (p. 11)."[91]

In a fairly lengthy review of the Baumol, Panzar, Willig [BPW] book, Spence makes a generally favorable assessment in connection with its contributions to the analysis of multiproduct firms and their cost structures, including the implications of these costs for strategy, structure, and performance.[92] However, Spence's review of contestability theory is less enthusiastic. He observes that BPW have eliminated elements of strategic interaction among firms that have generally been associated with entry deterrence and weakly defends this approach by noting that it is unfair to require economic models to capture all elements of reality. From this, he concludes that the debate over contestability will depend on the empirical importance of those aspects of industry structure that BPW intentionally neglect. Spence's analysis ultimately leads him to question a fundamental assumption of contestability theory as he notes ". . . I am not yet persuaded

---

90 Schwartz & Reynolds, *Contestable Markets: An Uprising in the Theory of Industry Structure: Comment*, 73 AMER. ECON. REV. 488–90 (1983).

91 *Id.* at 489.

92 Spence, *Contestable Markets and the Theory of Industry Structure: A Review Article*, 21 J. ECON. LIT. 981–90 (1983).

that sunk costs are negligible for most goods.''[93] This, of course, undermines the BPW assumption of costless exit. Thus, regarding the usefulness of the theory as a descriptive tool Spence argues ". . . that the range of applicability of the theory as a descriptive tool for analyzing short- and medium-run industry configurations is limited by the widespread existence of partial irreversibility of investment.''[94]

A review article by Brock warns the applied economist to handle contestability theory and its "happy'' implications (*i.e.*, a perfectly competitive outcome even in a monopoly) with care because of explicit and hidden assumptions.[95] He cites Dixit in noting that the economic conditions required for perfect contestability are very stringent. Brock expresses concern about the wholesale rejection of conjectural variations and reaction functions. Thus, Brock observes that in spite of its absence from contestability theory, there is some game between established firms and potential entrants forcing established firms to price competitively (assuming for the moment entry is costlessly reversible). In Brock's view, until this game is precisely defined ". . . contestability theory must be used with caution. Unpalatable hidden assumptions may be necessary to obtain Baumol *et al.*'s conclusions.''[96] Regarding the explicit assumptions of contestability, Brock notes that to achieve the competitive price in monopolies and oligopolies due to the presence of hit and run entry ". . . may require unpleasant assumptions.''[97] In particular, Brock notes that ". . . costlessly reversible entry needs incumbents to be sluggish relative to challengers and consumers must be quicker to respond to price changes than the incumbents whose very livelihood depends on rapid reaction. This seems implausible

---

93 *Id.* at 987.

94 *Id.* at 986.

95 Brock, *Contestable Markets and the Theory of Industry Structure: A Review Article*, 91 J. Pol. Econ. 1055–66 (1983).

96 *Id.* at 1059.

97 *Id.* at 1063.

unless regulators or some other force restrains the reaction time of incumbents."[98]

While applauding the analysis of multiple products and joint costs by BPW, Shepherd presents a criticism of contestability theory and its foundation, ultrafree entry.[99] Shepherd is critical from the start, arguing that contestability is presented as a whole new theoretical framework whereas in fact there are numerous important predecessors going back at least 30 years; a fact we noted earlier. Because of the large number of criticisms by Shepherd, we will simply enumerate them without any elaboration. Shepherd argues that ultrafree entry requires inconsistent assumptions; ultrafree entry lacks generality because of its extreme nature; it is eccentric to assume that external conditions dominate internal industry conditions; contrary to claims in the contestability theory, structure is not more endogenous than in earlier analyses; and a monopoly facing ultrafree entry is probably unstable. In connection with many of these criticisms, Shepherd cites empirical work to support his position. For example, he notes that a lot of empirical work indicates that internal conditions (*e.g.*, market share) are very important, and barriers to entry do exist and affect performance. Shepherd sees little practical use for contestability theory and concludes ". . . their analysis only treats a specialized, extreme set of conditions, which are probably found in no real markets which have significant internal market power. Little has been added to the existing entry and exit analysis."[100]

Schwartz argues that the threat of hit-and-run entry is the key element in contestability theory.[101] He notes that concern has been expressed by others over the basic structural assumptions, such as no sunk costs, that are a necessary condition for contestability.

---

98 *Id.* at 1065.

99 Shepherd, *'Contestability' vs. Competition*, 74 AMER. ECON. REV. 572–87 (1984).

100 *Id.* at 585.

101 Schwartz, *The Nature and Scope of Contestability Theory*, OXFORD ECONOMIC PAPERS, NS, 37–57 (Suppl. Nov. 1986).

However, Schwartz argues that these are not sufficient conditions. Contestability assumes that prices will be set at the competitive level by the incumbent because the incumbent is very slow at adjusting prices. Schwartz has serious reservations regarding this underlying assumption. He notes that if, in fact, incumbent firms can adjust prices rapidly in response to entry, markets will be uncontestable. Schwartz' theoretical analysis and review of some empirical evidence leads him to conclude that ". . . the ability of incumbent firms to change price rapidly in response to entry can offset ease of entry and exit and make markets noncontestable in the sense that pricing behavior becomes unaffected by the threat of entry. Available empirical evidence indicates that this is typically the case."[102]

This brief examination of some reviews and critiques of the theory of contestable markets reveals that numerous economists have serious reservations as to the generality and applicability of the theory. Fundamental questions have been raised regarding the relevance of crucial assumptions about sunk costs, the pricing response of incumbent firms, and the dominance of external over internal industry conditions. Under the circumstances, it is hard to argue that contestability theory per se provides a solid foundation for policy purposes. Apparently in reaction to the unusually strong and widespread criticism of contestability theory, the authors have recently emphasized the limitations of their theory for policy purposes. They state ". . . we will deny emphatically that it offers carte blanche to mindless deregulation and dismantling of antitrust safeguards." Furthermore, "Contestability theory does not, and was not intended to, lend support to those who believe (or almost seem to believe) that the unrestrained market automatically solves all economic problems and that virtually all regulation and antitrust activity constitutes a pointless and costly source of economic inefficiency."[103] And, recognizing the need for empirical testing they observe,

---

102 *Id.* at 55.

103 Baumol & Willig, *Contestability: Developments Since the Book*, Oxford Economic Papers, NS, 9 (Suppl. Nov. 1986).

> The economy of reality is composed of sectors which vary widely in the degree to which they approximate the attributes of contestability. Thus, the conclusion that *perfectly* contestable markets require no intervention requires little more than the possibility (which remains to be proven case by case) that *some* markets in reality may automatically perform in a very acceptable manner despite the small number of firms that inhabit them.[104]

Contestability theory is clearly useful in drawing attention back to the theory of potential competition and entry conditions in merger analysis. However, serious questions have been raised about the generality and applicability of the theory's results. The usefulness of contestability theory for policy purposes depends on the findings of empirical work, which is discussed below.

Contestable markets: empirical evidence

To date, empirical evidence on contestable markets generally tends to support the original theory of potential competition rather than the theory of contestable markets. This is the case even in those markets where the theory's authors believe the theory is most likely to apply, such as airlines where sunk costs are arguably very low (even though fixed costs are high) because airplanes may be moved quickly from one route to another.[105] One of the difficulties faced in attempting to test contestability theory is that the authors did not specify a research design or methodology for testing the theory. Moreover, it is not clear whether entry and exit (or the lack of it) or price (profit) performance should be the focus of analysis. Indeed, the difficulties faced in testing contestability theory are reminiscent of the difficulties formerly faced in efforts to test the theory of potential competition.

A study of 4-digit manufacturing industries by Kessides attempts to explain entry with a number of variables, including a

---

104 *Id.* at 10 (emphasis in original).

105 This case, of course, refers only to a special class of entry. Specifically, it involves entry by already established firms rather than by newly established firms.

proxy for sunk costs.[106] The results indicate that sunk costs have a significant negative influence on entry acting as an important entry barrier. While BPW cite Kessides' work, it appears to support the original theory of competition, with its emphasis on barriers to entry (an *internal* factor), rather than contestability theory. A study of the airline industry found that air fares in 1980 and 1981 were higher in high concentration markets than in low concentration markets; a finding that is inconsistent with contestability theory.[107] Another study of the airline industry finds a positive and statistically significant relationship between concentration and profits.[108] Moreover, the authors find that new entry does occur and that incumbents reduce fares in response to entry. This pattern of pricing and profits suggests that even in the airline industry prices are not automatically set to deter entry and that internal industry factors (*e.g.*, the number of competitors) are an important factor in determining prices.

A study of airline markets by Morrison and Winston uses a multinomial logit model in which both the actual number of competitors and the number of potential competitors are included to explain the deviation of observed consumer surplus from the optimum consumer surplus.[109] Both variables are positive and statistically significant but the actual number of competitors is quantitatively much more important. This result suggests that internal industry factors are more important than external factors which is not consistent with contestability theory but does support the theory of potential competition. An analysis of airline fares in Australia for 1979 and 1983 found no significant differ-

---

106 Kessides, Toward a Testable Model of Entry: A Study of the U.S. Manufacturing Industries (unpublished manuscript, Princeton University 1982).

107 Graham, Kaplan & Sibley, *Efficiency and Competition in the Airline Industry*, 14 BELL J. ECON. 118–38 (1983).

108 Call & Keeler, *Airline Deregulation, Fares, and Market Behavior: Some Empirical Evidence*, in ANALYTICAL STUDIES IN TRANSPORT ECONOMICS 221–47 (Andrew F. Daughety ed. 1985).

109 Morrison & Winston, *Empirical Implications and Tests of the Contestability Hypothesis*, 30 J. L. & ECON. 53–66 (1987).

ence in fares between routes served by a single operator and those served by multiple operators.[110] This finding is, of course, consistent with contestability theory. A recent study of the liner shipping industry analyzes entry and exit from shipping markets.[111] Based on his observations that there is frequent entry and exit in specific markets and that the industry has generally experienced low profits, the author concludes that there is some support for contestability theory in the liner shipping industry.[112]

The empirical studies outlined above suggest that contestability theory is not generally applicable.[113] Contrary to the predictions of the theory, it is apparent that internal factors are generally important determinants of pricing behavior. Thus, it appears that the numerous theoretical criticisms of the underlying assumptions, discussed earlier, are well founded. Nevertheless, at this point, contestability is essentially an empirical question and it will be useful to extend empirical work beyond airlines. In the section below, we examine the contestability notion in commercial banking.

---

110 Starkie & Starrs, *Contestability and Sustainability in Regional Airline Markets*, 60 ECON. REC. 274–83 (1984).

111 Davies, *Competition, Contestability, and the Liner Shipping Industry*, 20 J. TRANSPORT ECON. 299–312 (1986).

112 In addition to empirical investigations of contestability theory such as those outlined above, there have been a few that have used the experimental methodology. Because of the newness of and questions surrounding this methodology in economics, we have not discussed these studies. The interested reader may, however, refer to Coursey, Isaac, Luke, & Smith, *Market Contestability in the Presence of Sunk Entry Costs*, 15 RAND J. ECON. 69–84 (1984); Harrison & McKee, *Monopoly Behavior, Decentralized Regulation, and Contestable Markets: An Experimental Evaluation*, 16 RAND J. ECON. 51–69 (1985); and Harrison, *Experimental Evaluation of the Contestable Markets Hypothesis*, PUBLIC REGULATION: NEW PERSPECTIVES ON INSTITUTIONS AND POLICIES 191–225 (E. E. Bailey ed. 1987).

113 For further evidence of the inapplicability of contestable markets *see* Butler & Huston, *How Contestable Are Airline Markets?* ATLANTIC ECON. J. 27–35 (1989); and Reed & Waldman, *Mergers and Air Fares: Contestable Markets in the Airline Industry*, 20 ANTITRUST L. & ECON. REV. 15–20 (1988).

Contestable markets: new evidence from commercial banking

Two recent studies have tested the contestable markets hypothesis in local commercial banking markets. In the first of these studies, the rates of return of banks in markets containing only one, two, three, and four banks (monopolistically structured markets) are compared with rates of return of similar-sized banks in metropolitan statistical areas [MSAs] where there are a relatively large number of banks.[114] If banking markets are contestable, a monopolistic market structure will not enable banks to charge higher and/or pay lower interest rates than banks in more competitively structured markets. Thus, there would be no significant difference in rates of return between the two groups of markets. An OLS regression analysis using rate of return as the dependent variable, several control variables, and dummy variables to distinguish between monopolistically and competitively structured markets, led to a rejection of the contestable markets hypothesis. The analysis was based on a nationwide sample of banks.

The second study of contestability theory in banking used essentially the same methodology as the first study but limited the geographic scope of the study to the two states of Pennsylvania and Ohio rather than the nation as a whole.[115] Three time periods were used to test for the relationship between concentration and bank profitability both before and after legal barriers to geographic expansion by banks were lowered. It was observed that the disappearance of a positive relationship between concentration and profitability coincided with the liberalization of bank branching laws in Ohio and Pennsylvania and the expansion of

---

114 *See* Burke & Rhoades, *Profits and Contestability in Highly Concentrated Banking Markets*, 3 REV. INDUS. ORGAN. 82–97 (1987). For more recent evidence see Burke & Rhoades, *Profits and Contestability: State-by-State Evidence from Banking Markets*, 4 REV. INDUS. ORGAN. 59–77 (1989).

115 WHALEN, COMPETITION AND BANK PROFITABILITY: RECENT EVIDENCE (Economic Commentary, Federal Reserve Bank of Cleveland, Nov. 1, 1986).

S&L powers authorized by Congress in 1980 and 1982. Based on this finding, Whalen concluded that merger-related increases in concentration, in some states with minimal legal barriers to geographic expansion by banks, are unlikely to result in monopoly profits for institutions in those local markets. This policy conclusion is somewhat strong since it is based on findings from only two states.

Because of the differences in results between these two previous studies of banking markets and the likelihood that differences exist among states, we have tested for contestability in banking markets in each of 46 states separately. In particular, where data permit, rates of return of banks in one-, two-, three-, and four-bank markets are compared with rates of return for similar-sized banks in MSAs. We conclude that findings based on a sample that includes banks drawn from all states, while generally relevant, will not be relevant in all instances. Entry conditions and the perceived threat of entry by out-of-market competitors may differ significantly across different competitive environments. A complete listing, by state, of instances in which return on assets [ROA] is greater in small highly concentrated markets than in MSAs and vice versa is presented in tables 1–3. Tables 1–3 also separate those states that have statewide branching, limited branching, and unit banking, respectively, because branching powers are one of the obvious indicators of entry conditions.[116]

Tables 4–7 summarize the state findings and show the percentage of states where the average ROA for MSAs is greater than and less than that for one-, two-, three-, and four-bank markets, respectively. The frequency of statistically significant differences is also shown. There are a relatively small number of instances where average bank profits are greater in the competitively structured MSA markets than in markets with one to four banks, though these differences are not statistically significant. For

116 Whalen concluded that expanded branching powers caused the gradual lowering of entry barriers in Ohio and Pennsylvania and led to the disappearance of a positive relationship between concentration and profitability in local markets in those two states. *Id.*

example, when comparing MSA markets with one-bank markets (see table 4), in 18% of the states with statewide branching and 28% of states with limited branching, the unexpected relationship holds. To reiterate, however, the differences in bank profits are not statistically significant in any state. Conversely, in over 80% of states tested, average profits are higher in one-bank markets than in MSAs. More importantly, the differences are statistically significant in 21% of states with statewide branching, 38% of states with limited branching, and in two-thirds of the states with unit banking.

A similar pattern of relationships is found in markets with two, three, and four banks when they are compared to MSA markets (see tables 5–7). Although the expected relationship holds in many states (regardless of branching laws), it is generally strongest and occurs most frequently in unit branching states. There is not a single instance (regardless of branching laws) where the MSA ROA exceeds that of two-, three-, or four-bank markets—and where the difference is statistically significant. The percentage of states, however, in which ROAs in two- to four-bank markets exceeds those in MSAs (and where the differences are statistically significant) ranges from 13% to 100% and averages 56%.

Based on the test results presented in this section, it can be concluded that market structure (specifically the number of commercial bank competitors in a local market) very often has an effect on the profit performance of banking organizations.[117] Apparently, the competitive behavior of bankers in markets with a small number of banks is frequently not modified by the threat of hit-and-run entry or by the often-mentioned host of other potential or actual providers of financial services. However, these results also suggest that barriers to entry (a factor internal to an industry) do matter and that market structure alone is not indicative of the performance of firms in a market. Moreover, these results suggest that the original theory of potential competi-

---

117 These results are basically consistent with the findings of previous studies that have dealt with the issue of contestability.

Table 1

Instances in Which Average Return on Assets [ROA] Is Greater in Small Markets Than in MSAs, and Vice Versa, by State[†]

Statewide branching states	*Percent of state deposits held by multibank holding companies*	*ROA in one-bank markets > MSAs*	*ROA in two-bank markets > MSAs*	*ROA in three-bank markets > MSAs*	*ROA in four-bank markets > MSAs*
Arizona	27.9	*	NA	NA	NA
California	13.3	*	*	NA	NA
Connecticut	19.1	NA	NA	*	NA
Florida	68.5	*	*	*S	NA
Hawaii	8.5	NA	NA	NA	*S
Idaho	46.2	*	NA	NA	NA
Maine	69.4	*	*	NA	NA
Maryland	48.0	*	NA	*S	NA
Massachusetts	79.5	*	—	NA	—
Nevada	49.2	*	NA	NA	NA
New Hampshire	39.2	NA	NA	NA	—
New York	60.7	—	—	NA	NA
N. Carolina	3.5	*S	NA	*	NA
Oregon	72.8	*	NA	NA	NA
S. Carolina	0	*S	*	—	NA
S. Dakota	44.5	*S	*S	*S	*S
Utah	68.3	*	*	NA	NA

Vermont	0	—	*	*	—
Virginia	44.6	*	—	—	—
Washington	14.6	—	*	NA	NA

† No comparisons were possible, based on the criteria used for including markets in the analysis, for Alaska, Delaware, New Jersey, and Rhode Island.

NA means no data to permit comparison.

— means that the MSA rate of return is greater.

* means that the small market rate of return is greater.

S means the difference is statistically significant at least at the 90% level.

Table 2

Instances in Which Average Return on Assets [ROA] Is Greater in Small Markets Than in MSAs, and Vice Versa, by State

Limited branching states	*Percent of state deposits held by multibank holding companies*	*ROA in one-bank towns > MSAs*	*ROA in two-bank towns > MSAs*	*ROA in three-bank towns > MSAs*	*ROA in four-bank towns > MSAs*
Alabama	58.6	*	—	*S	—
Arkansas	9.0	*S	—	—	—
Georgia	52.3	*S	—	—	—
Indiana	27.7	—	—	*S	—
Iowa	3.2	—	—	—	*
Kentucky	9.2	*S	*	*	*
Louisiana	0.4	*S	*S	*	*
Michigan	69.5	*	*	*S	*S
Minnesota	57.6	*	*	*S	*S
Mississippi	0.0	*	—	—	NA
Nebraska	13.2	*	*S	*S	*S
New Mexico	48.1	—	*	*	—
Ohio	56.5	—	*	—	*
Oklahoma	1.3	*	*S	*	*
Pennsylvania	20.4	—	—	—	*
Tennessee	42.3	*	*	—	*S
W. Virginia	0.3	*S	*S	*S	*
Wisconsin	49.4	*	*	*S	*S

NA means no data to permit comparison.
— means that the MSA rate of return is greater.
* means that the small market rate of return is greater.
S means the difference is statistically significant.

Table 3

Instances in Which Average Return on Assets [ROA] Is Greater in Small Markets Than in MSAs, and Vice Versa, by State

Unit banking states	*Percent of state deposits held by multibank holding companies*	*ROA in one-bank towns > MSAs*	*ROA in two-bank towns > MSAs*	*ROA in three-bank towns > MSAs*	*ROA in four-bank towns > MSAs*
Colorado	68.2	*	*	*	—
Illinois	0.6	*S	*S	*S	*S
Kansas	3.2	equal	*	*S	*S
Missouri	64.0	*	—	—	*
Montana	55.6	*S	*	*S	*
N. Dakota	39.9	*S	*S	*S	*S
Texas	56.2	*S	*S	*	*S
Wyoming	47.2	NA	*S	*S	NA

NA means no data to permit comparison.
— means that the MSA rate of return is greater.
* means that the small market rate of return is greater.
S means the difference is statistically significant.

Table 4

Percentage of States With Average Return on Assets [ROA] for MSAs Greater Than and Less Than That for One-Bank Markets and Frequency of Statistically Significant Differences

Number of states observed	*State law*	*Percent of states with MSA ROA >one-bank markets*	*(Percent statistically significant)*	*Percent of states with one-bank markets ROA > MSA*	*(Percent statistically significant)*
17	S	18	(0)	82	(21)
18	L	28	(0)	72	(38)
6	U	0	(0)	100	(67)

Table 5

Percentage of States With Average Return on Assets [ROA] for MSAs Greater Than and Less Than That for Two-Bank Markets and Frequency of Statistically Significant Differences

Number of states observed	*State law*	*Percent of states with MSA ROA >two-bank markets*	*(Percent statistically significant)*	*Percent of states with two-bank markets ROA > MSA*	*(Percent statistically significant)*
11	S	27	(0)	73	(13)
18	L	39	(0)	61	(36)
8	U	13	(0)	88	(57)

Table 6

Percentage of States With Average Return on Assets [ROA] for MSAs Greater Than and Less Than That for Three-Bank Markets and Frequency of Statistically Significant Differences

Number of states observed	*State law*	*Percent of states with MSA ROA >three-bank markets*	*(Percent statistically significant)*	*Percent of states with three-bank markets ROA > MSA*	*(Percent statistically significant)*
8	S	25	(0)	75	(50)
18	L	39	(0)	61	(64)
8	U	13	(0)	88	(71)

Table 7
Percentage of States With Average Return on Assets [ROA] for MSAs Greater Than and Less Than That for Four-Bank Markets and Frequency of Statistically Significant Differences

Number of states observed	*State law*	*Percent of states with MSA ROA >four-bank markets*	*(Percent statistically significant)*	*Percent of states with four-bank markets ROA > MSA*	*(Percent statistically significant)*
6	S	67	(0)	33	(100)
17	L	29	(0)	71	(42)
7	U	14	(0)	86	(67)

tion, with its explicit recognition of entry barriers, is more useful for merger analysis than is contestability theory.

V. Consequences of the political and economic foundations

The political and economic thinking discussed above arguably provided the basis for more cautious enforcement of the antitrust laws and section 7 in particular. In this section, the commercial banking industry is used as an example of this more cautious approach to antitrust enforcement. The banking industry is particularly well suited for our investigation because local market data with which to calculate structural indexes are readily available, as is a consistent series of consummated mergers.

In commercial banking, the more cautious approach to section 7 enforcement has been implemented by recent court decisions, new merger guidelines, and other developments that have affected merger analysis conducted by the bank regulatory agencies and the Department of Justice. Factors influencing the actions of bank regulatory agencies are important because those agencies have the legal responsibility for the enforcement of laws that specify that section 7 criteria are to be applied to mergers in the commercial banking industry.[118]

---

118 Although the Comptroller of the Currency and the FDIC also have statutory responsibility for some bank mergers (under the Bank

This section examines the following developments in the bank regulatory area that reflect more cautious antitrust enforcement: (1) court decisions and legislation affecting bank merger analysis; (2) special Justice Department merger guidelines (1985) for use in bank merger analysis; and (3) potential as well as actual merger activity in banking. In addition, merger activity in the industrial sector, and resources devoted to antitrust enforcement in general are briefly discussed.

Judicial and legislative developments affecting bank merger analysis

The first in a series of recent developments leading to modifications in bank merger analysis was a court decision rendered in 1981. In that decision, the U.S. Court of Appeals for the Eighth Circuit (St. Louis) invalidated a 1979 Federal Reserve Board order denying the application of County National Bancorp., St. Louis, to acquire TG Bancshares Company, St. Louis. The case originally had been denied by the Federal Reserve Board on the basis that, despite the earlier *Washington Mutual* decision,[119] the Board had authority under the Bank Holding Company Act to deny proposals that would result in what it viewed as serious anticompetitive effects even though such proposals were not in violation of antitrust law standards. The court, however, relying in part on the *Washington Mutual* decision, reiterated that bank regulatory agencies could not deny merger proposals if the anticompetitive effects did not result in a violation of the antitrust laws.

Merger Act), most large merger proposals (which usually involve bank holding company organizations) are evaluated by the Federal Reserve Board under the Bank Holding Company Act.

119 In 1973, the U.S. Court of Appeals for the Ninth Circuit (San Francisco) overturned an FDIC order denying approval under the Bank Merger Act (which contains a standard identical to that in the BHC Act) on grounds of anticompetitive effects that the FDIC conceded did not rise to the level of an antitrust violation (Washington Mutual Savings Bank v. FDIC, 482 F.2d 459 [9th Cir. 1973]).

After the *County National* case was remanded to the Federal Reserve Board and later approved, the bank regulatory agencies adopted a more cautious approach to the analysis of the competitive effects of horizontal bank mergers. As a result, both the absolute deposit sizes and the market shares of banking organizations involved in horizontal mergers have increased significantly in recent years.[120] It has also become increasingly common for entire bank holding company systems to merge with each other. Moreover, since many such holding company mergers involve organizations with operations in states that have traditionally had liberal branching or holding company laws, the merging partners frequently compete with each other in many of the same local markets. Consequently, a single merger often results in the elimination of some existing competition in a large number of markets.[121]

More cautious merger enforcement policy by the bank regulatory agencies was further dictated by two other court decisions in the early 1980's. During the mid- and late-1970's, a large propor-

---

120 For example, the County National-TG (St. Louis) merger involved two firms that had market shares of 3.2% and 2.3%, respectively, and deposits of $333.7 million and $225.6 million, respectively. In contrast, the horizontal merger of First Chicago Corporation and American National Corporation (1984), involved market deposits of $13.3 billion and $2.0 billion, respectively, and market shares of 19.9% and 2.9%, respectively, in the Chicago market, 70 FED. RES. BULL. 351 (1984). Many recent mergers involved firms with combined market shares of over 30% and some reach 40% or even 50% (despite the absence of any financial or other supervisory problems). *For example, see Key Centurion Bankshares, Inc., Charleston, West Virginia*, 72 FED. RES. BULL. 719 (1986) and *AmSouth Bancorporation, Birmingham, Alabama*, 73 FED. RES. BULL. 351 (1987).

121 For example, the recent merger of First & Merchants National Bank, Richmond (deposits of $2.2 billion) and Virginia National Bank, Norfolk (deposits of $3.1 billion), approved by the Comptroller of the Currency, resulted in the elimination of existing competition in 10 local markets. (The two banks had offices in a total of 28 other markets.) Another 1983 merger, of Sun Banks, Orlando, and Flagship Banks, Miami, involved existing competition in 22 local markets. The recent merger of Wells Fargo, San Francisco, and Crocker, Los Angeles, resulted in the elimination of some existing competition in 36 markets.

tion of mergers were of the market-extension variety—that is, they involved banks that did not operate in the same local geographic markets. Due in large part to the application of a variant of the potential competition doctrine[122] by bank regulators, sizable bank holding companies [BHCs] were generally permitted to acquire only relatively small banks.[123] Then, in 1981, the Fifth Circuit Court (New Orleans) vacated two 1980 Federal Reserve Board orders denying two such relatively small acquisitions by large BHCs in Texas.[124] In remanding the cases, the court specified a demanding set of criteria that had to be met before future proposals could be denied because of the elimination of potential or probable future competition. After approval of the remanded cases, it became clear that bank regulatory agencies were no longer free to use their broad discretion to deny mergers because of the sheer size of the resulting banking organization or on grounds such as adverse statewide structural effects (increasing dominance by the largest institutions in a particular state) at least in cases where the acquired firm is small. Since 1980, no bank merger has been denied on such grounds despite the fact that some of the largest bank mergers in history have taken place.

---

122 For a discussion of the issue of potential competition, *see* Rhoades, *A Clarification of the Potential Competition Doctrine in Bank Merger Analysis*, 5 J. BANK RES. 35–42 (1975); and Winer, *Applying the Theory of Probable Future Competition*, 68 FED. RES. BULL. 527–33 (1982).

123 Several proposed acquisitions that were denied on grounds that they would eliminate significant potential competition and adversely affect statewide banking structure involved banks with deposits of less than $100 million. The following proposals are examples: First International, Dallas, to acquire Bank of Tyler, Tyler ($86 million in deposits), 60 FED. RES. BULL. 43 (1974); First City Bancorporation, Houston, to acquire Lufkin National Bank, Lufkin ($66 million in deposits), 60 FED. RES. BULL. 450 (1974).

124 *See* Mercantile Texas Corp. v. Board of Governors, 638 F.2d 1255 (5th Cir. 1981), and Republic of Texas Corp. v. Board of Governors, 649 F.2d 1026 (5th Cir. 1981). These cases involved the acquisition of banking organizations that held deposits of $623 million and $203 million, respectively.

Another important development that contributed to more cautious enforcement policy toward bank mergers was the passage of the Monetary Control Act (1980) and the Garn-St Germain Act (1982). Both laws expanded the powers of thrift institutions, enabling them to offer services previously supplied solely or primarily by commercial banks (*e.g.*, demand deposits and commercial loans). As a result, bank regulatory agencies and the Department of Justice now routinely include some thrift institution deposits in the relevant product market when calculating market shares and levels of concentration in local banking markets. This procedure effectively allows larger commercial banking organizations to merge with each other because market shares are diluted by the inclusion of some thrift deposits.

One other important factor that has contributed to the higher level of market share combinations that are acceptable to the bank regulatory agencies is the recent liberalization of the Department of Justice horizontal merger guidelines. Bank regulatory agencies have typically used the Justice Department guidelines as a benchmark for screening the competitive effects of all proposed mergers. The guidelines, which were revised in 1982, state that the Department will not challenge any merger in an unconcentrated market, but may challenge mergers that increase the Herfindahl-Hirschman index [HHI] in moderately concentrated and highly concentrated markets by 100 points and 50 points, respectively. Markets are classified as highly concentrated if the postmerger HHI exceeds 1,800, as moderately concentrated if it is between 1,000 and 1,800, and as unconcentrated if it is less than 1,000.

The guidelines for banking, in particular, were revised in a February 1985 letter from Acting Assistant Attorney General for Antitrust, Charles F. Rule, to the Comptroller of the Currency, C. Todd Conover.[125] The letter stated that bank mergers generally would not be challenged (absent other factors indicating an anticompetitive effect) unless the postmerger HHI *is at least 1,800*, and the increase in the HHI attributable to the merger *is at*

---

125 A similar letter was sent to Paul A. Volcker, Chairman of the Federal Reserve Board in May 1985.

least 200 (as opposed to an increase of 50 previously). It was explained that this higher-than-normal HHI threshold for banking is appropriate in order to account for the competitive effect of nonbank competitors, including limited-purpose lenders (*e.g.*, consumer finance companies) and other nondepository financial entities (*e.g.*, production credit associations). These revised guidelines have effectively permitted mergers among banking organizations with significantly higher market shares than in the past. The possible effect of strict adherence to the new horizontal merger guidelines on local banking market structure is examined below.

Potential horizontal merger activity among commercial banks—a simulation

To assess the possible effect of the new merger guidelines in banking, merger activity (following the new Department of Justice guidelines) is simulated in every one of the 315 MSAs and 2,383 non-MSA counties in the United States. The sequence of hypothetical mergers is designed to result in the upper limit of concentration and the lower limit of the number of remaining firms in each market. Thus, it is a mechanical exercise that reflects policy direction and not necessarily likely results.

The procedure allows the largest firm in the market to consummate as many mergers as possible (with acquisition targets proceeding from the largest to the smallest bank acceptable) without exceeding the levels specified in the guidelines. Then, in sequence from the largest to the smallest, each of the remaining firms in the market is allowed to consummate every merger permissible under the guidelines until the limits imposed by the guidelines proscribe further mergers. The particular sequence followed in this simulation results in the most highly skewed final distribution of deposit shares possible, given the assumption that the regulatory authorities follow the guidelines to the letter.[126]

---

126 In practice, the regulatory agencies frequently approve mergers that involve structural changes that exceed the levels specified in the guidelines because of other factors, such as thrift competition and the conditions of entry that indicate competition is more intense than banks-only structural measures suggest. *For example, see Hartford*

There are factors that might, in actuality, alter the final distribution of market shares and the number of firms remaining in any given market. For example, if some of the lower-ranked banks were either commonly owned or merged among themselves, their combined market shares might be too large to allow acquisition by one of the leading firms. The bias from this possibility is probably small because experience demonstrates that the largest firms in given markets are typically responsible for a very high proportion of acquisition activity. Also, the merger sequence might not be carried out to the limit, as it is in the simulation, because of financial limitations of the acquiring firms. In addition, several states have "cap" legislation that imposes a ceiling on the percentage of state deposits that an organization may control.[127] On the other hand, there may be other considerations, such as the poor financial condition of the firms being acquired, that would render antitrust considerations moot. The following two sections describe the hypothetical structural changes that are possible in banking markets in metropolitan areas and in counties.

Merger potential in MSAs[128]

The number of banks that could be merged in MSAs and the minimum number of banks remaining after all possible mergers

---

National Corporation, 73 FED. RES. BULL. 720 (1987); *Houghton Financial*, 73 FED. RES. BULL. 870 (1987); and *Fleet Financial Group Inc.*, 74 FED. RES. BULL. 62 (1988).

127 As of January 1988, 15 states had such legislation: Iowa, 10%; Missouri, 13%; New Hampshire, 15%; New Jersey, 13.5%; Tennessee, 16.5%; West Virginia, 20%; Nebraska, 9%; Oklahoma, 11%; Arkansas, 15%; Indiana, 12%; Kansas, 9%; Kentucky, 20%; Ohio, 20%; Mississippi, 18%; and Texas, 25%. Some of the caps include deposits of banks and thrift institutions combined.

128 NECMAS (New England County Metropolitan Areas) are used instead of MSAs for the states of Connecticut, Maine, Massachusetts, New Hampshire, Rhode Island, and Vermont. NECMAS assure that complete counties are used in the market definitions for the New

are presented in table 8. The 315 MSAs are classified by number of banks before the merger simulation. Since the number of banks in MSAs ranges from 3 to 247, various subgroups are formed to simplify the presentation. As shown in the table, more than half the MSAs in the country presently have fewer than 14 banking organizations, while only 6 have more than 100 banking organizations. Not surprisingly, the greatest number of mergers could occur in the group of MSAs having the largest number of banking organizations. For example, after the simulation, only 12 of the original 981 banks would remain in the group of 6 MSAs with more than 100 firms. Within this group, only 1 bank would remain in the market that started out with 247 firms; 2 would remain in the four markets that started out with 168, 160, 157, and 108 firms; and 3 would remain in the market with 141 firms. These markets include Chicago, Los Angeles, Dallas, Houston, Minneapolis, and Oklahoma City.

The present wide range of variation in the number of banks in MSAs throughout the country could be dramatically reduced if all mergers permissible under the 1985 merger guidelines were approved and consummated. As noted above, the reduction in the number of banking alternatives would be greatest in the largest markets. Thus, the Chicago and Los Angeles MSAs, with populations of more than 7 million each, conceivably could have fewer banks than most small MSAs, with populations of less than 100,000.[129] Moreover, MSAs covering thousands of square miles could have fewer banks than those covering only 100 or 200 square miles. After the simulation almost all MSAs had either 2 (104) or 3 (156) banks. In addition to the 8 MSAs that had only 1 surviving bank, 43 had 4 banks, 3 had 5 banks, and 1 had 6 banks. Thus, only 1 MSA in the nation would have 6 banks and all the rest would have between 1 and 5 banks. Using the 1985 guidelines for the simulation, the total number of banks in all

---

England states. This is done with the MSA definitions for all other areas of the country except New England. By using complete counties, market definitions remain consistent over time.

129 To be classified as an MSA, an area generally must have a central city with a population of at least 50,000.

MSAs would be reduced from 6,646 to 877. The average number of banks per MSA would fall from 21 to 2.8.

Table 8
Average Number of Firms Involved in Simulated Mergers in MSAs, by Number of Banking Organizations in the MSA

Number of banking organizations in MSA (number of MSAs in given range)	*Number of firms before mergers*		*Number of mergers*		*Number of firms after mergers*	
	Average	*Range*	*Average*	*Range*	*Average*	*Range*
101 or more (6)	163.5	108–247	161.5	106–246	2.0	1–3
61–100 (10)	73.6	62–94	71.9	60–93	1.7	1–2
41–60 (20)	48.3	41–58	46.2	39–56	2.1	1–3
31–40 (12)	34.8	31–38	32.3	29–36	2.6	2–4
26–30 (16)	28.4	26–30	26.2	24–29	2.2	1–3
21–25 (19)	23.1	21–25	20.7	18–23	2.4	1–3
18–20 (34)	18.8	18–20	16.3	14–20	2.5	2–4
15–17 (34)	15.9	15–17	13.1	11–15	2.7	2–4
12–14 (34)	12.7	12–14	10.0	8–12	2.7	2–4
9–11 (52)	10.1	9–11	7.0	5–9	3.1	2–4
6–8 (63)	7.1	6–8	3.8	2–5	3.3	2–6
5 or fewer (15)	4.4	3–5	1.1	0–2	3.3	2–4
Total, all MSAs (315)	21.1	3–247	18.3	0–246	2.8	1–6

In an earlier study, which included a simulation of potential merger activity using the 1982 Justice Department guidelines, it was shown that the total number of banks in MSAs could be reduced from 6,585 to 1,801. Thus, less than half as many independent banks would remain in MSAs using the current 1985 guidelines. Likewise, the average number of banks per MSA in the earliest simulation was reduced from 20.1 to 5.7.[130] Clearly, the 1985 guidelines for horizontal mergers in banking would theoretically allow a substantial consolidation of banking resources in the United States.

130 *See* BURKE, ANTITRUST LAWS, JUSTICE DEPARTMENT GUIDELINES, AND THE LIMITS OF CONCENTRATION IN LOCAL BANKING MARKETS 5 (Staff Study No. 138, Board of Governors of the Federal Reserve System, June 1984).

Merger potential in counties

The average and totals of banks that could be merged in county markets of various sizes are summarized in table 9. The 2,383 non-MSA counties in the country are classified by the number of banking organizations in operation before the merger simulation. Since the number of banks does not vary nearly so much in counties as in MSAs, only the 10 counties with 15 or more banks are presented as a group. Unlike the case in MSA markets, the range of the number of banks operating in county markets would not be dramatically narrowed by application of the guidelines. Many counties have so few banks that their potential merger activity is virtually nil. For example, 1,172 counties have only 1 to 3 banks; only 53 mergers among the 2,563 banking organizations that operate in these counties could possibly be approved under the guidelines. Thus, merger activity of any significance is likely in only about one-half (1,210) of all counties.

The simulation results indicate that 2 to 4 (2.9 average) banks would remain in most counties. The smallest number of banks in any county (excluding those that now have 3 or fewer banks) would be 2. At present, 9,917 banking organizations are represented in the 2,383 counties in the country. Mergers could reduce the number of organizations by 2,913 to a total of 7,004. The average number of banks in county markets is now 4.2, and the range is from 1 to 21; after the simulated mergers the average would be 2.9, and the range 1 to 6.[131] In the earlier simulation by Burke, *supra*, there were originally 10,050 banking organizations represented in the 2,408 counties in the country. Adherence to the 1982 guidelines could have reduced the number of organizations by 1,194 to a total of 8,856. The average number of banks in county markets was originally 4.2, and the range was from 1 to

---

131 If the 1,172 counties with 3 or fewer banks are excluded, the remaining 1,211 counties currently have an average of 6.1 banks, with a range of 21 to 4. After the simulated mergers, the average number falls to 3.7, with a range of 2 to 6 banks (only 6 counties in the nation would still have 6 banks).

22; after the simulated mergers the average was 3.7, and the range 1 to 10.

Table 9
Average Number of Firms Involved in Simulated Mergers in Counties by Number of Banking Organizations in the County

Number of banking organizations in county (no. of counties in given range)	*Number of firms before mergers*		*Number of mergers*		*Number of firms after mergers*	
	Average	*Range*	*Average*	*Range*	*Average*	*Range*
15 or more (10)	16.3	15–21	13.5	12–19	2.8	2–3
14 (6)	14.0	—	11.0	11–11	3.0	3–3
13 (13)	13.0	—	9.8	9–11	3.2	2–4
12 (17)	12.0	—	8.6	8–10	3.4	2–4
11 (25)	11.0	—	7.6	7–9	3.4	2–4
10 (34)	10.0	—	6.4	5–8	3.6	2–5
9 (51)	9.0	—	5.2	4–6	3.8	2–5
8 (87)	8.0	—	4.1	2–6	3.9	2–6
7 (139)	7.0	—	3.0	1–5	4.0	2–6
6 (199)	6.0	—	2.1	0–4	3.9	2–6
5 (277)	5.0	—	1.2	0–3	3.8	2–5
4 (353)	4.0	—	.5	0–2	3.5	2–4
3 (458)	3.0	—	.1	0–1	2.9	2–3
2 (475)	2.0	—	.0	0–1	2.0	1–2
1 (239)	1.0	—	—	—	1.0	—
Total, all counties (2383)	4.2	1–21	1.2	0–19	2.9	1–6

These changes in county structural characteristics appear small, when contrasted with the potential changes in metropolitan markets. However, considering the very small number of banks that currently operate in county markets, the potential merger activity is not insignificant. Moreover, some 1,700 more mergers could be allowed using the current (1985) guidelines than could have been allowed under the 1982 guidelines. In contrast to the hypothetical merger exercise just completed, the next section describes actual recent merger activity involving large banking organizations.

Recent merger activity and concentration in commercial banking

Following the political and economic developments that led to a modification in the standards applied to bank mergers, there was a significant increase in consolidation activity. Mergers involving banking organizations each holding domestic deposits in excess of $1 billion first occurred in 1982 and since then have become commonplace.[132] Prior to that time, the acquisition of a bank with deposits of even $500 million in deposits was a rare event.[133] As shown in table 10, there were 72 bank mergers (36 of which were interstate) between 1982 and December 2, 1987, where both partners held deposits in excess of $1 billion. The 72 acquiring firms held deposits of $618.2 billion while the deposits of acquired firms totaled $213.9 billion. The large mergers that have been completed, in addition to some that are pending or have been announced, indicate that, in terms of total resources involved, merger activity in 1987 surpassed that of any previous year by a considerable margin.

---

132 A critical event affecting the merger movement among very large banking organizations was the Supreme Court's 1982 action upholding the Federal Reserve Board's three decisions approving acquisitions pursuant to regional interstate banking statutes. Presently, 40 states and the District of Columbia have similar laws, and interstate acquisition activity is proceeding briskly. Most interstate merger activity to date has involved banking organizations that are among the largest in their respective states.

133 Although 4,805 bank mergers and acquisitions occurred between 1960 and 1983, the aggregate assets acquired were modest ($206.3 billion or approximately 25% of the industry's average assets over the 24-year period) because the acquired banks were generally small. *See*, S. A. RHOADES, MERGERS AND ACQUISITIONS BY COMMERCIAL BANKS, 1960–1983 (Staff Study No. 142, Board of Governors of the Federal Reserve System, Jan. 1985).

Table 10

Number of Approved Mergers of Large (Both Over $1 Billion in Domestic Deposits) Banking Organizations and Deposits by Year

Year	*Number of mergers*	*Domestic deposits of acquirers (in $ bil.)*	*Domestic deposits of acquired (in $ bil.)*	*Total*
1980	0	—	—	—
1981	1	$ 1.0	$ 1.0	$ 2.0
1982	2	6.5	3.1	9.6
1983	6	78.9	16.1	95.0
1984	15	97.6	37.8	135.4
1985	7	28.2	20.2	48.4
1986	20	167.8	49.7	217.5
1987*	21	238.2	86.0	324.2
Total	72	$618.2	$213.9	$832.1

Pending and Announced Mergers

Year	*Number of pending mergers*	*Domestic deposits of acquirers (in $ bil.)*	*Domestic deposits of acquired (in $ bil.)*	*Total*
1987*	13	$109.6	$ 45.6	$155.2

* As of December 1987

Table 11 shows the percentage of deposits held by the nation's top 10, 25, 50, and 100 banking organizations in 1980, 1986, and 1987. Although the percentage of deposits held by the top 10 and 25 firms in the nation has not changed appreciably during the relatively short time period between 1980 and 1987, the share of the top 50 and 100 organizations has risen rather markedly, especially by historical standards. These changes reflect the recent merger trend involving increasingly large regional banking organizations, which in turn reflects the implementation of more cautious section 7 enforcement.

Table 11
Percentages of Deposits Held by Largest Banking Organizations in the United States—1980, 1986, and 1987

Year	*Top 10*	*Top 25*	*Top 50*	*Top 100*
1980	18.56	29.12	37.05	46.75
1986	17.25	29.18	41.69	54.58
1987	18.19	30.40	42.59	55.45

Resources employed in recent antitrust enforcement policy

The resources devoted to antitrust enforcement in recent years are also indicative of effective implementation of more cautious section 7 enforcement. According to one article,[134] antitrust enforcement under the Reagan administration had been significantly reduced. It was noted that budgets and staff had fallen significantly. For example, the number of attorneys serving in the Antitrust Division fell from 429 in 1980 to 240 in February 1987. Altogether, full-time staff, which includes economists, paralegals and clerical and secretarial support, had fallen from 883 to 539; the total was expected to fall to 500 by 1988. In addition, at no time since 1980 have all the positions authorized been filled, a policy that was justified in the name of Gramm-Rudman-Hollings budget cutting.

A former assistant attorney general in charge of antitrust during President Ford's tenure recently stated that the cuts in Antitrust Division budgeting are "quite simply a disaster." Donald Baker, who now practices antitrust law, recently told the House Judiciary Subcommittee on Monopolies and Commercial Law:

> The stark truth is the Antitrust Division today is less than two-thirds its size when President Reagan took office. It is smaller than when I came to it first in October 1966, when the staff totaled 600. If the

---

134 Elias, *Scales Tip Against Antitrust Statutes*, INSIGHT, June 15, 1987, at 9–16.

fiscal year 1988 budget cuts are accepted by Congress, it would only be about 58 percent of its January 1981 strength.[135]

In the meantime, both the number of mergers and their size have been growing significantly. New York University's antitrust scholar, Eleanor M. Fox reported that:

> In 1983 the total number of mergers consummated was 2,533, the largest number since 1974. The 1983 merger deals amounted to $73.1 billion and included 187 transactions worth $100 million or more. In 1984 there were 2,543 mergers, worth $122.2 billion, including 200 mergers worth more than $100 million. In 1985 there were 3,001 mergers, which set a 12-year record and represented an 18 percent increase over 1984. The value of the transactions was $179.6 billion, nearly 50 percent higher than in 1984. Of the 1985 mergers, 268 were valued at $100 million or more and 36 were valued at or over $1 billion. During this period, the largest mergers in the nation's history have been consummated, including enormous horizontal mergers such as Gulf-Socal [Standard Oil of California] and Texaco-Getty.[136]

Another recent study[137] that focused on professional hours devoted to antitrust activity by the Justice Department and FTC from the beginning of the decade through 1985 also revealed similar trends. The findings clearly indicate an attenuation of antitrust under the Reagan administration. Overall professional time expended by the Antitrust Division declined by 14% from 1980 to 1985, while activity within the manufacturing industries dropped by 30% over the same period. FTC professional effort devoted to overall antitrust declined by 42% from 1981 to 1985 and decreased by 59% within the manufacturing industries only. From 1981 to 1985, the aggregate efforts of the two agencies declined by 40% overall and by 51% in the manufacturing industries only. Thus, antitrust matters in general attracted less

---

135 *Id.* at 12.

136 *Id.*

137 Preston & Conner, *Federal Antitrust Activity Under the Reagan Administration: New Evidence*, Paper presented at the Industrial Organization Society Sessions Annual Conference of the Southern Economic Association, Washington, D.C. (Nov. 22–24, 1987). We thank the authors for expeditiously sending us a copy of their paper.

attention by both agencies. Activity within the manufacturing industries in particular experienced more severe declines.

VI. Summary and conclusion

Even the most casual observation suggests that enforcement of section 7 of the Clayton Act became decidedly more cautious during the 1980's. We contend that a strong confluence of political and economic developments provided the foundation for this trend and present evidence supporting this position.

The political foundations for more cautious section 7 enforcement are clearly established in the widely publicized statements of numerous, high-level administration officials beginning in 1981. We present a collection of relevant quotations illustrating this point. The complementary economic developments are more diverse but they clearly have been an important factor in recent section 7 enforcement.

The economic developments that we regard as most directly influential generally appeared to undermine the findings of earlier structure-performance studies, which had formerly provided the foundation for a relatively vigorous, structural approach to section 7 enforcement. These developments are (1) Demsetz' reinterpretation of findings of the traditional structure-performance studies (*i.e.*, high profits in concentrated markets are due to efficiency rather than collusion); (2) theoretical and empirical developments in research on the structure-performance relationship that raised questions about the methodology and consequently the validity of earlier studies; and (3) publication of the theory of contestable markets, which holds that perfect competition may prevail regardless of the structure (*i.e.*, concentration or number of firms) of a market. These are all important developments in the field of industrial organization and all have stimulated substantial research.

Nevertheless, a review of significant literature in connection with these developments reveals that each has significant shortcomings and has been subject to serious questions. For one, Demsetz' reinterpretation of the structure-performance relationship, along with purportedly supporting evidence, have been plausibly reinterpreted to attribute high profits to collusion rather than to efficiency. Recent evidence on strategic groups and the persistence of profits also suggest a market power rather than efficiency explanation for high profits. Second, the new theoretical and empirical models that highlighted technical inadequacies of earlier structure-performance models have themselves been found to have important shortcomings. Additionally, results from the technically more sophisticated studies are often the same as the results from earlier studies. Consequently, about all that can be said is that the earlier studies had shortcomings. It cannot be said that they are wrong or have been disproven. The third economic development we discussed, contestable markets, has been subject to some sharp criticism for its extreme assumptions, and empirical studies of contestability generally have not supported the theory. We present new evidence on contestability in banking and do not find support. However, our findings are consistent with the theory of potential competition, which includes the concept of barriers to entry.

Examination of relevant evidence indicates that recent political and economic developments have been implemented effectively in the policy arena. For example, mergers have reached record levels during the 1980's, at least in banking and the industrial sector, and horizontal mergers have become much more common. Additionally, recently implemented merger guidelines for banking, by the Justice Department, substantially increase the opportunities for mergers according to a simulation we present. Finally, data indicate that resources devoted to federal antitrust enforcement have declined substantially during the 1980's.

In view of the shortcomings of the economic developments underlying more cautious section 7 enforcement, it is not clear that the economic foundation for more cautious enforcement is any stronger than the earlier economic foundation for enforcement. With such basic questions and uncertainty remaining, it is not at all clear what future section 7 enforcement should or will be like, though it appears to have become unduly cautious during the 1980's because of a strong belief in the theories of potential competition (contestability) and perfect markets.[138]

138 A discussion of the possible major long-term implications of very cautious enforcement may be found in STEPHEN A. RHOADES, POWER EMPIRE BUILDING AND MERGERS (1983).

13
Has antitrust outgrown dual enforcement? A proposal for rationalization

BY ERNEST GELLHORN, CHARLES A. JAMES, RICHARD POGUE and JOE SIMS*

I. Introduction

Antitrust enforcement has changed significantly in recent years. Per se rules and bright-line tests used to make antitrust a "pigeonhole" problem, with the ultimate outcome in a given case almost wholly dependent on how the conduct was characterized. Even merger analysis, which should be the most fact-sensitive of disciplines, fell to Derek Bok,[1] *Philadelphia Bank*[2] and the luxury of certainty. This simplistic approach started to change during

---

* Members of the law firm Jones, Day, Reavis & Pogue.

AUTHORS' NOTE: *We wish to thank William E. Swope, Tom D. Smith, Neil Roberts and Timothy J. Muris for their helpful comments and suggestions. Any errors are the responsibility of the authors.*

1 *See* Bok, *Section 7 of the Clayton Act and the Merging of Law and Economics*, 74 HARV. L. REV. 226 (1960).

2 United States v. Philadelphia National Bank, 374 U.S. 321 (1963).

the mid-to-late 1970's, and fell apart completely during the Reagan administration, where the laissez faire concepts of the Chicago school reached their primacy. Under the twin pressures of international competition and growing economic sophistication, the phrase "antitrust rule" became an oxymoron, and the reign of the so-called rule of reason became close to absolute.[3]

The net effect of this change in antitrust standards, ironically enough, was to transform noncriminal antitrust enforcement into a complex form of market regulation. This development in turn virtually disintegrated the "law enforcement" shield that antitrust regulators historically had used to distinguish themselves from the Interstate Commerce Commission, Civil Aeronautics Board *et al.* The antitrust "cop on the beat" was still alive, but only in the area of criminal prosecution of hard-core price fixing. During the 1980's, antitrust was epitomized by grand juries and merger regulation, the two polar extremes of the antitrust enforcement spectrum.

All of the early signs suggest that the Bush administration is retreating from the more extreme positions of the Chicago school. Indeed, the Reagan years are now being painted by some as a period of deregulatory excess, with everything from the savings and loan crisis to the malaise on Wall Street being blamed upon lax federal regulation. This sentiment has also spilled over into the antitrust arena, with the result being a strong impetus (in part from the antitrust bar itself) for more aggressive antitrust enforcement.

The Bush antitrust appointees are already talking tough, requesting harsher penalties and increased resources. At the Antitrust Division, Assistant Attorney General Rill promises that criminal enforcement will continue to be the top priority. Mr. Rill has stated that he will attempt to turn minor cases over to the states in order to free-up federal resources for bigger fish. He will

---

3 *See* Gellhorn and Tathum, *Making Sense Out of the Rule of Reason*, 35 Case W. Res. L. Rev. 155 (1984–85).

also push for tougher sentences and harsher fines.[4] Because the Federal Trade Commission [FTC] lacks criminal enforcement authority, it has limited targets for its increased aggressiveness outside the merger area. FTC Chairman Steiger, however, threatens more intensive scrutiny of trade association activities and continued pursuit of nonprice predation, which has been the agency's pet (and still unproven) theory in recent years. Chairman Steiger has also established a working group of her so-called best and brightest attorneys to look for new and innovative uses of section 5. Like Assistant Attorney Rill, Chairman Steiger also wants to "up the ante." She wants legislation to increase civil penalties for antitrust violations and statutory authority to seek consumer redress in antitrust cases.[5]

The greatest change will likely take place in the merger area. During the Reagan administration, antitrust enforcers did not believe that big was necessarily bad, and thus drew very weak presumptions from evidence of high market concentration. In essence, to justify a merger challenge the staffs of both agencies had to demonstrate high concentration *and* strong nonstructural evidence that the merger would increase the likelihood of collusion. The burden of persuasion fell on those urging action, and the inevitable result was that only a relatively few transactions were challenged. Given their apparent charter (and desire) to shift the burden of persuasion back to those defending a proposed transaction that falls within the traditional presumption, the Bush enforcers would largely eliminate theoretical defenses that were effective just a few years ago. This approach will guarantee more merger challenges, but it is still unclear how these challenges will fare in the federal courts, where roughly 50 percent of sitting

---

4 *See* Remarks of James F. Rill before the 23d Annual New England Antitrust Conference, Cambridge, Massachusetts (Nov. 3, 1989).

5 *See* Remarks of Janet Steiger before the 23d Annual New England Antitrust Conference, Cambridge, Massachusetts (Nov. 3, 1989).

judges are products of the Reagan administration.[6] The Antitrust Division's recent loss in *United States v. Baker Hughes, Inc.*[7] indicates that at least some courts will continue to require proof of something more than high concentration in order to sustain a government merger challenge.

Of course, the status quo ante cannot be replicated. We now know too much about market behavior to retreat entirely to the old presumptive rules, and much of the new economic learning has already become a part of the merger case law. Whether this is good or bad is irrelevant for our purposes; it is unlikely to change in any drastic way in the foreseeable future. In addition, criminal enforcement efforts will continue as long as they produce results, and there is no indication that horizontal price-fixing enforcement is approaching a point of diminishing returns. The deployment of more enforcement resources in the criminal area apparently means more cases, and there seems to be unanimous agreement from all points on the political compass that this enforcement effort is worth continuing (even if there are some quibbles about its focus).

All other enforcement efforts are necessarily quite complicated, because of both the intense focus on specific fact situations and the necessary economic analysis of those facts. There is much disagreement on results and conclusions here, but very little on methodology. Criminal enforcement will remain a simple game of "who-done-it," relying on straightforward and reasonably noncontroversial principles. By contrast, noncriminal (especially merger) enforcement will remain a heavily regulatory process. The dichotomy between these two forms of antitrust will remain, and may become even more stark over time.

---

6 According to statistics maintained by the Judicial Conference of the United States, Reagan appointees hold 292 of the 575 authorized seats on the federal district courts and 83 of the 168 authorized seats on the courts of appeals.

7 1990-1 Trade Cas. (CCH) ¶ 68,930 (D.D.C.), *aff'd*, No. 90-5060 (D.C. Cir. Jul. 6, 1990). *See also* FTC v. Promodes SA, 1989 Trade Reg. Rep. (CCH) ¶ 68,688 (N.D. Ga. 1989) (court rejects FTC challenge of merger resulting in a firm with 67%–76% of market due to ease of entry).

Despite the dramatic shifts in antitrust philosophy over the years, the basic procedural mechanisms for federal antitrust enforcement have remained substantially unchanged since 1914. The FTC, which was the product of the election of Woodrow Wilson and the brain of Louis Brandeis, was intended to be a general overseer of competition policy—a committee of experts who could be expected to do a better job than federal judges in protecting the public from the perils of big business. The Department of Justice [DOJ] had not been terribly active in the first quarter-century following the passage of the Sherman Act, and no doubt there was some fear (especially following the judicial creation of the rule of reason in 1911[8]) that conservative federal judges were not the ideal guardians of consumer welfare.

The idea underlying creation of the FTC was probably flawed in its inception, but dual enforcement survived without much controversy through most of the next 50-plus years, in large part because the FTC did not do much, and the DOJ was only sporadically active. However, following the Kirkpatrick Report in 1969,[9] and the subsequent installation of the report's author as Chairman, the FTC became much more aggressive. Earlier in that decade, the DOJ had rediscovered criminal enforcement, and for much of the rest of the 1960's and 1970's, the two competition agencies engaged in what seems in hindsight to have been a very aggressive competition of their own.

The bureaucratic excesses of the 1960's and 1970's are well-cataloged, and are not worth repeating here. Suffice it to say that the differences between the two agencies really did make a difference! The FTC used the vague language of section 5, and its administrative process, to attack virtually every form of industrial concentration, from mergers to distribution contracts.[10] If

---

8 *See* Standard Oil Co. v. United States, 221 U.S. 1 (1911); United States v. American Tobacco Co., 221 U.S. 106 (1911).

9 Report of the ABA Commission to Study the Federal Trade Commission (1969) [ABA Report].

10 During the 1970's and early 1980's, the FTC commenced a number of ill-fated but significant monopolization cases under section 5

there was ever a case to be made for dual enforcement, it was made in the 15 years between 1965 and 1980. For those who believe in dual enforcement, this was truly the golden age of federal antitrust enforcement.

The world is different now and, we would argue, better. Competition between the two federal antitrust agencies has largely subsided, and the two agencies are applying relatively similar substantive standards (although frequently in very different ways). The key word, unfortunately, is "largely." The bureaucratic imperative inevitably compels activity rather than inactivity, aggression rather than sloth. Despite the Reagan administration's initial instincts to consolidate the activities of the two agencies, the best that it was able to do was generally harmonize their output. Nonetheless, the Antitrust Division and the FTC still have different standards, different procedures, and very different mind sets. They still produce different results. And of greatest concern, the signs of relapse to the old ways were already present even as the Reagan administration wound to a close.[11] The ideological energy has been dissipated, but it has been replaced by the more enduring energy of bureaucratic imperative. The FTC is clearly not the CAB; it will not voluntarily expire.

---

such as Exxon Corp., 98 F.T.C. 453 (1981) (dismissed); Ethyl Corp., 101 F.T.C. 425 (1983), *rev'd*, 729 F.2d 128 (2d Cir. 1984); E.I. du Pont de Nemours & Co., 96 F.T.C. 650 (1980); and Reuben H. Donnelly Corp., 95 F.T.C. 1 (1980), *enforcement denied*, 630 F.2d 920 (2d Cir. 1980). The Commission even attempted to expand the law of vertical restraints in Russell Stover Candies, Inc., 100 F.T.C. 1 (1982), *rev'd*, 718 F.2d 256 (8th Cir. 1983).

11 For example, former FTC Bureau of Competition Director Jeffrey Zuckerman went to great pains to explain what he believed were significant differences in merger enforcement policy between the two agencies. *See* Remarks by Bureau of Competition Director Jeffrey Zuckerman before the ABA Section of Antitrust Law, Washington, DC (March 23, 1988), *reprinted in* FTC WATCH, No. 277 (May 2, 1988), at 5. To the extent that Mr. Zuckerman's remarks reflect the gradual emergence of substantially different standards between the two agencies, we could be headed backward toward the unfortunate time when the agency clearance decision was in many instances outcome-determinative.

In some respects, attacking dual enforcement today may seem both Sisyphean and unnecessary. Indeed, task forces of the ABA's Antitrust Section have just given both agencies clean bills of health, with only passing references to the problems stemming from dual enforcement.[12] Neither task force report evidences a consensus for addressing dual antitrust enforcement at the present time. There is value in repeating truth, however, even if few initially listen. It is true that the two federal agencies are probably closer today in enforcement policies than ever before, thus generating less friction in federal antitrust enforcement than in the past. But this parity is not guaranteed, and indeed is unlikely to continue, given the differences between the agencies, their functions and the selection process (and terms) of their managers. With the two agencies each gearing-up for a period of new assertiveness, we can reasonably expect an end to the present policy harmony between them, and the most obvious ill effects of dual antitrust enforcement may soon resume. Thus, this may in fact be the optimal time to deal with the issue.

Finally, there is a somewhat paradoxical rationale for ending dual enforcement now. In the old days, when antitrust rules were more rigid, the fact that the two agencies might apply different standards was somewhat less troublesome. The lowest common denominator was the standard for protected conduct. And given the size and strength of our domestic market, the U.S. economy could absorb the cost of inefficient and misguided antitrust

---

12 *See* REPORT OF THE AMERICAN BAR ASSOCIATION SECTION OF ANTITRUST LAW SPECIAL COMMITTEE TO STUDY THE ROLE OF THE FEDERAL TRADE COMMISSION (April 7, 1989); REPORT OF THE AMERICAN BAR ASSOCIATION SECTION OF ANTITRUST LAW TASK FORCE ON THE ANTITRUST DIVISION (July 1989). The ABA FTC Task Force Report indicates that the members had differing views on various subjects relating to dual enforcement, but states that there was no consensus among the group for a major restructuring of antitrust enforcement or the roles of either agency. The Task Force on the Antitrust Division opted not to address the question of dual enforcement, but expressed concern that the Division's focus on criminal matters was giving the FTC de facto primacy in the area of mergers. The Task Force, therefore, recommended that the Division reassert itself in the merger area. Antitrust Division Task Force Report at 44.

enforcement. Today, in a much more competitive world, and with considerably more subjective "rules," the presence of—and differences between—two decisionmakers can be dramatically more important. This is especially so if, as seems likely, the FTC is always going to be subject to a sometimes latent but never dead bureaucratic impulse to justify its existence by creating law (under section 5 or otherwise) that is somehow different from the antitrust law practiced at the Antitrust Division.

Much of the historical debate concerning dual antitrust enforcement has focused on perceived differences in enforcement policy. The FTC has generally fared poorly in comparative studies of the two agencies. The FTC's poor showing reflects a number of factors, not the least of which is the fact that the agency has swung back and forth between virtual inactivity and what former Chairman James Miller termed "Star Trek enforcement."[13] The efficacy and basic fairness of the Commission's administrative adjudicatory procedures have also been a continuing source of controversy. Indeed, most commentators who have studied the question of dual enforcement seem to favor transferring the FTC's antitrust enforcement authority to DOJ.[14]

---

13 The term "Star Trek enforcement" refers to the once popular television show in which a group of space explorers were given the mission to "go boldly where no man has gone before." During the 1970's, the FTC did just that by pursuing certain entirely new antitrust theories such as "shared monopoly" (Exxon Corp., 98 F.T.C. 453 (1981)—complaint filed in 1973 and dismissed in 1981) and noncollusive price signalling (Ethyl Corp., 101 F.T.C. 425 (1983), *rev'd*, 729 F.2d 128 (2d Cir. 1984)). *See* Gellhorn, *The Wages of Zealotry: The FTC Under Siege*, 4 REGULATION 33 (Jan./Feb. 1980).

14 Previous analyses of the dual enforcement question include: Blair, *A Suggestion for Improved Antitrust Enforcement*, 30 ANTITRUST BULL. 433 (1985); Handler, *Reforming the Antitrust Laws*, 82 COLUM. L. REV. 1287 (1982); Baker, *Dual Enforcement: Coordination, Competition or Confusion*, Nat'l L.J., Dec. 18, 1978, at 26–27; Roll, *Dual Enforcement of the Antitrust Laws by the Department of Justice and the FTC: The Liaison Procedure*, 31 BUS. LAW 2075 (1976); Rockefeller, *Antitrust Enforcement: Duopoly or Monopoly*, 1962 WISC. L. REV. 437 (1962); Simon, *The Case Against the Federal Trade Commission*, 19

Of course, the DOJ's enforcement record has not been free from criticism. During certain periods, the DOJ has also pursued antitrust theories that appear in retrospect misguided,[15] and at times has been criticized for being too accommodating to the political desires of the executive branch.[16]

This article looks at the question of dual enforcement in a slightly different way than some of the previous efforts. Rather than contributing further to the debate over which agency has pursued the most misguided enforcement policies in the past, we try to determine which agency has the structure and procedures most capable of carrying out the modern antitrust enforcement mission. The optimal antitrust enforcement agency should be able to develop a coherent enforcement policy, apply that policy consistently in the selection of cases and litigate its cases efficiently to final resolutions. Proceeding from that premise, we

---

U. CHI. L. REV. 297 (1951). Messrs. Gellhorn and Sims have also written previously on the subject of dual enforcement, both concluding that federal antitrust enforcement should be unified within DOJ. *See* Gellhorn, *Regulatory Reform and the Federal Trade Commission's Antitrust Jurisdiction*, 49 TENN. L. REV. 471 (1982); Sims, *Miller's FTC Chairmanship Merits High Marks*, Legal Times, Mar. 18, 1985, at 16.

15 DOJ, after all, was the agency that first established structural presumptions in merger litigation in United States v. Philadelphia National Bank, 374 U.S. 321 (1963), and moved to lower past the point of logic the structural enforcement thresholds in subsequent cases, such as United States v. Von's Grocery Co., 384 U.S. 270 (1966), and United States v. Pabst Brewing Co., 384 U.S. 546 (1966). DOJ was the agency most aggressively pursuing conglomerate merger theories. *See, e.g.* United States v. ITT, 1972 Trade Cas. (CCH) ¶ 74,093 (1972). DOJ was the agency that successfully placed many nonprice vertical restraints within the per se category in United States v. Arnold, Schwinn & Co., 388 U.S. 365 (1967). Indeed, it was DOJ that closed out the decade by filing United States v. International Business Machines, Inc. [1961-1970 Transfer Binder] Trade Reg. Rep. (CCH) ¶ 45,069 (Jan. 17, 1969), the massive and futile monopolization case ultimately dismissed after nearly 13 years of painful and expensive litigation.

16 Both agencies have generally been successful in avoiding the appearance of being subject to political influence in making enforcement determinations in individual cases. Nonetheless, both have been subject to occasional criticism on specific matters.

begin with a brief review of the substantive changes that have taken place in antitrust law and the manner in which those changes have influenced the nature of public antitrust enforcement. Next, we discuss the present enforcement scheme and how each agency's organizational and procedural characteristics have affected its relative performance. We conclude with an examination of the various options for rationalization.

II. The evolution of antitrust policy

Since the mid-1970's, the basic theories driving antitrust enforcement have been evolving rapidly. Prior to that time, antitrust enforcement had been primarily a game of characterization. Having been handed the principal responsibility for giving meaning to the vague statutory pronouncements of the Sherman and Clayton Acts, the courts responded by attempting to develop a series of per se rules and other bright-line tests that could simplify the task of distinguishing between legitimate business conduct and behavior that actually restrained competition. Once these rules were in place, antitrust analysis too often involved not much more than attempting to place business conduct in the appropriate legal pigeonhole. Although this approach may have been sensible as a matter of judicial economy, the per se rules and bright-line tests often drew less than perfect distinctions and sometimes resulted in decisions that were irrational, if not outright silly, as a matter of economic policy.

By the early 1970's, a view had begun to develop that overly simplistic antitrust principles were stifling, not promoting, competitive behavior in the U.S. economy. This view drew strong theoretical support from the writings of antitrust scholars, such as Phillip Areeda, Richard Posner and Robert Bork, and from the emerging economic literature concerning price theory, contestable markets, and cartel behavior. Proponents of this new view of antitrust argued that market power—*i.e.*, the ability to raise prices above competitive levels—was the principal antitrust risk and that market power could be exercised only under a limited set of economic conditions. Gradually, a consensus began to build that proper antitrust analysis required detailed evaluation of economic behavior.[17]

The translation of this largely academic consensus into actual enforcement policy has proven to be an uneven process. The early 1970's remained a period of antitrust activism, with both DOJ and the FTC generally continuing to pursue the simplistic structural theories that had characterized the 1960's. Nevertheless, a few Supreme Court decisions in the mid and late 1970's signaled the beginning of change.

The Supreme Court's 1974 decision in *United States v. General Dynamics Corp.*[18] was the first major step. Previous Supreme Court decisions under section 7 of the Clayton Act had condemned mergers upon a simple showing that the market shares of the merging parties exceeded a minimum level.[19] In response to those decisions, the Department of Justice promulgated merger guidelines in 1968 that indicated that the government would challenge mergers involving firms with combined market shares as small as eight percent, without regard to other economic evidence.[20] In *General Dynamics*, the Supreme Court declined to

---

17 There are, of course, divergent views concerning the magnitude of the antitrust risk, with scholars of different ideological persuasions disagreeing sharply over what should be the appropriate antitrust treatment for specific types of conduct. One such view, which is usually associated with the conservative economists and lawyers of the so-called Chicago school, asserts that markets are largely self-correcting and that "market failures" are relatively rare. Accordingly, proponents of this view advocate a permissive, noninterventionist antitrust enforcement policy that would prohibit little more than outright collusion. A more traditional view accepts the premise that economic analysis is necessary to ferret out instances of actual or incipient market power, but asserts that market forces cannot be expected to resolve most competitive problems. Both recognize the importance of careful factual analysis.

18 415 U.S. 486 (1974).

19 *See*, *e.g.*, United States v. Philadelphia National Bank, 374 U.S. 321 (1963).

20 *See* United States Department Justice 1968 Merger Guidelines, 2 Trade Reg. Rep. (CCH) ¶ 4510 (May 30, 1968).

block a merger solely on the basis of structural evidence, holding that a prima facie case based exclusively upon market shares could be rebutted by evidence of actual economic conditions in the relevant market.

A second major change came in 1977, when the Court decided *Continental T.V., Inc. v. GTE Sylvania Inc.*[21] The Court's earlier decision in *United States v. Arnold, Schwinn & Co.*[22] had held that most nonprice vertical restraints were per se unlawful under section 1 of the Sherman Act. In *GTE Sylvania*, the Court reversed *Schwinn* and held that a detailed competitive analysis was required before vertical restraints could be found illegal.

Finally, in *Broadcast Music, Inc. v. Columbia Broadcasting System, Inc.*,[23] the Supreme Court substantially opened the field for ancillary horizontal restraints imposed in connection with the formation of a joint enterprise. By declining to apply the per se rule to this conduct, the Court departed from prior decisions that slavishly condemned such arrangements as horizontal conspiracies.[24]

Consistent with this changing jurisprudence, the federal enforcement agencies were also changing. Thomas E. Kauper's tenure at the DOJ (1972–1976) marked the basic realignment of that agency's enforcement policies away from bare structuralism and toward a more sophisticated economically based analysis. It also marked the beginning of the "do-no-harm" approach to antitrust enforcement made so clear during the Reagan administration. Criminal enforcement, horizontal mergers and regulatory intervention became the focus, while attacks on conglomerate mergers, vertical restraints and other adventurous theories were basically abandoned. The Carter administration saw a few aberrations (shared monopoly investigations and a particularly misguided criminal resale price maintenance case), but the trend line

---

21 433 U.S. 36 (1977).

22 388 U.S. 365 (1967).

23 441 U.S. 1 (1979).

24 *See, e,g.*, United States v. Sealy, Inc., 388 U.S. 350 (1967).

in large part remained steady, and led quite naturally into the somewhat broader efforts of William Baxter and his successors.

The FTC took a slightly different tack. Its rejuvenation in 1969 soon took on a life of its own; more significant initiatives were enthusiastically and somewhat uncritically advanced. As discussed in more detail later, the FTC in the decade of the seventies was largely outside the antitrust mainstream, however defined. This no doubt led directly to the Reagan administration's effort to send a dramatic message through its initial antitrust appointments.

The appointment of conservative lawyers and economists to key antitrust enforcement posts in the Reagan administration accelerated the pace of change at the DOJ, and began it at the FTC. The initial Reagan appointees—William Baxter at the DOJ and James C. Miller at the FTC—were strong and vocal advocates of the noninterventionist view of antitrust. Both Baxter and Miller emphasized economic analysis. Baxter accelerated the growing emphasis on criminal antitrust enforcement at the DOJ,[25] and moved to halt the massive monopolization case against IBM.[26] Baxter also sought to initiate further judicial change by encouraging Supreme Court review in cases raising important antitrust issues.[27] Under Miller, the FTC ceased its fascination

---

25 The primacy of criminal enforcement within the Reagan administration Antitrust Division is revealed in its enforcement record. During the first 7 years of the Reagan administration, the Division filed 555 criminal antitrust complaints, compared to only 531 over the 59 years from 1890 to 1949. *See* "Criminal Enforcement of the Antitrust Laws: Targeting Naked Cartel Restraints," Remarks of Assistant Attorney General Charles F. Rule before American Bar Association's 36th Annual Antitrust Spring Meeting, Washington, D.C. (Mar. 24, 1988). Even considering different procedures that reduce the realistic comparability of the numbers, the comparison is striking.

26 Assistant Attorney General Baxter also settled DOJ's monopolization suit against AT&T through a controversial consent decree.

27 Amicus Curiae Brief for the United States (on Petition for Certiorari at 139; on the Merits at 485), *Copperweld Corp. v. Independence Tube Corp.*, Trade Reg. Series (BNA) Vol. 17, No. 3 (1983–84);

with vertical matters and terminated its shared monopoly cases against the oil and cereal industries. Like the DOJ under Baxter, the Miller FTC focused on horizontal collusion.[28] Both agencies adopted new, more permissive enforcement policies with regard to mergers.[29] Miller and Baxter also began the process of reducing the size of the federal enforcement agencies, a process that has continued under their successors. In 1979, the FTC consisted of approximately 1,750 employees; by 1987, the number decreased to 1,010.[30] Between 1980 and 1987, the Antitrust Division's legal staff declined from 429 to 240.[31] According to FTC Commissioner Andrew Strenio, the Commission has sustained a real budget cut of roughly 50 percent since 1980. By keeping the FTC's budget at about $66 million from 1980 to 1989, the

---

Amicus Curiae Brief for the United States (on Petition for Certiorari at 119; on the Merits at 767), *Monsanto Co. v. Spray-Rite Service Corp.*, Trade Reg. Series (BNA) Vol. 17, No. 2 (1983–84); Amicus Curiae Brief for the United States (on Petition for Certiorari at 93; on the Merits at 503), *Jefferson Parish Hospital District No. 2 v. Hyde*, Trade Reg. Series (BNA) Vol. 17, No. 1 (1983–84).

28 DOJ's exclusive jurisdiction over criminal antitrust matters effectively precludes the FTC from proceeding against many forms of hardcore collusion. Thus, Miller's efforts to direct the Commission toward increased emphasis on horizontal restraints led to collusion cases involving more complex economic issues. Examples of such cases are the FTC's suits against auto dealers in Detroit (Detroit Auto Dealers Assn., Inc., 108 F.T.C. 193 (1986)), title insurers (Ticor Title Ins. Co., D. 9190), municipal taxi regulations (The City of New Orleans, 105 F.T.C. 1 (1985)), and striking lawyers for indigent defendants (Superior Court Trial Lawyers Assn., 107 F.T.C. 510 (1986), *rev'd*, 856 F.2d 226 (D.C. Cir. 1988), *rev'd*, 110 S. Ct. 768 (1990)).

29 *See* Department of Justice 1982 Merger Guidelines, 2 Trade Reg. Rep. (CCH) ¶ 4500 (June 14, 1982); Federal Trade Commission Statement Concerning Horizontal Mergers, 2 Trade Reg. Rep. (CCH) ¶ 4516 (June 14, 1982).

30 A. Strenio, Remarks before the Antitrust Session of the Los Angeles Bar Ass'n (Sept. 17, 1987).

31 *Scales Tip Against Antitrust Statutes*, Washington Times, June 15, 1987, Insight Mag., at 8.

Commission has sustained a constant dollar cut of about $28 million.[32]

The Reagan administration's antitrust reform agenda was helped along in no small degree by a general deregulatory sentiment within the country. President Reagan had emphasized deregulatory themes during the 1980 election campaign, tying deregulation to the need to improve the competitiveness of domestic firms in global markets. With U.S. producers in many basic industries facing increasing competition from foreign vendors and U.S. manufacturing jobs being lost to foreign firms, the deregulatory theme drew wide grass roots support. Antitrust constraints were seen as another form of federal regulation to which foreign firms were not directly subject. Indeed, former Secretary of Commerce Malcolm Baldridge called for outright repeal of section 7,[33] and the administration forwarded a package of legislative reforms, one of which would have made economic efficiency the primary focus of merger enforcement.[34]

Most of the Supreme Court's antitrust decisions during the 1980's continued the liberalizing trend away from the wooden rules of the past. In *Monsanto Co. v. Spray-Rite Service Corp.*,[35] the Court reaffirmed the view that resale price maintenance was subject to the per se rule, but at the same time toughened the proof required for establishing a resale price maintenance agreement. In its subsequent decision in *Business Electronics Corp. v. Sharp Electronics Corp.*,[36] the Court took the *Monsanto* doctrine one step further by requiring that plaintiffs in resale price maintenance cases establish an actual agreement to affect prices.

---

32 *See The Budget in Perspective*, FTC WATCH, No. 285 (Oct. 10 1988), at 6.

33 Baldridge, *Luncheon Address*, 53 ANTITRUST L.J. 397 (1984).

34 Merger Modernization Act of 1986, S. 2161, 99th Cong., 2d Sess., 132 CONG. REC. 2268 (Mar. 7 1986).

35 465 U.S. 752 (1984).

36 108 S. Ct. 1515 (1988).

In *Copperweld Corp. v. Independence Tube Co.*,[37] the Court dispensed with the so-called intraenterprise conspiracy doctrine under which a corporation could be held to have conspired with its wholly owned subsidiary. In *Jefferson Parish Hospital District No. 2 v. Hyde*,[38] the Court held that tying arrangements were subject to per se treatment only after a finding that the defendant possessed market power in the tying product.[39] In *Cargill, Inc. v. Monfort of Colorado, Inc.*,[40] the Court sharply limited the ability of competitors of the merging parties to challenge a transaction under section 7 of the Clayton Act. Finally, in *Matsushita Electric Industrial Co v. Zenith Radio Corp.*,[41] the Court substantially increased the burden on a plaintiff attempting to show concerted action under section 1 of the Sherman Act, and greatly eased the difficulty of obtaining summary judgment in antitrust cases.

Not everyone shared the view that the new emphasis on economic analysis improved antitrust enforcement. Many in Congress, for example, were openly critical of the antitrust policies pursued by the Reagan administration. In 1983, Congress passed a resolution prohibiting the DOJ from seeking reversal of per se treatment for resale price maintenance,[42] and there have been recurring attempts in recent legislative sessions to repeal the

---

37 467 U.S. 752 (1984).

38 466 U.S. 2 (1984).

39 This form of analysis is tantamount to adopting a rule of reason approach in that the plaintiff must first perform an economic analysis to establish that the defendant possesses market power in the tying product. In fact, four Justices would have dispensed with the per se rule for tying arrangements entirely. *See* concurring opinion of Justice O'Connor.

40 107 S. Ct. 484 (1986).

41 106 S. Ct. 1348 (1986). 475 U.S. 574 (1986).

42 H.R. 3222, Pub. L. No. 98-166, § 510, 97 Stat. 1071, 1102-3 (1983).

Monsanto and *Sharp* decisions.[43] The National Association of Attorneys General adopted merger and vertical restraints guidelines that were far more restrictive than the comparable guidelines adopted by the DOJ.[44] Small business groups actively lobbied for more aggressive federal enforcement in the areas of predatory pricing, price discrimination and vertical restraints. Nevertheless, the new emphasis on economic analysis has clearly moved into the mainstream of antitrust policy, and the arguments now are largely over interpretations, not concepts.

Today's antitrust environment is thus very different from that of even 15 years ago, not to mention the 80 years before that time. The simple presumptive rules that once governed antitrust analysis have largely disappeared, and the few that remain are under direct attack.[45] However, much of the older case law (especially in the merger area, where there has been no Supreme Court opinion since 1975) remains in effect. And even in the substantive areas where the legal standards have become more flexible, the lower federal courts have broad discretion, and may apply or misapply the emerging economic theories as they see fit. Many federal judges have a good understanding of economics, while others either do not understand, or simply reject, economic

---

43 These efforts began in 1987 and continue to the present. The original House version, which was entitled H.R. 585, the Freedom From Vertical Price Fixing Act of 1987, was passed by that body on November 9, 1987. The Senate version, which was entitled S. 430, the Retail Competition Enforcement Act of 1987, never reached a final vote. Versions of these bills were introduced in 1989—H.R. 1236, the Price-Fixing Prevention Act of 1989, and S. 865, the Consumer Protection Against Price-Fixing Act of 1989.

44 NAAG Horizontal Merger Guidelines 52 (Supp.) A&TRR (BNA) 476 (Mar. 12, 1987); NAAG Vertical Restraints Guidelines, 49 A&TRR (BNA) 996 (Dec. 5, 1985).

45 In both *Monsanto* and *Hyde*, some Justices favored repealing per se treatment. With the appointment of Justices Scalia and Kennedy to the Court, there is probably now even less sympathy on the Court for broad use of per se rules, although their predecessors (Chief Justice Burger and Justice Powell) generally favored a rule of reason approach.

principles. Thus, the outcome in a particular case may depend significantly upon the extent to which the judge or appellate panel is willing to embrace the new economic theories.

In this environment, the natural regulatory tendencies of agencies applying economic concepts to complicated factual situations have been enhanced. Because of the risks and uncertainties of litigation, the agency decision is often the final decision. In the merger area, this accounts for the fact that few of the transactions the agencies decide to challenge ever proceed to litigation. Instead, most challenged transactions are either settled or abandoned. In the conduct area, the FTC has been able to obtain settlements in most of its major cases and those that have proceeded to trial have generally involved fact-specific issues relating to jurisdiction or the applicability of exemptions.[46]

The agencies have generally (at least until very recently) exercised this life or death power judiciously, becoming more willing than ever before to consider untried remedies that seek to minimize the impact of antitrust relief upon the normal functioning of the market. Thus, in the merger area, the agencies have been willing to accept partial divestitures where antitrust concerns can be dealt with in a way that enables the lion's share of a transaction to proceed.

---

46 For example, two of the most recent conduct cases the FTC has tried to a final agency determination are Superior Court Trial Lawyers Ass'n, 107 F.T.C. 510 (1986); Detroit Auto Dealers Ass'n, Inc., 108 F.T.C. 193 (1986); and Ticor Title Ins. Co., D. 9190. In *Superior Court Trial Lawyers*, the Commission challenged a boycott by local attorneys who were attempting to force the city council to raise the fees paid for defending indigent criminal defendants. The case raised the question whether the antitrust laws would apply to this type of quasi-political activity. In addition there were questions with respect to the *Noerr-Pennington* doctrine. In *Detroit Auto Dealers*, a group of auto retailers agreed to limit their hours of operation partially in response to threatened unionization by their sales personnel. This case raised issues under the labor exemption as well as issues concerning the FTC's authority to order certain affirmative relief. In cases of this type, legal questions are more likely to be dispositive than questions of economic policy, and respondent's likelihood of success is much greater.

These changes in antitrust policy have had several effects upon the manner in which the agencies go about their work. First, the flexible and largely open-ended nature of current enforcement standards permits the agencies to exercise substantial discretion in making enforcement decisions. The agencies now conduct comprehensive, fact-intensive investigations and ultimately make decisions based upon the weighing of complex economic criteria. This has made the decision-making process much more similar to the function of a typical regulatory agency than to that of a traditional federal prosecutor.

Second, current internal enforcement criteria foster conciliation more than litigation. This, too, is similar to the way in which regulatory agencies function, in the sense that litigation is pursued only when the agencies are believed to have abused their discretion or overstepped the bounds of their jurisdiction.

Third, the new emphasis on permitting markets to work without undue government interference has caused the agencies to be more receptive to innovative remedial approaches, particularly in the merger area. The process through which the agencies permit a company to acquire certain plants upon the actual or promised sale of other plants is essentially a regulatory process.

In short, the agencies no longer have the luxury of making legal determinations based upon the methodical application of simple prosecutorial criteria. Rather, they must make complex economic determinations that cast them in the role of economic regulators. Even with the renewed aggressiveness promised by the Bush administration, the agencies cannot totally retreat from the economic regulatory role mandated by our improved understanding of market behavior and the evolving case law that reflects it.

III. The current enforcement scheme

Antitrust enforcement is one of the few areas of federal regulatory activity in which two agencies share responsibility for enforcing what are, for all practical purposes, the exact same set of laws.[47] The current system of dual enforcement, however, is more the product of historical accident than a conscious decision to have separate enforcement agencies with directly overlapping responsibilities. Although dual enforcement has not generally resulted in the most obvious vices of duplication of effort and bureaucratic infighting between the two agencies, it has had the effect of complicating compliance with the antitrust laws and contributing substantial uncertainty to the antitrust enforcement process. In an increasingly competitive world, dual enforcement is a luxury we can no longer afford.

A. *The evolution of dual enforcement*

For nearly a quarter of a century, federal enforcement of the antitrust laws was solely the responsibility of the DOJ. By 1914, however, a view had emerged that additional antitrust legislation was necessary to address perceived weaknesses in the Sherman Act system of enforcement. One impetus for reform was the Supreme Court's 1911 decisions in *Standard Oil Co. v. United States*[48] and *United States v. American Tobacco Co.*,[49] which adopted the rule of reason approach for evaluating the legality of alleged restraints of trade. These decisions prompted concern that the courts would emasculate the Sherman Act. At the same time, there was concern that the antitrust laws should expressly prohibit certain practices believed to facilitate monopoly. The response to these concerns was enactment of the Clayton Act, which enumerated specific unlawful practices, and the Federal Trade Commission Act, which established an "expert" administrative agency to combat unfair methods of competition.

---

47 The situation in antitrust contrasts with the situation in securities regulation, where the prospect of regulation of "stock index figures" by the Commodity Futures Trading Commission [CFTC] has prompted calls for the merger of the CFTC into the Securities and Exchange Commission. *See The SEC vs. the CFTC: Takeover or Stalemate?*, Nat'l L.J., April 23, 1990, at 1.

48 221 U.S. 1 (1911).

49 221 U.S. 106 (1911).

As initially envisioned by President Wilson, the FTC was not to be a separate law enforcement agency. The Commission's principal function was to aid the DOJ and the courts in conducting investigations and supervising the dissolution of trusts found to be unlawful.[50] Even the DOJ supported the creation of the FTC as a supplemental investigative agency. Attorney General Harmon stated:

> If the Department of Justice is expected to conduct investigations of alleged violations of the present law or of the law as it may be amended, it must be provided with a liberal appropriation and a force properly selected and organized. . . . But I respectfully submit that the general policy which has hitherto been pursued of confining this department very closely to the court work is a wise one, and that the duty of detecting offenses and furnishing evidence thereof should be committed to some other department or bureau.[51]

Following upon this theme, the initial House version of the trade commission legislation would have created an agency with largely advisory powers. In the Senate, however, alternative legislation was developed, creating an independent regulatory agency with adjudicative authority. A bill more closely resembling the Senate version emerged from conference and the legislation was signed into law on September 26, 1914.

Most of the debate in the Senate and in the House-Senate conference centered on the definition of unfair methods of competition. Clearly, one area of concern was the rule of reason announced in the *Standard Oil* decision, which some felt gave the courts too much discretion to determine which business practices would be condemned under the Sherman Act. Some in Congress questioned whether the courts were an appropriate forum in

---

50 *See* Address by President Woodrow Wilson before Joint Session of Congress on Additional Legislation for the Control of Trusts and Monopolies, Jan 20, 1914, 51 CONG. REC. 1962–64, 1978–79 (1914).

51 REPORT OF THE HOUSE COMMITTEE ON INTERSTATE AND FOREIGN COMMERCE, H.R. REP. No. 533, 63 Cong., 2d Sess., pt.1, at 5 (Apr. 14, 1914). DOJ's views on the subject might have been different had it already created the Antitrust Division, which was not formed until 1933.

which to make these discretionary determinations.[52] An argument can be made that the FTC was intended to be an expert body that would supplant, or at least supplement, the courts in interpreting the rule of reason.[53] On the other hand, the congressional debate over the FTC act also indicates that there were concerns about specific business practices that may have been outside of the reach of the Sherman Act (as it was then interpreted). The FTC may have been intended to address those practices under the Commission's expansive power to define and to prohibit unfair methods of competition. Certain passages in the legislative history indicate that the FTC's "unfair methods" authority was created to enable the Commission to address common law unfair competition issues as well as other business practices believed to facilitate monopoly. These crosscurrents in the congressional debate make it difficult to assert definitively either that the FTC was intended to share concurrent enforcement authority with the DOJ or that it was instead to perform some other distinct function.

Whatever the initial intent, in practice the DOJ and the FTC enforcement responsibilities have tended to coalesce over the years. In *FTC v. Sperry & Hutchinson Co.*,[54] the Supreme Court held that section 5 of the FTC Act empowers the Commission to proscribe unfair methods of competition whether or not they violate the letter or spirit of the antitrust laws. Despite this expansive reading of the FTC's authority, the Commission's subsequent efforts to define classes of unlawful conduct outside the boundaries of the Sherman and Clayton Acts failed consistently.[55] Today, we know of no significant scholarship arguing that FTC Act jurisdiction is necessary to enable the enforcement

---

52 *See, e.g.*, House Debate re H.R. 15613, 63d Cong., 2d Sess. (1914), Remarks of Rep. Stevens, 51 CONG. REC. 1064 (1914).

53 *See* REPORT OF THE SENATE COMMITTEE ON INTERSTATE COMMERCE, S. REP. No. 597, 63d Cong., 2d Sess. (1914), at 9.

54 405 U.S. 233 (1972).

55 *See* note 9 *supra*. *See also* Gellhorn, *Trading Stamps, S&H and the FTC's Unfairness Doctrine*, 1983 DUKE L.J. 903 (1983).

agencies to reach any conduct they should appropriately reach. For the last decade or so, and certainly during the entirety of the Reagan administration, the FTC and DOJ have pursued very similar law enforcement agendas. Personalities and procedures have been the major differences between the agencies.

B. Organizational and procedural characteristics

Notwithstanding their common enforcement responsibilities and their common focus in recent years, the FTC and DOJ are two very different agencies in terms of the ways in which they approach their missions. The DOJ's Antitrust Division traces its roots to the creation of the post of Assistant Attorney General for Antitrust in 1903.[56] Some 30 years later, Attorney General Homer S. Cummings created the Antitrust Division as a separate operating unit within the Department of Justice.

Over the years, the Antitrust Division has undergone a number of structural reorganizations, the most recent of which took place in 1985 under Assistant Attorney General Douglas Ginsburg. Under the current organizational scheme, the Antitrust Division is divided into several litigation units or sections each with its own industry or subject matter expertise. The Division also has seven regional field offices. Direct supervision of staff investigations and matters in litigation is performed by an Operations Office, which reports to two Deputy Assistant Attorneys General for litigation. Reflecting the Division's new emphasis on economic analysis, its economic review and support functions are now under the supervision of a nonlawyer economist who holds the position of Deputy Assistant Attorney General. The Antitrust Division's structure, which is similar in many respects to that of other law enforcement divisions within the DOJ, is designed to centralize decision making and reduce the risk of inconsistent approaches to similar problems. It is hierarchical, reflecting the

---

56 The Assistant Attorney General is nominated by the President and must be confirmed by the Senate. The Assistant Attorney General serves at the pleasure of the President.

Division's perception of the importance of consistent and predictable enforcement patterns.

Other than some specific authority to comment on regulatory actions by other agencies, DOJ's functions are largely confined to criminal investigations and decisions on whether to bring lawsuits on behalf of the government as law enforcer or injured party.[57] The DOJ utilizes grand jury process in criminal investigations, and may exercise compulsory process in civil investigations pursuant to the Antitrust Civil Process Act.[58] Like the FTC, the DOJ conducts most merger investigations pursuant to the Hart-Scott-Rodino Antitrust Improvements Act of 1976,[59] which provides for premerger notification and specifies waiting periods and other requirements before a merger can be consummated. Criminal investigations are subject to procedures and oversight similar to those that apply in other parts of DOJ. All of DOJ's suits must be litigated in federal court. Settlements of pending DOJ cases must take place under court supervised consent decrees, which are subject to the notice and comment procedures of the Antitrust Procedures and Penalties Act.[60] Pursuant to section 5 of the Clayton Act,[61] a finding of violation in an antitrust suit brought by or on behalf of the government is prima facie evidence of a violation in any subsequent private suit challenging the same conduct.[62]

---

57 *See* section 4A of the Clayton Act, 15 U.S.C. § 15a.

58 15 U.S.C. §§ 1311-1314 (1982).

59 15 U.S.C. § 15A (1982). *See also* implementing regulations at 16 C.F.R. § 800.1 *et seq.*

60 15 U.S.C. § 16(b)-(h) (1982).

61 15 U.S.C. § 16(a) (1982).

62 FTC determinations have no such effect. The estoppel effect of DOJ proceedings is an important tool in encouraging settlements of cases brought by DOJ. While an adverse decision in an FTC matter will result only in a cease and desist order and perhaps consumer redress in an extraordinary case, the import of the prima facie evidence rule in treble damage cases could be significant.

The FTC, by contrast, is a self-contained, independent regulatory agency. The Commission itself consists of five Commissioners, who serve staggered terms of 7 years. No more than three Commissioners may be members of the same political party. Each Commissioner is nominated by the President and must be confirmed by the Senate.[63] A majority of the participating Commissioners is required for most Commission actions.[64] One of the five Commissioners is designated by the President to serve as Chairman. The Chairman's powers are set forth in Reorganization Plan No. 8 of 1950, 64 Stat. 1264, which delegates to the Chairman responsibility for the "executive and administrative" functions of the agency, including (1) the appointment of key management personnel; (2) the division of labor among operating units; and (3) the use and expenditure of funds. Under section (b)(1) of the Reorganization Plan, these powers must be carried out consistent with general policies, regulatory decisions, findings and determinations of the full Commission. Thus, the practical scope of the Chairman's rights and duties, as distinct from those of other Commissioners, is largely unclear.[65]

Structurally, the FTC's Bureau of Competition is organized much like the Antitrust Division, with a small group of staff

---

63 Pursuant to section 1 of the FTC Act, 15 U.S.C. § 41, a Commissioner may be removed only for "inefficiency, neglect of duty, or malfeasance in office." *See* Humphrey's Executor v. United States, 295 U.S. 602 (1935).

64 Certain functions, such as the issuance of subpoenas, have been delegated to single Commissioners.

65 The extent to which a FTC Chairman can "run" the Commission has largely been a question of the Chairman's management style and the extent to which other Commissioners have been willing to cede management functions to the Chairman and his appointees. Over the years, various Chairmen have had varying degrees of practical autonomy in management functions. For example, in 1987, *FTC Watch* reported that the Commission met in closed session to discuss whether a majority of Commissioners could remove the Bureau of Competition Director for pursuing enforcement policies at odds with those of the Commission majority (although presumably not those of the FTC Chairman). *Here Comes the Pendulum*, FTC WATCH, No. 256 (May 29, 1987), at 1.

divisions each focusing on particular substantive antitrust areas. The Bureau is headed by a director, who supervises the work of several litigating divisions comprised principally of attorneys. The Bureau of Competition also has a compliance division, which is responsible for insuring compliance with Commission antitrust orders, as well as divisions responsible for planning, case evaluation, and administration of the Hart-Scott-Rodino premerger notification program.[66] Economic review and support functions are provided by a separate Bureau of Economics.

The key difference between the DOJ and FTC is the decision-making process. The DOJ is a hierarchical agency with a single decision-maker. The staff has no independent existence, and all decisions are made by the Assistant Attorney General or his delegate. At the FTC, by contrast, the staff is organized in a similar way, but the Director of the Bureau of Competition—the analog to the Assistant Attorney General—does not have any independent authority from the Commission, which at any given time can be unified or divided, controlled by a majority or simply five unaligned duchys with occasional alliances of convenience.

Thus, at all times (except, perhaps, when the Chairman has a solid majority) the staff members can develop and implement personal enforcement agendas through manipulation of the agency's general political system. The end result is less organizational control, less policy consistency, more reliance on the individual judgment of individual staff lawyers and supervisors, and necessarily much more uncertainty in enforcement attitudes and procedures. If there is any doubt on this point, we refer the reader to the change between the relatively predictable Miller-Douglas-Calvani Commission of the early 1980's and the Commission of 1988, which had no set majority and certainly had no obvious hierarchy.[67]

---

66 Pursuant to the Hart-Scott-Rodino Antitrust Improvements Act of 1976, both DOJ and the FTC are responsible for review of reported transactions, but the FTC has principal responsibility for promulgating implementing regulations and for the various reporting obligations under the statute.

67 During the tenure of Chairman Daniel Oliver, the Commissioners reclaimed management control from the Chairman and Bureau of

As an independent regulatory agency, the FTC is empowered to conduct administrative enforcement proceedings and may issue cease and desist orders in connection with violations of section 5. This is another critical difference. The DOJ must convince a court that some relief is appropriate. The FTC, at least until the very last step, must only convince itself. The healthy influence of an independent arbiter is totally missing in the FTC structure, and this phenomenon seems to be the only explanation for some of the more extreme FTC actions of the past.

IV. Comparative performance

Attempting to measure the comparative performance of the DOJ and the FTC by any objective means is nearly an impossible task. Statistical measurements of the relative performance of each agency—*i.e.*, measures based upon the number of enforcement actions brought or orders obtained—ignore critical externalities, such as the competitive significance of individual cases or the level of antitrust activity within particular industries.[68] Subjective

---

Competition Director, such that all management decisions—down to whether or not to request documents in a merger investigation—were matters for Commission consideration. Because there was no cohesive voting block, this meant that every decision was the product of temporary and shifting alliances among the Commissioners.

68 For example, given the fact that the agencies have historically divided up industrial sectors under their liaison agreement, the statistical performance of each agency depends in part upon the level of antitrust activity within the industries for which it is responsible. Moreover, the level of case activity tells very little about the extent to which an agency is performing its assigned function. A low level of activity might reflect the deterrence value of prior enforcement actions, while a high level of activity might reflect a perceived weakness in agency enforcement programs. One good example of this phenomenon is the FTC's activity with respect to petroleum industry mergers in the early 1980's. The fact that the liaison agreement assigned the FTC principal responsibility for petroleum matters enabled it to get credit for several merger enforcement matters when the petroleum industry began to consolidate following a major decline in crude oil prices. The fact that these mergers were

measures of agency performance are equally suspect. Much of the criticism leveled at both agencies has involved disagreements with policy decisions reflected in individual enforcement matters. Policy decisions of this type will always be subject to vigorous debate, and critics holding different policy perspectives will always disagree with the enforcement policies the agencies are pursuing.

In 1969, the American Bar Association commissioned a major task force study of the FTC's antitrust enforcement activities.[69] The ABA Report concluded that the FTC was concentrating its efforts on trivial cases, such as those involving price discrimination, and failing to employ its broad powers under section 5 of the FTC Act. The ABA Report urged the Commission to refocus its activities upon cases where "issues of competitive effects turn essentially on complicated economic analysis, and where decided cases have not yet succeeded in fashioning a clear line marking the boundary between legal and illegal conduct."[70] The ABA recommendations were quickly embraced by supporters of aggressive antitrust enforcement in the Congress. FTC Chairmen Casper Weinberger and Miles W. Kirkpatrick were exhorted by Congress to energize the Commission's antitrust activities and to use the full measure of its broad powers under section 5.[71]

---

attempted could well have reflected economic forces within the industry or misperceptions that enforcement standards would permit these transactions to proceed unchallenged.

69 ABA Report at 1-3, 67-69.

70 *Id.* at 66. Quite interestingly, the 1989 ABA Task Force Report sounds a similar theme. In discussing suggested case selection criteria the Task Force states: "The cases may involve development and application of uncertain legal theories. The FTC is a less dangerous forum than the federal courts for testing legal theories and considering their application in difficult cases since the FTC's sanctions are civil and prospective and its decisions cannot be used as prima facie evidence to support treble damage awards." 1989 Task Force Report at 18.

71 *See Nomination of Casper W. Weinberger to be Chairman of the Federal Trade Commission: Hearings Before the Senate Committee on Commerce*, 91st Cong., 1st Sess. 5 (1970); *Agriculture, Environmental*

The FTC of the 1970's reflected many of the reforms suggested in the report, and ironically it was those reforms that led to the next round of criticisms leveled at the agency. During the early and mid-1970's, the FTC embarked upon an expansive enforcement program, featuring a host of monopolization cases,[72] as well as a number of innovative conduct cases.[73] By the late 1970's, however, many of the FTC's key supporters in Congress—Senators Hart, Moss, Hartke, McGee, Tunney and Pastore, among others—were no longer in office.[74] Moreover, the conservative antigovernment sentiment that would help to elect President Reagan had begun to manifest itself. As the 1970's drew to a close, the FTC was under direct attack from many industry groups and the Federal Trade Commission Improvements Act of 1980[75] removed entire industries from the Commis-

---

and Consumer Protection Appropriations for Fiscal Year 1972: Hearings Before a Subcommittee of the Senate Committee on Appropriations, 92d Cong., 1st Sess. 2673 (1971).

72 *See, e.g.*, Kellogg Co., 99 F.T.C. 8 (1982) (dismissed); Exxon Corp., 98 F.T.C. 453 (1981) (dismissed); Xerox Corp., 86 F.T.C. 364 (1975); Borden, Inc., 92 F.T.C. 669 (1978), *aff'd*, 674 F.2d 498 (6th Cir. 1982); ITT Continental Baking Co., 83 F.T.C. 865, *modified*, 83 F.T.C. 1105 (1973), *modified and enforced*, 532 F.2d 207 (2d Cir. 1976); Hertz Corp., 88 F.T.C. 715 (1976); General Foods Corp., 103 F.T.C. 204 (1984), *dismissed*, 103 F.T.C. 204 (1984); Reuben H. Donnelly Corp., 95 F.T.C. 1 (1980), *enforcement denied*, 630 F.2d 920 (2d Cir. 1980), *cert. denied sub nom.*, FTC v. Official Airline Guides Inc., 450 U.S. 917 (2d Cir. 1981).

73 *See, e.g.*, E.I. du Pont de Nemours & Co., 96 F.T.C. 650 (1980); Ethyl Corp., 101 F.T.C. 425 (1983), *rev'd*, 729 F.2d 128 (2d Cir. 1984); Russell Stover Candies, Inc., 100 F.T.C. 1 (1982), *rev'd*, 718 F.2d 256 (8th Cir. 1983).

74 For an analysis of this change, *see* Weingast & Moran, *Bureaucratic Discretion or Congressional Control? Regulatory Policymaking and the Federal Trade Commission*, 91 J. Pol. Econ. 765, 777 (1983).

75 Pub. Law 96-252, 94 Stat. 374 (1980).

sion's jurisdiction.[76] FTC bashing became a national pastime, and the *Washington Post* labeled the FTC the National Nanny.[77]

To the extent that the FTC's enforcement record since the early 1970's reflects its response to perceived congressional and public sentiment at that time,[78] it is clear that a performance analysis based upon a retrospective review of its cases will yield dubious conclusions at best. The analysis in this section, therefore, attempts to ignore differences in policy perspectives. Rather, this analysis attempts to address more basic structural and procedural questions concerning the way in which each agency goes about enforcing the antitrust laws. An effective antitrust enforcement agency should be able to develop a coherent enforcement policy, apply that policy consistently in the selection of cases, and litigate its cases efficiently to final resolutions. In this section, we discuss how the structure and procedures of each agency either facilitate or impede the performance of these basic functions.

A. *Policy development*

In today's world, the development of antitrust enforcement policy involves the translation of what are essentially value-based perspectives into both an overall enforcement agenda and analytical standards for evaluation of specific cases. Most substantial firms have access to sophisticated antitrust counsel, and the noncriminal antitrust questions the agencies typically confront involve complex issues that are at or close to the border between lawful and unlawful conduct. Given the broad range of policy perspectives that can be adopted with respect to antitrust issues,

---

76 Despite the anti-FTC sentiment that was prevalent at the time, organized medicine failed to win an exemption from FTC jurisdiction.

77 *The FTC as a National Nanny*, Washington Post, Mar. 1, 1978, at A22.

78 For a general discussion of the relationship between Congress and the FTC, *see* Kovacic, *The Federal Trade Commission and Congressional Oversight of Antitrust Enforcement*, 17 TULSA L.J. 587 (1982). *See also* Weingast & Moran, *supra* note 74.

policy development is one of the most sensitive areas of agency activity. Policy development is all the more sensitive because normally no single branch or agency of government is free to make economic policy independent of the policies being pursued by other branches or agencies. Thus, there are major questions concerning not only how antitrust policy should be made, but who should take the lead role in making it.

Under the present scheme of dual enforcement, it is often said that the DOJ is the enforcement agency of the executive branch and the FTC is Congress' antitrust enforcement agency. This view is overly simplistic. The fact is that neither the President nor Congress has complete control over either agency. Although it is true that the President has management control over the DOJ as an executive branch agency under the supervision of the Attorney General, Congress has input into the operation of the Antitrust Division through oversight procedures, the appropriations process, and most importantly through its ability to pass antitrust legislation. The resolution forbidding Assistant Attorney General Baxter from expending funds to seek repeal of per se treatment for resale price maintenance is an example of Congress' ability to affect DOJ enforcement practices. As an independent agency, neither Congress nor the President has asserted direct supervisory authority over the FTC, but the President has the appointment power—especially the power to appoint the Chairman—and Congress has the same powers over the FTC that it has over the DOJ; it can oversee, appropriate, and legislate.[79]

Notwithstanding the direct lines of authority over the agencies, if recent history is any indication, it is the executive branch that plays the principal role in setting antitrust policy, for it is the executive branch that is responsible for selecting the leadership of each agency. Both Baxter and Miller were able to bring their policies into effect despite protestations from many in Congress who disagreed. Carter administration FTC Chairman Michael Pertschuk was also able to set the policy agenda. Congress,

---

79 In point of fact, of course, most congressional intervention in agency affairs is less direct—*i.e.*, through staff contacts and other informal means—but nonetheless just as effective.

however, plays a significant advisory role and can step in with legislation if it believes that the agencies have gone too far in the wrong direction. Congressional criticism—or the threat thereof—certainly tempers administration policy, and Congress has not been shy in altering agency procedures and responsibilities through so-called improvement legislation.[80]

If we assume that the principal policy determinations will be made by presidential appointees subject to advisory or legislative input from Congress, the executive branch/independent agency distinction becomes less important and the principal question then becomes whether the single-leader format of the DOJ or the collegial body format of the FTC is the better policy development mechanism. On the surface, it might be argued that the FTC, with its bipartisan membership and collegial decision-making process, would be a superior mechanism for making the subjective judgments that go into antitrust policy. Nevertheless, several aspects of the collegial decision-making process have complicated, if not frustrated, policy development efforts within the FTC.

The most notable feature of a collegial body is that no one is in charge. Within the FTC structure, the Chairman has some control over staff functions, but any agency action requires a majority vote. The inability of the FTC Chairman to direct policies without the assent of other Commissioners complicates the development of a coherent enforcement agenda.

Any formal agenda or policy must come as the result of complicated, collective deliberations among the Commissioners. A majority of Commissioners must first decide that there is a policy issue worthy of Commission consideration and then must direct that some sort of staff analysis be performed. Once that is done, the Commissioners must then meet, analyze the issues and then synthesize the analysis into some written statement that can win a majority vote. Each one of these steps can require complex

---

80 The FTC Improvements Act of 1980, which removed Commission jurisdiction over entire industries, is an example of the ability of Congress to affect FTC enforcement policies through legislation.

negotiations among the Commissioners, and the resulting policy determination will very often reflect nothing more than a temporary compromise that will hold only until the next Commission vote.

In recent years, the Commission has had few, if any, formal policy review sessions in the antitrust area. Even when significant policy questions have been identified, the Commissioners have had difficulty in actually defining a policy stance. The Commission's efforts to develop a policy with respect to merger remedies is a notable example of the problems the agency has experienced in the policy development area.

Beginning with the decision in *Hospital Corp. of America*,[81] the Commission debated the question whether merger orders should as a matter of course require that the respondent obtain prior Commission approval of any subsequent acquisitions.[82] A staff study was requested in 1985. In 1988, the Commission finally announced a policy favoring the continued use of prior approval provisions.

Similarly, for nearly 6 years prior to announcing a policy in late 1987, the Commission debated the question whether it should adopt the DOJ's fix-it-first approach to curative divestitures.[83] Even when the Commission reached a policy decision, it took months before the decision was communicated to the public. The

---

81 106 F.T.C. 361 (1985).

82 Prior approval provisions were a standard part of the Commission remedial approach to mergers prior to enactment of the Hart-Scott-Rodino premerger notification requirements. Following Hart-Scott-Rodino, the continuing need for such provisions became subject to question. Moreover, there are questions as to whether such provisions are necessary in all cases and how long they should remain in effect. Given the speed at which competitive conditions change in some markets, the standard 10-year provision may be either too short or too long. Finally, there are questions concerning whether the Commission should seek prior approval provisions with respect to transactions abandoned after issuance of a preliminary injunction.

83 *See "Fix-it-First" Update*, FTC WATCH, No. 261 (Sept. 11, 1987); *Can We Talk?* FTC WATCH, No. 263 (October 5, 1987), at 5.

Commission issued its directive on December 7, 1987, but did not release it publicly until March of 1988. Through all of these machinations, parties to proposed transactions have had to wend their way through the Commission review procedure with little if any guidance concerning the remedial standards the Commission was following.

Policy development within the Commission is all the more difficult because of the different policy perspectives the various Commissioners bring to the agency and the infighting and bickering that results.[84] The Commission's bipartisan structure was supposed to insure that agency policy would reflect a true national consensus on trade regulation issues. In recent years, however, this structure has insured nothing but open partisan warfare among the Commissioners. Chairman Miller's first few years at the FTC are illustrative. When he first arrived at the agency, Miller faced vigorous opposition from former Chairman Pertschuk and fellow Carter appointee Patricia Bailey.[85] It was not until the President appointed Commissioners George Douglas and Terry Calvani that Miller had an effective working majority on the Commission—a majority that has apparently disappeared under his successors. In the interim, there was no real enforcement policy within the agency, and parties with matters before the Commission were at the mercy of case-by-case determinations that could go one way or the other depending upon shifting alliances among the Commissioners.

Not surprisingly, the Commission has issued very few formal policy statements in the antitrust area.[86] The most notable excep-

---

84 This problem is the inevitable result of the process through which FTC Commissioners are selected. *See* discussion *infra.*

85 *See* Leighton, *Miller, Pertschuk Battles Give FTC a Bad Name*, Legal Times, Aug. 20, 1984, at 8.

86 The ABA's task force on the FTC notes that the "Commission's recent use of policy statements is a positive development. They soften the image of an agency with unbridled discretion. The issuance of such statements should be encouraged." 1989 ABA Task Force Report at 63. While recognizing the importance of such guidance to the regulated

tion, the 1982 statement on horizontal mergers, lacks the precision and clarity of the DOJ merger guidelines that were issued at the same time—a fact that could well reflect the compromise nature of the FTC statement. By contrast, the DOJ process requires only that the Assistant Attorney General make a decision on the issue at hand.

Another problem with the Commission as a maker of policy is the fact that Commission policies are almost never communicated to the public in any meaningful way. Because it rarely issues formal policy statements on significant antitrust issues and relies primarily upon case-by-case determinations to announce policy stances, the FTC's policies and enforcement priorities are almost a total mystery to the public.[87] The FTC's use of case determinations as the primary indicia of its enforcement policies is all the more problematic because of the fact that many close issues are resolved in split opinions. With Commissioners moving in and out of office—some before their terms would otherwise expire—and Commissioners declining to participate in matters due to recusals and scheduling conflicts, the likely pattern of voting on a particular issue at any given point in time is nearly impossible to discern.

While the DOJ has issued few formal policy statements—the merger and vertical restraints guidelines being notable exceptions—the Assistant Attorney General's speeches and writings provide a substantial amount of guidance. The hierarchical nature of the agency insures that pronouncements have an institutional patina that generally escapes FTC speeches and other statements. FTC Commissioners often give speeches and write

---

public, the task force could only point to the Horizontal Merger Statement (1982) and the Enforcement Policy Regarding Physician Agreements to Control Medical Prepayment Plans (1981) as recent examples in the antitrust field.

87 Former Commissioner Phillip Elman suggested nearly 20 years ago that the Commission's various nonadjudicative decisions, such as decisions to commence or close investigations, amount to a body of "secret law" that the Commission guards far too closely. *See* Elman, *Administrative Reform of the Federal Trade Commission*, 59 Geo. L.J. 777 (1971).

articles, but it is impossible to know whether the views of any single Commissioner truly reflect the view of the majority.[88]

Under the theory that five minds are better than one, it would seem that the FTC would have an advantage over the DOJ in the policy development area. There is no indication, however, that in practice significant issues are subject to less complete analysis and evaluation within the DOJ than within the FTC. Indeed, the reality appears to be that the FTC is by its very nature vastly inferior to DOJ in resolving policy issues and in making its policy determinations known to the public.

B. Policy implementation

Many of the same problems attend the implementation of policy within the FTC. One major problem within the Commission structure is the absence of any direct-line management channel between those who set policy and those who are charged with implementing it. Under the Commission structure, the professional career staff is directed by a handful of political appointees who work under the general supervision of the Chairman.[89] As discussed above, the authority of any of the other Commissioners over these supervisory personnel is unclear. Thus, there is no direct management mechanism through which the Commission as a whole, which sets policy, can control the staff, which implements it.

---

88 This was recognized in the recent ABA Task Force Report where the authors stated: "[G]uidance is best provided by the Commission acting as a whole, rather than by individual commissioners or staff members. There is always a risk that the views of a collegial body will be ambiguous. Only by speaking with one voice (even with dissent) can the Commission give authoritative guidance to business and to its own staff. When the Commission speaks regularly, its staff only fills in the interstices in policy; when it speaks more rarely, the 'interstices' can be too large." 1989 ABA Task Force Report at 55.

89 In contrast, DOJ has frequently staffed positions below the level of Assistant Attorney General with career professionals.

When, as is often the case, the Commissioners are divided on questions of policy, the absence of a supervisory link between the Commission and the staff results in open and constant discord. Members of the professional staff, who disagree with policies set by the Chairman and his appointed managers, can often end-run senior management and get their views before the Commission where there could well be a majority for the staff position. Similarly, a bureau director who disagrees with some directive from a majority of the Commission can delay, if not totally avoid, Commission consideration of a matter simply by declining to pursue the types of matters the Commission majority desires.[90] Accusations and counter-accusations concerning these issues have become a regular part of FTC lore in recent years. From outside the agency, it often appears that the outcome in a specific case is more dependent upon the skill of particular factions within the agency in manipulating the internal processes of the agency than upon the substantive merits. This type of regulatory intrigue does nothing to increase public confidence in the regulatory process. Nor does it insure that the antitrust laws are applied in a consistent manner.

Even when all of the Commissioners are in apparent agreement with respect to policy issues, the FTC structure does not necessarily facilitate the smooth translation of policy into practice. In many ways, the Commissioners are as insulated from the staff as they are from parties subject to Commission investigations. In the absence of written directives or policy review sessions open to the staff, neither of which occurs often within the agency, staff members can only guess as to the policy preferences of the Commission. In attempting to guess about policy matters, the staff must consider not only the expressed views of the individual Commissioners but also the likely group

90 As Commissioner Calvani noted in a recent speech, the only real power of an FTC Commissioner is a negative one, *i.e.*, he or she can vote against a proposed enforcement initiative. A Commissioner has very little power to commence an investigation or to insure that it is pursued aggressively. *See* "A Proposal for Radical Change," Remarks of FTC Commissioner Terry Calvani before American Law Institute/American Bar Association, San Francisco, CA (May 6, 1988).

view, which will often reflect compromises and trading among the Commissioners. In short, in implementing Commission policy, the staff is often called upon to know the unknowable.

Finally, policy implementation within the FTC often suffers from a lack of accountability. The fact that no one is in charge of the agency also means that no one is individually responsible for its actions. When dealing with the FTC one is always forced to rely on the representations and suggestions of staff members who, by definition, cannot bind the Commission to any particular course of action. A party to a Commission investigation can spend untold time and money pursuing a course of action recommended or even demanded by a particular staff unit only to have an entirely different course recommended or demanded at the next level of review. Issues long since abandoned by the operating staff can suddenly reemerge as higher level staff or the Commission itself become involved. In the end, the Commissioners go behind closed doors for deliberations, and only limited fragments of the Commission's reasoning in nonadjudicative matters is ever communicated to the parties or public at large. With the exception of final orders in adjudicative matters, most Commission actions are either practically or legally unreviewable.

In contrast, the DOJ structure is designed to insure that policy directed by the Assistant Attorney General is implemented by the staff. The Assistant Attorney General has direct-line supervisory responsibility for staff functions. Factional disputes within the agency are of little consequence because the Assistant Attorney General has final say over all agency actions. Moreover, the Assistant Attorney General is directly accountable to the Attorney General and ultimately to the President. Finally, because the Antitrust Division has virtually no self-enforcing authority, most of its actions are directly reviewable by the courts, a fact that insures even greater accountability. Once again, the DOJ structure appears superior to that of the FTC.

C. Case management and litigation

One principal difference between the two agencies is that the FTC litigates primarily in administrative proceedings while DOJ cases are brought in federal court. The analysis in this section addresses the manner in which this basic difference between the two agencies affects the types of cases they bring and the way in which the cases are managed.

As an initial matter, the DOJ and the FTC must make significantly different determinations when they decide to initiate litigation. When the FTC initiates an administrative law enforcement proceeding, it need only find that it has "reason to believe" that the law has been violated and that a proceeding with respect to that alleged violation would be in the public interest. The Supreme Court has held that a FTC reason to believe determination is not immediately reviewable.[91] When the DOJ brings suit in federal court, it is like any other litigant, and the sufficiency of its case is subject to all of the standard preliminary challenges permitted under federal civil procedure, complete with all existing rights of appeal.

It seems likely that this basic procedural difference has a significant impact upon the types of cases each agency brings. For the Commission, the decision to bring suit is a low-risk proposition. Difficult issues can be resolved in favor of bringing suit in the hope that postcomplaint discovery and theory development will eliminate weaknesses in the initial staff work. If weaknesses cannot be cured during the course of proceedings before the administrative law judge [ALJ], the Commission can of course dismiss its own complaint prior to any review by the courts. DOJ, on the other hand, faces the immediate risk of summary dismissal, and cannot control the amount of latitude its litigators are afforded in firming up their case with postcomplaint discovery. Clearly, the FTC has greater latitude than the DOJ to bring speculative, less fully developed cases and to burden sound complaints with alternative theories of violation that are questionable at best.

Moreover, the *ex parte* rules, which are necessary to avoid issues of prejudgment in administrative litigation, hinder the FTC

---

91 *See* Standard Oil Co. of California v. FTC, 449 U.S. 232 (1980).

in effectively managing the cases that it brings. Once the complaint is issued, the Commission can have no further direct involvement in the management of the case. This fact, particularly when combined with the ALJ's incentive passively to permit the parties to develop whatever factual record they care to establish,[92] no doubt contributes to the ponderous and time-consuming nature of FTC administrative proceedings. The staff, which can only guess as to the type of record the Commission wants to have developed, usually feels compelled to preserve every possible theory conceivable under the complaint and to present evidence on every point that might be relevant to a Commissioner.[93]

Although the FTC system of administrative litigation has its drawbacks, the placement of all antitrust enforcement in the federal courts is not necessarily a panacea. The federal judiciary has been very uneven in its sophistication regarding antitrust issues. By the luck of the draw, judges with no prior economic, regulatory or antitrust experience whatsoever can be thrust into the role of deciding questions of major economic significance. The FTC was initially created to serve as an expert body to resolve what are essentially questions of economic policy. If this original concept had become reality, administrative litigation before the FTC might in theory be preferable to litigation in the

---

92 For a variety of reasons, not the least of which is the Commission's propensity to review the record on a de novo basis, FTC ALJs see their main function as supervising the development of whatever factual issues the parties wish to present. Although they have many of the same powers available to a federal judge, FTC ALJs have very little incentive to manage a proceeding aggressively by narrowing issues, dismissing frivolous allegations, and limiting irrelevant discovery. It is far easier for ALJs to preserve hard questions for the Commission, which in any event will ultimately decide them.

93 At times, it has been suggested that the Commission should issue some type of written staff directive prior to the vote on the complaint. In addition to the logistical problems that would be involved in preparing a definitive directive prior to a final vote, such a directive would open the Commissioners to claims of prejudgment.

federal courts. In practice, however, the FTC's expertise has been uneven at most and has certainly not been a sufficient positive factor to outweigh the negative elements of the administrative enforcement process.[94]

The FTC has seldom, if ever, lived up to its billing as a body of true experts in matters of trade regulation. Like most appointive boards and panels within government, political considerations and patronage have been ever-present in the selection of FTC Commissioners. Some individual Commissioners have been particularly able and others less so. As a consequence, the Commission's antitrust decisions are pretty much like those of the federal courts: some have been brilliant, some have been unintelligible, some have been upheld, some have been reversed.

One would be hard pressed to demonstrate any substantial advantages of administrative antitrust litigation over the litigation of comparable cases in the federal courts. Indeed, the 1989 ABA Task Force Report concedes that the Commission has generally failed to live up to its promise as a special-purpose forum for litigating complex antitrust cases:

> It is disappointing that the Commission, which ought to offer the potential for innovation and flexibility, and for custom-tailoring trial procedures, has lagged behind the federal courts in developing techniques for complex cases. It also is disappointing that the Commission continues to have problems of delay. . . . Particularly troubling is the length of time between oral argument and issuance of an opinion. Data provided to us by the FTC show that between 1975 and 1988 the Commission took an average of 15.1 months from oral argument to issuance of an FTC final order (not counting subsequent appeals). . . . There is no excuse for taking more than a year to write an opinion.[95]

---

94 For a more general discussion of the issue of agency expertise, *see* Freedman, *Expertise and the Administrative Process*, 28 ADMIN. L. REV. 363 (1976); Schwartz, *Legal Restriction of Competition in the Regulated Industries: An Abdication of Judicial Responsibility*, 67 HARV. L. REV. 436 (1954).

95 1989 Task Force Report at 113.

As a body of law, the FTC's decisions have been no more insightful or well-reasoned than those of the federal courts. Nor have there been any appreciable advantages in terms of expedition or procedural fairness. In fact, many would argue that federal court litigation is superior to administrative adjudication in all these respects.[96]

Theoretically, there is one way in which it could be argued that FTC antitrust decision making has the potential to be superior to that of the DOJ and the federal courts. Given the long and staggered terms of FTC Commissioners, and the required bipartisan appointments, it is at least arguable that at any given time, the FTC more clearly represents the current political consensus on antitrust policy than would either a federal court judge or an executive branch agency. Of course, many Commissioners do not serve a full term; bipartisan appointments may be in name only; and the potential ability of an administrator to gain quick (if temporary) control of the agency is apparent from history. Thus, this may be only a theoretical possibility, but it deserves mention.

V. A proposal for rationalizing antitrust enforcement

It seems clear that dual enforcement is at best inefficient, and at worst inconsistent with sound economic policy. It also seems clear that the FTC structure has considerably more problems than does that of the DOJ.

This, of course, does not mean that the DOJ structure and procedures are optimal. In fact, the combination of criminal and civil enforcement has a variety of effects, some desirable and some not. The necessity of seeking all relief in district court leaves both important and trivial economic policy decisions in a great many unequal hands, and also has led to such burdens as the Tunney Act procedure for settling cases. The DOJ has frequently tried to hide behind the mantle of "law enforcement," thus

---

96 *See, e.g.*, Elman, *supra* note 87; White, *FTC: Wrong Agency for the Job of Adjudication*, 61 A.B.A. J. 1242 (1975).

avoiding the necessity of defending what are essentially economic policy decisions within the administration. The decision to seek to break up AT&T is only the most obvious example of this particular phenomenon.

Thus, deciding the proper structure for modern antitrust enforcement is not a one-sided problem. It is important that various options for change be carefully explored and debated. The present state of policy harmony is not guaranteed to last, and we could once again see the agencies pursuing even more disparate policies, particularly in light of the flexible standards that have now become part of the law.

Defenders of dual enforcement argue that the current system has real benefits that go beyond a simple comparison of the two agencies. The 1989 ABA Task Force Report, for example, suggests that dual enforcement should be preserved to insure that ample resources are devoted to antitrust enforcement and to reassure the public and Congress that antitrust is important. It is hard to imagine two weaker reasons for continued dual enforcement. There is simply no reason to believe that Congress could not properly assess the resource requirements of a combined antitrust enforcement agency and give it the financial support required for the task. Moreover, if the number of federal agencies is some indication of the importance the federal government assigns to a particular governmental function, perhaps we should have 20 or 30 drug enforcement administrations and 50 or 60 environmental protection agencies.

FTC Commissioner Andrew Strenio, another vocal supporter of dual enforcement, asserts that the FTC should be preserved because of its flexible statutory powers and its expert, "multi-disciplinary" approach to antitrust policy issues.[97] These justifications simply do not hold up to close scrutiny.

The FTC has had only minimal success in using the broad powers conferred in section 5 to define antitrust violations that

---

97 A. Strenio, *Down But Not Out: The FTC Nears Its Diamond Jubilee*, 24th Annual Symposium on Association and Antitrust Law, D.C. Bar Ass'n (Mar. 2, 1988).

fall outside the bounds of the Sherman and Clayton Acts. Its major efforts to define such violations—*e.g.*, cases such as *Exxon*, *Ethyl*, *du Pont*, *Reuben H. Donnelly*, and *Russell Stover* (all of which have been discussed earlier)—have all ended in disaster, either at the Commission's own hand or in the courts. Those cases were all filed during the activist period of the 1970's. Since that time, the movement to expand the antitrust laws has all but died, and the emphasis today is on a more refined process of antitrust scrutiny, employing the traditional tools of Sherman and Clayton Act enforcement.

The FTC would be hard pressed to identify a single complaint among the more than 100 issued since 1981 that DOJ could not have brought under the Sherman or Clayton Acts. Even the FTC's current cutting-edge theory, nonprice predation, is no more than an allegation of attempted monopolization, which draws its theoretical underpinnings from the established Sherman Act law.[98] It is possible, of course, that we will one day enter a new age of antitrust expansionism. Whatever the likelihood or wisdom of that possibility, it does not justify keeping the FTC in business simply because there might be an opportunity to define some new antitrust violations in the future. Indeed, given the FTC's past success rate in such endeavors, it would clearly be better to leave that task to Congress.

Arguments concerning the FTC's unique expertise and multidisciplinary capability are equally flawed. The question of the Commission's expertise has always been a subject of dispute. The FTC, after all, is not an agency like the Federal Communications Commission or the Federal Energy Regulatory Commission, which can over time gain specific expertise in the affairs of a particular industry. At most, the FTC can lay claim to experience in the amorphous field of economic regulation. More to the point, however, the DOJ possesses the very same institutional expertise, and its approach to antitrust issues is every bit as multidisciplinary as that of the FTC.

---

[98] *See* In re Amerco, [1983-87 Transfer Binder] Trade Reg. Rep. (CCH) ¶ 22,434 (Feb. 26, 1987).

Commissioner Strenio also asserts that the FTC's administrative process "lends itself readily to the incorporation of the new economic learning."[99] But, if anything, the FTC has generally been slower than DOJ in moving to embrace new policy directions. While the DOJ began to make the transition into the new age of antitrust under Assistant Attorney General Kauper in the early 1970's, it took congressional attacks, adverse court decisions, and a new working majority on the Commission to drag the FTC, kicking and screaming, into the antitrust mainstream in the 1980's.

The DOJ structure, in which a single administrator directs policy, is more capable of making rapid and smooth policy transitions. Each new administration can set its own priorities and direct its own enforcement policies. Moreover, DOJ decisions are subject to more immediate testing in the courts. At the FTC, however, each new administration must fight a veritable war of attrition as new appointees attempt to implement policies over the objections of Commissioners appointed by prior administrations. In the early period of the Reagan administration, for example, Chairman Miller faced constant opposition from Carter appointees Pertschuk and Bailey as he attempted to incorporate the so-called new learning in Commission enforcement policy. Thus, there is no basis for asserting that the FTC is superior to DOJ in making policy transitions.

The case for unification of antitrust enforcement goes beyond the fact that there are few good reasons for continuation of the status quo. There are affirmative justifications as well. With the movement of antitrust policy toward a more regulatory framework, it has become increasingly difficult for antitrust enforcement to stand as an island unto itself. Markets have become more international in scope, and trade, national defense and other important policy issues have become intertwined with antitrust. The government has recognized the benefits of competition in government procurement, and antitrust issues have thus become more prominent in the government contracts sphere. Regulatory actions by other government agencies have come to impact more

---

99 A. Strenio, *supra* note 97.

directly the nature and quality of competition in many markets. As an independent agency with no strong tie-in to government-wide policy making, the FTC may bring too narrow a perspective to antitrust policy issues.[100] At a minimum, the FTC's status as an independent regulatory agency makes it difficult for it to participate fully in the economic policy decisions of the executive branch.

If we are to do away with dual enforcement, should we then simply sweep the FTC into the DOJ? This has the attraction of simplicity, but is not clearly the optimal solution. At least two other possibilities should be explored: (1) The creation of a new executive branch agency responsible only for civil antitrust enforcement or (2) the creation of a true regulatory agency responsible for antitrust regulation. Indeed, these two concepts could even be combined, but for discussion purposes we will treat them as separate alternatives.

A. The EPA approach

If the combination of criminal and civil enforcement authority makes the DOJ think and act too much like a prosecutor, and helps it avoid dealing with other economic policy agencies the way it should, then the two could be separated. Criminal enforcement could be left with the DOJ, either through the U.S. attorneys supervised by the Criminal Division or in a separate but smaller Antitrust Division divested of all noncriminal responsibilities. We suspect that there would be plenty to keep the DOJ busy within either structure, but the latter would more likely insure a continued focus on price fixing and bid rigging.

Noncriminal enforcement would be the responsibility of a new, single-administrator agency, with a separate enforcement arm to litigate complaints in the federal courts. The new agency should have the ability to reach administrative settlements without the necessity of a complaint or consent decree. It would be

---

100 *See* Elman, *A Modest Proposal for Radical Reform*, 56 A.B.A. J. 1045, 1047 (1970).

organized hierarchically and report directly to the President or his delegate.

B. The trade court approach

A totally different option would be the creation of a multi-member trade court, to hear complaints brought by an independent antitrust enforcement agency. The latter could be either the DOJ or a new EPA-type agency. The trade court could have an economic staff (and for that matter lawyers, too) who could produce studies and policy analysis, but basically it would exist to serve as the court of first resort for all civil antitrust prosecutions by the federal government. Decisions of the trade court would be appealable to the courts of appeals. It would have the power to issue preliminary injunctions.

A variant on this theme would be to utilize the existing FTC, but separate the Commission and the FTC staff. The Director of the Bureau of Competition, who would be a presidential appointee, would have the exclusive power to initiate proceedings. The Antitrust Division's civil authority would be eliminated. The FTC would serve only as a decisional body. This would largely eliminate the "judge and jury" quality of the FTC today, and most dual enforcement problems, while preserving whatever are seen as the benefits of the administrative process. FTC Commissioner Terry Calvani endorsed a similar proposal in a recent speech.[101] In addition to some of the benefits discussed above, Commissioner Calvani notes that such an approach would increase agency accountability and remove the concern about prejudgment inherent in the administrative litigation process.

While each of these options has merit, both have problems as well. The EPA alternative would require the creation of a new agency and probably new statutory authority. Given the current political climate, that would be a large legislative undertaking and

---

101 Calvani, "A Proposal for Radical Change," Remarks before American Law Institute/American Bar Association, San Francisco, CA, May 6, 1988, *reprinted in* Trade Reg. Rpts. (CCH) No. 860 (May 10, 1988).

no doubt would result in a number of unfortunate political compromises. Moreover, an independent antitrust agency would be much like the FTC: it would be isolated from the policy crosscurrents within the executive branch and thus could not act to harmonize antitrust policy with other aspects of the administration's economic agenda. Indeed, the EPA itself has just become a cabinet level department in order to develop a more coordinated national policy on environmental issues.

The trade court notion also has its problems. Presumably, such a court would replace the federal district courts as the basic trial forum for government antitrust cases; the courts of appeals would play the same role as they now play in appeals from FTC decisions. The federal district courts, however, have come a long way in learning to manage complex antitrust cases, and it would be difficult to recreate that expertise in a new court. Indeed, it might be very difficult to find prospective jurists with equal skills in both antitrust theory and complex trial management. In addition, the creation of such a court would do away with the independent perspective of nonspecialist judges, which some believe is an important leavening factor in this specialized area. Finally, it is unclear that there is enough government antitrust litigation to occupy a panel that had no other responsibilities. Despite the substantial period it takes the current FTC to write opinions, there is no indication that any significant percentage of a Commissioner's time is now spent performing adjudicatory functions. In the absence of broader jurisdiction, appointees to a trade court might find the position to be less than demanding. Over the longer term, this would dissuade qualified persons from serving.

In short, the creation of a specialized court to resolve government antitrust matters would be much more difficult than it sounds. Furthermore, there is no way to be certain that the resulting court would be any more effective than the current federal judicial system. Absent some reason to believe that a trade court would be vastly superior to the present system, the creation of such a court seems unwise.

In the end, we come down strongly in favor of simplicity. A new EPA-type agency would not differ substantially from the Antitrust Division, except in terms of its independence, which we do not necessarily see as a virtue. The trade court sounds good as a concept, but we have severe doubts that an effective trade court could be created. Moreover, the creation of a trade court would do little to solve the problems identified herein without the consolidation of the prosecutorial function into a single-administrator agency. Thus, we would eliminate the FTC as an antitrust enforcement agency. Its important consumer protection mission can be absorbed by other federal agencies.[102] The FTC's antitrust mission should be given to the DOJ. Section 5 can, if thought necessary, be retained as a fail-safe overflow in case the Sherman and Clayton Acts prove insufficient in the future, but we would repeal the statute. The DOJ's criminal enforcement should remain in the DOJ, but either U.S. attorneys or a specialized cadre of attorneys within the Department should investigate and prosecute criminal cases.

VI. Conclusion

An analysis of the relative strengths of the FTC and DOJ shows that, as between the two, the DOJ is better suited to the task of antitrust enforcement. The DOJ enforcement structure is more amenable to making policy and communicating its policy positions to the public. The DOJ enforcement structure is also preferable for the translation of policy into actual enforcement practice. While other options are possible, unification of all antitrust enforcement in the DOJ is the simplest way to improve results.

---

102 Alternatively, functions such as those performed by the Consumer Product Safety Commission could be placed into an expanded FTC.

14
The Justice Department and the antitrust laws: law enforcer or regulator?

BY THOMAS E. KAUPER*

The celebration of the Sherman Act's[1] first 100 years will bring forth encomiums from some, and brickbats from others. Some will applaud the Act as a bulwark against the oppression of economic and political liberty through the centralization of private economic power. If the Act has fallen short of this lofty ambition, the fault is not with the Congress or the now familiar language it enacted, but with courts and enforcement agencies that either failed to understand or chose to ignore Congress' intent.[2] Some may attack the Act as a futile gesture, a cynical and perhaps successful effort to prevent alternative, more effective

* Henry M. Butzel Professor of Law, University of Michigan.

AUTHOR'S NOTE: *Barry Hawk and Shirley Kauper offered helpful comments on an early draft of this article.*

1 15 U.S.C. § 1 (1982).

2 *See, e.g.*, Kramer, *Antitrust Today: The Baxterization of the Sherman and Clayton Acts*, 1981 WIS. L. REV. 1287.

measures against the use of corporate power.[3] Still others will view the Act, as interpreted, as a factor contributing significantly to inefficiency in the marketplace, and the loss of sales and jobs to foreign competitors. In their eyes, courts and enforcement agencies have been overzealous, and have taken the Act down paths both inappropriate and costly.[4]

Such disagreements are hardly surprising. The Congress of 1890 stood at a relatively early point in the growth of American industrialism. It lacked the experience and economic sophistication with which we at least think we approach the same issues today. While it did not like the trusts, it was relatively inarticulate in explaining why. The Sherman Act is in its language remarkably imprecise, and efforts to divine its purposes from legislative history have been inconclusive.[5] The debate over antitrust's goals has focused more on what these goals should be than on what Congress has said that they are.[6] The values and beliefs at issue go

---

3 For discussion of this point of view see Hofstadter, *What Happened to the Antitrust Movement?* in THE PARANOID STYLE IN AMERICAN POLITICS 188, 190 (1966).

4 *See, e.g.*, R. BORK, THE ANTITRUST PARADOX 407–16 (1978).

5 *Compare* Bork, *Legislative Intent and the Policy of the Sherman Act*, 9 J.L. & ECON. 7 (1966) (primary concern reflected in legislative history of the Sherman Act was efficiency) *with* Lande, *Wealth Transfers as the Original and Primary Concern of Antitrust: The Efficiency Interpretation Challenged*, 34 HASTINGS L.J. 65 (1982) (dominant purpose was to eliminate wealth transfers to monopolists from consumers).

6 I have discussed the debate over antitrust's goals elsewhere. *See* Kauper, *The Sullivan Approach to Horizontal Restraints*, 75 CALIF. L. REV. 893, 894–901 (1987); Kauper, *The Goals of United States Antitrust Policy—The Current Debate*, 136 ZEITSCHRIFT FÜR DIE GESAMTE STAATSWISSENSCHAFT 408 (1980) (in English). For relatively recent expressions of views, *compare* R. BORK, *supra* note 4, at 81–89 (the "consumer welfare" view); Baxter, *Responding to the Reaction: The Draftsman's View*, 71 CALIF. L. REV. 618, 619–21 (1983) (same); Easterbrook, *Is There a Ratchet in Antitrust Law?* 60 TEX. L. REV. 705, 714–17 (1982) (advocating economic goals) *with* Fox, *The Modernization of Antitrust Law: A New Equilibrium*, 66 CORNELL L. REV. 1140, 1146–55 (1981) (efficiency not sole goal); Pitofsky, *The Political Content of Antitrust*,

far beyond the boundaries of antitrust, encompassing broad issues of political and economic power that transcend the narrow issues with which antitrust must deal. Fear of economic concentration, faith in the ability of government to act responsibly and intelligently, and skepticism about the equation of private and public good, will lead some to seek a highly interventionist antitrust program that is,[7] in turn, anathema to those whose major fear is the government and whose faith in free markets is unshaken.[8] These values, however articulated, are born out of tradition, and the economic and political philosophies that we all hold. They are as much a matter of faith as demonstrable truth, however hard we may try to wrap antitrust in the trappings of science. Disagreements on these broad issues, which are central to the evaluation of the Sherman Act, the body of antitrust doctrine that it has spawned, and the performance of the institutions involved in its interpretation and enforcement, will not and cannot be resolved simply through the exercise of reason.

The subject of this article is the role played in antitrust enforcement by the United States Department of Justice and, after 1933, its Antitrust Division.[9] It will not be an analysis of the substance of antitrust. But substance and enforcement are hopelessly intertwined. Those who concur in the Division's view of antitrust policy at a given moment will find little in its conduct to condemn. Criticism of the Division's operations generally reflects

---

127 U. Pa. L. Rev. 1051, 1052–58 (1978) (antitrust analysis includes "political goals"); Sullivan, *Economics and More Humanistic Disciplines: What Are the Sources of Wisdom for Antitrust?* 125 U. Pa. L. Rev. 1214, 1232–41 (1977) (antitrust more fully "illuminated" by "humanistic" goals).

7 *See* Pitofsky, *Antitrust in the Next 100 Years*, 75 Calif. L. Rev. 817, 818–23 (1987); Fox, *Consumer Beware Chicago*, 84 Mich. L. Rev. 1714, 1718–19 (1986).

8 *See, e.g.*, Easterbrook, *Comparative Advantage and Antitrust Law*, 75 Calif. L. Rev. 983 (1987); Easterbrook, *The Limits of Antitrust*, 63 Tex. L. Rev. 1 (1984).

9 The Antitrust Division was not established until 1933. Prior to that time, the Department's antitrust operations were run by a Special Assistant to the Attorney General.

an underlying disagreement with the substance of that same policy. Because we cannot agree on what the Sherman Act was meant to do, or, in a broader policy sense, should do, we cannot expect a consensus about the performance of the Division. This article does not therefore pursue the question of whether the Division's substantive policies are "right" or "wrong" (although I find the policies of the Division of the 1980's generally "right"). I will examine instead how the Division operates, how and why its role and methods have changed over time, and whether further, more radical changes are either necessary or desirable. Doctrine is not irrelevant in this discussion. The focus, however, is on the relationship between doctrine and the various institutions of antitrust, rather than on doctrine for its own sake.[10]

In the 100 years following enactment of the Sherman Act, antitrust doctrine and enforcement activity have not followed a single, unwavering course. Antitrust's early concern with labor unions was quickly abandoned.[11] Following a flurry of activity against the major trusts, the antitrust of the 1920's faded into the background of a public euphoria about the virtues of American business.[12] America was doing well, and the government meant to keep its hands off. The depression brought a deep suspicion of the free market system, and a faith, born perhaps of desperation, that the government was better able than private enterprises to make a broad range of economic decisions. Antitrust, the guarantor of free markets, was displaced by formal and informal

---

10 A description of the Division over a period of nearly 100 years requires broad generalizations about antitrust doctrine, procedures and institutions. I will engage liberally in such generalizations, recognizing that at any given moment in history the generalization may seem inappropriate or may need considerable qualification. But the discussion that follows is directed toward trends, not moments, and should be taken in that vein.

11 *See* A. NEALE & D. GOYDER, ANTITRUST LAWS OF THE UNITED STATES OF AMERICA 19 (3d ed. 1980).

12 *Id.* at 19–20. The period from 1914 through 1937 in antitrust has been characterized as "the era of neglect." Hofstadter, *supra* note 3, at 197.

economic regulation that had as its premise the failure of those very market forces.[13] With the advent of the Second New Deal came a new commitment to antitrust and regulation through the market. Thurman Arnold became a legendary figure in the history of antitrust enforcement.[14] The young and energetic staff of the Antitrust Division, picked from the top graduates of the nation's law schools,[15] brought criminal prosecutions in large numbers.[16] World War II brought another halt to antitrust activity. With the conclusion of the war, public and private enforcement again increased. By the mid-1960's private actions dominated the statistics on antitrust cases filed.[17] Shifts in

---

13 The period from 1932 through 1938 saw the imposition of direct economic regulation with respect to motor and air carriers, telecommunications, natural gas and electrical power, and in a variety of other areas as well. Industry self-regulation inconsistent with reliance on free markets occurred pursuant to industry codes ("Blue Eagle codes") authorized by the National Industrial Recovery Act.

14 Thurman Arnold was Assistant Attorney General in charge of the Antitrust Division from 1938 until mid-1943. For a brief biography *see* G. GRESSLEY, VOLTAIRE AND THE COWBOY: THE LETTERS OF THURMAN ARNOLD 1–94 (1977).

15 *See* Letter of Thurman Arnold to Gordon Dean (October 15, 1938) in G. GRESSLEY, *supra* note 14, at 276–78, in which Arnold defended himself against the charge that the Division hired only "Yale, Harvard and Columbia men."

16 In the years 1940–1944 the Division filed 163 criminal cases. It filed only 173 criminal cases between 1890 and 1940. *See* Posner, *A Statistical Study of Antitrust Enforcement*, 13 J.L. & ECON. 365, 385 (1970). From time to time, the level of activity at the Division outran its budget. In 1939, for example, Division lawyers on the road were forced to pay their own hotel bills. *See* letter from Thurman Arnold to Dorothy Thompson (January 4, 1940) in G. GRESSLEY, *supra* note 14, at 300.

17 From 1890 to 1940 only 175 private cases were finally adjudicated. *See* Bicks, *The Department of Justice and Private Treble Damage Actions*, 4 ANTITRUST BULL. 5, 11 (1959). It has been estimated that during the same period only 423 such cases were filed. From 1960 through 1964, 3,354 private cases were filed. In the same period 215 cases were filed by the Antitrust Division. *See* Posner, *supra* note 16, at 366, 371. In the years from 1975 to 1980, the ratio of private cases to

enforcement activity have occurred since, but not in such dramatic fashion.

As enforcement activity has swung back and forth, antitrust doctrine has also seen significant, if somewhat less dramatic, changes. The use of per se rules, and of what might be called antitrust analysis by characterization, began with *United States v. Standard Oil Co.*[18] and reached its high point during the Warren Court era.[19] From the outset, antitrust courts struggled with two quite different perceptions of what the Sherman Act sought to protect, although they were slow to see that they were in fact different. If monopoly and cartels harmed consumers by raising prices, as has been clear from the beginning, antitrust's mission was to assure that unnecessary monopoly did not occur and that cartels did not succeed. The harm to be avoided was to the consuming public. But antitrust might also be viewed as protecting individuals and business enterprises—particularly small business enterprises—from conduct through which economic power was used against them in an arbitrary, coercive or unfair manner. So perceived, the Sherman Act gave individuals and firms the *right* to be free of such impositions. Antitrust, in this view, was a species of tort law, focused on individual harm as a measure of damage to the public at large. By the 1960's, this individual rights view of antitrust came to predominate. In language similar to the

---

Antitrust Division cases ranged as high as 20 to 1. *See* M. HANDLER, H. BLAKE, R. PITOFSKY & H. GOLDSCHMID, TRADE REGULATION 124, 129 (2d ed. 1983).

18 221 U.S. 1 (1911). In *Standard Oil* the Court laid the groundwork for the creation of per se rules, and thus for a process of adjudication by characterization, with the observation that in some cases the "nature and character" of the conduct may create "a conclusive presumption of illegality." *Id.* at 65.

19 The high point (or low point, depending on one's point of view) came with the declaration in United States v. Arnold, Schwinn & Co., 388 U.S. 365 (1967) that vertical territorial restraints were per se illegal. Courts thereafter were required to engage in an initial characterization process, inevitable with per se rules, to determine whether the arrangement in question fit the *Schwinn* "pigeonhole." *Schwinn* was overruled in Continental T.V., Inc. v. GTE-Sylvania, Inc., 433 U.S. 36 (1977).

civil rights cases of the same era, the Supreme Court used the antitrust laws to prevent economic coercion and to assure small business enterprises of equality of opportunity.[20] This "rights" approach has in turn given way to the onslaught of the Chicago school, and antitrust is now preoccupied with consumer welfare.[21] The common law method, which shaped the development of antitrust for eight decades and was dominated by lawyers, has given way to a mode of analysis in which economists, if not kings, are at least princes.[22] Although rules with respect to cartel behavior have remained constant, in most other questions antitrust doctrine has wavered.

Changes in doctrine, enforcement activity and the institutions within the antitrust system have been reflective, to some degree, of shifts in public perceptions about the relevance and purpose of antitrust. It is no accident, for example, that the rise of the Chicago school with its emphasis on economic efficiency has coincided with the growing public concern over the apparent inability of American business to fend off foreign competition. These changes have been made possible by the general language of the Sherman Act and the lack of consensus from the outset about its purpose. I do not suggest that such inconstancy is bad. Flexibility and adaptability of doctrine to change may well be a virtue. I suggest only that there may be few revealed truths, and that any evaluation of the appropriate role of antitrust and those involved in its formulation and enforcement, including the Anti-

---

20 *See* Kauper, *The "Warren Court" and the Antitrust Laws: Of Economics, Populism and Cynicism*, 67 MICH. L. REV. 325, 332–34 (1968).

21 *See* Gerhart, *The Supreme Court and Antitrust Analysis: The (Near) Triumph of the Chicago School*, 1982 SUP. CT. REV. 319. For a more general discussion and critique *see* Hovenkamp, *Antitrust Policy After Chicago*, 84 MICH. L. REV. 213 (1985).

22 For more detailed discussions of the relative roles of lawyers and economists in the "new" antitrust *see* ANTITRUST POLICY IN TRANSITION: THE CONVERGENCE OF LAW AND ECONOMICS 23–42 (E. Fox & J. Halverson eds. 1984); Kauper, *The Role of Economic Analysis in the Antitrust Division Before and After the Establishment of the Economic Policy Office: A Lawyer's View*, 29 ANTITRUST BULL. 111, 130–32 (1984).

trust Division, depends in large part on the point from which the evaluator begins, on faith as much as reason.

I. The institutions of antitrust

The Sherman Act has spawned a series of institutions and actors who play on its stage. The Antitrust Division [the Division] is the primary focus of the pages that follow. As perceptions of antitrust's goals have shifted, and doctrine has moved in different directions, the role played by the Division has also changed. The Division today bears little resemblance to the Division of the late 1930's, or even the 1970's. Fewer matters are resolved through litigation, although the threat of litigation remains the Division's primary weapon. No longer a simple "law enforcement" body, the Division now plays a more complex regulatory role, and has taken on more of the trappings of agencies charged with responsibility for direct economic regulation. The Division has changed gradually, as doctrine and antitrust's other institutions have changed.

The part played by the Division cannot be analyzed without regard to antitrust's other institutions. The Division is but one actor in the antitrust system. No actor's role can be assessed without consideration of the others who occupy the same stage, and the relationships that exist among them. In any production, every actor both supports and limits the performance of others. This, as we shall see, is true of those involved in antitrust. Roles have shifted with doctrine, and in response to the roles played by others.

Antitrust has a large cast. The central role is played by the federal courts and, more particularly, the Supreme Court of the United States. The significance of this obvious fact is sometimes neglected. Because the interpretation of the Sherman Act rests with the judiciary, no one else makes antitrust "rules." There is, and can be, no regulatory body that can give authoritative rulings. Change must come through legislation, or the judicial process. This process can be invoked only if there is a case or controversy. The courts cannot render advisory opinions; nor do they deliver a whole series of rules at once. Change is therefore slow, and comes piecemeal. Precedent that is inconsistent with the philosophy of later cases may remain without overruling for decades, to the consternation of lower courts and those who must make judgments about what the law is at a given moment. Enforcement agencies following the lead of modern decisions may appear to be flaunting older precedent more directly on point.[23] Cases cannot be brought to determine that *no* antitrust violation has occurred, a fact that has been particularly vexing to the Division of the 1980's.[24] Congress can of course work sudden and dramatic changes in antitrust policy, but has seldom done so. The generality of the Sherman Act's language has become a virtue that legislators have been reluctant to disturb.

While the federal courts occupy center stage, there are a number of supporting actors. These include the Division, the Federal Trade Commission [FTC], private plaintiffs (and their lawyers), defendants (and their lawyers) and state attorneys general.[25] The Congress lurks in the background, as does an academic community whose influence has been significant.[26] With

---

23 *See, e.g.*, Rothery Storage & Van Co. v. Atlas Van Lines, Inc., 792 F.2d 210, 226–27 (D.C. Cir.), *cert. denied*, 107 S. Ct. 880 (1986), where the court suggested that the Supreme Court's decision in United States v. Topco Associates, Inc., 405 U.S. 596 (1972) was no longer good law because inconsistent with the philosophy, albeit not the holdings, of a number of subsequent decisions. *Compare* Hospital Corp. of America v. FTC, 807 F.2d 1381, 1385 (7th Cir. 1986).

24 For example, the Antitrust Division in recent years has expressed the view that vertical price-fixing ought not be per se illegal. But the Division cannot file a case to establish that a particular form of conduct is lawful. It is therefore confined to filing amicus briefs on behalf of defendants in order to present its position, as it did with a singular lack of success in Monsanto Co. v. Spray-Rite Service Corp., 465 U.S. 752 (1984).

25 State attorneys general not only may bring suit under the federal antitrust laws where the state has suffered antitrust injury, but in some cases may also sue on behalf of the state's citizens on a parens patriae basis. Clayton Act § 4C, 15 U.S.C. § 15c (1982).

26 In recent years, for example, academics of the Chicago school have dominated antitrust thinking, not only in academe but in the courts

the exception of Congress, each of these groups performs the same basic role. They give input to the judiciary, initiating the process that the rulemakers cannot begin on their own, and providing the facts and arguments upon which doctrine is based.[27] At any given moment, one group of actors may be more persuasive than others. But in a technical legal sense, their views are equally authoritative. The advice given by the Division is more compelling than contrary advice of private counsel only if it is more in accord with contemporary judicial thought on the same question. The Division's views may give assurance that it will not act, a matter of some consequence to those who would prefer that their actions not be questioned. But it cannot prevent private parties from challenging precisely the same conduct.

II. The Antitrust Division, 1890–1980: law enforcement or economic regulation?

While the roles of the supporting cast are in a broad sense the same, their prominence has varied substantially over time. Between 1890 and World War II, antitrust doctrine was largely the result of interplay between the Justice Department and the judiciary.[28] Private equitable and treble damage actions were relatively rare.[29] Until well into the 1960's, the majority of such actions were "follow-ons," cases seeking damages caused by

---

as well. *See generally* Gerhart, *supra* note 21; Hovenkamp, *supra* note 21.

27 *See* Kauper, *Competition Policy and the Institutions of Antitrust*, 23 So. Dak. L. Rev. 1, 5–6 (1978).

28 The FTC, created in 1914, filed a substantial number of restraint of trade complaints between 1915 and 1940. But a high percentage of these complaints were dismissed by the Commission. Very few ended up in court. *See* Posner, *supra* note 16, at 369, 382. And when FTC cases were judicially reviewed, the Commission was represented by the Department of Justice.

29 *See* note 19 *supra*.

conduct that had already been challenged by the Division.[30] Such actions added significantly to the deterrent effect of the Division's enforcement program, but were not a major independent factor in the formulation of doctrine. The FTC, preoccupied with its consumer protection responsibilities and, after 1936, enforcement of the Robinson-Patman Act,[31] played a lesser role in mainstream antitrust enforcement. As a practical matter, the decisions and policies of the Justice Department during this period had a degree of authoritativeness to them that has weakened over the years. If Justice decided not to proceed with a given matter, it was not likely anyone else would.

The role of the Justice Department during this period was generally described as "law enforcement." Antitrust was commonly described as the alternative to economic regulation, rather than as a species of it. The Division's primary tool was litigation. Criminal prosecutions were common. Like any law enforcement agency, the Division exercised discretion in initiating investigations and filing cases, if for no other reason than the presence of budget constraints. But the discretion it exercised operated within a far more narrow range than appears to be the case today. By Thurman Arnold's day, the Division was also issuing "prosecution policy" statements intended to provide guidance to the business community,[32] a practice that grew into the far more elaborate "guidelines" and business review procedures of recent years.

By the mid-1960's roles had begun to change. The number of private actions increased dramatically.[33] Over the next two decades, private cases outnumbered cases filed by the government

---

30 One estimate is that before 1960 75% of all treble damage actions were follow-on cases. Comment, *Consent Decrees and Private Actions: An Antitrust Dilemma*, 53 CALIF. L. REV. 627, 628 n.7 (1965).

31 15 U.S.C. §§ 13–13b, 21a (1982).

32 *See* letter of Thurman Arnold to Arthur Sulzberger (August 25, 1939) in G. GRESSLEY, *supra* note 14, at 291-94.

33 *See* Posner, *supra* note 16, at 371; Salop & White, *Economic Analysis of Private Antitrust Litigation*, 74 GEO. L.J. 1001, 1002 (1986).

by a ratio of better than ten to one.[34] The percentage of these cases that followed successful government litigation declined steadily.[35] Thus more and more private litigants brought *new* issues to the federal courts, providing additional opportunities for the formulation of doctrine without the participation of the Division at all. Antitrust policy that had developed primarily through the interplay between the Division, defendants and the judiciary was displaced by policy that resulted from the relationship between the courts and private litigants. The Division could, and did, participate in a few of these cases, usually on an amicus basis at the Supreme Court level. But it played no role in their initiation, and was forced to influence the formulation of doctrine in litigation it did not prepare and on records it did not shape.

There are many possible reasons for the dramatic increase in private antitrust litigation. Expanded concepts of standing and other procedural changes facilitated private litigation of all sorts. Prosperity may increase litigiousness, especially on the part of those who feel that they do not share in it. A number of other explanations may be offered. One fundamental reason stands out. Success encourages emulation, particularly when damages are trebled. And during the Warren Court era private plaintiffs at least appeared to succeed in ever-increasing numbers and amounts.[36] The "individual rights" approach to antitrust, with its focus on individual harm, was not new, but now came to the forefront, easing the burden on plaintiffs who for one reason or another felt aggrieved. This was particularly true in cases involv-

---

34 *See* note 17 *supra*.

35 *See* Kauper & Snyder, *An Inquiry Into the Efficiency of Private Antitrust Enforcement: Follow-on and Independently Initiated Cases Compared*, 74 GEO. L.J. 1163, 1221 (1986) (estimating that in the period 1973–1983 follow-on cases, represented no more than 24% of all private actions filed).

36 In the period 1965–1969, for example, plaintiffs won 11 of 12 private antitrust cases decided by the Supreme Court. *See* Posner, *supra* note 16, at 384.

ing vertical restraints, where the "rights" theory of antitrust was most often employed.[37]

It is not farfetched, I believe, to suggest that underlying these procedural and substantive changes were many of the same forces that drove the civil rights movement and the general expansion of the federal judicial role. Federal courts became the protectors of those who felt oppressed by the exercise of political and economic power. I have already noted the similarity in the language of civil rights and antitrust opinions of the Warren Court period. Nor, I believe, is it mere coincidence that the increase in private antitrust litigation tracked the rise in private actions under 42 U.S.C. § 1983, the private remedial section of the Civil Rights Act of 1871.[38] No longer prepared to rely on protection through actions of the government, private parties in growing numbers went to court on their own. In antitrust cases, this tendency was bolstered by the incentive created by the lure of treble damages.

Whatever the reasons underlying the large increases in private antitrust actions, the role of the Division in areas of traditional antitrust concern was diminished, except with respect to mergers. The impact of its statements of policy was weakened by the ability and willingness of private parties to challenge the very conduct the Division found unobjectionable. The primary antitrust concern of the business community became exposure to treble damages. The Division's business review procedure,[39] which permitted parties contemplating a future action to obtain a statement of its enforcement intentions, was valuable in some cases but was utilized most frequently where private suit was

---

37 *See* Kauper, *supra* note 20, at 333–34.

38 *See* Whitman, *Constitutional Torts*, 79 Mich. L. Rev. 5, 6 (1980).

39 28 C.F.R., Ch. 1, Part 50, § 50.6 (1987), 42 Fed. Reg. 11831 (March 1, 1977). The business review procedure is described more fully in Sullivan, *The Antitrust Division as a Regulatory Agency: An Enforcement Policy in Transition*, 64 Wash. U.L.Q. 997, 1033–34 (1986).

unlikely. At the same time, increased reliance on detailed economic analysis within the Division, facilitated by creation of the Economic Policy Office in 1973,[40] moved its enforcement policy further away from the "rules" formulated by courts in private and earlier government litigation,[41] further diminishing the authoritativeness of its pronouncements. The Division of the late 1960's and 1970's was an influential voice in the formulation of antitrust policy, but was hardly an agency with anything akin to direct regulatory power.

The story with respect to merger enforcement is somewhat different. The effect of the 1950 amendments to section 7 of the Clayton Act[42] was not immediate, but following the decision in *Brown Shoe Co. v. United States*,[43] the Division became increasingly active in policing merger activity. The Warren Court's merger decisions opened the door to an extremely restrictive merger policy, a policy more extreme than that sought by the Division.[44] While as a theoretical matter section 7 might be enforced through private actions (although there has been some disagreement on the point),[45] private actions were rare. If the

---

40 *See generally* Kauper, *supra* note 22.

41 For example, the Division brought no cases challenging vertical territorial restriction cases despite the then-governing per se rule adopted in United States v. Arnold, Schwinn & Co., 388 U.S. 365 (1987), a decision inconsistent with economic thought.

42 15 U.S.C. § 18 (1982 and Supp. IV 1986) (original version at Ch. 323, § 7, 38 Stat. 730, 731–32 (1914)).

43 370 U.S. 294 (1962).

44 For example, in United States v. Von's Grocery Co., 384 U.S. 270 (1966), the Court condemned a horizontal merger between two competitors with a combined 7.5% market share, on grounds other than those advanced by the Division. The Division's 1968 Merger Guidelines (*reprinted in* 4 Trade Reg. Rep. (CCH) ¶ 13,101) do not represent as extreme an approach as that found in *Von's*.

45 The disagreement has been over the ability to obtain treble damages under section 7. The issue is discussed in 2 P. Areeda & D. Turner, Antitrust Law ¶ 335d (1978). Private parties who meet standing and antitrust injury requirements may seek injunctive relief. Cargill, Inc. v. Monfort of Colorado, Inc., 479 U.S. 104 (1986).

Division decided not to attack a given acquisition it was unlikely to be challenged by anyone. And given the accuracy of Mr. Justice Stewart's observation that in section 7 cases "the government always wins,"[46] the Division's decision to file was critical. In these circumstances, the Division was in a position to control merger activity directly, subject only to its ability to continue to convince the courts that mergers it challenged were anticompetitive.[47] The 1968 Merger Guidelines,[48] while formally simply a statement of prosecution policy, thus had significant normative consequences. The FTC, with concurrent authority under section 7, did serve as some check on the Division, but only in an indirect way. While it could have challenged mergers that the Division found unobjectionable, it generally did not.[49] The assignment of particular mergers to one agency or the other through the FTC–Antitrust Division clearance process assured that this would not occur. The FTC served as a check on the Division only because FTC merger cases ended up in federal court, where its views might lead to the development of doctrine that bound the Division as much as the FTC. But even this indirect effect was limited because throughout much of this period the FTC's views in court were presented by the Justice Department, its courtroom lawyer.[50]

---

46 United States v. Von's Grocery Co., 384 U.S. 270, 301 (1966) (Stewart, J. dissenting).

47 When the Division was required to consider the "failing company" defense, its decisions generally controlled outcome simply because of the practical difficulties inherent in the defense. *See* discussion in Kauper, *The 1982 Merger Guidelines: Of Collusion, Efficiency and Failure*, 71 CALIF. L. REV. 497, 529–31 (1983).

48 *Reprinted in* 4 Trade Reg. Rep. (CCH) ¶ 13,101.

49 *But see* Hospital Corp. of America v. FTC, 807 F.2d 1381 (7th Cir. 1986), where the FTC challenged an acquisition after the Antitrust Division decided to take no action, on the basis of likely effect in a geographic market that was not the focus of the Division's investigation.

50 The Commission did not receive broad authority to represent itself in court until 1975. Act of January 4, 1975, Public Law 93-637, § 204(a), 88 Stat. 2199, amending section 16 of the Clayton Act, 15 U.S.C. § 56 (1982) (as amended).

The key to a successful merger, in antitrust terms, was to convince the government not to proceed. So long as the Division (and the FTC) adhered to their own policy statements, those statements began to operate like formal antitrust rules.

The relationship between the Division and private plaintiffs was, and still is, an uneasy one. A simple-minded view of antitrust would suggest that they were necessarily allies. In a good many cases their interests did coincide. When private litigants proceeded against conduct the Division believed anticompetitive, Division resources could be employed elsewhere. In follow-on cases treble damages provided a deterrent effect that Division enforcement efforts lacked, at least until the increase in criminal penalties in 1974.[51] The Division was generally cooperative with private plaintiffs in such cases, at least to the point where cooperation might frustrate its own enforcement efforts. In a number of matters, however, the interests of the Division and private plaintiffs diverged, sometimes to the point of opposition. The Division might believe the conduct at issue in private litigation was procompetitive. Even if an outcome in plaintiff's favor seemed sound, the arguments plaintiffs offered in support, and which might shape doctrine, were objectionable. The relief sought by plaintiffs in private cases might interfere with relief sought by the Division or, worse yet, be considered anticompetitive. In some circumstances, the availability of treble damages worked to prevent the Division from filing cases it believed meritorious.[52] As the Division pursued enforcement objectives consistent with contemporary economic thinking and its emphasis on consumer welfare and private plaintiffs continued to assert the

---

51 From 1890 to 1974 violation of the Sherman Act was a misdemeanor. In 1974 maximum fines and jail sentences were increased. Violation became a felony. Antitrust Procedures and Penalties Act, Pub. L. 93-528, 88 Stat. 1708 (codified at 15 U.S.C. § 1 (1982)).

52 The awarding of treble damages following successful and innovative government civil litigation might undermine the relief obtained by the government, or in some other way be at cross-purposes from what the government sought to achieve. In such cases, the mandatory treble damage remedy has deterred the Division from proceeding in the first instance, a fact to which I can personally attest.

protection of their individual rights, the divergence between public and private enforcement grew.[53] The Division more frequently found itself allied with defendants.

Even in such cases, however, private litigation on occasion served a useful purpose for the Division. The availability of private relief permitted the Division to avoid cases that it thought economically unwise but that under existing precedent involved conduct likely to be held unlawful. The Division thus could insist that it was pursuing economically rational policies, while at the same time the "law" was being faithfully executed (albeit by others). For example, in the years I served as Assistant Attorney General, vertical territorial restrictions were per se illegal, according to the Supreme Court's decision in *United States v. Arnold, Schwinn & Co.*[54] The rule made no economic sense. We brought no such cases, explaining that the conduct was overt, that those allegedly harmed knew that they were "victims" and had all the facts necessary for application of a per se rule at their disposal, that a private remedy was readily available and there was therefore no reason to expend the Division's resources on such cases. *Schwinn* was not yet ripe for overruling, and the private remedy provided the Division with an excuse for inaction. In a similar vein, the Division used its understanding with the FTC that the latter would be responsible for government enforcement of the Robinson-Patman Act to avoid any involvement under a statute it thought economically unwise.

As private enforcement activity increased throughout the years between 1965 and 1980, the Division's response was ambivalent. Private actions were often seen as valuable, freeing Divi-

---

53 During the period 1969–1971, the Division under Assistant Attorney General Richard W. McClaren pursued policies with respect to large conglomerate mergers and reciprocity that had little foundation in economic analysis. The Division thus deviated for a brief period from the emphasis on economic analysis that characterized its enforcement efforts under Assistant Attorney General Donald F. Turner (1965–1968).

54 388 U.S. 365 (1967), *overruled* in Continental T.V., Inc. v. GTE-Sylvania, Inc., 433 U.S. 36 (1977).

sion resources, providing additional deterrent and, occasionally, permitting the Division to avoid taking actions that it thought unsound but might otherwise have been required to undertake. Yet as the Division moved in the direction of a consumer welfare model of antitrust, the conflict in goals between the Division and private plaintiffs increased, particularly with respect to vertical restraints. Over time, the Division increased its efforts to influence and, to some extent control, the outcomes of private cases and the impact of those cases on the development of doctrine.

The Division was not always prepared to cooperate with plaintiffs whose cases it viewed as economically unsound. Amicus filings in private cases increased, as the Division sought to have its views presented even when it was not a party. On rare occasions, the Division filed amicus briefs on behalf of defendants.[55] The Division acted in the belief that its own enforcement program was sound, and should not be jeopardized by private actions inconsistent with it. But it also acted as a bureaucracy might be expected to act. Threatened with a loss of influence, and with a diminution of its previously predominant role among antitrust's supporting cast, the Division sought to exert its influence over that which threatened it.[56] The response was similar to that of agencies administering programs of direct economic regulation. Where unregulated activity threatens the system of economic regulation, the regulator invariably seeks to influence, and then control, the unregulated activity as well.

I do not mean to suggest that the Division was opposed to all private litigation or preoccupied with its control. It was neither. Much of the Division's work was either consistent with or unaffected by private actions. The Division's criminal prosecutions for horizontal price-fixing and bid-rigging increased

---

55 *See, e.g.*, Worthen Bank & Trust Co. v. National Bank Americard, Inc., 485 F.2d 119 (8th Cir. 1973), *cert. denied*, 415 U.S. 918 (1974).

56 The Division retained a degree of influence over the FTC during this period through the Justice Department's control of FTC litigation. *See* note 50 *supra*.

through this same period.[57] Treble damages in these cases provided a valuable deterrent. A substantial percentage of the Division's resources went to merger enforcement, where, as already noted, private enforcement did not significantly threaten government policy. The Division was also actively pursuing its regulatory intervention program, which had its genesis in the regime of Donald Turner and expanded considerably thereafter.[58] Through intervention in various ways in formal regulatory proceedings before agencies such as the Interstate Commerce Commission and Federal Communications Commission, and in councils of the executive branch as well, the Division sought to minimize the creation of monopoly power by government itself. Such intervention can hardly be characterized as "law enforcement"; in virtually none of these proceedings is there a plausible argument that the antitrust laws have been violated. The same suspicion of economic regulation led to the Division's heavy involvement in the decade of the 1970's in the deregulation movement. The Economic Policy Office gave the Division a body of expertise, and therefore an influence, in these efforts beyond what many might have expected.[59] Each of these activities involved the Division in broad issues of public policy, with little connection to its traditional law enforcement function. Private litigation had little impact on these programs.

Nevertheless, concern over private litigation involving vertical restraints and those horizontal restraints not normally the subject of criminal prosecution was real. While a good deal of this concern was on the merits, *i.e.*, based on the belief that positions

---

[57] *See* M. HANDLER, H. BLAKE, R. PITOFSKY & H. GOLDSCHMID, *supra* note 17, at 124.

[58] For fuller descriptions of the program *see* Kauper, *supra* note 27, at 22–25; Baker, *The Antitrust Division, Department of Justice: The Role of Competition in Regulated Industries*, 11 BOSTON COLL. IND. & COMM. L. REV. 571 (1970). The program is now simply taken as a given. *See generally* Ginsburg, *The Appropriate Role of the Antitrust Enforcement Agencies*, 9 CARDOZO L. REV. 1277, 1284–88 (1988); Shenefield, *Open Letter to the New President of the United States*, 9 CARDOZO L. REV. 1295, 1302 (1988).

[59] *See* Kauper, *supra* note 22, at 124–25.

taken by private litigants were unsound, and in some cases anticompetitive, it also manifested a frustration over the Division's inability to shape the development of antitrust doctrine. This frustration has become more apparent in the Division of the 1980's, the years of the Reagan administration.

III. The Division as economic regulator: the era of the 1980's

By 1980, the Division no longer fit a simple "law enforcement" model. It had not done so for some time. Through its regulatory intervention program it had extended its influence into markets to which the antitrust laws did not even apply. Its heavy involvement in the deregulation movement gave it a voice on a variety of economic policy issues in higher executive branch levels. The Division continued to maintain an active litigation program, but its litigation decisions were governed more by economic analysis than by existing legal rules. The Division spoke as much of competition policy,[60] which it described in economic terms, as it did of "the law." Movement away from the "law enforcement" model accelerated during the Reagan administration, with a more pronouncedly regulatory stance taking its place.

As the Reagan administration took office, a number of factors suggested further changes in the Division's posture and methods. Among these were the following. First, in a series of decisions beginning with *Continental T.V., Inc. v. GTE-Sylvania, Inc.*,[61] the Supreme Court has virtually abandoned the "individual rights" approach to antitrust, and relied instead upon an economic analysis of efficiency effects. Lower courts have fol-

---

60 *See* Kauper, *supra* note 27, at 26–28.

61 433 U.S. 36 (1977). For succeeding cases relying on efficiency analysis *see* Broadcast Music, Inc. v. Columbia Broadcasting Sys., 441 U.S. 1 (1979); NCAA v. Board of Regents, 468 U.S. 85 (1984); Jefferson Parish Hosp. District No. 2 v. Hyde, 466 U.S. 2 (1984); Northwest Wholesale Stationers, Inc. v. Pacific Stationery & Printing Co., 472 U.S. 284 (1985); Business Electronics Co. v. Sharp Electronics Co., 108 S. Ct 1515 (1988).

lowed suit.[62] As a result of this movement, which began in the courts well before 1980, the Division's economics-based enforcement policy was more in accord with existing precedent. The divergence between the Division and judicially formulated rules was narrowing, not widening.

Second, private litigation was being gradually impeded not only by a redirection of substantive antitrust policy toward consumer welfare analysis, but also by the decision in *Illinois Brick v. Illinois*,[63] the requirement of "antitrust injury,"[64] and more restrictive views on standing generally.[65] Taken in conjunction, these two factors suggested a weakening in the role played by private enforcement. The numbers of private cases filed flattened out and then declined slightly.[66] The Division's role was correspondingly strengthened. Its enforcement policies, however strongly opposed by members of Congress[67] and private parties,

---

62 *See, e.g.*, Rothery Storage & Van Lines, Inc. v. Atlas Van Lines, Inc., 792 F.2d 210 (D.C. Cir. 1986), *cert. denied*, 107 S. Ct. 880 (1987); Vogel v. American Society of Appraisers, 744 F.2d 598 (7th Cir. 1984); Cowley v. Braden Industries, Inc., 613 F.2d 751 (9th Cir.), *cert. denied*, 446 U.S. 765 (1980).

63 431 U.S. 720 (1977) (indirect purchasers from violator may not maintain suit for damages).

64 *See* Brunswick Corp. v. Pueblo Bowl-O-Mat, Inc., 429 U.S. 477 (1977); Cargill, Inc. v. Monfort of Colorado, Inc., 479 U.S. 104 (1986).

65 *See, e.g.*, Solinger v. A&M Records, Inc., 718 F.2d 298 (9th Cir. 1983), interpreting the decision in Associated General Contractors of California v. California State Council of Carpenters, 459 U.S. 519 (1983) as a retreat from earlier, more expansive concepts of standing. *Compare* Crimpers Promotions, Inc. v. Home Box Office, Inc., 724 F.2d 290 (2d Cir. 1983), *cert. denied*, 467 U.S. 1252 (1984).

66 *See* Salop & White, *supra* note 33, at 1002.

67 Congress could, of course, change the Division's enforcement policies through enactment of substantive legislation or, as it has done in recent years, through the denial of funds for particular purposes. In 1983, for example, the Division's appropriation did not permit the Division to use funds for any activities directed against the per se rule

were more likely to have normative effects as the likelihood of successful private challenges lessened.

Third, the Division's movement away from the law enforcement model, and toward a more direct regulatory role, had already been underway for some time, particularly with respect to mergers. The stage for the 1982 and 1984 Merger Guidelines[68] was already set with the 1968 Merger Guidelines, the Division's business review procedure and, in a broader sense, the Division's longstanding policy of issuing policy statements in order to clarify and give guidance concerning enforcement policy. The Division's regulatory stance concerning mergers was strengthened by the 1976 enactment of the premerger notification requirements of the Hart-Scott-Rodino Act.[69] Premerger notification, requiring submission of data in advance of acquisition, resembles the notification and prescreening requirements common to regulatory bodies.[70] By establishing close contact and identification of areas of concern well in advance of closing, it virtually invites negotiation as the method for conforming the acquisition to the Division's standards.[71]

---

against vertical price-fixing. Departments of Commerce, Justice, and State, the Judiciary and Related Agencies Appropriation Act, 1984, Pub. L. No. 98-166, § 501, 97 Stat. 1071 (1983). This provision prevented the Division from presenting oral argument in Monsanto Co. v. Spray-Rite Service Corp., 465 U.S. 752 (1984), urging that the per se rule be overturned. Legislation enacted in 1985 contains a similar prohibition, and further states the sense of the Congress that the Division's 1985 Vertical Restraints Guidelines do not accurately express federal antitrust principles or congressional intent, should not be treated by courts as binding or persuasive, and should be recalled by the Attorney General. Departments of Commerce, Justice, and State, the Judiciary and Related Agencies Appropriation Act, 1986, Pub. L. No. 99-180, § 605, 99 Stat. 1136 (1985).

68 The 1982 and 1984 Merger Guidelines are *reprinted in* 4 Trade Reg. Rep. (CCH) ¶¶ 13,102, 13,103.

69 Pub. Law No. 94-435, § 201, 90 Stat. 1383 (1976) (adding a new § 7A to the Clayton Act) (codified at 15 U.S.C. § 18a (1982)).

70 For a detailed discussion *see* Sullivan, *supra* note 39, at 1022–24.

71 *Id.* at 1034–35.

Fourth, the Division's growing involvement in regulatory processes and executive branch economic policy making, contributed to the perception that the Division's mission was not simply law enforcement but the implementation of competition policy. Its activities in regulated markets were not themselves regulatory. It functioned as an advocate, not as a regulator. But participation in economic policy making unbounded by the substantive and procedural limitations of the Sherman and Clayton Acts has changed the way the Division thinks of itself, and has encouraged a reexamination of its role.

The Division's leadership in the 1980's took office committed to an antitrust policy based on the single goal of economic efficiency, to the continuing development of the Division's capability for economic analysis and to the use of its resources as an affirmative force in assuring that antitrust doctrine conformed to that goal.[72] Further change in the Division's role and operations was inevitable.

In criminal matters the Division today continues to function as a traditional prosecutor. But in other matters, and particularly with respect to mergers, the Division more closely resembles a regulatory agency, with administrative "rules" and processes that seldom involve litigation. There are in effect two Divisions. One, the criminal prosecutor, handles price-fixing and bid-rigging cases, utilizing detective work, grand juries, indictments, criminal trials and jail sentences. These activities are fully in accord with better than 50 years of existing precedent. Economic analysis plays virtually no role with respect to criminal matters, and the Division exercises little discretion in determining whether cases should be brought. The other Division, which handles mergers and a variety of other restraints, regulatory interventions and legislative issues, has little in common with the first. Litigation is uncommon, although the threat of litigation continues to be the Division's ultimate sanction. Decisions are made pursuant to

---

[72] *See* Address of Attorney General William French Smith at the Annual Meeting of the District of Columbia Bar, June 24, 1981, *reprinted in* [1969–1983 Transfer Binder, Current Comment], Trade Reg. Rep. (CCH) ¶ 50,430.

published guidelines, which retain a broad range of discretion to proceed on the basis of economic analysis in individual cases. Procedures are informal, relying heavily on negotiation to resolve disputes. The Division, in true regulatory fashion, has taken further steps to control and minimize private litigation that threatens its view of appropriate antitrust rules. Its guidelines enforcement policy have regained some of the authoritativeness of earlier years, giving it significant regulatory control over a number of transactions.

The Division's merger enforcement policies provide the best example. The Hart-Scott-Rodino premerger notification requirement has become a kind of informal screening process of a type familiar to a number of regulatory bodies. The process begins with filing of the prescribed "notification." Absent some preliminary indication from the Division that the proposed merger may present a significant competitive issue, an indication typically reflected in a "second request" for information, the merger is generally taken to be legitimate (in the sense that the Division will not take the matter to court). If Division concern about the transaction is expressed, a process of negotiation begins. Such negotiations are likely to start with the question of whether the merger actually poses a significant threat to competition. To this point, the process would be familiar to any law enforcement agency. Discussions between prosecutors and counsel for defendants about whether the law has been broken are commonplace. They also occur regularly in the Division's handling of criminal prosecutions. Even in this early stage of discussion, however, the Division's merger enforcement program differs from that of the typical law enforcement agency in one significant respect. Discussion is bounded by the Division's Merger Guidelines, with scant attention paid to "the law" as embodied in precedent.[73] The standards are those of the Division, not of the courts, and the focus is on economic analysis more than the state of the law. Given the practical normative effect of a decision by the Division not to proceed against a merger, the Guidelines' standards are in

---

73 Except, of course, to the extent the Guidelines themselves embody such precedent.

fact the operative rules of the game. This part of the process is not new. The Division has discussed competitive issues with the parties in advance, and has done so in the context of published guidelines, for the past two decades. But it is now more common, if for no other reason than the greater Division involvement required as a practical matter by the premerger notification process.

The next step in the process begins once it is clear that the Division believes some element of the merger is anticompetitive. Under the "fix it first" procedure employed in recent years, the Division notifies the parties of the specific anticompetitive effects of the merger, and of ways in which the transactions could be restructured to eliminate the problem. Negotiations will now focus on restructuring that will satisfy the Division's concerns. If the merger is restructured in a manner acceptable to the Division prior to consummation, no action is filed and the parties are free to proceed with the restructured merger. If the restructuring cannot be satisfactorily achieved before consummation, an agreement to do so after consummation may be embodied in a consent decree. A complaint charging that the merger violates section 7 and the consent decree are filed simultaneously, and the merger is permitted to proceed.[74]

The "fix it first" policy is not unprecedented. The Division has consistently recognized that if the parties restructure to eliminate all competitive issues prior to closing, there is no reason to seek an injunction. There is simply nothing to enjoin. The simultaneous filing of a complaint and negotiated consent decree is a practice referred to in earlier days as "pre-filing," employed with some frequency in the late 1960's and early 1970's (although the practice was terminated in 1974). The "fix it first" policy has been pursued more aggressively since 1980, and has now become

---

74 The "fix it first" policy is discussed in detail in Sullivan, *supra* note 39, at 1034–40. For the current version, *see* Rule, *Merger Enforcement Policy: Protecting the Consumer*, 56 ANTITRUST LAW J. 739, 745–46, (1987). For examples *see* United States v. LTV Corp., 1984-2 Trade Cas. (CCH) ¶ 66,235 (D.C. Cir. 1984); United States v. Stroh Brewery Co., 1982-2 Trade Cas. (CCH) ¶ 65,627 (D.D.C. 1983).

a relatively routine process. Taken together with the prescreening process, the process now resembles a regularized form of regulation through negotiation.

The 1982 and 1984 Merger Guidelines have also contributed to this regulatory process. The Guidelines establish three horizontal merger zones, depending upon the structure of the market in which the merger takes place. These zones are based upon the numerical standards of the Herfindahl-Hirschman index. At the low end is the "safe harbor," the zone in which the Division "will not challenge mergers . . . except in extraordinary circumstances."[75] At the high end is the zone in which challenge is "likely."[76] In the broad middle range, the decision to challenge is based upon a complex weighing of a large number of economic factors. The 1982 and 1984 Guidelines are phrased entirely in terms of economic analysis. As I have stated elsewhere, "the Guidelines read, in places, more like a chapter in an industrial organization economics treatise than a simple set of guiding principles."[77] This emphasis on economic policy, and the phrasing of standards in terms neither previously used nor recognized by the courts, is itself a manifestation of the degree to which the Division has departed from the simple "law enforcement" model.

The regulatory effects of these Guidelines vary depending upon the zone in which a given merger falls. The "safe harbor" provisions are in practical effect normative, unless there is some significant risk of private challenge. Even if courts are willing to apply a different standard, there is no one to present the case to them.[78] The upper zone is normative in a different sense. A

---

[75] U.S. Dept. of Justice Merger Guidelines, 49 Fed. Reg. 26,823 (1984) § 3.11(a), *reprinted in* 4 Trade Reg. Rep. ¶ 13,103.

[76] *Id.* at § 3.11(c).

[77] Kauper, *supra* note 47, at 508.

[78] Cargill, Inc. v. Monfort of Colorado, Inc., 479 U.S. 104 (1986) severely curtails the ability of competitors to challenge mergers of two other competitors, although it does not entirely eliminate the possibility. *See* Tasty Baking Co. v. Ralston Purina Inc., 653 F. Supp. 1250 (E.D.

decision by the Division to file suit is often outcome determinative. The merger may well be abandoned. If it is not, and suit is filed, the courts have the opportunity to apply standards that differ significantly from those of the Division. But the authoritativeness of the upper level standard will increase if the courts over time adopt the Division's standards as their own. This now seems to be occurring.[79] As a practical matter, such litigated cases begin to resemble actions to review regulatory agency rulings, with a presumption in the Division's favor.[80]

For mergers in the middle zone the Guidelines have a different effect. The Division retains a broad range of discretion in such cases. I have previously noted that "It would not be far off the mark to characterize the horizontal merger provisions as guidelines for the high and low ends, with an essay in the middle."[81] Today the Guidelines at high and low ends more closely resemble governing rules; in the middle zone, however, the Guidelines remain "an invitation to talk, with some advance indication of the agenda."[82] The Guidelines in middle and upper zone cases provide the foundation for negotiation over restructuring of

---

Pa. 1987). There are at least serious questions whether targets of hostile takeovers may maintain suit under section 7. *See* H.H. Robertson Co. v. Guardian Industries Corp., 1986 Trade Cas. (CCH) ¶ 66,911 (3d Cir.) (opinion withdrawn and case settled); Burlington Industries, Inc. v. Edelman, 666 F. Supp. 799 (M.D.N.C. 1987). While customers may apparently challenge mergers of their suppliers, such actions seem highly unlikely. And, as already noted, the FTC is not likely to proceed where the Antitrust Division has investigated and decided that a challenge is inappropriate.

79 *See, e.g.*, FTC v. PPG Industries, Inc., 798 F.2d 1500 (D.C. Cir. 1986).

80 The Division may also expect to lose cases when courts use the standards of its own guidelines against it, just as other regulatory bodies may lose in court when their own rules have not been met. *See* United States v. Waste Management, Inc., 743 F.2d 976 (2d Cir. 1984).

81 Kauper, *supra* note 47, at 513.

82 *Id.*

transactions. They are an integral part of a highly regulatory structure.

The Division's role with respect to civil matters other than mergers reflects some of these same tendencies, albeit to a lesser degree. It has issued guidelines for international operations[83] and research and development joint ventures.[84] Like the Merger Guidelines, the latter are an exercise in economic analysis. The International Guidelines rely more on legal precedent, but they are soon to be replaced by a revised version that will undoubtedly more closely resemble the other guidelines of the 1980's. The Research and Development Guidelines, now repudiated,[85] could have had a substantial standard-setting impact because of the absence of judicial precedent dealing with research joint ventures. Private litigation challenging such ventures is highly unlikely, not only because of increasing barriers with respect to standing and antitrust injury, but because of the elimination of the added incentive of trebling in cases involving such ventures.[86]

As the Division offers more guidance, through guidelines, business review letters and less formal public pronouncements, its regulatory stance increases, not just with respect to mergers but in other areas as well. The normative quality of its pronouncements is of course dependent on the inability and unwillingness of either the FTC or private litigants successfully to attack conduct that

---

83 U.S. DEPARTMENT OF JUSTICE, ANTITRUST ENFORCEMENT GUIDELINES FOR INTERNATIONAL OPERATIONS (1988), *reprinted in* 4 Trade Reg. Rep. (CCH) ¶ 13,109.

84 U.S. DEPARTMENT OF JUSTICE, ANTITRUST GUIDE CONCERNING RESEARCH JOINT VENTURES, *reprinted in* No. 466, Part II, Trade Reg. Rep. (CCH) (December 10, 1980).

85 *See* Rule, *The Administration's Views on Joint Ventures*, 54 ANTITRUST LAW J. 1121, 1129 (1985).

86 The National Cooperative Research Act of 1984, Pub. L. No. 98-462, 98 Stat. 1815 (1984) (codified at 15 U.S.C. §§ 4301–05 (Supp. IV 1986)) limits plaintiffs challenging research joint ventures notified to federal enforcement agencies to single damages. One effect is to place the Division more firmly in control of antitrust policies concerning such ventures.

the Division finds unobjectionable. Firms will not rely on the Division's standards if doing so invites a risk of liability. But the FTC's policy views have in recent years been remarkably similar to those of the Division.[87] And private litigants have found the going increasingly difficult in recent years, except in cases where their positions are in accord with those of the Division. Standing and procedural barriers have made private litigation more difficult even in cases where judicial doctrine has *not* been in accord with Division policy. And while the courts have not fully embraced the views of the Division, they have moved, with a few notable exceptions, much closer to them. The Division's standards are more likely to be seen as normative if they accord with established doctrine.

The most significant threat to the Division's ability to regulate remains the threat of private litigation. And in true regulatory fashion, the Division of the 1980's has actively sought to curtail this threat, except where private litigation reinforces Division policies. The Division embarked on a much publicized program of amicus participation in the lower courts, often siding with defendants.[88] Appearing as amicus, the Division has not only urged the courts to adopt substantive doctrine in accord with its own views,[89] but to tighten standing and similar rules to the detriment of private plaintiffs.[90] Its Vertical Restraints Guide-

---

87 For example, the FTC Statement Concerning Horizontal Mergers (June 14, 1982) (*reprinted in* 4 Trade Reg. Rep. (CCH) § 13,200), issued the same day as the Justice Department's 1982 Merger Guidelines, is in most respects similar to those guidelines. More recently, the FTC has appeared to embrace the Department's 1984 Merger Guidelines. *See, e.g.*, Weyerhaeuser Co., 3 Trade Reg. Rep. (CCH) § 22,315 (1985).

88 *See* Address of Attorney General William French Smith, *supra* note 72.

89 *See, e.g.*, Kreuzer v. American Academy of Periodontology, 735 F.2d 1479 (D.C. Cir. 1984).

90 *See, e.g.*, Cargill, Inc. v. Monfort of Colorado, Inc., 479 U.S. 104 (1986).

lines,[91] which contain standards significantly different from established doctrine,[92] are less an attempt to provide guidance than an effort to influence the reshaping of doctrine in cases in which the Division is not a party.[93] The Division has also sought legislation to eliminate treble damages, and thus reduce the incentives for private litigation, in all cases except those brought by customers seeking recovery of overcharges.[94] The cases in which treble damages would still be allowed are those involving cartels or other output-restricting conduct, cases that supplement the Division's own enforcement policies. These actions go well beyond efforts to persuade the courts that the substantive positions taken by private litigants are wrong. The Division has sought to curtail the ability of such litigants to have their views heard at all.

The Division's amicus position in *Cargill, Inc. v. Monfort of Colorado, Inc.*,[95] is a classic example of its efforts to maintain a firm grip on antitrust policy, in this instance with respect to mergers. In *Monfort*, the Division urged the Court to hold that competitors lacked standing to challenge horizontal mergers

---

91 UNITED STATES DEP'T OF JUSTICE GUIDELINES ON VERTICAL DISTRIBUTION RESTRAINTS (January 23, 1985) (*reprinted in* 4 Trade Reg. Rep. (CCH) ¶ 13,105).

92 The extent to which the Vertical Distribution Restraints Guidelines vary from existing doctrine is discussed at length in *Panel Discussion, Vertical Restraints Guidelines*, 54 ANTITRUST L.J. 319 (1985). *See also* H.R. REP. No. 99-399, 99th Cong., 1st Sess. 12–16 (1985).

93 "The Committee views [the Vertical Restraints Guidelines] more in the nature of an amicus brief 'form book,' designed primarily to influence courts in private cases to which the Division is not a party and with the further intended effect of reducing the incidence of such cases in the future. The Committee also fails to see the need for a clarification of the Division's enforcement intentions in an area where it has unmistakably shown its intention not to enforce the law during the past five years." H.R. REP. No. 99-399, *supra* note 92, at 11. *See also* Slater, *supra* note 92, at 326.

94 *See* proposed Antitrust Remedies Improvement Act, S. 2162 & H.R. 4250, 99th Cong., 2d Sess. (1986). The bill would also permit recovery of undercharges by suppliers.

95 479 U.S. 104 (1986).

among other firms in the same market. Had the Court agreed (it did not), attacks on mergers by private parties would effectively have come to an end; customers would seldom have sufficient interest to sue. Except for those cases being handled by the FTC, the Division would have been left in full regulatory control of mergers, in the sense that its decision *not* to proceed would have been final.

The Division's programs to influence the outcome of private actions and to reshape the private remedy itself have not been the result of any openly stated desire to exert a greater control over antitrust policy. There are other sound reasons for curtailing the remedy in some cases, reasons that the Division has regularly advanced.[96] Litigation is costly, and the threat of litigation, whether successful or not, deters firms from conduct that may be desirable. Private actions brought by competitors may protect inefficiency, and be an effective anticompetitive weapon. The Division also honestly believes that its own enforcement policy is wise, and that actions not in accord with it are unsound. But whether the Division's actions reflect a conscious effort to strengthen its regulatory position (and my own experience suggests that the Division is not unconscious to what it is doing), that has been the effect. It is a form of behavior familiar to any student of regulatory agencies.

IV. Conclusion

The Division of today is not the Division of the 1930's. There is no reason why it should be. Changes in doctrine, and in the public perception of what antitrust is meant to be, have brought changes in the roles of all of the institutions of antitrust. These institutions are interrelated, and the roles of each, including the Division, change correspondingly over time.

The Division today bears some resemblance to the antitrust operations of the Justice Department 80 years ago. With no FTC in existence, and private litigation uncommon, the Department

---

96 *See* Ginsburg, *supra* note 58, at 1283–84; Kauper, *supra* note 27, at 27–28.

sat firmly astride antitrust policy. Courts might check Department excesses in cases it filed, but its decisions not to file, its statements concerning what was not in its view unlawful, were as a practical matter controlling. The Division of the 1980's was in a similar position, particularly with respect to mergers. It had regained much of the control over antitrust policy that it lost during the era of the Warren Court and the years immediately following.

In another sense, however, the Division has departed from the role of its earlier counterparts. Once operated pursuant to a "law enforcement" model, with the exercise of discretion bounded by consideration of factors already judicially recognized, the Division has moved steadily into a more regulatory posture, and has expanded its sphere of influence into markets not subject to the antitrust laws at all. Its economics-based competition policy, which has evolved over decades, has often rested uneasily alongside established precedent, suggesting to many an unwillingness to enforce the law.[97] Today the Division exercises discretion based as much on its perception of sound economic policy as on governing legal standards, in a manner similar to that of regulatory bodies charged with implementing broad public-interest standards. The use of guidelines, prescreening procedures, and negotiations in lieu of litigation also bears a strong resemblance to the rule-making and related procedures employed by such agencies.[98]

---

97 *See, e.g.*, Litvack, *Government Antitrust Policy: Theory Versus Practice and the Role of the Antitrust Division*, 60 TEX. L. REV. 649, 651–52 (1982) (". . . the Division recognizes no obligation to enforce the law's established prohibitions"). For a detailed response, *see* Baxter, *Separation of Powers, Prosecutorial Discretion, and the "Common Law" Nature of Antitrust Law*, 60 TEX. L. REV. 661 (1982). *Compare* Kauper, *supra* note 27, at 9–13.

98 The same point is made with respect to merger policy in greater detail in Sullivan, *supra* note 39, at 1025–44. He concludes that "the Antitrust Division has become, at least in a de facto sense, an economic regulator of mergers." *Id.* at 1043–44, a conclusion with which I agree. But I believe the same may be said of the Division's treatment of virtually all civil matters, although merger policy is the best example.

This is all, of course, a matter of degree. Every law enforcement agency is in a sense a regulator, and every regulatory body may be said to enforce the law. The regulatory/law enforcement dichotomy is not sharp. And at any given moment, the Division may be more on one side of the line than the other. The Division's current handling of criminal matters conforms closely to the traditional law enforcement model. Even its merger policy, which most closely resembles direct regulation, cannot be divorced from law enforcement. Nevertheless, the dichotomy is a useful way of describing changes in the way the Division does its business, and of trends over a long period of time.[99]

Whether the changes in the Division's role, influence and methods that I have described in very broad terms are for the good, and whether further, more dramatic changes should be made with respect to the Division and antitrust's other institutions, are the hard questions. Answers are likely to turn on one's views about the Division's enforcement policies. Those opposed to the Division's policies would prefer to see its influence diminished, and are likely to press for strengthening of the treble damage remedy. To those who applaud these policies, a further weakening of the private remedy is the logical next step. But at least some evaluation of the Division's role should be possible without assessment of the soundness of its substantive views. Whether the Division now makes better informed decisions, and operates in an efficient manner, for example, are issues that do not turn on whether its substantive policies are right or wrong.

Some of these changes in the Division's operations have been inevitable, a necessary response to shifts in doctrine and the increasing emphasis in the formulation of doctrine on economic analysis. The economics approach to antitrust does not provide simple rules and ready answers. Through a process built upon

---

99 To compare the Division's processes to those of other regulatory bodies is not of course to suggest that the Division is engaged in direct economic regulation of the sort typified by control of output, prices or entry. The Division has strenuously resisted such a role, particularly in recent years.

guidelines and negotiated solutions, the Division has mitigated the uncertainty inherent in this approach. Moreover, this "regulatory" process is likely to be better adapted to evaluation of a wide range of economic factors than litigation. If the consumer welfare model continues to dominate antitrust thinking, the Division's regulatory methods will continue (except in criminal cases).

Continued reliance on the consumer welfare model is not itself inevitable. But this approach is now too well-ingrained in judicially formulated doctrine to be changed by the Division itself. Whether lawyers like it or not, economics is here to stay. The Division, of course, has a role to play in shaping doctrine. Much of the criticism of the Division in recent years rests on its attempts to do so, bringing charges that it has failed to execute the law. But to the degree the Division is persuasive, its views become the law that it is obligated to enforce. The gap between its policies and established doctrine narrows, and perhaps disappears, and it is once again enforcing the "law." This leadership role is appropriate to the development of a well-informed antitrust policy, even though the Division can hardly be expected to enthusiastically enforce rules that it is seeking to change. For the foreseeable future, however, it is unlikely that the Division will seek to redirect antitrust policy back in the direction of the more populist-oriented policies of the 1960's. Nor would it be likely to succeed if it tried.

The Division's regulatory posture, particularly with respect to mergers, has not only been dictated by the substance of its enforcement policies and established doctrine, but has also resulted in a more rapid and efficient resolution of disputes over particular transactions. Guidelines and carefully defined policy statements may provide deterrence without any further elaboration. Negotiated settlements, and other informal methods of dispute resolutions, have lessened the costs of delay and saved resources, including judicial resources. Antitrust litigation is particularly costly and time consuming. Its avoidance frees judicial resources to handle matters which cannot be effectively resolved through other means (including antitrust cases). If this efficiency is attained without impairing the reliability and accuracy of the decisions to be made, and without threatening the public's confidence in the process, it is to be applauded.[100]

Today the Division's enforcement decisions are undoubtedly better informed than its decisions in the past. Expansion of its civil investigative demand authority[101] and creation of the premerger notification requirements in 1976 gave the Division access to far more information upon which to base its decisions. The Economic Policy Office has institutionalized the consideration of economic factors, and provided the Division with a great deal of economic expertise. For the same reasons, the Division's decisions are at least as well-informed as those of the judiciary. Given the limitations of the judicial process, I believe the Division is capable of exceeding the judiciary in the quality of decision making. The question remains whether the Division will make decisions in the highly professional way which has characterized its decisions in the past. The critical issue is the integrity of the process, and the public's faith in it.

The Division's current posture and influence may promote efficiency and enhance the quality of antitrust decision making, but may also be abused. In the past, the private remedy served to check Division policy making when it departed too far from established norms. But this check has been weakened. As a result, the Division is freer to make regulatory decisions in accord with its own perceptions of sound policy, or even on purely political grounds. The public is now more dependent on the Division's own judgments, and upon its willingness to keep the exercise of its discretion within the bounds of legislative intention and established doctrine. At the same time, as the Division's policies move further in the direction of economic policy making, its ability to make professional judgments free from outside inter-

---

100 *See* Sullivan, *supra* note 39, at 1046–53.

101 In the Hart-Scott-Rodino Act, Pub. L. No. 94-435, §§ 101–104, 90 Stat. 1383 (1976) (codified at 15 U.S.C. §§ 1311–1314 (1982)), the Division's authority to compel production of information in civil matters through issuance of a civil investigative demand was expanded to include depositions and interrogatories from both targets and non-targets of investigations.

vention is jeopardized. In the past, those both within and without government who sought to influence Division decisions were deterred from doing so by the perception that it was simply a law enforcement agency. That perception was a shield against intrusion, a shield that has been weakened. If the Division is seen as an economic policy maker, other agencies with a legitimate interest in national economic policy are more likely to intervene, and to insist that Division programs be coordinated with their own.[102] And once the shield is lowered, illegitimate partisan intervention may also increase, jeopardizing public confidence.[103] Thus, as the Division's independence has been strengthened through the weakening of the private remedy, it may be lessened through direct outside intervention in its operations. Only time will tell whether this danger is real. Whether such intervention occurs will depend upon the Division's stature within the executive branch. As I have said elsewhere, "its expertise, to the extent it exists, must provide its protection."[104]

There is another, more severe risk in the Division's current posture. While consumer welfare analysis is currently in the ascendancy, the "individual rights" approach of the 1960's remains waiting in the wings. It has strong supporters and considerable political appeal. In the past, the private remedy has been the vehicle for presentation of this point of view, even when the Division found such cases groundless. Courts were to some degree receptive. Today, neither the Division nor the courts are likely to find claims based on values other than efficiency meritorious. With more restrictive views of standing and antitrust injury, success is even less likely. The Division's efforts to further curtail treble damage actions add to the frustration of those advocating this point of view. In an antitrust world of the Division's making, such claims ought not be recognized and

---

102 *See* Kauper, *supra* note 27, at 20–26; Kauper, *supra* note 22, at 132.

103 *See* references in note 102, *supra*. Such intervention may also jeopardize continuity in the Division's enforcement programs.

104 Kauper, *supra* note 27, at 29.

should simply go away. The danger is that they will instead be brought in a different forum, and with different actors.

This is now beginning to happen. State attorneys general are becoming more active participants in the antitrust system. Their views, reflected *inter alia* in their own merger and vertical restraints guidelines,[105] often conflict sharply with those of the Division. They are the inheritors of the more populist strand of the antitrust tradition. Their discontent extends not only to the substance of the Division's policies (and to the corresponding changes in judicial doctrine), but to its regulatory posture as well.[106] If their enforcement efforts are confined to federal court actions under the Sherman and Clayton Acts, they may threaten the Division's control of merger policy and impair its influence in a variety of other areas but pose little danger to a uniform, federal antitrust policy. The federal judiciary will remain the standard setter.

The more ominous development is the resurgence in actions initiated by both state attorneys general and private parties under state antitrust laws.[107] Born of the same frustrations, such actions could result in a second-level antitrust system, a system in which results may vary from state to state. This "backlash" is not

---

105 Horizontal Merger Guidelines of the National Association of Attorneys General (March 10, 1987) *reprinted in* 4 Trade Reg. Rep. (CCH) ¶ 13,405; National Association of Attorneys General Vertical Restraints Guidelines (December 4, 1985) (*reprinted in* 4 Trade Reg. Rep. (CCH) ¶ 13,400).

106 *See* Constantine, *Current Antitrust Enforcement Initiatives by State Attorneys General*, 56 ANTITRUST LAW J. 111, 120 (1987).

107 For a description of this renewed effort by state attorneys general under both federal and state law *see id.* at 111–17. Private litigants are turning to use of state antitrust laws as a means of avoiding federal court rulings they view as unduly restrictive. For a particularly clear example, *see* Louisiana Power & Light Co. v. United Gas Pipe Line Co., 493 So. 2d 1149 (La. 1986), concluding that contrary to the federal decision in Copperweld Corp. v. Independence Tube Corp., 467 U.S. 752 (1984), a parent and wholly owned subsidiary are legally capable of conspiring under Louisiana's state antitrust statute.

entirely the result of actions of the Division; it presumably would not occur if federal courts were not following a similar course. But the Division policies have contributed significantly to it. Preemption doctrine may work to control this development,[108] but there is a real risk that the uniform national antitrust policy that has evolved over the past century could be seriously disrupted.

The Division's role on the antitrust stage has evolved over decades. It is better informed, and its regulatory methods are more efficient, than in the past. The quality of its decisions has been substantially enhanced. Through its advocacy of a broad national competition policy, it has forced a reexamination of regulatory schemes that have created and preserved monopoly power. So, too, it has been an effective advocate of doctrinal reform. On the debit side, the Division now seems more vulnerable to outside intervention. Its enforcement policies and efforts to curtail private litigation have contributed to the resurgence of state antitrust statutes, although doctrinal changes have been a more significant factor.

What does the Division's history suggest for its future? Presumably the Division's role will continue to shift with doctrine, and with the roles of antitrust's other institutions. A resurrection of the "individual rights" approach to antitrust, for example, would significantly weaken the Division's influence. Absent amendment of the Sherman Act or the passage of new substantive antitrust legislation, however, major shifts in doctrine over the next decade or two appear highly unlikely. State antitrust actions may complicate the further development of doctrine, but there is no reason to believe that a return to either the doctrine or the Antitrust Division of an earlier day would be an intelligent or foreseeable response. Given an antitrust policy predicated upon economic efficiency, the Division may be expected to continue much as it has over the past decade.

---

108 *But see* California v. ARC American Corp., 109 S. Ct. 1661 (1989) (state antitrust laws permitting recoveries by indirect purchasers preempted by the Sherman Act, as interpreted in Illinois Brick Co. v. Illinois, 431 U.S. 720 (1977)).

Assuming that antitrust of the next several decades continues to be dominated by economic analysis, with little use of relatively simple per se rules, should there be further changes made in its institutions? Could complex economic decisions be made more wisely in another way, or by another institution? The Division has accommodated itself to changing antitrust doctrine well. But could it be done better?

Several alternative models might be considered. The Division's criminal prosecution activity presumably must remain with the Justice Department.[109] But responsibility for criminal antitrust actions could be given to United States attorneys, who handle most federal criminal prosecutions, or with a unit of the Criminal Division (perhaps even an Antitrust Section within this Division). Criminal antitrust actions involve detective work and the normal criminal processes. Little detailed economic analysis or expertise is required. While it is logical to keep responsibility for both civil and criminal actions together if the civil responsibility is to be in the Justice Department at all, the need to retain criminal authority in the Department ought not prevent consideration of transferring civil responsibility to some other body.

In 1914 Congress created the Federal Trade Commission, in part in the belief that complex economic issues could be more efficiently and expertly resolved through administrative rather than judicial processes. During the years since, the overlapping jurisdiction of the FTC and Justice has been examined and reexamined, with many urging that the FTC's antitrust jurisdiction be transferred to the Antitrust Division.[110] The critical issue

---

109 With minor exceptions (such as special prosecutors), the Justice Department alone has authority to appear before grand juries, sign indictments and, in general, to conduct criminal trials.

110 *See, e.g.*, Gellhorn, *Distinguished Alumni Lecture—Regulatory Reform and the Federal Trade Commission's Antitrust Jurisdiction*, 49 Tenn. L. Rev. 471 (1982); Roll, *Dual Enforcement of the Antitrust Laws by the Department of Justice and the FTC: The Liaison Procedure*, 31 Bus. Lawyer 2075, 2082 (1976); Posner, *The Federal Trade Commission*, 37 U. Chi. L. Rev. 47 (1969) (urging that FTC be abolished altogether).

in this debate has been the utility of section 5 of the Federal Trade Commission Act, a provision thought by many, including the Congress that enacted it, to be too undefined for enforcement through judicial processes.[111] The time may now have come to consider the transfer of the Division's antitrust jurisdiction, other than its criminal jurisdiction, to the FTC.

The wisdom of transferring all government civil antitrust responsibility to the FTC, or of transferring the civil responsibility of both the Division and the FTC to a new agency, turns on a comparison of the ability of judicial and administrative processes to resolve complex issues accurately and efficiently, and upon the desirability of keeping the initial decision-making authority in the hands of generalists. These questions are well beyond the scope of this article. But it should be noted that given the Division's current regulatory stance, particularly with respect to mergers, the judicial process has already been substantially displaced. The real question, then, may be whether the Division's highly informal internal procedures should be replaced with a somewhat more formal administrative process.

In the short run, these are purely academic questions. The executive branch is not likely to surrender the influence over antitrust policy that it can currently exert through the Justice Department. Few believe that the FTC's procedures have been superior to those of courts in antitrust cases. On the face of it, there is little reason to believe that a new antitrust agency would perform any better. For the foreseeable future, then, the Division will continue on its present course. Its methods will continue to evolve, and its influence may wax and wane. But it will remain on stage, if not in the central role at least as the leading character actor.

---

111 *See* Atlantic Refining Co. v. FTC, 381 U.S. 357, 367 (1965); Gellhorn, *supra* note 110, at 503. *See generally* R. CUSHMAN, THE INDEPENDENT REGULATORY COMMISSIONS 177–213 (1941).

15
Cycles of antitrust zeal: predictability?

BY LOUIS B. SCHWARTZ*

The idea of cycles of antitrust vitality is obvious, attractive, and dubious. One knows in a general way that antitrust languished in the twenties, nearly expired under NRA in the early thirties, experienced an extraordinary resuscitation under Thurman Arnold and Walton Hamilton in the Antitrust Division in the late thirties, was put in cold storage during World War II, etc. It is also a commonplace belief that we were at a zenith in the sixties in Chief Justice Warren's era, and that we have been at a nadir under the Burger-Rehnquist Court and the Reagan administration. There is talk of a turnaround ahead. Professor Eleanor Fox writes—if only ironically—of "The Phoenix Ris[ing] From Its Ashes," after "The Great Calm."[1]

---

* Professor of Law, University of California, Hastings College of the Law, Emeritus Benjamin Franklin and University Professor of Law, University of Pennsylvania.

AUTHOR'S NOTE: *I am indebted, for comments on earlier drafts, to the following colleagues: L. Sullivan; H. Hovenkamp; H. First.*

1 E. Fox, *Antitrust in Its Second Century: The Phoenix Risen From Its Ashes*, 31 ANTITRUST BULL. 383 (1986).

Like a conception of cyclicality in business activity[2] and in history,[3] the notion of periodic revitalization of antitrust has a fascination for reflective minds. It satisfies the human hunger for a perceived order in the chaos. It offers hope to those who want to renew the drive for deconcentration of economic power and elimination of restraints of trade that handicap small business and mulct consumers. Cyclicality would comfort lawyers professionally—not only those whose incomes from prosecuting and defending antitrust suits would be enhanced by an increase in public and private litigation in the field, but also those who would like a firmer rational basis for counseling clients about management decisions valid in today's legal environment but potentially disastrous: after the next election? . . . decades later?[4]

The question is not whether there have been great tides in antitrust enforcement, as there obviously have been, but whether the periodicity of the crests and troughs can be measured with any precision, whether the great waves should be seen as composites of many smaller oscillations that require independent analysis, and whether for prediction purposes account can be taken of major exogenous influences such as wars and fundamental technological change. It is a daunting task. I shall attempt to measure periodicity and isolate the subsets of oscillations that make up the great waves. I disavow forthwith any pretense of power to forecast wars or fundamental technological revolutions. That is not an insignificant concession. It means giving up long-range forecasting. Short-range forecasting, *e.g.*, estimating the antitrust risk of a given management decision during the Reagan presidency or in a successor Republican administration, is too easy to

---

2 W. C. MITCHELL, BUSINESS CYCLES (1927).

3 A. J. TOYNBEE, A STUDY OF HISTORY (12 vols. 1935–1961); A. SCHLESINGER, JR., THE CYCLES OF AMERICAN HISTORY (1986); T. S. KUHN, THE STRUCTURE OF SCIENTIFIC REVOLUTIONS (1962).

4 U.S. v. E.I. Du Pont de Nemours & Co., 353 U.S. 586, 597, 607 (1957) (acquisition of controlling shares invalidated where prejudice to competition exists "at the time of suit").

engage in. Accordingly, the focus of the inquiry becomes "What can a close look at the cyclicality of past antitrust enforcement tell us about probabilities 5 or 10 years hence?" We shall certainly not achieve the reliability of astronomers' predictions of eclipses. Can we do better than the *Farmer's Almanac* on the weather of the future?

I start by dating the crests and troughs of the great waves of antitrust's first century, never losing sight of the fact any such date represents a zone not a point.[5] A plus mark beside a named year, below, indicates a crest in antitrust zeal. A minus indicates a trough.

+ 1890

Although legislative *enactment* of the Sherman Act cannot of course be identified as an *enforcement* peak, it is appropriate to use 1890 as the starting point of our wave analysis since federal enforcement rather than change in substantive law was the chief novelty of the Sherman Act.[6] Federal executive and judicial power was marshaled to confront corporate power which had grown beyond the resistance capabilities of the states. Criminal penalties and treble damage sanctions were added to common law

---

[5] The analysis in this article should be compared with that of Kramer, *The Antitrust Division and the Supreme Court*, 40 VA. L. REV. 433 (1954). Kramer focused on percentages of government victory in cases carried to the Supreme Court, and arrived at five "more or less distinctive periods:" 1890–1898; 1899–1915; 1916–1933; 1934–1948; and 1948 to and beyond the date of his article. 40 VA. L. REV. at 435. He did not try to specify peak and trough years, thus making it difficult to compare his periodicity with mine. *See also* Kramer, *The Supreme Court and Tying Arrangements: Antitrust as History*, 69 MINN. L. REV. 1013 (1985). Flynn, *Monopolization Under the Sherman Act: The Third Wave and Beyond*, 26 ANTITRUST BULL. 1 (1981), considered "waves" or "eruptions" of monopolization litigation under section 2 of the Sherman Act. He identified periods of high activity but without specifying peaks or troughs so that periodicity cannot be quantified.

[6] H. B. THORELLI, THE FEDERAL ANTITRUST POLICY 53, 229 (1955).

civil remedies. It was a high moment in the evolution of "populism," less equivocal than the precursor Interstate Commerce Act of 1887. That Act imposed federal regulation on the railroads, but could be interpreted as a bulwark against more radical state intervention to compel competition or to nationalize.[7]

- 1895

This is the date of the failure of the Sugar Trust case in *United States v. E.C. Knight Co.*, 156 U.S. (1895). Holding that local manufacture was not interstate commerce, the Supreme Court sustained the creation and continued dominance of a single-firm monopoly of 98% of the sugar refining in the country. Chief Justice Fuller's opinion evoked the "economic and political literature" supporting the "clear distinction" between manufacture and commerce, and voiced shock at the notion that uniform nationwide legislation might be made applicable to "production in this vast country with its many different climates and opportunities . . . at the sacrifice of the peculiar advantages . . . of the localities,"[8] merely because the producer intended to market the product interstate. The decision went very far toward reinstating a pre-Sherman decentralized and ineffectual antitrust regime. At approximately the same time, the Court was turning the Sherman Act in an unexpected direction by vindicating its use against unions,[9] thus turning the act to the advantage of the very interests it was to have constrained.

---

7 *See* T. K. McCraw, Prophets of Regulation (1984), at chapter 1: *Adams and the Sunshine Commission*, recounting the career of Charles Francis Adams as proponent of regulatory suppression of competition among railroads.

8 156 U.S. at 15.

9 Loewe v. Lawler, 208 U.S. 274 (1908). Cf. *In re* Debs, 158 U.S. 564 (1895) (Sherman Act relied on, but contempt conviction sustained on broader ground of federal power to prevent obstruction of interstate commerce).

Addyston in 1898 marked the beginning of a turnaround with its resounding affirmation by Taft, a conservative judge later to be Chief Justice, that price conspiracies could not be defended on the ground that noncompetitive pricing, "reasonably" exercised, served the public interest in economic stabilization.[10] In *Northern Securities Co. v. United States*, 193 U.S. 197 (1904), the first Justice Harlan spoke for the majority of the Court in asserting the applicability of the Sherman Act to combinations of competing transcontinental railroads. Holmes' dissent was the voice of Massachusetts oligarchs who for a generation had regulated railroads precisely to restrain competition.[11] "The [Sherman] act says nothing about competition,"[12] observed Holmes, illustrating the myopia that can afflict even venerated "liberal" sages. Given his eminence and persuasive power, Holmes' dissent could have become the charter for unlimited "voluntary" consolidation of industry.

Holmes' opinion was noteworthy also for its reactionary exaltation of state incorporation law over federal antitrust constraints: for him it was enough that the state would have been free to incorporate both railroads as one, thus creating an entity that could not be charged with "combining."[13] He seemed not to realize that antitrust was a limitation of legal rights of every description:[14] "contract" most obviously but also "property,"[15] "patent,"[16] "agency,"[17] "free speech,"[18] to name only a few.

---

10 U.S. v. Addyston Pipe & Steel Co., 87 Fed. 271 (6th Cir. 1898), affirmed with a modification in Addyston Pipe & Steel Co. v. United States, 178 U.S. 211 (1899).

11 *See* McCraw, *supra* note 7.

12 193 U.S. at 403.

13 193 U.S. at 407–409.

14 ". . . the Sherman Law is not only a prohibition against the infliction of a particular type of public injury. It is a limitation of rights . . . which may be pushed to evil consequences. . . ." Stone, J. in U.S. v. Trenton Potteries, 273 U.S. 392, 398 (1927).

15 U.S. v. Terminal Railroad Ass'n, 224 U.S. 383 (1912) (exclusive control of jointly owned "bottleneck" facilities); Gamco, Inc. v.

(*footnotes 16, 17, 18 appear on following page*)

On the other hand, Holmes' reading of Sherman as directed against "ferocious extreme of competition," suppression of rivals rather than union of competitors,[19] contained the seed of the doctrine, later much developed by antitrust activists, that "unfair" competitive tactics are a concern of antitrust whatever the state of competition in the relevant markets. That doctrine would be excoriated by antitrust conservatives on the ground that it "protects competitors not competition." Be that as it may, Harlan's opinion for the Court in *Northern Securities* is a harbinger of the new springtime of antitrust to which I assign the central date:

+ 1911

The years before World War I manifested an obvious high tide in antitrust zeal. An extraordinary explosion of major antitrust prosecutions began under the Progressive Republican President Theodore Roosevelt and continued under President Taft,[20] although these prosecutions were to a degree frustrated at the end of the line by decisions of the U.S. Supreme Court from 1918 onward narrowly circumscribing remedies.[21]

Four decisions capture the spirit of this activist era. Resale price maintenance contracts were roundly repudiated (Holmes dissenting) in *Dr. Miles Medical Co. v. John D. Park & Sons Co.*, 220 U.S. 373 (1911). Joint ventures by which collaborating

---

Providence Fruit & Produce Building, 194 F.2d 484 (1st Cir. 1952) (landlords' right to select tenant).

16 Hartford Empire Co. v. U.S., 323 U.S. 386 (1945).

17 U.S. v. Masonite Corp., 316 U.S. 265 (1942).

18 American Column & Lumber Co. v. U.S., 257 U.S. 377 (1921), Holmes dissenting; U.S. v. Container Corp., 393 U.S. 333 (1969).

19 193 U.S. at 405.

20 *See* JONES, THE TRUST PROBLEM IN THE UNITED STATES 443–44 (1921).

21 *Id.* at ch. 28.

railroads preempted "bottleneck" facilities were compelled to afford access to competing carriers in *U.S. v. Terminal Railroad Ass'n*, 224 U.S. 383 (1912). The oil trusts and the tobacco trusts were broken,[22] and although the sometimes enfeebling "rule-of-reason" was strongly affirmed in the oil case, that gave impetus to congressional enactment in 1914 of the Clayton and Federal Trade Commission Acts.

The Clayton Act repudiated the rule-of-reason for specified practices: price discrimination (Clayton § 2), exclusive dealing and tying (Clayton § 3), certain types of merger (Clayton § 7), and interlocking directorships (Clayton § 8). Regulatory agencies were explicitly directed to enforce the Act (Clayton § 11). The rule-of-reason was supplanted by a criterion that turned on potential ("where the effect may be") rather than realized harm to competition. The Federal Trade Commission Act supplemented the enforcement authority of the Department of Justice by empowering a complementary administrative agency to proscribe "unfair methods of competition," a phrase that included not only direct violations of the antitrust laws but also practices deemed to violate the "spirit" or "policies" of antitrust.[23]

But with World War I the political pendulum swung once more to the right. Foreign powers displaced domestic oligarchs as the target of concern. Brandeis' 1918 opinion in *Chicago Board of Trade v. U.S.*, 246 U.S. 231 (1918), is an early signal of what lay ahead, with its retreat from per se condemnation of price fixing and its acceptance of the fiction that collective setting of prices for trades after exchange hours was merely a regulation of hours of trading. The *Colgate* opinion of 1919[24] is of the same genre, a disingenuous retreat from *Dr. Miles'* proscription of

---

22 Standard Oil Co. of New Jersey v. U.S., 221 U.S. 1 (1911); U.S. v. American Tobacco Co., 221 U.S. 106 (1911). As to the arguable inadequacy of the remedies granted in these cases, *see* Jones, *supra* note 20, at 461 ff.

23 Federal Trade Commission v. Sperry & Hutchinson Co., 405 U.S. 233 (1972); F.T.C. v. Cement Institute, 333 U.S. 683, 708 (1948).

24 250 U.S. 300.

resale price maintenance, based on a fiction of unilateral dictation by the supplier to his passive distributors.

The turnaround from 1911 is exemplified by the 1920 *Steel* decision,[25] where a plurality of the Court refused to divest a giant holding company concededly formed to suppress competition and long engaged in price stabilization activities. The plurality opinion rested upon the failure of the company to achieve monopoly, the abandonment of restrictive practices prior to suit, the absence of predatory behavior against competitors, and the purported necessity of promoting export trade through the holding company, notwithstanding the availability of the Webb-Pomerene Act for joint export by otherwise competing entities. It should be noted that the steel litigation was initiated in the prewar antitrust activist period of 1911, only to come a cropper in the postwar reaction.

We are on our way to the Republican Harding-Coolidge-Hoover era of "normalcy," of minimum governmental interference with business managers' decisions.

- 1930

This dating of the next trough of antitrust enforcement ties it to the incredible decision in *International Shoe Co. v. FTC*, 280 U.S. 291 (1930), which was virtually a judicial repudiation of both the Federal Trade Commission Act and the Clayton Act. The Court, overruling the FTC decision, sustained a merger of two leading shoe manufacturers on the ground that no competition existed between them: their products did not compete because one made "dress" shoes and the other "work" shoes; and their customers differed in that one company sold direct to retailers while the other sold through distributors who supplied many of the same retailers. The Court unhesitatingly substituted its own judgment for that of the administrative agency with regard to significant rivalry between close substitutes in product

---

25 U.S. v. United States Steel Corp., 251 U.S. 417 (1920).

and distribution systems. The Court ignored the critical distinction between Sherman and Clayton formulations by which the latter was extended to potential as well as realized impairments of competition. Finally, the Court assigned a broad exemption for "failing companies" which would be much utilized in future antitrust ideological struggles. Under that dispensation, a financially embarrassed firm could be acquired by a powerful competitor with little or no regard for its long-term viability as a rival, *e.g.*, through survival of temporary economic difficulties, through reorganization, or through sale to alternative buyers who were not dominant competitors.

The Harding-Coolidge-Hoover trough presents enough anti-antitrust decisions to have persuaded most observers that antitrust was dead. In the *General Electric* lamp case,[26] the Supreme Court fashioned a great loophole for resale price maintenance by sustaining the concept of "consignment" distribution as a basis for escaping the *Dr. Miles* ban against manufacturers' control of resale prices. G.E. had devised contracts under which it "retained title" to lamps as they moved down the ladder of distribution through distributors and wholesalers to thousands of hardware, grocery, and general stores and finally to the household purchaser. The intermediaries became "agents" through whom the mighty G.E. dealt "directly" with household consumers who could thus be compelled to pay prices untainted by competition among retailers.

This exaltation of property, contract, and agency law over antitrust realities was accompanied by an extraordinary vindication of patent rights as a means of regulating not only a competitor's production of the patented article, but also its distribution system: Westinghouse, too, was required to follow the consignment, resale-price-maintenance scheme.

Lovers of paradox and legal realists should recall that 40 years later Justice Fortas based an opinion *favorable* to competition upon the same distinction between sale and consignment;[27] it

---

26 U.S. v. General Electric Co., 272 U.S. 476 (1926).

27 U.S. v. Arnold, Schwinn & Co., 388 U.S. 365 (1967).

evoked a storm of criticism and was soon disavowed in a landmark decision of the Burger-Reagan antitrust trough, *Continental T.V., Inc. v. GTE Sylvania Inc.*[28] Continental used the asserted artificiality of the distinction to align the law of vertical territorial resale restraints, which had been thought illegal per se, with similar restraints in a consignment-agency context.

The government's defeat in the cement and flooring trade association decisions of 1925[29] fit the paattern of the twenties although the decisions were partially explicable in terms of the first amendment, since the challenged activity was exchange of price information. The liberals' sensitivity to free speech issues coincided with Holmes' penchant favoring voluntary cooperation among businesses, thus yielding a majority against antitrust. A generation would pass before a new Supreme Court grasped the reality that a trade association's promotion of a schedule of artificial prices was not merely dissemination of news but also an effort to stabilize the price structure.[30]

One Supreme Court decision of the twenties that seems hard to fit into the "trough" hypothesis is *United States v. Trenton Potteries*, 273 U.S. 392 (1927). There Justice Stone resoundingly reaffirmed the rule of per-se illegality of horizontal price fixing, in the face of the seemingly pervasive scope of Brandeis' opinion in *Chicago Board of Trade.* One should probably view this "anomaly" as a statement of the ineradicable minimum content of the Sherman Act, going back to *Addyston*,[31] that would persist even into the Reagan-Burger era of nonenforcement.

---

28 433 U.S. 36 (1977). See text at note 54, *infra*.

29 Cement Manufacturers Protective Association v. U.S., 268 U.S. 588 (1925); Maple Flooring Mfrs. Ass'n v. U.S., 268 U.S. 563 (1925). American Column and Lumber Co. v. U.S., 257 U.S. 377 (1921), was also a trade association exchange-of-information case, which the government had won. In the interim between 1921 and 1925 new appointments had shifted the balance of power on the Court strongly to the right.

30 F.T.C. v. Cement Institute, 333 U.S. 683 (1948).

31 *Supra* note 10.

The hospitality of the thirties to "cooperation" culminated in *Appalachian Coals, Inc. v. U.S.*, 288 U.S. 344 (1933), and in congressional enactment of the National Industrial Recovery Act (NIRA).[32] The coal decision, like the G.E. lamp decision of 1926, embodied a gigantic pretense that a system of regional coal marketing sales "cooperatives," in which cooperation was virtually limited to unified price decisions, had no power to influence prices since each coop faced competition from others in the consuming markets.

NIRA, embodying the principle of industry self-regulation, was the ultimate affirmation of cooperation and trade association values; only a shell remained of antitrust. NIRA was soon brought down by a combination of adverse legal and political circumstances.[33] But the antitrust legislative tide continued to run out as exemplified by the Motor Carrier Act of 1935[34] (designed to restrain competition in motor transportation, especially for the protection of railroads); the Guffey Coal Act of 1935 and Bituminous Coal Act of 1937,[35] and the Miller-Tydings Act of 1937[36] (amending the Sherman Act to validate resale price maintenance contracts). On the other hand, eddies in the tidal current were already visible. The Public Utility Holding Company Act of 1935,[37] with its provisions mandating break-up of oversized indiscriminately conglomerate utility empires, passed after a mighty struggle in Congress.

I well remember an employment interview I had late in 1935 with John Dickinson, who had been my professor at the University of Pennsylvania Law School and was now Assistant Attorney

---

32 Act of June 16, 1933, 48 Stat. 195.

33 Schechter Poultry Corp. v. U.S., 295 U.S. 495 (1935).

34 Act of Aug. 9, 1935, 49 Stat. 543.

35 50 Stat. 72, sustained as constitutional in Sunshine Anthracite Coal Co. v. Adkins, 310 U.S. 381 (1940).

36 Act of Aug. 17, 1937, 50 Stat. 693.

37 Act of Aug. 26, 1935, 49 Stat. 803, 15 U.S.C.A. § 79 *et seq.*

General in charge of the Antitrust Division. He was kindly disposed toward me and I needed a job, which he offered me. With hubris I now cringe to recall, I let this distinguished man know that a career in his moribund division was not for me: the exciting new Securities and Exchange Commission was my choice.

+ 1940

The post-NIRA resurgence of antitrust was brief but spectacular until halted by conservative influences generated by World War II. Justice Douglas' opinion in *U.S. v. Socony-Vacuum Oil Co.*, 310 U.S. 150 (1940), beat back implications of *Appalachian Coals* that price stabilization arrangements could be validated by structuring them as joint ventures in purchasing "distress" supplies. In *U.S. v. Masonite Corp.*, 316 U.S. 265 (1942), antitrust prevailed despite the "agency" guise in which rival manufacturers dressed their market collaboration. *Fashion Originators' Guild v. Federal Trade Commission*, 312 U.S. 457 (1941), gave Justice Black an opportunity to declare in the strongest terms that private boycotts—for whatever "ethical" goals—would not be allowed to replace or supplement public regulation of commerce.

Two decisions may be assigned to this period, although they came at the end of World War II. *Alcoa*[38] was Judge Learned Hand's powerful assertion that section 2 of the Sherman Act covered the purposeful acquisition and maintenance of monopoly power whether or not the means employed were otherwise legal and regardless of the beneficent use of the power so maintained. Of equal significance was Hand's readiness to draw the commonsense conclusion that a three-decade reign as sole producer of virgin aluminum ingot demonstrated monopoly, whether or not recycled aluminum and foreign imports could in some sense be regarded as competing with virgin. For Hand, the easily manipulated numbers describing markets and shares were clearly no more than illuminating rather than decisive.

---

38 U.S. v. Aluminum Co. of America, 148 F.2d 416 (2d Cir. 1945).

The *Associated Press* case,[39] gave Justices Black, Douglas and Frankfurter an opportunity to extricate antitrust from the tangle of first amendment issues that had entrapped the Court in the trade-association information-exchange decisions of the twenties. Freedom of the press was not to be accepted as a defense against prosecution for conspiring to disadvantage competitors; the first amendment did not immunize the press from governmental controls only to turn control over to private groups. Yet the decision was, in the final analysis, a Pyrrhic victory because of the limitations on relief granted. In a setting where the essence of the restraint lay in barriers to entry both in the newspaper field and the press association field, nothing was done about either. A.P. was not required to admit new members to its unique facilities. A.P. remained free to reject an application on the ground that an existing member was already supplying all the spot news needed by the association. A.P. retained its exclusive arrangements with powerful foreign news associations, so that competing American press associations would operate at the disadvantage of having to create prohibitively expensive duplicate newsgathering networks to obtain foreign news. Domestic newsgathering remained obstructed by continuance of A.P.'s exclusive contracts with its powerful members.

The shortfall in relief secured in the A.P. case marks it as a transition decision inaugurating the new era of declining antitrust zeal, which may be dated from:

- 1948

This is the year of *Columbia Steel.*[40] A post-war corporate acquisition by the U.S. Steel Corp. was upheld by vote of 5 to 4, despite substantial anticompetitive effects both in Big Steel's competition as a fabricator and in its competition for sales of rolled steel to the acquired fabricator. It mattered not that the

---

39 Associated Press v. U.S., 326 U.S. 1 (1945).

40 U.S. v. Columbia Steel Co., 334 U.S. 495 (1948).

Steel Corporation's avowed purpose was to acquire a "firm" market, *i.e.*, an assured buyer that would become unavailable to rival sellers of rolled steel. "Normal business purpose," said the majority opinion, hailing the "welcome westward extension" of the industry without a glimmer of understanding that acquisition of a firm already operating in California was not a contribution to expansion of manufacture in the West, as an original entry might have been, but simply an expansion of control by an already dominant firm. Anticompetitive impact on rival sellers was discounted by the usual manipulation of "market" boundaries and on the basis of "production flexibility," *i.e.*, the theoretical possibility that competitors could adapt to market restrictions by producing different products.

The majority opinion in *Columbia Steel* also manifested the recurrent tendency of the Court to defer to presidential tolerance of corporate concentration.[41] In this case, President Truman had approved the sale to U.S. Steel of the government's Geneva, Utah, rolling mill built for military purposes during World War II. In the opinion of many of us in the Antitrust Division at the time, that approval flew in the face of very strong anticoncentration provisions in the Surplus Property Act of 1944. There were widely credited rumors that the approval was politically tied to the controversy over President Truman's seizure of the steel plants to settle a nationwide steelworkers' strike.[42] The whole episode reminds one of the weight assigned by the *U.S. Steel* Court of 1920 to earlier presidential approval of Big Steel's acquisition of Tennessee Coal and Iron Co.[43] One can add to this list of episodes illustrating the proindustry weight of the executive in the scales of antitrust justice.[44]

---

41 334 U.S. at 505.

42 *See* Kramer, *Of Plates and Shapes: An Antitrust Vignette*, 64 MINN. L. REV. 143, 145 (1979).

43 251 U.S. at 446.

44 See President Nixon's intervention to prevent the Department of Justice from appealing the I.T.T. conglomerate merger case to the

The post-World-War-II decade of reaction saw, also, the enactment of the McGuire Act of 1952, restoring the vitality of the state resale price-maintenance laws by making fair trade "contracts" enforceable against nonsigners.[45] In 1955, the Eisenhower "National Committee to Study the Antitrust Laws" issued its strongly conservative report.[46] In 1956, came the government's surrender by consent decree to A.T. & T., following Attorney General Brownell's unguarded comment during negotiations that "a way ought to be found to get rid of the case" and that A.T. & T. "could readily find practices that [they] might agree to have enjoined with no real injury to their business."[47]

+ 1965

The midpoint of the sixties is selected not because it dates a particular antitrust peak but rather as the mathematical middle of the notable decade in which every year contributed to an unprecedented antitrust swell. The decade opens with *U.S. v. Parke, Davis & Co.*, 362 U.S. 29 (1960), drastically narrowing the *Colgate* doctrine that a supplier might engage in resale price maintenance by refusing to deal with price-cutters or with distributors who sold to price-cutters. The Court adopted an expansive view of "combination" and discerned an illegal conspiracy where creative lawyers and exuberant sales managers had envisioned only unilateral selection of customers. Other decisions of the

---

Supreme Court. U.S. v. I.T.T., 349 F. Supp. 22 (D. Conn. 1972), *aff'd per cur. sub. nom.*, Nader v. U.S., 410 U.S. 919 (1973). See also the White House attempt to force the DOJ to drop the suit against A.T. & T. S. COLL, THE DEAL OF THE CENTURY: THE BREAKUP OF A.T. & T. 212, 222, 245 (1984).

45 Act of July 14, 1952, 66 Stat. 631.

46 REPORT OF THE ATTORNEY GENERAL'S NATIONAL COMMITTEE TO STUDY THE ANTITRUST LAWS (1955) and Schwartz, *The Complete Dissenting Opinion of Professor Louis B. Schwartz*, 1 ANTITRUST BULL. 37 (1955).

47 *See* U.S. v. A.T. & T., 552 F. Supp. 131, 137 (D.D.C. 1982).

decade undermined the *G.E.* consignment method of avoiding the *Dr. Miles* ban against resale price maintenance,[48] and extended the per se ban to suppliers' setting of *maximum* resale prices, as well as minimum.[49]

On the structural side, *Brown Shoe*[50] and *PNB*[51] gave full effect to section 7 of the Clayton Act, emphasizing the purpose of Congress to halt trends toward oligopoly by antitrust intervention at the "incipiency" stage. Vertical mergers were brought squarely within the ambit of antitrust, because of their potential to squeeze independent suppliers out of the market. Of all the merger cases, *U.S. v. Von's Grocery Co.*, 384 U.S. 270 (1966), would later arouse the greatest hostility from opponents of "excessive" enforcement. The decision vetoed the merger of two smallish supermarket chains operating in adjoining sectors of Los Angeles. They were in direct competition at some points and unquestionably were potential entrants in each other's markets. Whatever might be said about misallocation of prosecutors' resources to this relatively trivial violation of the Clayton Act, in a quite competitive market context, the correctness of this judicial interpretation of the statute seems clear. Moreover, welfare consequences of the decision were certainly not baneful: grocery competition thrives in Los Angeles and the decision preserved a choice for consumers. The chief significance of *Von's* was its continuing utility as punching bag for enemies of antitrust and as an opportunity for some friends of antitrust to acquire a degree of respectability by disavowing this "extreme" decision while defending against major assaults on antitrust.

Utah Pie Co. v. Continental Baking Co., 386 U.S. 685 (1967), is another instance of defensible high-tide antitrust jurisprudence of the sixties which has nevertheless been thrown to the wolves by some friends of antitrust who wish to distance themselves from

---

48 Simpson v. Union Oil Co., 377 U.S. 13 (1964).

49 Albrecht v. Herald Co., 390 U.S. 145 (1968).

50 Brown Shoe Co. v. U.S., 370 U.S. 294 (1962).

51 U.S. v. Philadelphia National Bank, 374 U.S. 321 (1963).

"extremes." Critics of the decision treat it as affirming some such propositions as "Hard competition that injures a competitor is unlawful under the price-discrimination provisions of the Robinson-Patman Act." There was evidence in the case that national producers of frozen pies engaged in strenuous competition in Salt Lake City, to the point of pricing below cost. Other evidence pointed toward a plan specifically directed to undermining the local transitorily-leading producer, Utah Pie, by industrial espionage and other unfair competitive practices. The Supreme Court merely held, by a vote of 7 to 2, that there was enough of the latter sort of evidence to sustain a jury verdict for the plaintiff. This vindication of jury trial illustrates the confluence of relatively independent jurisprudential oscillations to make up the composite wave motion that is the subject of this article. In an era of respect for jury trial that coincides with an era of antitrust vitality, decisions like *Utah Pie* are to be expected. A neatly contrasting case is *Matsushita Elec. Ind. Co., Ltd. v. Zenith Radio Corp.*, 475 U.S. 574 (1986). There, in an era of antitrust ebb, jury trial was precluded by means of summary judgment in which the Court decided that plaintiff's theory was implausible.

- 1982

Nineteen eighty-two represents the midpoint of a decade of declining antitrust, extending roughly from 1977 to the present. *General Dynamics*[52] of 1974 may be regarded as a precursor, announcing a retreat from the great structural decisions of the preceding decade. In a context where there were the usual disputes about definition of "market" and calculation of market shares, the Supreme Court, by a vote of 6 to 3, sustained the trial court's determination that "other pertinent factors" outweighed any conclusion derivable from the market share statistics. The other pertinent factors were alleged exhaustion of the available coal reserves of one of the merger partners and alleged difficulties

52 U.S. v. General Dynamics Corp., 415 U.S. 486 (1974).

in obtaining new reserves by switching from surface deposits to deep shaft mining.

The significance of *General Dynamics* is easily exaggerated. Doctrinally, it was no great departure from precedent, since *Brown Shoe* had merely made substantial market share a presumptive basis for inferring prejudice to competition, leaving open further inquiry and such defenses as "failing company." Moreover, the Court would probably have sustained a trial court decision condemning the merger. In that view, *General Dynamics* becomes simply deference to a trial court's appraisal. Thus *General Dynamics* can be paired with *Utah Pie*'s deference to jury trial. Yet there is a warning of things to come in the majority's willingness to accept implausible hypotheses (of course, supported by "expert" testimony) such as the technological barrier against a surface mining company expanding into deep shaft operations.

Accepting implausible (fictional?) barriers so as to deny competitive significance of a merger is the hallmark of a remarkable decision that opens the new era of antitrust regression, *British Oxygen Corp. International Ltd. v. Federal Trade Commission*, 557 F.2d 24 (2d Cir. 1977). Here the Commission had condemned the acquisition of a leading American industrial gas firm by the dominant British producer, which the Commission regarded as a potential entrant into the American market. To the contrary, the Court held that the difficulties of entering a new remote national market made British Oxygen's potential entry only an "ephemeral possibility." This, despite the fact that British Oxygen was already established in Canada. The willingness of the Court to substitute its own judgment for that of an administrative agency is simply a reversion to the standards of the twenties as exemplified in *International Shoe.*[53]

Nineteen hundred and seventy-seven was the year when the antitrust ebb tide first manifested its full strength. Vertical restraints received the full blessing of a rule-of-reason opinion that undermined even the ban against resale price mainte-

---

53 See text following section titled "- 1930."

nance.[54] Private enforcement was cut back by *Illinois Brick*,[55] holding that indirect purchasers, *i.e.*, consumers who purchased from middlemen, were not injured by a price hike engineered by a producer cartel and passed down the chain of distribution. Moreover, in *Pueblo Bowl-O-Mat*, middlemen whose injury was palpably caused by supplier-subsidized competition lost their treble damage action on the subtle ground that "competition" is not an antitrust-type offense compensable under the Sherman Act.[56] The depth of the current antitrust trough will be sufficiently indicated by a short list of more recent antitrust disasters:

Russell Stover Candy, Inc. v. Federal Trade Commission, 718 F.2d 256 (8th Cir. 1983) (reversing F.T.C. appraisal of resale price maintenance operation as systematic coercion through threats of termination; *Colgate*'s immunity for mere refusal to deal prevails).

Monsanto Co. v. Spray-Rite Service Corp., 460 U.S. 1010 (1984) (supplier's cut-off of price-cutting distributor upon complaint of competing distributor insufficient evidence of conspiracy to maintain resale prices; "there must be evidence that tends to *exclude possibility*" [emphasis added] of independent decision).

Copperweld Corp. v. Independence Tube Corp., 467 U.S. 752 (1984) ("conspiracy" between parent and wholly-owned subsidiary not actionable).

---

54 Continental T.V., Inc. v. GTE Sylvania, Inc., 433 U.S. 36 (1977).

55 Illinois Brick Co. v. Illinois, 431 U.S. 720 (1977). *Cf.* Associated General Contractors v. California, 459 U.S. 519 (1983) (union lacks standing to maintain antitrust action based on employer's coercion of other employers to resist unionization).

56 Brunswick Corp. v. Pueblo Bowl-O-Mat, 429 U.S. 477 (1977). *But cf.* Photovest Corp. v. Fotomat Corp., 606 F.2d 704 (7th Cir. 1979), *cert. denied*, 445 U.S. 917 (1980) (saturating rival's market by opening competing stores in order to compel rival to sell out violates Sherman Act: "Otherwise lawful practices may become unlawful if they are part of an illegal scheme.").

Matsushita Elec. Ind. Co., Ltd. v. Zenith Radio Corp., 475 U.S. 574 (1986) (summary judgment for defendants sustained on ground that "predatory pricing conspiracies [are] self-deterring" —according to theoretical writings of Chicago school economists—and hence "implausible").

Broadcast Music, Inc. v. Columbia Broadcasting System, Inc., 441 U.S. 1 (1979), should perhaps be added to the list since it sustained the right of ASCAP to insist on blanket licensing of its entire portfolio of performance rights to music copyrighted by thousands of composers. The arrangement, of course, meant the end of price competition among individual licensors although they had retained the legal right to negotiate individual licenses. However, the decision did not as some have feared espouse a rule-of-reason approach to price fixing. Instead, the Court justifiably viewed the arrangement as a joint venture, not merely to *market* collaboratively potentially competitive products as in *Appalachian Coals*[57] but to *produce* a unique and useful product, low-cost easy access to a vast portfolio of music. The vice of the decision lay, as Justice Stevens, noted in dissent, in its failure to require less restrictive alternatives, *e.g.*, offering consumers reasonable subdivisions of the entire portfolio.

Nonjudicial developments also manifest the era's retreat from antitrust. This is the age when a "joint venture" can easily elude condemnation as a combination to restrain trade. This is best, or worst, exemplified in the government's approval of General Motors–Toyota collaboration to produce small cars in California. The preposterous justification that this was an educational experience for General Motors to learn mysterious Japanese management techniques satisfied the moribund Antitrust Division and Federal Trade Commission.[58] Congress also curtailed the impact of antitrust on joint research[59] and joint export.[60]

---

57 See text accompanying note 32, *supra*.

58 *See* Schwartz, *Justice, Expediency, and Beauty*, 136 U. Pa. L. Rev. 141, 161 (1987).

59 National Cooperative Research Act of 1984, 15 U.S.C.A. § 4303.

60 Export Trading Company Act of 1982, 15 U.S.C.A. § 4001 *et seq.*; Horizons International, Inc. v. Balridge, 811 F.2d 154 (3d Cir. 1987).

However, there are in this era several proantitrust decisions that either presage a turnabout or bring into question the theory that antitrust zeal goes in distinct waves. Among them are *Professional Engineers*,[61] *Maricopa Medical*,[62] *Aspen Skiing*,[63] *NCAA*,[64] and *Indiana Dentists*.[65] These decisions must be considered in terms of whether they express the bedrock minimum of antitrust, which may be expected to survive all periods of adversity, or whether they are harbingers of a new rise of antitrust zeal to follow the present already prolonged ebb. I believe the 1978 unanimous decision in *Professional Engineers* expresses bedrock antitrust. The engineers' code of ethics barred competitive bidding or even the submission of cost estimates by an engineer until he or she had been selected for the job. It is impossible to reconcile such an arrangement with the Sherman Act command to compete. Rejection of the alleged justification—that noncompetitive pricing promoted responsible safety-concerned engineering—can be traced back to *Trenton Potteries*,[66] which likewise in an era of antitrust recession rejected alleged public benefits from private price fixing. *Maricopa Medical* of 1982 is another story. The doctors' agreement on *maximum* prices to be charged to a third-party provider was invalidated, but only by a bare plurality vote of 4 to 3. Considering subsequent changes in the composition of the Court, *Maricopa Medical* credibly presages further retreats, *e.g.*, from Albrecht's per se rule against fixing maximum resale prices.[67]

---

61 National Society of Professional Engineers v. U.S., 435 U.S. 679 (1978).

62 Arizona v. Maricopa County Medical Society, 102 S. Ct. 2466 (1982).

63 Aspen Skiing Co. v. Aspen Highlands Skiing Corp., 105 S. Ct. 3346 (1985).

64 National Collegiate Athletic Association v. Board of Regents, 104 S. Ct. 2948 (1984).

65 F.T.C. v. Indiana Federation of Dentists, 106 S. Ct. 2009 (1986).

66 See discussion under heading "- 1930" *supra*.

67 Albrecht v. Herald Co., 390 U.S. 145 (1968).

Aspen Skiing[68] and *Indiana Dentists*[69] would give a cycle theorist grounds to believe that the cycle has recently passed the nadir. But they are shaky grounds, especially after recent changes in the composition of the Court. *Aspen Skiing* did reaffirm that the *Colgate* right to select the people with whom one deals is not absolute; in particular, a monopolist may not suddenly invoke the right to terminate an ongoing trade relationship with a smaller rival if the purpose is to undermine the competitive viability of that rival. The jury was allowed to infer such purpose where defendant did not advance any "normal business purpose," did not offer to prove efficiency gains from the termination of the joint sale arrangement, and acted contrary to its current business interest in a way that would pay off only through harm done to the competitor, a harm that actually materialized. Moreover, the termination actually prejudiced consumers, who were deprived of the all-slopes ticket alternative theretofore available. That concatenation of circumstances will be rare. The unanimity of the Court attests to the egregious character of the violation. It will not be difficult for the new majority to distinguish a case in which "efficiency" and "normal business purpose" are advanced with any plausibility. Still, even the *Aspen Skiing* facts might have supported a finding of normal business purpose in view of the pretermination disagreement between the partner enterprises as to the sharing of revenues. It is not abnormal for a partner who feels underrewarded to wish to dissolve the partnership. Would summary judgment for the defendant in a like case be sustained by the current Court on the ground that the possibility of lawful purpose was not "excluded" by the totality of the evidence.[70] The crystal ball clouds.

The 1986 decision in *Indiana Dentists*,[71] like *Aspen Skiing*, presented an unexpected unanimity in support of a Federal Trade

---

68 Aspen Skiing Co. v. Aspen Highlands Skiing Corp., 105 S. Ct. 3346 (1985).

69 F.T.C. v. Indiana Federation of Dentists, 106 S. Ct. 2009 (1986).

70 *Cf.* Monsanto Co. v. Spray-Rite Service Corp., 104 S. Ct. 1464, 1471 (1984); Matsushita Elec. Ind. Co. Ltd. v. Zenith Radio Corp., 475 U.S. 574 (1986).

71 *Supra* note 69.

Commission finding against a dentists' "boycott" of third-party payers who desired access to the dental X-rays supporting reimbursement claims. Although the decision can support a hypothesis of ebb-tide turnaround, there is more ambiguity than the unanimity suggests. In the first place, a concerted refusal to deal, where the purpose was demonstrably to disadvantage a competing supplier, might well have been condemned per se, but Justice White's opinion declined to do so. Instead, it confined per se boycotts "generally" to cases where the boycotters have "market power" and employ it with the purpose of discouraging rivals from doing business.[72] In the second place, although the opinion expresses a conventional deference to administrative expertise, including a reference to the power of the F.T.C. to ban a practice as an "unfair method of competition" even if it does not amount to an antitrust violation, the Court, *as did the Commission*, analyzed the case under the requirements of the Sherman Act. Such a crabbed approach to the administrative power has ominous implications for the health of antitrust as the administrative agencies become predominantly staffed with conservative Republican appointees.[73]

Wave frequency and prediction

Accepting the foregoing rough chronology, one can calculate a wave frequency of approximately 25 years. It is a remarkable coincidence that the historian, Arthur Schlesinger, Jr., linking up with an earlier analysis by his father and one by Henry Adams, finds similar periodicity in the cycles of American politics, identifying the oscillations as "conservative/liberal," "private-interest/public-action," or "commerce/virtue."[74] Schlesinger also supplies a theory to explain and help forecast the oscillations. Each phase generates conditions that lead to reactions bringing on the next phase. The crisis of a war or economic

---

72 106 S. Ct. 2009, 2018.

73 See text at note 78 *infra*.

74 A. SCHLESINGER, *supra* note 3, at 24–26 (1986).

recession evokes consensus and demand for political solutions. Eventually loyalties weaken, government falters, privatization takes over. Antigovernment governments then come to power. They are in turn weakened by exacerbation of class conflicts and exposure of the corruption that seems endemic in private commercial dominance. And so on. Periodicity is also promoted by "intergenerational conflict." People who come to political consciousness at critical periods carry forward the imprint of those times, doing battle with predecessors and their successors until the latter in turn become the "establishment" against which rebellion must be carried on. That brings Schlesinger to this forecast:

> If the thirty-year rhythm [that is, of generational wave] holds, then the 1980s will witness the burnout of the most recent conservative ascendancy, and the age of Reagan, like its earlier versions in the 1950s, 1920s and 1890s, will fade into historical memory. . . . We may conclude that public purpose will have at least one more chance. At some point, shortly before or after the Year 1990, there should come a sharp change in the national mood and direction—a change comparable to those bursts of innovation and reform that followed the accessions to office of Theodore Roosevelt in 1901, of Franklin Roosevelt in 1933 and of John Kennedy in 1961. The 1990s should be the turn in the generational succession for the young women and men who came of political age in the Kennedy years.[75]

The interrelation between my calculation of waves of antitrust zeal and Schlesinger's political waves is obvious. The 1890 antitrust crest follows the long deflationary crises of the 1870's and 1880's, which evoked the political responses of the Granger and Progressive movements.[76] The crest of 1911 coincides roughly with the victory of the "New Freedom" in Wilson's election in 1912. The trough of 1930 (and the twenties) seems clearly related to the conservative influences of World War I and the Republican hands-off-business era of Harding, Coolidge, and Hoover. The

---

75 *Id.* at 45, 47.

76 2 S. E. Morison & H. S. Commager, The Growth of the American Republic, 1865–1950 chaps. v, vi, ix, xi, and xv (1950).

trough of 1948 likewise occurs in the wake of a war, when allegiance to political leadership crumbles into irritation with government. Financial and industrial barons replace governors and legislators as role models for "freedom's" organizers.

It is harder to relate the crest of the sixties or the depth and duration of the current trough to political sea-changes. One is tempted to look at the changes in the composition of the Supreme Court itself. The appointment of that surprising Republican Warren and the more predictable Democrats Brennan, Marshall, White, Goldberg, and Fortas restored the primacy of the antitrust views of Black and Douglas, staunch survivors of the heyday of the forties. Of course, appointments to the Supreme Court are themselves a reflection of contemporaneous politics, but in the late fifties and sixties the antitrust outlook of candidates for the Court counted for little as compared with their expected positions on civil rights and government regulation. On the other hand, there can be little doubt that the Bork candidacy for the Supreme Court first came to public and academic attention through his idiosyncratic diatribe against antitrust, *The Antitrust Paradox*, and Scalia's views of government regulation were likewise crucial to his nomination.

The Supreme Court has once again been basically reconstituted in the late seventies and eighties. With Douglas and Black gone, a phalanx of antitrust conservatives—Burger, Powell, Rehnquist, Scalia, O'Connor—overwhelmed the proantitrust survivors. The advent of Kennedy strengthened the conservative alliance.[77] Interestingly, the most powerful voice among the survivors is that of another surprising Republican, John Paul Stevens. Like Warren, Stevens combines deep concerns for civil liberties with the not-unrelated concern for diffusion of economic power and prevention of private restraint of trade. If the pendulum swings again during his tenure in the Court, Justice Stevens may well become the name associated with the new era, as Warren's was with his.

---

77 *See* Schwartz, *Kennedy: The Newest Justice Stakes Out His Position,* Los Angeles Daily Journal, September 30, 1988, at 2.

The pendulum is unlikely to swing back in the years immediately ahead. Rolling back antitrust was a high priority of the Reagan administration. Nominations like those of Scalia, Bork, and Kennedy were made with antitrust in mind. The first two are clearly activist. Bork's book, *The Antitrust Paradox*, was a caricature of scholarship in its learned and disingenous "demonstration" that the Congress of 1890 directed the Sherman Act exclusively at economic efficiency (measured by Chicago-school economics invented more than 60 years later) rather than at broader political and social goals. Justice Scalia's activist dedication to a similar goal, the vindication of private economic power against governmental controls, is sufficiently manifested in his argument that close judicial review of administrative action, once the pillar of conservative resistance to governmental "excesses," should be abandoned since Reagan appointees now dominate the administrative agencies. Those appointees favor "deregulation," and should be given a free hand by conservative judges.[78] It is not an accident that recent appointees combine antitrust conservatism with a generally restrictive view of civil rights.[79] Authoritarianism embraces both positions.

It will be many years before the Reagan sabotage of the antitrust laws can be undone. The earliest prospective retirements from the Supreme Court will be those of the proantitrust survivors. Their replacements would not change the balance of the Court. Moreover, there will survive into the new era a powerful slogan of "international competitiveness" to restrain any executive inclination to enforce the American antitrust laws.

Despite the total demolition by Adams and Brock of the fantasy that nonenforcement of antitrust enhances American

---

78 Scalia, *Regulatory Reform—The Game Has Changed*, Regulation, Jan./Feb. 1981, p. 13.

79 For a review of conservative activism in the field of civil rights, *see* Wright, *The Judicial Right and the Rhetoric of Restraint: A Defense of Judicial Activism in an Age of Conservative Judges*, 14 HASTINGS CONST. L.Q. 487, 495 *et seq.* (1987).

foreign trade,[80] the impact of the "international competitiveness" slogan on the domestic antitrust scene may be far reaching. (1) The notion of "market" may change dramatically so that enterprises of enormous power, from a national perspective, will be made to seem innocuous because of the rivalry of remote European or Asian giants; the influence of "submarket" analysis will tend to diminish. (2) Joint ventures and other restraints of competition will be made to appear justifiable to overcome adverse trade balances and to "preserve jobs" (in the protected industries, of course). (3) The reach of the American antitrust laws will be constricted by an increasingly liberal exemption for foreign trade not deemed to affect American commerce substantially and adversely, and for arrangements entered into abroad under putative compulsion of a foreign sovereign. The Departments of State, Commerce and Defense will have increasing and often secret influence against potential intervention by the Department of Justice. The spectacle of giant American industrial firms eluding American antitrust norms by sidling into the virtually unregulated international arena is reminiscent of and carries the same dangers as the ancient narrow definitions of "commerce" that created a states' rights refuge from effective federal antitrust.[81]

The sloganists of "international competitiveness" exhibit a remarkable ignorance of history in picturing the world as suddenly become the major arena of competitive commerce and "new technology" as requiring giantism.[82] At the very time when

---

80 Adams & Brock, *The "New Learning" and the Euthanasia of Antitrust*, 74 CAL. L. REV. 1516, 1520 ff. (1986). A similar demonstration had been made 66 years earlier in JONES, *supra* note 20, at 522 ff.

81 U.S. v. E.C. Knight Co., 156 U.S. 1 (1895); Federal Baseball Club v. National League, 259 U.S. 200 (1922). For a parallel constriction of federal power by the new Court expansively interpreting the eleventh amendment, *see* Welch v. State Department of Highways, 55 U.S.L.W. 5046 (1987).

82 *See* Harris & Sullivan, *Horizontal Merger Policy: Promoting Competition and American Competitiveness*, 31 ANTITRUST BULL. 871 (1986).

the Sherman Act was debated and enacted, the dominant view of professional economists, dubious about antitrust, was that international free trade was the only effective restrainer of domestic monopoly. A century earlier Hamiltonians had argued for protective tariffs to stimulate American industry. Already in 1894, Congress showed its sensitivity to the "world market" by specifically enacting legislation against import conspiracies.[83] The Webb-Pomerene Act of 1918 likewise reflected Congress' awareness of the international competitiveness dimension of world trade. Against that background, Congress and the Courts recurrently reaffirmed the antitrust tradition. The rediscovery of the "world market" is disingenuous.

As for the "New Learning" discovery of rapid technological advance as distinctive of our era, thus justifying inroads on antitrust, one has only to recall the fundamental innovations of the past to realize that "new technology" is a pretext rather than a reason to alter our institutions.[84] Not electronic data processing nor any other development of recent decades compares for impact with the steam engine, the mechanization of agriculture, the electric motor and the electric lamp, the telephone, the automobile, the airplane, and nuclear energy.

One other wave-like phenomenon must be recognized as a possible offset against entrenched judicial conservatism. There are waves of fashion in economic ideas, and there are signs that the Chicago-school fad is passing. The generation of non-Chicago economists is coming into its own.[85] It would be ironic if

---

83 Wilson Tariff Act, 15 U.S.C. § 8.

84 Adams & Brock, *supra* note 80, at 1556 ff.

85 *See* Hovenkamp, *Antitrust Policy After Chicago*, 84 MICH. L. REV. 213 (1985). Among other economists and lawyer-economists leading the anti-Chicago troops, I would list: Adams & Brock, *supra* note 80; Flynn, *The Misuse of Economic Analysis in Antitrust Litigation*, 12 SW.U.L. REV. 335, 361 (1981); Fox & Sullivan, *Antitrust Retrospective and Prospective—Where Are We Coming From? Where Are We Going?* 62 N.Y.U. L. REV. 936 (1987); Harrison, *Egoism, Altruism, and Market Illusions: The Limits of Law and Economics*, 33 UCLA L. REV. 1309

the exaggerated free-market notions survived mainly on the Supreme Court, where some justices would have to be reminded that the Sherman Act did not enact the political views of Professors Director, Easterbrook, Posner and Bork.[86]

Conclusion

There is little useful predictive value in the cycle theory of antitrust. The regularities we perceive are largely retrospective subjective projections. There is some synchronicity with major politicoeconomic trends, but who can predict those with any reliability? The waves of antitrust zeal are composites of many ideological oscillations: federalism vs. states' rights, business vs. political leadership, judicial supremacy vs. executive and legislative powers, judicial activism vs. deference to administrative decisions, respect for jury trial, etc. Moreover, there are no "leading indicators" such as those sometimes relied on with notorious fallibility by financial forecasters. The periods of the antitrust pendulum and the interrelated political pendulum differ from each other and each is quite variable.

My own approximation of 25 years for the antitrust cycle must be compared with 30 years for Schlesinger's political-generational cycle.[87] Frequently, these influences would cancel each other out, and we would experience neap tides. When the crests of the two waves coincide we will experience spring tides.

(1986); Kaplow, *Extension of Market Power Through Leverage*, 85 Colum. L. Rev. 515 (1985); Mueller, *A New Attack on Antitrust: The Chicago Case*, 1986 L. & Econ. Rev. 29; F. Scherer, Industrial Market Structure and Economic Performance (2d ed. 1980); Shepard, *The Twilight of Antitrust*, 18 Antitrust Law & Econ. Rev. 21 (1985).

86 Cf. Justice Holmes' admonition to his colleagues in Lochner v. New York, 198 U.S. 45, 75 (1905). ("This case is decided upon an economic theory which a large part of the country does not entertain. . . . The 14th Amendment does not enact Mr. Herbert Spenser's Social Statics.").

87 A. Schlesinger, *supra* note 3, at 45.

Schlesinger suggests a turnaround by the end of this decade, a peak of liberalism in the 1990's, and a decline towards neo-Reaganism by 2010 (under the auspices of "the young people who came of political age in the Reagan years"[88]). Using my 25-year periodicity, one arrives at 1990 for the next antitrust crest, by adding 25 to 1965. A spring tide? I doubt it.

88 *Id.* at 47.

16
The Sherman Act and the economic power problem

BY WALTER ADAMS* and JAMES W. BROCK**

Controlling power in a free society and guarding against its usurpation and abuse are the core of the American politico-economic experience.

In the political realm, the new American nation was born as a protest against arbitrary power, symbolized by the British Crown. The nation's founders understood that in framing a governance structure for a free society, they must provide for a government strong enough to prevent individuals from infringing on the rights and liberties of one another, and at the same time a government that was not so powerful that it could oppress the citizenry. As sons of the Enlightenment, the founders had a dyspeptic view of human nature; they recognized (as Thomas Burke expressed it in 1777) that "Power of all kinds has an irresistible propensity to increase a desire for itself," that "Power will sometime or other be abused unless men are well watched, and checked by something they cannot remove when they

* Distinguished University Professor and Past President, Michigan State University.

** Professor of Economics, Miami University (Ohio).

please," and that "The root of the evil is deep in human nature."[1]

The Constitution crafted by the founders was predicated on two transcendental political principles: First, that it is in the *structure* of government, and not the personal predilections of those who govern, that liberty must be vouchsafed; and second, in Jefferson's words, that "it is not by the consolidation or concentration of powers, but by their distribution, that good government is effected."[2] Above all, the Constitution was to be, and is, a power-control structure—a system of governance for controlling political power, and for guarding against its abuse, by dispersing decision making among three coordinate and coequal branches, each designed to act as a built-in check and balance to the others in order to protect the people.

Subsequent events, however, indicated that in a free society, the power problem is not confined to the political arena. A century after the Constitution was ratified—during the post-Civil War era—the proliferation of pools, trusts, and monopolies indicated the need for controlling economic as well as political, private as well as public concentrations of power. People began to see a need to prevent (what Senator Sherman called) the autocrats of trade from fashioning an *economic* feudalism.[3] They

---

1 Quoted in W. ADAMS & J. BROCK, THE BIGNESS COMPLEX 87 (1986).

2 T. JEFFERSON, JEFFERSON: WRITINGS 74 (Library of America ed. 1984).

3 Quoted in H. THORELLI, FEDERAL ANTITRUST POLICY 180 (1955). For informative surveys of the trust movement in America, *see* H. LLOYD, WEALTH AGAINST COMMONWEALTH (1894); Andrews, *Trusts According to Official Investigations*, 3 Q.J. ECON. 117 (1889); J. MOODY, TRUTH ABOUT TRUSTS (1904); E. JONES, TRUST PROBLEM IN THE UNITED STATES (1922); H. SEAGER & C. GULICK, TRUST AND CORPORATION PROBLEMS (1929); and M. JOSEPHSON, THE ROBBER BARONS (1934).

These sources show that prior to the enactment of the Sherman Act in 1890, a large segment of American industry fell under centralized control by trusts. These include the meatpacking trust of 1880; the Standard Oil trust of 1879 (reorganized in 1882 with the combination of 40 firms controlling 90%-95% of the nation's refining capacity); the

feared the "irresponsible rulers of industry, whose power, like that of the feudal barons, burdens the people, and even overshadows the government which gave it existence."[4] They hearkened to the warning of Senator Sherman, a stalwart Republican, that if Congress failed to address the problem, there would "be a trust for every production and a master to fix the price for every necessity of life."[5]

In theory, Adam Smith seemed to have demonstrated the competitive market system would regulate and neutralize economic power. It would decentralize and disperse decision making in the hands of a multitude of rivals, and would force each to perform well in the public interest. In theory, the competitive market would channel freedom of economic decision making into socially beneficial outlets. It would *compel* innovation, technological advance, and efficiency in production, and would allocate

---

cotton oil trust of 1884 (controlling 75% of the market); the linseed oil trust of 1885; the whiskey trust of 1887 (combining 80 producers, commanding 85% of the market); the sugar trust of 1887 (combining 17 firms and controlling 78% of the nation's sugar refining capacity); the lead trust of 1887; the cordage trust of 1887; the match trust of 1889 (eventually controlling 85% of the market); and the tobacco trust of 1890 (controlling 90% of the field).

As summarized by one economic analyst of the day, there was "scarcely a single industry in the country which has not, either bodily or in some of its phases or departments, passed under this or that form of associate management." Andrews, at 121.

[4] Hudson, *Modern Fuedalism*, 144 N. AM. REV. 277, 290 (1887).

In 1890, David Millon argues, Congress "was concerned about power, not efficiency. The legislators confronted the concentration crisis from the perspective of an ideological tradition that equated excessive economic power with political corruption as well as oppression of competitors and consumers. This tradition grew out of classical liberal assumptions about the threat to individual liberty inherent in public and private power. . . . Just as separation and balance within government prevented concentration of power in any single constituent element, so too was atomization of economic power the solution to the crisis brought on by the concentrated power of the trusts." *The Sherman Act and the Balance of Power*, 61 S. CAL. L.R. 1219, at 1287, 1288.

[5] Quoted in Thorelli, *supra* note 3, at 180.

resources in accordance with society's collective preferences. In theory, it would maintain economic freedom and opportunity for all, while insuring that private economic decision making was continuously accountable to the public.

In reality, however, the trust movement demonstrated that, as a system of governance, the competitive market is neither a self-perpetuating nor an immutable artifact of nature. Without strictly enforced rules of the game, the competitive market can be eroded and subverted from within—through agreements not to compete, as well as through consolidations of industrial control in the hands of dominant firms and private power complexes. In the words of Lord Robbins, "The invisible hand which guides men to promote ends which were no part of their intention, is not the hand of some god or some natural agency independent of human effort; it is the hand of the lawgiver, the hand which withdraws from the sphere of pursuit of self-interest those possibilities which do not harmonize with the public good."[6]

Preserving the competitive market as the primary regulator of economic affairs was the central objective of the Sherman Act of 1890. Undoubtedly, it sought to promote good economic performance by proscribing contracts, combinations, and conspiracies in restraint of trade (sec. 1), as well as monopolization and attempts to monopolize (sec. 2). But its purpose was broader. Like the Constitution, the Act was animated by a fundamental distrust of concentrated power.[7] Like the Constitution, it sought

---

6 L. Robbins, The Theory of Economic Policy in English Classical Political Economy 56 (1952).

7 Justice Douglas articulated antitrust's traditional hostility to concentration of economic power. Such power, he wrote, "can be benign or it can be dangerous. The philosophy of the Sherman Act is that it should not exist. For all power tends to develop into a government in itself. . . . Industrial power should be decentralized. It should be scattered into many hands so that the fortunes of the people will not be dependent on the whim or caprice, the political prejudices, the emotional stability of a few self-appointed men. The fact that they are not vicious men but respectable and social-minded is irrelevant. That is the philosophy and the command of the Sherman Act. It is founded on

to provide for a structure of governance—a social blueprint—for controlling power. Like the Constitution, it sought to disperse power into many hands, so that the fortunes of the people would not be in the hands of an irresponsible (*i.e.*, not accountable) oligarchy. In sum, as the purpose of the Constitution was to prevent cartels, monopolies and "factions" from controlling the coercive power of the state, so the basic objective of the Sherman Act was to prevent private power groups from controlling economic decision making in a free society.

Clearly, the objectives that the Sherman Act was designed to attain are as relevant today as they were 100 years ago. It is fitting, therefore, to examine the anatomy and contours of economic power—particularly some of the consequences of unaccountable discretion for a democratic, free enterprise society.

I. The consequences of economic power

Broadly construed, economic power is the capacity to control and to regulate economic affairs and the fortunes of others, and to allocate society's resources, outside the checks and balances of an effectively competitive market. It is the capacity to control markets, industries and sectors of the economy, but without assurance that the public interest will be protected. It is arbitrary, unaccountable—and hence, irresponsible—discretion.

---

a theory of hostility to the concentration in private hands of power so great that only a government of the people should have it." United States v. Columbia Steel Co., 334 U.S. 495, 536 (1948).

The broader purposes of antitrust were forcefully expressed by Judge Hand. He observed that "possession of economic power deadens initiative, discourages thrift and depresses energy; that immunity from competition is a narcotic, and rivalry a stimulant, to industrial progress; that the spur of constant stress is necessary to counteract an inevitable disposition to let well enough alone." But more broadly, he pointed out, Congress in enacting the Sherman Act "was not necessarily motivated by economic motives alone. It is possible, because of its indirect social or moral effect, to prefer a system of small producers, each dependent for his success upon his own skill and character, to one in which the great mass of those engaged must accept the direction of a few." United States v. Aluminum Co. of America, 148 F.2d 416, 427 (2d Cir. 1945).

Economic power can derive from the large relative size of one or a few participants in a particular market or industry, such as monopoly or oligopoly. Or it can flow from disproportionately large absolute size relative to broad sectors of the economy. It may be exerted singly, or it may be exercised jointly in concert, either through outright agreement among rivals or via tacit collusion and conscious parallelism. It may be exerted privately without government support; or it may be bolstered by private subversion and corruption of the power of the state and its use for anticompetitive ends.

A. Artificially inflated prices

"The price of monopoly," Adam Smith observed, "is upon every occasion the highest which can be got. The natural price, or the price of free competition, on the contrary, is the lowest which can be taken. . . . The one is upon every occasion the highest which can be squeezed out of the buyers. . . . The other is the lowest which the sellers can commonly afford to take, and at the same time continue their business."[8] Empirical evidence affirms the validity of Smith's observation.

In the 1920's, for example, the formation of an international cartel to eliminate competition empowered General Electric and other producers to inflate the price of tungsten carbide by 806%, from $50 per pound to $453, at a time when the cost to manufacture the material was estimated to be approximately $8 per pound.[9]

In the 1930's, in the midst of the Great Depression and with farm prices and consumer incomes at all-time lows, tacit collusion enabled the American cigarette oligopoly to impose sizable price boosts, and to enjoy one of their most profitable years.[10]

---

8 A. SMITH, WEALTH OF NATIONS 61 (Modern Lib. ed. 1937).

9 G. STOCKING & M. WATKINS, CARTELS OR COMPETITION 132–33 (1948).

10 Am. Tobacco Co. v. United States, 328 U.S. 781 (1946).

In the 1950's, the great electrical conspiracy, involving the major U.S. manufacturers of electrical power generating equipment and apparatus, operated to inflate prices to utilities and ratepayers by as much as 21% for major products like turbine generators.[11]

In the early 1960's, data gathered during the course of a congressional investigation revealed the pricing power of prescription drug producers. In the case of one drug, Orinase, for example, the manufacturer's wholesale price was $83.40 per thousand tablets—compared to a manufacturing cost of $6.86 per thousand. Defended by one producer as only "pennies a day," the annual cost to the patient amounted to $150 for a substance produced at a cost of about $14.[12] For another drug, Meprobmate, the price charged to druggists and wholesalers was found to be $52–$65 per thousand tablets, compared to a production cost of $7–$15.[13]

Noncompetitive prices have in recent years been notoriously in evidence in the procurement of defense weapons and allied equipment. On the one hand, defense contractors have charged the military $640 for toilet covers,[14] $660 apiece for ashtrays,[15] $7,622 for a 10-cup coffee brewer,[16] and $10,169 for a kit of tools which could be procured from a neighborhood hardware store for less than $100.[17] For major weapons systems, on other hand,

---

11 D. Greer, Industrial Organization and Public Policy 302–305 (1980).

12 Administered Prices, Drugs, Report of the Subcomm. on Antitrust and Monopoly of the Senate Comm. on the Judiciary, 87th Cong., 1st Sess. 20 (1961).

13 *Id.* at 18.

14 *Toilet Covers on Plane Cost Navy $640 Each*, N.Y. Times, Feb. 5, 1985, at 5.

15 Keller, *2 Ashtrays Cost Navy $660 Apiece*, N.Y. Times, May 29, 1985, at 16.

16 D. Rasor, Pentagon Underground 154 (1985).

17 W. Adams & J. Brock, The Bigness Complex 341 (1986).

economic power has enabled contractors to raise prices far in excess of contracted-for levels, and to obtain lucrative follow-on contracts to repair defects in overpriced, underperforming weapons.[18]

Years of collusion and bid-rigging among highway contractors across the country are estimated to have cost governments—and taxpayers—at least several hundred million dollars annually in artificially inflated prices.[19]

These findings are neither isolated nor atypical. Numerous studies and analyses confirm that economic power, and noncompetitive market structures, permit excessive prices to be extracted in a variety of fields, including food processing,[20] grocery retailing,[21] banking and gasoline marketing.[22]

B. Capture and subversion of government power

When unable to adequately control markets unilaterally, powerful private interests can reach out to capture government power, and pervert it to the end of eliminating competition at the public's expense.

---

18 *Id.* at 331–44.

19 Flax, *Crackdown on Colluding Roadbuilders*, FORTUNE, Oct. 3, 1983, at 79.

20 *See* J. CONNOR ET AL., THE FOOD MANUFACTURING INDUSTRIES: STRUCTURE, STRATEGIES, PERFORMANCE, and POLICIES 296 (1985).

21 *See Impact of Market Concentration on Rising Food Prices: Hearings Before the Subcomm. on Antitrust, Monopoly and Business Rights of the Senate Comm. on the Judiciary*, 96th Cong., 1st Sess. 68–69. (1979); Cotterill, *Market Power in the Retail Food Industry: Evidence from Vermont*, 68 REV. ECON. & STAT. 379 (1986); B. MARION, ORGANIZATION AND PERFORMANCE OF THE U.S. FOOD SYSTEM 320–24 (1986).

22 For comprehensive surveys, *see* L. WEISS, CONCENTRATION AND PRICE (1989); and *idem*, "*Concentration and Price: A Progress Report*," in ISSUES AFTER A CENTURY OF FEDERAL COMPETITION POLICY 317–30 (R. Wills, J. Caswell, and J. Culbertson eds. 1987).

The "public utility" field traditionally has provided fertile soil for the full flowering of economic power. By a process so brilliantly analyzed by Horace Gray, in a number of instances

> public utilities status was to be the haven of refuge for all aspiring monopolists who found it too difficult, too costly, or too precarious to secure and maintain monopoly by private action alone. Their future prosperity would be assured if only they could induce government to grant them monopoly power and to protect them against interlopers, provided always, of course, that government did not exact too high a price for its favors in the form of restrictive regulation.[23]

Trucking and airlines provide two prime examples of this aspect of the economic power problem.[24] Although inherently competitive fields, established carriers in these industries lobbied for, and successfully obtained, public utilities status beginning in the 1930's. Thereafter, government effectively cartelized both fields by restricting entry, by suppressing competition, by promoting consolidation and concentration, and by permitting—nay, indeed, by actively encouraging—collusion and price-fixing. The results were scarcely in the public interest: inefficiency, waste, lack of technological progress, and artificially inflated fares of 30%-50% in airlines, and 20%-40% in trucking.

Protectionist government restrictions on foreign competition in the form of quotas, "voluntary" export restraints, and "orderly marketing agreements" afford a second tantalizing arena for the exercise of economic power and the subversion of the state. They conveniently mask the inefficiencies and technical backwardnesses of private power complexes—but at exhorbitant cost to society.

Confronted with the inevitable consequences of decades of noncompetitive structure, noncompetitive conduct and noncom-

---

23 Gray, *Passing of the Public Utility Concept*, 16 LAND ECON. 8 (1940).

24 Generally, *see* W. ADAMS & J. BROCK, *supra* note 17, chapters 17 and 18.

petitive performance,[25] the "bigness complex" in automobiles—big management and big labor—succeeded in lobbying for government restrictions on Japanese imports that since 1981 have raised new-car prices in the U.S. possibly as much as $2,500 per car, with an aggregate cost to American consumers of perhaps as much as $5.8 billion annually, and at the expense of $240,000 per U.S. auto job saved.[26]

In steel, two decades of import restraints and government protectionism elicited at the behest of big management and big labor have inflated U.S. steel prices 12%-40% above international levels, have cost consumers (including American steel-using firms) an estimated minimum of $1.1 billion to as much as $6.8 billion annually, and have amounted to a staggering expense of nearly $750,000 per job saved in steel while, according to one calculation, causing a considerable net loss in employment in the rest of American industry.[27]

For Henry C. Simons, this capacity of private economic power blocs to capture the state, and to pervert it to antisocial ends, posed one of the most serious threats of monopoly in a free enterprise democracy. The state, he pointed out, "rarely will permit private monopolies to bear the consequences of their own actions. Monopolists will run to the government for protection against any threat to their unstable equilibrium." Hence, "every suppression of competition gives rise to an apparent need for regulation; and every venture in regulation creates the necessity of more regulation; and every interference by government on behalf of one group necessitates, in the orderly routine of

---

25 *See* Adams & Brock, *The Automobile Industry*, in STRUCTURE OF AMERICAN INDUSTRY 101-27 (W. Adams ed. 8th ed. 1989).

26 G. HUFBAUER, D. BERLINER, & K. ELLIOTT, TRADE PROTECTION IN THE UNITED STATES: 31 CASE STUDIES 256-58 (1986); Crandall, *Detroit Rode Quotas to Prosperity*, Wall St. J., Jan. 29, 1986, at 28.

27 G. HUFBAUER, D. BERLINER, & K. ELLIOTT, *supra* note 26, at 178-79; ORGANIZATION FOR ECONOMIC COOPERATION AND DEVELOPMENT, COSTS AND BENEFITS OF PROTECTIONISM 48 (1985); A. DENZAU, HOW IMPORT RESTRAINTS REDUCE EMPLOYMENT (Center for the Study of American Business, June 1987).

democratic corruption, additional interference on behalf of others." The outcome, he warned, would feature "all the afflictions of socialization and none of its possible benefits; an enterprise economy paralyzed by political control; the moral disintegration of representative government in the endless contest of innumerable pressure groups for special political favors. . . ."[28]

C. Administered pricing and macroeconomic instability

More broadly, economic power and the administered pricing power concomitant therewith exacerbates macroeconomic instability in the economy generally. This is especially the case during recessionary periods, when powerful firms (typically in concert with powerful labor unions) rigidly hold prices and wages constant, or even perversely raise them in the face of sales declines, thereby further depressing production, sales and employment levels. It is particularly troublesome when it occurs in major industries that affect broad segments of the economy.

The automobile industry, for example, exerts a sizable influence on the American economy: As many as one-fifth of all U.S. manufacturing workers are employed in jobs tied directly or indirectly to auto production; the auto industry is one of the nation's largest buyers of a broad array of industrial products; and automobile purchases account for approximately one-fifth of total national retail sales of goods and services.[29] Hence, it is all the more significant that in this industry, as the figure below shows, the short-run pattern of U.S. new-car prices over the course of business cycles is one in which prices are persistently—and significantly—raised in the face of sales declines, thereby inducing even greater falloffs in production and employment, not only in autos, but across the vast congery of allied industries.

---

28 H. C. SIMONS, ECONOMIC POLICY FOR A FREE SOCIETY 87–88 (1948).

29 *See* Adams & Brock, *Corporate Power and Economic Sabotage*, 20 J. ECON. ISSUES 919, 931 (1986), and the sources cited therein.

Prices and New-Car Registrations

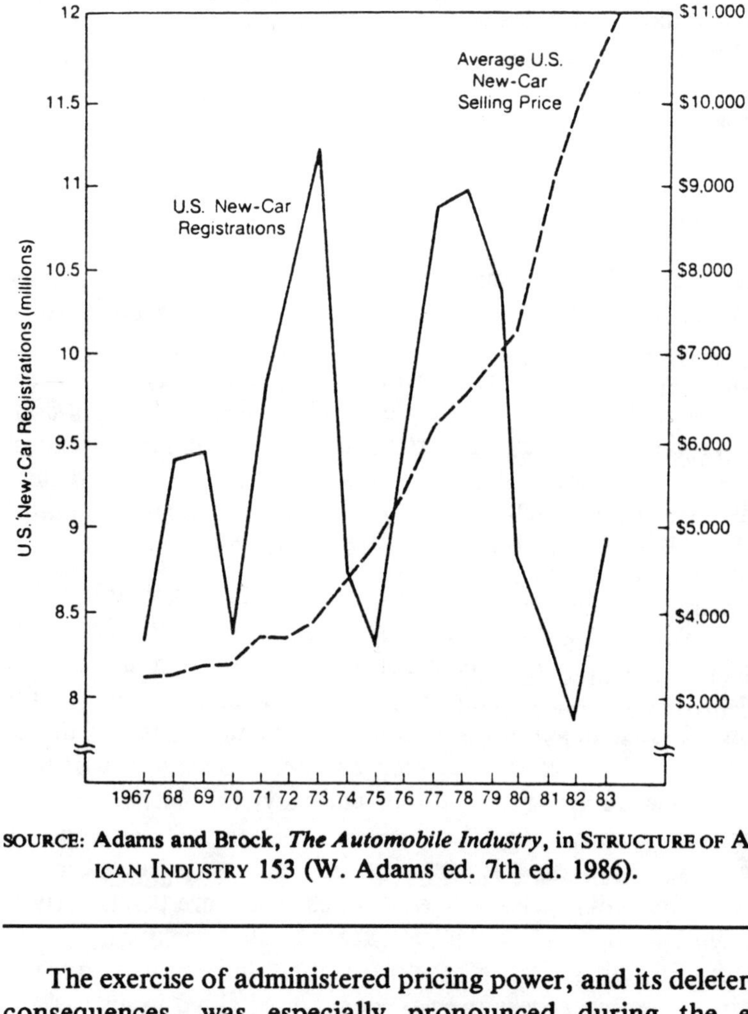

SOURCE: Adams and Brock, *The Automobile Industry*, in STRUCTURE OF AMERICAN INDUSTRY 153 (W. Adams ed. 7th ed. 1986).

The exercise of administered pricing power, and its deleterious consequences, was especially pronounced during the early 1980's.[30] In 1980, on the eve of what would prove to be the worst

For a detailed documentation of similar pricing patterns in the industry during the 1950's, *see* ADMINISTERED PRICES, AUTOMOBILES, REPORT OF THE SUBCOMM. ON ANTITRUST AND MONOPOLY OF THE SENATE COMM. ON THE JUDICIARY, 85th Cong., 2d Sess. (1958).

national recession since the Great Depression, with an unemployment rate of 26% in the motor vehicle industry, and with another 350,000 to 650,000 layoffs in auto-related industries, the domestic oligopoly disclosed price increases that the *Wall Street Journal* incredulously reported as "rivaling anything in modern Detroit history."[31] Another round of price increases shortly thereafter prompted one dealer to exclaim the auto companies "don't know what's going on in the market. They defy the law of supply and demand."[32] As the recession deepened, and as auto sales continued to plummet, "General Motors Corp. slapped an exceptionally sharp price boost on its 1982 models"—a price hike matched by Ford and Chrysler.[33] That this display of administered pricing power in action was less than desirable was obvious: "After pushing through a stiff 6% price increase last fall on 1982 models, GM spent much of the year suffering through the deepest sales plunge of the three-year-old auto-industry recession," the *Wall Street Journal* later reported.[34]

Steel is another major sector afflicted by administered pricing power. Steel, of course, is an important basic input to the manufacture of a myriad of products throughout the economy, from plants, factories and producer goods, to consumer durables like automobiles and appliances. It is a concentrated, noncompetitively structured industry that (like automobiles) poses the problem of perverse administered pricing—a pattern of pricing that exacerbates instability in steel and, thus, in the economy at large.

---

31 Koten, *Steep Price Increases for Detroit's '81 Autos May Dissuade Buyers*, Wall St. J., Oct. 3, 1980, at 1.

32 *Ford and Chrysler Response to Price Rise by GM Is Unclear; Dealers Urge Restraint*, Wall St. J., Jan. 5, 1981, at 5.

33 *GM Increases 1982 Car Prices an Average of 6%*, Wall St. J., Aug. 10, 1981, at 2; Koten, *Ford to Boost 1982 Car Prices as Much as 7%*, Wall St. J., Sept. 1, 1981, at 2.

34 Simpson, *GM May Curb Price Increases on Its 1983 Cars*, Wall St. J., June 29, 1982, at 2.

From 1947 to the end of the 1950's, for example, steel prices were steadily increased at regular intervals regardless of costs of demand.[35] The untoward macroeconomic consequences were pointed out by President Johnson's Council of Economic Advisors in a 1965 report:

> Steel prices played an important role in the general price increases of the 1950s. Between 1947 and 1951, the average increase in the price of basic steel products was 9 percent per year, twice the average increase of all wholesale prices. The unique behavior of steel prices was most pronounced in the mid-1950s. While the wholesale price index was falling an average of 0.9 percent annually from 1951 to 1955, the price index was falling an average of 0.9 percent annually from 1951 to 1955, the price index for steel was rising an average of 4.8 percent per year. From 1955 to 1958, steel prices were increasing 7.1 percent annually, or almost three times as fast as wholesale prices generally. No other major sector shows a similar record.[36]

With only occasional exceptions when foreign competition has been permitted to operate, this perverse recession-magnifying pattern of pricing has persisted: "In the two recessions during the 1970s, steel prices rose 6.4 percent in 1970 and 26.8 percent in 1974, while output fell. During the 1980 recession, steel production fell by 18 percent and steel prices increased by 6.8 percent."[37] In 1982–83, with steel demand at its lowest level since the Great Depression, and with nearly one-half of the nation's steelworkers laid off, the steel oligopoly raised prices 6% on sheet and strip steel products used widely throughout American industry.[38] It was

---

35 *See* ADMINISTERED PRICES IN STEEL, REPORT OF THE SUBCOMM. ON ANTITRUST AND MONOPOLY OF THE SENATE COMM. ON THE JUDICIARY, 85th Cong., 2d Sess. 17–26 (1958).

36 COUNCIL OF ECONOMIC ADVISERS, REPORT TO THE PRESIDENT ON STEEL PRICES 8–9 (1965).

37 Z. ACS, CHANGING STRUCTURE OF THE U.S. ECONOMY: LESSONS FROM THE STEEL INDUSTRY 93 (1984).

38 Chavez, *Bethlehem Steel to Cut 7,300 Jobs at Upstate Plant*, N.Y. Times, Dec. 28, 1982, at D3; Bonner, *U.S. Steel, Armco Inc. and Inland Raise Prices*, N.Y. Times, Jan. 21, 1983, at 36.

an impressive display of what *Business Week* called "steel pricing that ignores the market."[39]

But the problem is broader than that. Administered pricing power has public policy consequences as well. The ability of economic power complexes to rigidly hold prices constant, and to raise them in the face of slack sales and employment, compounds the challenge of formulating macrostabilization policy, as inflation arises at less than full employment, as anti-inflation policies produce price increases (rather than price decreases) in key sectors of the economy, and as the "bite"—and hence, the risks—of macropolicies must be increased in intensity in the struggle to combat the business cycle.[40]

D. Obstruction of technological advance

A fourth dimension of the economic power problem is the capacity to control technology and technical advance and, when desirable or necessary, to suppress, restrain or obstruct it.

In oil, for example, Standard Oil of New Jersey (now Exxon) obtained in the 1920's worldwide ownership and control of an important German breakthrough in the synthetic production of gasoline from coal.[41] Standard's objective was clearly something

---

39 *Steel Pricing that Ignores the Market*, BUS. WK., Feb. 2, 1981, at 26. For additional evidence of the problem in American industry generally, *see* J. BLAIR, ECONOMIC CONCENTRATION 405–66 (1972); *idem*, *Market Power and Inflation: A Short-Run Target Return Model*, 8 J. ECON. ISSUES 453 (1974); and Ross and Krousz, *Buyers' and Sellers' Prices and Administered Behavior*, 68 REV. ECON. & STAT. 369 (1986).

40 Indeed, the "most important macroeconomic policy implication" Mancur Olson draws from his recent examination of stagflation, unemployment, and business cycles "is that the best macroeconomic policy is a good microeconomic policy. . . . If combinations dominate markets throughout the economy and the government is always intervening on behalf of special interests, there is no macroeconomic policy that can put things right." M. OLSON, THE RISE AND DECLINE OF NATIONS 233 (1982).

41 This account is drawn from G. STOCKING & M. WATKINS, CARTELS IN ACTION 91–93, 491–95 (1946).

other than vigorously developing synthetic gasoline at the expense of its extensive crude oil holdings, however. According to a Twentieth Century Fund study, the manner in which the firm subsequently utilized its rights clearly revealed that its goal was to suppress this technological development in order to protect its oil interests. Former Standard Oil president Walter Teagle admitted as much in an internal company document. Addressing the firm's handling of its synthetic gasoline rights and technology, he wrote: "There is little doubt in our minds but what, if other than oil companies had dominated the situation, the management's conduct of the business would have been along lines better calculated to secure the maximum return on the capital invested."[42]

Restraint of alternative-fuels technology continues to characterize "big oil's" behavior. In the 1970's, in a company document uncovered by Canadian antitrust authorities, an official of Humble (an Exxon subsidiary) summarized the firm's efforts to forestall synthetic fuel development in the following terms:

> It is therefore desirable for Humble to do research work on shale and coal to know where the processes are headed. . . .
>
> In the meantime, it should not itself initiate commercial production, or take other action or make announcements that would motivate other companies to initiate commercial production or even development.
>
> It is felt that there is a fair amount of mass psychology in the industry and that, while many companies would prefer to go slow because of their domestic crude interests . . . they would feel compelled to start plans if others did and particularly so if a company with the stature of Humble did.[43]

In the medical field of pain control, the evidence reveals that Johnson & Johnson succeeded in acquiring control of a promising nondrug method for ameliorating pain, and suppressing its

---

42 Quoted in *id.* at 493.

43 Mintz, *Synfuel Development Delay Laid to Exxon*, Wash. Post, Aug. 11, 1981, at A2.

commercialization, in order to protect the firm's lucrative sales of Tylenol tablets. Ruling that Johnson & Johnson had unlawfully restrained trade and innovation, Judge Miles Lord found that

> Johnson & Johnson's actions resulted in countless individuals having to suffer the debilitating side effects of pain-killing drugs because a product which can afford them the relief they seek without such adverse [drug] effects was withheld from competition. . . . The evidence is such that had [the non-drug technology] not been suppressed, it could have benefitted millions of people throughout the world.[44]

In automobiles, the Big Three triopoly tacitly delayed development and commercialization of small fuel-efficient cars in order to protect their oligopoly profits in big cars.[45] They tacitly colluded to delay safety features known to them for decades.[46] And they created a cartel in order to delay the adoption of pollution control devices and technologies.[47]

In amateur photography, the Eastman Kodak Company for decades blocked the development of easy-to-use cartridge-loading cameras and held back commercial introduction of new flash

---

44 McDonald v. Johnson & Johnson Co., 537 F. Supp. 1282, 1338 (D. Minn. 1982).

45 *See* White, *The American Automobile Industry and the Small Car, 1945–1970*, 20 J. IND. ECON. 179 (1972). "In this behavior," according to White, "the Big Three definitely realized their mutual interdependence, since in the absence of retaliation by rivals a single firm contemplating the production of a small car should have expected to gain more profits from stealing the dissatisfied customers from other firms than he would lose from dissatisfied customers of his own large cars. . . . But the Big Three mutually contemplating a small car could only see lost profits from reduced sales of large cars." *Id.* at 180.

46 *See* Adams & Brock, *Bigness and Social Efficiency: A Case Study of the U.S. Auto Industry*, in CORPORATIONS AND SOCIETY: POWER AND RESPONSIBILITY 226–28 (W. Samuels and A. Miller eds., 1987).

47 *See Smog Control Antitrust Case*, 117 CONG. REC. 15,626 (May 18, 1971).

technologies,[48] while incandescent lamp manufacturers devoted themselves to impeding the development and commercialization of competitive fluorescent lighting.[49] In telephony, AT&T—with the aid of government regulatory commissions—obstructed the availability of new services and equipment.[50]

Clearly, concentrated power includes discretionary control, not only over price, but over technology and the rate of technical advance as well.

E. Private planning power

Private planning power is the capacity of economic power blocs to privately plan the allocation of society's resources, and to arrange and to rearrange the economic landscape, but without assurance that such private planning is in the public interest. It is the power to operate beyond and behind supply and demand.

For example, as the nation's dominant producer of buses and automobiles, and as one of its very largest industrial concerns, General Motors understood at an early date that if urban rail transit systems could be eliminated as a viable option, a huge market would open up for additional sales of its buses and cars. Anything that reduced the attractiveness of mass urban rail transportation would be perceived as a desirable development from GM's private perspective—adverse public consequences for urban congestion, smog and fuel inefficiency to the contrary notwithstanding.

Thus, according to the findings of a federal court (sustaining a conviction for criminal conspiracy to violate the nation's

---

48 *See* Brock, *Structural Monopoly, Technological Performance, and Predatory Innovation: Relevant Standards Under Section 2 of the Sherman Act*, 21 AM. BUS. L.J. 291 (1983).

49 Edwards, *Commercial and Political Aspects of International Cartels, Study Made for the Subcomm. on War Mobilization of the Senate Comm. on Military Affairs*, 78th Cong., 2d Sess. 17–18 (1946).

50 *See* Judge Greene's masterful discussion in United States v. Am. Tel. & Tel. Co., 524 F. Supp. 1336 (D.D.C. 1981).

antitrust laws[51]), General Motors was instrumental in organizing National City Lines, an operating company that engineered the demise of 46 electric rail transit systems in 45 cities in 16 states across the country. Through its National City Lines subsidiary, GM and its coconspirators (a tire manufacturer and an oil company) acquired control of urban rail systems, literally destroyed them, and replaced them with GM buses.

The impact of GM's private planning power on one city, Los Angeles, was described in 1974 as follows:

> Thirty-five years ago Los Angeles was a beautiful city of lush palm trees, fragrant orange groves and ocean-clean air. It was served then by the world's largest electric railway network. In the late 1930's General Motors and allied highway interests acquired the local transit companies, scrapped their pollution-free electric trains, tore down their power transmission lines, ripped up their tracks, and placed GM buses on already congested Los Angeles streets. The noisy, foul-smelling buses turned earlier patrons of the high-speed rail system away from public transit and, in effect, sold millions of private automobiles. Largely as a result, the city is today an ecological wasteland: the palm trees are dying of petrochemical smog; the orange groves have been paved over by 300 miles of freeways; the air is a septic tank into which 4 million cars, half of them built by General Motors, pump 13,000 tons of pollutants daily.[52]

After surveying the evidence, another transportation expert concluded that street "railways and trolley bus operations, even if better suited to traffic needs and the public interest, were doomed in favor of the vehicles and material produced by the [National City Lines] conspirators."[53]

Private planning power, and the absence of effective checks and balances to insure economic decision making in the public interest, is also apparent in the nuclear commercial electric power

---

51 United States v. National City Lines, 186 F.2d 562 (7th Cir. 1951).

52 Snell, *American Ground Transport*, in *Hearings Before the Subcomm. on Antitrust and Monopoly of the Senate Comm. on the Judiciary*, 93d Cong., 2d Sess., pt. 4A, A2–3 (1974).

53 G. Smerk, Urban Transportation 50 (1965).

field.[54] Here, powerful producers of nuclear plants and fuels (including Westinghouse, General Electric, and Exxon), allied with a coterie of zealous supporters in government and shrouded from meaningful public oversight, pushed and planned for decades for a "nuclear option." They have suppressed and distorted information, and misled the public. They have been the beneficiaries of tens of billions of dollars in government funding, subsidy, and support. The result? An economically nonviable energy source, wherein scores of plants representing billions of dollars of investments have been abandoned, that has become more—not less—dependent on government largesse, that has generated large amounts of highly toxic wastes for which no permanently safe method of disposal is known, and that has prodigiously consumed public monies that might well have been better devoted to the development of less risky (and more job generating) renewable energy sources such as solar power and conservation. It has been planning. But planning by whom? For what? With what consequences? And with what accountability to the national interest?

F. The sabotage problem

Some 40 years ago, Henry Simons pointed out that in a highly developed economy, with an intricate division of labor and functional interdependence between sectors, "every large organized group is in a position at any time to disrupt or stop the whole flow of social income." The system, he warned, "must soon break down if groups persist in exercising that power or if they must continuously be bribed to forgo its disastrous exercise." A free society, he foresaw, "must not concede to any functional group the power ('right') to withold its contribution to an elaborate production process or to exact tribute by threat of such collective action."[55]

---

54 Generally, *see* W. Adams & J. Brock, *supra* note 17, at 274–90. *See also* M. Hertsgaard, Nuclear Inc. (1983), and D. Barlett & J. Steele, Forevermore: Nuclear Waste in America (1985).

55 H. C. Simons, *supra* note 28, at 122, 218.

This sabotage power—the capacity of giant firms (and labor unions) to threaten to shut down operations, and to thereby inflict economic catastrophe on a nation if their demands are not met—is a potent dimension of the economic power problem.

In automobiles, for example, the American auto giants have recently honed their sabotage power into a venerable art form. In the area of automotive pollution control, a recent Brookings Institution treatise observes that the auto giants "can easily argue that their inability [or unwillingness] to meet a deadline will force them to abandon production altogether. Such a threat catches the attention of politicians; hence [auto smog control] delays were granted in 1973, 1974, and 1977. . . . Announcements by the major domestic manufacturers that they could not [or would not] comply have at times forced changes in the law, most recently in the Clean Air Act Amendments." In this way, they "have found they can obtain waivers, postponements, or changes."[56]

In fuel economy, GM and Ford exercised their sabotage power in their successful machinations in 1985–86 to force government to relax auto mileage standards. They threatened Congress with plant closings, layoffs and unemployment on a massive scale—in a crucial sector of the economy at a critical stage in the economic recovery—unless government relaxed the standards. Unless this were done, a GM vice president told Congress, "full-line manufacturers [*i.e.*, GM and Ford] face the prospect of restricting product availability." This, she pointedly noted for a Congress facing upcoming elections, "translates into plant closings, job losses, and lower economic growth." Failure to bow to GM's demand, she warned, "would lead to potentially serious economic upheavals, including massive layoffs." To drive home the point, GM submitted an extensive list of 88 plants—specifying the city and state location for each—that could be adversely impacted should the government refuse to act.[57] The

---

56 R. Crandall, H. Gruenspecht, T. Keeler, & L. Lave, Regulating the Automobile 29, 90 (1986).

57 *Automobile Fuel Economy Standards: Hearings Before the Subcomm. on Energy Regulation and Conservation of the Senate Comm.*

industry's sabotage campaign succeeded. The mileage requirements were lowered (according to a government spokeswoman) for fear of "adverse economic consequences, including job losses in the tens of thousands in the auto industry, if the standard was not lowered."[58]

The sabotage power is also evident in defense weapons procurement. For example, in forcing the Navy to pay for cost overruns on Trident submarines produced by its Electric Boat division, General Dynamics—one of the nation's very largest weapons conglomerates—found the

> threat that Electric Boat might shut down . . . was fully appreciated in Washington. Quite apart from the fact that the submarine builder was the largest employer in both Connecticut and Rhode Island, there was only one other qualified submarine builder in the country, and that [firm] lacked the experience and the facilities to produce the new Trident submarines, the planned mainstay of the nation's seaborne nuclear deterrent into the next century. The confrontationist approach produced results. Although the Settlement Board had recommended only $125 [million] in additional payments, Electric Boat managed to obtain all of $486 million.[59]

It was "nothing if not blackmail."[60] Addressing the problem in defense procurement more generally, a military officer confesses: "It would be swell if I could say 'You're a naughty boy and I'm

---

on Energy and Natural Resources, 99th Cong., 1st Sess. 57, 284–88 (1985); *Rollback of CAFE Standards and Methanol Vehicle Incentives Act of 1985: Hearings Before the Senate Comm. on Commerce, Science, and Transportation*, 99th Cong., 1st Sess. 76 (1985) (testimony of Marina von Neumann Whitman, vice president, General Motors Corp.).

58 *Fuel Economy Rules Relaxed for 1986 Cars*, N.Y. Times, Oct. 2, 1985, at 11.

It should be pointed out that in contrast to these dire warnings before Congress, General Motors assured its stockholders that "the ultimate liability under these regulations is *not expected to have a material adverse effect on the Corporation's consolidated financial position*." GENERAL MOTORS CORP. ANNUAL REPORT 38 (1985) (emphasis added).

59 R. FRANKLIN, THE DEFENDER 278 (1986).

60 *Id*. at 310.

going to cast you into oblivion.' But if I do, where am I going to buy the submarines and tanks and planes that I need?''[61]

G. *Manipulation of government for favors and privileges*

"It is a necessary outcome of human nature," economist Richard T. Ely once observed, "that those people who are to be controlled should enter politics in order that they may either escape the control, or shape it to their own ends."[62] Indeed, an Ely contemporary noted as early as 1902 that the "seasonal migration to Washington of representatives of all the great commercial interests [had] become a salient datum in political zoology."[63]

The capacity of economic power to manipulate the state, and to obtain favors, privileges and dispensations, is evident on a number of fronts. The following examples are merely illustrative of a pervasive phenomenon.

First, in taxation, large powerful groups are strategically positioned by virtue of their size and influence to demand, and frequently to obtain, tax favors, tax loopholes and tax privileges from government.

---

61 Quoted in Halloran, *Making Arms Makers Do It Right*, N.Y. Times, June 15, 1986, § 3, at 4.

62 R. T. Ely, Studies in the Evolution of Industrial Society 231 (1903). In 1901, *Bankers' Magazine* made this frank admission: "The growth of corporations and of combinations tends to strengthen the forces which seek to control the machinery of the government and the laws in behalf of special interests. . . . The productive forces are the purse-bearers. The businessman, whether alone or in combination with other businessmen, seeks to shape politics and government in a way conducive to his own prosperity. As the business of the country has learned the secret of combination, it is gradually subverting the power of the politician and rendering him subservient to its purposes. That government is not entirely controlled by these interests is due to the fact that business organization has not reached full perfection." Quoted in L. Corey, The House of Morgan 289 (1930).

63 W. Ghent, Our Benevolent Feudalism 33 (1902).

At the federal level, this dimension of economic power has been described by Charls Walker, one of Washington's most influential tax lobbyists, and a person whose clientele features a number of the nation's largest corporations. Asked about his remarkable record of success in influencing federal tax legislation, Mr. Walker explains that members of Congress

> will listen to me, let me in, when I am coming to talk about jobs, payrolls, economic growth in their districts. . . . If you [represent] twelve major multinational corporations and you look over the country, you have got operations, employment, in most of the states and many of the congressional districts. . . . And so you have a coalition to begin with.[64]

At the state and local government level, the economic power to extract tax privileges and favors is equally potent, if not more so. Carl Kaysen explains:

> The large national-market firm has available to it the promise of locating in a particular area or expanding its operations there, the threat of moving or contracting its operations as potent bargaining points in its dealings with local and even state political leaders. The branch manager of the company whose plant is the largest employer in a town or the vice-president of the firm proposing to build a plant which will become the largest employer in a small state treats local

---

64 Quoted in R. NADER & W. TAYLOR, THE BIG BOYS: POWER AND POSITION IN AMERICAN BUSINESS 269 (1986).

Evidence recently compiled by the Citizens for Tax Justice corroborates Mr. Walker's observations. An analysis of corporate tax records for the years 1981–84 reveals that for 275 large profitable firms, 129 of them (or almost half) either paid *no* federal taxes or received rebates from the government in at least 1 of the 4 years analyzed; 74 of them paid no taxes or received rebates in at least 2 years; 26 paid no taxes or received rebates in at least 3 of the 4 years analyzed; and 9 firms (including ITT, General Dynamics, and Transamerica) either paid no taxes or received rebates from the federal government in all 4 years surveyed. CITIZENS FOR TAX JUSTICE, CORPORATE TAXPAYERS & CORPORATE FREELOADERS 2 (Aug. 1985). For the entire sample, "the overall four-year effective tax rate was only 15 percent, less than one-third of the 46 percent tax rate that the tax code purportedly requires major corporations to pay." *Id.* at 4. In fact, a mother of three earning $12,000 paid more taxes in 1983 than the *combined* tax payments of Boeing, General Electric, DuPont, and Texaco. J. BIRNBAUM, & A. MURRAY, SHOWDOWN AT GUCCI GULCH 12 (1987).

> government not as a citizen but as a quasi-sovereign power. Taxes, zoning laws, roads, and the like become matters of negotiation as much as matters of legislation.[65]

General Motors' recent exploitation of its Saturn small-car plant to whipsaw states and communities to obtain a bonanza of tax holidays, free land and subsidized government loans is an obvious case in point.[66]

Second, private power complexes are at times able to immunize themselves from prosecution for corporate outlawry. For example, the government sought in 1969 to challenge as unlawful a number of large acquisitions made by ITT. The case was subsequently abandoned, however, in the face of dire warnings that continued prosecution of ITT might irreparably damage the nation's international balance of payments and (some warned) might even precipitate a collapse on Wall Street.[67] (A timely contribution of $400,000 to the President's reelection campaign did not hurt the firm's cause.)[68]

Similar privileges obtain in the defense industry. For example, a small defense contractor was recently disbarred from all government business for 3 years after offering a federal employee a $200 television set and a *Playboy* subscription.[69] For a defense

---

65 Kaysen, *The Corporation: How Much Power? What Scope?* in THE CORPORATION IN MODERN SOCIETY 100 (E. Mason ed. 1966).

66 For a more detailed examination of GM's extraction of favors and concessions from state and local governments in recent years, *see* Adams & Brock, *Corporate Size and the Bailout Factor*, 21 J. ECON. ISSUES 61, 76 (1987).

67 *See Richard J. Kleindienst: Hearings Before the Senate Comm. on the Judiciary*, 92d Cong., 2d Sess., pt. 2, at 114 and 651, and pt. 3, at 1409–11 (1972).

68 *See* Mueller, *The ITT Settlement: A Deal With Justice*, 1 IND. ORG. REV. 67 (1973), and Blake, *Beyond the ITT Case*, HARPER'S, June 1972, at 74–78.

69 Hitchens, *Minority Report*, THE NATION, Dec. 15, 1984, at 638.

giant like General Dynamics, however, the consequences of criminality are quite different. In a front-page expose (carrying the subtitle "Beating the Rap"), the *Wall Street Journal* reported:

> Along with two indictments for fraud on Pentagon contracts, General Dynamics won notoriety for billing the government for dog-kennel fees incurred by one executive and country-club dues paid by another. It even got the Pentagon to bail out a corporate barbershop that had suffered financial losses.
>
> Navy Secretary John Lehman characterized the company's corporate philosophy as "catch us if you can." The Pentagon's chief spokesman called the company's actions "nauseating."[70]

The consequences? A fleeting "suspension" (during which bidding periods for billion-dollar contracts were extended to enable General Dynamics to participate), followed by defense awards to the firm of "$1 billion of arms contracts, six times the $166.8 million contracts the company had won in August 1984. Another $1.4 billion came in September." As a result, "General Dynamics emerged as the year's most successful contractor."[71]

Third, the ultimate privilege of economic power is the capacity to obtain assured survival, and to be publicly bailed out, regardless of how incompetent, inefficient, and unprogressive the firm might be. Once a corporation attains the absolute size of a Lockheed, a Chrysler, or a Continental Illinois, its fortunes reverberate throughout the economy. Then the imminent demise of such a firm is no longer a private failure, but a social catastrophe. Once a democratic free enterprise society allows itself to become dependent on such corporate giants, it becomes their captive. It becomes a hostage to economic power. It confronts the intractable dilemma of what Walter Lippmann saw as "the problems and the tragedies of semi-obsolete corporate leviathans that are unable to live and unable to die."[72] The

---

70 Koten & Carrington, *For General Dynamics, Scandal Over Billing Hasn't Hurt Business*, Wall St. J., Mar. 29, 1986, at 1.

71 *Id.* at 20.

72 W. LIPPMANN, THE GOOD SOCIETY 224 (1937).

community's ability to absorb private mistakes is eroded, and it becomes less stable and more vulnerable as a result.

H. Undermining of national security

At times, the discretion inherent in economic power can be exercised in ways and toward private ends that operate to jeopardize national security.

One apt case in point is the extensive web of global cartels spun during the interwar years of the 1920's and 1930's. Comprising collusion between American producers and their foreign rivals, these international cartels operated in practice to retard the development of a number of strategic American industries in the years leading up to World War II.

In synthetic rubber, a cartel agreement not to compete, struck between Standard Oil in the U.S. and Farben in Germany, caused the development of the field in the U.S. to lag behind that in Germany. Indeed, "not only did Standard Oil agree with I.G. Farben that the latter should control the exploitation of synthetic rubber, but it cooperated in preventing anyone else from producing."[73]

In the case of synthetic gasoline produced from coal, Standard's "marriage" agreement with Farben enabled Standard to suppress the development of this alternative energy source in order to protect its crude oil holdings. Farben, on the other hand, vigorously promoted this new technology, with the result that synthetic gasoline provided at times upwards of 90% of the aviation fuel required to power Hitler's Luftwaffe.[74]

Likewise, the "production of Diesel engines in the United States was apparently retarded by the arrangements between American Bosch and Robert Bosch of Germany." Similarly, in

---

73 W. Berge, Cartels: Challenge to a Free World 212 (1944).

74 B.H.L. Hart, History of the Second World War 610 (1982).

the case of magnesium, restrictive cartel agreements enabled Nazi production to outstrip that in America.[75]

But this problem of discretionary economic power is not the relic of a bygone day.

For example, restrictions on the importation of foreign oil—restraints lobbied for and obtained from government by "big oil" over the years 1957–73—artificially accelerated consumption of American crude oil reserves. They rendered the U.S. *less* self-sufficient in petroleum, *more* vulnerable to the oil embargoes of the 1970's, and thus compounded the problem of energy insecurity. As Professor Alfred Kahn explained to Congress at the height of the 1973–74 oil crisis, "big oil's" protectionism "accelerated the exhaustion of our cheap and readily available sources of energy, so that now, when the rainy day comes, we are less well off than before."[76]

So, too, in the noncompetitive world of weapons procurement, where monopoly prices, cost overruns, deficient weapons performance, "revolving doors" between buyer and seller, and technological "gold-plating" have combined to *reduce* the American arsenal at the same time that defense spending skyrockets.[77] The result is what Marine Lieutenant Colonel David Evans describes as "self-imposed disarmament," whereby U.S. forces

---

75 Edwards, *supra* note 49, at 60–61.

76 *Market Performance and Competition in the Petroleum Industry: Hearings Before the Senate Special Subcomm. on Integrated Oil Operations*, 93d Cong., 2d Sess., pt. 1, at 325 (1974).

77 For a more detailed treatment, *see* W. Adams & J. Brock, *supra* note 17, chapter 24.

One analyst provides the following calculations: "the Army is now spending roughly the same amount on new tanks as it did during the Korean War. But that amount buys one-tenth the tanks it used to—700 today compared to almost 7,000 in 1953. Similarly, we built over 6,000 fighter planes in 1951 with $7 billion, but can build only about 300 with $11 billion today." P. Navarro, The Policy Game 267 (1984).

"will be increasingly outnumbered as we reluctantly spend more on defense."[78]

I. Erosion of economic freedom

Coercion is the coin of control. Hence, a final important dimension of the economic power problem is the erosion of economic freedom and opportunity that such control inevitably entails—for producers and consumers alike.

Above all else, the turn-of the century trusts were coercive, concentrated systems for control. When necessary, they brought their power to bear in order to restrict, prevent and eliminate the freedom of others to compete. In oil, for example, Rockefeller's Standard Oil trust dictated who would be permitted to remain in the industry, and who would not; who would be permitted to serve particular regions of the country, and which areas were out of bounds; and who would be permitted to produce particular petroleum products and which products were off-limits.[79] The Standard dictated the transportation fees to be paid by others, and when they received forbidden supplies, it commanded the railroads to "turn another screw."[80] It dictated the prices to be charged, the profits that "independents" would be permitted to retain, and the bounties to be remitted to the Standard.[81] As the Supreme Court later ruled, no disinterested mind could survey the field "without being irresistibly driven to the conclusion" that the trust operated to "drive others from the field and to exclude them from their right to trade. . . ."[82]

In amateur photography, the Eastman trust enforced exclusive dealership arrangements on more than 95% of all photo-

---

[78] Evans, *'Technological Bloat' Plagues the Pentagon*, Wall St. J., Aug. 15, 1983, at 12.

[79] H. Lloyd, *supra* note 3, at 61-63.

[80] M. Josephson, *supra* note 3, at 268.

[81] H. Lloyd, *supra* note 3, at 61-63.

[82] Standard Oil Co. v. United States, 221 U.S. 1, 76 (1911).

graphic dealers across the country, visiting recalcitrants with Kodak representatives accompanied on occasion by "a low-browed looking party with a club."[83] The whiskey trust, on the other hand, opted at times for a more explosive approach, relying a few well-placed sticks of dynamite in order to exert control.[84]

The problem persists in our own day. Economic regulation of the airline and trucking industries denied freedom of choice, not only for consumers, but for potential competitors who sought in vain to enter or to expand in the industry. So, too, has collusive control eroded freedom of enterprise in roadbuilding, where honest contractors have been warned by conspirators: "If you don't go along we can always move an asphalt plant into your town and take turns bidding below cost against you. Pretty soon we won't have you to worry about."[85]

For this reason, concern for freedom of enterprise and opportunity has from the outset been an integral element in American antitrust policy. After its enactment into law, Senator Sherman described the Sherman Act as a "charter of liberty"—an economic bill of rights designed to insure that "occupations were to be kept open to all who wished to try their luck, that the individual was to be protected in his 'common right' to choose his calling and that hindrances to equal opportunity were to be eliminated."[86]

---

83 *See* Brock, *Persistent Monopoly and the Charade of Antitrust: The Durability of Kodak's Monopoly Power*, 14 Tol. L. Rev. 653, 661, n.38 (1983).

84 H. Lloyd, *supra* note 3, at 20–22.

85 Quoted in Flax, *supra* note 19, at 80. For an analysis of the persistence of this problem in the video entertainment field, including motion pictures, cable and broadcast television, *see* Adams & Brock, *Vertical Integration, Monopoly Power and Antitrust: A Case Study of Video Entertainment*, 36 Wayne L. Rev. (forthcoming 1990).

86 Quoted in H. Thorelli, *supra* note 3, at 226.

II. Conclusion

The primary purpose of the Sherman Act is to perpetuate and preserve a system of governance for a competitive, free enterprise economy. Economic efficiency, progress and consumer welfare are important benefits that derive from it. But they are ancillary to a broader objective. Like the political framework prescribed by the Constitution, the Sherman Act calls for a dispersion of power—and a system of competitive checks and balances—in order to guard against the abuse of economic power.

In the centennial year of the Sherman Act, the challenge of controlling economic power is as persistent and vexing as ever. The aim of sound public policy, as John Stuart Mill observed long ago, should be "to surround any given society with the greatest possible number of circumstances of which the tendencies are beneficial, and to remove or counteract, as far as practicable, those of which the tendencies are injurious."[87] That, we submit, is the philosophy of antitrust in a free society.

---

87 J.S. MILL, A SYSTEM OF LOGIC 490 (1868). The challenge of fashioning the right economic rules is extensively treated in W. ADAMS & J. BROCK, DANGEROUS PURSUITS: MERGERS AND ACQUISITIONS IN THE AGE OF WALL STREET (1989) 162–82.

Abbreviations

Every accredited law school in the United States publishes at least one journal or law review on a regular basis. Many years ago, the editors of the leading publications agreed on a uniform, abbreviated system of citation which differed from that used in other disciplines. We have utilized this format for *The Antitrust Impulse*. To facilitate checking a footnote, please consider the following example:

X. Smith, *Antitrust Now and Then*, 99 ANTITRUST BULL. 949 (1999).
Author: X. Smith
Article title: Antitrust Now and Then
Journal: *The Antitrust Bulletin*—see explanation below.
Volume: 99
Year of publication: 1999
Page: 949.

The law review abbreviations usually include standard state or university abbreviations. Listed below are some of the less obvious ones and several recurring ones:

ABA (sometimes separated with periods) = American Bar Association

J	=	Journal
L	=	Law
Rev	=	Review
Q	=	Quarterly
U	=	University

Other abbreviations:

AAG	=	Assistant Attorney General
BNA	=	Bureau of National Affairs, Inc.
BOC	=	Bell Operating Company

CAB	=	Civil Aeronautics Board
CCH	=	Commerce Clearing House
CES	=	Center for Economic Studies at the U. S. Bureau of the Census
Cir.	=	Circuit
CIS	=	Consumer Information System
cert.	=	*certiorari*
D	=	District (but see below)
DOE	=	Department of Energy
DOJ	=	Department of Justice
DOT	=	Department of Transportation
EEC	=	European Economic Community
EPO	=	Economy Policy Office at the DOJ (see above)
ETC	=	Export Trading Company (Act)
EWG	=	Executive Working Group on Antitrust
FCC	=	Federal Communications Commission
FERC	=	Federal Energy Regulatory Commission (successor to the FPC)
FPC	=	Federal Power Commission (predecessor of the FERC)
FTC	=	Federal Trade Commission (sometimes referred to as the "Commission")
GATT	=	General Agreement on Tariffs and Trade
HHI	=	Herfindahl–Hirschman Index
HSR	=	Hart Scott Rodino (sometimes referred to as the Antitrust Improvements Act)
ICC	=	Interstate Commerce Commission
LBO	=	Leveraged Buyout
LRD	=	Longitudinal Research Database of the CES (see above)
L.S.E.	=	London School of Economics
MFJ	=	Modification of Final Judgment (usually referring to the AT&T Divestiture settlement)
NAAG	=	National Association of Attorneys General
NIRA	=	National Industrial Recovery Act
NRA	=	National Recovery Administration
NRC	=	Nuclear Regulatory Commission

OECD	=	Organization for Economic Cooperation and Development
R&D	=	Research and Development
RPM	=	Resale Price Maintenance
Reg.	=	Regulation *or* Register
SEC	=	Securities and Exchange Commission
SIC	=	Standard Industry Classification
TNEC	=	Temporary National Economic Committee
U.S.C.	=	United States Code
§	=	Section
¶	=	Paragraph

Index